INTERNATIONAL BUSINESS LAW:
Cases and Materials

George D. Cameron III
Emeritus Professor of Business Law
Ross School of Business
The University of Michigan

Published by Van Rye Publishing, LLC
www.vanryepublishing.com

ISBN-10: 0-9903671-1-8
ISBN-13: 978-0-9903671-1-6

About the Author

George Cameron is Emeritus Professor of Business Law at the University of Michigan's Ross School of Business. He earned a B.A. and an M.A. at Kent State University, and a J.D. and Ph.D. (Political Science) at the University of Michigan. He taught for 53 years—the last 43 at Michigan, including teaching visits in Beijing, Helsinki, Hong Kong, and Sao Paulo. The three Business Law texts that he authored or co-authored have gone through a combined total of 17 editions. He has won a number of teaching and research awards, including students' first (1982) "Best Professor" award at the University of Michigan's business school, listing as a noteworthy professor by *Business Week* in its 1986 ranking of the Top Ten Business Schools, a State of Michigan Undergraduate Teaching Award in 1990, the Bernard Teaching Leadership Award from his business school colleagues in 2003, and the Outstanding Senior Professor for 2004 by the Academy of Legal Studies in Business.

International and comparative law has always been a high priority with Professor Cameron. The *Business Law: Text and Cases* (1982) that he co-authored was the first to include a full chapter on International Law, in addition to cases dealing with international transactions. He developed special courses for his teaching assignments at China University of Political Science and Law, and at Helsinki School of Economics and Business Administration (now the Aalto University School of Business). He co-taught a special international class in the University of Michigan's joint program with Erasmus University (the Netherlands) for three years, and also co-taught in the U/M's Global MBA program—teaching twice each in Hong Kong and Sao Paolo.

The UN Convention on Contracts for the International Sale of Goods (addressed in Chapter III of *International Business Law: Cases and Materials*) became a regular part of all the University of Michigan courses Professor Cameron taught dealing with Contract Law and Sale of Goods Law. He felt it was important for future business managers to be aware of the risks of lawsuits in other nations, so he insisted on covering "long-arm" jurisdiction (addressed in Chapter II of this book) in every course he taught—for the last 40+ years. He also developed a separate International Law course for MBAs, and teaching materials from that course became the starting point for this text (with the encouragement of his colleague Professor George Siedel). *International Business Law: Cases and Materials* thus brings together a considerable history of teaching and research, to provide some significant insights into an increasingly important subject-matter.

Dedication

To the many wonderful colleagues with whom I have had the privilege and pleasure of working during my lengthy academic career;

To the several thousand students with whom I have had the challenge and the stimulation of classroom interaction;

and

To my family and friends—especially my wife Julie, for your love and support through the tribulations and the triumphs.

Thank you all.

"How can he explain to him? The world is not run from where he thinks. Not from his border fortresses, not even from Whitehall. The world is run from Antwerp, from Florence, from places he has never imagined; from Lisbon, from where the ships with sails of silk drift west and are burned up in the sun. Not from castle walls, but from countinghouses, not by the call of the bugle but by the click of the abacus, not by the grate and click of the mechanism of the gun but by the scrape of the pen on the page of the promissory note that pays for the gun and the gunsmith and the powder and shot."

—Thomas Cromwell (counsellor to King Henry VIII of England): thoughts on Lord Harry Percy.
—in *WOLF HALL*, Hilary Mantel (2009).

Contents

Preface

International Business Law: Cases and Materials is a timely and useful book. Uncounted millions of "international" transactions occur daily, as goods and services are purchased across the national boundaries of some 200 political units. Capital flows from nation to nation, and so—to a lesser extent—do jobs, as companies seek more favorable locations for their business operations. The "rules" (laws) governing these exchanges quickly become complex, as persons (and governments) from different countries are involved. If problems arise in a cross-border relationship, whose rules apply? What forums are available to resolve disputes? Are there tax implications to the transaction? If so, where? These and similar questions need to be factored into the decision to "go overseas."

Each of the six Chapters begins with a brief overview of the subject-matter, followed by short previews of the chosen case examples. The primary content of the Chapters consists of some 120 court and arbitration decisions in real disputes, between real parties. The actual texts of the decisions in these cases have been edited; some excerpts are quite brief, others are more substantial. Most "background" facts have been summarized by the author, but the edited-decision part of each case is quoted from the actual recorded text of the court or arbitrator who decided it. Clearly, a minute sample from tens of thousands of cases cannot provide comprehensive coverage of what all the world's legal rules are. Our objectives here are simply to indicate some of the major potential "flash points" of doing international business, to illustrate some of the significant differences in the applicable legal rules, and to provide an exposure to the language and process by which international business disputes are resolved. "Fore-warned is fore-armed." Being aware of these potential trouble spots, a sensible business manager will presumably consider them in making the decision to engage in cross-border transactions, and take appropriate steps to avoid or minimize potential adverse consequences.

Chapter I introduces International Law—its course of development and its two major sources (custom and treaties). Chapter II examines the use of national and international courts and arbitrators to resolve cross-border disputes. Chapter III provides basic coverage of the United Nations Convention on Contracts for the International Sale of Goods: when it applies;

how the sale contract is formed; when risk of loss on the goods passes from Seller to Buyer; what responsibilities the Seller has for the quality of the goods sold. Chapter IV looks at some of the legal questions that may arise in conducting cross-border commercial operations— employment issues, intellectual property issues, and investment issues. Chapter V considers potential questions regarding taxation of international activities, and the regulation of adverse environmental effects. Chapter VI reviews the efforts by national governments to apply their competition regulations to international business transactions, and the difficulties that private parties may have in attempting to enforce legal claims against governments and their agencies. While these are surely not the only legal issues that may arise in connection with international business, they do constitute a significant set of concerns of which managers need to be aware as they venture into the international "stream of commerce."

CHAPTER I

Sources of International Law—Custom, Treaties, Cases, and Texts

OVERVIEW:

History. The peoples of the earth have been interacting with each other for millennia. Much of that interaction has involved commerce, especially trading in goods. Initially, overland routes were readily available for trade among the Eurasian civilizations, and with Africa. Alternate sea routes were soon developed—across the Mediterranean Sea, the Red Sea, the Persian Gulf, and the Indian Ocean. The 4000-mile long "Silk Road" linked China to India, Persia, Arabia, Egypt, and ultimately, Europe—and to ports in those countries, for trans-shipment of goods. (The *Wall Street Journal* of March 28, 2015 featured a report of China's current plans to construct a 21st-Century "Silk Road": a land/water economic connection across Eurasia. *See also*, Chapter 2 "The New Silk Road," in David Eimer, *The Emperor Far Away*, New York: Bloomsbury, 2014.) The desire of Western European nations for alternate trade routes to Asia motivated much of the exploration that led to the sea routes around Africa and to the "discovery" of the American continents. (*See, e.g.,* Charles Corn, *The Scents of Eden*, New York: Kodansha International, 1998—a history of the spice trade and its impact on the making of the modern world.)

Inevitably, some of these interactions led to disputes, up to and including wars. It must have become evident to at least some of these early traders and diplomats that a regular mechanism for dispute resolution would be useful. In the sixth edition of his extensive text *International Law*, Malcolm Shaw notes the existence of two ancient treaties: the boundary agreement (c. 2100 BC) between the Sumerian cities of Lagash and Umma, and the peace treaty between Rameses II of Egypt and the Hittite king Hattusili III (c. 1258 BC). Shaw also refers to the "numerous treaties" that bound together the Greek city-states. Treaties have been, and continue to be, one of the primary sources of international law—both as binding rules for the nations that consent to them, and as specific examples of international "custom" (what nations have accepted as legal rules in prior situations). One of the most fundamental principles of international law is "*pacta sunt servanda*": (Latin) "promises must be kept" = treaties must be performed as agreed.

While two or more governing bodies might agree on specific rules to be binding as between themselves, day-to-day exchanges—diplomatic, cultural, commercial—were also occurring. Behavior patterns developed and were repeated; patterns which eventually came to be expected in similar situations. The sanctity of a government's representatives in another country, for example, came to be recognized as a practical rule that was useful to all nations. In the absence of an international legislature, it was the long-continued usage by the international community of customary rules that created much of international law.

At various times, efforts were made to codify these accepted customary rules, or at least parts of them, so that they were more readily available to participants in cross-border exchanges. The island of Rhodes, in the Aegean Sea, became a major maritime power in the Mediterranean between 1000 and 800 BC, and evidently produced a sea-law compilation—the *Lex Rhodia*, although no copy of that work has ever been found. (Some commentators doubt that it ever really existed at all. *See, e.g.,* Robert D. Benedict, *The Historical Position of the Rhodian Law,* 18 YALE L.J. 223 [1909].) Much later (c. 800 A.D.), there was a "Rhodian Sea Law," parts of which were incorporated in similar maritime codes. One such code, the "Rules of Oleron," was promulgated c.1266 A.D. by Eleanor of Acquitaine, France. Located in the Bay of Biscay just off the west coast of France, and about halfway between Brittany and Spain, the island of Oleron was an important part of inter-European Atlantic trade. A third group of island traders—from Visby, Sweden—also produced a codification of the customary rules of the sea. Visby's position on the island of Gotland, off the east coast of Sweden, helped to make it a center of the English/German/Russian trading done by the collection of cities known as the Hanseatic League. (Visby's influence on sea-law has continued into modern times, in the 1924 International Convention dealing with bills of lading, amended in 1968 as the "Hague-Visby Rules." Nearly 100 nations have adopted one or more of the three versions of this maritime rule-set, and it was also the basis for the English Carriage of Goods by Sea Act of 1971.)

Meanwhile, Roman jurists had been busy for several centuries, constructing the great Roman legal system. Founded in 753 BC, Rome was governed by a series of seven kings, the last being overthrown in 509 BC and replaced by the "Republic." The legal system was provided by unwritten custom, interpreted in specific cases by a limited set of patricians learned in the law. There was allegedly some feeling among the popular classes ("plebeians") that the law should be accessible to all citizens, and so in 451/450 BC a commission drafted a rudimentary legal code—the "Twelve Tables." The rules were then posted in the city's forum, for all to see. They applied only to citizens, and were more a restatement than a reform of the law.

Nevertheless, according to the editors of the *Encyclopedia Brittanica* (digital entry as of January 20, 2014), the stated rules for contract law and estate law had a "remarkable liberality for their time," "probably the result … of the progress that had been made in commercial customs in Rome…." The law for Roman citizens continued to develop, and came to be known as the "*ius civile*"—civil law.

More directly relevant for our purposes was the development by the third century BC of a second body of Roman law: the "*ius gentium*"—law of nations—applicable to relationships with and between non-citizens. The basic idea was to discover and apply the legal principles that were common to all "civilized" nations. The underlying assumption was that, if everyone (or nearly everyone) was using a particular legal rule, that rule must be basically fair—at least in the sense that the rule was producing desirable results. A rule's adoption by a wide variety of European, Asian and African cultures would seem to indicate that it was not based on any localized bias or developmental quirk. A next logical step would be to infer that such a universally-recognized rule was part of something necessary to our species' existence—a **"natural law,"** either of divine origin or capable of discovery via human reason. By the time empire-wide citizenship was granted in the third century AD, the *ius gentium* was also being applied to Roman citizens, and the two parts of Roman Law had become one unified system. It was then that this rule-set was codified as the *Corpus Juris Civilis*—in 534 AD—by Byzantine scholars, for the eastern Roman emperor Justinian.

The eastern Roman Empire lasted until 1453 AD, when the capital Byzantium-Constantinople-Istanbul was captured by the Ottoman Turks. The developed Roman law was thus available to the emerging nations of Europe during their formative years, for intellectual study and for actual use. Roman law was also used as the basis for the **"Law Merchant,"** which became a kind of alternate system for European traders doing business in other nations, particularly in England.

Shaw traces the beginnings of the "new approach to international law" back to the 1532 work of Francisco Vitoria—a professor of theology at the University of Salamanca, Spain: *De Indis*. Vitoria criticized Spanish treatment of South American natives on the basis that it violated the universal standards of international law. In 1625, the great Dutch jurist Hugo Grotius published *De Jure Belli ac Pacis* ("The Law of Wars and Peace"), for which he is generally regarded as the "father of International Law." (For the influence of his advocacy of freedom of the seas on the spice trade, and his role in negotiating the Anglo-Dutch truce in 1620, *see* Corn, *The Scents of Eden*, cited above—Chapters 11, 12 and 14.) This emphasis on the activities of nations and the relations between them continued through most of the next three centuries: **"public international law,"** as opposed to **"private international law"**—which was largely confined to questions of which nation's law applied to international commercial disputes, and where such disputes could be litigated. (To some extent, that emphasis continues to the present day: the 2014 third edition of Peter Stone's *EU Private International Law* is described on its Amazon webpage as dealing exclusively with choice of law and choice of forum questions.)

There were considerable efforts during the late nineteenth century and throughout the twentieth century to provide settlement mechanisms for nation-v-nation disputes, to limit armaments, to avoid war, and to regulate military tactics if war did occur. The First Hague Peace Conference in 1899, for example, set up the Permanent Court of Arbitration, and the Permanent Court for International Justice was established in 1920 by the League of Nations, pursuant to the Versailles Peace Treaty that ended World War I. Of course, neither of these "rational-settlement" mechanisms had the authority or the power to prevent the world wars that followed their creation. Neither did the various agreed-on (or imposed—by the Versailles Treaty—in the case of Germany) limits on armaments. Attempts to guarantee humane treatment of prisoners of war may have had some limited effect, but there are seemingly endless stories of savagery and atrocities—especially during World War II, and not necessarily confined to crimes against P.O.W.'s.

The war-crimes trials held by the victorious Allies in 1945-1949 (and in some nations both before and after those dates) established new principles of international law. Although criticized by some as "victors' justice," the rule by now seems well-agreed that individuals (including companies and their managers) can be held criminally responsible—under international law—for acts which violate basic principles of human conduct. As noted in Chapter II, *infra*, ad hoc international criminal courts were set up in the 1990's to deal with such occurrences in two nations, and over 100 countries indicated their approval of the creation of the permanent International Criminal Court ("ICC"). The ICC came into being in 2002, after 60 nations ratified the Rome Statute creating it, and it has been hearing cases and issuing arrest warrants against defendants.

Also created in 1945, of course, was the United Nations ("UN") itself, including the International Court of Justice ("ICJ"). (*See* Chapter II, *infra*.) Of the 51 original UN members, 37 were from Europe and the Americas. There are now 193 members, and relative voting strength in the UN's General Assembly has shifted significantly in favor of African and Asian nations. While the General Assembly does not have legislative authority in the traditional sense, its "resolutions" are generally seen as representing a consensus of the international community— and in that sense, evidence of international "custom." The ICJ's opinions are generally accepted as authoritative statements of international law, as for example the *Australia v. Japan* whaling case in Chapter V, *infra*. The UN is thus an ongoing source for the development of international law.

During the 40+ years of the Cold War, the main focus of the international system was directed to the prevention of the unimaginable horror of an all-out nuclear war. In addition to direct negotiations between the two major protagonists—the USA and the USSR (sometimes also including China, France and the UK), there were multi-nation agreements to try to limit the spread of nuclear weapons to additional nations. These latter efforts continue to the present day, as illustrated by the *New York Times* headline of April 3, 2015, announcing an international agreement limiting Iran's nuclear activities. As the Iran case illustrates, one of the difficulties in preventing access to nuclear weapons is the technological linkage to nuclear generation of electricity. Another point frequently raised is the seeming unfairness of having an exclusive nuclear club: "We've got ours, but you can't have yours." That perceived unfairness becomes even sharper if the nuclear-wannabe nation feels that it is being threatened by a sworn enemy that does have "the bomb."

In any event, the world has thus far managed to avoid nuclear war, although there have been some very close calls. Certainly the best-known of these was the Cuban Missile Crisis—the 13 days in October 1962 when it seemed that the USA and the USSR were headed for mutual annihilation. Thankfully, that high point of tension passed, and the crisis was resolved without nuclear war. That (unsuccessful) "nuclear adventurism" may have played a part in Nikita Khrushchev's replacement by Leonid Brezhnev in 1964. Brezhnev was supposedly a Khrushchev protégé, but he negotiated the Anti-Ballistic Missile Treaty and an Interim Agreement on Strategic Offensive Arms with President Richard Nixon in 1969, and signed the 1975 Helsinki Accords—with all the other European nations except Albania, plus the USA and Canada. The policy of *détente* between the USA and the USSR at the very least worked to reduce animosity between the two superpowers, and thus to lessen the possibility of nuclear war through accident or misunderstanding. Further "normalization" of the international system occurred in 1972, when President Nixon went to China to meet with Chairman Mao Tse-Tung and sign the world-changing agreement that led to China's re-establishment as a leading political and economic power.

A negotiated settlement signed in January 1973 finally ended the U.S. direct military involvement in the Vietnam War, and U.S. combat units were withdrawn. Standing alone, the South Vietnamese government was unable resist for long when hostilities recommenced. President Nixon had evidently promised the return of U.S. forces if necessary to enforce the terms of the agreement, but he had been forced to resign in August 1974, as a result of the "Watergate" scandal. The U.S. Congress had indicated its intent to prevent any re-engagement, and there seemed little popular support for such further U.S. involvement. North Vietnamese troops occupied the southern capital of Saigon in April 1975, and the country was at last reunified.

Even though Brezhnev was still the leader of the USSR when Ronald Reagan became the U.S. President in 1981, the Cold War seemed to be heating up again. Reagan's foreign policy seemed more solidly anti-communist, and he ratcheted up the USA's military expenditures and proposed new technological developments. His rhetoric was much stronger than his predecessor's, describing the USSR as an "evil empire" in a 1983 speech. At that point, Brezhnev having died in 1982, the General Secretary of the USSR Communist Party was Yuri Andropov, former head of the KGB (the Soviet Secret Police) and a key player in the brutal suppression of the 1956 Hungarian Revolution. It seemed as if there was to be a regression to earlier international face-offs. Andropov, however, died after a little more than a year as leader, and so did his immediate successor, Konstantin Chernenko. Chernenko was succeeded as General Secretary by Mikhail Gorbachev, a reformer. Reagan challenged Gorbachev even more directly than he had Brezhnev. In a speech in front of the Brandenberg Gate in Berlin, on June 12, 1987, Reagan used the Berlin Wall to symbolize the East/West divide: "General Secretary Gorbachev, if you seek peace, if you seek prosperity for the Soviet Union and Eastern Europe, if you seek liberalization, come here to this gate. Mr. Gorbachev, open this gate. Mr. Gorbachev, tear down this wall!" Less well-publicized, but also in the speech, was Reagan's proposal to end the arms race: "[T]oday we have within reach the possibility, not merely of limiting the growth of arms, but of eliminating, for the first time, an entire class of nuclear weapons from the face of the earth."

Sure enough, six months later (December 8, 1987), President Reagan and General Secretary Gorbachev signed the Intermediate-Range Nuclear Forces Treaty—in Washington, DC—eliminating their nations' intermediate-range missiles. And on November 9, 1989—some 29 months after the "tear-down" challenge—East Germany opened the Berlin Wall, and the Cold War was effectively over. Reagan was no longer President at that point, having been replaced by his Vice-President George H. W. Bush in January 1989. The (first) Bush presidency also saw the dissolution of the USSR in 1991, with the three Baltic SSRs (Estonia, Latvia, Lithuania) declaring their independence in September, and the other 12 SSRs ending the federation completely on December 26.

While the threat of nuclear war had been minimized—if not eliminated, new challenges faced the international community and its policy-makers. In August 1990, Iraq invaded, conquered, and then annexed Kuwait. Twelve UN resolutions demanding that Iraq withdraw from Kuwait were ignored. President Bush sent an ultimatum, demanding withdrawal by January 1991—otherwise there would be war. Eventually some 32 nations contributed personnel to the USA-led coalition that liberated Kuwait in about six weeks of fighting. Iraq's army was badly mauled, but Iraq retained its independence and Saddam Hussein remained in power.

The 1990s also saw major reoccurrences of genocide—in Bosnia in 1994 and in Rwanda in 1992; in each instance, as noted above, an ad hoc international criminal court was convened to hear charges against those responsible. There was a series of terrorist attacks: bombings of the World Trade Center in New York City in 1994 and a government building in Oklahoma City in 1995, and the 1995 discharge of deadly sarin nerve-gas in the Tokyo subway. The "nuclear club" added two members in 1998, as both India and Pakistan tested nuclear devices.

Year 2000—the much-feared "Y2K"—arrived without the world-wide computer meltdown anticipated by some forecasters. But on January 3 there was an attempted suicide attack on a U.S warship at the port of Aden, Yemen, and a successful attack there against the *USS Cole* on October 12. Then came 9/11/2001! An incredibly complex terrorist plot involved the hijacking of at least four large airliners, loaded with fuel for their scheduled flights across the USA. One plane was flown into each of the two towers of the World Trade Center in New York City, and one was flown against the military's Pentagon Building in Washington, DC; the fourth plane crashed in rural Pennsylvania as the passengers fought the hijackers for control. Over 2700 were killed as the twin towers of the WTC disintegrated, nearly 200 were killed at the Pentagon, and 40 passengers and crew died in the Pennsylvania crash.

Tracing responsibility for the 9/11 attacks to the al-Qaeda leader Osama bin Laden and his Taliban sponsors in Afghanistan, the USA—joined by the U.K. and eventually NATO and other nations—invaded Afghanistan in October 2001. With the assistance of the Afghan "Northern Alliance," the ouster of the Taliban government was achieved rather quickly, but the establishment of a democratic republic proved much more difficult. When NATO formally ended its military operations in December 2014, there were still questions about the long-term viability of the new Afghan government.

Long before that date, the USA (with some 39 allied nations) extended the conflict by invading Iraq on March 20, 2003—alleging that Iraq had "weapons of mass destruction" and was prepared to use them, and that perhaps Iraq was also partially responsible for the 9/11 attacks, due to president Saddam Hussein's sponsorship of al-Qaeda and Osama bin Laden. Once again, there was quick success against the government's conventional military forces, and President George W. Bush publicly declared "mission accomplished" on May 1. However, the presence of US and European troops occupying the country, and the lack of any real local government quickly led to guerilla attacks against the foreign military units and violence between the Sunnis and the Shiites (two competing branches of Islam). Extensive looting and destruction of cultural and other valuables also occurred. Saddam Hussein was captured in December 2003, tried in 2005-2006, and executed in 2006. Osama bin Laden was killed in Pakistan in 2011 by USA special forces. The USA officially withdrew (most of) its military forces in 2011, but the nature and survivability of the new Iraqi government is still not clear.

In addition to the continued violence in Afghanistan and Iraq, the new millennium saw periodic terrorist attacks in the Middle East and around the world. The popular tourist destination of Bali, Indonesia was targeted in 2002: over 200 dead and another 200+ injured, and again in 2005: 20 dead, over 100 injured. Bombs killed 56 and injured some 700 persons in London in 2005. Suicide bombers killed nearly 800 people in Mosul, Iraq in 2007. In 2009, Indonesia was hit yet again: the toll was 7 dead and over 50 injured in a bombing in its capital city, Jakarta. More recently, Islamic militants massacred 147 persons—mostly students—at Garissa University in Kenya in April 2015. International tensions were also heightened when North Korea conducted its first test of a nuclear device in 2006, and then related tests in subsequent years.

What seems to be the most serious threat to the post-Cold-War international system of trade and peaceful development involves the Ukraine and Russia. Using verbal justifications that sounded like a re-run of the 1930s, in March 2014 Russia invaded and annexed the Crimean peninsula—part of the sovereign nation of Ukraine. While the Crimea invasion was essentially bloodless, Russia was not satisfied and continued its aggression against its much smaller neighbor. Hostilities broke out in the eastern Ukraine, with some of the Russian minority population in revolt against the Ukrainian government. While Russia has denied involvement in this part of the dispute, the use of Russian military equipment seems to indicate rather clearly that there is an ongoing attempt to re-incorporate part or all of the Ukraine into a greater Russia. There is an eerie parallel to Hitler's policies toward the Rhineland, Austria, and Czechoslovakia prior to World War II. Thus far, at least, the world's response to this gross violation of international law has been the same sort of mystical blather epitomized by Neville Chamberlain at Munich, Germany in 1938.

There were high hopes that the inclusion of nearly all the nations in the United Nations, the World Trade Organization, and similar international bodies would be a basis for the avoidance of aggression and war. (*See, e.g.,* Chrystia Freeland, "Globalization Bites Back," *The Atlantic,* [May 2015], pp. 82-85.) For a time, those hopes seemed realistic, as both China and Russia joined, with most of the other nations. Russian President Putin has put these assumptions in serious doubt. (And there is similar international concern over some of the recent repressive policies adopted by China. *See, e.g.,* Evan Osnos, "Born Red," *The New Yorker,* [April 6, 2015], pp. 42-55; and Howard French, "China's Dangerous Game," *The Atlantic,* [November 2014], pp. 96-109.) Limited sanctions have been imposed against Russia, but they do not seem to be effective. Many European nations have a significant dependence on Russian oil and gas exports, and would be colder and darker if Russia retaliated against serious trade sanctions. International *Law*, it seems, is still very much subject to international *politics*—at least with respect to the conduct of large, powerful nations.

Sources.   As indicated by the very brief historical review above, the two major sources of international law are custom and treaties. The inter-relationship between these two major sources is rather complex, and is still subject to some uncertainty and debate—even after (at least) four millennia.

Custom, as used here, means the accepted norms of conduct in international relations. Originally, since international law had to do with dealings between and among nations, customary rules were discovered by examining the historical record to see what sorts of national behavior were accepted and expected. Custom was therefore the general rule-set that was applicable to all nations in their dealings with each other. A *treaty*, by contrast, is an agreement between two or more nations regulating the relationships between and among only those nations who signed it. A treaty might be used as a specific example of what the customary rule was, but it would presumably not by itself prove a customary rule—at least not unless it had so many signatory nations as to be a clear consensus on the point at issue. A treaty might also be an attempt by the signatory nations to specifically state and/or to clarify a customary rule; but again, it presumably would not *per se* be binding on non-signatories.

A treaty can also be used to change a customary rule; but once again, the change would be binding only between the signing nations—unless and until enough other nations had accepted the change so as to make it the new customary rule. There is one important exception to this "amendment by treaty" process: the international law concept of *jus cogens*. Just as in a "common-law" (case-law) system, where a statute can change a case-law rule but *cannot* change a constitutional rule, so also in international law, a treaty can change a customary rule, but cannot change a rule which is considered *jus cogens*—fundamental law. A treaty could not, for example, legitimize genocide or torture, or the unprovoked invasion of another nation.

Where there is no customary rule, the signatory parties could by treaty create an international rule which would be binding as between them as to all future relationships covered by the rule. This sort of treaty "legislation" seems particularly appropriate for situations where the treaty partners are attempting to promote trade by providing a uniform set of commercial rules among themselves, as with, for example, the United Nations Convention on Contracts for the International Sale of Goods ("UNC/CISG"). With some 200 separate nations existing, there are likely to be numerous differences on specific points of commercial law. To take just one instance: the domestic law in many nations provides that acceptances of contract offers become effective to form contracts only if and when received by the person making the offer; but the rule in some common-law nations (UK, USA, *et al.*) is that an acceptance is effective when sent. So UNC/CISG includes a provision resolving this conflict. (*See* Chapter III, *infra*.) UNC/CISG was prepared by the United Nations Commission on International Trade Law, a group created by the UN General Assembly in 1947 and tasked with the job of developing international law.

There are similar projects for other trade-law areas under development.

In addition to treaties and custom, Article 38 of the Statute creating the ICJ provides that the Court "shall apply ... c. the general principles of law recognized by civilized nations; d. subject to the provisions of Article 59, judicial decisions and the teachings of the most highly qualified publicists of the various nations, as subsidiary means for the determination of rules of law." Further, section 2 of Article 38 states: "This provision shall not prejudice the power of the Court to decide a case *ex aequo et bono*, if the parties agree thereto." Article 59 specifically repudiates the common-law **doctrine of precedent**: "The decision of the Court has no binding force except between the parties and in respect of that particular case." In other words, other courts hearing other cases are not required to follow a prior ICJ ruling in a similar case. The ICJ's reasoning in a prior case may or may not be persuasive in the eyes of another court. As noted above, an ICJ decision may be some evidence of a customary international-law rule for the type of issue involved.

What is meant by the phrase "**general principles of law**"? The intent of including this additional source is to provide a basis for deciding international cases not covered by a treaty and where there does not appear to be any operative international custom. Some commentators interpret the phrase as a reference to the fundamental rules underlying international law: national sovereignty, equality of nations, and the like. Others take it as meaning the universal legal truths embodied in an over-riding system of natural law (either discoverable by human reason or provided by a divine being): human dignity must be respected; war, killing and torture are always wrong; etc. Here again, whatever the theoretical underpinning, the actual use of a legal rule in a large assortment of nations would seem to indicate that the rule qualifies as a "general principle of law." The ICJ's 1970 decision in the *Barcelona Traction* case, excerpted in Chapter IV, provides one example of this last point. The ICJ used the widespread recognition of the separate legal personality of limited-liability companies in national laws as part of the basis for its decision.

Also in 1970, a resolution by the UN General Assembly reaffirmed the duty imposed on all UN members by Article 2(2) of the UN Charter to "fulfill in good faith the obligations assumed by them in accordance with the present Charter." As explained by the ICJ in 1988 and 1998 decisions, however, the "good faith" requirement does not of itself create any additional "obligations"; it merely requires good faith in the performance of already-existing obligations. To that extent, good faith operates as a general principle of law.

The inclusion of "**judicial decisions**" as a source seems clear enough. Although one might argue that "judicial decisions" was not intended to include arbitrators' rulings as well as those of courts, and rulings by national courts as well as those of the ICJ and PCIJ, it seems well established that both broader categories are included. As a practical matter, a strict interpretation of the phrase would not have provided very much of a supplementary resource, in view of the scarcity of "international court" rulings until quite recently. However, it is interesting that the Article 59 limitation on the binding effect of a judicial decision is exclusively applicable to decisions of "the Court," i.e., the ICJ. Common sense would seem to indicate that if decisions by the ICJ itself have no binding effect on future courts, neither should those of other courts. Arbitration decisions are generally not considered to have binding effects on future arbitrators anyway; they may or may not be persuasive examples of how the applicable international rule should be applied.

Similarly, "**teachings of publicists**"—textbooks and treatises on general and specialized international law topics—are not binding in specific disputes. They are, however, frequently used as source materials, as summaries of what practice has been, what specific decisions have been made, and what customs have been recognized. Some commentators' works are generally recognized as authoritative statements of the international rules of the game, such as those by Grotius and Vitoria—noted above. More recently, texts by Hersch Lauterpacht and Lassa Oppenheim have been influential.

Finally, section 2 of Article 38 of the ICJ Statute permits the Court to decide cases on the basis of its sense of **fundamental fairness**: "This provision shall not prejudice the power of the Court to decide a case *ex aequo et bono*, if the parties agree thereto." The key part of this sentence is the qualifying clause ("if…."); the grant to the Court of an extra measure of decision-making flexibility is important enough to require the specific assent of the parties. Of course, because of the indefiniteness inherent in International Law itself, the ICJ already has a considerable degree of discretion in arriving at a decision. The Court must decide what counts as evidence of a customary rule, whether there is enough such evidence to constitute such a rule, and then how the discovered rule applies to the facts of the case before it. Giving the Court the additional power to extend, modify—or disregard (?)—the legal rule, on the basis that it would not produce a "fair" result, should surely require the specific consent of both of the concerned parties. Just as Margaret Hungerford said (in her novel, *Molly Bawn*) that "beauty is in the eyes of the beholder," fairness is likely to be in the eyes of the judge—and quite different from judge to judge.

While supplementary sources discussed above are specifically listed for the ICJ, in its Statute, they are generally accepted means of determining the content and correct application of International Law. They are not all, however, specifically illustrated by our example cases.

EXAMPLE CASES PREVIEW:

REPUBLIC OF CROATIA & YUCYCO: The first two cases—from the Austrian Supreme Court and the U.S. District Court for the Southern District of New York—raise a classic international-law problem: the rights and liabilities of successor Nation-States. Where one Nation is succeeded by two or more new Nations, who owns the assets of the former Nation and who is liable for its debts? More precisely, for our immediate purposes, where do the deciding courts find the rules to decide these questions? (Note the impact of United Nations resolutions on the courts' analyses.) The "business" implications of these issues would seem to be obvious—at least to bankers and to holders of government bonds.

NOTTEBOHM: The *Nottebohm* case highlights the difference between national law and its effect, and international law and its effect. Each sovereign nation surely has the power to define for itself which persons it considers to be its "citizens"—and what the rights and duties of such persons are. Those "in-house" definitions, however, are not necessarily binding on other members of the international community. *International* law sets the standards for deciding the international effectiveness of "citizenship." Again, the relevance of such questions to our increasingly internationalized commercial world should be self-evident. Both human persons and "legal persons" (corporations and various other such forms) are doing business and transferring property in many Nations other than their "home" state.

LA JEUNE EUGENIE: The 1822 U.S. case involving the USA government seizure of the French-registered ship *La Jeune Eugenie* also demonstrates the national-law/international-law difference. International Law is something more than just the "lowest-common-denominator" of existing national laws. (Note Justice Story's use of what is generally called "Natural Law.")

KIOBEL: The *Kiobel* case deals with a uniquely-USA problem for international business. The very first Congress of the United States, as part of the Judiciary Act of 1789, passed what has come to be known as the Alien Tort Statute (or Alien Tort Claims Act). The ATS gives the U.S. District Courts the power to hear tort (civil injury) cases brought by aliens (non-USA persons), where the claim is based on violation of a treaty signed by the USA, or of "the law of nations" (i.e., international law). The question for U.S. courts thus becomes one of definition: what sorts of (alleged) conduct by businesses and their agents violates "the law of nations" so as to invoke the ATS and permit the use of the plaintiff-friendly USA court system?

CHILDREN OF THE CHIPPEWA: Just as is true for statutes passed by a legislature and rules adopted by an executive or administrative body, treaties need to be interpreted as to their application to specific factual contexts. Our first three selections illustrate the tremendous range of topics that are subject to treaties.

The various Native American tribes living in what became the USA were initially treated as foreign Nations (or at least analogous to such—at least for some purposes). Thus, numerous "treaties" were entered into between the USA and the various tribes. One such treaty produced the lawsuit against The University of Michigan. The Native American tribes asked the Michigan court to enforce the treaty involved—by imposing an obligation on the University to provide free education to the children of the treaty-tribes.

HONG KONG S.A.R.: The second treaty case involves the status of the "Common Law" which had (presumably) existed in the British Crown Colony of Hong Kong prior to its "return" to the People's Republic of China ("PRC"). Did the "Common Law" survive after the effective date of the PRC/UK treaty that provided for the return of sovereignty over Hong Kong to the PRC? (The case deals with a specific criminal liability, but surely there might be similar issues with respect to civil rights and liabilities.)

DIGITAL RIGHTS IRELAND: The third treaty example shows the impact of treaties on the national laws of the ratifying Nation-States, and ultimately, on the rights of individuals within them. It is generally assumed that a treaty should be given (at least) the same legal force as locally-adopted laws, and indeed, may be interpreted as superseding them. Failure to recognize and enforce the provisions of a treaty by agencies of a ratifying Nation-State would of course normally be a breach of the treaty/agreement. One of the most basic rules of International Law is "*Pacta sunt servanda*"—"Treaties must be observed." (The potential impact of this decision for the sellers and users of information technology is staggering!)

AIR FRANCE, STOVALL, CATHAY PACIFIC, ZICHERMAN, AQUINO: The next five cases all interpret the same multi-nation treaty—the Warsaw Convention. This sequence is intended to provide some appreciation of the depth involved in treaty interpretation. Millions of us fly internationally each year, for pleasure as well as for business reasons. Most such flights are covered by the Convention, and most of us are delivered to destination without adverse incident. But what if things do go wrong? The Philippine Supreme Court's decision in the *Cathay Pacific* case describes a classic "business-trip" problem—lost luggage. Does that decision seem consistent with those of the USA courts in the other four cases?

GOLDWATER: *Goldwater v. Carter* presents a USA-specific question on treaties: if the U.S. Senate has approved the treaty (by a required two-thirds majority vote), can the President, acting alone, terminate it? The treaty involved was a mutual-defense treaty, but the same rule applied there would presumably also apply to commercial treaties—NAFTA, for example. The stability of a nation's investment climate could be seriously disrupted if *one* decision-maker, acting alone, can drastically change the rules.

CASE EXAMPLES:

REPUBLIC OF CROATIA, ET AL. v.
GIROCREDIT BANK A.G. DER SPARKASSEN
4 Ob 2304/96v (Austrian Supreme Court) [trans. 36 I.L.M. 1520 (1997)]

BACKGROUND: The Socialist Federal Republic of Yugoslavia (SFRY) was dissolved in 1991, and succeeded by five nations—Bosnia-Herzegovina, Croatia, Macedonia, Slovenia, and a new "Federal Republic of Yugoslavia" (consisting of Serbia and Montenegro). The new Yugoslavia claimed to be a continuation of the old SFRY, and therefore the owner of all of its predecessor's state-owned property, including the funds on deposit in the Girocredit Bank in Austria. The Republic of Croatia and its national bank (plaintiffs one and two) and the Republic of Macedonia and its national bank (plaintiffs three and four) sued in the Austrian courts for an injunction against Girocredit Bank, to prevent its disbursing any funds to the FRY until the five successor nations had worked out a distribution agreement. The Vienna Commercial Court granted the injunction, and the Higher Provincial Court of Vienna affirmed that ruling. Girocredit Bank then appealed to the Supreme Court of Austria.

THE COURT: *(translation)*

"While the rights and obligations resulting from the banking contract itself are to be judged under the law of the place of the establishment of the credit institution ... i.e. under Austrian law, the question as to whether the assets invested by the National Bank of the SFRY in Austria were held by the National Bank as an independent legal entity or constituted State property (in terms of international Law) are to be assessed according to the then domestic law of the SFRY.

"It is in this sense that Art.8 of the 1983 'Vienna Convention on Succession of States in Respect of State Property, Archives and Debts', prepared by the International Law Commission, defines 'State property of the predecessor State' as property and rights which, at the date of the succession of States, were, according to the internal law of the predecessor State, owned by that State. The purpose of this codification was to formulate existing customary international law....

"The National Bank Act of the SFRY ... which is relevant for this question, shows that the National Bank of that State had to fulfill the typical tasks of a bank of issue.... The main objective of the activities of the then National Bank of the SFRY according to the National Bank Act of the SFRY was to secure monetary stability as well as to maintain liquidity towards foreign countries….

"Under Art. 17 of the SFRY National Bank Act, the National Bank of the SFRY, when purchasing or selling foreign exchange on the general foreign exchange market, had to act in conformity with federal laws and the prescribed monetary and foreign exchange policy of the State….

"The legal personality of the National Bank of the SFRY is defined in Art. 91 of said Act. It was a 'socialized' legal person, which is to be seen in contrast to a legal person under private law. Its organs were appointed by the Federal parliament and responsible to it. The Parliament also adopted the Statute of the National Bank as the basis of its organization…. The National Bank performed its activities in political dependence; it had no political autonomy. It was directly subject to political influence….

"All these provisions taken together show that the National Bank of the SFRY—although it enjoyed legal personality as a 'socialized company'—formed part of State property of the SFRY according to international law, which in the case of a 'dismembratio' has to be distributed among the successor States….

"While the Federal Republic of Yugoslavia considers itself to be the sole successor State to the SFRY and identical with it, the international community unanimously views the disintegration of the SFRY as a case of 'dismembratio'. In international law this means the complete dissolution of the predecessor State and replacement by several successor States….

"The opinion of the international community is expressed in the following documents: In Security Council Resolution 757 (1992) it was stated that the claim of the successor States of Serbia and Montenegro to continue automatically the membership of the former SFRY in the United Nations was not recognized. In Security Council Resolution 777 (1992) the view is expressed that the SFRY had ceased to exist, that there was no identity of the Federal Republic of Yugoslavia, consisting of Serbia and Montenegro, with the former State of the SFRY. The Federal Republic of Yugoslavia could not participate in the General Assembly of the United Nations and would have first to apply for membership….

"The Arbitration Commission set up by the Members of the European Community … also dealt with the question of State succession and in its Opinions No. 1, 8 and 10 (1992) held the view that the SFRY had been dissolved and had ceased to exist, that the Federal Republic of Yugoslavia was one of the successor States and not the sole legal successor. This view was also supported in a declaration of the European Political Cooperations of 20 July 1992 as well as the

EU Declaration of 9 April 1996 on the Recognition of the Federal Republic of Yugoslavia as a successor State.

"On the basis of this, Austria recognized the Federal Republic of Yugoslavia as one of the successor States of the SFRY and as an independent and sovereign Member of the community of States....

"In terms of international law, the disintegration of the SFRY therefore is to be regarded as a case of 'dismembration'. The SFRY as a subject of international law has ceased to exist; its State territory has been divided among five successor States, which have in the meantime been recognized by Austria.

"Under customary international law, in the case of 'dismembratio' State property is to be distributed according to the international principle of 'equity'.... In such a case Art. 18 of the [1983 Vienna Convention] provides for the passing of movable State property to the successor States in 'equitable proportions'. Thus, the successor States have an international law title to distribution recognized by the community of States....

"Also the EU Arbitration Commission ... states in its Opinion No. 9 that State property of the SFRY located in third countries must be distributed equitably among the successor States in accordance with an agreement to be reached among them....

"This right can be secured by an interim injunction according to S.381(1) of the Enforcement Code [of Austria]....

"However, only the first and third Plaintiffs in their capacity as legitimate successor States to the SFRY are to be regarded as members of this joint-ownership community.... Proof of the fact that the National Banks of Croatia and Macedonia are entitled to bring a claim against said funds and assets was ... not submitted by Plaintiffs.

"The [Defendant's] appeal for revision ... therefore had to be partly granted, i.e. with respect to the claims of the second and fourth Plaintiffs, and the latter's petition for an injunction had to be dismissed....

"The first and third Plaintiffs have fully prevailed, whereas the second and fourth Plaintiffs have lost.... Thus, the Defendant is entitled to compensation by the second and fourth Plaintiffs of half the costs of the appeal proceedings."

YUCYCO, LTD. v. REPUBLIC OF SLOVENIA, et al.
984 F. Supp. 209 (S.D. NY 1997)

BACKGROUND: Yucyco, Ltd., a Cyprus corporation, is the owner of $29.5 million in loans made to certain Yugoslavian banks and guaranteed by Yugoslavia under a refinancing agreement, the New Financing Agreement of 1988 (the "NFA"). In June 1996, after the dissolution of Yugoslavia and the creation of the five new republics, Slovenia agreed to assume a share of the former Yugoslavia's debts by offering creditors the opportunity to exchange a portion of their loans for newly-issued Slovenian obligations. Slovenia did so in an effort to normalize its relations with the world financial community. Certain creditors, however, were not permitted to participate in the exchange because they had been placed by the United States on a list of entities identified as connected with one of the other new republics, the Federal Republic of Yugoslavia ("Serbia-Montenegro"), which the United States had concluded presented a threat to the national security, foreign policy, and economy of the United States. Yucyco was one of these listed entities.

Yucyco commenced this action against Slovenia, the central bank of Slovenia (Banka Slovenije), four other Slovenian banks (Ljubljanska Banka d.d., Kreditna Banka Maribor d.d., Nova Ljubljanska Banka d.d., and Nova Kreditna Banka Maribor d.d.) (collectively, the "Slovenian defendants"), as well as Chase Manhattan Bank ("Chase"). Ljubljanska Banka d.d. and Kreditna Banka Maribor d.d. were original signatories to the NFA, and Nova Ljubljanska Banka d.d. and Nova Kreditna Banka Maribor d.d. are alleged to be their successors-in-interest. Chase is sued solely in its capacity as agent under the NFA; Yucyco asks the Court to order Chase to declare the loans in default and to accelerate the payment date.

Yucyco seeks to hold the Slovenia defendants liable for the $29.5 million in loans. Alternatively, it contends that the Slovenian defendants should be ordered to permit Yucyco to participate in the exchange on the same terms as other creditors under the NFA. Finally, Yucyco asserts an alternative claim for tortious interference with contract. The defendants move to dismiss the complaint.

JUDGE CHIN:

"Defendants insist that Yucyco's claims against Slovenia should be dismissed as a matter of law because (a) Slovenia is not and never has been a party to the NFA, and (b) whether Slovenia is liable under the Guaranty presents a nonjusticiable political question concerning the issue of state succession…. In response, Yucyco makes two principal arguments: first, Slovenia effectively became a party to the NFA through its actions in effecting the Exchange, and second, Slovenia is liable on the Guaranty and no political question is implicated….

"It is well established that a plaintiff in a breach of contract action 'may not assert a cause of action to recover damages for breach of contract against a party with whom it is not in privity.'... ('As a general rule, privity or its equivalent remains the predicate for imposing liability for nonperformance of contractual obligations.') Here, Yucyco acknowledges that Slovenia is not a signatory to the NFA, but contends that Slovenia transformed itself into an obligor under the NFA by playing an 'integral role' in the restructuring of the NFA debt and by assuming a portion of the debt....

"This argument fails. Slovenia's involvement in the Exchange is no basis for holding it liable under the NFA in general. Slovenia agreed to the terms of the Exchange and nothing more. It agreed to accept only a limited portion of the former Yugoslavia's obligations; it did not agree to assume any further obligations, under the NFA or otherwise. Because 'a non-signatory to a contract cannot be named as a defendant in a breach of contract action unless it has thereafter assumed or been assigned the contract,' plaintiff may not assert its NFA-based claims against Slovenia....

"Finally, Yucyco suggests in its papers in opposition to defendants' motions that Slovenia is liable for the actions of Slovenian Obligers on an alter ego or 'piercing the corporate veil' theory.... The argument must be rejected as well, for Yucyco did not allege such a theory in its amended complaint, and it is well-settled that a 'claim for relief "may not be amended by the briefs in opposition to a motion to dismiss".'... Nor has Yucyco offered sufficient facts to support such a claim. Although Slovenia was intimately involved in the Exchange, that fact alone does not suggest that Slovenia 'exercised general control over the day-to-day activities' of the Slovenian banks or that it engaged in conduct that would trigger alter ego liability.... In short, Yucyco has not sufficiently alleged a basis for a breach of contract claim against Slovenia under the NFA....

"Yucyco's claims against Slovenia based on the Guaranty similarly fail as a matter of law. Under principles of international law, a successor state such as Slovenia is not bound by its predecessor's agreements. Furthermore, Yucyco fails to allege any facts suggesting that Slovenia has voluntarily assumed Yugoslavia's financial duties under the Guaranty.

"'International law sharply distinguishes the succession of state, which may create a discontinuity of statehood, from a succession of government, which leaves statehood unaffected.'... Although a mere change in 'government, regime or ideology has no effect on that state's international rights and obligations ..., where one sovereign succeeds another, and a new state is created, the rights and obligations of the successor state are affected.'... A full successor state, unlike a state that has experienced a mere change in government or ideology, is not bound by the contracts executed by the former sovereign.... ('When the state ceases to exist, its capacities, rights, and duties terminate.'); … ('When part of a state becomes a new state, the new state does not succeed to the international agreements to which the predecessor state was party, unless, expressly or by implication, it accepts such agreements and the other party or parties thereto agree or acquiesce.')...

"In the instant case, Yucyco does not deny that Slovenia is one of five successor states to the now-dissolved Yugoslavia…. Slovenia clearly constitutes a successor state within the meaning of the law. The Yugoslav government did not merely see its power taken over by a new government. Rather, Yugoslavia has been dismembered, its boundaries have been dramatically redrawn, and multiple sovereigns exist where once there stood a single nation. There can be little doubt that Slovenia exists today 'because of the dismemberment of the state of which it had been a part.'…

"As a successor state, Slovenia is not legally bound by any contract executed by the former Yugoslavia unless Slovenia has voluntarily 'assumed' the responsibilities of the predecessor state and 'the other party or parties thereto agree or acquiesce.'…

"Yucyco does not allege that Slovenia has explicitly assumed Yugoslavia's role as NFA Guarantor. Indeed, the amended complaint is devoid of any such factual allegations. Because Slovenia does not automatically succeed Yugoslavia as NFA Guarantor and there are no indications that Slovenia has voluntarily substituted itself as NFA Guarantor, Yucyco is not in privity with this defendant.

"To the extent Yucyco now argues that Slovenia is liable for an 'equitable' share of the former state's obligations under the Guaranty, such a claim poses a nonjusticiable political question…. Courts have held that certain intractable issues involving state succession may pose such problems of justiciability….

"In the instant case, the Court lacks 'judicially discoverable and manageable standards for resolving' Yucyco's claims against Slovenia. While the international norm may arguably be that a successor state should be held liable for a share of its predecessor's liabilities, plaintiff has not offered any basis by which this Court may 'equitably' apportion Slovenia's liability, if any, under the Guaranty. Yucyco does not allege the existence of any controlling agreement, treaty, or similar instrument allocating the economic liabilities of the former nation under the Guaranty among the various successor states. As a result, this Court lacks 'satisfactory criteria for a judicial determination' of Yucyco's equitable claims against Slovenia…. Under the circumstances, I am unable to properly 'take into account . . . the property, rights and interests which pass to the successor States' to properly determine the fair share of debt that should be borne by Slovenia….

"In addition, without the benefit of such legal instruments, resolution of Yucyco's claims would require this Court to make policy determinations—including, for example, apportionment of responsibility among the five new republics—for which the Court is ill-suited and 'of a kind clearly for nonjudicial discretion.'… To the contrary, the settlement of foreign debts falls squarely within the ambit of the President's and Congress's constitutional authority…. This Court should not thrust itself into a role 'textually committed' to the political branches by the Constitution….

"In short, Yucyco is unable to state a claim against Slovenia under the Guaranty or the NFA. Accordingly, all claims against Slovenia must be dismissed….

"Defendants further argue that plaintiff has failed to plead any claims against Banka Slovenije. Plaintiff acknowledges that it has not articulated claims specific to this defendant. Instead, Yucyco argues that Banka Slovenije, as the Paying Agent during the Exchange, must be retained in the lawsuit because its 'presence may be necessary to afford Yucyco complete relief' in the event that this Court were to decide that Yucyco is entitled to participate in the transaction…. Construing the amended complaint liberally in plaintiff's favor, I conclude that Yucyco has failed to plead claims against Banka Slovenije….

"The Slovenian defendants seek dismissal of plaintiffs' fifth and sixth claims on the ground that NFA creditors are not entitled to immediate acceleration of their loans without approval of the Majority Creditors…. Defendants argue that acceleration is an unavailable remedy as consent by the creditors was neither sought nor granted in this case. Chase similarly contends that the fourth claim seeking an order 'directing the Agent [Chase] under the NFA to declare [an event of default and] . . . the Refinancing Loans outstanding to be . . . forthwith due and payable' … should be dismissed….

"Here, the plain terms of the NFA coupled with Yucyco's failure to obtain approval by the majority lenders preclude plaintiff from obtaining the relief it seeks. As plaintiff itself has acknowledged, the NFA does not provide a single creditor with the authority to unilaterally accelerate its loans…. Under the unambiguous provisions of the agreement, NFA creditors and their successors in interest have expressly given up their right to unilaterally declare an event of default or insist upon acceleration for failure to make payments….

"More important, Yucyco never even sought the creditors' approval for loan acceleration. Thus, the complaint provides no reasonable basis for believing that compliance with this provision was 'impossible,' especially during the period before the transaction was approved and consummated. Finally, while participating creditors surely would derive some benefit from the transaction, 'adverse' interest alone does not rise to the level of futility….

"Accordingly, Yucyco's fourth claim is dismissed in its entirety. Additionally, plaintiff's fifth and sixth claims are dismissed to the extent that Yucyco seeks immediate payment of its refinancing loans.

"Finally, the Slovenian defendants contend that Yucyco's alternative claim of tortious interference with contract should be dismissed on the grounds that (a) the FSIA bars the action because 28 U.S.C. § 1605(a)(5)(B) expressly immunizes foreign agencies or instrumentalities from any claim arising out of 'interference with contract rights'; (b) plaintiff pleads insufficient facts as to how the specific banks allegedly interfered with Yucyco's contractual rights under the NFA; and (c) to the extent the Slovenian banks did anything at all, they were protecting 'legitimate economic interests.' In response, plaintiff argues that defendants are not immune from suit because the alleged conduct at issue falls within the 'commercial activity' exception under 28 U.S.C. § 1605(a)(2), and that plaintiff has alleged sufficient facts to sustain a claim of tortious interference....

"The Slovenian defendants contend that Yucyco's claim is barred by Section 1605(a)(5)(b) even if the conduct in question constitutes 'commercial activity' within the meaning of Section 1605(a)(2). Section 1605(a)(5) provides in pertinent part that immunity shall not be afforded a sovereign entity in any case:

> not otherwise encompassed in paragraph (2) above, in which money damages are sought against a foreign state for personal injury or death, or damage to or loss of property, occurring in the United States and caused by the tortious act or omission of that foreign state or of any official or employee of that foreign state while acting within the scope of his office or employment; except this paragraph shall not apply to . . . (b) any claim arising out of malicious prosecution, abuse of process, libel, slander, misrepresentation, deceit, or interference with contract rights ....

In essence, defendants argue that subsection (a)(5)(b) serves as a double exception limiting not only subsection (a)(5) but also subsection (a)(2). In defendants' view, subsection (a)(5)(b) restores sovereign immunity as to all torts listed therein, and therefore no viable claim for interference with contract rights can ever be made against a foreign state, agency or instrumentality.

"Neither the Supreme Court nor the Second Circuit has ever explicitly decided whether the limitations in section 1605(a)(5)(b) restrict the 'commercial activity' exception in section 1605(a)(2). Although the language of the FSIA is far from clear, several factors suggest that the limitations on sovereign liability in subsection (a)(5)(b) apply only to noncommercial torts.

"First, subsection (a)(5) expressly states that its provisions apply to torts 'not otherwise encompassed' in subsection (a)(2)—in other words, commercial torts. Hence, subsection (a)(5) provides an exception to sovereign immunity solely for noncommercial torts....

"Second, most courts have interpreted the various exceptions to immunity set forth in section 1605 as mutually exclusive....

"Third, numerous courts, including those in this Circuit, have addressed tort claims involving commercial activity under subsection (a)(2) without finding that subsection (a)(5)(b) posed any particular difficulties....

"For all of these reasons, I conclude that the language of section 1605(a)(5) does not limit the commercial activity exception to sovereign immunity. Consequently, Section 1605(a)(5)(b) does not preclude plaintiff's tortious interference claim....

"The next question is whether Yucyco has alleged with sufficient particularity facts supporting its claim of tortious interference.... Construing all reasonable inferences in plaintiff's favor, I hold that Yucyco has failed to plead sufficient facts to sustain its tortious interference claim. Neither side disputes the existence of the NFA as a valid contract or defendants' awareness of the agreement.... And, of course, Yucyco claims that it suffered damages as a result of defendants' allegedly tortious conduct. Nevertheless, plaintiff does not allege facts that, if true, would demonstrate an 'intentional procuring' of a breach of contract.... Yucyco fails to support [its] assertion by specifying which defendants intentionally procured such a breach and describing the conduct of each defendant allegedly 'inducing' the parties to breach their obligations.... Without such critical details, the amended complaint merely alleges that the remaining Slovenian defendants are 'responsible for negotiating and proposing' the Exchange.... Assuming the allegation to be true, this fact alone would fail to establish that the Slovenian banks intentionally procured a breach of contract. Yucyco's tortious interference claim is therefore inadequately pled and must be dismissed....

"For the foregoing reasons, the Slovenian defendants' motion is granted in part and denied in part. Chase's motion is granted in all respects. Because no claims remain against Slovenia, Banka Slovenije, or Chase, these parties are dismissed from the action. The claims for acceleration are also dismissed. The only claims that remain are the breach of contract and breach of good faith claims contained in the first, second, fifth, and sixth causes of action against Ljubljanska Banka d.d., Kreditna Banka Maribor d.d., Nova Ljubljanska Banka d.d., and Nova Kreditna Banka Maribor d.d. Plaintiff is granted leave to replead the seventh cause of action within 20 days hereof.

NOTTEBOHM CASE (LIECHTENSTEIN v. GUATEMALA)
I.C.J. Reports 1955, p. 4

BACKGROUND: By the Application filed on December 17, 1951, the Government of Liechtenstein instituted proceedings before the Court in which it claimed restitution and compensation on the ground that the Government of Guatemala had "acted towards the person and property of Mr. Friedrich Nottebohm, a citizen of Liechtenstein, in a manner contrary to international law." In its Counter-Memorial, the Government of Guatemala contended that this claim was inadmissible on a number of grounds, and one of its objections to the admissibility of the claim related to the nationality of the person for whose protection Liechtenstein had applied to the Court.

Guatemala has referred to a well-established principle of international law that "it is the bond of nationality between the State and the individual which alone confers upon the State the right of diplomatic protection." This sentence is taken from a Judgment of the Permanent Court of International Justice, which relates to the form of diplomatic protection constituted by international judicial proceedings. Liechtenstein considers itself to be acting in conformity with this principle and contends that Nottebohm is its national by virtue of the naturalization conferred upon him.

Nottebohm was born at Hamburg on September 16, 1881. He was German by birth, and still possessed German nationality when, in October 1939, he applied for naturalization in Liechtenstein. In 1905 he went to Guatemala. He took up residence there and made that country the headquarters of his business activities. Having been an employee in the firm of Nottebohm Hermanos, which had been founded by his brothers Juan and Arturo, he became their partner in 1912 and later, in 1937, he was made head of the firm. After 1905 he sometimes went to Germany on business and to other countries for holidays. He continued to have business connections in Germany. He paid a few visits to a brother who had lived in Liechtenstein since 1931. Some of his other brothers, relatives and friends were in Germany, others in Guatemala. He himself continued to have his fixed abode in Guatemala until 1943, that is to say, until the occurrence of the events which constitute the basis of the present dispute.

In 1939, after having provided for the safeguarding of his interests in Guatemala by a power of attorney given to the firm of Nottebohm Hermanos on March 22, he left that country at a date fixed by Counsel for Liechtenstein as at approximately the end of March or the beginning of April, when he seems to have gone to Hamburg, and later to have paid a few brief visits to Vaduz, Liechtenstein where he was at the beginning of October 1939. It was then, on October 9th, a little more than a month after the opening of the second World War marked by Germany's attack on Poland, that his attorney, Dr. Marxer, submitted an application for naturalization on behalf of Nottebohm.

The Liechtenstein Law of January 4th, 1934, lays down the conditions for the naturalization of foreigners, specifies the supporting documents to be submitted and the undertakings to be given and defines the competent organs for giving a decision and the procedure to be followed. The Law specifies certain mandatory requirements, namely, that the applicant for naturalization should prove: (1) "that the acceptance into the Home Corporation … of a Liechtenstein commune has been promised to him in case of acquisition of the nationality of the State"; (2) that he will lose his former nationality as a result of naturalization, although this requirement may be waived under stated conditions. It further makes naturalization conditional upon compliance with the requirement of residence for at least three years in the territory of the Principality, although it is provided that "this requirement can be dispensed with in circumstances deserving special consideration and by way of exception." In addition, the applicant for naturalization is required to submit a number of documents, such as evidence of his residence in the territory of the Principality, a certificate of good conduct issued by the competent authority of the place of residence, documents relating to his property and income and, if he is not a resident in the Principality, proof that he has concluded an agreement with the Revenue authorities, "subsequent to the revenue commission of the presumptive home commune having been heard." The Law further provides for the payment by the applicant of a naturalization fee, which is fixed by the Princely Government and amounts to at least one half of the sum payable by the applicant for reception into the Home Corporation of a Liechtenstein commune, the promise of such reception constituting a condition under the Law for the grant of naturalization.

As to the consideration of the application by the competent organs and the procedure to be followed by them, the Law provides that the Government, after having examined the application and the documents pertaining thereto, and after having obtained satisfactory information concerning the applicant, shall submit the application to the Diet. If the latter approves the application, the Government shall submit the requisite request to the Prince, who alone is entitled to confer nationality of the Principality. Finally, the Law empowers the Princely Government, within a period of five years from the date of naturalization, to withdraw Liechtenstein nationality from any person who may have acquired it if it appears that the requirements laid down in the Law were not satisfied; it likewise provides that the Government may at any time deprive a person of his nationality if the naturalization was fraudulently obtained.

A document dated October 15, 1939, certifies that on that date the Commune of Mauren conferred the privilege of its citizenship upon Mr. Nottebohm and requested the Government to transmit it to the Diet for approval. A certificate of October 17, 1939, evidences the payment of the taxes required to be paid by Mr. Nottebohm. On October 20, 1939, Mr. Nottebohm took the oath of allegiance, and a final arrangement concerning liability to taxation was concluded on October 23. A certificate of nationality has also been produced, signed on behalf of the Government of the Principality and dated October 20, 1939, to the effect that Nottebohm was naturalized by Supreme Resolution of the Reigning Prince dated October 13, 1939. Having obtained a Liechtenstein passport, Nottebohm had it visa-ed by the Consul General of Guatemala in Zurich on December 1, 1939, and he returned to Guatemala at the beginning of 1940, where he resumed his former business activities and in particular the management of the firm Nottebohm Hermanos.

THE COURT:

"The Law reveals concern that naturalization should only be granted with knowledge of all the pertinent facts, in that it expressly provides for an enquiry into the relations of the applicant with the country of his former nationality, as well as into all other personal and family circumstances, and adds that 'the grant of nationality is barred where these relations and circumstances are such as to cause apprehension that prejudice of any kind may enure to the State by reason of the admission to nationality'....

"The Court does not propose to go beyond the limited scope of the question which it has to decide, namely whether the nationality conferred on Nottebohm can be relied upon as against Guatemala in justification of the proceedings instituted before the Court. It must decide this question on the basis of international law; to do so is consistent with the nature of the question and with the nature of the Court's own function....

"Since no proof has been adduced that Guatemala has recognized the title to the exercise of protection relied upon by Liechtenstein as being derived from the naturalization which it granted to Nottebohm, the Court must consider whether such an act of granting nationality by Liechtenstein directly entails an obligation on the part of Guatemala to recognize its effect, namely, Liechtenstein's right to exercise its protection. In other words, it must be determined whether that unilateral act by Liechtenstein is one which can be relied upon against Guatemala in regard to the exercise of protection. The Court will deal with this question without considering that of the validity of Nottebohm's naturalization according to the law of Liechtenstein.

"It is for Liechtenstein, as it is for every sovereign State, to settle by its own legislation the rules relating to the acquisition of its nationality, and to confer that nationality by naturalization granted by its own organs in accordance with that legislation. It is not necessary to determine whether international law imposes any limitations on its freedom of decision in this domain. Furthermore, nationality has its most immediate, its most far-reaching and, for most people, its only effects within the legal system of the State conferring it. Nationality serves above all to determine that the person upon whom it is conferred enjoys the rights and is bound by the obligations which the law of the State in question grants to or imposes on its nationals. This is implied in the wider concept that nationality is within the domestic jurisdiction of the State.

"But the issue which the Court must decide is not one which pertains to the legal system of Liechtenstein. It does not depend on the law or on the decision of Liechtenstein whether that State is entitled to exercise its protection, in the case under consideration. To exercise protection, to apply to the Court, is to place oneself on the plane of international law. It is international law which determines whether a State is entitled to exercise protection and to seise the Court.

"The naturalization of Nottebohm was an act performed by Liechtenstein in the exercise of its domestic jurisdiction. The question to be decided is whether that act has the international effect here under consideration.

"International practice provides many examples of acts performed by States in the exercise of their domestic jurisdiction which do not necessarily or automatically have international effect, which are not necessarily and automatically binding on other States or which are binding on them only subject to certain conditions: this is the case, for instance, of a judgment given by the competent court of a State which it is sought to invoke in another State….

"Naturalization is not a matter to be taken lightly. To seek and to obtain it is not something that happens frequently in the life of a human being. It involves his breaking of a bond of allegiance and his establishment of a new bond of allegiance. It may have far-reaching consequences and involve profound changes in the destiny of the individual who obtains it. It concerns him personally, and to consider it only from the point of view of its repercussions with regard to his property would be to misunderstand its profound significance. In order to appraise its international effect, it is impossible to disregard the circumstances in which it was conferred, the serious character which attaches to it, the real and effective, and not merely the verbal preference of the individual seeking it for the country which grants it to him.

"At the time of his naturalization does Nottebohm appear to have been more closely attached by his tradition, his establishment, his interests, his activities, his family ties, his intentions for the near future to Liechtenstein than to any other State?...

"At the date when he applied for naturalization Nottebohm had been a German national from the time of his birth. He had always retained his connections with members of his family who had remained in Germany and he had always had business connections with that country. His country had been at war for more than a month, and there is nothing to indicate that the application for naturalization then made by Nottebohm was motivated by any desire to dissociate himself from the Government of his country.

"He had been settled in Guatemala for 34 years. He had carried on his activities there. It was the main seat of his interests. He returned there shortly after his naturalization, and it remained the centre of his interests and of his business activities. He stayed there until his removal as a result of war measures in 1943. He subsequently attempted to return there, and he now complains of Guatemala's refusal to admit him. There, too, were several members of his family who sought to safeguard his interests.

"In contrast, his actual connections with Liechtenstein were extremely tenuous. No settled abode, no prolonged residence in that country at the time of his application for naturalization: the application indicates that he was paying a visit there and confirms the transient character of this visit by its request that the naturalization proceedings should be initiated and concluded without delay. No intention of settling there was shown at that time or realized in the ensuing weeks, months or years-on the contrary, he returned to Guatemala very shortly after his naturalization and showed every intention of remaining there. If Nottebohm went to Liechtenstein in 1946, this was because of the refusal of Guatemala to admit him. No indication is given of the grounds warranting the waiver of the condition of residence, required by the 1934 Nationality Law, which waiver was implicitly granted to him. There is no allegation of any economic interests or of any activities exercised or to be exercised in Liechtenstein, and no manifestation of any intention whatsoever to transfer all or some of his interests and his business activities to Liechtenstein. It is unnecessary in this connection to attribute much importance to the promise to pay the taxes levied at the time of his naturalization. The only links to be discovered between the Principality and Nottebohm are the short sojourns already referred to and the presence in Vaduz of one of his brothers: but his brother's presence is referred to in his application for naturalization only as a reference to his good conduct. Furthermore, other members of his family have asserted Nottebohm's desire to spend his old age in Guatemala.

"These facts clearly establish, on the one hand, the absence of any bond of attachment between Nottebohm and Liechtenstein and, on the other hand, the existence of a long-standing and close connection between him and Guatemala, a link which his naturalization in no way weakened. That naturalization was not based on any real prior connection with Liechtenstein, nor did it in any way alter the manner of life of the person upon whom it was conferred in exceptional circumstances of speed and accommodation. In both respects, it was lacking in the genuineness requisite to an act of such importance, if it is to be entitled to be respected by a State in the position of Guatemala. It was granted without regard to the concept of nationality adopted in international relations.

"Naturalization was asked for not so much for the purpose of obtaining a legal recognition of

Nottebohm's membership in fact in the population of Liechtenstein, as it was to enable him to substitute for his status as a national of a belligerent State that of a national of a neutral State, with the sole aim of thus coming within the protection of Liechtenstein but not of becoming wedded to its traditions, its interests, its way of life or of assuming the obligations-other than fiscal obligations-and exercising the rights pertaining to the status thus acquired.

"Guatemala is under no obligation to recognize a nationality granted in such circumstances. Liechtenstein consequently is not entitled to extend its protection to Nottebohm vis-a-vis Guatemala and its claim must, for this reason, be held to be inadmissible....

"*For these reasons,*

"THE COURT, by eleven votes to three,

"Holds that the claim submitted by the Government of the Principality of Liechtenstein is inadmissible.

"Done in French and English, the French text being authoritative, at the Peace Palace, The Hague, this sixth day of April, one thousand nine hundred and fifty-five, in three copies, one of which will be placed in the archives of the Court and the others will be transmitted to the Government of the Principality of Liechtenstein and to the Government of the Republic of Guatemala, respectively.

(Signed) GREEN H. HACKWORTH, President.

(Signed) J.LOPEZ OJIVAN, Registrar."

UNITED STATES v. SCHOONER *LA JEUNE EUGENIE*
26 F.Cas. 832 (Cir.Ct. MA 1822)

BACKGROUND: A U.S. warship seized the French-owned schooner *La Jeune Eugenie* off the coast of Africa, and brought it to the USA. The U.S. government filed an action in a USA national court to forfeit ownership of the ship because it was being used for criminal activity—transporting slaves from Africa. The French owners claimed that only a French court could decide—using French law—whether the ship should be forfeited because it was being used for criminal activity. The United States government claimed that USA courts had jurisdiction because slavery violated the "Law of Nations" as well as French national law.

JUSTICE STORY:

"[T]he first question naturally arising out of the asserted facts is, whether the African slave trade be prohibited by the law of nations; for, if it be so, it will not, I presume, be denied, that confiscation of the property rights ought to follow, for that is the proper penalty denounced by that law for any violation of its precepts....

"I shall take up no time in the examination of the history of slavery, or of the question, how far it is consistent with the natural rights of mankind.... That it has existed in all ages of the world, and has been tolerated by some, encouraged by others, and sanctioned by most, of the enlightened and civilized nations of the earth in former ages, admits of no reasonable question. That it has interwoven itself into the municipal institutions of some countries, and forms the foundation of large masses of property in a portion of our own country, is known to all of us. Sitting, therefore, in an American court of judicature, I am not permitted to deny, that under some circumstances it may have a lawful existence; and that the practice may be justified by the condition, or wants, of society, or may form a part of the domestic policy of a nation.... But this concession carries us but a very short distance towards the decision of this cause. It is not, as the learned counsel for the government have justly stated, on account of the simple fact that the traffic necessarily involves the enslavement of human beings, that it stands reprehended by the present sense of nations; but that it necessarily carries with it a breach of all the moral duties, of all the maxims of justice, mercy, and humanity, and of the admitted rights, which independent Christian nations now hold sacred....

"Now the law of nations may be deduced, first, from the general principles of right and justice, applied to the concerns of individuals, and thence to the relations and duties of nations; or, secondly, in things indifferent or questionable, from the customary observances and recognitions of civilized nations; or, lastly, from the conventional or positive law, that regulates intercourse between states.... [N]o practice ... can obliterate the fundamental distinction between right and wrong....

"[T]he African slave trade ... is repugnant to the great principles of Christian duty, the dictates of natural religion, the obligations of good faith and morality, and the eternal maxims of social justice.

"After listening to the very able, eloquent, and learned arguments delivered at the bar on this occasion—after weighing the authorities, which bear on the case, with mature deliberation—after reflecting anxiously and carefully upon the general principles, which may be drawn from the law of nations to illustrate or confirm them, I have come to the conclusion, that the slave trade is a trade prohibited by universal law, and by the law of France, and that, therefore, the claim of the asserted French owners must be rejected. That claim being rejected, I feel myself at perfect liberty, with the express consent of our own government, to decree, that the property be delivered over to the consular agent of the king of France, to be dealt with according to his own sense of duty and right."

KIOBEL et al. v. ROYAL DUTCH PETROLEUM CO. et al.
133 S. Ct. 1659 (2013)

BACKGROUND: Petitioners, a group of Nigerian nationals residing in the United States, filed suit in federal court against certain Dutch, British, and Nigerian corporations. Petitioners were residents of Ogoniland, an area of 250 square miles located in the Niger delta area of Nigeria and populated by roughly half a million people. When the complaint was filed, Royal Dutch Petroleum Company and Shell Transport and Trading, p.l.c., were holding companies incorporated in the Netherlands and England, respectively. Their joint subsidiary, respondent Shell Petroleum Development Company of Nigeria, Ltd. (SPDC), was incorporated in Nigeria, and engaged in oil exploration and production in Ogoniland. According to the complaint, after concerned residents of Ogoniland began protesting the environmental effects of SPDC's practices, respondents enlisted the Nigerian Government to violently suppress the burgeoning demonstrations. Throughout the early 1990's, the complaint alleges, Nigerian military and police forces attacked Ogoni villages, beating, raping, killing, and arresting residents and destroying or looting property. Petitioners further allege that respondents aided and abetted these atrocities by, among other things, providing the Nigerian forces with food, transportation, and compensation, as well as by allowing the Nigerian military to use respondents' property as a staging ground for attacks. Following the alleged atrocities, petitioners moved to the United States where they have been granted political asylum and now reside as legal residents.

Petitioners sued under the Alien Tort Statute, 28 U.S.C. § 1350, alleging that the corporations aided and abetted the Nigerian Government in committing violations of the law of nations in Nigeria. The United States Court of Appeals for the Second Circuit dismissed the complaint, reasoning that the law of nations did not recognize corporate liability. Certiorari was granted.

CHIEF JUSTICE ROBERTS:

"… The question presented is whether and under what circumstances courts may recognize a cause of action under the Alien Tort Statute, for violations of the law of nations occurring within the territory of a sovereign other than the United States….

"The ATS provides, in full, that '[t]he district courts shall have original jurisdiction of any civil action by an alien for a tort only, committed in violation of the law of nations or a treaty of the United States.' According to petitioners, respondents violated the law of nations by aiding and abetting the Nigerian Government in committing (1) extrajudicial killings; (2) crimes against humanity; (3) torture and cruel treatment; (4) arbitrary arrest and detention; (5) violations of the rights to life, liberty, security, and association; (6) forced exile; and (7) property destruction. The District Court dismissed the first, fifth, sixth, and seventh claims, reasoning that the facts alleged to support those claims did not give rise to a violation of the law of nations. The court denied respondents' motion to dismiss with respect to the remaining claims, but certified its order for interlocutory appeal pursuant to §1292(b).

"The Second Circuit dismissed the entire complaint, reasoning that the law of nations does not recognize corporate liability…. We granted certiorari to consider that question…. After oral argument, we directed the parties to file supplemental briefs addressing an additional question: 'Whether and under what circumstances the [ATS] allows courts to recognize a cause of action for violations of the law of nations occurring within the territory of a sovereign other than the United States.'… We heard oral argument again and now affirm the judgment below, based on our answer to the second question….

"Passed as part of the Judiciary Act of 1789, the ATS was invoked twice in the late 18th century, but then only once more over the next 167 years…. The statute provides district courts with jurisdiction to hear certain claims, but does not expressly provide any causes of action. We held in *Sosa* v. *Alvarez-Machain* … however, that the First Congress did not intend the provision to be 'stillborn.' The grant of jurisdiction is instead 'best read as having been enacted on the understanding that the common law would provide a cause of action for [a] modest number of international law violations.'… We thus held that federal courts may 'recognize private claims [for such violations] under federal common law.'… The Court in *Sosa* rejected the plaintiff's claim in that case for 'arbitrary arrest and detention,' on the ground that it failed to state a violation of the law of nations with the requisite 'definite content and acceptance among civilized nations.'…

"The question here is not whether petitioners have stated a proper claim under the ATS, but whether a claim may reach conduct occurring in the territory of a foreign sovereign. Respondents contend that claims under the ATS do not, relying primarily on a canon of statutory interpretation known as the presumption against extraterritorial application. That canon provides that '[w]hen a statute gives no clear indication of an extraterritorial application, it has none,' …

"This presumption 'serves to protect against unintended clashes between our laws and those of other nations which could result in international discord.'… As this Court has explained:

'For us to run interference in . . . a delicate field of international relations there must be present the affirmative intention of the Congress clearly expressed. It alone has the facilities necessary to make fairly such an important policy decision where the possibilities of international discord are so evident and retaliative action so certain.'... The presumption against extraterritorial application helps ensure that the Judiciary does not erroneously adopt an interpretation of U.S. law that carries foreign policy consequences not clearly intended by the political branches.

"We typically apply the presumption to discern whether an Act of Congress regulating conduct applies abroad.... The ATS, on the other hand, is 'strictly jurisdictional.'... It does not directly regulate conduct or afford relief. It instead allows federal courts to recognize certain causes of action based on sufficiently definite norms of international law. But we think the principles underlying the canon of interpretation similarly constrain courts considering causes of action that may be brought under the ATS.

"Indeed, the danger of unwarranted judicial interference in the conduct of foreign policy is magnified in the context of the ATS, because the question is not what Congress has done but instead what courts may do. This Court in *Sosa* repeatedly stressed the need for judicial caution in considering which claims could be brought under the ATS, in light of foreign policy concerns. As the Court explained, 'the potential [foreign policy] implications . . . of recognizing . . . . causes [under the ATS] should make courts particularly wary of impinging on the discretion of the Legislative and Executive Branches in managing foreign affairs.'... (Since many attempts by federal courts to craft remedies for the violation of new norms of international law would raise risks of adverse foreign policy consequences, they should be undertaken, if at all, with great caution.) ('[T]he possible collateral consequences of making international rules privately actionable argue for judicial caution.') These concerns, which are implicated in any case arising under the ATS, are all the more pressing when the question is whether a cause of action under the ATS reaches conduct within the territory of another sovereign.

"These concerns are not diminished by the fact that *Sosa* limited federal courts to recognizing causes of action only for alleged violations of international law norms that are 'specific, universal, and obligatory.'... As demonstrated by Congress's enactment of the Torture Victim Protection Act of 1991 ... identifying such a norm is only the beginning of defining a cause of action.... Each of these decisions carries with it significant foreign policy implications.

"The principles underlying the presumption against extraterritoriality thus constrain courts exercising their power under the ATS....

"Petitioners contend that even if the presumption applies, the text, history, and purposes of the

ATS rebut it for causes of action brought under that statute. It is true that Congress, even in a jurisdictional provision, can indicate that it intends federal law to apply to conduct occurring abroad…. But to rebut the presumption, the ATS would need to evince a 'clear indication of extraterritoriality.'… It does not.

"To begin, nothing in the text of the statute suggests that Congress intended causes of action recognized under it to have extraterritorial reach. The ATS covers actions by aliens for violations of the law of nations, but that does not imply extraterritorial reach—such violations affecting aliens can occur either within or outside the United States. Nor does the fact that the text reaches '*any* civil action' suggest application to torts committed abroad; it is well established that generic terms like 'any' or 'every' do not rebut the presumption against extraterritoriality….

"Petitioners make much of the fact that the ATS provides jurisdiction over civil actions for 'torts' in violation of the law of nations. They claim that in using that word, the First Congress 'necessarily meant to provide for jurisdiction over extraterritorial transitory torts that could arise on foreign soil.'… For support, they cite the common-law doctrine that allowed courts to assume jurisdiction over such 'transitory torts,' including actions for personal injury, arising abroad….

"Under the transitory torts doctrine, however, 'the only justification for allowing a party to recover when the cause of action arose in another civilized jurisdiction is a well founded belief that it was a cause of action in that place."'… The question under *Sosa* is not whether a federal court has jurisdiction to entertain a cause of action provided by foreign or even international law. The question is instead whether the court has authority to recognize a cause of action under U.S. law to enforce a norm of international law. The reference to 'tort' does not demonstrate that the First Congress 'necessarily meant' for those causes of action to reach conduct in the territory of a foreign sovereign. In the end, nothing in the text of the ATS evinces the requisite clear indication of extraterritoriality.

"Nor does the historical background against which the ATS was enacted overcome the presumption against application to conduct in the territory of another sovereign…. We explained in *Sosa* that when Congress passed the ATS, 'three principal offenses against the law of nations' had been identified by Blackstone: violation of safe conducts, infringement of the rights of ambassadors, and piracy.'… The first two offenses have no necessary extraterritorial application….

"Two notorious episodes involving violations of the law of nations occurred in the United States shortly before passage of the ATS. Each concerned the rights of ambassadors, and each involved conduct within the Union. In 1784, a French adventurer verbally and physically assaulted Francis Barbe Marbois—the Secretary of the French Legion—in Philadelphia. The assault led the French

Minister Plenipotentiary to lodge a formal protest with the Continental Congress and threaten to leave the country unless an adequate remedy were provided.... And in 1787, a New York constable entered the Dutch Ambassador's house and arrested one of his domestic servants.... At the request of Secretary of Foreign Affairs John Jay, the Mayor of New York City arrested the constable in turn, but cautioned that because 'neither Congress nor our [State] Legislature have yet passed any act respecting a breach of the privileges of Ambassadors,' the extent of any available relief would depend on the common law.... The two cases in which the ATS was invoked shortly after its passage also concerned conduct within the territory of the United States....

"These prominent contemporary examples—immediately before and after passage of the ATS— provide no support for the proposition that Congress expected causes of action to be brought under the statute for violations of the law of nations occurring abroad.

"The third example of a violation of the law of nations familiar to the Congress that enacted the ATS was piracy. Piracy typically occurs on the high seas, beyond the territorial jurisdiction of the United States or any other country. ('The offence of piracy, by common law, consists of committing those acts of robbery and depredation upon the high seas, which, if committed upon land, would have amounted to felony there.') This Court has generally treated the high seas the same as foreign soil for purposes of the presumption against extraterritorial application.... Petitioners contend that because Congress surely intended the ATS to provide jurisdiction for actions against pirates, it necessarily anticipated the statute would apply to conduct occurring abroad.

"Applying U.S. law to pirates, however, does not typically impose the sovereign will of the United States onto conduct occurring within the territorial jurisdiction of another sovereign, and therefore carries less direct foreign policy consequences. Pirates were fair game wherever found, by any nation, because they generally did not operate within any jurisdiction.... We do not think that the existence of a cause of action against them is a sufficient basis for concluding that other causes of action under the ATS reach conduct that does occur within the territory of another sovereign; pirates may well be a category unto themselves....

"Finally, there is no indication that the ATS was passed to make the United States a uniquely hospitable forum for the enforcement of international norms. As Justice Story put it, 'No nation has ever yet pretended to be the custos morum of the whole world.... *United States* v. *The La Jeune Eugenie*.... It is implausible to suppose that the First Congress wanted their fledgling Republic—struggling to receive international recognition—to be the first. Indeed, the parties offer no evidence that any nation, meek or mighty, presumed to do such a thing.

"We therefore conclude the presumption against extraterritoriality applies to claims under the ATS, and that nothing in the statute rebuts that presumption. '[T]here is no clear indication of extraterritoriality here,' and petitioners' case seeking relief for violations of the law of nations occurring outside the United States is barred…

"On these facts, all the relevant conduct took place outside the United States. And even where the claims touch and concern the territory of the United States, they must do so with sufficient force to displace the presumption against extraterritorial application…. Corporations are often present in many countries, and it would reach too far to say that mere corporate presence suffices. If Congress were to determine otherwise, a statute more specific than the ATS would be required.

"The judgment of the Court of Appeals is affirmed.

"*It is so ordered.*"

CHILDREN OF THE CHIPPEWA, OTTAWA, & POTAWATOMY TRIBES v. THE UNIVERSITY OF MICHIGAN
305 N.W.2d 522 (MI App. 1981)

BACKGROUND: The newly-formed United States government treated the various Native American tribes as sovereign nations (at least for some purposes), and negotiated a number of treaties with different tribes. In 1817, the Treaty of Fort Meigs was entered into between the USA and the Chippewa, Ottawa, and Potawatomy tribes. The treaty was drafted entirely by a U.S. government representative. The University of Michigan ("U of M") was not a party to the treaty, but was mentioned ("the college at Detroit") as receiving a large grant of land from the tribes.

Descendants of the signatory tribes filed a lawsuit in Washtenaw County Circuit Court, to have an educational trust declared against the U of M, based on the provisions of the treaty. Article 16 of the Treaty of Fort Meigs states: "Some of the Ottawa, Chippewa, and Potawatomy Tribes, being attached to the Catholic religion, and believing they may wish some of their children hereafter educated, do grant to the rector of the Catholic church of St. Anne of Detroit, for the use of the said church, and to the corporation of the college at Detroit, for the use of the said college, to be retained or sold, as the said rector and corporation may judge expedient, each, one-half of three sections of land, to contain 640 acres, on the river Raisin, at a place called Macon; and three sections of land not yet located, which tracts were reserved, for the use of the said Indians, by the treaty of Detroit, in 1807; and the superintendent of Indian affairs, in the territory of Michigan, is authorized, on the part of the said Indians, to select the said tracts of land." Plaintiffs interpreted Article 16 to mean that the land had been given so that Native American children would receive a U of M education (without cost). The trial court (Judge Edward Deake) denied plaintiffs' request for a declaration of a trust in their favor. Plaintiffs asked the Michigan Court of Appeals to review the decision.

THE COURT:

"The inclusion of St. Anne's Church in the complaint was occasioned by the plaintiffs' assertion that the treaty compelled the church to provide for the primary and secondary education of the Indians. The complaint then contends that the treaty imposed a concomitant duty upon defendant [U of M] to ensure the Indians' college education. It is then claimed that the ... conveyance by the church to the defendant merged the foregoing duties wholly into defendant's realm of responsibility....

"... During the [1978] trial, numerous exhibits were received along with much expert testimony from all sides.... [T]he trial judge issued a meticulously researched and well drafted written opinion, thoroughly discussing the historical and procedural facets of this novel action and carefully setting forth the law which he believed controlling of this case. The opinion denied relief on all counts.

"We have painstakingly reviewed the findings of fact in the opinion and agree with the trial judge in respect to those findings. The task of leaping back over 160 years in time is most difficult, and the trial judge is to be commended for his efforts in that regard....

"[The main] issue raised by plaintiffs is whether the trial court was justified in holding that Article 16 of the Treaty of Fort Meigs constituted a gift of lands to Father Richard and to defendant. We believe that it did....

"Clearly, the grant itself is a completed one and not conditional in nature. Nor do its terms encompass more than one transaction. The land is donated jointly to the church, and to the corporation. The later division of the parcels was a consequence of Father Richard's discretion, a discretion Article 16 allowed him to exercise.

"The evidence points to an almost reverential attitude toward Father Richard on the Indians' part. This attitude was commingled with an attitude of filial affection. The evidence also points to a clear donative intent on the Indians' part as regards Father Richard and encompasses a similar attitude toward the educational institution which the Indians very properly regarded as an extension of Father Richard's personality and influence....

"The last claim on appeal concerns the issue of a constructive trust. The trial court rejected this theory for several reasons…. We agree.

"In a pristinely humane world, it might be honorable and fair to compel defendant to offer comprehensive scholarships in gratitude for the 1817 conveyance. Certainly, the cost of higher education is subject to the rigors of inflation as are all other things, and the plaintiffs, like everyone else, could benefit by the financial assistance they seek. However, constructive trusts are not used to requite obligations imposed by conscience alone. Rather, they are imposed solely where a balancing of equities discloses that it would be unfair to act otherwise. Where, as here, the language of the treaty and the historical evidence reflect a gift *inter vivos* and nothing more, the imposition of a constructive trust is neither equitably nor legally desirable.

"Based on the foregoing, it is readily apparent that the judgment of the trial court should be and the same is hereby affirmed."

HONG KONG S.A.R. v. MA WAI KWAN & ORS.
1997-2 HKC 315 (Hong Kong Court of Appeal 1997)

BACKGROUND: In 1841, as part of the settlement of the "First Opium War"—between China and Britain, China ceded the island of Hong Kong to the British. At the time, there was only a small fishing village on the island. In 1898, after China was defeated in a war with Japan, Britain was given a 99-year lease on Hong Kong, some 200 other nearby islands and two adjoining peninsulas. Over the next century, organized as a "Crown Colony," Hong Kong grew into an economic powerhouse—one of the world's main financial centers and largest ports, with a population of some 1.6 million by 1941—and, all by itself, by the 1990s, one of the USA's largest trading partners.

As a result of negotiations begun in 1984, and culminating in a "Joint Declaration" signed by the United Kingdom and the People's Republic of China ("PRC"), the PRC regained sovereignty over Hong Kong as of July 1, 1997. However, the Joint Declaration also specified that the existing legal system would remain in effect for 50 years in the "Hong Kong Special Autonomous Region" ("HKSAR"). A "Basic Law" embodying these principles was prepared by a committee with members from Hong Kong and China, and was adopted by the PRC's National People's Congress—to become effective on July 1, 1997.

Criminal charges against Ma Wai Kwan and two other persons, for the "common-law" (i.e., non-statutory) crime of "conspiracy to pervert the course of public justice," were pending in the Hong Kong courts on July 1. On July 3, defendants' lawyers suggested to the trial court that the common-law crime with which they were charged no longer existed in the HKSAR, now part of the PRC. The prosecution requested a ruling on that point from the Hong Kong Court of Appeal.

CHIEF JUDGE CHAN: *(translation)*

The Basic Law is a unique document. It reflects a treaty between two nations. It deals with the relationship between the National Government and an autonomous region using a different system. It provides for the organizations and functions of the different branches of government. It sets out the rights and duties of the citizens. Therefore it has at least three dimensions—international, domestic and constitutional. It must also be noted that it was not drafted by common-law lawyers, but was drafted in Chinese—with an official English version, but with the Chinese version taking precedence in case of discrepancies. That being its background and features, there will obviously be difficulties in interpreting the various provisions of the Basic Law.

The intent of the Basic Law is clear. There is to be no change in our laws and legal system (except those which contravene the Basic Law). These legal rules are the very fabric of our society. Legal continuity is the key to stability. Any disruption would be disastrous. Even a single moment of legal vacuum might produce chaos. Every part of the laws and the legal system except those provisions which contravene the Basic Law has to continue in force. The existing legal system must already be in place when the transfer of sovereignty occurs on 1 July 1997. That must have been the intent of those who drafted the Basic Law.

The wording is equally clear. The Basic Law is the constitution of the HKSAR. It is our most important legal document. It states clearly what the law is as of 1 July 1997. The word "shall" in these provisions can only have been used in the mandatory and declaratory sense. It means this: on 1 July 1997, when the HKSAR comes into existence and the Basic Law comes into effect, these are the laws and legal system in force and the principles in place. There is no express or implied requirement in any of these provisions that the laws previously in force or the legal system previously in place need any further formal adoption before they continue to be applicable. To the contrary, the use of the terms "shall be maintained," "shall continue" and "shall be" leaves absolutely no doubt that there is no need of any act of adoption. These terms are totally inconsistent with such a requirement….

The defendants' argument is based mainly on the words "shall be adopted" in Article 160. They suggest that "shall" in this phrase is used in the future tense. But that provision cannot be read in isolation; it must be considered in the light of the rest of the Basic Law, including in particular the articles referred to above. It cannot be construed to have a meaning which is inconsistent with the other articles relating to the adoption of the existing laws and legal system....

For the reasons listed above, I conclude that a true interpretation of the Basic Law's relevant provisions means that the laws previously in force in Hong Kong, including the common law, have been adopted and became the laws of HKSAR on 1 July 1997, that the judicial system and the principles applicable to court proceedings have continued, and that any indictments and pending court proceedings have continued to be valid.

The answers to the questions reserved for this court are that the common law has survived the change of sovereignty, and that the three respondents are liable to answer to and be tried under the amended indictment.

DIGITAL RIGHTS IRELAND LTD. v.
MINISTER FOR COMMUNICATIONS, MARINE & NATURAL RESOURCES, et al.
C-293/12 & C-594/12 (European Court of Justice 2014)

BACKGROUND: These requests for a preliminary ruling concern the validity of Directive 2006/24/EC of the European Parliament and of the Council of March 15, 2006, on the retention of data generated or processed in connection with the provision of publicly available electronic communications services or of public communications networks and amending Directive 2002/58/EC (OJ 2006 L 105, p. 54). The request made by the Ireland High Court (Case C-293/12) concerns proceedings between (i) Digital Rights Ireland Ltd. and (ii) the Minister for Communications, Marine and Natural Resources, the Minister for Justice, Equality and Law Reform, the Commissioner of the Garda Síochána, Ireland and the Attorney General, regarding the legality of national legislative and administrative measures concerning the retention of data relating to electronic communications. The request made by the Verfassungsgerichtshof (Austrian Constitutional Court)—Case C-594/12—concerns constitutional actions brought before that court by the Kärntner Landesregierung (Government of the Province of Carinthia) and by Mr. Seitlinger, Mr. Tschohl and 11,128 other applicants regarding the compatibility with the Federal Constitutional Law (Bundes-Verfassungsgesetz) of the law transposing Directive 2006/24 into Austrian national law.

The object of Directive 95/46/EC of the European Parliament and of the Council of 24 October 1995 on the protection of individuals with regard to the processing of personal data and on the free movement of such data (OJ 1995 L 281, p. 31), according to Article 1(1) thereof, is to protect the fundamental rights and freedoms of natural persons, and in particular their right to privacy with regard to the processing of personal data.

The aim of Directive 2002/58/EC of the European Parliament and of the Council of 12 July 2002 concerning the processing of personal data and the protection of privacy in the electronic communications sector (Directive on privacy and electronic communications), as amended by Directive 2009/136/EC of the European Parliament and of the Council of 25 November 2009 (OJ 2009 L 337, p. 11, 'Directive 2002/58), according to Article 1(1) thereof, is to harmonize the provisions of the Member States required to ensure an equivalent level of protection of fundamental rights and freedoms, and in particular the right to privacy and to confidentiality, with respect to the processing of personal data in the electronic communication sector and to ensure the free movement of such data and of electronic communication equipment and services in the European Union. According to Article 1(2), the provisions of that directive particularize and complement Directive 95/46 for the purposes mentioned in Article 1(1).

The Declaration on Combating Terrorism adopted by the European Council on March 25, 2004 instructed the Council to examine measures for establishing rules on the retention of communications traffic data by service providers. On July 13, 2005, the Council reaffirmed, in its declaration condemning terrorist attacks on London, the need to adopt common measures on the retention of telecommunications data as soon as possible.

Directive 2006/24 lays down the obligation on the providers of publicly available electronic communications services or of public communications networks to retain certain data which are generated or processed by them. "Article 3. Obligation to retain data. 1. By way of derogation from Articles 5, 6 and 9 of Directive 2002/58/EC, Member States shall adopt measures to ensure that the data specified in Article 5 of this Directive are retained in accordance with the provisions thereof, to the extent that those data are generated or processed by providers of publicly available electronic communications services or of a public communications network within their jurisdiction in the process of supplying the communications services concerned…. Article 6. Periods of retention. Member States shall ensure that the categories of data specified in Article 5 are retained for periods of not less than six months nor more than two years from the date of the communication."

On August 11, 2006, Digital Rights brought an action before the Ireland High Court in which it claimed that it owned a mobile phone which had been registered on June 3, 2006, and that it had used that mobile phone since that date. It challenged the legality of national legislative and administrative measures concerning the retention of data relating to electronic communications and asked the national court, in particular, to declare the invalidity of Directive 2006/24 and of Part 7 of the Criminal Justice (Terrorist Offences) Act 2005, which requires telephone communications service providers to retain traffic and location data relating to those providers for a period specified by law in order to prevent, detect, investigate and prosecute crime and safeguard the security of the State. The High Court, considering that it was not able to resolve the questions raised relating to national law unless the validity of Directive 2006/24 had first been examined, decided to stay proceedings and to refer the case to the European Court of Justice for a preliminary ruling. By decision of the President of the Court of June 11, 2013, Cases C-293/12 and C-594/12 were joined for the purposes of the oral procedure and the judgment.

THE COURT:

"By the second question, parts (b) to (d), in Case C-293/12 and the first question in Case C-594/12, which should be examined together, the referring courts are essentially asking the Court to examine the validity of Directive 2006/24 in the light of Articles 7, 8 and 11 of the Charter [of Fundamental Rights of the European Union]….

"The obligation, under Article 3 of Directive 2006/24, on providers of publicly available electronic communications services or of public communications networks to retain the data listed in Article 5 of the directive for the purpose of making them accessible, if necessary, to the competent national authorities raises questions relating to respect for private life and communications under Article 7 of the Charter, the protection of personal data under Article 8 of the Charter and respect for freedom of expression under Article 11 of the Charter.

"In that regard, it should be observed that the data which providers of publicly available electronic communications services or of public communications networks must retain, pursuant to Articles 3 and 5 of Directive 2006/24, include data necessary to trace and identify the source of a communication and its destination, to identify the date, time, duration and type of a communication, to identify users' communication equipment, and to identify the location of mobile communication equipment, data which consist, inter alia, of the name and address of the subscriber or registered user, the calling telephone number, the number called and an IP address for Internet services. Those data make it possible, in particular, to know the identity of the person with whom a subscriber or registered user has communicated and by what means, and to identify the time of the communication as well as the place from which that communication took place. They also make it possible to know the frequency of the communications of the subscriber or registered user with certain persons during a given period.

"Those data, taken as a whole, may allow very precise conclusions to be drawn concerning the private lives of the persons whose data has been retained, such as the habits of everyday life, permanent or temporary places of residence, daily or other movements, the activities carried out, the social relationships of those persons and the social environments frequented by them. In such

INTERNATIONAL BUSINESS LAW

circumstances, even though ... the directive does not permit the retention of the content of the communication or of information consulted using an electronic communications network, it is not inconceivable that the retention of the data in question might have an effect on the use, by subscribers or registered users, of the means of communication covered by that directive and, consequently, on their exercise of the freedom of expression guaranteed by Article 11 of the Charter.

"The retention of data for the purpose of possible access to them by the competent national authorities, as provided for by Directive 2006/24, directly and specifically affects private life and, consequently, the rights guaranteed by Article 7 of the Charter. Furthermore, such a retention of data also falls under Article 8 of the Charter because it constitutes the processing of personal data within the meaning of that article and, therefore, necessarily has to satisfy the data protection requirements arising from that article....

"Whereas the references for a preliminary ruling in the present cases raise, in particular, the question of principle as to whether or not, in the light of Article 7 of the Charter, the data of subscribers and registered users may be retained, they also concern the question of principle as to whether Directive 2006/24 meets the requirements for the protection of personal data arising from Article 8 of the Charter....

"By requiring the retention of the data listed in Article 5(1) of Directive 2006/24 and by allowing the competent national authorities to access those data, Directive 2006/24 ... derogates from the system of protection of the right to privacy established by Directives 95/46 and 2002/58 with regard to the processing of personal data in the electronic communications sector, directives which provided for the confidentiality of communications and of traffic data as well as the obligation to erase or make those data anonymous where they are no longer needed for the purpose of the transmission of a communication, unless they are necessary for billing purposes and only for as long as so necessary.

"To establish the existence of an interference with the fundamental right to privacy, it does not matter whether the information on the private lives concerned is sensitive or whether the persons concerned have been inconvenienced in any way.... As a result, the obligation imposed by Articles 3 and 6 of Directive 2006/24 on providers of publicly available electronic communications services or of public communications networks to retain, for a certain period, data relating to a person's private life and to his communications, such as those referred to in Article 5 of the directive, constitutes in itself an interference with the rights guaranteed by Article 7 of the Charter. Furthermore, the access of the competent national authorities to the data constitutes a further interference with that fundamental right.... Likewise, Directive 2006/24 constitutes an interference with the fundamental right to the protection of personal data guaranteed by Article 8 of the Charter because it provides for the processing of personal data…. Furthermore … the fact that data are retained and subsequently used without the subscriber or registered user being informed is likely to generate in the minds of the persons concerned the feeling that their private lives are the subject of constant surveillance….

"It is apparent from the case-law of the Court that the fight against international terrorism in order to maintain international peace and security constitutes an objective of general interest…. The same is true of the fight against serious crime in order to ensure public security…. Furthermore, it should be noted, in this respect, that Article 6 of the Charter lays down the right of any person not only to liberty, but also to security.

"In this respect, it is apparent … that, because of the significant growth in the possibilities afforded by electronic communications, the Justice and Home Affairs Council of 19 December 2002 concluded that data relating to the use of electronic communications are particularly important and therefore a valuable tool in the prevention of offences and the fight against crime, in particular organised crime. It must therefore be held that the retention of data for the purpose of allowing the competent national authorities to have possible access to those data, as required by Directive 2006/24, genuinely satisfies an objective of general interest.

"In those circumstances, it is necessary to verify the proportionality of the interference found to exist. In that regard, according to the settled case-law of the Court, the principle of proportionality requires that acts of the EU institutions be appropriate for attaining the legitimate objectives pursued by the legislation at issue and do not exceed the limits of what is appropriate and necessary in order to achieve those objectives….

"In the present case, in view of the important role played by the protection of personal data in the light of the fundamental right to respect for private life and the extent and seriousness of the interference with that right caused by Directive 2006/24, the EU legislature's discretion is reduced, with the result that review of that discretion should be strict…. In that regard, it should be noted that the protection of personal data resulting from the explicit obligation laid down in Article 8(1) of the Charter is especially important for the right to respect for private life enshrined in Article 7 of the Charter…. Consequently, the EU legislation in question must lay down clear and precise rules governing the scope and application of the measure in question and imposing minimum safeguards so that the persons whose data have been retained have sufficient guarantees to effectively protect their personal data against the risk of abuse and against any unlawful access and use of that data…. The need for such safeguards is all the greater where, as laid down in Directive 2006/24, personal data are subjected to automatic processing and where there is a significant risk of unlawful access to those data….

"… [W]hilst seeking to contribute to the fight against serious crime, Directive 2006/24 does not require any relationship between the data whose retention is provided for and a threat to public security and, in particular, it is not restricted to a retention in relation (i) to data pertaining to a particular time period and/or a particular geographical zone and/or to a circle of particular persons likely to be involved, in one way or another, in a serious crime, or (ii) to persons who could, for other reasons, contribute, by the retention of their data, to the prevention, detection or prosecution of serious offences.

"Secondly, not only is there a general absence of limits in Directive 2006/24 but [it] also fails to lay down any objective criterion by which to determine the limits of the access of the competent national authorities to the data and their subsequent use for the purposes of prevention, detection or criminal prosecutions concerning offences that, in view of the extent and seriousness of the interference with the fundamental rights enshrined in Articles 7 and 8 of the Charter, may be considered to be sufficiently serious to justify such an interference. On the contrary, Directive 2006/24 simply refers, in Article 1(1), in a general manner to serious crime, as defined by each Member State in its national law.

"Furthermore, Directive 2006/24 does not contain substantive and procedural conditions relating to the access of the competent national authorities to the data and to their subsequent use. Article 4 of the directive, which governs the access of those authorities to the data retained, does not expressly provide that that access and the subsequent use of the data in question must be strictly restricted to the purpose of preventing and detecting precisely defined serious offences or of conducting criminal prosecutions relating thereto; it merely provides that each Member State is to define the procedures to be followed and the conditions to be fulfilled in order to gain access to the retained data in accordance with necessity and proportionality requirements.

"In particular, Directive 2006/24 does not lay down any objective criterion by which the number of persons authorised to access and subsequently use the data retained is limited to what is strictly necessary in the light of the objective pursued. Above all, the access by the competent national authorities to the data retained is not made dependent on a prior review carried out by a court or by an independent administrative body whose decision seeks to limit access to the data and their use to what is strictly necessary for the purpose of attaining the objective pursued and which intervenes following a reasoned request of those authorities submitted within the framework of procedures of prevention, detection or criminal prosecutions. Nor does it lay down a specific obligation on Member States designed to establish such limits.

"Thirdly, so far as concerns the data retention period, Article 6 of Directive 2006/24 requires that those data be retained for a period of at least six months, without any distinction being made between the categories of data set out in Article 5 of that directive on the basis of their possible usefulness for the purposes of the objective pursued or according to the persons concerned.

"Furthermore, that period is set at between a minimum of 6 months and a maximum of 24 months, but it is not stated that the determination of the period of retention must be based on objective criteria in order to ensure that it is limited to what is strictly necessary.

"It follows from the above that Directive 2006/24 does not lay down clear and precise rules governing the extent of the interference with the fundamental rights enshrined in Articles 7 and 8 of the Charter. It must therefore be held that Directive 2006/24 entails a wide-ranging and particularly serious interference with those fundamental rights in the legal order of the EU, without such an interference being precisely circumscribed by provisions to ensure that it is actually limited to what is strictly necessary.

"Moreover, as far as concerns the rules relating to the security and protection of data retained by providers of publicly available electronic communications services or of public communications networks, it must be held that Directive 2006/24 does not provide for sufficient safeguards, as required by Article 8 of the Charter, to ensure effective protection of the data retained against the risk of abuse and against any unlawful access and use of that data. In the first place, Article 7 of Directive 2006/24 does not lay down rules which are specific and adapted to (i) the vast quantity of data whose retention is required by that directive, (ii) the sensitive nature of that data and (iii) the risk of unlawful access to that data, rules which would serve, in particular, to govern the protection and security of the data in question in a clear and strict manner in order to ensure their full integrity and confidentiality. Furthermore, a specific obligation on Member States to establish such rules has also not been laid down.

"Article 7 of Directive 2006/24, read in conjunction with Article 4(1) of Directive 2002/58 and the second subparagraph of Article 17(1) of Directive 95/46, does not ensure that a particularly high level of protection and security is applied by those providers by means of technical and organisational measures, but permits those providers in particular to have regard to economic considerations when determining the level of security which they apply, as regards the costs of implementing security measures. In particular, Directive 2006/24 does not ensure the irreversible destruction of the data at the end of the data retention period.

"In the second place, it should be added that that directive does not require the data in question to be retained within the European Union, with the result that it cannot be held that the control, explicitly required by Article 8(3) of the Charter, by an independent authority of compliance with the requirements of protection and security, as referred to in the two previous paragraphs, is fully ensured. Such a control, carried out on the basis of EU law, is an essential component of the protection of individuals with regard to the processing of personal data....

"Having regard to all the foregoing considerations, it must be held that, by adopting Directive 2006/24, the EU legislature has exceeded the limits imposed by compliance with the principle of proportionality in the light of Articles 7, 8 and 52(1) of the Charter. In those circumstances, there is no need to examine the validity of Directive 2006/24 in the light of Article 11 of the Charter.

"Consequently, the answer to the second question, parts (b) to (d), in Case C-293/12 and the first question in Case C-594/12 is that Directive 2006/24 is invalid....

"It follows from what was held in the previous paragraph that there is no need to answer the first question, the second question, parts (a) and (e), and the third question in Case C-293/12 or the second question in Case C-594/12....

"On those grounds, the Court (Grand Chamber) hereby rules:
Directive 2006/24/EC of the European Parliament and of the Council of 15 March 2006 on the retention of data generated or processed in connection with the provision of publicly available electronic communications services or of public communications networks and amending Directive 2002/58/EC is invalid."

AIR FRANCE v. SAKS
470 U.S. 392 (1985)

BACKGROUND: Valerie Saks sued Air France in California state court, alleging that she had sustained injury during her flight from Paris to Los Angeles. She had boarded an Air France jet in Paris for the 12-hour flight to Los Angeles. There were no unusual incidents during the flight, but as the plane descended for landing in Los Angeles, Valerie felt severe pressure and pain in her left ear. The pain continued after landing, but Valerie said nothing about it to any Air France personnel. When she consulted a doctor five days later, he told Valerie that she had become permanently deaf in her left ear. She alleged that her condition was caused by Air France's negligent maintenance of the plane's pressurization system. The case was removed to U.S. District Court, since a question of international law was involved. After extensive investigation indicated that the pressurization system had operated in the normal manner, Air France moved for summary judgment, since no "accident" within the meaning of the Warsaw Convention had caused Valerie's injury. The U.S. District Court granted the motion, but the U.S. Ninth Circuit reversed. Air France asked for U.S. Supreme Court review.

JUSTICE O'CONNOR:

"Air France is liable to a passenger under the terms of the Warsaw Convention only if the passenger proves that an 'accident' was the cause of her injury…. The narrow issue presented is whether [Saks] can meet this burden by showing that her injury was caused by the normal operation of the aircraft's pressurization system. The proper answer turns on interpretation of a clause in an international treaty to which the United States is a party. '[T]reaties are construed more liberally than private agreements, and to ascertain their meaning we may look beyond the written words to the history of the treaty, the negotiations, and the practical construction adopted by the parties.'… The analysis must begin, however, with the text of the treaty and the context within which the written words are used….

"Article 17 of the Warsaw Convention establishes the liability of international air carriers for harm to passengers. Article 18 contains parallel provisions regarding liability for damage to baggage…. Th[is] … portion of the text … reads as follows: 'Article 17: The carrier shall be liable for damage sustained in the event of the death or wounding of a passenger or any other bodily injury suffered by a passenger, if the accident which caused the damage so sustained took place on board the aircraft or in the course of any of the operations of embarking or disembarking." [emphasis by the Court] 'Article 18: (1) The carrier shall be liable for damage sustained in the event of the destruction or loss of, or damage to any checked baggage or any goods, if the occurrence which caused the damage so sustained took place during the transportation by air.' [emphasis by the Court]

"Two significant features of these provisions stand out in both the French and the English texts. First, Article 17 imposes liability for injuries to passengers caused by an 'accident,' whereas Article 18 imposes liability for destruction or loss of baggage caused by an 'occurrence.' This difference in the parallel language of Articles 17 and 18 implies that the drafters of the Convention understood the word 'accident' to mean something different than the word 'occurrence,' for they otherwise logically would have used the same word in each article….

"Second, the text of Article 17 refers to an accident *which caused* the passenger's injury, and not to an accident which *is* the passenger's injury. In light of the many senses in which the word 'accident' can be used, this distinction is significant….

"In Article 17, the drafters of the Warsaw Convention apparently did make an attempt to discriminate between 'the cause and the effect'; they specified that air carriers would be liable if an accident *caused* the passenger's injury. The text of the Convention thus implies that, however, we define 'accident,' it is the *cause* of the injury that must satisfy the definition rather than the occurrence of the injury alone. American jurisprudence has long recognized this distinction between an accident that is the *cause* of an injury and an injury that is itself an accident....

"This interpretation of Article 17 is consistent with the negotiating history of the Convention, the conduct of the parties to the Convention, and the weight of precedent in foreign and American courts....

"The judgment of the Court of Appeals is reversed, and the case is remanded for further proceedings consistent with this opinion."

STOVALL v. NORTHWEST AIRLINES, INC.
595 N.E.2d 330 (MA App. 1992)

BACKGROUND: The Warsaw Convention holds an airline strictly liable, up to $75,000, for injuries sustained by a passenger on an international flight, including the "operations of embarking or disembarking." Dawn Stovall was injured, and her mother Esther Shaleen was killed, when they fell out of the back doors of a Massachusetts Port Authority bus. They had purchased round-trip tickets on Northwest Airlines for their Minneapolis/London journey. The flights each way required a stop in Boston, with a change of planes. The return flight landed in Boston, and the passengers were processed through immigration and customs at the international terminal. Stovall and Shaleen were processed, their baggage was taken by Northwest personnel, and they were given vouchers for an M.P.A. bus which would take them to the domestic terminal. The bus was crowded. The back doors opened when it rounded a curve, and the two women fell out.

Plaintiffs' lawsuit was filed against Northwest, based on the Warsaw Convention. The trial judge denied Northwest's motion for summary judgment, and ordered summary judgment for the plaintiffs. Northwest asked for review by the Massachusetts Court of Appeals.

JUSTICE FINE:

"Neither the text of the Convention, nor its history, clearly defines the scope of liability for accidents in and around an airport terminal.

"[C]ourts have held that coverage would depend upon the particular facts analyzed on the basis of a number of factors: (1) the activity in which the passenger was engaged at the time of the accident, (2) the degree of control the airline had over the passenger at the time, (3) the physical proximity of the passenger to the aircraft, and (4) the closeness of the time of the accident to the passenger's entering or leaving the airplane....

"Even under the more expansive ... test, which is nor routinely applied whether the issue relates to embarkation or debarkation, the plaintiff in this case may not prevail. The accident occurred while the two women were engaged in the activity of traveling on a public bus from one terminal to another. True, they were required to travel between terminals to continue their flight, but the activity in which they were engaged presented none of the dangers generally associated with air travel with which the Warsaw Convention was concerned.... Airline personnel exerted some restrictions and control over Stovall and Shaleen's activities by providing them with vouchers and escorting them to the Massachusetts Port Authority bus. The airline did not tell them they were required to take that particular bus, however, and they were free to proceed by any means of transportation to the domestic terminal.... If any agency was directly in control of the two women at the time of the accident, it was the Massachusetts Port Authority, operating the bus, rather than Northwest. With regard to the time factor, more than one hour had elapsed since the flight from London had landed and the Minneapolis flight was not scheduled to depart for yet another two and one-half hours....

"The plaintiff emphasizes the facts ... that at the time of the accident Stovall and Shaleen remained passengers on the Northwest flight from London to Minneapolis, they were in possession of their boarding cards, their baggage was in custody of the airline, and Northwest had made arrangements for their transportation between terminals. The Plaintiff contends, therefore, that the women were on one continuous journey to their final destination. The entire duration of a stop-over in the course of such a journey, however, is not necessarily included within 'the operations of embarking and disembarking' as that phrase is used in the Warsaw Convention.... Where an accident occurs, as this one did, outside any airport terminal building while the passengers are on a public bus, substantially removed both in time and space from their flight, we think the uniform result in courts throughout this country would be that the accident is not covered by the Warsaw Convention. The risk that materialized was not a risk of aviation."

CATHAY PACIFIC AIRWAYS, LTD. v.
COURT OF APPEALS & TOMAS L. ALCANTARA
(G.R. No. L-60501 March 5, 1993, Philippine Supreme Court)

BACKGROUND: On October 19, 1975, Tomas L. Alcantara was a first class passenger of Cathay Pacific Airways, Ltd. (Cathay) on its Flight No. CX-900 from Manila to Hong Kong and then to Jakarta on Flight No. CX-711. The purpose of his trip was to attend, the following day, a conference with the Director General of Trade of Indonesia (Alcantara being Executive Vice-President and General Manager of Iligan Cement Corporation, Chairman of the Export Committee of the Philippine Cement Corporation, and representative of the Cement Industry Authority). He checked in his luggage, which contained not only his clothing and articles for personal use but also papers and documents he needed for the conference. Upon his arrival in Jakarta, he discovered that his luggage was missing. When he inquired about his luggage from Cathay's representative in Jakarta, he was told that his luggage was left behind in Hong Kong. For this, Alcantara was offered $20.00 as "inconvenience money" to buy his immediate personal needs until the luggage could be delivered to him. His luggage finally reached Jakarta more than 24 hours after his arrival. However, it was not delivered to him at his hotel but was instead required by Cathay Pacific to be picked up by an official of the Philippine Embassy.

On March 1, 1976, Alcantara filed his complaint against Cathay Pacific with the Court of First Instance of Lanao del Norte asking for temperate, moral and exemplary damages, plus attorney's fees. On April 18, 1978, the trial court rendered its decision ordering Cathay to pay plaintiff P20,000 for moral damages, P5,000 for temperate damages, P10,000 for exemplary damages, and P25,000 for attorney's fees and costs. Both parties appealed to the Court of Appeals. Cathay assailed the conclusion of the trial court that the airline was accountable for breach of contract, and the non-application by the court of the Warsaw Convention, as well as the excessive damages awarded on the basis of its finding that Alcantara was rudely treated by its employees during the time that his luggage could not be found. For his part, Alcantara assigned as error the failure of the trial court to grant the full amount of damages sought in his complaint. On November 11, 1981, respondent Court of Appeals rendered its decision affirming the findings of fact of the trial court but modifying its award by increasing the moral damages to P80,000, exemplary damages to P20,000 and temperate or moderate damages to P10,000. The award of P25,000 for attorney's fees was maintained. Review by the Philippine Supreme Court was requested.

JUSTICE BELLOSILLO:

"The same grounds raised by petitioner in the Court of Appeals are reiterated before Us. Cathay contends that: (1) the Court of Appeals erred in holding petitioner liable to … Alcantara for moral, exemplary and temperate damages as well as attorneys fees; and, (2) the Court of Appeals erred in failing to apply the Warsaw Convention on the liability of a carrier to its passengers.

"On its first assigned error, Cathay argues that although it failed to transport … Alcantara's luggage on time, the one-day delay was not made in bad faith so as to justify moral, exemplary and temperate damages. It submits that the conclusion of respondent appellate court that

[Alcantara] was treated rudely and arrogantly when he sought assistance from Cathay's employees has no factual basis, hence, the award of moral damages has no leg to stand on.

"Petitioner's [Cathay's] first assigned error involves findings of fact which are not reviewable by this Court. At any rate, it is not impressed with merit. Petitioner breached its contract of carriage with [Alcantara] when it failed to deliver his luggage at the designated place and time, it being the obligation of a common carrier to carry its passengers and their luggage safely to their destination, which includes the duty not to delay their transportation, and the evidence shows that petitioner acted fraudulently or in bad faith.

"Moral damages predicated upon a breach of contract of carriage may only be recoverable in instances where the mishap results in death of a passenger, or where the carrier is guilty of fraud or bad faith.

"In the case at bar, both the trial court and the appellate court found that Cathay was grossly negligent and reckless when it failed to deliver the luggage of petitioner at the appointed place and time. We agree. Cathay alleges that as a result of mechanical trouble, all pieces of luggage on board the first aircraft bound for Jakarta were unloaded and transferred to the second aircraft which departed an hour and a half later. Yet, as the Court of Appeals noted, petitioner was not even aware that it left behind [Alcantara's] luggage until its attention was called by the Hong Kong Custom authorities. More, bad faith or otherwise improper conduct may be attributed to the employees of petitioner. While the mere failure of Cathay to deliver respondent's luggage at the agreed place and time did not *ipso facto* amount to willful misconduct since the luggage was eventually delivered to [him], albeit belatedly, We are persuaded that the employees of Cathay acted in bad faith. We refer to the deposition of Romulo Palma, Commercial Attache of the Philippine Embassy at Jakarta, who was with … Alcantara when [he] sought assistance from the employees of Cathay. This deposition was the basis of the findings of the lower courts when both awarded moral damages to [Alcantara]. Hereunder is part of Palma's testimony—

Q. What did Mr. Alcantara say, if any[thing]?

A. Mr. Alcantara was of course . . . . I could understand his position. He was furious for the experience because probably he was thinking he was going to meet the Director-General the following day and, well, he was with no change of proper clothes and so, I would say, he was not happy about the situation.

Q. What did Mr. Alcantara say?

A. He was trying to press the fellow to make the report and if possible make the delivery of his baggage as soon as possible.

51

Q. And what did the agent or duty officer say, if any[thing]?

A. The duty officer, of course, answered back saying What can we do, the baggage is missing. I cannot do anything, something like it. 'Anyhow you can buy anything you need, charged to Cathay Pacific.'

Q. What was the demeanor or comportment of the duty officer of Cathay Pacific when he said to Mr. Alcantara 'You can buy anything chargeable to Cathay Pacific'?

A. If I had to look at it objectively, the duty officer would like to dismiss the affair as soon as possible by saying indifferently 'Don't worry. It can be found.'

"Indeed, the aforequoted testimony shows that the language and conduct of petitioner's representative towards respondent Alcantara was discourteous or arbitrary to justify the grant of moral damages. The Cathay representative was not only indifferent and impatient; he was also rude and insulting. He simply advised Alcantara to buy anything he wanted. But even that was not sincere because the representative knew that the passenger was limited only to $20.00 which, certainly, was not enough to purchase comfortable clothings appropriate for an executive conference. Considering that Alcantara was not only a revenue passenger but even paid for a first class airline accommodation and accompanied at the time by the Commercial Attache of the Philippine Embassy who was assisting him in his problem, petitioner or its agents should have been more courteous and accommodating to [him], instead of giving him a curt reply, 'What can we do, the baggage is missing. I cannot do anything . . . . Anyhow, you can buy anything you need, charged to Cathay Pacific.' Cathay's employees should have been more solicitous to a passenger in distress and assuaged his anxieties and apprehensions. To compound matters, Cathay refused to have the luggage of Alcantara delivered to him at his hotel; instead, he was required to pick it up himself [via] an official of the Philippine Embassy. Under the circumstances, it is evident that petitioner was remiss in its duty to provide proper and adequate assistance to a paying passenger, more so one with first class accommodation.

"Where in breaching the contract of carriage the defendant airline is not shown to have acted fraudulently or in bad faith, liability for damages is limited to the natural and probable consequences of the breach of obligation which the parties had foreseen or could have reasonably foreseen. In that case, such liability does not include moral and exemplary damages. Conversely, if the defendant airline is shown to have acted fraudulently or in bad faith, the award of moral and exemplary damages is proper.

"However, respondent Alcantara is not entitled to temperate damages, contrary to the ruling of the court [below], in the absence of any showing that he sustained some pecuniary loss. It cannot be gainsaid that respondent's luggage was ultimately delivered to him without serious or appreciable damage.

"As regards its second assigned error, petitioner airline contends that the extent of its liability for breach of contract should be limited absolutely to that set forth in the Warsaw Convention. We do not agree. As We have repeatedly held, although the Warsaw Convention has the force and effect of law in this country, being a treaty commitment assumed by the Philippine government, said convention does not operate as an exclusive enumeration of the instances for declaring a carrier liable for breach of contract of carriage or as an absolute limit of the extent of that liability. The Warsaw Convention declares the carrier liable for damages in the enumerated cases and under certain limitations. However, it must not be construed to preclude the operation of the Civil Code and other pertinent laws. It does not regulate, much less exempt, the carrier from liability for damages for violating the rights of its passengers under the contract of carriage, especially if willful misconduct on the part of the carrier's employees is found or established, which is clearly the case before Us. For the Warsaw Convention itself provides in Art. 25 that— (1) The carrier shall not be entitled to avail himself of the provisions of this convention which exclude or limit his liability, if the damage is caused by his willful misconduct or by such default on his part as, in accordance with the law of the court to which the case is submitted, is considered to be equivalent to willful misconduct. (2) Similarly the carrier shall not be entitled to avail himself of the said provisions, if the damage is caused under the same circumstances by any agent of the carrier acting within the scope of his employment.

"When petitioner airline misplaced respondent's luggage and failed to deliver it to its passenger at the appointed place and time, some special species of injury must have been caused to him. For sure, the latter underwent profound distress and anxiety, and the fear of losing the opportunity to fulfill the purpose of his trip. In fact, for want of appropriate clothings for the occasion brought about by the delay of the arrival of his luggage, to his embarrassment and consternation respondent Alcantara had to seek postponement of his pre-arranged conference with the Director General of Trade of the host country.

"In one [previous] case, this Court observed that a traveler would naturally suffer mental anguish, anxiety and shock when he finds that his luggage did not travel with him and he finds himself in a foreign land without any article of clothing other than what he has on.

"Thus, respondent is entitled to moral and exemplary damages. We however find the award by the Court of Appeals of P80,000.00 for moral damages excessive, hence, We reduce the amount to P30,000.00. The exemplary damages of P20,000.00 being reasonable is maintained, as well as the attorney's fees of P25,000.00 considering that petitioner's act or omission has compelled Alcantara to litigate with third persons or to incur expenses to protect his interest.

"WHEREFORE, the assailed decision of respondent Court of Appeals is AFFIRMED with the exception of the award of temperate damages of P10,000.00 which is deleted, while the award of moral damages of P80,000.00 is reduced to P30,000.00. The award of P20,000.00 for exemplary damages is maintained as reasonable together with the attorney's fees of P25,000.00. The moral and exemplary damages shall earn interest at the legal rate from 1 March 1976 when the complaint was filed until full payment.

"SO ORDERED."

ZICHERMAN v. KOREAN AIR LINES CO.
516 U.S. 217 (1996)

BACKGROUND: With the "Cold War" still very much in process, Korean Air Lines ("KAL") flight KE007, en route from Anchorage, Alaska, to Seoul, Korea, strayed into Soviet air space on September 1, 1983. It was shot down by the USSR's air defenses, over the Sea of Japan. All 269 persons on board were killed, including Muriel Kole. Kole's sister (Majorie Zicherman) and Kole's mother (Muriel Mahalek) sued KAL. Part of the damages they requested were for "their grief and mental anguish," "the loss of the decedent's society and companionship," and "the decedent's conscious pain and suffering." Their case was joined with others in the U.S. District Court for the District of Columbia.

A jury found that "willful misconduct" by the KAL flight crew had caused the mishap, and awarded $50 million in punitive damages to the claimants as a group. The D.C. Court of Appeals reversed, stating that the Warsaw Convention does not permit the award of punitive damages, even though willful misconduct removes the $75,000 cap on actual damages. The jury then awarded "loss-of-society" damages of $70,000 to Zicherman and $28,000 to Mahalek. These awards were also set aside by the Court of Appeals. Zicherman and Mahalek asked the Supreme Court for further review.

JUSTICE SCALIA:

"Article 17 of the Warsaw Convention ... provides as follows: 'The carrier shall be liable for *damage sustained* in the event of the death or wounding of a passenger or any other bodily injury suffered by a passenger, if the accident took place on board the aircraft or in the course of any of the operations of embarking or disembarking.' [Emphasis added by the Court.] The first and principal question before us is whether loss of society of a relative is made recoverable by this provision.

"It is obvious that the English word 'damage' or 'harm'—or in the official text of the Convention, the French word '*dommage*'—can be applied to an extremely wide range of phenomena, from the medical expenses incurred as a result of Kole's injuries (for which every legal system would provide tort compensation), to the mental distress of some stranger who reads about Kole's death in the paper (for which no legal system would provide tort compensation). It cannot seriously be maintained that Article 17 uses the term in this broadest sense, thus exploding tort liability beyond what any legal system in the world allows, to the farthest reaches of what could be denominated 'harm.' We therefore reject petitioners' initial proposal that we simply look to English dictionary definitions of 'damage' and apply that term's 'plain meaning.'...

"There are only two thinkable alternatives to that. First, what petitioners ultimately suggest: that *'dommage'* means what French law, in 1929, recognized as *legally cognizable* harm, which petitioners assert included not only *'dommage materiel'* (pecuniary harm of various sorts) but also *'dommage moral'* (non-pecuniary harm of various sorts, including loss of society)....

"The other alternative, and the only one we think realistic, is to believe that *'dommage'* means (as it does in French legal usage) 'legally cognizable harm,' but that Article 17 leaves it to adjudicating courts to specify what harm is cognizable....

"That this is the proper interpretation is confirmed by another provision of the Convention. Article 17 is expressly limited by Article 24, which ... provides: '(1) In the cases covered by articles 18 and 19 any action for damages, however founded, can only be brought subject to the conditions and limits set out in this convention. (2) In the cases covered by article 17 the provisions of the preceding paragraph shall also apply, *without prejudice to the questions as to who are the persons who have the right to bring suit and what are their respective rights.*' [Emphasis by the Court.] The most natural reading of this Article is that, in an action brought under Article 17, the law of the Convention does not affect the substantive questions of who may bring suit and what they may be compensated for. Those questions are to be answered by the domestic law selected by the courts of the contracting states....

"Having concluded that compensable harm is to be determined by domestic law, the next question to which we would logically turn is that of *which sovereign's* domestic law.... We have been spared that inquiry, however, because both parties agree that if the issue of compensable harm is ... unresolved by the Convention itself, it is governed ... by the law of the United States....

"That leaves a final question unresolved: which particular law of the United States provides the governing rule?...

"The death that occurred here falls within the literal terms of [the Death on the High Seas Act], and it is well established that those literal terms apply to airplane crashes.... Section 762 of DOHSA provides that the recovery in a suit under S.761 'shall be a fair and just compensation for the pecuniary loss sustained by the persons for whose benefit the suit is brought.'... Thus, petitioners cannot recover loss-of-society damages under DOHSA."

AQUINO v. ASIANA AIRLINES INC.
105 Cal.App.4th 1272 (CA App. 2003)

BACKGROUND: Modesta and David Aquino bought round-trip tickets for an Asiana flight from San Francisco to the Philippines. On the departure date, November 29, 1999, their daughter took them to the airport. At the check-in desk, an Asiana manager asked how old they were, and when their daughter said they were 90, he said they could not fly without a doctor's certificate stating it was safe for them to do so. They walked to the airport medical clinic, but did not get a medical clearance. They then went back to the Asiana check-in, where their daughter insisted they be permitted on the plane anyway. The Asiana manager threatened to call the police, who arrived shortly. At that point, the Aquinos gave up, and left the airport. They later took another airline to the Philippines, where David died on February 5, 2000.

Modesta Aquino sued for herself and for David's estate, alleging several tort and contract claims against Asiana. Asiana moved for summary judgment, because the state-law tort and contract claims were preempted by the Warsaw Convention and/or by the USA's Airline Deregulation Act of 1978. The California trial court granted Asiana's motion. Modesta asked for review by the California Court of Appeals.

JUDGE RIVERA:

"Where it is applicable, the Warsaw Convention provides the exclusive remedy for personal injuries....

"However, in order for the Warsaw Convention to govern a claim, the incident giving rise to the claim must take place 'on board the aircraft or in the course of any of the operations of embarking or disembarking.'...

"The question of whether a passenger is involved in any of the operations of embarking is a question of law to be decided based on the facts of each case.... In making this determination, courts focus on several factors, in particular '(1) Activity of the passengers at the time of the accident; (2) the restrictions, if any, on their movements; (3) the imminence of actual boarding;

[and] (4) the physical proximity of the passengers to the gate.'…

"Courts have found the Warsaw Convention inapplicable … where passengers were still in common areas, were not under the control of airline personnel, or were not physically near the departure gate….

"Based on the record presented, we conclude the Aquinos were not engaged in the operations of embarking. At the time of the events giving rise to this action, they were in a common passenger area, attempting to check in. They had not checked their luggage or received their boarding passes. They had not progressed through security to an area restricted to passengers. Indeed, their claim is that they were not allowed to begin the operations of embarkation. The record does not show that they ever became engaged in those operations. Asiana does not direct us to any case extending the reach of the Warsaw Convention to the stage of attempting to check in, and our independent research does not disclose any….

"Asiana argues that even if the Warsaw Convention does not preempt this action, the Airline Deregulation Act of 1978 does….

"The scope of this preemption, particularly as it relates to 'service,' has been the subject of considerable dispute, although it is clear that the Act does not preempt all state law based actions related to an airline's conduct….

"The federal circuit courts have not devised a uniform test for determining whether a state law action is related to an airline's 'service.'…

"We agree with both the [U.S.] Ninth Circuit Court of Appeals and the [California] Second District Court of Appeals that the Act does not preempt state law personal injury and discrimination claims that have only a peripheral effect on deregulation….

"The Aquinos have also alleged a cause of action for breach of contract. The United States Supreme Court has concluded that the Act does not preempt routine breach of contract claims….

"Accordingly, we conclude the Act does not preempt any of the Aquinos' claims….

"We affirm the judgment of the superior court to the extent it granted summary judgment on the cause of action for intentional infliction of emotional distress. In all other respects, we reverse the judgment and remand for further proceedings consistent with this opinion."

GOLDWATER, et al. v. CARTER, et al.
617 F.2d 697 (D.C. Cir. 1979)

BACKGROUND: In the aftermath of the Chinese Revolution and the Korean War, the United States and the Republic of China ("ROC") negotiated a Mutual Defense Treaty, primarily directed against the perceived threat from the People's Republic of China ("PRC"). The Treaty was signed by representatives of both nations on December 2, 1954. It was approved by the Senate, and finally signed by the President on February 11, 1955. Article X of the Treaty provided that it would remain in force "indefinitely," but said that "(e)ither Party may terminate it one year after notice has been given to the other Party."

At that time both the ROC and PRC claimed, and still claim, to be the sole legitimate government of China; both considered Taiwan a part of China. Since then over 100 nations, including all of the USA's NATO allies and Japan, have officially recognized the PRC as the sole government of China, breaking off relations with Taiwan. In 1971 the United Nations admitted delegates from the PRC to the seats reserved for China in the General Assembly and Security Council, and expelled those from the ROC.

In the early 1970's the United States began to pursue a policy of closer relations with the PRC. The early stage of this effort culminated in President Nixon's visit to the mainland of China, during which the two nations released the "Shanghai Communique," declaring the goal of "normalization of relations between China and the United States." The PRC stipulated that full mutual diplomatic recognition was preconditioned on United States agreement to cease all diplomatic and other official relations with the ROC, to withdraw United States military units from Taiwan, and to terminate the Mutual Defense Treaty with the ROC.

In September 1978 Congress passed and the President signed the International Security Assistance Act. Section 26 of that Act provided: "It is the sense of the Congress that there should be prior consultation between the Congress and the executive branch on any proposed policy changes affecting the continuation in force of the Mutual Defense Treaty of 1954." On December 15, 1978, President Carter announced that the United States would recognize the PRC as the sole government of China, effective January 1, 1979, and would simultaneously withdraw recognition of the ROC. In addition, the United States announced that the ROC would be notified that "the Mutual Defense Treaty is being terminated in accordance with the provisions of the Treaty." On December 23, 1978, the State Department formally notified the ROC that the Treaty would terminate on January 1, 1980.

While severing all official ties with the ROC, the United States has sought to preserve "extensive, close, and friendly commercial, cultural, and other relations between the people of the United States and the people of Taiwan." The Taiwan Relations Act (1979) established the statutory framework for such relations. It provided: "3.... Relations between the United States Government and the authorities on Taiwan are conducted through a nonprofit corporation, the American Institute in Taiwan...." Section 3 of the Act authorizes the United States to provide defense material to Taiwan, and says that "(t)he President and the Congress shall determine the nature and quantity of such defense articles and services based solely upon their judgment of the needs of Taiwan." It further directs the President to report to the Congress on "any threat to the security or the social or economic system of the people of Taiwan and any danger to the interests of the United States arising therefrom." The President and the Congress then "shall determine * * * appropriate action by the United States in response to any such danger.'... For all purposes, including actions in any court in the United States, the Congress approves the continuation in force of all treaties and other international agreements, including multilateral conventions, entered into by the United States and the governing authorities on Taiwan recognized by the United States as the Republic of China prior to January 1, 1979, and in force between them on December 31, 1978, unless and until terminated in accordance with law."

On December 22, 1978 plaintiffs-appellees filed this suit in U.S. District Court, seeking declaratory and injunctive relief to prevent termination of the Treaty without senatorial or congressional consent. The complaint alleged that the President violated his sworn duty to uphold the laws, including the treaties, of the United States. It asserted that the President has no unilateral power under the Constitution to abrogate treaties, and that the United States, not the President, is the party invested by Article X of the Treaty with the power of termination.

On June 6, 1979, the District Court dismissed the suit, without prejudice, for lack of "standing." The court observed that three resolutions then pending in the Senate might resolve the controversy without need for judicial intervention. Within hours of the District Court order the Senate called up Senate Resolution 15 which, as amended by the Foreign Relations Committee, would have recognized some fourteen grounds that would justify unilateral action by the President to terminate treaty obligations of the United States. By a vote of 59 to 35 the Senate substituted for its consideration an amendment: "That it is the sense of the Senate that approval of the United States Senate is required to terminate any mutual defense treaty between the United States and another nation." Later that day, during the course of debate on the amended resolution, a dispute arose among the Senators over whether the resolution would have retrospective, or merely prospective effect. No final vote was ever taken on the resolution, and the Majority Leader returned the resolution to the calendar.

On June 12, 1979, after the amendment was voted on, the plaintiffs filed a motion in District Court for alteration or amendment of the June 6 order of dismissal. They contended that the Senate's action on the amendment satisfied the court's stated criteria for creating a justiciable controversy. On October 17, 1979, the District Court granted this motion, ruling that the plaintiffs had suffered the requisite injury in fact because of the denial of their right to be consulted and to vote on treaty termination. The court also ruled that the case did not present a nonjusticiable political question. Reaching the constitutional question, the court granted plaintiffs' cross-motion for summary judgment. President Carter appealed to the U.S. Court of Appeals for the District of Columbia.

THE COURT:

"The court en banc has before it for review the judgment of the District Court that the notice of termination given by the President pursuant to the terms of the Mutual Defense Treaty with the Republic of China is ineffective absent either (1) a manifestation of the consent of the Senate to such termination by a two-thirds vote or (2) an approving majority vote therefor by both houses of Congress. The preliminary questions we confront are, first, whether the District Court was without jurisdiction because appellees lacked standing, and, second, whether it should in any event have declined to exercise jurisdiction by reason of the political nature of the question it was called upon to decide. Since a majority of the court does not exist to dispose of the appeal on either of these bases, we reach the merits and reverse.

"Amici ['Friends' of the Court (other interested parties) who were permitted to file arguments] submit that the President's action in recognizing the People's Republic of China and in withdrawing recognition of the Republic of China, arising out of changed circumstances, of its own force under international law brought an end to the Mutual Defense Treaty between the latter and the United States. This end, so it is said, occurred automatically, and thus there is no necessity for the court to rule upon the validity of the notice of termination which in substance had no meaning or effect.

"Without intimating any view on the accuracy of the amici's premises, we do not pursue the mootness claim for the reason that the President did not purport to rely on international law as a possible defense against any future claim that the Treaty was a continuing obligation of the United States despite the events enumerated by the amici. Instead, the President elected to assert, on behalf of the United States, the privilege of terminating the Treaty by appropriate notice as provided by its own terms. A proper functioning of such a mutual termination clause is to permit a party to a treaty to respond to a change in circumstances without becoming embroiled in disputes as to the reach of international law doctrines. As we hold hereinafter, this course of action was, on the facts in this record, within the constitutional authority of the President.

"In doing so, however, we think it important at the outset to stress that the Treaty, as it was presented to the Senate in 1954 and consented to by it, contained an explicit provision for termination by either party on one year's notice. The Senate, in the course of giving its consent, exhibited no purpose and took no action to reserve a role for itself by amendment, reservation, or condition in the effectuation of this provision. Neither has the Senate, since the giving of the notice of termination, purported to take any final or decisive action with respect to it, either by way of approval or disapproval. The constitutional issue we face, therefore, is solely and simply the one of whether the President in these precise circumstances is, on behalf of the United States, empowered to terminate the Treaty in accordance with its terms. It is our view that he is, and that the limitations which the District Court purported to place on his action in this regard have no foundation in the Constitution.

"For purposes of the standing issue, we accept, as we must, appellees' pleaded theories as valid. A majority of the court is of the view that, at least as their principal theory has evolved that the Senate has a constitutional right to vote on the President's proposed treaty termination and to block such termination with a one-third plus one vote the appellee Senators have standing....

"The crucial fact is that, on the record before us, there is no conceivable senatorial action that could likely prevent termination of the Treaty. A congressional resolution or statute might at most have persuasive effect with the President; it could not block termination if he persisted in his present interpretation of the Constitution giving him unilateral power to terminate. That appellee Senators have no power to enact a remedy is especially clear in light of the nature of their constitutional claim. They claim the right to block termination with only one-third plus one of their colleagues. There is no way that such a minority can even force a resolution to the floor, let alone pass it. To pretend that effective remedies are open to appellees is to ignore that, first, their alleged right would enable them to block termination with a minority, and, second, that even if they could muster a majority, any legislative action they might take under the present circumstances could well be futile. The only way the Senate can effectively vote on a treaty termination, with the burden on termination proponents to secure a two-thirds majority, is for the President to submit the proposed treaty termination to the Senate as he would a proposed treaty. This is the concrete remedy appellees seek. For the court to require of them some other legislative action before allowing them standing to pursue this claim would be to require a useless act....

"Various considerations enter into our determination that the President's notice of termination will be effective on January 1, 1980. The result we reach draws upon their totality, but in listing them hereinafter we neither assign them hierarchical values nor imply that any one factor or combination of factors is determinative.

"We turn first to the argument, embraced by the District Court, drawn from the language of Article II, § 2, of the Constitution. It is that, since the President clearly cannot enter into a treaty without the consent of the Senate, the inference is inescapable that he must in all circumstances seek the same senatorial consent to terminate that treaty. As a matter of language alone, however, the same inference would appear automatically to obtain with respect to the termination by the President of officers appointed by him under the same clause of the Constitution and subject to Senate confirmation. But the Supreme Court has read that clause as not having such an inevitable effect in any and all circumstances.... In the area of foreign relations in particular, where the constitutional commitment of powers to the President is notably comprehensive, it has never been suggested that the services of Ambassadors appointed by the President, confirmed by the Senate, and of critical importance as they are to the successful conduct of our foreign relations may not be terminated by the President without the prior authorization of that body....

"Expansion of the language of the Constitution by sequential linguistic projection is a tricky business at best. Virtually all constitutional principles have unique elements and can be distinguished from one another. As the Supreme Court has recognized with respect to the clause in question, it is not abstract logic or sterile symmetry that controls, but a sensible and realistic ascertainment of the meaning of the Constitution in the context of the specific action taken.

"The District Court's declaration, in the alternative, that the necessary authority in this instance may be granted by a majority of each house of Congress presumably has its source in the Supremacy Clause of Article VI. The argument is that a treaty, being a part of the "supreme Law of the Land," can only be terminated at the least by a subsequent federal statute.

"The central purpose of the Supremacy Clause has been accepted to be that of causing each of the designated supreme laws Constitution, statute, and treaty to prevail, for purposes of domestic law, over state law in any form. Article VI speaks explicitly to the judges to assure that this is so. But these three types of supreme law are not necessarily the same in their other characteristics, any more than are the circumstances and terms of their creation the same. Certainly the Constitution is silent on the matter of treaty termination. And the fact that it speaks to the common characteristic of supremacy over state law does not provide any basis for concluding that a treaty must be unmade either by (1) the same process by which it was made, or (2) the alternative means by which a statute is made or terminated.

"The constitutional institution of advice and consent of the Senate, provided two-thirds of the Senators concur, is a special and extraordinary condition of the exercise by the President of certain specified powers under Article II. It is not lightly to be extended in instances not set forth in the Constitution. Such an extension by implication is not proper unless that implication is unmistakably clear.

"The District Court's absolutist extension of this limitation to termination of treaties, irrespective of the particular circumstances involved, is not sound. The making of a treaty has the consequences of an entangling alliance for the nation. Similarly, the amending of a treaty merely continues such entangling alliances, changing only their character, and therefore also requires the advice and consent of the Senate. It does not follow, however, that a constitutional provision for a special concurrence (two-thirds of the Senators) prior to entry into an entangling alliance necessarily applies to its termination in accordance with its terms.

"The Constitution specifically confers no power of treaty termination on either the Congress or the Executive. We note, however, that the powers conferred upon Congress in Article I of the Constitution are specific, detailed, and limited, while the powers conferred upon the President by Article II are generalized in a manner that bespeaks no such limitation upon foreign affairs powers. 'Section 1. The executive Power shall be vested in a President . . . .' Although specific powers are listed in Section 2 and Section 3, these are in many instances not powers necessary to an Executive, while 'The executive Power' referred to in Section 1 is nowhere defined. There is no required two-thirds vote of the Senate conditioning the exercise of any power in Section 1....

"The President is the constitutional representative of the United States with respect to external affairs. It is significant that the treaty power appears in Article II of the Constitution, relating to the executive branch, and not in Article I, setting forth the powers of the legislative branch. It is the President as Chief Executive who is given the constitutional authority to enter into a treaty; and even after he has obtained the consent of the Senate it is for him to decide whether to ratify a treaty and put it into effect. Senatorial confirmation of a treaty concededly does not obligate the President to go forward with a treaty if he concludes that it is not in the public interest to do so....

"Ultimately, what must be recognized is that a treaty is sui generis. It is not just another law. It is an international compact, a solemn obligation of the United States and a 'supreme Law' that supersedes state policies and prior federal laws. For clarity of analysis, it is thus well to distinguish between treaty-making as an international act and the consequences which flow domestically from such act. In one realm the Constitution has conferred the primary role upon the President; in the other, Congress retains its primary role as lawmaker. The fact that the Constitution, statutes, and treaties are all listed in the Supremacy Clause as being superior to any form of state law does not mean that the making and unmaking of treaties can be analogized to the making and unmaking of domestic statutes any more than it can be analogized to the making or unmaking of a constitutional amendment....

"If we were to hold that under the Constitution a treaty could only be terminated by exactly the same process by which it was made, we would be locking the United States into all of its international obligations, even if the President and two-thirds of the Senate minus one firmly believed that the proper course for the United States was to terminate a treaty. Many of our treaties in force, such as mutual defense treaties, carry potentially dangerous obligations. These obligations are terminable under international law upon breach by the other party or change in circumstances that frustrate the purpose of the treaty. In many of these situations the President must take immediate action. The creation of a constitutionally obligatory role in all cases for a two-thirds consent by the Senate would give to one-third plus one of the Senate the power to deny the President the authority necessary to conduct our foreign policy in a rational and effective manner.

"Even as to the formal termination of treaties, as the District Court pointed out, 'a variety of means have been used to terminate treaties.' There is much debate among the historians and scholars as to whether in some instances the legislature has been involved at all; they are agreed that, when involved, that involvement with the President has taken many different forms. It appears moreover that the Senate may wish to continue to determine the nature of its involvement on a case by case basis.

"The District Court concluded that the diversity of historical precedents left an inconclusive basis on which to decide the issue of whether the President's power to terminate a treaty must always be 'shared' in some way by the Senate or Congress. We agree. Yet we think it is not without significance that out of all the historical precedents brought to our attention, in no situation has a treaty been continued in force over the opposition of the President....

"How the vital functions of the President in implementing treaties and in deciding on their viability in response to changing events can or should interact with Congress' legitimate concerns and powers in relating to foreign affairs is an area into which we should not and do not prematurely intrude. History shows us that there are too many variables to lay down any hard and fast constitutional rules.

"We cannot find an implied role in the Constitution for the Senate in treaty termination for some but not all treaties in terms of their relative importance. There is no judicially ascertainable and manageable method of making any distinction among treaties on the basis of their substance, the magnitude of the risk involved, the degree of controversy which their termination would engender, or by any other standards. We know of no standards to apply in making such distinctions. The facts on which such distinctions might be drawn may be difficult of ascertainment; and the resolution of such inevitable disputes between the two Branches would be an improper and unnecessary role for the courts. To decide whether there was a breach or changed circumstances, for example, would involve a court in making fundamental decisions of foreign policy and would create insuperable problems of evidentiary proof. This is beyond the acceptable judicial role. All we decide today is that two-thirds Senate consent or majority consent in both houses is not necessary to terminate this treaty in the circumstances before us now....

"Reversed."

CHAPTER II

Jurisdiction of International and National Courts, International Choice of Law, and International Arbitration

OVERVIEW:

Jurisdiction is a crucial concept in the litigation process. Without jurisdiction both as to the type of case being litigated (subject-matter jurisdiction) and as to the parties to the dispute (personal jurisdiction), the court should dismiss the case. If it proceeds to hear and decide the case anyway, the court's judgment is not entitled to enforcement by courts in other states or nations.

International jurisdiction rules have many similarities to U.S. rules, but also some notable differences. Unlike the USA, where most or all State-v-State controversies can be resolved by the U.S. Supreme Court, there is no final legal "umpire" for the conflicting authorities of nations. Resolution of such disputes, in the end, depends on diplomacy, or economic or military sanctions.

Secondly, since the principle of territorial sovereignty is the bedrock of International Law (and international relations), any attempt by one nation to exercise legal authority over persons and things within the territory of another may provoke a serious negative reaction. Such extra-territorial application of a nation's laws is in a sense a direct challenge to the legitimacy and integrity of the other, affected nation. The exchanges of views on these points can thus get quite heated, as we will see in some of our examples.

Nations have historically been very reluctant to surrender any of their sovereign powers to an international body. Whereas within a nation the courts can be given power to adjudicate claims between litigants, international courts hearing nation-v-nation disputes have only the powers conferred on them by agreement of the litigants. Governments may grant power to an international body to hear a certain type of dispute, or may agree to have only a particular case heard. Arbitrations are also frequently used to settle international disputes—both disputes involving Governments and disputes between private parties.

International Courts. Established under the United Nations ("UN") Charter, the ***International Court of Justice*** ("ICJ") hears cases and claims between nations. Investors and companies who have claims against a host nation for violations of international law must have their claims submitted to the court by their home country; they cannot themselves file a claim with the ICJ. The home country's government decides whether to pursue the claim, and what to do with any monetary settlement. The ICJ also issues advisory opinions on legal questions submitted to it by certain UN agencies.

There are fifteen judges on the ICJ; no more than two can be from the same nation. Five are elected by the UN General Assembly and the Security Council each third year, for nine-year terms. The General Assembly now has 193 members. The Security Council is made up of the U.S., the U.K., Russia, China, and France as permanent members, and 10 other nations elected for terms. These two bodies hold independent elections. A person chosen by both bodies is automatically elected to the ICJ. Two additional separate ballots may be cast. If there are still not five persons agreed on, the selection will be made by a committee consisting of three members from each body.

Under the provisions of the 1958 Treaty of Rome, a "supranational" court—the (European) ***Court of Justice***—was also established for the European Economic Community ("EEC"). Most of Europe, including its largest economies, is included in what is now the European Union, and membership has expanded from the original six nations to the present 28. The original treaty has been revised several times to take account of the expanding membership, and of the desire for closer policy coordination and greater citizen voice. These policy objectives are observable to some extent in changes made to the EU's supranational court structure. As described by the website for the "Court of Justice of the European Union": "To help the Court of Justice cope with the large number of cases brought before it, and to offer citizens better legal protection, a ***'General Court'*** deals with cases brought forward by private individuals, companies, and some organizations, and cases relating to competition law." The EU thus provides direct access to its supranational court for individuals and companies with competition-law complaints. (*See* the example cases in Chapter VI, *infra*.)

The Court of Justice is the court of last resort on matters of Community law. It hears appeals in cases in which a party alleges that national courts did not follow Community law, and also responds to questions from national courts. Community law supersedes national law, to the extent of any conflict, in much the same way as a treaty supersedes the law of an individual State in the USA. Since the EU is now by far the largest trading bloc in the world, its multi-national rules are a very important part of international law.

Separately from the EU court structure, as the enforcement body for the European Convention on Human Rights, there exists the ***European Court of Human Rights*** ("ECHR"). Established in 1959, and a full-time court since 1998, it has delivered some 18,000 judgments on alleged human rights violations in Europe. Its jurisdiction covers the member-states of the Council of Europe—nations with a combined population of some 800 million, according to the ECHR website. While its name does not suggest a particular relevance to business operations, the listings of rights protected and practices prohibited do indicate the necessity of managerial awareness. "The Convention secures in particular:" the right to life; the right to a fair hearing; the right to respect for private and family life; freedom of expression; freedom of thought, conscience and religion; and the protection of property. Except perhaps for the first of these, it does not seem to require much deep thought to imagine business policies or decisions that might be an alleged violation of the Convention, and thus subject to litigation in the ECHR. On the negative side, "[t]he Convention prohibits in particular:" torture and inhuman or degrading treatment or punishment; slavery and forced labor; death penalty; arbitrary and unlawful detention; and discrimination in the enjoyment of the rights and freedoms set out in the Convention. Again, except for the "death penalty," the possibility of one or more of the prohibited behaviors occurring in a business setting seems all too real. (*See*, for example, the *Kiobel* case in Chapter I.)

In the Western Hemisphere, the ***Inter-American Court of Human Rights*** ("IACHR") was established in 1979, with a similar mission. Twenty of the 35 American nations have agreed to accept the IACHR's jurisdiction over alleged violations of human rights. Unlike the European CHR, however, individuals do not have direct access to the Court. Claims must first be presented to a relevant nation's regular dispute mechanisms. Claims still unresolved after ordinary remedies have been exhausted may then be filed with the Inter-American Commission on Human Rights. If the Commission decides that the claim is valid, it will send the offending nation a list of recommended curative steps to be taken. The Commission brings the case before the IACHR only if the offending nation refuses to perform the recommended remedies, or if the Commission thinks that the case is important enough to require a formal ruling by the IACHR. At this point in time, it seems fair to conclude that the IACHR has not had the same level of impact on American human rights as its European counterpart has had on human rights in Europe.

Although the North American Free Trade Agreement between Canada, Mexico, and the USA ("NAFTA") did not set up its own court, similar to the EU's Court of Justice, the NAFTA treaty does contain several sections on dispute resolution. For investment disputes, NAFTA Chapter 11 gives the complainant the option of using one of three international arbitration systems (the World Bank's International Centre for the Settlement of Investment Disputes—ICSID, ICSID'S Additional Facility Rules, United Nations Commission for International Trade Law—UNCITRAL), or the normal domestic courts of the host nation. Chapter 11 provides that any such arbitration awards will be enforceable in domestic courts of the three member-nations.

For disputes involving "antidumping" and "countervailing duty" determinations by designated domestic agencies in the three countries, Article 1904 of NAFTA Chapter 19 provides for review by *Independent Binational Panels*—as an alternative to review by the designated domestic court of the same member-nation (the Federal Court of Canada, the Mexican Tribunal Fiscal de la Federacion, the U.S. Court of International Trade). The penalized industry (importing from a NAFTA nation to a NAFTA nation) files a request for review with the NAFTA Secretariat. Panel members are chosen from lists of qualified persons prepared by each member-nation. Each of the two parties to the dispute chooses two panel members, in consultation with the other party; the fifth panel member is from one of the two parties, usually alternating dispute by dispute. The panel's decision is final, subject to limited review. Where a party believes that a panel decision has been "materially affected" by a panel member's conflict of interest or by the panel's violation of a fundamental procedural rule or the scope of its authority, that nation may require review by an *Extraordinary Challenge Committee* ("ECC"). The three-person ECC will be composed of judges and former judges, chosen from lists prepared by each NAFTA member. Under Article 1905, review by a three-person "*Special Committee*" is also possible where one of the parties alleges that the application of the other's domestic law has interfered with the panel system's functioning.

NAFTA Chapter 20 provides a dispute settlement mechanism for all questions related to the interpretation or application of NAFTA. The emphasis is on trying to reach an agreed settlement, starting with consultations between the two disputing nations themselves. If they are unable to reach an agreement, the next step is to request a meeting with the NAFTA Free-Trade Commission: the Trade Ministers of all three nations. If there is still no resolution, either disputing nation may request *arbitration* by a five-person panel. The selection of a Chapter 20 panel is a bit different than that under Chapter 19—each disputing party chooses two panel members who are citizens of the *other* nation, and the *chair* (chosen by the two disputants) may be a citizen of *any* nation. Within about five months after the initiation of the process, a Chapter 20 panel is to produce a report with findings of fact, a decision on whether the action complained of violates NAFTA, and any recommendations suggested by the panel.

As of January 1, 1995, the General Agreement on Tariffs and Trade ("GATT") was reconstituted as the World Trade Organization ("WTO"). The WTO now includes nearly all the world—as of mid-2014, 160 members and 24 "observers" (nations who must begin negotiations for membership within five years after being granted observer status). While the WTO's primary mission is the lowering of trade barriers and the encouragement of international commerce, its website notes that it serves protective functions as well—such as protecting consumers and preventing "the spread of disease."

To quote the WTO website: "Agreements, including those painstakingly negotiated in the WTO system, often need interpreting. The most harmonious way to settle these differences is through some neutral procedure based on an agreed legal foundation. That is the purpose behind the dispute settlement process written into the WTO agreements."

WTO's General Council, composed of all its member-nations, also functions as its **Dispute Settlement Body** ("DSB"). The DSB has exclusive power to establish the panels of experts that hear disputes, to approve or disapprove the panels' decisions, to monitor implementation of any recommendations, and to authorize "retaliation" against the violator-nation by the nation/s affected by the wrongful trade tactics.

The nations involved in the dispute are first given 60 days to resolve the problem themselves. If they are unsuccessful in doing so, they can request assistance from the WTO Director-General. Failing an agreed settlement, the complaining nation can request the DSB to "establish" a panel to investigate the dispute. The "defending" nation can block the first request, but cannot prevent establishment if the DSB so decides a second time. The actual members of the three-person (or five-person) panel are selected by the parties to the dispute, from lists of experts nominated by WTO members. Other persons with similar qualifications can also be chosen. If the parties cannot agree on panel members, the WTO Director-General selects the panel.

The panel holds hearings, investigates and evaluates the evidence, and interprets the applicable laws. Its final report is a decision on the merits of the case—who's right and who's wrong. The report is circulated to the parties, and then to all WTO members. While in theory the panel is merely "advising" the WTO on how the dispute ought to be decided, the panel's final report becomes the ruling of the WTO itself unless the WTO members *unanimously* reject it, within 60 days. (Under the previous GATT procedure, a panel ruling only became the official decision if it was unanimously *approved* by GATT's member-nations—including the defendant-nation!)

Either party can, however, appeal a panel's decision—on points of law. Any appeals are heard by three members of a standing seven-person **Appellate Body** ("AB"). AB members are persons of "recognized standing" in international law and international trade, who serve 4-year terms on the AB. The AB panel can affirm, reverse or modify the hearing panel's legal interpretations. It has an "absolute maximum" of 90 days in which to do so. The DSB has 30 days to accept or reject the appellate report, and again, rejection must be a unanimous decision by the WTO members.

If the defending nation has been found guilty of a trade violation, it must inform the DSB—within 30 days of the report's adoption—of its intention to follow any recommendations in the panel's decision. It may be given a reasonable time to implement the required policy changes. If the nation fails to do so, it must discuss other possible forms of compensation with the complaining nation. If after 20 days the parties cannot agree on some alternate compensation, the complaining nation can ask the DSB for permission to "retaliate" against the wrongdoer—by blocking its imports or raising tariffs on them, for example. The DSB has the difficult job of enforcing its rulings, while also avoiding the escalation of such disputes into a full-fledged "trade war"—a delicate balance, requiring a refined judgment and a steady hand.

In large part as an outgrowth of the "war crimes" trials following the end of World War II, over 100 nations agreed in 1998 to the creation of an ***International Criminal Court*** ("ICC"). *Ad hoc* criminal courts had been established in 1993 for alleged violations of international law in Yugoslavia in 1993 and in Rwanda in 1994. The diamond wars in Sierra Leone and the genocide in Cambodia may yet merit their own criminal panels. The idea behind the ICC is to provide an ongoing forum for the prosecution of similar atrocities, without the necessity of establishing specific panels for each such occurrence—with all the procedural difficulties that entails.

While the stated goals for the ICC sound noble and unobjectionable, there are still some unanswered questions about the details and thus some remaining national reluctance to "hop on the bandwagon." One troubling point seems to be the tendency on the part of some of its supporters to equate "human rights" violations with "war crimes." It's one thing to state that violation of international standards of criminal procedure (whatever those may be) would give other nations the "right," under international law, to refuse extradition of a criminal suspect or convicted criminal fugitive. But it hardly seems proportional to equate an over-extended interrogation period, or a failure to notify the accused's embassy of the criminal charge, with the sort of ethnic genocide that was the main subject-matter of the Nuremberg trials. One nation's tactics "in defense of national security" may be acceptable to persons in other nations, or may be condemned as "human rights violations." Further, the past history of inclusion of some of the worst national violators of "human rights" on various UN human rights commissions and tribunals raises questions about the potential membership of the ICC. Perhaps these points—and similar uncertainties—help explain the USA's failure to ratify the ICC treaty. (*See, e.g.,* "The ICC's Limits," *Time,* [June 29, 2015], p. 12.) It seems unlikely that a majority of the U.S. Senate will vote to ratify until they have a substantially higher level of confidence that these issues will be resolved satisfactorily. Even without the USA's participation, the acceptance of the ICC by a large number of nations means that managers need to be aware of its existence and its relevance to international business operations. Three of the Nuremberg Trials held by USA military courts featured business managers (at I.G. Farben, Krupp, and Fritz KG); 27 of the 42 total defendants were convicted of one or more war crimes. And at least some of the offenses alleged in the various international tort cases would also seem to be justifiably characterized as "crimes against humanity." Doing business with totalitarian regimes does carry significant additional downside risks.

National Courts and Jurisdictional Questions. Since there are no "world-wide" trial courts in which private parties can directly file lawsuits, they are forced to use national courts when disputes arise. The plaintiff will naturally try to select a court where it thinks it can receive a fair hearing, at least. Often, the plaintiff will try to bring the litigation in its home country, feeling that it may have some advantage there over the alien defendant. A plaintiff seeking damages will probably try to select a court where larger awards are possible. If the claim is based on a new or unestablished theory of liability, the plaintiff will try for a sympathetic or innovative court.

The defendant, wishing to avoid liability if it can, will in many cases object to plaintiff's choice of **forum** (the court where the case has been filed). The defendant may also object to the use of the body of law which plaintiff says applies to the case. These two issues arise with considerable frequency in international disputes.

Forum Jurisdiction. On the first issue, the forum court will have to decide if it does have jurisdiction over the defendant, and if so, whether there are other factors which would prevent it from hearing the case. The basic test is whether the defendant has had sufficient contacts with the forum nation to justify its being sued there. Modern rules are generally quite liberal on this point, even though cases still deny jurisdiction in some instances. Commission of a tort within the forum nation is generally considered a sufficient basis for a lawsuit based on that wrong. Entering into or performing a contract in the forum state would normally also be a sufficient basis for claims arising out of that contract. Ownership of property within the forum state is clearly enough basis for a lawsuit related to that property. (Under German law, it seems to be a sufficient basis for suing the owner there for any claim, regardless of amount.) Organization of a business in the forum state would certainly give it jurisdiction to hear any claims related to the operation of the business, or to its internal management.

One's **"presence"** in the forum state or nation may be another alternative basis for jurisdiction, depending on the local rules. The physical presence of a human person is simply his or her location at any given point in time—recognizing that each of us can be "present" in only one place at a time, although we are surely able to change locations from time to time. The "presence" of a "legal person" (corporation or other such fictional being) is a bit more difficult to define, since the legal person has no physical form at all. It may own things which have physical form—such as buildings, vehicles and other property—but those things are not themselves the legal person. The legal person is created by some government's approval of its certificate of incorporation or some similar document that has physical form (unless it is only a set of electrical impulses on someone's "cloud" file—which may or may not constitute a "physical" presence). But the corporate (physical?) "birth certificate" in Delaware is not the Ford Motor Company any more than my birth certificate in Ohio is *me*. So where is the Ford Motor Company "present" for court jurisdiction purposes? The rule adopted by the U.S. Supreme Court says that it is present anywhere it is doing, or attempting to do, "a systematic and regular part of its general business operations." What this means in plain language is that the Ford Motor Company can be sued in lots and lots of places around the world—by anybody, from anywhere, for anything. That general rule on jurisdiction is, of course, subject to significant limitations—the *forum non conveniens* rule, and others.

Applicable Law. The second issue on which a defendant may object to forum—choice of the applicable law—is even more complicated. Much of private international law is still concerned with this basic question: whose law applies to the dispute? Over the centuries, some general rules have become widely accepted, but the development of modern commercial practices has required some updating of these rules. (*See, e.g.*, the careful balancing of "technicalities" and "practicalities" by Bankruptcy Judge Gassen in the *L.M.S.* case in Chapter III.) It is generally agreed that the validity of a contract is determined according to the law of the country where it was made. Contract performance will normally be judged according to the law of the nation where performance was to occur. Questions relating to the internal management of an organization are nearly always determined by the law of the place of organization. Tort liability may be based on the law of the place where the alleged wrongful act occurred, or where its effects were felt. Using a newer "grouping of contacts" approach, some courts use the law of the country which, overall, has the major relationship to the alleged wrong and the parties involved. Since the forum court uses its own nation's procedural law, there are many tough questions as to whether a particular point is "procedural" or "substantive" (and thus subject to some other law under the above tests). Much time, effort, and money can be expended just in deciding these two preliminary issues, before the court ever gets to the merits of the dispute. Meanwhile, the attention of the involved companies' managers may be diverted from ongoing business operations, and litigation expenses are affecting the companies' economics.

Arbitration of International Disputes. To avoid these extended preliminary wrangles, many international contracts contain arbitration clauses. An arbitration clause permits the parties to select a person or panel of persons who are experienced in the type of problem at issue and who are trusted by both sides. Quite often, a nation respected for its impartiality, such as Sweden or Switzerland, will be selected as the site for the hearing. Arbitrators, and established procedures, are available in such locations. Either party is thus able to refer any problem to a specific place, for hearing and resolution. As a preliminary matter, there may be a dispute over whether the parties did in fact agree to arbitrate any future contract disputes, and if so, to what extent.

Arbitration also has the great advantage of being private, as opposed to having the publicity associated with a court trial. The parties can make concessions and work out a compromise settlement, without having to worry about playing to the press and the public. Arbitrators are also selected for their expertise in dealing with commercial problems. In contrast, litigants take the luck of the draw with judges and juries.

Arbitration awards are today generally enforceable in USA courts, in the event the parties do not voluntarily comply. The lawsuit in court does not retry the whole case on the merits, but only makes sure that the dispute was properly subject to arbitration and that the arbitrator followed the rules. There may be considerable variation from nation to nation as to what sorts of disputes are arbitrable, and also as to the enforceability of arbitration awards and the procedure for doing so. To remove many of these possible inconsistencies, 149 nations have agreed to the New York Convention on the Enforceability of Foreign Arbitration Awards, whereby they will (generally) enforce such awards according to the rules of the place under whose laws the award was made.

Because of the lack of international courts with jurisdiction over normal business disputes, arbitration has been widely used for such cases for many years. (It has of course also been used in many nation-to-nation disputes.) The parties may include an agreement to arbitrate any future disputes as part of a business contract, or may so agree after a contractual or any other dispute arises between them. Customary arbitration practices have gradually developed into some generally-agreed-on "rules"—both within nations and internationally. Since arbitration is generally a matter of agreement between the disputing parties, they usually are free to adopt whatever rules they wish to use for the resolution of their dispute.

Cross-Border Enforcement of Judgments. Since there is no international parallel to the "Full Faith and Credit" clause found in the USA's national Constitution, cross-border enforcement of court judgments is discretionary. As a starting point, each nation's courts are free to decide which judgments from other nations they will enforce locally. The idea of "comity" (mutual respect for each other's judgments) will operate to permit enforcement in many cases—"We will recognize yours, if you will recognize ours." This sort of understanding may be somewhat easier if the two nations have the same type of legal system—common-law to common-law, civil-law to civil-law. (The civil codes and commercial codes in many nations are based on those originating in France and Germany.) Nations may also specifically agree by treaty to enforce each other's judgments. As noted above, the New York Convention requires enforcement of *arbitration* decisions in any of the signatory nations, with only a few limited exceptions. Nations will generally refuse to enforce a foreign judgment where the law or policy underlying it violates a strongly-held local principle. (*See* the *Spink & Son* and *Matusevich* cases, below.)

EXAMPLE CASES PREVIEW:

JP MORGAN CHASE BANK: The USA's national trial courts are given the power to hear civil cases between persons who are citizens of different USA States, or between a citizen of a USA State and a citizen or subject of a foreign nation. Since USA State courts may have different procedural systems than the national courts, there may be perceived advantages is using the latter. The USA's national intermediate appellate court for New York had decided in an earlier case that the national courts were not available to a Hong Kong corporation suing to collect for merchandise sold to New York persons. Following its precedent, the same court refused to hear Chase Bank's suit against a British Virgin Islands corporation. Chase Bank asked the U.S. Supreme Court to review that denial.

WILES: Floyd Wiles sustained a serious on-the-job injury in Illinois, while using a machine manufactured in Japan and sold to his USA employer company. The Japanese manufacturer-seller claimed it could not be sued in the Illinois State courts, since it had no connection with Illinois other than the presence there of two machines it had manufactured and sold in Japan.

ASAHI METAL: A motorcycle tire valve, manufactured in Japan and sold to the Taiwanese tire manufacturer, allegedly malfunctioned in California resulting in an accident that seriously injured the motorcycle driver and killed his passenger. A lawsuit was filed in the California courts. The manufacturers settled the claims of the injured humans, but the Taiwanese tire manufacturer claimed recourse against the Japanese valve manufacturer (for the damages the tire-maker had paid to the victims). The Japanese company said the tire-maker's claim should not be heard in the California courts.

CLUNE: An employee was killed in Missouri when he fell off a construction hoist. His family filed a lawsuit there, against the Swedish company that manufactured the hoist, claiming that it was defective in design and/or manufacture. The Swedish manufacturer claimed that it could not be sued in Missouri—essentially the same litigation pattern as in *Wiles* (and in about two-thirds of all the tens of thousands of product-liability lawsuits filed in the USA—think asbestos). The U.S. Eighth Circuit Court of Appeals held that the lawsuit could proceed. Checking the facts, there *may* be enough difference to justify the different result here than in *Wiles*. In any event, this decision was the first one cited by U.S. Supreme Court Justice Ginsburg in her dissenting opinion in *J. McIntyre* (below).

PREWITT: Anyone who wonders how the Organization of the Petroleum Exporting Countries ("OPEC") continues to escape the legal consequences of its seemingly illegal manipulations of the supply and pricing of petroleum needs to read this opinion.

BLIMKA: Here's a nice example of how these "long-arm" jurisdictional rules apply to Web-based transactions. It's not a purely Internet case, however, since the seller's employee also lied to buyer Blimka over the telephone.

J. MCINTYRE MACHINERY: This is a classic "good news/bad news" decision from the U.S. Supreme Court. The good news for overseas manufacturers is that six of the nine Justices agreed that the U.K. manufacturer could not be sued in New Jersey just because one of its machines was there and had allegedly caused injury there. The bad news is that two of those six decided the case on the basis of "fairness" (*not fair* to force McIntyre to defend in New Jersey), as did the three dissenting Justices (it would be *fair* to force McIntyre to defend in New Jersey). Thus a majority of five Justices is deciding the case on the basis of an extremely vague and subjective "standard," rather than on the basis of more predictable and controllable criteria (what specifically had McIntyre done intentionally to connect it with New Jersey?)

STANGVIK: Usually in these "long-arm" cases, the plaintiff wants to sue in its home State (*Wiles*; *Clune*), and the defendant manufacturer/seller wants to defend in its home State. Each party is looking for its own "home-field advantage"—just as is true in many sports contests. In this case, however, things are reversed—the Scandinavian plaintiffs are willing to travel several thousand miles to sue in California, and the defendant California manufacturer is claiming that the courts in Scandinavia would be a more "convenient" (i.e., appropriate) location. Why?

PAREX BANK: The same "convenience" argument, as in *Stangvik*, is made here—with a different result. To get a court to transfer a case that it has the power to hear if it wants to, to a court in another State or Nation, the party in favor of the transfer has to convince the transferring court that the alternative is preferable. This means that, at least, the alternative court can provide an appropriate remedy if the claim is proved and that the "convenience" of all the stakeholders favors the alternative location.

CONGREGATION B'NAI SHOLOM: Most little civil litigations don't make the newspapers, but this one did—because of the *implied* choice-of-law rule that the Michigan Supreme Court used. The Court was convinced by the affidavit of the expert on Jewish religious law, to the effect that State court enforcement of a pledge to the church would violate fundamental religious precepts, and that the parties making the pledge(s) "must have intended" application of Jewish law as to their enforceability.

FINNISH FUR SALES: The Shulof Fur Company is bankrupt, without funds to pay for the furs it bought from Finnish Fur Sales ("FFS"). FFS is thus attempting to impose personal liability on George Shulof; and the bank that financed part of the transaction is suing Juliette Shulof. The two claims are based on different theories of liability—George, on the basis that he was the agent who bought the furs at an auction in Finland; Juliette, on the basis that she signed a payment instrument in an ambiguous fashion, not clearly indicating that she was signing *only* as an agent. Since George was personally present at the auction in Finland, he is bound by Finnish law as to the personal liability of an agent. (We may take our own toothbrush with us on our overseas business trip, but we do not take our own country's laws with us—at least not unless we so specify in our contract, and get the other contracting party to agree thereto.) Juliette signed the negotiable instrument in New York, and so she is liable on it (to the financing bank) as per the rules in Article 3 of New York's version of the USA's Uniform Commercial Code.

SPINK & SON: There's a different twist to this choice-of-law case. The alleged oral contract was supposedly made in the U.K., with agents for both parties personally present there. Thus the general rule would be that U.K. contract law (which does not require a signed writing as proof of such a contract) should apply. The alleged buyer (now back in New York) is trying to argue that enforcement of the oral contract by the New York court would violate a strong "public policy" here, since Article 2 of the Uniform Commercial Code does require a signed writing (or one of the four alternatives) for enforcement of a contract for the sale of goods with a contract price of $500 or more. (Compare the result in the *Matusevich* case.)

CARNIVAL CRUISE LINES: The relatively simple and innocuous choice-of-law point in this case is in fact very important, and has been seized on by many businesses in the USA (and perhaps elsewhere). At least in some nations, for some types of contracts, the parties are free to decide where any lawsuits arising out of their relationship will be litigated, and to choose which nation's law will be applied. In the USA, this freedom to choose has been strongly supported by the Supreme Court for at least four decades. So when Mr. and Mrs. Shute accept and use a cruise ticket which states that any lawsuits resulting from their cruise *must* be heard in Florida courts, they are prevented from suing in their home State of Washington.

MATUSEVICH: The USA court granted an injunction against the enforcement here of an English court's libel judgment, because the statements made by Matusevich in the U.K. would have been protected by the First Amendment's "freedom of speech" principle if made in the

USA. "Freedom of speech" is one of the most important principles in the USA's political/ constitutional structure. Enforcement here of a court decision that contradicted that principle would violate the USA's fundamental public policy. (Note the difference between the USA/UK policies here and the "oral vs. written contract" contrast in *Spink*.)

IVEY: The Canadian Supreme Court followed the general "comity" here, and decided to enforce the USA court's judgment. Ivey was held accountable by the USA court for activities in the USA (Michigan), and the USA plaintiff (government) was merely seeking Canadian enforcement of the established liabilities.

KARAHA BODAS: The plaintiff is seeking USA court enforcement of a "Swiss" arbitration decision, which the defendant claims was nullified by an Indonesian court. International arbitration rules indicate that naming a location for arbitration implies use of that place's arbitration rules, and that a challenge to the validity of any arbitration award must be processed through that nation's courts. Thus, while Indonesian courts could refuse to enforce the Swiss award in Indonesia, they did *not* have the authority to nullify the award itself. The USA court enforced the award.

FORD MOTOR: Although USA courts had previously held that Mexican courts were proper venues for trying liability cases involving USA-made products, the plaintiffs here had strong motivation to get their case tried in the U.S. (probability of higher awards), and thus constructed an elaborate scheme to get the Mexican courts disqualified. Some complicated procedural steps were necessary to straighten things out.

YAYASAN MELIKA: While this case did involve an international joint venture, the default judgment entered and the appeal filed later to try to overturn it were both processed by the national courts. It is thus a sort of counter-point to several of the prior cases. (The judgment in default ["JID"] was in fact overturned by the appellate court, due to the fraudulent conduct of the majority partner.) The case could also be used as a nice example of the fiduciary duty that one joint venturer owes to the other/s.

BHATIA INT'L: There is a general assumption that a valid arbitration agreement preempts all court proceedings. The arbitration process is presumed to be the exclusive mechanism for resolution of the rights and wrongs of the dispute. It is, however, also recognized that there may be a necessity for certain supplementary court processes to *aid* in the arbitration process. The Supreme Court of India did recognize that "exception," and interpreted the relevant Indian statute to permit such supplementary assistance. (The Supreme Court also explained the contrary holdings of several appellate courts by indicating that the statute had used some ambiguous wording.)

KOREA SUPREME COURT: The Supreme Court of Korea is reviewing lower courts' handling of a Vietnamese arbitration award, to make sure that the requirements of the New York Convention on the Recognition and Enforcement of Foreign Arbitral Awards have been met.

STOLT-NIELSON S.A.: If an arbitration agreement does not specify whether it authorizes arbitration on behalf of a class of claimants, in a group proceeding, should a court require that such a "class arbitration" be held? Although the U.S. Supreme Court has been strongly supportive of arbitration agreements for the last several decades, it answered this question in the negative.

GLOBAL TRADING: Established by a multi-nation treaty, the International Centre for the Settlement of Investment Disputes provides a neutral arbitration forum for the resolution of such cases. That forum was not available to hear disputes arising out of ordinary sale-of-goods transactions between USA sellers and Ukrainian buyers. The fact that the Ukrainian prime minister had "sponsored" these sales as being necessary for the economy did not change a sale of goods into an "investment" for the purposes of the ICSID treaty (or for purposes of the USA-Ukrainian *Investment* Treaty).

BG GROUP: BG Group requested arbitration of its claim against Argentina; Argentina said no arbitration could occur until after the "local litigation" requirement specified in the arbitration agreement had been met. The arbitration occurred in Washington, DC; the arbitrators agreed with BG's position and made an award. Court review of the decision reached the U.S. Supreme Court, which decided that the arbitrators had acted within their authority and that their decision was not arbitrary or unreasonable.

CASE EXAMPLES:

JPMORGAN CHASE BANK v. TRAFFIC STREAM (BVI)
  536 U.S. 88 (2002)

BACKGROUND: The USA's national courts have jurisdiction (authority/power) to hear ordinary civil cases governed by State law if there is "diversity of citizenship" between the parties to the dispute, and if at least $75,000 is at stake in the litigation. In 1997, the U.S. District Court for the Southern District of New York dismissed a contract dispute between a plaintiff Hong Kong corporation and New York defendants for lack of the required "diversity." Hong Kong was at the time not an independent nation, and the U.K. citizenship statute said that

Hong Kong corporations were not citizens of the U.K. Disagreeing with several other U.S. Courts of Appeal, the U.S. Second Circuit affirmed that decision. The U.S. Supreme Court did not review that case.

In 1998, Chase Manhattan Bank (now JPMorgan Chase) agreed to finance some—rather extensive—ventures that Traffic Stream had organized to build and operate toll roads in China. Traffic Stream is a corporation organized under the laws of the British Virgin Islands (BVI), an Overseas Territory of the United Kingdom. The contract provided that it would be governed by the laws of New York and that Traffic Stream agreed to be subject to the jurisdiction of the federal courts there.

Chase sued Traffic Stream for breach of contract, in the U.S. District Court in New York. The court granted Chase's motion for summary judgment, but on appeal the Second Circuit ordered that the case be dismissed. As per the earlier Second Circuit decision, the national courts did not have subject-matter jurisdiction—since Traffic Stream was not the citizen or subject of an "independent foreign nation." The U.S. Supreme Court granted Chase's petition for certiorari.

JUSTICE SOUTER:

"Title 28 U.S.C. s.1332(a)(2) provides district courts with 'original jurisdiction of all civil actions where the matter in controversy exceeds the sum or value of $75,000 ... and is between ... citizens of a State and citizens or subjects of a foreign state.' A 'corporation of a foreign state is, for purposes of jurisdiction in the courts of the United States, to be deemed, constructively, a citizen or subject of such State.'... 'For purposes of international law, a corporation has the nationality of the state under the laws of which the corporation is organized.'...

"The argument that the status of the BVI renders the statute inapplicable begins by assuming that Traffic Stream, organized under BVI law, must be a citizen or subject of the BVI alone. Since the BVI is a British Overseas territory, unrecognized by the United States Executive Branch as an independent foreign state, it is supposed to follow that for purposes of alienage jurisdiction Traffic Stream is not a citizen or subject of a 'foreign state' within the meaning of s.1332(a)(2).

"Even on the assumption, however, that a foreign state must be diplomatically recognized by our own Government to qualify as such under the jurisdictional statute ..., we have never held that the requisite status as citizen or subject must be held directly from a formally recognized state, as distinct from such a state's legal dependency. On the contrary, a consideration of the relationships of the BVI and the recognized state of the United Kingdom convinces us that any such distinction would be entirely beside the point of the statute providing alienage jurisdiction....

"The relationship between the BVI's powers over corporations and the sources of these powers in Crown and Parliament places the United Kingdom well within the range of concern addressed by Article III and s.1332(a)(2). The United Kingdom exercises ultimate authority over the BVI's statutory law, including its corporate law and the law of corporate charter, and it exercises responsibility for the BVI's external relations. These exercises of power and responsibility point to just the kind of relationship that the Framers believed would bind sovereigns 'by inclination, as well as duty, to redress the wrongs' against their nationals.'...

"Traffic Stream's alternative argument is that BVI corporations are not 'citizens or subjects' of the United Kingdom. Traffic Stream begins with the old fiction that a corporation is just an association of shareholders, presumed to reside in the place of incorporation ... with the result that, for jurisdictional purposes, a suit against the corporation should be understood as a suit against the shareholders.... Traffic Stream proceeds to read the British Nationality Act, 1981, as a declaration by the United Kingdom that BVI residents are not its citizens or subjects, but mere 'nationals,' without the rights and privileges of citizens or subjects.... Traffic Stream insists that because it is legally nothing more than a collection of noncitizen individuals, the corporation itself cannot be treated as deserving of access to the courts of the United States under a statute that opens them to foreign citizens and subjects.

"The less important flaw in the argument is its reliance on the outdated legal construct of corporations as collections of shareholders linked by contract ... a view long since replaced by the corporations as independent legal entities.... Thus, Traffic Stream's whole notion of corporate citizenship derived from natural persons is irrelevant to jurisdictional inquiry in the United States today....

"But the argument's more significant weakness is its failure to recognize that jurisdictional analysis under the law of the United States is not ultimately governed by the law of the United Kingdom, whatever that may be.... [O]ur jurisdictional concern here is with the meaning of 'citizen' and 'subject' as those terms are used in s.1332(a)(2)....

"Traffic Stream concedes that BVI are at least 'nationals' of the United Kingdom.... Given the object of the alienage statute ... there is no serious question that 'nationals' were meant to be amenable to the jurisdiction if the federal courts, leaving it immaterial for our purposes that the law of the United Kingdom may provide different rights of abode for individuals in the territories.

"... [T]he United Kingdom's retention and exercise of authority over the BVI renders BVI citizens, both natural and juridic, 'citizens or subjects' of the United Kingdom under 28 U.S.C. s.1332(a). We therefore reverse the judgment of the Court of Appeals."

WILES v. MORITA IRON WORKS CO. LTD.
530 N.E.2d 1382 (Illinois, 1988)

BACKGROUND: Astro Packaging—a USA company—purchased four machines in Japan from Morita Iron Works, a Japanese manufacturer. Two machines went to Astro's Illinois plant, and two went to its New Jersey plant. Floyd Wiles, an employee at the Illinois plant, was using one of the Morita machines when he was injured. (The machine evidently went through an operating cycle when Floyd thought he had it turned off.) Claiming that a defect in the machine's design and/or manufacture had caused his injury, he sued Morita for damages. Morita filed a motion to dismiss the case, "due to lack of personal jurisdiction," since it had no personnel or property in Illinois and did no business there. The case was dismissed, but the Illinois Appellate Court reversed the trial court. Morita appealed to the Illinois Supreme Court.

JUSTICE CLARK:

"The sole issue presented in this appeal is whether the defendant's contacts with the State of Illinois are sufficient to subject the defendant to the *in personam* jurisdiction of the Illinois courts....

"By 'purposefully availing' itself of opportunities in the forum State, such as by purposefully directing itself to forum residents, a defendant subjects itself to the possible exercise of that forum's jurisdiction. Satisfaction of this 'purposeful availment' requirement ensures that an alien defendant will not be forced to litigate in a distant or inconvenient forum solely as a result of 'random,' 'fortuitous,' or 'attenuated' contacts, or the unilateral act of a consumer or some other third person. Jurisdiction will only be proper where the contacts proximately result from actions by the *defendant himself* that create a 'substantial connection' with the forum State.... Only in situations 'where the defendant "deliberately" has engaged in significant activities within a State ... or has created "continuing obligations" between himself and residents of the forum ... [has] he manifestly . . . availed himself of the privilege of conducting business there, and . . . it is not presumptively unreasonable to require him to submit to . . . litigation in that forum.'

"Applying these principles to the facts before us, we hold that MIW did not have the requisite minimum contacts with the State of Illinois to subject it to the personal jurisdiction of the circuit court.

"The thrust of the plaintiff's due process argument here is that MIW should have reasonably anticipated being sued in Illinois because it directly sold its products to a New Jersey corporation that had an industrial plant in Illinois. Specifically, the plaintiff alleges that MIW must have had either 'actual or constructive knowledge' that Astro had a plant in Illinois and therefore should have anticipated that the product may find its way into Illinois. According to the plaintiff MIW's intentional act of placing its products into the stream of commerce by delivering the air cell formers to Astro in Japan, coupled with MIW's 'actual or constructive' knowledge that some of these products would eventually find their way to Illinois, is sufficient to form the basis for State court jurisdiction under the due process clause.

"[W]e believe that even under the broader version of the stream of commerce theory there were no minimum contacts between defendant Morita and the State of Illinois. Under the facts presented in the instant case, an exertion of personal jurisdiction over this defendant by the Illinois courts would still be inconsistent with due process. Under either interpretation of the stream of commerce theory, it is dear that purposeful availment of the forum's market requires, at a minimum that the alien defendant is 'aware that the final product is being marketed in the forum State.' The record in this case is totally devoid of any evidence that the defendant was aware either during contract negotiations or at the time of delivery of the products to Astro in Japan that Astro intended to transport two of the air cell formers to Illinois, or that Astro even had a plant in Illinois. Without any evidence of such knowledge on the part of the defendant, on this basis alone we would have to conclude, under either theory, that [MIW] made no effort, directly or indirectly, to serve the market for its product in Illinois and that the air cell formers were, therefore, brought into Illinois solely by the unilateral act of Astro. 'The unilateral activity of those who claim some relationship with a nonresident defendant cannot satisfy the requirement of contact with the forum state.' The fact that the defendant now knows the machines were sent to Illinois, as revealed in the defendant's affidavit, is of no consequence in the determination of whether this defendant has purposefully availed itself of the privilege of conducting activities within Illinois.

"For the foregoing reasons the judgment of the appellate court is reversed and the judgment of the circuit court is affirmed."

ASAHI METAL IND. v. SUPERIOR COURT OF CALIFORNIA, SOLANO
480 U.S. 1026 (1987)

BACKGROUND: Between 1978 and 1982 Asahi Metal—a Japanese manufacturer of tire valve assemblies—sold them to tire manufacturers, including Cheng Shin (a Taiwanese company). Cheng Shin sold its motorcycle tires all over the world, including in California. California resident Gary Zurcher was injured riding his motorcycle; his wife (a passenger) was killed. He filed a product liability action against Cheng Shin, alleging that its tire was defective. Cheng Shin claimed that Asahi's defective tire valve caused the accident and that Asahi should reimburse any liability that Cheng Shin owed to Zurcher. Zurcher settled his claims. Cheng Shin continued its action against Asahi. When the California courts refused to dismiss this cross-complaint, Asahi petitioned for review by the United States Supreme Court.

JUSTICE O'CONNOR:

"The Due Process Clause of the Fourteenth Amendment limits the power of a state court to exert personal jurisdiction over a nonresident defendant. '[T]he constitutional touchstone' of the determination whether an exercise of personal jurisdiction comports with due process 'remains whether the defendant purposefully established "minimum contacts" in the forum State.'...

"Most recently we have reaffirmed the oft-quoted reasoning of Hanson v. Denckla ... that minimum contacts must have a basis in 'some act by which the defendant purposefully avails himself of the privilege of conducting activities within the forum State, thus invoking the benefits and protection of its laws.' ... 'Jurisdiction is proper ... where the contacts proximately result from actions by the defendant himself that create a substantial connection with the forum State.'...

"The placement of a product into the stream of commerce, without more, is not an act of the defendant purposefully directed toward the forum State. Additional conduct of the defendant may indicate an intent or purpose to serve the market in the forum State, for example, designing the product for the market in the forum State, advertising in the forum State, establishing channels for providing regular advice to customers in the forum State, or marketing the product through a distributor who has agreed to serve as the sales agent in the forum State. But a defendant's awareness that the stream of commerce may or will sweep the product into the forum State does not convert the mere act of placing the product into the stream into an act purposefully directed toward the forum State.

"Assuming ... that respondents have established Asahi's awareness that some of the valves sold to Cheng Shin would be incorporated into tire tubes sold in California, respondents have not demonstrated any action by Asahi to avail itself of this market. It has no office, agents, employees, or property in California. It does not advertise or otherwise solicit business in California. It did not create or employ the distribution system that brought its valves to California.... There is no evidence that Asahi designed its product in anticipation of sales in California.... On the basis of these facts the exertion of personal jurisdiction over Asahi by the Superior Court of California exceeds the limits of Due Process.

"The strictures of the Due Process Clause forbid a state court from exercising personal jurisdiction over Asahi under circumstances that would offend 'traditional notions of fair play and substantial justice.'...

"We have previously explained that the determination of the reasonableness of the exercise of jurisdiction in each case will depend on an evaluation of several factors....

"Certainly the burden on the defendant in this case is severe. Asahi has been commanded by the Supreme Court of California not only to traverse the distance between Asahi's headquarters in Japan and the Superior Court of California in and for the County of Solano, but also to submit its dispute with Cheng Shin to a foreign nation's judicial system. The unique burdens placed upon one who must defend oneself in a foreign legal system should have significant weight in assessing the reasonableness of stretching the long arm of personal jurisdiction over national borders.

"When minimum contacts have been established, often the interests of the plaintiff and the forum in the exercise of jurisdiction will justify even the serious burdens placed on the alien defendant. In the present case, however, the interests of the plaintiff and the forum in California's assertion of jurisdiction over Asahi are slight. All that remains is a claim for indemnification asserted by Cheng Shin, a Taiwanese corporation, against Asahi. The transaction on which the indemnification claim is based took place in Taiwan; Asahi's components were shipped from Japan to Taiwan. Cheng Shin has not demonstrated that it is more convenient for it to litigate its indemnification claim against Asahi in California rather than in Taiwan or Japan.

"Because the plaintiff is not a California resident, California's legitimate interests in the dispute have considerably diminished. The Supreme Court of California argued that the State had an interest in 'protecting its consumers by ensuring that foreign manufacturers comply with the state's safety standards.'... The State Supreme Court's definition of California's interest, however, was overly broad. The dispute between Cheng Shin and Asahi is primarily about indemnification rather than safety. Moreover, it is not at all clear at this point that California law should govern the question whether a Japanese corporation should indemnify a Taiwanese corporation on the basis of a sale made in Taiwan and a shipment of goods from Japan to Taiwan.

"Considering the international context, the heavy burden on the alien defendant, and the slight interests of the plaintiff and the forum State, the exercise of personal jurisdiction by a California court over Asahi in this instance would be unreasonable and unfair.

"Because the facts of this case do not establish minimum contacts such that the exercise of personal jurisdiction is consistent with fair play and substantial justice, the judgment of the Supreme Court of California is reversed, and the case is remanded for further proceedings not inconsistent with this opinion.

"It is so ordered."

CLUNE v. ALIMAK AB & INDUSTRIVARDEN SERVICE AB
233 F.3d 538 (8th Cir. 2000)

BACKGROUND: In February 1996, Joseph Clune died when he fell off a construction hoist at a worksite in Kansas City, Missouri. Alimak AB, a Swedish corporation, had manufactured the hoist in Sweden. Industrivarden is one of two successor corporations to Alimak; it exists solely to handle Alimak's liabilities.

Esco Corporation, one of Alimak's two U.S. distributors, bought the hoist in 1972. Alimak later bought its other U.S. distributor, renamed it Alimak, Inc., and made it the exclusive U.S. distributor. While the two Alimak companies were separate entities, they did have some common directors, and subsidiary personnel went to Sweden for product discussions and service training. Some 700 Alimak construction hoists were sold in the U.S.; about 20 to 40 of them were in Missouri.

Clune's wife and two children filed a wrongful death lawsuit in U.S. District Court in Missouri. The case was dismissed by the U.S. District Court due to lack of personal jurisdiction over the Swedish defendants. The plaintiffs asked for review by the U.S. Eighth Circuit Court of Appeals.

JUDGE LAY:

"We apply a two-part test to the jurisdictional issue. First, whether the state's long-arm statute is satisfied, and second, whether the exercise of jurisdiction comports with due process....

"The Missouri long-arm statute confers jurisdiction over nonresidents who commit tortious acts within the state.... Missouri courts have interpreted the statute broadly to cover those cases where the Due Process Clause permits the assertion of personal jurisdiction.... Thus, the critical factor in our analysis is whether the exercise of personal jurisdiction in this case comports with due process.

"The Due Process Clause establishes the parameters of a state's power to assert personal jurisdiction over a nonresident defendant.... Due process requires that the defendant 'have certain minimum contacts' with the forum state 'such that the maintenance of the suit does not offend traditional notions of fair play and substantial justice.'... The Supreme Court has rejected 'talismanic' formulas to personal jurisdiction.... Rather, we must carefully consider the facts of each case to assess the nature of the contacts between the defendant and the forum state.... The factors we weigh include: the burden on the defendant, the interests of the forum state in adjudicating the dispute, the plaintiff's interest in obtaining convenient and effective relief, the interstate judicial system's interest in obtaining the most efficient resolution of controversies, and the shared interest of the several states in furthering fundamental substantive social policies....

"The baseline for minimum contacts is 'some act by which the defendant purposefully avails itself of the privilege of conducting activities in the forum state, thus invoking the benefits and protections of its laws.'... The defendant's conduct must be such that he or she 'should reasonably anticipate being haled into court there.'... In other words, personal jurisdiction may be exercised consonant with due process 'over a corporation that delivers its products into the stream of commerce with the expectation that they will be purchased by consumers in the forum state.'...

"In the present case, Alimak did more than simply set a product adrift in the international stream of commerce. The record shows ... Alimak AB created the distribution system that brought the hoist to Missouri....

"... Alimak AB designed its construction hoists for the United State market. The company had exclusive distribution agreements with United States distributors. The Swedish parent's logo was displayed on products that were sold in the United States.... Alimak AB also conducted training seminars in the United States for technicians employed by Alimak, Inc., who serviced hoists that were sold by the subsidiary. Of the 700 construction hoists that were sold in the United States to the company's distributors, between twenty and forty ended up in Missouri. This fact alone makes it difficult for us to characterize the hoist's location in Missouri as random, attenuated or fortuitous.... Additionally, the Swedish parent provided sales brochures and instruction manuals to its distributors for use in promoting and servicing its products in the United States. Members of the Swedish parent's board of directors also served as directors of the subsidiary. Any of these facts, taken alone, might fall short of purposeful availment, however, when taken together they show that ... Alimak AB engaged in a series of activities that were designed to generate profits to the parent from its subsidiar[y's] sales across the United States....

"The Supreme Court has noted that 'the unique burdens placed upon one who must defend oneself in a foreign legal system should have significant weight in assessing the reasonableness of stretching the long arm of personal jurisdiction over national borders.'... As we have noted, Industrivarden is a shell corporation that has no employees or products to sell. Essentially, the company exists through its insurance company. The overwhelming majority of the evidence in this case will be found in Missouri or the surrounding area, such as the construction hoist, eyewitnesses, medical records and documents material to the incident. As a result, Industrivarden would have to come to Missouri to investigate and gather evidence no matter where a trial were to take place. With the help of modern technology and transportation, Industrivarden easily will be able to collect any relevant documents that are in Sweden and transport them to the United States. For these reasons, any burden Industrivarden might undertake in defending itself in Missouri will be minimal.

"It is readily apparent that Missouri has the strongest interest of any forum in adjudicating this dispute. The accident that gave rise to the case occurred in Missouri. Joseph Clune was an employee of the Missouri company, he worked and paid taxes in that state, and his death occurred there as a result of a product sold in that forum. No other state has a more compelling connection to this case.

"The Clunes' interest in obtaining convenient and effective relief is best satisfied by adjudicating this dispute in Missouri. Although they are residents of Kansas, Kansas is not a viable venue for this case and Missouri is the closest choice. In any event, Missouri is abundantly more convenient for the Clunes than if this case were to be tried in Sweden. Our decision today in no way guarantees the Clunes['] success in this suit. However, it likely would be impossible for this family of three who ha[ve] lost their husband and father to travel abroad to seek restitution for his death.

"Trying this case in Missouri federal court also satisfies the judicial system's interest in obtaining the most efficient resolution of this controversy. We exercise caution when subjecting a foreign corporation to jurisdiction in the United States, but are satisfied that ... Alimak AB affirmatively took on the risk of liabilities here.

"Finally, the adjudication of this dispute in Missouri ensures the fundamental social policy of safety in goods that enter our marketplace. As commercial borders are dismantled in the increasingly global marketplace, more products are available to consumers in the United States. It is essential that our laws designed to protect the health and safety of human beings not be lost in this flurry of commerce.

"The judgment of dismissal by the district court is vacated and the cause is remanded for further proceedings."

PREWITT ENTERPRISES INC. v.
ORGANIZATION OF PETROLEUM EXPORTING COUNTRIES
353 F.3d 916 (11th Cir. 2003)

BACKGROUND: Prewitt Enterprises, Inc. appeals from the dismissal of its complaint against the Organization of the Petroleum Exporting Countries ("OPEC") for insufficient service of process and from the denial of its motion for alternative service of process. Prewitt's complaint against OPEC alleged a violation of the Sherman Act for illegal price-fixing agreements on production and export of crude oil and claimed equitable relief pursuant to the Clayton Act. Because OPEC initially did not respond to the complaint, the district court entered a default final judgment against OPEC enjoining it from entering into, implementing or enforcing any agreements to fix and control the production and export of crude oil for one year. OPEC then appeared and moved to vacate the default judgment and injunction on the grounds that OPEC had never been properly served with process and that, thus, the court lacked jurisdiction over it. The district court concluded that, because OPEC resides in Austria and the applicable Austrian law prohibits service without OPEC's consent, Prewitt's complaint must be dismissed for lack of jurisdiction.

JUDGE BARKETT:

"Prewitt filed a complaint with the district court against OPEC on behalf of itself and as the representative of all persons or entities who have indirectly purchased petroleum or petroleum products in the United States since March 1999. Prewitt claimed that OPEC has been coordinating an international conspiracy through agreements among its Member States and non-OPEC members to limit the production and export of oil in order to fix world oil prices above competitive levels. Prewitt argued that these agreements constitute violations of United States antitrust laws, specifically the Sherman and Clayton Acts, and have resulted in a substantial and adverse impact on United States trade and commerce. Prewitt claimed that as a result of OPEC's illegal conduct, its own acquisition and inventory costs for gasoline have increased significantly. Consequently, Prewitt requested that the court declare the OPEC-coordinated agreements illegal under United States law, enjoin implementation of the agreements, grant any other appropriate equitable relief, and award costs of the suit against OPEC for injuries sustained by Prewitt.

"Prewitt attempted service on OPEC by requesting that the trial court send a copy of the complaint to OPEC by international registered mail, return receipt requested. The court clerk did so, mailing Prewitt's summons and complaint to OPEC at its headquarters in Vienna. The pleadings were signed for, stamped 'received' by OPEC's Administration and Human Resources Department, and forwarded to the Director of OPEC's Research Division as well as other departments including the Secretary General's office. Ultimately, the Secretary General decided that the OPEC Secretariat would not take any action with regard to the summons and complaint.

"Without the participation of OPEC, the district court certified a class defined as all persons or entities who purchased refined petroleum products in the United States from March 1999 to the present and entered a default final judgment and order of injunction against OPEC. The court found that there was a conspiracy between OPEC, its Member States, and non-OPEC members, namely Norway, Mexico, the Russian Federation and Oman, to fix and control crude oil prices; that the agreements coordinated and implemented by OPEC were illegal under United States antitrust laws; that OPEC's illegal conduct has resulted in substantial and adverse impact on United States trade and commerce of approximately $80-120 million per day; and that OPEC and those acting in concert with OPEC should be enjoined from entering into, implementing, and enforcing any further oil price-fixing agreements for a period of twelve months. Copies of the court's orders were delivered to each of the United States embassies for the Member States of OPEC.

"In response, OPEC made a special appearance and filed a motion to set aside the default judgment and stay its enforcement ... which the district court granted, vacating the default judgment and injunction. OPEC then filed a motion to dismiss Prewitt's complaint on various grounds including insufficient service of process.... The district court dismissed the case without prejudice, finding that Prewitt had failed to serve OPEC its summons and complaint properly under the Federal Rules. Prewitt then filed a motion to pursue alternative means of effecting service or to amend the judgment. The district court denied the motion finding that, in this case, OPEC cannot be effectively served with process....

"The threshold issue in this case is whether OPEC has been effectively served under the Federal Rules of Civil Procedure. If it has not, we must then determine whether extraterritorial service of process on OPEC may be effectuated at all under the circumstances here. By definition, 'service of summons is the procedure by which a court having venue and jurisdiction of the subject matter of the suit asserts jurisdiction over the person of the party served.'... A court is required to have personal jurisdiction under the Due Process Clauses of the Fifth and Fourteenth Amendments to the United States Constitution 'as a matter of individual liberty' so that 'the maintenance of the suit . . . [does] not offend "traditional notions of fair play and substantial justice".'...

"There are two rules of federal civil procedure that apply to service of process upon an international entity located outside of United States jurisdiction: Fed.R.Civ.P. 4(f) (Service Upon Individuals in a Foreign Country) and Fed.R.Civ.P. 4(h) (Service of Process Upon Corporations and Associations). The latter governs service on unincorporated associations located outside of the United States and provides that: 'Unless otherwise provided by federal law, service upon an .

. . unincorporated association that is subject to suit under a common name, and from which a waiver of service has not been obtained and filed, shall be effected: . . . (2) in a place not within any judicial district of the United States *in any manner prescribed for individuals by subdivision (f)* except personal delivery....' (Emphasis added [by the Court]).... Thus, an 'unincorporated association' headquartered outside of the United States that is (1) subject to suit under a common name and (2) has not waived service may be served in any manner authorized under Fed.R.Civ.P. 4(f) for individuals in a foreign country except for personal delivery....

"Turning to Fed.R.Civ.P. 4(f), the first relevant section provides that: 'Unless otherwise provided by federal law, service upon an individual from whom a waiver has not been obtained and filed, other than an infant or an incompetent person, may be effected in a place not within any judicial district of the United States: (1) by any internationally agreed means reasonably calculated to give notice, such as those means authorized by the Hague Convention on the Service Abroad of Judicial and Extrajudicial Documents.... In this case, no other means of service has been 'otherwise provided by federal law' nor is there an 'internationally agreed means reasonably calculated to give notice such as those means authorized by the Hague Convention on the Service Abroad of Judicial and Extrajudicial Document.'... The federal laws pertaining to service of process on a foreign entity are codified in 28 U.S.C. §§ 1602 *et seq.*, the Foreign Sovereign Immunities Act ('FSIA'), and 22 U.S.C. §§ 288 *et seq.*, the International Organizations Immunities Act ('IOIA'). The parties agree that neither of these federal laws apply to OPEC in this case. The parties likewise agree that there is no international agreement that stipulates the appropriate means of service.

"Thus, we must look to the remainder of Fed.R.Civ.P. 4(f), which provides for other methods by which an unincorporated association may be served in the absence of relevant federal law or international agreements: '(2) if there is no internationally agreed means of service or the applicable international agreement allows other means of service, provided that service is reasonably calculated to give notice:
(A) in the manner prescribed by the law of the foreign country for service in that country in an action in any of its courts of general jurisdiction; or
(B) as directed by the foreign authority in response to a letter rogatory or letter of request; or
(C) unless prohibited by the law of the foreign country, by
(i) delivery to the individual personally of a copy of the summons and the complaint; or
(ii) any form of mail requiring a signed receipt, to be addressed and dispatched by the clerk of the court to the party to be served; or
(3) by other means not prohibited by international agreement as may be directed by the court.'...

"Prewitt originally chose to attempt service of process on OPEC under Fed.R.Civ.P. 4(f)(2)(C) (ii). However, the method set forth under that provision applies only if it is not prohibited by the law of the foreign country. Based on the evidence presented, the district court correctly found that service on OPEC was prohibited by the law of Austria. Article 5(2) of the Austrian/OPEC Headquarters Agreement provides that: 'the service of legal process . . . shall not take place within the [OPEC] headquarters seat except with the express consent of, and under conditions approved by, the Secretary General.' Since the Headquarters Agreement was enacted into law by resolution of the Austrian Parliament and published in the Austrian Official Gazette pursuant to the Austrian Constitution, the district court found it to be an integral part of Austrian law. Thus, because service was prohibited by Austrian law, Prewitt could not have effectively served OPEC under Fed.R.Civ.P. 4(f)(2)(C)(ii)....

"Prewitt nonetheless suggests that we should liberally construe the formal requirements for service under the Federal Rules because OPEC received actual notice but simply chose to 'ignore the whole thing.'... However, we find no support for such an argument. Due process under the United States Constitution requires that 'before a court may exercise personal jurisdiction over a defendant, there must be *more than* notice to the defendant . . . there also must be a *basis* for the defendant's amenability to service of summons. Absent consent, this means there must be *authorization* for service of summons on the defendant.'... In other words, an individual or entity 'is not obliged to engage in litigation unless [officially] notified of the action . . . under a court's authority, by formal process.' In this case, Fed.R.Civ.P. (f)(2)(C)(ii) clearly states that service of process by registered mail is only authorized where it is not prohibited by foreign law. Here, the Headquarters Agreement constitutes Austrian law and, under Article 5(2), expressly prohibits all service of process upon OPEC within the headquarters seat that has not been consented to by its Secretary General. Thus, we agree with the district court that even though OPEC had actual notice of the filing of the suit, service of process was ineffective because it was clearly not in substantial compliance with the requirements of Fed.R.Civ.P. 4(f)(2)(C)(ii)....

"Alternatively, Prewitt argues that even if service failed under Fed.R.Civ.P. 4(f)(2)(C)(ii), service by registered mail upon OPEC nonetheless complied with Fed.R.Civ.P. 4(f)(2)(A), which permits service if it is effectuated 'in the manner prescribed by the law of the foreign country for service in that country in an action in any of its courts of general jurisdiction.' The provisions of Austrian law that Prewitt references from Austria's Civil Procedure Code and regulations for service of process by mail relate to service by Austrian courts on persons resident in Austria and abroad. None of these Austrian law provisions directly pertain to service mailed *from abroad* upon international organizations resident in Austria. Prewitt argues that we should look only to the approved 'method' of service within the foreign jurisdiction and not to the substance of Austrian law. However, the substance of the law specifically relating to service of process cannot be divorced from the 'method' of service. Indeed, §§ 12(1) and 11(2) of the Austrian Service Act specifically address service from authorities abroad upon residents in Austria and trump the more general provisions cited by Prewitt from the Austrian Code of Civil Procedure and regulations for service of process by Austrian courts on residents in Austria or abroad. Moreover, the Regulation Regarding the Service of Process by Mail upon Persons Abroad in Civil Proceedings that Prewitt argues applies in this case specifically states that it *does not* apply to service on entities specified under § 11(2) of the Austrian Service Act…. Section 12(1) … of the Austrian Service Act requires that: 'The service of documents generated by authorities abroad to recipients in Austria shall be carried out in accordance with the existing international conventions, *in the absence of which it has to be done in accordance with this law.*'… (Emphasis added [by the Court]).

"Section 11(2) … of the Austrian Service Act directly addresses service from abroad upon international organizations such as OPEC requiring that: 'the mediation of the Federal Ministry for Foreign Affairs shall be enlisted in undertaking service of process on foreigners or international organizations that enjoy privileges and immunities under international law, regardless of their place of residence or headquarters.'

"There would be no way for Prewitt to serve OPEC under § 11(2) of the Austrian Service Act because we must assume that if it had gone to the Austrian Federal Ministry of Foreign Affairs, the Ministry would have applied the laws of its own country and obeyed the dictates of the Austrian/OPEC Headquarters Agreement prohibiting service without OPEC's consent….

"In response, Prewitt again argues that actual notice can cure defective service of process pursuant to Section 7 of the Austrian Service Act, which provides: 'Should defects in service of process occur, service shall be deemed effectuated at the time when the document has actually reached the recipient designated by the authority.'… However, this section has specifically been interpreted in Austria not to apply to defects in service of process that are in breach of the requirements for service under an international agreement such as the Austrian/OPEC Headquarters Agreement. Moreover, Section 7 may not cure a failure to obtain OPEC's express consent because under the Austrian law of *lex specialis*, the more specific provision in the Headquarters Agreement for service of process upon OPEC takes precedence over the more general language of the Austrian Service Act…. Finally, Prewitt contends that even if its service by registered mail on OPEC could not be effectuated pursuant to any of the provisions of Fed.R.Civ.P. 4(f)(2), the district court still had the discretion to order service of process pursuant to Fed.R.Civ.P. 4(f)(3), which provides that service may be effected 'by *other means* not prohibited by international agreement as may be directed by the court.' (Emphasis added [by the Court]). We agree with Prewitt that a district court's denial of relief under 4(f)(3) is reviewed under an abuse of discretion standard. However, there is no abuse of discretion here; on the contrary, any circumvention of 4(f)(2)(C)(ii) by the district court in directing service again by registered mail would constitute such an abuse. On these facts, we cannot read 4(f)(3) as permitting that which has already been specifically prohibited under 4(f)(2)….

"Prewitt then argues that, even if service by registered mail is prohibited by 4(f)(2), other means of giving actual notice, such as fax or e-mail, that are not mentioned in the rule or prohibited by international agreement could be employed to serve OPEC under Fed.R.Civ.P. 4(f)(3), even if the service is contrary to the laws of Austria. However, the 1993 Advisory Committee Notes to Fed.R.Civ.P. 4(f)(3) instruct that: 'Paragraph (3) authorizes the court to approve other methods of service not prohibited by international agreements…. Inasmuch as our Constitution requires that reasonable notice be given, *an earnest effort* should be made to devise a method of communication that is *consistent with due process* and *minimizes offense to foreign law.*' (Emphasis added [by the Court]). Rather than minimizing offense to Austrian law, the failure to obtain OPEC's consent would constitute a substantial affront to Austrian law. We can find no support permitting such a consequence in the face of Austria's direct prohibition of service on OPEC without its consent….

"Austrian law clearly provides protection to OPEC as an international organization from all methods of service of process without its consent and also requires that any service of process from abroad be effected through Austrian authorities. In this case, OPEC has made clear that it refuses to consent expressly to service of process by Prewitt; thus, the district court did not abuse its discretion in denying Prewitt's motion to authorize alternative means of service….

"Based on the foregoing, we **AFFIRM** the district court's motion to dismiss this case for insufficient service of process and its denial of alternative service of process on OPEC."

BLIMKA v. MY WEB WHOLESALER, LLC.
152 P.2d 594 (ID 2007)

BACKGROUND: My Web, a Maine limited liability company, uses its website to wholesale salvaged and "distressed" merchandise. Mike Blimka—an Idaho resident and a subscriber to My Web's "listserv"—received an email offering to sell jeans to him, in bulk. He had telephone conversations with several My Web employees, including the manager—Lisa DePalma, and agreed to buy 26,500 pairs of jeans at 79 cents per pair. He sent the money, and received the jeans. After examining the jeans, Blimka claimed that they had been misrepresented (both on the web, and by DePalma over the phone) as to quality, value, and wrapping. Blimka sued My Web and Lisa DePalma for fraud and for breach of warranties.

My Web and DePalma received proper notice of the lawsuit, but did not appear in the Idaho court to defend the case. The Idaho trial court entered a default judgment in favor of Blimka. Defendants later asked the court to declare the judgment void, since they were not subject to jurisdiction in Idaho. The court refused to do so, so the defendants appealed to the Idaho Supreme Court.

JUSTICE JONES:

"The proper exercise of personal jurisdiction over non-resident defendants by an Idaho court involves satisfying two criteria.... First, the court must determine that the non-resident defendant's actions fall within the scope of Idaho's long-arm statute.... Second, the court must determine that exercising jurisdiction over the non-resident defendant comports with the constitutional standards of the Due Process Clause of the U.S. Constitution....

"Since we conclude that jurisdiction existed on the fraud claim, both with respect to My Web and DePalma, and because that claim supports all relief granted in the judgment, we need not address the issue of jurisdiction over the contract claims.

"Idaho's long-arm statute extends jurisdiction to 'the commission of a tortious act within this state.'... This court has held that 'an allegation that an injury has occurred in Idaho in a tortious manner is sufficient.'... This is remedial legislation designed to provide a forum for Idaho residents and should be liberally construed to effectuate that purpose....

"In this case, the allegedly fraudulent representations were directed at an Idaho resident and the injury occurred in this state. Thus, we hold that Blimka's allegation of fraud was sufficient to invoke the tortious acts language of Idaho Code S. 5-514(b) with respect to both defendants.

"Next, the defendants contend that their contacts with Idaho were insufficient under the Due Process Clause of the U.S. Constitution to permit personal jurisdiction in this case. The Fourteenth Amendment to the U.S. Constitution permits a state to exercise personal jurisdiction over a non-resident defendant when that defendant has certain minimum contacts with the state such that the maintenance of the suit does not offend 'traditional notions of fair play and substantial justice. '...

"Blimka's complaint alleged that the defendants committed the intentional tort of fraud. In the Calder case, the U.S. Supreme Court distinguished 'untargeted negligence' from intentional, and allegedly tortious, acts expressly aimed at the forum, and adopted an 'effects' test to address what contacts are necessary to satisfy minimum contacts in the context of an intentional tort expressly aimed at the forum state.... The Court held that minimum contacts were satisfied where the defendants allegedly committed the intentional tort of libel outside of the forum state, but the effects of the tort were directed to, and suffered in, the forum state....

"Like the defendants in Calder, the defendants in this case were not charged with mere 'untargeted negligence.' Rather, they were charged with the commission of a fraud in Idaho. Blimka alleged that the defendants intentionally misrepresented facts regarding the quality, value, and packaging of the jeans during telephonic and electronic communications. At all times during the communications, the defendants knew that Blimka was residing in Idaho. Therefore … 'their intentional, and allegedly tortious actions were expressly aimed' at Idaho, and they realized that the brunt of the damage resulting from these actions would occur in Idaho…. Where an Idaho resident alleges that a defendant in Maine intentionally directed false representations to, and caused injury in Idaho, that resident need not travel to Maine to pursue his or her claim against the perpetrator of the fraud…. The defendants' actions satisfy minimum contacts with respect to the fraud allegations.

"Additionally, because the defendants purposefully directed their allegedly false representations into Idaho, the exercise of personal jurisdiction is presumed not to offend traditional notions of fair play and substantial justice…. Idaho has an ever-increasing interest in protecting its residents from fraud committed on them from afar by electronic means. Given the fact, the defendants should have reasonably anticipated being haled into Idaho courts….

"In sum, neither the Idaho long-arm statute nor the Due Process Clause precluded the district court from exercising personal jurisdiction over the defendants and entering a binding judgment against them in this case. As a result, the district court's decision to deny the defendants' motion for relief from judgment was not an abuse of that court's discretion and will not be disturbed by this court….

"The decision of the district court is affirmed. Blimka is awarded attorney fees and costs on appeal."

J. McINTYRE MACHINERY LTD. v. NICASTRO
131 S.Ct. 2780 (U.S. 2011)

BACKGROUND: Robert Nicastro, an employee of Curcio Scrap Metal—a New Jersey firm, was working with a three-ton metal-shearing machine when it severed four fingers from his right hand. The machine had been manufactured in the U.K. by J. McIntyre Machinery ("JMM"), and sold to Curcio by McIntyre America, an independent exclusive distributor based in Ohio. Nicastro sued JMM in New Jersey state court, and JMM filed a motion to dismiss, claiming that it was not subject to jurisdiction in New Jersey.

JMM has no operations, personnel, property, or inventory in New Jersey. JMM executives have attended trade shows in the USA, but not in New Jersey. Curcio's machine and (perhaps) three others are located in New Jersey. At least some machines were sold on consignment to the Ohio distributor, and the Ohio distributor did try to structure its advertising and sales efforts with JMM "whenever possible." The New Jersey courts held that JMM could be sued there, and JMM asked for U.S. Supreme Court review.

THE COURT (4 Justices):

"The Due Process Clause protects an individual's right to be deprived of life, liberty, or property only by the exercise of lawful power…. This is no less true with respect to the power of a sovereign to resolve disputes through judicial process than with respect to the power of a sovereign to prescribe rules of conduct for those within its sphere…. As a general rule, neither statute nor judicial decree may bind strangers to the State….

"A court may subject a defendant to judgment only when the defendant has sufficient contacts with the sovereign 'such that the maintenance of the suit does not offend "traditional notions of fair play and substantial justice".'… Freeform notions of fundamental fairness divorced from traditional practice cannot transform a judgment rendered in the absence of authority into law. As a general rule, the sovereign's exercise of power requires some act by which the defendant 'purposefully avails itself of the privilege of conducting activities within the forum State, thus invoking the benefits and protections of its laws,'…though in some cases, as with an intentional tort, the defendant might well fall within the State's authority by reason of his attempt to obstruct its laws. In products liability cases like this one, it is the defendant's purposeful availment that makes jurisdiction consistent with 'traditional notions of fair play and substantial justice.'

"A person may submit to a State's authority in a number of ways. There is, of course, explicit consent…. Presence within a State at the time suit commences through service of process is another example…. Citizenship or domicile—or, by analogy, incorporation or principal place of business for corporations—also indicates general submission to a State's powers…. Each of these examples reveals circumstances, or a course of conduct, from which it is proper to infer an intention to benefit from and thus an intention to submit to the laws of the forum State…. These examples support exercise of the general jurisdiction of the State's courts and allow the State to resolve both matters that originate within the State and those based on activities and events elsewhere…. By contrast, those who live or operate primarily outside a State have a due process right not to be subjected to judgment in its courts as a general matter.

"There is also a more limited form of submission to a State's authority for disputes that 'arise out of or are connected with the activities within the state.'… Where a defendant 'purposefully avails itself to the privilege of conducting activities within the forum State, thus invoking the benefits and protections of its laws,' … it submits to the judicial power of an otherwise foreign sovereign to the extent that power is exercised in connection with the defendant's activities touching on the State. In other words, submission through contact with and activity directed at a sovereign may justify specific jurisdiction 'in a suit arising out of or related to the defendant's contacts with the forum.'…

"In *Asahi*, an opinion by Justice Brennan for four Justices outlined a different approach. It discarded the central concept of sovereign authority in favor of considerations of fairness and foreseeability. As that concurrence contended, 'jurisdiction premised on the placement of a product into the stream of commerce [without more] is consistent with the Due Process Clause, for [a]s long as a participant in this process is aware that the final product is being marketed in the forum State, the possibility of a lawsuit there cannot come as a surprise.'… It was the premise of the concurring opinion that the defendant's ability to anticipate suit renders the assertion of jurisdiction fair. In this way, the opinion made foreseeability the touchstone of jurisdiction.…

"Since *Asahi* was decided, the courts have sought to reconcile the competing opinions. But Justice Brennan's concurrence, advocating a rule based on general notions of fairness and foreseeability, is inconsistent with the premises of lawful judicial power. This Court's precedents make clear that it is the defendant's actions, not his expectations, that empower a State's courts to subject him to judgment.…

"In this case, petitioner [JMM] directed marketing and sales efforts at the United States. It may be that, assuming it were otherwise empowered to legislate on the subject, the Congress could authorize the exercise of jurisdiction in appropriate courts. That circumstance is not presented in this case, however, and it is neither necessary nor appropriate to address here any constitutional concerns that might be attendant to that exercise of power.…

"Respondent [Nicastro] has not established that J. McIntyre engaged in conduct purposefully directed at New Jersey. Recall that respondent's claim of jurisdiction centers on three facts: The distributor agreed to sell J. McIntyre's machines in the United States; J McIntyre officials attended trade shows in several States but not in New Jersey; and up to four machines ended up in New Jersey. The British manufacturer had no office in New Jersey; it neither paid taxes nor owned property there; and it neither advertised in, nor sent any employees to, the State. Indeed, after discovery the trial court found that the 'defendant does not have a single contact with New Jersey short of the machine in question ending up in this state.'… These facts may reveal an intent to serve the U.S. market, but they do not show that J. McIntyre purposefully availed itself of the New Jersey market.…

"Due process protects petitioner's [JMM's] right to be subject only to lawful authority. At no time did petitioner engage in any activities in New Jersey that reveal an intent to invoke or benefit from the protection of its laws. New Jersey is without power to adjudge the rights and liabilities of J. McIntyre, and its exercise of jurisdiction would violate due process. The contrary judgment of the New Jersey Supreme Court is
Reversed."

JUSTICE GINSBURG, dissenting with SOTOMAYOR & KAGAN:

"The modern approach to jurisdiction … gave prime place to reason and fairness. Is it not fair and reasonable, given the mode of trading of which this case is an example, to require the international seller to defend at the place its products cause injury? Do not litigational convenience and choice-of-law considerations point in that direction? On what measure of reason and fairness can it be considered undue to require McIntyre UK to defend in New Jersey as an incident of its efforts to develop a market for its industrial machines anywhere and everywhere in the United States? Is not the burden on McIntyre to defend in New Jersey fair, *i.e.*, a reasonable cost of transacting business internationally, in comparison to the burden on Nicastro to go to Nottingham, England to gain recompense for an injury he sustained using McIntyre's product at his workplace in Saddle Brook, New Jersey?"

STANGVIK v. SHILEY, INC.
1 Cal.Rptr.2d 556 (Calif. 1991)

BACKGROUND: Shiley, Inc. is incorporated in California, where it manufactures artificial heart valves. Shiley's valves were implanted in two men who died after their surgeries—in Norway and Sweden. Plaintiffs are the wives and children of the two men—the Stangvik family from Norway, and the Karlsson family from Sweden. A product liability lawsuit was filed in California, against Shiley and its parent, a Delaware corporation. The defendants filed a motion to dismiss, on the basis of *forum non conveniens*. They claimed the cases should be tried in Norway and Sweden. The trial court and the appeals court so held, and the plaintiffs asked the state supreme court for review.

JUSTICE MOSK:

"Forum non conveniens is an equitable doctrine invoking the discretionary power of a court to decline to exercise the jurisdiction it has over a transitory cause of action when it believes that the action may be more appropriately and justly tried elsewhere.... 'There are manifest reasons for preferring residents in access to often overcrowded Courts, both in convenience and in the fact that broadly speaking it is they who pay for maintaining the Court concerned.'... [T]he injustices and the burdens on local courts and taxpayers, as well as on those leaving their work and business to serve as jurors, which can follow from an unchecked and unregulated importation of transitory causes of action for trial in this state ... require that our courts ... exercise their 'discretionary power to decline to proceed with those causes of action which they conclude, on satisfactory evidence, may be more appropriately and justly tried elsewhere.'...

"In determining whether to grant a motion based on forum non conveniens, a court must first determine whether the alternate forum is a 'suitable' place for trial. If it is, the next step is to consider the private interests of the litigants and the interests of the public in retaining the action for trial in California. The private interest factors are those that make trial and the enforceability of the ensuing judgment expeditious and relatively inexpensive, such as ease of access to sources of proof, the cost of obtaining attendance of witnesses, and the availability of compulsory process for the attendance of witnesses. The public interest factors include avoidance of overburdening local courts with congested calendars, protecting the interests of potential jurors so that they are not called upon to decide cases in which the local community has little concern, and weighing the competing interest of California and the alternate jurisdiction in the litigation....

"We come, then, to an assessment of the factors discussed above. We are confronted with the somewhat anomalous situation that the parties seek to try the action in a jurisdiction which would appear to violate their interest in a convenient place for trial. Both plaintiffs and defendants are willing, indeed, eager—to litigate the matter in a jurisdiction separated by an ocean and a continent from their places of residence. Although both claim that they are motivated by the convenience of the place of trial, this court, like others before it, recognizes that an additional motivating factor—and perhaps the major one—relates to the circumstances that trial in California will enhance the possibility of substantial recovery. Plaintiffs seek and defendants resist trial in California courts substantially for this reason. In the service of this goal, they are willing to transport numerous witnesses and documents many thousand miles....

"The public interest factors clearly favor defendants' position. If we hold that the present cases may be tried in California, it will likely mean that the remaining 108 cases involving the Shiley valve will also be tried here. The burden on the California courts of trying these numerous complex actions is considerable. Moreover, California's interest in deterring future improper conduct by defendants would be amply vindicated if the actions filed by California resident plaintiffs resulted in judgments in their favor. Under all the circumstances, we hold that the Court of Appeals was correct in concluding that there was substantial evidence to support the trial court's determination that the private and public interest factors, on balance, justified the stays granted in these actions."

PAREX BANK v. RUSSIAN SAVINGS BANK
116 F.Supp.2d 415 (S.D. NY 2000)

BACKGROUND: Parex Bank is a Latvian company. Russian Savings Bank is a Russian open joint-stock company known by various names, but usually referred to as Sberbank. The dispute stems from Sberbank's failure to honor a non-deliverable forward exchange contract. NFE contracts enabled foreign investors to hedge their investments in ruble-denominated Russian securities. A bank contracts to convert rubles into dollars at a specified rate, on a specified date. When the Russian financial system collapsed in 1998, and the ruble was substantially devalued, Parex demanded payment of $3,755,642.01 under the terms of its contract.

Parex sued in New York state court for breach of contract and for deceptive business practices, under New York law. Sberbank had the case removed to U.S. District Court. Sberbank then moved to dismiss the case for lack of personal jurisdiction, *forum non conveniens*, and failure to state a claim.

JUDGE SWEET:

"Sberbank's actions surrounding this currency transaction were sufficient to establish the constitutionally requisite minimum contacts to support the exercise of personal jurisdiction. Sberbank consented to make payment in dollars to Parex's Bank of New York account in the event that the exchange rate changed unfavorably, and to receive payment into its New York account if the rate changed favorably. In addition, Sberbank accepted Parex's security deposit into its own Bank of New York account as security for the repayment of the NDF contract when it was due…. Sberbank 'routinely conducts exchange deals through and in New York state.'…

"In combination, Sberbank's use of accounts at Bank of New York for this particular transaction and its practice of conducting other similar transactions using New York banks establishes Sberbank's 'minimum contacts' with this jurisdiction….

"The equitable doctrine of forum non conveniens allows a court to dismiss even if the court is a permissible venue and has proper jurisdiction over the claim…. This inquiry involves two steps (1) determining whether there is an adequate alternate forum for the dispute … and (2) balancing the public and private interest factors the Supreme Court described in *Gilbert*….

"The first step of the forum non conveniens inquiry requires the Court to determine whether Russia would be an adequate alternative forum in which to adjudicate the dispute. A foreign forum is not inadequate merely because its justice system differs from that of the United

States.... [C]omity requires that this Court abstain from adversely judging the quality of Russia's justice system unless Parex makes a showing of inadequate procedural safeguards.... Absent such a showing, it is 'rare' that courts find ... an alternative forum to be inadequate....

"Russia is an adequate alternative forum if (1) Sberbank is subject to service of process there, and (2) the forum permits a satisfactory remedy.... Both parties agree that Sberbank is subject to service of process in Russia....

"The question thus becomes whether the Moscow City Arbitration Court permits a satisfactory remedy.... [W]hile an alternate forum's less favorable substantive law should ordinarily not weigh heavily against dismissal, this factor increases in significance when 'the remedy provided by the alternative forum is so clearly inadequate or unsatisfactory that it is no remedy at all.'...

"Even if Russia employs different procedures than the United States courts, Sberbank has met its burden of proving that Russia's judicial system affords adequate procedural protections upon the face of its statutory provisions....

"Parex argues that Russia is not an adequate alternate forum because, unlike New York law, Russian law does not recognize NDF contracts as legally enforceable. In support of this proposition, Parex submits a recent decision from the highest arbitration court in Russia, the Supreme Arbitrazh Court....

"Sberbank's motion to dismiss for forum non conveniens is denied at this time for lack of proof that Russia will permit any litigation of the NDF contract....

"Parex has made no showing that the currency exchange between the party banks in this case is 'consumer-oriented' under [New York law]....

"For the foregoing reasons, the motions to dismiss for lack of personal jurisdiction and forum non conveniens are denied, and the motion to dismiss Count II is granted."

CONGREGATION B'NAI SHOLOM v. MARTIN
173 N.W.2d 504 (MI 1969)

BACKGROUND: Morris Martin was named chairman of the building committee for the new synagogue in January 1959. The Congregation hired a professional fund-raiser on April 22, to assist in gathering pledges for the project. In June, Morris Martin turned in four pledge cards—his own, and one signed by each of his brothers (Irving Martin and Jack Martin). Morris had signed the fourth one, in the name of Bessie Martin Steinberg (his sister). None of the four pledge cards had been filled out as to amount. Morris had written the words, "Total Donation $25,000.00" on an attached scrap of paper. Later in 1959, Morris Martin and the congregation had a serious disagreement, and Morris indicated he was withdrawing the $25,000 pledge.

The Congregation sued all four Martins in 1962, to enforce the pledge. The Martins filed a motion to amend their answer to the complaint to add a defense based on the Jewish law relating to such pledges. The trial judge denied the motion. The trial judge then granted judgment in favor of the Congregation against Morris for the full sum of $25,000, plus interest. Morris Martin could then try to force contributions from Jack and Irving. (The case against Bessie was dismissed—she had signed nothing and there was no other evidence that she had agreed to make a pledge.) The Court of Appeals affirmed. Morris appealed to the Michigan Supreme Court.

JUSTICE ADAMS:

"The defendants' motions to amend were supported by the affidavit of a Dr. Rabbi Bernard D. Perlow, a rabbi and a scholar. After stating his qualifications as an expert witness, he included the following points in his opinion: '5. That the religious customs, practices, and laws binding on all Jews are codified in the work known as the *Shulchan Aruch;* that this code is generally regarded as binding as a matter of religious faith by both Orthodox and Conservative Jews.... 6. That in the opinion of this deponent, the *Shulchan Aruch,* as well as the custom and tradition for more than a thousand years, prohibits the bringing of a suit in the civil courts of any state by a synagogue against any of its members or vice versa and is contrary to Jewish law and is prohibited; that any such civil controversy must be first brought before the Jewish religious court known as the Beth Din (a Jewish rabbinical court); that under Jewish law, matters of charity to the synagogue go to the heart of the Jewish religion; that a charitable contribution to a synagogue is considered a religious matter by and between the synagogue and the member; that for a synagogue to file a suit against one of its members upon an alleged charitable contribution without submitting it to a Beth Din is what is known in Jewish law as a 'Chillul Hashem' which is a profanation of God's name and such action is such a grave sin in Jewish law, that it warrants excommunication.... 7. That it is expressly stated in Hyman E. Goldin's translation of Rabbi Solomon Ganzfried's Code of Jewish Law, Kidzur Schulchan Aruch ... that it is forbidden to bring a suit in the civil courts even if their decision would be in accordance with the law of Israel; that even if the two litigants are willing to try the case before such a court, it is forbidden; that even if they make an oral or a written agreement to that effect, it is of no avail; that whoever takes a case against another Jew involving religious matters, is a Godless person and he has violated and defiled the law of Moses....'

"Nothing appears in the record before us in this case to warrant the trial judge's denial of the motion. When the rights of the parties are being tested on motions for summary judgment filed, not at the election of the parties themselves but at the behest of the trial judge, a defendant should most certainly be allowed to amend to assert any defense he may have before the court has ruled."

FINNISH FUR SALES v. JULIETTE SHULOF FURS
770 F.Supp. 139 (S.D. NY 1991)

BACKGROUND: Finnish Fur Sales ("FFS") is a limited company organized under Finnish law. It sells fur pelts raised by Finnish breeders, at public auction, several times a year. The auctions are conducted under certain "Conditions of Sale," which are listed in the auction catalogue, a copy of which is given to each prospective bidder in advance of the auction. A one-page English translation of the Conditions appears on the inside front cover of the catalogue.

Juliette Shulof Furs ("JSF") is a New York corporation engaged in fur dealing. George Shulof, an officer of JSF, has been in the fur business since 1935. In January and May 1987, he attended FFS auctions in Vantaa, Finland. He bought over $500,000 worth of skins in January and some $700,000 worth in May. JSF paid for most of these skins, but a dispute arose over 2,469 fox pelts, worth $290,048.17. JSF paid part of the disputed amount, leaving $202,416.85 due, plus interest. FFS then sold the rest of the skins at its auctions in May and September 1989, at a loss. FFS says George is also personally liable for the $153,502.39 balance still due, based on Finnish law, custom in the fur trade, and Section 4 of the Conditions of Sale. Section 4 says: "Any person bidding at the auction shall stand surety as for its own debt until full payment is made for the purchased merchandise. If he has made the bid on behalf of another person, he is jointly and severally liable with the person for the purchase."

The claim against Juliette Shulof is by Okobank Osuuspankkien Keskuspankki Oy, based on her signature on a bill of exchange which JSF had used to make a part payment on the skins. Juliette signed "Juliette A. Shulof," above the printed name "Juliette Shulof Furs Inc." Okobank bought the bill of exchange as a holder in due course, but the bill was dishonored by Bank Leumi in New York City, when it was presented for payment. $37,480.90 is due on the bill of exchange.

George and Juliette each moved for summary judgment; the plaintiff in each case also moved for summary judgment.

JUDGE LEISURE:

"Finland's contacts with the transactions at issue are substantial, rendering the choice of law clause enforceable unless a strong public policy of New York is impaired by the application of Finnish law....

"FFS's expert, Vesa Majamaa ... a Doctor of Law and Professor of the Faculty of Law at the University of Helsinki, gives as his opinion that the provision of Section 4 of the Conditions imposing personal liability upon the bidder, regardless of whether he bids on behalf of another, is valid both as a term of the particular auctions at issue and as a general principle of Finnish and Scandanavian auction law....

"According to Majamaa, it is commonly accepted in Scandanavia that a bidder, by making a bid, accepts those conditions which have been announced at the auction....

"Majamaa also notes that under Danish law, which he maintains would be applied by a Finnish court in the absence of Finnish decisional or legislative law on point, 'it is taken for granted that someone who has bid on merchandise on someone else's account is responsible for the transaction, as he would be for his own obligation, together with his superior...'.

"[A] perusal of the Conditions reveals that their entire text is only a single page long, and that all of the Conditions, including Section 4, are printed in the same size print, which, although small, is legible. The catalogue was made available to Mr. Shulof at the beginning of the four-day period prior to the auction during which potential bidders were allowed to inspect the furs. Although Mr. Shulof contends that the urgent need to inspect large numbers of furs prevented him from reading the one-page list of Conditions, he admits that he knew where they were located in the catalogue and that he did read some of the Conditions before bidding. Further, Mr. Shulof does not dispute the fact that he was given a copy of the same Conditions at the time of the 1986 auction he attended.

"Under these circumstances, it seems unlikely that a New York court would refuse to enforce Section 4 in an arm's length commercial transaction involving a sophisticated defendant accustomed to bidding at fur auctions....

"Thus, Mr. Shulof must be held jointly and severally liable with JSF for any damages owed to FFS....

"The parties agree that New York law governs the issue of the liability of Juliette Shulof on the Bill of Exchange, which was executed and payable in New York. The parties do not dispute that the Bill of Exchange is a negotiable instrument, and therefore subject to the provisions of Article

3 of the [UCC]....

"The relevant section of the [UCC] is S.3-403, which governs signatures by authorized representatives....

"Mrs. Shulof's signature on the Bill of Exchange did not give notice that she signed in a representative capacity only, and therefore she is personally liable for the amount of the bill."

SPINK & SON, LTD. v. GENERAL ATLANTIC CORPORATION
637 N.Y.S.2d 921 (NY 1996)

BACKGROUND: In June 1991, Edwin Cohen, General Atlantic Corporation's ("GAC") chairman, attended an antiques fair in London, England. Cohen spoke with an employee of Spink & Son about a possible purchase of six pieces of the exhibited art, but he denies that he made a commitment to buy any. He never took possession of any art or signed any writing with respect thereto. Back in New York, Cohen and GAC received an invoice requesting $33,968 as the contract price for six art pieces. Defendants did not respond to the invoice. On June 25, 1993, after notice to the defendants, Spink & Son sold one of the pieces and reduced the amount allegedly owing to $32,768.

Spink & Son sued in U.S. District Court in New York, with claims under both New York and English law. Cohen and GAC moved to dismiss the claims under New York law as barred by the Uniform Commercial Code's ("UCC") "Statute of Frauds" sections—which require goods contracts for $500 or more to be proved by a signed writing (or one of four listed alternatives). Plaintiff claims that English law (which no longer requires written proof for such contracts) governs; and defendants claim New York's UCC applies.

JUDGE LEHNER:

"The central issue on this motion by defendants for summary judgment is whether New York or English law is applicable to determine the enforceability of an alleged oral contract for the purchase of artwork made in England between a New York resident and an English art gallery....

"In determining the law applicable to matters bearing upon the execution, interpretation, validity, and performance of a contract, the modern approach is to apply the law of the jurisdiction having the greatest interest in the litigation.... [T]he theory of 'grouping of contacts,' 'instead of regarding as conclusive the parties' intention or the place of making or performance, lays emphasis rather upon the law of the place "which has the most significant contacts with the matter in dispute."... The merit of [this] approach is that it gives to the place "having the most interest in the problem" paramount control over the legal issues arising out of a particular factual context, thus allowing the forum to apply the policy of the jurisdiction "most intimately concerned with the outcome of [the] particular litigation".'...

"… [W]hen determining choice of law, the 'five generally significant contacts in a contract case [are]: the places of contracting, negotiation, and performance; the location of the subject matter of the contract; and the domicile of the contracting parties.'

"Applying these criteria, it appears that, on balance, England has a greater interest in this matter. While defendants are New York residents, the place of the alleged negotiation and contracting is England, and the art is located there, as is plaintiff's place of incorporation and place of business. Cohen traveled there to attend the antiques fair, and England has an interest in enforcing contracts made there by its citizens doing business in the country. When a person travels abroad, it is not unfair that they subject themselves to the laws of the land to which they visit.

"While the court finds that England has a greater interest in the subject of this litigation, defendants assert that such law (which allegedly does not require a writing for the enforcement of the subject contract) should not be applied in light of the public policy of New York requiring a writing in order to enforce a contract for the sale of goods for a price in excess of $500 (UCC 2-201).

"It is recognized that notwithstanding that a proper application of conflict of laws principles suggests the application of foreign law, New York law may still be applied if the foreign law violates a strong public policy of this State. With respect to the Statute of Frauds ... our Court of Appeals wrote: 'Whether or not a contract, valid and enforceable in the jurisdiction where made, is subject to the Statute of Frauds of a jurisdiction where an action is brought upon the contract is a question not yet settled in this State.' In that case ... the Court criticized the test of examining whether the foreign Statute of Frauds was substantive or procedural, finding that such characterization 'does little more than restate the problem and has even less relevance to our modern approach to the conflict of laws.'... There the Court traced the legislative history of the statute and, noting that it 'is common knowledge that New York is a national and international center for the purchase and sale of businesses and interests therein' … concluded that the statute contributed to New York's economic development, which it opined constituted a strong State interest. In that case, however, most of the negotiations took place in New York and the Court ruled that '[t]hese contacts give New York a substantial interest in applying its own law in view of the policy underlying the applicable provision of our Statute of Frauds to protect principals in business transactions from unfounded claims and thereby encourage use of New York as a national and international business center.'…

"'In search of the public policy of the State, courts of course are not free to indulge in mere individual notions of expediency and fairness but must look to the law as expressed in statute and judicial decisions.'… [I]t was recently stated that 'if New York statutes … were routinely read to express fundamental policy, choice of law principles would be meaningless.' The Court concluded that in 'view of modern choice of law doctrine, resort to the public policy exception should be reserved for those foreign laws that are truly obnoxious.'…

"… [I]n *Finnish Fur Sales Co. v. Juliette Shulof Furs* … it was ruled that the section [UCC 2-201] would not be a bar to a purchase of personal property at auction in Finland in that its requirements 'do not constitute a "fundamental policy" for the purpose of choice of law analysis.'…

"The Court concludes that the UCC provision pertaining to the enforcement of a contract for the sale of goods does not represent such a strong public policy that the courts of this State should deny enforcement of an oral contract that is enforceable where made. There is nothing, per se, 'obnoxious' in granting enforcement of an oral agreement…. Hence, since it cannot be said that the policy underlying our law on sales outweighs the interest of England in enforcing oral contracts made in that country by merchants doing business there, English law will determine the enforceability of the oral contract sued upon herein.

"Accordingly, defendants' motion is granted solely to the extent of dismissing the causes of action asserted under New York law, and this action shall proceed applying the substantive law of England…."

CARNIVAL CRUISE LINES, INC. v. SHUTE
499 U.S. 585 (1991)

BACKGROUND: Eulala Shute and her husband sued Carnival for injuries she sustained when she slipped on a deck while touring the galley of the cruise ship *Tropicale*. The Shutes bought their cruise tickets from a travel agent in their home State—Washington. The travel agent sent payment to Carnival's headquarters in Miami, Florida. Carnival sent the tickets to the Shutes. On the face of each ticket was a statement indicating that it was subject to the conditions on the back. Statements on the back of the ticket said that the customers accepted all printed terms by accepting the ticket, and that any disputes "shall be litigated, if at all, in and before a Court located in the State of Florida, USA, to the exclusion of the Courts of any other state or country."

The Shutes boarded *Tropicale* in Los Angeles, for the cruise to Puerto Vallarta, Mexico. Eulala's accident occurred while the ship was in international waters off the Mexican Coast. The Shutes filed their lawsuit in the U.S. District Court in the State of Washington. Carnival asked the court for summary judgment, on the basis of the forum-selection clause on the tickets. It also claimed that it was not subject to personal jurisdiction in Washington. The District Court ruled in its favor on the jurisdiction argument. The U.S. Court of Appeals reversed, holding that there was jurisdiction, and that the forum-selection clause was not enforceable because it was not freely bargained for. Carnival asked the U.S. Supreme Court for further review.

JUSTICE BLACKMUN:

"In this context, it would be entirely unreasonable for us to assume that [the Shutes]—or any other cruise passenger—would negotiate with [Carnival] the terms of a forum-selection clause in an ordinary commercial cruise ticket. Common sense dictates that a ticket of this kind will be a form contract the terms of which are not subject to negotiation, and that an individual purchasing the ticket will not have bargaining parity with the cruise line....

"Including a reasonable forum clause in a form contract of this kind may well be permissible for several reasons: First, a cruise line has a special interest in limiting the fora in which it potentially could be subject to suit. Because a cruise ship typically carries passengers from many locales, it is not unlikely that a mishap on a cruise could subject the cruise line to litigation in several different fora.... Additionally, a clause establishing ... the forum for dispute resolution has the salutary effect of dispelling any confusion about where suits arising from the contract must be brought and defended, sparing litigants the time and expense of pretrial motions to determine the correct forum, and conserving judicial resources that otherwise would be devoted to deciding these motions.... Finally, it stands to reason that passengers who purchase tickets containing a forum clause like that at issue in this case benefit in the form of reduced fares reflecting the savings that the cruise line enjoys by limiting the fora in which it may be sued....

"In the present case, Florida is not a 'remote alien forum,' nor—given the fact that Mrs. Shute's accident occurred off the coast of Mexico—is this dispute an essentially local one inherently more suited to resolution in the State of Washington than in Florida. In light of these [factors], and because [the Shutes] do not claim lack of notice of the forum clause, we conclude that they have not satisfied the 'heavy burden of proof' ... required to set aside the clause on the grounds of inconvenience.

"It bears emphasis that forum-selection clauses contained in form passage contracts are subject to judicial scrutiny for fundamental fairness. In this case, there is no indication that [Carnival] set Florida as the forum in which disputes were to be resolved as a means of discouraging cruise passengers from pursuing legitimate claims. Any suggestion of such a bad-faith motive is belied by two facts: [Carnival] has its principal place of business in Florida, and many of its cruises depart from and return to Florida ports. Similarly, there is no evidence that [Carnival] obtained [the Shutes'] accession to the forum clause by fraud or overreaching. Finally, [the Shutes] have conceded that they were given notice of the forum provision and, therefore, presumably retained the option of rejecting the contract with impunity. In the case before us, therefore, we conclude that the Court of Appeals erred in refusing to enforce the forum-selection clause."

MATUSEVICH v. TELNIKOFF
877 F.Supp. 1 (D. DC 1995)

BACKGROUND: Telnikoff described himself as a "prominent activist" for human rights in the USSR since 1955. When Matusevich published a critical commentary on Telnikoff and his activities, Telnikoff sued for libel and was awarded a money judgment for damages by a U.K. court. Matusevich (the U.K. defendant) filed his own lawsuit in the USA, asking the U.S. court to declare the U.K. judgment unenforceable in the USA. He has filed a motion for summary judgment in his favor.

JUDGE URBINA:

"Before a party can enforce a judgment from a foreign country in the United States, the moving party must have the foreign judgment recognized by the state in which he is seeking to enforce the judgment. In the State of Maryland, the Uniform Foreign-Money Judgments Recognition Act of 1962 ... and the Uniform Enforcement of Foreign Judgments Act of 1964 ... govern the procedure for the recognition and enforcement of a foreign judgment....

"Section 10-704 lists a number of grounds for non-recognition of a foreign judgment.... Therefore, before a party can enforce a foreign-country judgment, the Recognition Act requires a proceeding to determine preliminarily whether the court should recognize the foreign-country judgment....

"Once the court recognizes the foreign-country judgment, the moving party can simply file that judgment in order to enforce it....

"Section 10-704(b)(2) states that a foreign judgment need not be recognized if 'the cause of action on which the judgment is based is repugnant to the public policy of the State.'...

"Although principles of comity, defined by the Supreme Court as 'the recognition which one nation allows within its territory to the legislative, executive, or judicial acts of another nation, having due regard both to international duty and convenience, and to the rights of its own citizens or of other persons who are under the protection of its laws,' are taken under consideration, the Supreme Court has ruled that comity 'does not require, but rather forbids [recognition] where such a recognition works a direct violation of the policy of our laws, and does violence to what we deem the rights of our citizens.'…

"Although the court recognizes that there is case law rejecting arguments for non-recognition of a foreign judgment based on public policy grounds, those cases are distinguishable in that they concern minor differences in statutory law and in the rules of civil procedure or corporate or commercial law.…

"In this case, libel standards that are contrary to U.S. libel standards would be repugnant to the public polices of the State of Maryland and the United States. Therefore, pursuant to section 10-704(b)(2) of the Recognition Act, this court declines to recognize the foreign judgment.…

"British law on libel differs from U.S. law. In the United Kingdom, the defendant bears the burden of proving allegedly defamatory statements true and the plaintiff is not required to prove malice on the part of the libel defendant.… As a result, a libel defendant would be held liable for statements the defendant honestly believed to be true and published without any negligence. In contrast, the law in the United States requires the plaintiff to prove that the statements were false and looks to the defendant's state of mind and intentions. In light of the different standards, this court concludes that recognition and enforcement of the foreign judgment in this case would deprive the plaintiff of his constitutional rights.…

"Speech similar to the plaintiff's statements ha[s] received protection under the First Amendment to the Constitution and are therefore unactionable in U.S. courts.… [T]he Supreme Court [has] held that hyperbole is not actionable. Plaintiff contends that his statements were plainly hyperbolic because they were stated in an attempt to portray defendant's extremist position.

"In addition, in the United States, courts look to the context in which the statements appeared when determining a First Amendment question.…

"In the case at hand, the court notes that the British judgment was based on jury instructions which asked the jury to ignore context. Therefore, this court finds that if the statements were read in context to the original article or statement and in reference to the location of the statements in the newspaper, a reader would reasonably be alerted to the statements' function as opinion and not as an assertion of fact.…

"The Supreme Court in *New York Times v. Sullivan* ... explained that a public figure must show by clear and convincing evidence that the libel defendant published defamatory statements with actual malice.... [T]he Supreme Court extended this standard to a nonpublic person who is 'nevertheless intimately involved in the resolution of important public questions or, by reason of their fame, shape events in areas of concern to society at large.'...

"During the trial in England, because of British libel standards for the defense of 'fair comment,' the court never looked to the degree of fault or the accused party's intentions. Also, the British court determined that the plaintiff's use of inverted commas around certain words may have falsely mislead [sic] a reader to believe that the defendant actually wrote those words, the [U.S. Supreme] court in *Masson* concluded that 'a deliberate alteration of the words uttered by a plaintiff does not equate with knowledge of falsity.... The use of quotations to attribute words not in fact spoken bears in a most important way on that inquiry, but it is not dispositive in every case.'... As a result, since there appears to be no proof that the plaintiff made the statements with actual malice, the plaintiff enjoys the constitutional protection for speech directed against public figures.

"For the reasons stated herein, the court grants summary judgment in favor of the Plaintiff. A separate order shall follow."

UNITED STATES OF AMERICA v. IVEY
[1996] O.J. No. 3360 (Ontario Court of Appeal, 1996)

BACKGROUND:

"1   The defendants appeal the decision of Sharpe J. ... enforcing in Ontario the judgments of the United States District Court for the Eastern District of Michigan ordering the defendants to pay the cost of cleaning up a Michigan waste disposal site pursuant to their liability under U.S. environmental law....

"3   The appellants submit that the ... judge erred in his appreciation of the evidence and made findings of fact that were not supported by the evidence:
1.   That the defendants engaged in the waste disposal business in Michigan;
2.   That the EPA notified Ivey and the LDI's trustee in bankruptcy before undertaking each removal action, and thus gave them an opportunity to respond;
3.   That the defendants caused the harm that created the cleanup cost;
4.   That the defendants had the opportunity in the U.S. action to raise the issue of their

alleged inability to take any remedial action as a result of the temporary restraining order.

"4 The appellants also submit that the … judge erred in law in the following respects:
1. In his interpretation and application, to the U.S. environmental legislation, of the 'penal, revenue or other public law' test;
2. In his interpretation and application of the Morguard test of real and substantial connection between the defendants and the subject matter or the place of the U.S. action;
3. In his conclusion that the American proceedings satisfied the requirements of natural justice."

THE COURT:

"I. The Factual Issues

"Did the Defendants Engage in the Waste Disposal Business?

"5 In Ivey's day to day control of the operations of LDI, in Maziv's share interest and mortgage and banking and other financial arrangements with LDI, in Ineco's assumption of Maziv's liabilities, and in the findings of fact by Judge Zatcoff, there is ample support for the conclusion of Sharpe J. that the defendants engaged in the waste disposal business in Michigan so as to give them a real and substantial connection with the subject matter of the action.

"Notification Before Cleanup?

"6 Sharpe J. found that the E.P.A. notified Ivey and LDI's trustee in bankruptcy before each of the removal actions, and gave them an opportunity to respond to the environmental problems identified by E.P.A. Because Ivey did not receive personal notice of the first two removals, it is more technically precise to say that the trustee received actual notice, and that Ivey received constructive notice of the second two removals.

"7 Because Ivey was working so closely with the trustee, notice to the trustee was constructive notice to Ivey. In any case, it is far from clear that notification before cleanup was essential to the American judgment or its Canadian enforcement.

"8 To the extent, however, that pre-cleanup notice is relevant, Ivey received constructive notice.

"Did the Defendants Cause the Harm?

"9 Sharpe J. noted that the American judgments went no further than to hold the defendants to account for the cost of remedying the environmental harm that their waste disposal activities caused.

"10   This finding is not essential for American liability or Canadian enforcement, because liability under the relevant U.S. environmental legislation depends on ownership or operation at the time of disposal, and it is not necessary to prove that the defendants caused the harm.

"11   Even though the finding of causation is not essential, there is ample evidence of causation in the evidence admitted by Judge Zatcoff of the pre-accident environmental violations by LDI, and in the failure of the defendants to abate the environmental problems by shipping the liquid contaminants to other available disposal sites when on-site incineration was no longer available.

"Opportunity to Argue Lack of Control?

"12   The defendants argued that the U.S. legislation (C.E.R.C.L.A.) was unfairly applied because they lacked control as a result of Judge Daner's temporary restraining order. Sharpe J. said the defendants had an opportunity to argue the point before Judge Zatcoff but they chose not to do so.

"13   The defendants' argument appears to be unsupported by the evidence. Although the defendants preferred to incinerate the material on site, the temporary restraining order did not prevent them from shipping it to another disposal site.

"14   A further answer to the appellant's argument, that the statute gave them no opportunity to raise that issue before Judge Zatcoff, is that they never defended the case, they never tried to raise that issue, and we will therefore never know whether or not the argument would have been received, or how it would have been received. To say they could not have made an argument they did not try to make is to speculate.

"15   In any event, as Sharpe J. pointed out, even if Judge Zatcoff erred in holding the defendants liable, that is no ground for refusing enforcement.

"II. The Legal Issues

"Penal, Revenue, or Other Public Law?

"16   For the reasons given by Sharpe, J., we conclude that the U.S. environmental legislation (C.E.R.C.L.A.) is not a penal or revenue statute.

"17   The public law exception to the enforceability of foreign judgments rests, as Sharpe J. pointed out in rejecting it, on a shaky doctrinal foundation.

"18 It is not, however, necessary to close the door on the possible existence of such an exception. As Sharpe J. pointed out, the doctrine would have to be extended beyond its present scope in order to apply to this case.

"19 We adopt the reasoning of Sharpe J. in this regard and simply note the following: The United States did not seek to enforce any laws against extraterritorial conduct. It simply sought financial compensation for actual costs incurred in the United States in remedying environmental damage inflicted in the United States on property in the United States. It is no extension of U.S. sovereign jurisdiction to enforce its domestic judgments against those legally accountable for an environmental mess in the United States by reason of their ownership or operation of American waste disposal sites.

"20 In this case the cost recovery action is unlike the laws typically associated with the 'other public law' public law exception, such as import and export regulations, trading with the enemy legislation, price control and anti-trust legislation.

"21 The cost recovery action, although asserted by a public authority, is so close to a common law claim for nuisance that it is, in substance, of a commercial or private law character.

"22 The cost recovery action under this statutory regime is not the unique right of government; it may be asserted against government and it may be asserted by between private parties.

"23 Many jurisdictions including Ontario have adopted similar statutes which strengthen common law compensation remedies. International comity supports the mutual enforcement of such similar statutory regimes.

"24 Real and Substantial Connection to the Action?

"25 Appellants' counsel, by saying he 'does not advance the argument that Morguard should not be followed' concedes the applicability of the 'real and substantial connection' test.

"26 For the reasons given by Sharpe J., we conclude that he correctly applied and interpreted the Morguard test.

"Was Natural Justice Satisfied?

"27 For the reasons given by Sharpe, J., we conclude that the American proceedings satisfied the requirements of natural justice."

KARAHA BODAS CO., LLC v.
PERUSAHAAN PERTAMBANGAN MINYAK DAN GAS
364 F.3d 274 (5th Cir. 2004)

BACKGROUND: Karaha Bodas ("KBC") sued in U.S. District Court in Texas to enforce against defendant PPMDGBN ("Pertamina"), an arbitration award made in Switzerland, involving contracts to be performed in Indonesia. KBC, a Cayman Islands firm, signed a "Joint Operation Contract" ("JOC") with Pertamina, by the terms of which KBC was to develop geothermal energy sources in Indonesia. Pertamina, a government-owned energy company, was to manage the project and receive the electricity thus produced. Under a second contract (an "Energy Sales Contract"—"ESC") Pertamina was to sell the electricity to another Indonesian government entity—PLN. Both contracts contained virtually identical clauses specifying arbitration in Switzerland using the United Nations Commission on International Trade Law ("UNCITRAL") Rules. When Indonesia suspended the project for lack of funds, KBC requested arbitration. There was a hotly contested dispute over whether KBC could have gotten other financing to complete the project, after the Indonesian government cancelled its backing. The panel ruled in favor of KBC, and the Swiss courts upheld the award. The U.S. District Court then enforced the award, and Pertamina appealed. Meanwhile, Pertamina had asked an Indonesian court to annul the award, which it did; and KBC also filed enforcement lawsuits in Hong Kong and Canada. The Canadian lawsuit discovered that investors in KBC had received a $75 million settlement from Lloyd's of London on a "political risk" insurance policy, as a result of Indonesia's cancellation of the project.

JUDGE ROSENTHAL:

"Thirty years ago, the United States Supreme Court recognized that '[a] contractual provision specifying in advance the forum in which disputes shall be litigated and the law to be applied is … an almost indispensable precondition to achievement of the orderliness and predictability essential to any international business transaction…. Such a provision obviates the danger that a dispute under the agreement might be submitted to a forum hostile to the interests of one of the parties or unfamiliar with the problem area involved.' When, as here, parties to international commercial contracts agree to arbitrate future disputes in a neutral forum, orderliness and predictability also depend on the procedures for reviewing and enforcing arbitral awards that may result….

"The New York Convention [United Nations Convention on Recognition and Enforcement of Foreign Arbitral Awards] provides a carefully structured framework for the review and enforcement of international arbitration awards. Only a court in a country with primary jurisdiction over an arbitral award may annul that award. Courts in other countries have secondary jurisdiction; a court in a country with secondary jurisdiction is limited to deciding whether the award may be enforced in that country. The Convention 'mandates very different regimes for the review of arbitral awards (1) in the [countries] in which, or under the law of which, the award was made, and (2) in other [countries] where recognition and enforcement are sought.' Under the Convention, 'the country in which, or under the [arbitration] law of which, [an] award was made' is said to have primary jurisdiction over the arbitration award. All other signatory states are secondary jurisdictions, in which parties can only contest whether that state should enforce the arbitral award. It is clear that the district court had secondary jurisdiction and considered only whether to enforce the Award in the United States.

"Article V enumerates specific grounds on which a court with secondary jurisdiction may refuse enforcement. In contrast to the limited authority of secondary jurisdiction courts to review an arbitral award, courts of primary jurisdiction, usually the courts of the country of the arbitral situs, have much broader discretion to set aside an award. While courts of a primary jurisdiction country may apply their own domestic law in evaluating a request to annul or set aside an arbitral award, courts in countries of secondary jurisdiction may refuse enforcement only on the grounds specified in Article V.

"The New York Convention and the implementing legislation, Chapter 2 of the Federal Arbitration Act … provide that a secondary jurisdiction court must enforce an arbitration award unless it finds one of the grounds for refusal or deferral of recognition or enforcement specified in the Convention. The court may not refuse to enforce an arbitral award solely on the ground that the arbitrator may have made a mistake of law or fact. 'Absent extraordinary circumstances, a confirming court is not to reconsider an arbitrator's findings.' The party defending against enforcement of the arbitral award bears the burden of proof. Defenses to enforcement under the New York Convention are construed narrowly, 'to encourage the recognition and enforcement of commercial arbitration agreements in international contracts.'…

"Article V(1)(e) of the Convention provides that a court of secondary jurisdiction may refuse to enforce an arbitral award if it 'has been set aside or suspended by a competent authority of the country in which, or under the law of which, that award was made.' Courts have held that the language '"the competent authority of the country … under the law of which, that award was made" refers exclusively to procedural and not substantive law, and more precisely, to the regimen or scheme of arbitral procedural law under which the arbitration was conducted, and not the substantive law … applied to the case.' In this appeal, Pertamina and the Republic of Indonesia … argue that the Tribunal and the district court erred in finding that Swiss procedural law, rather than Indonesian procedural law, applied…. KBC responds that the Tribunal properly interpreted the parties' contracts in deciding that Swiss procedural law applied and the district court properly applied the New York Convention in affirming that decision. This court agrees with KBC.

"Under the New York Convention, the rulings of the Tribunal interpreting the parties' contract are entitled to deference. Unless the Tribunal manifestly disregarded the parties' agreement or the law, there is no basis to set aside the determination that Swiss procedural law applied. The parties' arbitration agreements specified that the site of the arbitration was Geneva, Switzerland and that the arbitration would proceed under the UNCITRAL rules. Those rules specify that the 'arbitral tribunal shall apply the law designated by the parties as applicable to the substance of the dispute.' It is undisputed that the parties specified that Indonesian substantive law would apply. It is also undisputed that the contracts specified the site of the arbitration as Switzerland. The contracts did not otherwise expressly identify the procedural law that would apply to the arbitration. The parties did refer to certain Indonesian Civil Procedure Rules in the contracts. Pertamina and the Republic argue that these references evidence an intent that while Switzerland would be the place of the arbitration, Indonesian procedural law would apply as the lex arbitri.

"Under the New York Convention, an agreement specifying the place of arbitration creates a presumption that the procedural law of that place applies to the arbitration. Authorities on international arbitration describe an agreement providing that one country will be the site of the arbitration but the proceedings will be held under the arbitration law of another country by terms such as 'exceptional'; 'almost unknown'; a 'purely academic invention'; 'almost never used in practice'; a possibility 'more theoretical than real'; and a 'once-in-a-blue-moon set of circumstances.' Commentators note that such an agreement would be complex, inconvenient, and inconsistent with the selection of a neutral forum as the arbitral forum.

"In the JOC and the ESC, the parties expressly agreed that Switzerland would be the site for the arbitration. This agreement presumptively selected Swiss procedural law to apply to the arbitration. There is no express agreement in the JOC or ESC that Indonesia would be the country 'under the law of which' the arbitration was to be conducted and the Award was to be made. The Tribunal recognized the parties' selection of Switzerland by issuing the Award as 'made in Geneva.' In selecting Switzerland as the site of the arbitration, the parties were not choosing a physical place for the arbitration to occur, but rather the place where the award would be 'made.' Under Article 16(1) of the UNCITRAL Rules, the 'place' designated for an arbitration is the legal rather than physical location of the forum. The arbitration proceedings in this case physically occurred in Paris, but the award was 'made in' Geneva, the place of the arbitration in the legal sense and the presumptive source of the applicable procedural law....

"Pertamina correctly observes that the Convention provides two tests for determining which country has primary jurisdiction over an arbitration award: a country in which an award is made and a country under the law of which an award is made. The New York Convention suggests the potential for more than one country of primary jurisdiction. Courts and scholars have noted as much. Pertamina cites one such scholar as support for its position….

"Although an arbitration agreement may make more than one country eligible for primary jurisdiction under the New York Convention, the predominant view is that the Convention permits only one in any given case. 'Many commentators and foreign courts have concluded that an action to set aside an award can be brought only under the domestic law of the arbitral forum.' Pertamina's expert on international arbitration filed a report in the district court, stating that 'there can be only one country in which the courts have jurisdiction over an annulment.' In its motion to the district court to set aside judgment under Rule 60(b), Pertamina conceded that '[a] primary jurisdiction has exclusive authority to nullify an award on the basis of its own arbitration law.' Such 'exclusive' primary jurisdiction in the courts of single country is consistent with the New York Convention's purpose; facilitates the 'orderliness and predictability' necessary to international commercial agreements; and implements the parties' choice of a neutral forum.

"In this case, both the New York Convention criteria for the country with primary jurisdiction point to Switzerland—and only to Switzerland. The Award was made in Switzerland and was under Swiss procedural law. The parties' arbitration agreement designated Switzerland as the site for the arbitration. This designation presumptively designated Swiss procedural law as the lex loci arbitri, in the absence of any express statement making another country's procedural law applicable.

"Pertamina's own conduct during and after the arbitration evidences its intent to have Swiss procedural law apply and to have Switzerland be the country of primary jurisdiction over the Award. During the arbitration, Pertamina asserted that Swiss procedural law applied. When it lost the arbitration, Pertamina asked the Swiss court to set aside the Award, acknowledging that the Swiss courts had primary jurisdiction. While that appeal was pending, Pertamina urged the district court in the enforcement proceeding that the Swiss courts had exclusive primary jurisdiction—until the Swiss courts rejected Pertamina's appeal.

"Under the New York Convention, the parties' arbitration agreement, and this record, Switzerland had primary jurisdiction of the Award. Because Indonesia did not have primary jurisdiction to set aside the Award, this court affirms the district court's conclusion that the Indonesian court's annulment ruling is not a defense to enforcement under the New York Convention.

"Pertamina's challenges to the district court's decision affirming the Award are without merit.

The summary judgment enforcing the Award is AFFIRMED."

FORD MOTOR CO. & BRIDGESTONE/FIRESTONE N.AM. TIRE v. MENDOZA et al.
591 F.3d 406 (7th Cir. 2009)

BACKGROUND: Ford Motor Company, and Bridgestone/Firestone North American Tire LLC, requested that the district court reconsider a pretrial *forum non conveniens* ("FNC") motion that had been denied by a multidistrict litigation ("MDL") court. The district court declined the request, so petitioners seek a writ of mandamus. Plaintiffs (Mendoza) are several Mexican citizens who were injured in Mexico in vehicle accidents involving Ford sport utility vehicles and Firestone tires. They sued these Petitioners in Val Verde County, Texas, state court, and petitioners removed to the U.S. Western District of Texas. The case was transferred to the U.S. MDL court in the Southern District of Indiana, which had been established to deal with the more than 700 similar cases against Ford and Firestone. At about the same time that plaintiffs filed this suit, another case, *Manez*, involving similar circumstances, was also transferred to the MDL court. Before considering the plaintiffs' case, the MDL court examined the merits of a FNC motion in *Manez*. Petitioners (who were also the defendants in *Manez*) filed the FNC motion, claiming that Mexico was an available—and more appropriate—forum. The defendants stipulated that they would submit to personal jurisdiction in Mexico. The court stated, relying on Fifth Circuit precedent, that "[n]umerous cases have held Mexico to be an adequate forum for tort litigation involving American-made products, despite differences in Mexican and U.S. substantive and procedural law." The MDL court granted the FNC motion in *Manez*.

The *Manez* plaintiffs appealed to the Seventh Circuit Court of Appeals, as is proper under MDL procedure. On appeal, the court noted that the district court's FNC decision was "quite reasonable" and said that "this case looks like an easy candidate for a straightforward affirmance." The court then noted, however, that there was a "wrinkle" that prevented the easy affirmance: two *ex parte* Mexican court decisions that stated the case could not be tried in Mexican courts. The court noted that it had "substantial misgivings about the plaintiffs' actions" in submitting the orders but held that it did "not have an adequate record to assess whether the plaintiffs' actions were taken in good faith." It remanded for the MDL district court "thoroughly [to] explore the circumstances" surrounding the Mexican decisions.

On remand, the district court "conducted an evidentiary hearing to thoroughly explore the circumstances surrounding the [Mexican] courts' decisions." The court concluded that in seeking the Mexican dismissal order, "the attorneys for Plaintiffs acted with the clear purpose of having the case dismissed[] and, in seeking that result, manipulated the process to insure that the dismissal would be based on a particular reason that was calculated to improve the chances of the dismissal being sustained on appeal." Specifically, it noted e-mails between attorneys discussing how one Mexican judge "confirmed that she will throw out the suit according to what we planned." The MDL court dismissed the case on FNC grounds, and the decision was not appealed. The MDL court later sanctioned the *Manez* plaintiffs' expert witness, Dr. Leonel Pereznieto, noting that he was "the apparent mastermind behind these frauds on the U.S. and Mexican courts."

After that dismissal, the MDL court asked all parties to show cause why their cases should not be dismissed. Plaintiffs did not initially respond, but another plaintiff did submit a reply. Petitioners responded to that reply and specifically asked that plaintiffs' case be dismissed. Plaintiffs then filed a response, insisting that Mexico was not an available forum. Filed with the response were several dismissal orders, obtained *ex parte* from Mexican courts, that allegedly claimed that foreign defendants cannot be sued in Mexico for tort cases, even if they submit to jurisdiction there. The MDL court agreed with plaintiffs that Mexico is not an available forum; it denied petitioners' motion to dismiss. The court then ordered a conditional return of the case to the Western District.

Petitioners filed a motion for reconsideration, an alternative motion to certify the issue for interlocutory appeal to the Seventh Circuit, and an objection to the conditional remand order. Plaintiffs opposed all the motions; the MDL court did not rule on any of them before the MDL panel returned the case to the Western District. Six weeks after that occurred, the MDL court dismissed all of the motions as moot.

After the case had been returned to the Western District, Petitioners again filed a motion for reconsideration of the MDL court's FNC decision. They submitted new evidence regarding the *ex parte* dismissal orders, allegedly showing that they had been fraudulently obtained. Judge Hudspeth, of the Western District, denied the motion, opining that "[w]hen a civil action has been through the MDL process and has been remanded . . . the pretrial rulings made by the transferee court should be reconsidered, if at all, under only the most extraordinary circumstances. To do so would go a long way toward defeating the entire purposes of the MDL process." Judge Hudspeth expressed his view that such extraordinary circumstances are not present in this case and that he believed the petitioners did not actually want to have their case tried in Mexico but only wanted to delay the trial. Also, he denied an interlocutory appeal to this court because, in his opinion, this was a delay tactic. Petitioners asked the Seventh Circuit to grant mandamus on the FNC issue.

THE COURT:

"Treating the petition for rehearing en banc as a petition for panel rehearing, the petition for panel rehearing is DENIED. No member of the panel or judge in regular active service having requested that the court be polled on rehearing en banc, the petition for rehearing en banc is DENIED.

"The following opinion is substituted for the original opinion for the purpose of correcting minor factual errors and providing additional explanation. No further request for rehearing or rehearing en banc will be permitted....

JUDGE SMITH:

"The issue—whether we can grant mandamus on a district court's refusal to reconsider a pretrial MDL decision—is one of first impression in this circuit. We examine the question in two parts. First, we see whether the district court improperly denied the motion for reconsideration. If we decide that the district court did err, we next look to see whether we can properly grant mandamus in the procedural posture of Judge Hudspeth's denial of reconsideration....

"We begin by addressing how MDL transferor courts review the pretrial determinations of transferee MDL courts. We have not established a standard for review of this question, though we note that authorities are unanimous that some deference must be given to the transferee court's decisions....

"The better view is ... that transferor courts should use the law of the case doctrine to determine whether to revisit a transferee court's decision. Moreover, a bright-line rule cannot be reconciled with our precedent in similar situations: 'The revisitation by the court of [an] earlier order . . . was not error because . . . a court may correct its own errors. The fact that [the judge] was not correcting his own error, but that of another judge who initially had been in charge of the case, is no moment.'...

"The law of the case doctrine requires that courts not revisit the determinations of an earlier court unless '(i) the evidence on a subsequent trial was substantially different, (ii) controlling authority has since made a contrary decision of the law applicable to such issues, or (iii) the decision was clearly erroneous and would work . . . manifest injustice.'... Since the MDL court's ruling, no new controlling authority has overruled the decision. Though petitioners have presented new evidence that calls into question the plaintiffs' *ex parte* orders from Mexico, we need not decide whether that evidence is enough to invoke the law of the case doctrine.... Instead, we conclude that the transferee court's FNC decision is so clearly erroneous that it would work manifest injustice in this case. Because the transferor court should have recognized its serious error, its decision not to vacate its decision regarding FNC was also clearly erroneous....

"We have held in numerous cases that Mexico is an available forum for tort suits against a defendant that is willing to submit to jurisdiction there....

"These many decisions create a nearly airtight presumption that Mexico is an available forum. We have held that if a defendant submits to jurisdiction, there is a presumption of forum availability; petitioners have done so here. We have held in tort cases (even one case involving nearly identical facts) that Mexico is an available forum for tort suits against foreign defendants. Our rule of orderliness 'forbids one of our panels from overruling a prior panel.'... Thus, unless this court en banc or the Supreme Court decides otherwise, petitioners' willingness to submit to jurisdiction in Mexico makes it an available forum for FNC purposes, based on the binding precedent of this court....

"Along with failing to consider our earlier binding opinions, the MDL court erred when it relied solely on the plaintiffs' *ex parte* orders from Mexican courts without any expert testimony. At oral argument, plaintiffs' counsel conceded that they had submitted only two experts to the MDL court: Leonel Pereznieto and Mexican Judge Garcia Estrada. Counsel also admitted that the MDL court struck both Pereznieto's and Estrada's testimony. Thus, plaintiffs had no experts on whom to rely. Instead, they submitted only *ex parte* orders allegedly showing Mexico is not an available forum. The MDL court relied on those orders in denying petitioners' FNC motion.

"The MDL court erred twice in using the *ex parte* orders to reach its decision. First, the court should have required expert testimony to analyze the *ex parte* orders and other important materials, such as Mexican code provisions and Mexican Supreme Court or appellate decisions.... Second, relying solely on these *ex parte* orders was error. We recognize that in Mexican courts, jurisdictional decisions *can* be given *ex parte* without necessarily violating any rules. Plaintiffs, however, have not submitted any evidence to show that these orders *must* be issued without the opposing counsel's being present. Especially in a case such as this—where other similarly situated plaintiffs have acted fraudulently—the MDL court should have asked for orders that were issued in courts in which both parties were present, to ensure there was no fraud. By not having expert testimony, and by relying on *ex parte* orders obtained without the presence of opposing counsel, the MDL court again erred....

"Finally, but importantly, we note that petitioners were and are willing to submit to a return jurisdiction clause. As we noted [in another case], '[t]here is no guarantee that [Mexico] will remain an available forum or that defendants will submit to its jurisdiction. A return jurisdiction clause remedies this concern by permitting parties to return to the dismissing court should the lawsuit become impossible in the foreign forum.'... Petitioners stated that they will accept a return jurisdiction clause, and this weighs heavily in favor of finding that the MDL court erred.

"The evidence put before the MDL court was rather equivocal on whether Mexico was an available forum; both sides submitted experts, code provisions, court decisions, and orders showing Mexico to be either an available or unavailable forum. With such uncertainty, a return-jurisdiction clause must weigh heavily in favor of granting the FNC motion. That clause will allow both sides—rather than just plaintiffs—to go before a judge in Mexico and find out whether *this specific suit* can be tried there. If Mexico will not hear the case, plaintiffs can re-file in Texas and proceed to trial. In the face of evidence and caselaw showing Mexico to be an available forum, it was clear error for the MDL court to reject this option....

"For all of these reasons, under the law of the case doctrine, the transferor court should have reconsidered the MDL court's FNC decision for manifest injustice. In light of the binding caselaw, the lack of expert evidence, and the willingness of the petitioners to submit to a return jurisdiction clause, Mexico was the proper forum. Having found that there was manifest injustice and that the transferor court clearly erred in not reconsidering the MDL court's FNC decision, we now must see whether this case meets our criteria for granting mandamus relief.

"Mandamus is an appropriate remedy for 'exceptional circumstances amounting to a judicial usurpation of power or a clear abuse of discretion.'... Plainly, a transferor court's refusal to reexamine a transferee court's FNC decision can be one of the 'exceptional circumstances,' so long as the refusal meets our stringent criteria for granting mandamus.... Showing that there was a clear abuse of discretion, however, is not enough: The Supreme Court has established three requirements that must be met before a writ may issue: (1) the party seeking issuance of the writ must have no other adequate means to attain the relief he desires—a condition designed to ensure that the writ will not be used as a substitute for the regular appeals process; (2) the petitioner must satisfy the burden of showing that [his] right to issuance of the writ is clear and indisputable; and (3) even if the first two prerequisites have been met, the issuing court, in the exercise of its discretion, must be satisfied that the writ is appropriate under the circumstances....

"For the reasons we have explained, there was a clear abuse of discretion, because the transferor court refused to alter a transferee court's decision that relied on an erroneous conclusion of law. Petitioners submitted to jurisdiction in Mexico, and our caselaw plainly holds that Mexico is an available forum. It was patently erroneous for the MDL court to ignore this binding precedent and equally erroneous for the transferor court to accept that decision.

"We additionally find comfort in granting mandamus in light of the fact that this is an extraordinary case. Snippets of the record that counsel that result include, in no particular order of significance, the fact that plaintiffs' expert on Mexican law was the same person who had been employed by the *Manez* plaintiffs and who had been sanctioned by the MDL court for bad faith and fraudulent conduct. Moreover, to show that Mexico was unavailable, plaintiffs submitted *ex parte* dismissal orders that were suspiciously similar to orders proffered in *Manez*, in which the MDL court had declared that those plaintiffs had deliberately and fraudulently obtained the dismissals for the express purpose of defeating an FNC motion. Then, on the same day it denied the FNC motion, the MDL court suggested to the JPML that the cases be remanded immediately to the district courts….

"As a result of that remand, the MDL court never ruled on petitioners' motion to reconsider, but just dismissed the motion as moot long after the matter had been remanded to the transferor court and after the MDL court no longer had jurisdiction…. The transferor court never considered the merits of the motion to reconsider, but only denied that motion on the mistaken belief that the court lacked discretion to reach the merits….

"Petitioners also lack any other adequate means to attain relief. They attempted to have the MDL court's decision certified for appeal to the Seventh Circuit and asked for reconsideration by both the MDL court and the transferor court. All of these attempts were rejected….

"… [I]n these FNC cases, mandamus is appropriate on this prong because, if the issue is argued only on any eventual direct appeal, there is no way to show that the outcome of the case would have been different, and any inconvenience to the parties 'will already have been done by the time the case is tried and appealed.'… '[T]he writ is not here used as a substitute for an appeal, as an appeal will provide no remedy for a patently erroneous failure to transfer venue.'

"Additionally, the petitioners have a clear and indisputable right to the writ. That follows from our finding of a clear abuse of discretion: 'If the district court clearly abused its discretion . . . in denying [the] motion, then [the petitioners'] right to issuance of the writ is necessarily clear and indisputable.'… There was a clear abuse of discretion, so petitioners are entitled to a writ of mandamus.

"Finally, we must be satisfied that the writ is appropriate in this circumstance…. [O]ther suits may be filed in our district courts involving the question whether Mexico is an available forum in our circumstances. This issue is not specific to this case but is relevant for a variety of similar cases that have arisen or may arise in the district courts of this circuit. Recognizing this, a writ of mandamus is called for here. Considering the return-jurisdiction clause and our … binding precedent, it is plain that this trial should not take place in American courts unless a Mexican forum is unavailable.

"For all of the above reasons, the district court erred in not overruling the MDL court's FNC decision, and that error is serious enough to require mandamus as the appropriate relief. We direct the district court to render a judgment of dismissal without prejudice, because Mexico is an available and appropriate forum. Plaintiffs can re-file this suit and proceed to trial in the Western District of Texas on a sufficient showing that the Mexican courts are unavailable for this litigation despite petitioners' submission to jurisdiction there. Plaintiffs must litigate in good faith in Mexican courts, and evidence showing otherwise may justify sanctions against plaintiffs and their counsel.

"The petition for writ of mandamus is GRANTED."

YAYASAN MELAKA v. PHOTRAN CORP SDN BDN & ANOR.
[2012] 7 MLJ I (High Court—Kuala Lumpur, Singapore 2012)

BACKGROUND: Bryn Williams and Lim Lek Yan (D2) agreed with the state government of Melaka and Zeron Sdn Bhd to establish a joint venture (Photran—D1) which would manufacture optical products in Malaysia. The parties agreed to contribute various proportions of the capital needed for licenses from Photran USA, for machinery, and for working capital. When plaintiff was required to make a further contribution of RM4,600,000 in June 1997, it refused to do so unless that amount and an equal amount previously contributed were treated as loans to Photran, and Lim Lek Yan signed an agreement personally guaranteeing payment. In need of the money for operations, Photran and Yan so agreed. On June 30, 2003 plaintiff filed the present lawsuit to collect the RM9,200,000 "loan," and on August 12, 2003 plaintiff entered a judgment in default ("JID") against both Defendants (D1 and D2). On January 31, 2011 Photran (D1) applied to set aside the JID, but the senior assistant registrar (SAR) dismissed the application. Photran appealed.

JUDGE JC LEE SWEE SENG:

"The first thing that is obvious is the long delay between the date of the JID on 12 August 2003 and the date of the application to set aside the JID on 31 January 2011. There was a seven year gap. Is such a delay fatal or it all depends on the reasons for the delay? ... [T]he Federal Court case of *Muniandy a/l Thamba Kaundan & Anor v D&C Bank BHd & Anor* ... observed: 'Lapse of time is no bar to a defendant's application to set aside a judgment which is a nullity. Further, under its inherent jurisdiction to prevent an abuse of proceedings, the court has power to set aside a judgment in default despite the defendant's application being out of time if the particular circumstances of the case require it....'

"When is a judgment in default said to be an irregular judgment? ... [T]he Federal Court case of

Tuan Haji Ahmed Rahman v Arab-Malaysian Finance Bhd ... gives this succinct summary: 'It is elementary that an irregular judgment is one which has been entered otherwise than in strict compliance with the rules or some statute or is entered as the result of some impropriety which is considered to be so serious as to render the proceedings a nullity....'

"Here the JID had been entered because the board of D1 through its action or more particularly its inaction allowed no appearance to be entered and thus by design allowed a default judgment to be entered against D1. The final seal of silence or so the board of D1 thought, was by the same silent strategy of allowing Perbadanan Melaka to obtain a judgment in default against it and then to sit still and fold its arms in a deliberate inaction to suffer it being wound up by Perbadanan Melaka for a paltry sum of RM1,505....

"Such an irregularity where the plaintiff was fully aware of and by its overpowering presence controls the board of D1 to the extent of stultifying and silencing it to inaction, leads to the inevitable result that any judgment in default entered can only be entered 'otherwise than in strict compliance with the rules or some statute or is entered as a result of some impropriety which is considered to be so serious as to render the proceedings a nullity'....

"As D1 has maintained that there is a valid arbitration clause in the loan agreement by S.15 thereof, D1 was careful not to be seen to have taken a step in the proceeding by the proposed defence, set-off and counterclaim that it intended to file. Whilst it had referred to its various defences, set-off and counterclaim in its affidavits filed in support of its application to set aside the JID, it had also in Part C of its submission set out the whole of its defence, set-off and counterclaim....

"The crux of this defence is that D1 was induced and coerced in entering into the loan agreement by illegitimate pressure brought to bear upon it by the plaintiff and/or that in any event that loan agreement was void and unenforceable by reason of the various issues raised in the proposed defence, set-off and counterclaim....

"Viewed in the light of the history of the case in the events that led to the joint venture, the defence of undue influence and coercion should be allowed to be ventilated. This is not a stage to analyse with minute examination or microscopic precision the strength or likelihood of success of this defence which on the face of it is not totally frivolous....

"Under the shareholders' agreement the plaintiff undertook to assist D1 to apply and obtain from any banks or financial institutions an irrevocable letter of credit. The plaintiff agreed to contribute to funds required for the purpose of the business of D1. The plaintiff further agreed to take all necessary steps to give full effect to the provisions of the agreement and to procure through its directors that D1 and the directors do perform and observe the provisions of the agreement. Under the land transfer agreement, the plaintiff was to, inter alia, transfer the land to D1 to enable D1 to utilise the same as a security for facilities required by D1. D1 asserted in the proposed defence that the plaintiff had to-date failed to transfer the said land to D1....

"D1 further pleaded that the plaintiff by compelling D1 to execute the loan agreement ... was clearly in breach of its fiduciary duties to D1 vis-à-vis the shareholders' agreement. D1 argued that the shareholders' agreement is in essence and substance a joint venture between the plaintiff, Bryn Williams and D2 and that D1 was in fact the joint venture vehicle. In the circumstances, D1 contended the plaintiff owes a fiduciary duty to its other joint venturers as well as D1. Further, being in a joint venture, there is an express and/or implied duty on the plaintiff to use his best endeavours to ensure the success of the venture....

"Taking the cue from the above observations as to the fiduciary position that joint venturers stand towards one another, when as in here D1 alleges breach of the shareholders' agreement and the land transfer agreement, the very least is to give D1 the opportunity to be heard rather than allowing a JID to remain which was entered against it when it was voiceless and powerless to act for itself.

"In the light of the reasons given above, I [have] allowed D1's appeal against the decision of the SAR and I allowed the judgment in default against D1 to be set aside with costs in the cause."

BHATIA TRADING v. BULK TRADING S.A. & ANOR.
[2002] 1 LRI 703 (Supreme Court of India 2002)

BACKGROUND: The parties entered into a contract which included an arbitration clause providing that any arbitration proceeding would be conducted in accordance with the rules of the International Chamber of Commerce ("ICC"). When problems arose, Bhatia filed a request for arbitration with the ICC. The parties agreed that the arbitration would be held in Paris, with the ICC as the sole arbitrator. Bhatia then filed a request with an Indian District Court, pursuant to section 9 of India's Arbitration and Conciliation Act of 1996, for an injunction restraining Bulk Trading and another involved company from disposing of their business assets. Bulk Trading argued that Part I of the Act did not apply to arbitrations occurring outside India, but the district judge held that it did apply. That decision was affirmed by the High Court of Madhya Pradesh, even though several other High Courts had made contrary rulings. Bulk Trading asked for further review by the Supreme Court of India.

JUSTICE VARIAVA:

"Section 1 of the Act reads as follows: ... 'This Act may be called the arbitration and Conciliation Act of 1996. It extends to the whole of India: Provided that Parts I, III, and IV shall extend to the state of Jammu and Kashmir only in so far as they relate to international commercial arbitration or, as the case may be, international commercial conciliation.'

"The words 'this Act' means the entire Act. This shows that the entire Act, including part I, applies to the whole of India. The fact that all parts apply to the whole of India is clear from the proviso which provides that parts I, III and IV will apply to the State of Jammu and Kashmir only so far as international commercial arbitrations/conciliations are concerned. Significantly the proviso does not state that part I would apply to Jammu and Kashmir only if the place of the international commercial arbitration is in Jammu and Kashmir....

"That the legislature did not intend to exclude the applicability of part I to arbitrations which take place outside India, is further clear from certain other provisions of the said Act. Subsection (7) of s.2 reads as follows: 'An arbitral award made under this part shall be considered as a domestic award.'

"As is set out hereinabove the said Act applies to (a) arbitrations held in India between Indians and (b) international commercial arbitrations. Outside India an international commercial arbitration may be held in a convention country or in a non-convention country. The said Act however only classifies awards as 'domestic awards' or 'foreign awards'.... [P]rovisions of part II makes it clear that 'foreign awards' are only those where the arbitration takes place in a convention country. Awards in arbitration proceedings which take place in a non-convention country are not considered to be 'foreign awards' under the said Act. They would thus not be covered by part II. An award passed in an arbitration which takes place in India would be a 'domestic award'. There would thus be no need to define an award as a 'domestic award' unless the intention was to cover awards which would otherwise not be covered by this definition. Strictly speaking an award passed in an arbitration which takes place in a non-convention country would not be a 'domestic award'. Thus the necessity is to define a 'domestic award' as including all awards made under part I....

"Unless the parties have otherwise agreed, as soon as the file is transmitted to it, the arbitral tribunal may, at the request of a party, order any interim or conservatory measure it deems appropriate. The arbitral tribunal may make the granting of any such measure subject to appropriate security being furnished by the requesting party. Any such measure shall take the form of an order, giving reasons, or of an award, as the arbitral tribunal considers appropriate....

"Thus art.23 of the ICC rules permits parties to apply to a competent judicial authority for interim and conservatory measures. Therefore, in such cases an application can be made under s.9 of the said Act.

"Lastly it must be stated that the said Act does not appear to be a well drafted legislation. Therefore the High Court[s] of Orissa, Bombay, Madras, Delhi and Calcutta cannot be faulted for interpreting it in the manner indicated above. However, in our view a proper and conjoint reading of all the provisions indicates that Part I is to apply also to international commercial arbitrations which take place out of India, unless the parties by agreement, express or implied exclude it or any of its provisions. Such an interpretation does not lead to any conflict between any of the provisions of the said Act. On this interpretation there [are] no lacunae in the said Act. This interpretation also does not leave a party remedyless. Thus such an interpretation has to be preferred to the one adopted by the [other] High Courts.... It will therefore have to be held that the contrary view taken by these High Courts is not good law.

"In this view of the matter we see no reason to interfere with the impugned judgment. The appeal stands dismissed. There will be no order as to costs throughout."

SUPREME COURT DECISION 2001Da20134
Gong2003.6.1.(179).1148 (Korea 2003)

BACKGROUND: An arbitration case was submitted to the Vietnamese Commercial Arbitration Board with respect to the present case in which the plaintiff sued the defendant on the ground of a defective embroidery machine, produced and supplied by the defendant. On February 6, 1999, an arbitral award was issued such that the defendant should install a new embroidery machine as a replacement for the defective one (section 1.1 of the arbitral award), pay damages in the amount of $17,010.88 US dollars with additional damages for deferred payment, calculated based on the interest rate published by the Vietnamese bank, as the case may be (section 1.2 of the arbitral award), and costs of the arbitration proceeding in the amount of $5,336 US dollars (section 2 of the arbitral award). In accordance with the arbitral award, on March 13 of the same year, the defendant transferred by wire the total sum of $22,346.88 US dollars—composed of damages in the amount of $17,010.88 US dollars and costs of the arbitration proceeding in the amount of $5,336 US dollars.

Thereafter, the defendant produced a replacement embroidery machine, and on the 26th of the same month, had it transported to Vietnam where it completed an import customs clearance process. However, on May 17 of the same year, when the defendant brought a replacement machine to the plaintiff's factory for its installation, as well as import clearance documents required for the transfer of ownership title, the plaintiff refused the installation of a replacement machine, claiming that there existed problems with respect to defective import procedures, etc. Additionally, the court below acknowledged that from that time on to the present, the replacement embroidery machine and documents for title transfer have remained in the custody of a Vietnamese import agent designated by the defendant. Thus, the court below held the view that as far as the defendant offered to carry out its obligatory duties in accordance with the arbitration award of the present case on May 17 of the same year, and from then on continued to hold the replacement embroidery machine with documents for title transfer in the hands of an import agent, the defendant had fulfilled its duty to replace an embroidery machine.

Having scrutinized the above facts, the court below decided for enforcement of only the unfulfilled part, i.e., section 1.2 of the arbitral award, which stipulates additional damages for deferred payment accrued up until the complete performance date of replacing a machine and paying damages. On the other hand, the court below refused to enforce parts of the arbitral award, which was found to be already fulfilled by the defendant, i.e., section 1.1 for replacement of a machine and section 2 assessing costs of arbitration upon the defendant, on the basis of the following reasons: a ground for objection to the claim occurred after the issuance of the arbitral award and, in light of circumstances extending from the issuance of the arbitral award to the claim for enforcement, its enforcement would be contrary to public policy as an abusive exercise of rights under Paragraph 2 Item (b) of Article 5 of the New York Convention on the Recognition and Enforcement of Foreign Arbitral Awards.

THE COURT:

"We reverse, with respect to section 1.1 of the arbitral award of the present case, the part of the judgment of the court below against the plaintiff and remand that part of the case to Seoul High Court and dismiss the plaintiff's remaining grounds for appeal....

"Since the arbitral award of the present case is a foreign arbitral award issued under Convention on the Recognition and Enforcement of Foreign Arbitral Awards (hereinafter referred to as 'New York Convention'), its enforcement shall be decided upon by the New York Convention pursuant to Paragraph 1 of Article 37 and Paragraph 1 of Article 39 of the Arbitration Act. New York Convention limited grounds to refuse enforcement of awards to ones listed under the provision of Article 5, and among them, Paragraph 2 Item (b) of Article 5 provides that recognition and enforcement of an arbitral award may be refused by a court of law in the country where recognition and enforcement is sought if the recognition or enforcement of the award would be contrary to public policy of that country. Such ground for refusal is provided to the effect that recognition and enforcement of a foreign arbitral award does not negatively influence fundamental moral norms and social order of the enforcing country so that they shall be preserved as unharmed. However, a court of law should consider not only internal circumstances of the enforcing country, but also aspect of ensuring the stability of international transactions in rendering a judgment to refuse recognition and enforcement. Accordingly, grounds for refusing recognition or enforcement must be narrowly interpreted, and thus, recognition and enforcement of an arbitral award shall be refused only if concrete results of its recognition would be contrary to good public morals and social order of the enforcing country....

"Furthermore, a judgment of execution provides legality to a foreign arbitral award so that a compulsory execution procedure under the Korean laws is made available to an execution of a foreign arbitral award, and a judgment for or against the legality of a foreign arbitral award shall be rendered at the end of hearings. Therefore, in case where a ground for objection to claim under the Civil Execution Act such as the extinguishment of an obligation occurred after a[n] arbitral award had been issued, enforcement of the award may be refused as being contrary to public policy as provided by Paragraph 2 Item (b) of Article 5 of New York Convention if arguments heard in the hearing revealed that to allow a compulsory execution procedure merely based on the arbitral award would be against the fundamental principles of our laws. Such interpretation complies with the idea of economical conduct of a lawsuit more than any other interpretations, which may mandate another separate proceeding for raising an objection to claim even though a judgment of execution was already issued, and it is also justified in view of our legal systems which stipulate that a formal hearing shall be held before a judgment of execution is rendered.

"... In accordance with the above, with respect to an obligation of replacing a machine under section 1.1 of the arbitral award, the court below established facts that even though the defendant offered to perform its obligation of replacing a machine, it could not replace a machine of the present case and install a new one due to the plaintiff's refusal to accept its offer and the new machine still remains as of today in the hands of an import agent. However, merely based on the aforementioned facts, let alone the contention that the plaintiff unduly procrastinated the acceptance of duly offered performance on the side of the defendant, we cannot hold the view that an obligation to replace a machine was extinguished due to the defendant's completed performance of replacing a machine, and therefore, we cannot accept the contention that a ground for raising an objection to the plaintiff's claim was established. Furthermore, a scrutiny of the records did not reveal any other grounds for justifying an objection to the plaintiff's claim.

"Nonetheless, with respect to an obligation to replace a machine under section 1.1 of the arbitral award, the court below applied the provision of Paragraph Item (b) of Article 5 of New York Convention under the presumption that a ground for raising an objection to the plaintiff's claim was established. Thus, in such a holding, there were errors of misconceiving facts against the rules of evidence and misunderstanding legal principles as to 'contrary to public policy' provision of Paragraph 2 Item (b) of Article 5 of New York Convention, which affected the conclusion of the judgment. Therefore, the contention pointing out this issue as the ground for appeal is justified.

"... The plaintiff failed to submit in a timely manner an appellate brief supporting the ground for appeal against the court below's dismissal of a claim for execution of section 2 of the arbitral award.

"... Therefore, without reviewing the remaining grounds for appeal, we reverse the part of the judgment of the court below against the plaintiff as to section 1.1 of the arbitral award of the present case, and remand the case for a new trial and determination of the aforementioned part of the case, and dismiss other grounds for appeal for lack of supporting reasons, and it is decided as per Disposition with the assent of all Justices who reviewed the appeal."

STOLT-NIELSEN S. A., et al. v. ANIMALFEEDS INTERNATIONAL CORP.
559 U.S. 662 (2010)

BACKGROUND: Petitioners are shipping companies that serve a large share of the world market for parcel tankers—seagoing vessels with compartments that are separately chartered to customers wishing to ship liquids in small quantities. One of those customers is AnimalFeeds International Corp., which supplies raw ingredients, such as fish oil, to animal-feed producers around the world. AnimalFeeds ships its goods pursuant to a standard contract known in the maritime trade as a charter party. Numerous charter parties are in regular use, and the charter party that AnimalFeeds uses is known as the "Vegoilvoy" charter party. Petitioners assert, without contradiction, that charterers like AnimalFeeds, or their agents—not the shipowners— typically select the particular charter party that governs their shipments. The Vegoilvoy charter party contains the following arbitration clause: "Arbitration. Any dispute arising from the making, performance or termination of this Charter Party shall be settled in New York, Owner and Charterer each appointing an arbitrator, who shall be a merchant, broker or individual experienced in the shipping business; the two thus chosen, if they cannot agree, shall nominate a third arbitrator who shall be an Admiralty lawyer. Such arbitration shall be conducted in conformity with the provisions and procedure of the United States Arbitration Act [*i.e.*, the FAA], and a judgment of the Court shall be entered upon any award made by said arbitrator."

In 2003, a Department of Justice criminal investigation revealed that petitioners were engaging in an illegal price-fixing conspiracy. When AnimalFeeds learned of this, it brought a putative class action against petitioners in the District Court for the Eastern District of

Pennsylvania, asserting antitrust claims for supracompetitive prices that petitioners allegedly charged their customers over a period of several years.

In 2005, AnimalFeeds served petitioners with a demand for class arbitration, designating New York City as the place of arbitration and seeking to represent a class of "[a]ll direct purchasers of parcel tanker transportation services globally for bulk liquid chemicals, edible oils, acids, and other specialty liquids from [petitioners] at any time during the period from August 1, 1998, to November 30, 2002." The parties entered into a supplemental agreement providing for the question of class arbitration to be submitted to a panel of three arbitrators who were to "follow and be bound by Rules 3 through 7 of the American Arbitration Association's Supplementary Rules for Class Arbitrations (as effective Oct. 8, 2003)." Class Rule 3 requires an arbitrator, as a threshold matter, to determine "whether the applicable arbitration clause permits the arbitration to proceed on behalf of or against a class."

The parties selected a panel of arbitrators and stipulated that the arbitration clause was "silent" with respect to class arbitration. Counsel for AnimalFeeds explained to the arbitration panel that the term "silent" did not simply mean that the clause made no express reference to class arbitration. Rather, he said, "[a]ll the parties agree that when a contract is silent on an issue there's been no agreement that has been reached on that issue."

After hearing argument and evidence, including testimony from petitioners' experts regarding arbitration customs and usage in the maritime trade, the arbitrators concluded that the arbitration clause allowed for class arbitration. The arbitrators stayed the proceeding to allow the parties to seek judicial review. The District Court vacated the award, concluding that the arbitrators' decision was made in "manifest disregard" of the law insofar as the arbitrators failed to conduct a choice-of-law analysis. AnimalFeeds appealed to the Court of Appeals, which reversed. The Supreme Court granted certiorari.

JUSTICE ALITO:

"We granted certiorari in this case to decide whether imposing class arbitration on parties whose arbitration clauses are 'silent' on that issue is consistent with the Federal Arbitration Act (FAA)....

"Petitioners contend that the decision of the arbitration panel must be vacated, but in order to obtain that relief, they must clear a high hurdle. It is not enough for petitioners to show that the panel committed an error—or even a serious error. 'It is only when [an] arbitrator strays from interpretation and application of the agreement and effectively "dispense[s] his own brand of industrial justice" that his decision may be unenforceable.'... In that situation, an arbitration decision may be vacated under § 10(a)(4) of the FAA on the ground that the arbitrator 'exceeded

[his] powers,' for the task of an arbitrator is to interpret and enforce a contract, not to make public policy. In this case, we must conclude that what the arbitration panel did was simply to impose its own view of sound policy regarding class arbitration....

"In its memorandum of law filed in the arbitration proceedings, AnimalFeeds made three arguments in support of construing the arbitration clause to permit class arbitration: 'The parties' arbitration clause should be construed to allow class arbitration because (a) the clause is silent on the issue of class treatment and, without express prohibition, class arbitration is permitted under *Bazzle*; *(b) the clause should be construed to permit class arbitration as a matter of public policy*; and (c) the clause would be unconscionable and unenforceable if it forbade class arbitration.'... (emphasis added).

"The arbitrators expressly rejected AnimalFeeds' first argument ... and said nothing about the third. Instead, the panel appears to have rested its decision on AnimalFeeds' public policy argument. Because the parties agreed their agreement was 'silent' in the sense that they had not reached any agreement on the issue of class arbitration, the arbitrators' proper task was to identify the rule of law that governs in that situation. Had they engaged in that undertaking, they presumably would have looked either to the FAA itself or to one of the two bodies of law that the parties claimed were governing, *i.e.*, either federal maritime law or New York law. But the panel did not consider whether the FAA provides the rule of decision in such a situation; nor did the panel attempt to determine what rule would govern under either maritime or New York law in the case of a 'silent' contract. Instead, the panel based its decision on ... arbitral decisions that 'construed a wide variety of clauses in a wide variety of settings as allowing for class arbitration.'... The panel did not mention whether any of these decisions were based on a rule derived from the FAA or on maritime or New York law....

"Rather than inquiring whether the FAA, maritime law, or New York law contains a 'default rule' under which an arbitration clause is construed as allowing class arbitration in the absence of express consent, the panel proceeded as if it had the authority of a common-law court to develop what it viewed as the best rule to be applied in such a situation. Perceiving a ... consensus among arbitrators that class arbitration is beneficial in 'a wide variety of settings,' the panel considered only whether there was any good reason not to follow that consensus in this case.... The panel was not persuaded by 'court cases denying consolidation of arbitrations,' by undisputed evidence that the Vegoilvoy charter party had 'never been the basis of a class action,' or by expert opinion that 'sophisticated, multinational commercial parties of the type that are sought to be included in the class would never intend that the arbitration clauses would permit a class arbitration.'... Accordingly, finding no convincing ground for departing from the ... arbitral consensus, the panel held that class arbitration was permitted in this case. The conclusion is inescapable that the panel simply imposed its own conception of sound policy....

"It is true that the panel opinion makes a few references to intent, but none of these shows that the panel did anything other than impose its own policy preference…. [T]he panel had no occasion to 'ascertain the parties' intention' in the present case because the parties were in complete agreement regarding their intent….

"In sum, instead of identifying and applying a rule of decision derived from the FAA or either maritime or New York law, the arbitration panel imposed its own policy choice and thus exceeded its powers. As a result, under § 10(b) of the FAA, we must either 'direct a rehearing by the arbitrators' or decide the question that was originally referred to the panel. Because we conclude that there can be only one possible outcome on the facts before us, we see no need to direct a rehearing by the arbitrators….

"From these principles, it follows that a party may not be compelled under the FAA to submit to class arbitration unless there is a contractual basis for concluding that the party *agreed* to do so. In this case, however, the arbitration panel imposed class arbitration even though the parties concurred that they had reached 'no agreement' on that…. The panel's conclusion is fundamentally at war with the foundational FAA principle that arbitration is a matter of consent.

"In certain contexts, it is appropriate to presume that parties that enter into an arbitration agreement implicitly authorize the arbitrator to adopt such procedures as are necessary to give effect to the parties' agreement….

"An implicit agreement to authorize class-action arbitration, however, is not a term that the arbitrator may infer solely from the fact of the parties' agreement to arbitrate. This is so because class-action arbitration changes the nature of arbitration to such a degree that it cannot be presumed the parties consented to it by simply agreeing to submit their disputes to an arbitrator. In bilateral arbitration, parties forgo the procedural rigor and appellate review of the courts in order to realize the benefits of private dispute resolution: lower costs, greater efficiency and speed, and the ability to choose expert adjudicators to resolve specialized disputes….

"Consider just some of the fundamental changes brought about by the shift from bilateral arbitration to class-action arbitration. An arbitrator chosen according to an agreed-upon procedure … no longer resolves a single dispute between the parties to a single agreement, but instead resolves many disputes between hundreds or perhaps even thousands of parties…. Under the Class Rules, '[t]he presumption of privacy and confidentiality' that applies in many bilateral arbitrations 'shall not apply in class arbitrations' … thus potentially frustrating the parties' assumptions when they agreed to arbitrate. The arbitrator's award no longer purports to bind just the parties to a single arbitration agreement, but adjudicates the rights of absent parties as well…. And the commercial stakes of class-action arbitration are comparable to those of class-action litigation … even though the scope of judicial review is much more limited…. We think that the differences between bilateral and class-action arbitration are too great for arbitrators to presume, consistent with their limited powers under the FAA, that the parties' mere silence on the issue of class-action arbitration constitutes consent to resolve their disputes in class proceedings….

"For these reasons, the judgment of the Court of Appeals is reversed, and the case is remanded for further proceedings consistent with this opinion.

"It is so ordered."

GLOBAL TRADING RESOURCE CORP. v. REPUBLIC OF UKRAINE
50 I.L.M. 289 (International Center for Settlement of Investment Disputes 2011)

BACKGROUND: After Ukraine's 2007 national elections, Yulia V. Timoshenko—the new premier—held a meeting in Kiev between USA poultry exporters, an official of the U.S. embassy, and Ukrainian government officials. She proposed a poultry "purchase and import program" as an initiative of her new government to deal with the short supply of domestic poultry products. Contracts were signed, but, for unspecified reasons, the Ukraine buyers refused to take delivery and pay for most of the poultry shipped. Global Trading sustained losses as a result, and filed for arbitration with the International Center for Settlement of Investment Disputes ("ICSID"), basing jurisdiction on the ICSID Convention (a multi-nation treaty) and the U.S.-Ukraine Bilateral Investment Treaty ("BIT"). A panel of "leading arbitrators" was constituted to hear the case. Ukraine promptly moved for dismissal of the claim, on the basis that no "investment" was involved—only an ordinary sale of goods. When the ICSID revised its rules in 2006, it had adopted a provision (Rule 41[5]) which stated that a party could file for a dismissal on the basis that a claim was "manifestly without legal merit," and that the arbitral Tribunal "shall" consider that objection at its first meeting. There had been only two previous decisions applying the new Rule—*Brandes Investment* and *Trans-Global Petroleum*.

THE ARBITRATORS:

"As the Brandes Tribunal remarked …: 'There exist no objective reasons why the intent not to burden the parties with a possibly long and costly proceeding when dealing with such unmeritorious claims should be limited to an evaluation of the merits of the case and should not also englobe an examination of the jurisdictional basis on which the tribunal's powers to decide the case rest.' The present Tribunal respectfully agrees, and indeed the Parties in this case appear to have taken the same view in their conduct of the present proceedings. The Brandes Tribunal was of course careful to assure itself that the jurisdictional objection before it was one based on the legal merits and not on disputed issues of fact, but declined, in the event, to uphold the objection itself….

"Rule 41(5) is sparse in its indications to a tribunal as to the procedure to be followed when an objection is lodged. It says no more than that 'the parties' (in the plural) must have 'the opportunity to present their observations on the objection,' and that the Tribunal is required to notify the parties of its decision 'at its first session or shortly thereafter.' To the extent that the Rule leaves the question of procedure there, it is no doubt for each individual Tribunal to fill in the gaps by exercising the general procedural powers given to it by Rule 19. On the other hand, it should be noted that—if a Tribunal does in the event decide that all claims are manifestly without legal merit—it is then required by Rule 41(6) to render 'an award' to that effect, thus attracting all those elements of the Rules and the ICSID Convention that relate to the rendering of an award…. The problem is, of course, that a tribunal will by definition not know in advance whether or not the events to come are likely to lead to the objection being upheld and therefore to the rendering of an award striking out the claimant's claims. The very possibility that they might, however, raises an important question about what opportunities ought to be offered to the parties to present their arguments and counter-arguments, and in what form….

"That brings one, however, in the opinion of the Tribunal, to a different question, one that lies half-way between procedure and substance, namely, under what circumstances ought a tribunal to consider it proper to dispose of an objection summarily, at the pre-preliminary stage, under Rule 41(5)? It should be made clear that this is not the same question as the standard to be applied by a tribunal in deciding whether or not the legal demerits of a claim are 'manifest'…. It is, rather, the question: when can a tribunal properly be satisfied that it is in possession of sufficient materials to decide the matter summarily? Here, a balance has to be struck between the right (however qualified) given to the objecting party under Rule 41(5) to have a patently unmeritorious claim disposed of before unnecessary trouble and expense is incurred in defending it, and the duty of the tribunal to meet the requirements of due process. Once again, the matter seems to this Tribunal to present itself differently according to whether the outcome is to be to reject the objection, or to uphold it. In the former eventuality, a tribunal that is in doubt as to whether the claim is 'manifestly' without legal merit can decide not to determine the issue summarily, but to leave it over for decision later on, at a more developed stage of the proceedings…. In the latter eventuality, it would seem that the tribunal is under an obligation, not only to be sure that the claim is 'manifestly without legal merit,' but also to be certain that it has considered all of the relevant materials before reaching a decision to that effect, with all the consequences that flow from it…. The Tribunal is … satisfied that the conditions are met for it to dispose of the Respondent's objection pursuant to Article 41(5) of the ICSID Rules….

"Article I of the [Bilateral Investment] Treaty defines 'investment' as 'every kind of investment in the territory of one Party owned or controlled directly or indirectly by nationals or companies of the other Party, such as equity, debt, and service and investment contracts,' including '(iii) a claim to money or a claim to performance having economic value and associated with an investment' and '(v) any right conferred by law or contract, and any licenses and permits pursuant to law.' The Request for Arbitration sought to enforce 'the right to be paid for performance of contractual obligations' and was premised mainly upon Article I(a)(v)....

"It needs no elaboration that the concept of what does—or rather what does not—constitute an 'investment' for the purposes of Article 25 of the ICSID Convention has turned out to be one of the most highly contested issues in the development of practice under the Convention. The Claimant invokes the decisions of earlier ICSID tribunals ... in support of two propositions: that the determination of jurisdiction is fact-specific to each particular case; and that the correct approach to this exercise is a flexible and pragmatic one, which should not properly be tied to a priori distinctive marks defining what makes up an investment. To which the Respondent counterposes [other] decisions ... as a reminder that, however pragmatic the examination in individual cases, there is still an outer limit; and that purely commercial transactions, such as contracts for the sale of goods, were never intended to fall within ICSID's jurisdiction.

"The Tribunal does not consider it necessary to analyze each of those arbitral decisions in detail. The existing case law has thrown up no uniform approach as to the identification and respective importance of the criteria that may be resorted to by ICSID tribunals having to define an investment for the purposes of Article 25(1). More to the point, the question before this Tribunal in the present case is a simpler and more straightforward one than that with which most earlier ICSID tribunals have been faced, namely: is the supplier's outlay of money in performing a contract for the transboundary purchase and sale of goods capable of constituting an 'investment'? As to that limited, but precise, question, the tribunal in Joy Mining Machinery decided that even a more complex contract of that kind (which contained other elements in addition) would not satisfy the test of an 'investment' for the purposes of Article 25 of the ICSID Convention. The ad hoc Committee in the recent Malaysian Historical Salvors v. Malaysia decision likewise concluded ... that '[i]t appears to have been assumed by the Convention's drafters that the use of the term "investment" excluded a simple sale and like transient commercial transactions from the jurisdiction of the Centre.' The Committee concluded that: 'These fundaments, and the equally fundamental assumption that the term "investment" does not mean "sale," appear to comprise "the outer limits," the inner content of which is defined by the terms of the consent of the parties to ICSID jurisdiction.'

"In the present instance, the Tribunal considers that the purchase and sale contracts entered into by the Claimants were pure commercial transactions and therefore cannot qualify as an investment for the purposes of Article 25 of the Convention. When the circumstances of the present case are examined and weighed, it can readily be seen that the money laid out by the Claimants towards the performance of these contracts was no more than is typical of the trading supplier under a standard CIF contract. The fact that the trade in these particular goods was seen to further the policy priorities of the purchasing State does not bring about a qualitative change in the economic benefit that all legitimate trade brings in its train. Nor can an undertaking by officials of the State to honour the contractual commitments to be concluded transform a sale and purchase agreement into an investment. In the present case, having viewed the contracts concluded by Global and by Globex with Alan-Trade as nominee for the Ukrainian State Reserve, and having heard the parties' answers to the questions raised by it during the oral hearing, the Tribunal is compelled to the conclusion that these are each individual contracts, of limited duration, for the purchase and sale of goods, on a commercial basis and under normal CIF trading terms, and which provide for delivery, the transfer of title, and final payment, before the goods are cleared for import into the recipient territory; and that neither contracts of that kind, nor the moneys expended by the supplier in financing its part in their performance, can by any reasonable process of interpretation be construed to be 'investments' for the purposes of the ICSID Convention.

"The Tribunal accordingly decides that the claims brought in the present arbitration by Global Trading Resource Corp. and Globex International, Inc. against Ukraine are manifestly without legal merit, within the meaning of Article 41(5) of the ICSID Arbitration Rules, and renders the present Award to that effect."

BG GROUP plc v. REPUBLIC OF ARGENTINA
134 S. Ct. 1198 (2014)

BACKGROUND: An investment treaty between the United Kingdom and Argentina authorizes a party to submit a dispute "to the decision of the competent tribunal of the Contracting Party in whose territory the investment was made," i.e., a local court; and permits arbitration "where, after a period of eighteen months has elapsed from the moment when the dispute was submitted to [that] tribunal . . . , the said tribunal has not given its final decision."

BG Group plc, a British firm, belonged to a consortium with a majority interest in MetroGAS, an Argentine entity awarded an exclusive license to distribute natural gas in Buenos Aires. At the time of BG Group's investment, Argentine law provided that gas "tariffs" would be calculated in U.S. dollars and would be set at levels sufficient to assure gas distribution firms a reasonable return. But Argentina later amended the law, changing (among other things) the calculation basis to pesos. MetroGAS' profits soon became losses.

BG Group asked for arbitration, which the parties agreed would occur in Washington, DC. BG Group claimed that Argentina's new laws and practices violated the Treaty, which forbids the "expropriation" of investments and requires each nation to give "fair and equitable treatment" to investors from the other. Argentina denied those claims, but also argued that the arbitrators lacked "jurisdiction" to hear the dispute because BG Group had not complied with Article 8's local-litigation requirement. The arbitration panel concluded that it had jurisdiction, finding, among other things, that Argentina's conduct (such as also enacting new laws that hindered recourse to its judiciary by firms in BG Group's situation) had excused BG Group's failure to comply with Article 8's requirement. On the merits, the panel found that Argentina had not expropriated BG Group's investment but had denied BG Group "fair and equitable treatment." It awarded damages to BG Group. Both sides sought review in federal district court: BG Group to confirm the award under the New York Convention and the Federal Arbitration Act ("FAA"), and Argentina to vacate the award, in part on the ground that the arbitrators lacked jurisdiction under the FAA. The District Court confirmed the award, but the Court of Appeals for the District of Columbia Circuit vacated. BG Group filed a petition for review by the U.S. Supreme Court.

JUSTICE BREYER:

"Article 8 of an investment treaty between the United Kingdom and Argentina contains a dispute-resolution provision, applicable to disputes between one of those nations and an investor from the other....

"This case concerns the Treaty's arbitration clause, and specifically the local court litigation requirement set forth in Article 8(2)(a). The question before us is whether a court of the United States, in reviewing an arbitration award made under the Treaty, should interpret and apply the local litigation requirement de novo, or with the deference that courts ordinarily owe arbitration decisions. That is to say, who—court or arbitrator—bears primary responsibility for interpreting and applying the local litigation requirement to an underlying controversy? In our view, the matter is for the arbitrators, and courts must review their determinations with deference....

"In late December 2007, the arbitration panel reached a final decision. It began by determining that it had 'jurisdiction' to consider the merits of the dispute. In support of that determination, the tribunal concluded that BG Group was an 'investor,' that its interest in MetroGAS amounted to a Treaty-protected 'investment,' and that Argentina's own conduct had waived, or excused, BG Group's failure to comply with Article 8's local litigation requirement.... The panel pointed out that in 2002, the President of Argentina had issued a decree staying for 180 days the execution of its courts' final judgments (and injunctions) in suits claiming harm as a result of the new economic measures.... In addition, Argentina had established a 'renegotiation process' for public service contracts, such as its contract with MetroGAS, to alleviate the negative impact of the new economic measures.... But Argentina had simultaneously barred from participation in that 'process' firms that were litigating against Argentina in court or in arbitration.... These measures, while not making litigation in Argentina's courts literally impossible, nonetheless 'hindered' recourse 'to the domestic judiciary' to the point where the Treaty implicitly excused compliance with the local litigation requirement.... Requiring a private party in such circumstances to seek relief in Argentina's courts for 18 months, the panel concluded, would lead to 'absurd and unreasonable result[s].'... On the merits, the arbitration panel agreed with Argentina that it had not 'expropriate[d]' BG Group's investment, but also found that Argentina had denied BG Group 'fair and equitable treatment.'... It awarded BG Group $185 million in damages....

"In March 2008, both sides filed petitions for review in the District Court for the District of Columbia.... BG Group sought to confirm the award under the New York Convention [on the Recognition and Enforcement of Foreign Arbitral Awards] and the Federal Arbitration Act.... Argentina sought to vacate the award in part on the ground that the arbitrators lacked jurisdiction.... The District Court denied Argentina's claims and confirmed the award.... But the Court of Appeals for the District of Columbia Circuit reversed. BG Group filed a petition for certiorari. Given the importance of the matter for international commercial arbitration, we granted the petition....

"As we have said, the question before us is who—court or arbitrator—bears primary responsibility for interpreting and applying Article 8's local court litigation provision. Put in terms of standards of judicial review, should a United States court review the arbitrators' interpretation and application of the provision de novo, or with the deference that courts ordinarily show arbitral decisions on matters the parties have committed to arbitration? ...

"In answering the question, we shall initially treat the document before us as if it were an ordinary contract between private parties. Were that so, we conclude, the matter would be for the arbitrators. We then ask whether the fact that the document in question is a treaty makes a critical difference. We conclude that it does not.

"Where ordinary contracts are at issue, it is up to the parties to determine whether a particular matter is primarily for arbitrators or for courts to decide. ('[A]rbitration is a matter of contract and a party cannot be required to submit to arbitration any dispute which he has not agreed so to submit.') If the contract is silent on the matter of who primarily is to decide 'threshold' questions about arbitration, courts determine the parties' intent with the help of presumptions. On the one hand, courts presume that the parties intend courts, not arbitrators, to decide what we have called disputes about 'arbitrability.' These include questions such as 'whether the parties are bound by a given arbitration clause,' or 'whether an arbitration clause in a concededly binding contract applies to a particular type of controversy.'... ('Unless the parties clearly and unmistakably provide otherwise, the question of whether the parties agreed to arbitrate is to be decided by the court, not the arbitrator')....

"On the other hand, courts presume that the parties intend arbitrators, not courts, to decide disputes about the meaning and application of particular procedural preconditions for the use of arbitration.... These procedural matters include claims of 'waiver, delay, or a like defense to arbitrability.'... And they include the satisfaction of 'prerequisites such as time limits, notice, laches, estoppel, and other conditions precedent to an obligation to arbitrate.'... ('An arbitrator shall decide whether a condition precedent to arbitrability has been fulfilled.')…

"The provision before us is of the latter, procedural, variety. The text and structure of the provision make clear that it operates as a procedural condition precedent to arbitration. It says that a dispute 'shall be submitted to international arbitration' if 'one of the Parties so requests,' as long as 'a period of eighteen months has elapsed' since the dispute was 'submitted' to a local tribunal and the tribunal 'has not given its final decision.'... It determines when the contractual duty to arbitrate arises, not whether there is a contractual duty to arbitrate at all.... Neither does this language or other language in Article 8 give substantive weight to the local court's determinations on the matters at issue between the parties. To the contrary, Article 8 provides that only the 'arbitration decision shall be final and binding on both Parties.'... The litigation provision is consequently a purely procedural requirement—a claims-processing rule that governs when the arbitration may begin, but not whether it may occur or what its substantive outcome will be on the issues in dispute.

"Moreover, the local litigation requirement is highly analogous to procedural provisions that both this Court and others have found are for arbitrators, not courts, primarily to interpret and to apply....

"Finally ... we can find nothing in Article 8 or elsewhere in the Treaty that might overcome the ordinary assumption. It nowhere demonstrates a contrary intent as to the delegation of decisional authority between judges and arbitrators. Thus, were the document an ordinary contract, it would call for arbitrators primarily to interpret and to apply the local litigation provision....

"We now relax our ordinary contract assumption and ask whether the fact that the document before us is a treaty makes a critical difference to our analysis. The Solicitor General argues that it should. He says that the local litigation provision may be 'a condition on the State's consent to enter into an arbitration agreement.'...

"We do not accept the Solicitor General's view as applied to the treaty before us. As a general matter, a treaty is a contract, though between nations. Its interpretation normally is, like a contract's interpretation, a matter of determining the parties' intent. Air France v. Saks ... (courts must give 'the specific words of the treaty a meaning consistent with the shared expectations of the contracting parties.')... And where, as here, a federal court is asked to interpret that intent pursuant to a motion to vacate or confirm an award made in the United States under the Federal Arbitration Act, it should normally apply the presumptions supplied by American law....

"In any event, the treaty before us does not state that the local litigation requirement is a 'condition of consent' to arbitration. Thus, we need not, and do not, go beyond holding that, in the absence of explicit language in a treaty demonstrating that the parties intended a different delegation of authority, our ordinary interpretive framework applies. We leave for another day the question of interpreting treaties that refer to 'conditions of consent' explicitly.... And we apply our ordinary presumption that the interpretation and application of procedural provisions such as the provision before us are primarily for the arbitrators.

"A treaty may contain evidence that shows the parties had an intent contrary to our ordinary presumptions about who should decide threshold issues related to arbitration. But the treaty before us does not show any such contrary intention. We concede that the local litigation requirement appears in ¶(1) of Article 8, while the Article does not mention arbitration until the subsequent paragraph, ¶(2). Moreover, a requirement that a party exhaust its remedies in a country's domestic courts before seeking to arbitrate may seem particularly important to a country offering protections to foreign investors. And the placing of an important matter prior to any mention of arbitration at least arguably suggests an intent by Argentina, the United Kingdom, or both, to have courts rather than arbitrators apply the litigation requirement. These considerations, however, are outweighed by others. As discussed supra ... the text and structure of the litigation requirement set forth in Article 8 make clear that it is a procedural condition precedent to arbitration—a sequential step that a party must follow before giving notice of arbitration. The Treaty nowhere says that the provision is to operate as a substantive condition on the formation of the arbitration contract, or that it is a matter of such elevated importance that it is to be decided by courts. International arbitrators are likely more familiar than are judges with the expectations of foreign investors and recipient nations regarding the operation of the provision.... And the Treaty itself authorizes the use of international arbitration associations, the rules of which provide that arbitrators shall have the authority to interpret provisions of this kind.... The upshot is that our ordinary presumption applies and it is not overcome. The interpretation and application of the local litigation provision is primarily for the arbitrators. Reviewing courts cannot review their decision de novo. Rather, they must do so with

144

considerable deference....

"Argentina correctly argues that it is nonetheless entitled to court review of the arbitrators' decision to excuse BG Group's noncompliance with the litigation requirement, and to take jurisdiction over the dispute. It asks us to provide that review, and it argues that even if the proper standard is 'a [h]ighly [d]eferential' one, it should still prevail.... Having the relevant materials before us, we shall provide that review. But we cannot agree with Argentina that the arbitrators 'exceeded their powers' in concluding they had jurisdiction....

"The arbitration panel made three relevant determinations: (1) 'As a matter of treaty interpretation,' the local litigation provision 'cannot be construed as an absolute impediment to arbitration,' ... (2) Argentina enacted laws that 'hindered' 'recourse to the domestic judiciary' by those 'whose rights were allegedly affected by the emergency measures' ... ; that sought 'to prevent any judicial interference with the emergency legislation' ... ; and that 'excluded from the renegotiation process' for public service contracts 'any licensee seeking judicial redress' ... ; (3) under these circumstances, it would be 'absurd and unreasonable' to read Article 8 as requiring an investor to bring its grievance to a domestic court before arbitrating....

"The first determination lies well within the arbitrators' interpretive authority. Construing the local litigation provision as an 'absolute' requirement would mean Argentina could avoid arbitration by, say, passing a law that closed down its court system indefinitely or that prohibited investors from using its courts. Such an interpretation runs contrary to a basic objective of the investment treaty. Nor does Argentina argue for an absolute interpretation.

"As to the second determination, Argentina does not argue that the facts set forth by the arbitrators are incorrect. Thus, we accept them as valid.

"The third determination is more controversial. Argentina argues that neither the 180-day suspension of courts' issuances of final judgments nor its refusal to allow litigants (and those in arbitration) to use its contract renegotiation process, taken separately or together, warrants suspending or waiving the local litigation requirement. We would not necessarily characterize these actions as rendering a domestic court-exhaustion requirement 'absurd and unreasonable,' but at the same time we cannot say that the arbitrators' conclusions are barred by the Treaty. The arbitrators did not 'stra[y] from interpretation and application of the agreement' or otherwise 'effectively "dispens[e]"' their 'own brand of . . . justice.'...

"Consequently, we conclude that the arbitrators' jurisdictional determinations are lawful. The judgment of the Court of Appeals to the contrary is reversed.

"It is so ordered."

CHAPTER III

International Sales of Goods—Contract Formation, Transfer of Ownership, Seller Liability, and Financing and Bankruptcy Issues

OVERVIEW:

Turning to substantive law, one major area stands out: international contracts for the sales of most types of "**goods**" (tangible, movable personal property). There is now in place a multi-nation treaty ("convention")—open for all nations to join; over 70 have done so—the United Nations Convention on Contracts for the International Sale of Goods ("CISG"). If the CISG is applicable to an international sale of goods, its provisions supersede those of any national law, to the extent of any inconsistency. So if our business manager is buying or selling goods, s/he needs to know if the CISG applies, and if so, what its rules are. Do we have a contract at all? If so, as of when? If so, what are its terms? When do the risks of ownership of the contracted-for goods transfer from the Seller to the Buyer? What are the Seller's obligations with respect to the quality of the goods? The CISG's rules on these and other points are not necessarily the same as those of the parties' national laws. To take just two simple examples: the traditional common-law rule says that the acceptance of a contract offer takes legal effect to form the contract when the acceptance is *sent* (mailed or telegraphed, or—perhaps—emailed), while the CISG says it is not effective unless and until *received* by the person making the offer; and the USA's Uniform Commercial Code ("UCC") says that a positive response via a pre-printed form containing non-negotiated additional or different terms is still an acceptance and that the "extra" terms are not part of the contract unless *expressly* agreed to by the original offeror, while the CISG says that there is no contract at all on anyone's terms if the changes are material ones. (It would be difficult to imagine a more important difference than that—"deal, or no deal!")

Of course, these two rule sets do not disagree on every point. Of special note is the unique exception in UCC 2-209(1): "An agreement modifying a contract within this Article needs no consideration to be binding." In other words, a later agreed modification of a previous sale of goods contract can be completely one-sided, and still be enforceable. Since the CISG follows the civil-law principle and does not require "consideration" at all, just an agreement, the net results of the two legislations are consistent on this point. But, just to complete the contract "enforceability" picture, the UCC does require a signed writing (or one of the four listed alternative methods of compliance) in order for a goods contract with a price of $500 or more to be enforced in court, while the CISG has no such requirement.

Application of CISG. How do we know whether the CISG applies? The key is not the nationalities of the companies involved (their places of formation, or location of their respective principal places of business). CISG's application is determined by the location of each party's office that is most closely connected to the transaction in question. If those two most relevant offices are located in different nations, each of which has ratified the CISG, it applies to their international sale of goods. Alternatively, if one office is located in a nation that has ratified, and one is located in a nation that has not ratified, CISG still does apply if the normal international "choice-of-law" rules indicate that the law of the ratifying nation should apply. For example, Seller's most relevant office is in Japan, which has ratified, and Buyer's most relevant office is in the U.K., which has not. The contract terms indicate that the Seller is only required to "ship" (send) the goods to the Buyer at the indicated address, and that Buyer's payment must be received by the Seller within 15 days of the shipment. Since both parties' respective performances are to occur in Japan, there would be a strong argument that Japanese law (which now includes CISG) should apply to this transaction. For whatever combination of reasons, when the USA ratified CISG, it refused to accept this second alternative; so if the relevant office of one trading partner is in the USA, CISG will not apply unless the other party's relevant office is in another nation that has also ratified.

The CISG permits the parties to exclude its application to their contract, but they must do so with clear language. There is no similar provision permitting the parties to opt "in"—i.e., to have CISG apply to their contract even though it would not apply under the test/s in CISG itself. Presumably, the decision to have the Convention applicable to contracts within a nation is a matter for the sovereign governing powers in each country, not for private persons. Governments ratify treaties; individual citizens don't have that power. But since CISG does not cover this point specifically, it's certainly possible for a court to rule the other way—especially if the relevant office of one of the contracting parties is located in a nation that has ratified. In the U.K./Japan example above, for instance, suppose that the international choice-of-law rules pointed to the U.K.'s law—thus no CISG. Would the parties' contract clause choosing Japan's law (with the CISG) be effective? The answer to this question awaits further development through case decisions, except perhaps in the USA. Since the USA's ratification specified that

CISG was to apply to international contracts only where the other party's relevant office was also located in a ratifying nation, the answer seems a rather clear "No!"

Coverage. International sales of some types of "goods" (tangible, movable personal property) are not covered by CISG—ships, vessels, hovercraft or aircraft. Nor are sales of electricity (which may be defined as "goods" in some nations). If the contract requires the seller to perform services as well as to deliver goods, CISG does not apply if the service obligations constitute the "predominant part" of the contract. Nor does it apply where a buyer ordering the production of specific goods itself supplies a "substantial part of the materials necessary for such manufacture or production." To avoid misunderstandings, sales of "stocks, shares, investment securities, negotiable instruments or money" are likewise specifically excluded. Some types of international sales are also not covered—goods bought for personal, family or household use; goods bought "by auction" (on eBay, for *business* use?); goods bought "on execution or otherwise by authority of law" (through a bankruptcy proceeding?)

Article 4 of CISG specifies that it covers only the formation of the sale contract and the rights and obligations of the parties. It does not regulate "the validity of the contract or of any of its provisions or of any usage." (The validity of a contract clause purporting to disclaim the seller's obligations as to the quality of the goods sold, for example, would still be subject to the relevant national law of sales.) A second very significant limitation here indicates that CISG "is not concerned with … the effect which the contract may have on the property in the goods sold"—i.e., what is usually referred to as the "title" to the goods (the basic right of ownership). Again, reference to the relevant national law of sales will be necessary to resolve title disputes (such as whether a good faith purchaser can ever become the owner of stolen goods).

Article 5 of CISG states that it "does not apply to the liability of the seller for death or personal injury caused by the goods to any person." This is obviously a very important exclusion, since employee lawsuits for on-the-job injuries frequently include claims against the manufacturer/seller of industrial goods (raw materials, machinery, vehicles, supplies) involved in the accident.

Contract Formation. CISG defines an offer as a "sufficiently definite" proposal to one or more specific persons, indicating "the intention of the offeror to be bound in case of acceptance." To be sufficiently definite, it must "indicate[] the goods and expressly or implicitly fix[] or make[] provision for determining the quantity and the price." If the proposal is not addressed to one or more specific persons, it is "considered merely an invitation to make offers, unless the contrary is clearly indicated by the person making the proposal." (Thus: ads, webpages, catalogs and the like are usually not considered offers; the would-be buyer makes the offer by sending an order to the seller, or going to the seller's place of business and doing so.)

An offer becomes effective when it "reaches" the offeree. Even if the offer is otherwise "irrevocable," it can be withdrawn if the withdrawal reaches the offeree before or at the same time as the offer itself. Offers are generally revocable as long as the revocation "reaches" the offeree before the offeree has "dispatched" an acceptance. An offer is irrevocable if it indicates a fixed time for acceptance or otherwise so indicates—or if the offeree has reasonably relied on its being irrevocable. However, even an irrevocable offer is terminated when a rejection reaches the offeror.

A statement or conduct by the offeree indicating assent to the offer is an acceptance. In contrast to the "effective-when-mailed" presumption in most common-law nations, the "indication-of-assent" is effective under CISG rules only when it "reaches" the offeror. This seemingly trivial timing differential has potentially serious legal consequences. Bad things may happen between the sending of an acceptance and its receipt by the other party—flood, fire, worker strike, material shortage, war! What looked like a "good deal" when the acceptance was sent may look very different under the new market conditions. Can the offeror still revoke the offer, by sending a revocation which the offeree receives before the offeror receives the acceptance? Under the common-law rule, the answer is a clear "No!" Under CISG, the answer would appear to be "Yes," since the contract has not yet been "made" because the acceptance has not yet taken legal effect to form the agreement. Article 18 does not specifically spell out that result, but Article 22 states: "An acceptance may be withdrawn if the withdrawal reaches the offeror before or at the same time as the acceptance would have become effective." If the offeree is not bound by its sending of an acceptance and still has the option of changing its mind, it would seem not only non-sensible but also grossly unfair to prevent the offeror from doing the same. Article 23 does provide: "A contract is concluded at the moment when an acceptance of an offer becomes effective in accordance with the provisions of this Convention." Presumably, if there is still "no contract," the offeror can still revoke its offer, so long as the revocation is communicated to (i.e., received by) the offeree before the acceptance "becomes effective," i.e., "reaches" the offeror. A telephone call, fax, or email prior to receipt of the acceptance would seem to do the trick.

Even if nothing bad happens and market conditions do not change, there is still the question of *where* the contract was made, for jurisdictional and conflict-of-laws purposes. Many aspects of this contract may be subject to local, non-CISG law—of *one* of the parties, and the place where the contract was "made," i.e., where the acceptance took effect to form the agreement, has a very strong argument for its law to be considered as the proper choice.

As previously noted, there is also a very significant difference in the bottom-line results that occur when the offeree sends a positive response to the offer which contains different terms. The USA rule (UCC, section 2-207) says that the positive response is to be treated as an acceptance, and that there is a contract on the terms of the original offer. The different language is to be treated as proposals for amendment of the contract which has already been made on the offeror's terms. The offeror is not bound to respond to these proposals, and they only become part of the contract if the offeror *expressly* agrees to their inclusion as modifications. Under CISG, if the changes are "material," there is *no contract at all*—on anyone's terms! If the changes are not material ones, there is a contract which includes the non-material changes— "unless the offeror, without undue delay, objects orally to the discrepancy or dispatches a notice to that effect." (Presumably, if the offeror does so object, there is no contract on anyone's terms.) As being material, Article 19 (3) lists "among other things" changes relating to "the price, payment, quality and quantity of the goods, place and time of delivery, extent of one party's liability to the other or the settlement of disputes."

Again, as noted above, there is no "consideration" requirement listed in the "Formation" sections of CISG. Perhaps there are two reasons for this omission. First, most of the world's legal systems do not follow the common-law system, which has that "consideration" requirement. And second, in an international sale of goods, there is by definition a "bargained-for exchange of values": the Goods for the Price! The one aspect where the "consideration" requirement may still be relevant occurs when the parties wish to modify their contract. The common-law rule would require that each party receive some new benefit in order for the modification to be contractually enforceable. But in the USA, this problem in solved by UCC 209-1: "An agreement modifying a contract within this Article needs no consideration to be binding." Thus, as noted above, USA sales law is consistent with the CISG on this point.

While CISG Article 4(a) specifically says it is "not concerned" with the "validity" of the contract, it also says in Article 11 that the contract "need not be concluded in or evidenced by writing and is not subject to any other requirements as to form." This dichotomy also raises some questions. Article 4(a) seems to defer this issue to local law; but Article 11 provides its own rule. Perhaps the seeming inconsistency is resolved by Article 12, which states that Article 11 does not apply if a ratifying nation has made a declaration under Article 96 that local law (requiring a writing) prevails. Article 12 also provides that the parties may not, by agreement, override this provision.

Finally, CISG permits the parties to prove their actual intent by all available relevant evidence. There is no "parol evidence rule" excluding outside evidence inconsistent with a complete signed writing. (*See* the *MCC-Marble Ceramic* case, excerpted below.)

Transfer of Ownership. As previously noted, CISG has no provisions regarding passage of title from the seller to the buyer. Such questions remain subject to relevant local law. Issues regarding legal ownership of goods will still need to be decided according to non-CISG rules. These are primarily questions regarding the rights of third parties—not seller and buyer—against the goods.

The "seller-v-buyer" issues are predominately (if not exclusively) questions regarding loss or damage to the goods without the fault of either party. Who bears the loss? When does the "risk of loss" transfer from the seller to the buyer? Articles 66 through 70 discuss CISG's rules for the risk-of-loss disputes.

Article 66 merely states that loss or damage occurring after risk has passed to the buyer does not discharge the obligation to pay the contract price, unless the loss/damage "is due to an act or omission of the seller." Article 70 states a complementary rule: if the seller has committed a "fundamental breach of contract," the risk of loss rules in Articles 67, 68 and 69 "do not impair the remedies available to the buyer on account of the breach."

Article 67 includes two rules for contracts in which some transportation of the goods is required. If the contract does not specify a particular place at which the seller is required to "hand over" the goods, risk passes to the buyer when the seller gives them to the first carrier. If the contract does specify a particular place for the handing-over, risk stays with the seller until that occurs. For clarity in such a situation, which evidently arises with some frequency, Article 67 also states that the passage of risk is not affected by the fact that the seller is authorized to retain documents controlling the disposition of the goods. In addition, section (2) of Article 67 says that risk cannot pass until the goods "are clearly identified to the contract." This last rule is obviously intended to cover those cases where loss occurs as to a larger mass of shipped goods, and the seller tries to collect the contract price from the buyer by claiming "yours were in there somewhere." (*See* the classic USA case of *Lamborn v. Seggerman Bros.*, 240 N.E. 118 [NY 1925].)

Article 68 adds a rule that seems particularly applicable to shipment by sea carrier: the goods are already in transit to the buyer's general location when a sale is made for some or all of them. A German vintner sends a shipment of wine to the USA, intending to sell it there. An order for 1000 cases is received from a USA customer; the seller replies that the order can be filled in three days, since a shipment is already on the way. At least if that buyer's 1000 cases are somehow identified (e.g., by the number of a cargo container containing 1000 cases of the specified wine), Article 68 says that risk passes to the buyer "from the time of the conclusion of the contract." However, if the circumstances so indicate, the buyer assumes the risk from the time the goods were handed over to the carrier issuing the documents covering the ongoing transportation. But if at the time the contract was made the seller knew of the loss and did not so inform the buyer, the risk of that loss stays with the seller.

Article 69 provides two rules for situations where the goods are already at the location where they are to be turned over to the buyer. If that location is the seller's place of business, risk passes to the buyer when it does in fact "take over" the goods. If the buyer commits a breach of contract by failing to take the goods that have been placed at its disposal, the buyer has the risk as of the time when it commits the breach. In the other situation, where the goods are at the delivery location, but that location is not the seller's place of business, risk passes to the buyer when "delivery is due and the buyer is aware of the fact that the goods are placed at his disposal at that place." Section (3) of Article 69 reaffirms the necessity of the goods being identified. Goods are not considered to be "at the disposal of the buyer until they are clearly identified to the contract."

These CISG rules on risk of loss seem quite consistent with those contained in the USA's Uniform Commercial Code. (*See* UCC Section 2-509.) CISG's two "movement-of-goods" rules and the two "no-move" rules use some different terminology than the parallel rules in the UCC; but they would seem to provide closely matching results in most, if not all, cases. CISG's "in-transit" rule in Article 68 has no obvious parallel in the UCC. Given the massive tonnage of goods currently carried by sea, and therefore "in transit" for some period of time, the need for such an international rule seems obvious.

Seller's Quality Obligations. Here again, though CISG does not use the term "warranty" in describing the seller's quality obligations, its rules seem very similar to those found in the UCC's warranty sections. Article 35 of the CISG defines the nature of the seller's quality obligations. Articles 36 and 37 have to do with timing issues.

Article 35 (1) states the seller's obligation to deliver goods which conform to the contract terms as to "quantity, quality, and description" and which are "contained or packaged in the manner required." Section (2) then provides some specific requirements for "conformity." The goods must be "fit for the purposes for which goods of the same description would ordinarily be used." They must also be "fit for any particular purpose expressly or implicitly made known to the seller at the time of conclusion of the contract, except where the circumstances show that the buyer did not rely or that it was unreasonable for him to rely, on the seller's skill and judgment." Further, if the seller has "held out" a sample or model of the contracted-for goods, the delivered goods must "possess the qualities" of the sample or model. Finally, sub-section (2)(d) in effect restates the packaging conformity requirement from Section (1): the goods must be "contained or packaged in the manner usual for such goods or, where there is no such manner, in a manner adequate to preserve and protect the goods." Section (3), however, says the seller is not liable for any Section (2) nonconformity "if at the time of the conclusion of the contract the buyer knew or could not have been unaware of such lack of conformity."

Article 36 (1) holds the seller liable for any nonconformity existing "at the time risk passes to the buyer, even though the lack of conformity becomes apparent only after that time." Section (2) provides that the seller is also liable for a nonconformity occurring after risk has passed, if that nonconformity is due to the seller's breach of any of its quality obligations, including any guarantee that for a period of time the goods will remain fit for ordinary purposes or for a particular purpose, or that they "will retain specified qualities or characteristics."

Article 37 gives the seller a "second chance"—an opportunity to correct a nonconforming delivery of goods—if the specified delivery date has not yet passed, and if this re-delivery "does not cause the buyer unreasonable inconvenience or unreasonable expense." Even if a correction is made, the buyer "retains any right to claim damages" (caused by nonconforming delivery). This rule parallels a similar provision in the USA's UCC, although that "second chance" provision is stated somewhat more broadly.

EXAMPLE CASES PREVIEW:

ENTORES: In this 1955 case, the English court refused to apply the "mailbox rule"—a well-established presumption that a letter of acceptance is legally effective to form the contract when it is deposited with the Post Office—to a telex message. The decision seems very strange, since the telex would seem to be a much faster and surer means of communication than traditional "snail mail." Presumably, if the English rule is that a telex must be "received" to be effective, the same rule would apply to emails. That result seems equally bizarre. The court was good enough to note that the USA's rule on this specific point seems to be different: the mailbox rule applies.

ASANTE: The parties are making initial arguments about whether their lawsuit can be heard in U.S. District Court. Asante's principal place of business ("PPB") is California, and PMC's is British Columbia—but both are Delaware corporations, so there is no diversity of citizenship. Interpretation of a treaty raises a point of national ("federal") law, so the U.S. District Court has power to hear the case if the UNC/CISG applies. There are fact arguments about whether

PMC's "most relevant office" is in the USA or in Canada. When the court decides that it's Canada, CISG applies, and the case remains in U.S. District Court for trial.

USINOR: Usinor, a French steel seller, sued in the USA to recover possession of 18 shipments of steel for which the Illinois buyer had not paid, or alternatively, to cancel the contract. The U.S. District Court in Illinois has to sort out French law, Illinois' version of Article 9 of the UCC, and the UNC/CISG.

CHWEE KIN KEONG: Digilandmall.com, a Singapore company, advertised various products for sale on its website—among them, a laser printer for US $3,854. By mistake, the price was changed to $66. Nearly 800 buyers sent in over 1000 orders, for over 4000 of the printers. DMC refused to deliver the computers at the $66 price, and several buyers sued. DMC claimed the contract was invalid due to a "unilateral mistake." The implicit question for us is: "Why didn't the Singapore court apply the UNC/CISG?" (There are at least two obvious reasons.)

OLEFINS: CISG does not apply to the Olefins/Han Yang sale of goods, since the contract is made by Han Yang through its USA office, and by Olefins through its USA office. The arguments concern application of section 2-207 of the USA's State-adopted UCC, which section has the effect of excluding the Seller's non-negotiated terms in a pre-printed form that "accepts" the Buyer's offer to buy. That section does not apply on the facts of this case, since the parties had explicitly (though orally) agreed to a modification of their prior contract. Han Yang's president admitted as much on cross-examination during the trial.

FILANTO: CISG does seem applicable to the Filanto/Chilewich sale of goods, although the court does not really decide that, or even decide whether any contract at all had been formed. (Under the CISG, a non-"mirror-image" positive response to an offer operates as a counter-offer [= no contract], whereas under the UCC a contract is formed on the basis of the terms in the Buyer's "offer" document.) Even though Filanto had attached a cover letter with several objections to the Buyer's proposal, it had in fact signed the Buyer's document—which contained an agreement to arbitrate any disputes. Since all that the multi-nation Arbitration Convention requires is a signed agreement to arbitrate, the USA court held that arbitration in Moscow—as "agreed"—was required.

MCC-MARBLE: Somehow the U.S. District Court missed the application of CISG to this contract. It gave the defendant Italian seller (Ceramica) a summary judgment, on the basis that Florida buyer MCC was prevented from proving that the parties had orally agreed that the terms on the back of the pre-printed (in Italian) form which it signed were not to be part of the contract. That ruling is correct under the UCC's version of the Parol Evidence Rule (which excludes extraneous ["parol"] evidence that would "vary or contradict" the terms of a complete written contract). CISG, however, permits admission of any evidence which is relevant to determination of the parties' true intent.

FEINBACKEREI: Feinbackerei, a German maker of chocolate products, bought 12,000 apple rings from Rhumveld W&K, a Dutch seller of nuts and dried fruits. Part of the product delivered was not fit for human consumption. Buyer and its insurance company sued for damages. The seller claimed that their agreement was subject to arbitration since there had been a reference to the Netherlands Association rules, and those rules did provide for arbitration of disputes. The UNC/CISG clearly applies, so the Dutch courts need to interpret its meaning on the facts of this case.

RHEINBERG (I): This case pre-dates the CISG, but on the facts, CISG would not apply anyway, since Rheinberg made the contract in the USA, through its USA agents. UCC rules apply to determine whether risk of loss on the goods had already passed to the Buyer (Vineyard) when the ship carrying the wine was lost in a North Sea storm. If the specific contracted-for goods have been identified as the Buyer's, and the sale contract only requires the seller to ship or send the goods, risk is presumed to pass to the buyer when the goods are turned over to the carrier for shipment. However, there is also a requirement that the seller "promptly" so notify the buyer (presumably so that the buyer can get insurance covering the goods during shipment). Since Rheinberg failed to send such notice until some time after the ship had already sunk, risk had not passed—and the buyer did not owe contract price for the goods. (The result would seem to be essentially the same under the slightly different wording of the CISG.)

RHEINBERG (II): Rheinberg is still trying to sell product in the USA. There is another problem with lack of notice—but this time, the other way around. Risk of loss had clearly passed to the Texas buyer; but that company was bankrupt, and the wine had spoiled after sitting on the dock for some time. Seller thus sued Brookfield Bank, which had been involved in financing the buyer's purchase. Brookfield was required by its contract to notify Seller's bank if there was any refusal or "difficulty" of payment. The Buyer had told Brookfield that it needed some extra time to raise the contract price, but Brookfield had not passed along news of that "difficulty." Not knowing of the problem, Rheinberg was unable to take steps to prevent spoilage of the goods. Brookfield Bank was liable for the loss.

ST. PAUL GUARDIAN: Another risk of loss case, this one concerning a shipment of machinery from Germany to a USA customer. The contract specification "CIF New York" meant that risk of loss passed to the USA buyer when the goods passed over the ship's railing as they were being unloaded in New York. If the goods were undamaged at that time (which they evidently were), any damages caused while the goods were being transported from New York to their ultimate destination in Illinois would fall on the buyer—and *its* insurance company (St. Paul).

KUNSTSAMMLUNGEN ZU WEIMAR: This case also pre-dates the CISG, which would not be applicable anyways, since the ISSUE here is title to the goods, not risk of loss. Not knowing what they really were, Edward Elicofon bought two Durer paintings in New York in 1946, from an ex-serviceman who had allegedly bought them at a sale in Germany. Elicofon displayed them in his apartment for some 20 years before they were identified as Durer's work—and claims of ownership were made by the German museum from which they had been stolen. While there was (still is?) a German legal rule that permits ownership to be acquired by the good faith purchaser of stolen goods after 10 years of uncontested possession, the U.S. Second Circuit said that New York law applied, since the goods were in New York and had been sold there to Elicofon. He had to return them to the true owner. (Over two decades later, with the claimants reversed—the individual as the former owner from whom the artworks were stolen and the museum claiming to be the new owner—a panel of Austrian arbitrators reached the same result in the *Altmann* case, excerpted in Chapter VI.)

WILLIAMS DENTAL: The ISSUE here was the amount due from the transport company (Air Express) for loss of the (dental) gold that was part of the shipment from New York to Sweden. The Warsaw Convention has a posted limit of liability per pound of goods shipped, unless a higher value is declared and paid for at a higher rate. Air Express argued that gold shipments were also prohibited. Unfortunately, they had accepted the gold for shipment—and at a declared higher value, for an agreed higher rate.

VIMAR SEGUROS: This is a great international example on the facts—nearly $1 million in damages to a shipment of citrus fruit from a Moroccan seller to a USA buyer, while crossing the Atlantic Ocean in a Japanese-chartered freighter owned by a Panamanian company. The shipment contract provided that any disputes would be arbitrated in Tokyo. The risk of loss on the cargo had clearly passed to the USA buyer (Bacchus), so its insurer (Vimar Seguros) paid it for the part of the loss covered by the policy, and then sued the freighter and its operator. The defendants argued that the contract required Tokyo arbitration; but Vimar Seguros claimed that the arbitration clause was invalid because it violated the USA's Carriage of Goods by Sea Act, which prohibited clauses that "lessened liability." The majority of the U.S. Supreme Court said that a choice-of-forum clause did not really lessen liability, and that all ongoing participants in international commerce were aware of the use of arbitration agreements.

ALAFOSS: The ISSUE here involves the seller's quality guarantees relating to the goods sold. This is another pre-CISG case, but the results should be the same as under the UCC. When the seller supplies a sample of the goods, the bulk of the goods must conform to the sample. The fur pieces here did not so conform, so the seller was liable on the buyer's counter-claim for damages. (The seller had brought the lawsuit to collect the unpaid contract price. The buyer was responsible for paying for the goods received, offset by the buyer's damages—which in fact exceeded the balance of the price.)

MESMAN: The Mesman case illustrates the application of local law to product liability cases dealing with personal injuries—which cases are not covered by CISG. The USA's 7th Circuit Court of Appeals—a national court—applied the relevant State's law (Indiana) to determine the result. The case is typical, in that as many as two-thirds of all such product liability cases filed in the USA involve claims by workers for on-the-job injuries allegedly caused by interaction with some product. Note that in this case the "producer" of the allegedly defective product is not the actual manufacturer of it, but rather an engineering firm hired to renovate it for further use.

BP OIL: This is a risk of loss case, where the CISG rules do apply (although the trial court mistakenly did not apply it). If the contract is "CIF port of shipment," risk of loss is presumed to pass from the seller to the buyer when the goods pass over the ship's rail—onto the ship—at that port. If the goods meets the contract requirements at that point, any loss occurring later is the buyer's problem. The gasoline here had been inspected by the buyer's agent, and cleared for shipment, so the seller should presumably win the litigation. The buyer here raised an additional claim—that the seller had omitted to add a "gum inhibitor" which would have prevented the loss that occurred. The appeals court did not decide this part of the case, but remanded it to the trial court for further findings of fact. It sounds as if the seller should still win—since the buyer's agent cleared the goods for shipment, any loss should fall on the buyer.

LMS ASSOCIATES: The question here involves the correct place for filing the UCC-required public notice of claims against the buyer's inventory purchases. The facts present an unusual series of complications, since the buyer operates gift shops on cruise ships, and the ships will thus be carrying the goods in and out of several different nations. The UCC applies, since CISG does not cover any questions of "title" to the goods (and this would seem to be a question of "clear title" to the goods, rather than a question of "risk of loss"). Not all nations have such filing requirements for creditors' claims against goods, so the UCC does have a provision for filing in the District of Columbia if the applicable nation's law is one of those without such a requirement. This was an early UCC case, and the Florida court tried to do the best it could without many (any?) precedents for guidance. It decided that Florida was the best place to file; since that was the home port of the cruise ships, that was where most of the goods were delivered to the buyer (gift shop operator), and that would be the logical place for third parties to check on the status of the gift shop inventories. Unanswered are the complications of the UCC's re-filing requirement after the goods have been out of the original (filing) jurisdiction for more than 4 months, and of the other "obvious" place to check for filings—the nation where each ship is officially registered (its "flag" nation).

CONDOR INSURANCE: Condor, a corporation formed in the island-nation of Nevis, had been forced into a bankruptcy proceeding there. Its court-appointed liquidators filed a claim in the USA, asking for the USA court's assistance in recovering funds allegedly transferred illegally by Condor to a related company. Condor alleged that such recovery of funds was only available as part of a USA bankruptcy proceeding.

CASE EXAMPLES:

ENTORES LIMITED v. MILES FAR EAST CORPORATION
[1955] 2 QB 327 (England and Wales Court of Appeal, 17 May 1955)

BACKGROUND: Entores, an English company, filed a breach of contract lawsuit in England against Miles Far East—a USA corporation headquartered in New York—and its Dutch-company agent. The Dutch company negotiated the contract in question with Entores, using a "telex" system. The telex system was described by the court as requiring the Post Office to connect the teleprinter machine each company had in its office with the other party's machine, via the respective telephone-like numbers; as one party typed in the message, the message was "instantaneously passed" to the other's machine, and printed out on paper. The parties exchanged the following telexes:

> On September 8, 1954: Dutch agent—"Offer for account our associates Miles Far East Corporation Tokyo up to 400 tons Japanese cathodes sterling 240 longton c.i.f, shipment Mitsui Line September 28th or October 10th payment by letter of credit. Your reply Telex Amsterdam 12174 or phone 31490 before 4 p.m. invited".

> Entores—"Accept 100 longtons cathodes Japanese shipment latest October 10th sterling 239. 10. 0. longton c.i.f. London/ Rotterdam payment letter of credit stop please confirm latest tomorrow".

> Dutch agent—"We received O.K. Thank you".

> On September 9: Entores—"Regarding our telephone conversation a few minutes ago we

note that there is a query on the acceptance of our bid for 100 tons payment in sterling and you are ascertaining that your Tokyo office will confirm the price to be longton we therefore await to hear from you further".

On September 10: Entores—"Is the price for the sterling cathodes understood to be for longton by Japan as you were going to find this out yesterday?"

Dutch agent—"Yes, price 239.10.0. for longton".

Claiming that the contract was "made" in England, Entores asked the court for authorization to serve court process on the defendant Miles Far East—in New York. Permission was granted to do so, and the defendant's appeal of that decision was rejected. Defendant Miles then filed this further appeal.

LORD JUSTICE DENNING:

"This is an application for leave to serve notice of a writ out of the jurisdiction. The grounds are that the action is brought to recover damages for breach of a contract made within the jurisdiction or by implication to be governed by English law....

"[As of September 10] there was a completed contract by which the Defendants agreed to supply 100 tons of cathodes at a price of £239. 10s. 0d. a ton. The offer was sent by Telex from England offering to pay £239. 10s. 0d. for 100 tons and accepted by Telex from Holland. The question for our determination is where was the contract made?

"When a contract is made by post it is clear law throughout the common law countries that the acceptance is complete as soon as the letter is put into the post box, and that is the place where the contract is made. But there is no clear rule about contracts made by telephone or by Telex. Communications by these means are virtually instantaneous and stand on a different footing.

"The problem can only be solved by going in stages. Let me first consider a case where two people make a contract by word of mouth in the presence of one another. Suppose, for instance, that I shout an offer to a man across a river or a courtyard but I do not hear his reply because it is drowned by an aircraft flying overhead. There is no contract at that moment. If he wishes to make a contract? [H]e must wait till the aircraft is gone and then shout back his acceptance so that I can hear what he says. Not until I have his answer am I bound. I do not agree with the observations of Mr. Justice Hill in Newcomb v. De Roos (1859) 2, Ellis & Ellis at page 275.

"Now take a case where two people make a contract by telephone. Suppose, for instance, that I make an offer to a man by telephone and, in the middle of his reply, the line goes 'dead' so that I do not hear his words of acceptance. There is no contract at that moment. The other man may not know the precise moment when the line failed. But he will know that the telephone conversation was abruptly broken off: because people usually say something to signify the end of the conversation. If he wishes to make a contract, he must therefore get through again so as to make sure that I heard. Suppose next that the line does not go dead, but it is nevertheless so indistinct that I do not catch what he says and I ask him to repeat it. He then repeats it and I hear his acceptance. The contract is made, not on the first time when I do not hear, but only the second time when I do hear. If he does not repeat it, there is no contract. The contract is only complete when I have his answer accepting the offer.

"Lastly take the Telex. Suppose a clerk in a London office taps out on the teleprinter an offer which is immediately recorded on a teleprinter in a Manchester office, and a clerk at that end taps out an acceptance. If the line goes dead in the middle of the sentence of acceptance, the teleprinter motor will stop. There is then obviously no contract. The clerk at Manchester must get through again and send his complete sentence. But it may happen that the line does not go dead, yet the message does not get through to London. Thus the clerk at Manchester may tap out his message of acceptance and it will not be recorded in London because the ink at the London end fails or something of that kind. In that case the Manchester clerk will not know of the failure but the London clerk will know of it and will immediately send back a message 'not receiving'. Then, when the fault is rectified, the Manchester clerk will repeat his message. Only then is there a contract. If he does not repeat it, there is no contract. It is not until his message is received that the contract is complete.

"In all the instances I have taken so far, the man who sends the message of acceptance knows that it has not been received or he has reason to know it. So he must repeat it. But suppose that he does not know that his message did not get home. He thinks it has. This may happen if the listener on the telephone does not catch the words of acceptance, but nevertheless does not trouble to ask for them to be repeated: or the ink on the teleprinter fails at the receiving end, but the clerk does not ask for the message to be repeated: so that the man who sends an acceptance reasonably believes that his message has been received. The offeror in such circumstances is clearly bound, because he will be estopped from saying that he did not receive the message of acceptance. It is his own fault that he did not get it. But if there should be a case where the offeror without any fault on his part does not receive the message of acceptance—yet the sender of it reasonably believes it has got home when it has not—then I think there is no contract.

"My conclusion is that the rule about instantaneous communications between the parties is different from the rule about the post. The contract is only complete when the acceptance is received by the offeror; and the contract is made at the place where the acceptance is received.

"In a matter of this kind, however, it is very important that the countries of the world should have the same rule. I find that most of the European countries have substantially the same rule as that I have stated. Indeed they apply it to contracts by post as well as instantaneous communications. But in the United States of America it appears as if instantaneous communications are treated in the same way as postal communications. In view of this divergence, I think we must consider the matter on principle: and so considered, I have come to the view I have stated, and I am glad to see that Professor Winfield in this country (55 Law Quarterly Review, 514) and Professor Williston in the United States of America (Contracts I S. 82, 239) take the same view.

"Applying the principles which I have stated, I think that the contract in this case was made in London where the acceptance was received. It was therefore a proper case for service out of the jurisdiction.

"Apart from the contract by Telex, the Plaintiffs put the case in another way. They say that the contract by Telex was varied by letter posted in Holland and accepted by conduct in England: and that this amounted to a new contract made in England. The Dutch company on 11th September, 1954, wrote a letter to the English company saying: 'We confirm having sold to you for account of our associates in Tokyo: 100 metric tons: electrolitic copper in cathodes: £239. 10s. 0d. for longton c.i.f. U.K./Continental main ports: prompt shipment from a Japanese port after receipt of export licence: payment by irrevocable and transferable letter of credit to be opened in favour of Miles Far East Corporation with a first class Tokyo Bank. The respective import licences to be sent directly without delay to Miles Far Last Corporation.'

"The variations consisted in the ports of delivery, the provisions of import licence and so forth. The English company says that they accepted the variations by dispatching from London the import licence and giving instructions in London for the opening of the letter of credit, and that this was an acceptance by conduct which was complete as soon as the acts were done in London.

"I am not sure that this argument about variations is correct. It may well be that the contract is made at the place where first completed, not at the place where the variations are agreed. But whether this be so or not, I think the variations were accepted by conduct in London and were therefore made in England. Both the original contract and ensuing variations were made in England and leave can properly be given for service out of the jurisdiction.

"I am inclined to think also that the contract is by implication to be governed by English law, because England is the place with which it has the closest connection.

"I think the decisions of the Master and the Judge were right and I would dismiss the appeal. …

"MR DENNIS LLOYD [for Entores]: I would ask your Lordships that the appeal should be dismissed with costs.

"LORD JUSTICE DENNING: Yes, appeal dismissed with costs in any event.

"MR COOKE [for Miles Far East]: Would your Lordships give me leave to take the matter further? It is a matter of some considerable importance. It appears that communications of this kind are on the increase and your Lordships have at any rate disposed of a certain amount of authority. I think your Lordships have also indicated that the Courts here may depart from the rule which the American Courts have observed with regard to the telephone.

"LORD JUSTICE DENNING: This is an interlocutory appeal. It means that the trial of the action will be still further held up.

"MR COOKE: We do not wish to hold up the trial of the action further than necessary. On the other hand, it is an American corporation trading all over the world. It is a matter of considerable importance to them and others in like position as to what their position really is.

"(Their <u>Lordships</u> conferred).

"LORD JUSTICE DENNING: On the whole we do not think that we ourselves should give leave to appeal.

"MR COOKE: I am much obliged, my Lord."

ASANTE TECHNOLOGIES, INC. v. PMC-SIERRA, INC.
164 F.Supp.2d 1142 (N.D. CA 2001)

BACKGROUND: Both parties are Delaware corporations. Asante's principal place of business is California. It makes network switchers, an electronic component used to connect multiple computers to one another and to the Internet. It buys application-specific integrated circuits (ASICs) from PMC-Sierra. PMC-Sierra's principal place of business is British Columbia, Canada. It also has an engineering office in Portland, Oregon. Its products are sold in California by an authorized distributor, Unique Technologies, located in California. Four of the five batches of ASICs involved here were purchased through Unique; the fifth purchase order was sent directly to PMC-Sierra in Canada. PMC-Sierra shipped the goods from Canada directly to Asante; payment was made through Unique. Asante's purchase orders specified that California law was applicable; PMC-Sierra's shipment documents specified British Columbia and Canada law.

Asante, claiming that some ASICs did not meet specifications, filed a breach of contract claim in California state court. PMC-Sierra had the case removed to U.S. District Court, on the basis that a "federal question" (the interpretation of a treaty—the UNC/CISG) was involved. Claiming that the UNC/CISG was not applicable, Asante asked to have the case remanded back to the California state court.

JUDGE WARE:

"The Complaint asserts ... two claims for breach of contract and a claim for breach of express warranty based on the failure of the delivered ASICs to conform to the agreed technical specifications.... In support of these claims, Plaintiff relies on multiple representations allegedly made by Defendant regarding the technical specifications of the ASICs products at issue.... It appears undisputed that each of these alleged representations ... was issued from Defendant's headquarters in British Columbia, Canada....

"Rather than challenge the Canadian source of these documents, Plaintiff shifts its emphasis to the purchase orders submitted by Plaintiff to Unique Technologies, a nonexclusive distributor of Defendant's products. Plaintiff asserts that Unique acted in the United States as an agent of Defendant, and that Plaintiff's contacts with Unique establish Defendant's place of business in the U.S. for the purposes of this contract.

"Plaintiff has failed to persuade the Court that Unique acted as the agent of Defendant. Plaintiff provides no legal support for this proposition. To the contrary, a distributor of goods for resale is normally not treated as an agent of the manufacturer.... 'One who receives goods from another for resale to a third person is not thereby the other's agent in the transaction.'... Plaintiff has produced no evidence of consent by Defendant to be bound by the acts of Unique. To the contrary, Defendant cites the distributorship agreement with Unique, which expressly states that the contract does not 'allow Distributor to create or assume any obligation on behalf of [Defendant] for any purpose whatsoever.'... Furthermore, while Unique may distribute Defendant's products, Plaintiff does not allege that Unique made any representations regarding technical specifications on behalf of Defendant. Indeed, Unique is not even mentioned in the Complaint. To the extent that representations were made regarding the technical specifications of the ASICs, and those specifications were not satisfied by the delivered goods, the relevant agreement is that between Plaintiff and Defendant. Accordingly, the Court finds that Unique is not an agent of Defendant in this dispute. Plaintiff's dealings with Unique do not establish Defendant's place of business in the United States.

"Plaintiff's claims concern breaches of representations made by Defendant from Canada. Moreover, the products in question are manufactured in Canada, and Plaintiff knew that Defendant was Canadian, having sent one purchase order directly to Defendant in Canada by fax…. Anthony Contos, Plaintiff's Vice President of Finance and Administration … states that Plaintiff's primary contact with Defendant 'during the development and engineering of the ASICs at issue … was with [Defendant's] facilities in Portland, Oregon.'… The Court concludes that these contacts are not sufficient to override the fact that most if not all of Defendant's alleged representations regarding the technical specifications of the products emanated from Canada…. Moreover, Plaintiff directly corresponded with Defendant at Defendant's Canadian address…. In contrast, Plaintiff has not identified any specific representation or correspondence emanating from Defendant's Oregon branch. For these reasons, the Court finds that Defendant's place of business that has the closest relationship to the contract and its performance is British Columbia, Canada. Consequently, the contract at issue in this litigation is between parties from two different Contracting States, Canada and the United States….

"Plaintiff argues that, even if the Parties are from two nations that have adopted the CISG, the choice of law provisions in the 'Terms and Conditions' set forth by both Parties reflect the Parties' intent to 'opt out' of the application of the treaty…. Defendant asserts that merely choosing the law of a jurisdiction is insufficient to opt out of the CISG, absent express exclusion of the CISG. The Court finds that the particular choice of law provisions in the 'Terms and Conditions' of both parties are inadequate to effectuate an opt out of the CISG….

"Although the CISG is plainly limited in its scope … the CISG nevertheless can and does preempt state contract law to the extent that the state causes of action fall within the scope of the CISG…. For the foregoing reasons, Plaintiff's Motion to Remand is DENIED."

USINOR INDUSTEEL v. LEECO STEEL PRODUCTS, INC.
209 F. Supp.2d 880 (E.D. IL 2002)

BACKGROUND: On January 25, the Court entered a restraining order without prejudice as to any of the parties' legal positions. On February 20, the Court granted LaSalle National Bank's unopposed right to intervene, and granted injunctive relief preserving the steel shipments until the Court could rule on Usinor's replevin motion.

Usinor is a French corporation and has its principal place of business there. Usinor and its parents and sister companies constitute a global leader in steel production, and produce, process and distribute stainless and flat carbon steels serving customers in the automotive, mining, construction, packaging and household appliance industries. One of Usinor's specialty steels is a brand of steel plate, Creusabro 8000, which is an advanced homogeneous, lightweight, anti-abrasive steel plate for applications involving extreme wear and tear.

Leeco is an Illinois corporation that has its principal place of business in Illinois, with operations in several other States. Leeco is an independent steel center, specializing in securing, processing and delivering sheet and plate grades of steel.

In early February 2000, Leeco began placing orders with Usinor for the purchase and shipment of certain tonnage of Creusabro 8000. Leeco ordered the steel in order to participate in a proposed new project of Caterpillar relating to large mining vehicles. Leeco intended to sell the steel it had ordered from Usinor to either Caterpillar or Caterpillar suppliers. Caterpillar and its supplier facilities are located in, among other places, Wyoming, Mexico and Peru. Caterpillar and its suppliers intended to fabricate the steel into ultra-light truck beds for use at mining facilities throughout the world.

Under Paragraph 7 of the sales agreement between Usinor and Leeco for the steel shipments, Usinor "remains the owner of the goods up to the complete and total payment of all sums due." Also, pursuant to the terms of the Agreement, Leeco was obligated to pay Usinor within 60 days following receipt of the steel. In addition, Leeco agreed that any dispute regarding the steel shipments would be resolved in the French court system.

Usinor states that Leeco's early enthusiasm for the Caterpillar project resulted in extraordinary demands on Usinor to deliver substantial quantities of Creusabro 8000 steel plate. Therefore, beginning in December 2000 and continuing until April 20, 2001, Usinor produced and exported multiple shipments of the steel, valued at $1,188,817.30, from France to Leeco's designated locations, in accordance with Leeco's delivery schedule.

At some time in the year 2000, Caterpillar notified its own suppliers, as well as Leeco and Usinor, that it was halting, or considering halting, the fabrication of truck beds in the mining vehicle program. Leeco now has possession of Creusabro 8000 steel that Leeco was unable to sell to Caterpillar, although Usinor asserts that the steel has many alternate uses. Leeco took delivery of the steel shipments, and Usinor asserts that Leeco has used portions of the steel in its operations and/ or sold portions to others. Leeco has made a partial payment on the total value of only one of the steel shipments for the portions that it has used in its operations or sold to others. Leeco has not made a complete and total payment for the steel shipments, and has not returned the steel shipments, after demand by Usinor to do so. Currently, Leeco still owes Usinor at least $988,817.36 of the total value of the steel shipments. Usinor asserts that the value of the remaining steel in the possession of Leeco is worth substantially less than the amount of money that Leeco owes Usinor. Instead of making complete and total payment, Usinor asserts that Leeco has instead sought to use its control over the improved steel to force Usinor to provide Leeco a refund on the steel it had purchased, but not used.

Leeco purchased the steel using a line of credit (the "loan") from LaSalle Bank. Usinor asserts that Leeco is in default on the loan and has been urged by LaSalle Bank to sell the steel to pay off any remaining debt owed by Leeco to that lender under the loan. Usinor asserts that Leeco may be facing insolvency through its default on the loan and would not be able to pay any damages that Usinor might recover from Leeco for breach of the sales agreement.

JUDGE LINDBERG:

"Usinor seeks to exercise its replevin right under [UCC]9-101 *et seq.* to recover possession of the eighteen unpaid shipments of Creusabro 8000 steel (the 'Steel Shipments'), valued in excess of one million dollars, that Usinor sold and delivered to Leeco Steel Products, Inc.... If Usinor is unable to replevin the steel, it seeks its right to avoid the contract under the UN Convention on Contracts for the International Sale of Goods (the CISG). For the reasons described below, the Court denies Usinor's motion for replevin and its motion to avoid the contract under the CISG....

"This Court has subject matter jurisdiction pursuant to 28 U.S.C. § 1332, in that this dispute is between a citizen of a foreign state and a citizen of the United States and the amount in controversy exceeds $75,000....

"The conflict that the Court must face in its determination is one between maintaining the purpose of the CISG and the purpose of the UCC. As Usinor correctly argues, Article 7 of the CISG states 'in the interpretation of this Convention, regard is to be had to its international character and to the need to promote uniformity in its application and the observance of good faith in international trade.' Usinor argues that applying Article 2 of the UCC would increase the burden on parties to examine local sales law, which would not promote the purposes of the CISG. Application of the UCC, on the other hand, requires parties to bear the burden of inspecting the local law of wherever the goods involved in the contract might be shipped....

"To recover under replevin, Usinor must have the right to possession, or title, in the Steel Shipments. The issue of first impression facing the Court is whether the CISG applies to a transaction between a buyer and seller when a third party has an interest in the goods. The Court needs to determine whether or not when a third party is involved, if local law, the UCC, preempts the interest given to the seller by the CISG....

"… While there are few cases in the U.S. dealing with the CISG, it is clear that the CISG governs the transaction between Usinor and Leeco such that if LaSalle were not a party to this controversy, the resolution would be clear: under the Supremacy Clause of the United States Constitution, the Convention, would displace any contrary state sales law such as the UCC….

"However, the text of the CISG and analysis by commentators suggest that the CISG applies only to buyer and seller, not to third parties. Therefore, application of the CISG here requires a court to resolve an issue for first impression. To wit, the court must determine whether the CISG governs a controversy if a third party has a security interest in the goods….

"The key provision of the CISG which is at issue here is Article 4, which states that the CISG:
'governs only the formation of the contract of sale and the rights and obligations of the seller and the buyer arising from such a contract. In particular, except as otherwise expressly provided in this Convention, it is not concerned with: (a) the validity of the contract or of any of its provisions or of any usage; (b) the effect which the contract may have on the property in the goods sold.'…

"The 'conceivable' but 'unlikely' … is what occurred in the transaction at hand. The remedy of avoidance under the CISG is not available to Usinor if LaSalle has a right to the Steel Shipments under domestic law. The remedy of replevin is not available if Usinor does not have title to the Steel Shipments under domestic law. Therefore, the question the Court next needs to determine is whether domestic law grants LaSalle such a right, a right to the Steel Shipments that supersedes that of Usinor's….

"First, the Court needs to determine which domestic law applies, that of France or Illinois. Under French law, the seller of goods has an absolute right to contract for title until payment, and therefore the retention of title clause in the Agreement would be determinative. However, under the UCC, Usinor would only have a reservation of a security interest.

"Under the 'most significant contacts rule' of the Restatement (Second) which Usinor asks the Court to apply, and the UCC choice of law provision which Leeco argues should be the governing test, the Court finds the same result: Illinois law applies. The 'most significant contacts rule' states there are five relevant factors to consider: 1) place of contracting; 2) place of negotiating; 3) place of performance; 4) location of subject matter of the contract; 5) domicile, residence, place of incorporation and business of the parties…. Comment e to Section 188 of the Restatement (Second) on Conflicts states that the place of negotiation is of little importance when the parties do not meet but conduct negotiations via mail or telephone (and in this case facsimile). Comment e also states that when the contract deals with a specific physical thing, the location of the thing is significant: 'The state where the thing or the risk is located will have a natural interest in transactions affecting it.... Indeed, when the thing or the risk is the principal subject of the contract, it can often be assumed that the parties, to the extent that they thought about the matter at all, would expect that the local law of the state where the thing or risk was located would be applied to determine many of the issues arising under the contract.' Here, the goods are located in Illinois. Therefore, the most significant contacts are in Illinois.

"Application of the UCC choice of law provision leads to the same result. Section 1-105 of the UCC states 'when a transaction bears a reasonable relation to this state and also to another state or nation the parties may agree that the law either of this state or of such other state or nation shall govern their rights and duties. Failing an agreement this Act applies to transactions bearing an appropriate relation to this state.' To define the meaning of 'appropriate relation', commentary 3 to this Section states, 'Where a transaction has significant contacts with a state which has enacted the Act and also with other jurisdictions, the question what relation is "appropriate" is left to judicial decision. In deciding that question, the court is not strictly bound by precedents established in other contexts.'... Here, the steel is located in Illinois, and so the transaction has the most appropriate relation to Illinois.

"Therefore, the Court finds that the UCC governs the determination of whether LaSalle has title in the Steel Shipments, or, to phrase it in a different way, application of the UCC determines the validity of the retention of title provision in the contract....

"Under UCC Section 2-401(2)(a), Usinor has a reservation of a security interest only. Title retention contracts are construed as creating only security interests under the U.C.C. ... (Section 2-401(2)(a), 'Any retention or reservation by the seller of the title in goods shipped or delivered to the buyer is limited in effect to a reservation of a security interest. Subject to these provisions and to the provisions of the Article on Secured Transactions, title to goods passes from the seller to the buyer in any manner and on any conditions explicitly agreed on by the parties.') Therefore, under domestic law, Usinor's retention of title in the contract did not effectively retain title in Usinor. Rather, transfer of title was effected upon delivery to Leeco.... ('Unless otherwise explicitly agreed title passes to the buyer at the time and place at which the seller completes his performance with reference to the physical delivery of the goods, despite any reservation of a security interest...'.)

"A seller who retains a security interest by reservation of title under section 2-401(1) must file a financing statement if the interest is to continue to be perfected.... Usinor never filed a financing statement, so it never perfected its security interest....

"Once title passed to Leeco, Leeco possessed sufficient 'rights in the collateral' to give LaSalle a security interest under U.C.C. § 9-203. This security interest was not perfected, however, until the filing of the second financing statement on November 15, 2001.

"Through the Credit Agreement and Security Agreement ('Credit Agreement') entered into on February 4, 1997 by and between LaSalle and Leeco, LaSalle extended secured loans to Leeco. The financing statement dated February 11, 1997 (the 'First Financing Statement') shows that LaSalle holds a security interest in Leeco's collateral which it defines as:

> 'all inventory in all of its forms, including, but not limited to, (i) all goods held for sale or lease or to be furnished under contracts of service or so leased or furnished, (ii) all raw materials, work in process, finished goods, supplies and materials used or consumed in the processing, packing, shipping, advertising, selling, leasing, furnishing or production of such inventory or otherwise used or consumed in the Company's business, (iii) goods in which [Leeco] has an interest in mass or a joint or other interest or right of any kind, whether in the possession of the Company or of a bailee or other Person for sale, storage, transit, processing, use or otherwise, and (iv) goods which are returned to or repossessed or shipped in transit by the Company and all additions and accessions thereto and replacements thereof.'

"The Steel Shipments are 'goods held for sale or lease' under (i) but were not yet held by Leeco at that time, (and they were not 'to be furnished under contracts of service'). The Credit Agreement and the First Financing Statement do not have a clause providing for a security interest in after-acquired property. The financing statement dated November 15, 2001 continued the effectiveness of the First Financing Statement, thereby including within the definition of inventory the Steel Shipments that were at that time in the possession of Leeco.

"At the date of the sale of the Steel Shipments to Leeco, LaSalle did not have a perfected security interest in the Steel Shipments; its perfected interest arose only on November 15, 2001, after the sale of the Steel Shipments, once it was in the possession of Leeco, and LaSalle filed the continuing financing statement. Usinor's Complaint was filed on January 23, 2002, after LaSalle's security interest was perfected.

"Usinor does not have title in the Steel Shipments, only a reservation of a security interest. Therefore, the remedy of replevin is unavailable to Usinor. ('"Replevin" is a possessory action and the plaintiff must recover, if at all, on the strength of his own title or his right to immediate possession.')

"Usinor has a security interest in the Steel Shipments, but it is not perfected. A perfected security interest prevails over the retained interest of an unpaid seller who did not perfect a security interest. Therefore, LaSalle's perfected security interest prevails over the retained interest of Usinor in the Steel.

"ORDERED: Usinor's motion for replevin is denied. Usinor's motion to avoid the sales agreement between Usinor and Leeco under the CISG is denied."

CHWEE KIN KEONG and Others v. DIGILANDMALL.COM PTE. LTD.
[2005] 1 SLR(R) 502; [2005] SGCA 2 (Singapore Court of Appeal, 2005)

BACKGROUND: The respondent, Digilandmall.com Pte. Ltd. ("DPL"), is a Singapore company which is involved in the business of selling information technology ("IT") products over the Internet. For that purpose, the respondent established its own website ("the D Website"), which it used to advertise and offer its various IT products for sale. It also operated another website owned by Hewlett Packard ("the HP Website"), which it used for a similar purpose. Purchasers could place orders and conclude transactions through either website. One of the products which DPL advertised for sale was a Hewlett Packard laser printer with the description "HPC 9660A Color LaserJet 4600" priced at $3,854 (goods and services tax not included).

On January 8, 2003, sometime in the afternoon, through an error on the part of one Samuel Teo, who was working on a training template, the price for the printer was accidentally altered to just $66 on the websites. In addition, the product description, which should have been "HPC 9660A Color LaserJet 4600", was inadvertently altered to just the numeral "55." These mistakes, including the price, were not noted by any of the employees of DPL until after the orders were placed by the appellants. It was not in dispute that Samuel Teo was not authorized to alter the price and that the mistake was a bona fide one.

The first appellant was informed of this most extraordinary low price at 1:17 a.m. on January 13, 2003, and he in turn advised the second and third appellants about it. The second appellant then informed the fourth and fifth appellants about the offer, and the third appellant informed the sixth appellant. The first and fifth appellants each ordered a hundred printers, while the other appellants ordered more than a hundred printers each. As for the third appellant, he ordered a total of 760 printers. During the period when the mistaken price appeared on the websites, 784 persons made a total of 1,008 purchase orders for 4,086 printers.

It was only at about 9:15 a.m. on the same day, when a prospective customer checked with a DPL employee whether the posted price of $66 for the printer was correct, that the error was discovered. Immediately, steps were taken to remove the printer from the websites. On January 14, 2003, the respondent informed all the purchasers via e-mail that it would not honor the orders. The present proceedings were instituted by the appellants to enforce the contracts made pursuant to the purchase orders placed by them through the Internet.

JUDGE CHAO HICK TIN:

"This is an appeal against a decision of the High Court ... [which] held that various orders for the purchase of a model of Hewlett Packard laser printers placed by the six appellants through the Internet were void under the common law doctrine of unilateral mistake....

"We will now proceed to describe briefly how each of the appellants came to make the orders, including their state of mind, in order to determine whether the contract which each purchase order brought about should be declared void on the ground of unilateral mistake on the part of the respondent or should be set aside under equity.

"The first appellant, who holds a degree in business studies from the Nanyang Technological University ("NTU"), is a person of considerable business experience. He began his working life as a banker with a leading British bank in Singapore for a period of four years. He then started his own business carrying out multi-level marketing of aromatherapy products. In the early hours of 13 January 2003, at about 1.17am, a friend of his, Desmond Tan, left him a message on the Internet. Later, they began chatting on the Internet.

"From these exchanges between the first appellant and Desmond, the former knew that the offer of $66 per printer was too good to be true and that it must have been a mistake. The first appellant wanted to buy more to make more easy money. He even asked Desmond why the latter only bought three printers. Eventually, when the first appellant managed to obtain access into the HP Website, he placed an order for 100 printers. We agree with the trial judge when he held that the first appellant was 'fully aware of the likely existence of an error.' The first appellant is no longer appealing against the decision of the judge in holding that the contract was void for unilateral mistake, and is only appealing against certain orders on costs.

"At about the time the first appellant made his purchase order, he called the second and third appellants. He also sent to each of them an e-mail which was marked 'high importance' with the caption 'go load it now.' He claimed that he merely told the second and third appellants to check their e-mails and did not tell them much more. Later, at 2.58am, he sent a mass e-mail to 54 friends and business associates, including the second, fourth and fifth appellants and the third appellant's girlfriend, Tan Cheng Peng. The material part of this e-mail reads: 'Someone referred me to the HP website which shows the price of this HP Colour LaserJet 4600 Series as S$66.00. I do not know if this is an error or whether HP will honour this purchase. No harm trying right? I hope by the time you see this email, the price is still at S$66.00 [because] they might change it anytime. Good luck!' ...

"The second appellant is an accountancy graduate working in the taxation department of an international accounting firm. After receiving the call from the first appellant and being told of the good deal, the second appellant visited the two relevant websites and carried out checks on the Internet to ascertain whether such a model existed and whether it could be re-sold at a profit.... In all, the second appellant ordered 180 units. He admitted having at some point wondered whether the price of $66 per printer was a mistake. At the time, he had established from the Internet that such a printer would cost $3,000 and he had also discussed with the other appellants how much they would make by buying more units....

"The third appellant, aged 32, an economics graduate of a leading British university, runs his own network marketing business. Before this, he was working in the IT Project Development Department of a leading international bank. He made such a huge purchase [760 units] because he saw an opportunity to make gigantic profits, which would exceed a million dollars. He also received an e-mail from the fifth appellant containing research on what companies, which had made similar Internet errors, did.

"Another factor which went to show the third appellant's then state of mind was the fact that he woke up his brother, the sixth appellant, and ordered 330 units on his brother's behalf. His brother left it entirely to him to decide how many printers he would order on his behalf.

"The third appellant's girlfriend, Tan Cheng Peng, also ordered 32 units, 12 of which were ordered on behalf of her sister.

"The fourth appellant, an accountancy graduate, started working life with a major international accounting firm for three years. He then, together with the second appellant, went into the Internet business.... On that eventful morning, after receiving the call from the second appellant, the fourth appellant went into the Internet and established that the printer was offered by the respondent at $66. He also made other searches and ascertained that the normal price of the printer was in the region of US$2,000. At about 2.58am, after talking to the second appellant, he placed an order for 50 units on the HP Website.... This was followed by a second order for the same quantity.... Thereafter, he accessed the D Website and ... placed a third order for 25 units at 3.29am on the D Website. Interestingly, at 4.16am he made a fourth order on the HP Website for just one printer.... Lastly, at 4.21am, also on the HP Website, he placed an order for ten printers and charged the purchase to his credit card....

"The fifth appellant, aged 30, is an advocate and solicitor who started legal practice in 2000. It was at about 2.30am that morning when he learnt from the second appellant of the printer being available at such a huge discount. As far as the [trial] judge was concerned, he could not accept the fifth appellant's assertion that he did not realise that there was a mistake on the website. He analysed the position as follows … : 'It is pertinent he too made web searches using the "Google" search engine. I find it inconceivable, to say the least, that the fifth [appellant] would have placed an order for 100 laser printers without the conviction that it was in fact a current market model with a real and substantial resale value. After all, what would he do with 100 obsolete commercial laser printers?'

"Finally, the sixth appellant, aged 29 and an accountant with an international accounting firm, was awakened by his brother, the third appellant, at about 3.00am. On being advised of the opportunity to make money, the sixth appellant simply asked his brother to order some printers for him without stating the number of printers or the method of payment to be used for the purchase. The third appellant placed two orders for the sixth appellant, the first for 30 units and the second for 300 units…. In the circumstances it would be reasonable, as far as the sixth appellant is concerned, to impute the knowledge of the third appellant to him.

"Another material fact which the judge took into account in assessing the credibility of the appellants was their conduct after the event. Upon being told that the respondent did not intend to fulfill its obligations pursuant to the sales made on the Internet, they took the matter to the media. There were reports in The Straits Times and Channel News Asia ('CNA') both on 15 January 2003. The first to fifth appellants exhibited these reports in their affidavits, without any qualification, to substantiate their case…. We agree with the trial judge that these reports not only failed to substantiate the appellants' claim of innocence, but they also corroborated the respondent's contention that the appellants knew that there was a mistake in the price of the product.

"In his judgment, Rajah JC found that the appellants had constructive knowledge that there was an error in the pricing on the websites. He held that as the mistake related to a fundamental term, the apparent contracts formed were thereby void under the common law. In this appeal, the appellants do not dispute this statement of the law but have questioned whether the judge had correctly applied the law to the facts….

"It is common ground that the principles governing the formation of written or oral contracts apply also to contracts concluded through the Internet. In the present case, it is not in dispute that prima facie a contract was concluded each time an order placed by each of the appellants was followed by the recording of the transaction as a 'successful transaction' by the automated system. The system would also send a confirmation e-mail to the person who placed the order within a few minutes of recording a 'successful transaction.'…

"It is trite law that, as a general rule, a party to a contract is bound even though he may have made a mistake in entering into the contract. The law looks at the objective facts to determine whether a contract has come into being. The real motive or intention of the parties is irrelevant …. The raison d'etre behind this rule is the promotion of commercial certainty.

"However, there is an exception to this rule when the offeree knows that the offeror does not intend the terms of the offer to be the natural meaning of the words…. The reason behind this exception is self-evident, as a party who is aware of the error made by the other party cannot claim that there is consensus ad idem. The law should not go to the aid of a party who knows that the objective appearance does not correspond with reality. It would go against the grain of justice if the law were to deem the mistaken party bound by such a contract….

"However, it does not follow that every mistake would vitiate a contract. It has to be a sufficiently important or fundamental mistake as to a term for that to happen. There is no doubt that the error in the present case as to the price is a fundamental one….

"Accordingly, the law will declare void a contract which was purportedly entered into where the non-mistaken party was actually aware of the mistake made by the mistaken party. This proposition is not in dispute. But should this rule also apply to a case where the non-mistaken party did not have actual knowledge of the error but ought to have known about the other party's mistake, i.e., where there is constructive knowledge? The judge below thought that it should be the case.

"Rajah JC found … that the appellants had actual knowledge that the price stated on the websites was a mistake. However, he also found, in the alternative, that the appellants had constructive knowledge … : 'I find, in the alternative, that the [appellants], given each of their backgrounds, would in any event, each have separately realised and appreciated, before placing their purchase orders, that a manifest mistake had occurred—even if no communications on the error had taken place between them. Further, the character of the mistake was such that any reasonable person similarly circumstanced as each of the[m] would have had every reason to believe that a manifest error had occurred. ... If the price of a product is so absurdly low in relation to its known market value, it stands to reason that a reasonable man would harbour a real suspicion that the price may not be correct or that there may be some troubling underlying basis for such a pricing. ...'

"As is so often alluded to in the cases, in the absence of an express admission or incontrovertible evidence, the fact of knowledge would invariably have to be inferred from all the surrounding circumstances, including the experiences and idiosyncrasies of the person and what a reasonable person would have known in a similar situation. If a court, upon weighing all the circumstances, thinks that the non-mistaken party is probably aware of the error made by the mistaken party, it is entitled to find, as a fact, that the former party has actual knowledge of the error. Following from that holding, the court should declare the contract so formed as void on the ground of unilateral mistake....

"It is not possible to reconcile the cases or the reasoning in each case.... The case of Riverlate Properties Ltd. v Paul [1975] ... is instructive as it illustrated the circumstances under which the court should exercise its equitable jurisdiction. There, the plaintiff lessor, through its agent, had mistakenly omitted to insert a clause to place the defendant lessee under an obligation to bear a part of the cost of the exterior and structural repairs of the demised premises. The lessor sought rectification, or, alternatively, rescission in equity on the ground that the lessor had made a mistake which the lessee and/or her agent knew. The English Court of Appeal held that as the error was purely that of the lessor and/or its solicitors and the lessee and/or her solicitors had no knowledge of such error and were not guilty of anything approaching sharp practice, there were no grounds to intervene. Russell LJ said ... : 'If reference be made to principles of equity, it operates on conscience. If conscience is clear at the time of the transaction, why should equity disrupt the transaction? If a man may be said to have been fortunate in obtaining a property at a bargain price, or on terms that make it a good bargain, because the other party unknown to him has made a miscalculation or other mistake, some high-minded men might consider it appropriate that he should agree to a fresh bargain to cure the miscalculation or mistake, abandoning his good fortune. But if equity were to enforce the views of those high-minded men, we have no doubt that it would run counter to the attitudes of much the greater part of ordinary mankind (not least the world of commerce), and would be venturing upon the field of moral philosophy in which it would soon be in difficulties.'...

"In view of the difficulties, one may be tempted to take a clear simplistic approach, namely, where there is actual knowledge, the contract would be void at common law. But where there is no actual knowledge, the contract ought to be performed. There would then be no room for equity to operate. But we believe that simplicity may not always lead to a just result, especially where innocent third parties are involved....

"We do not think this court should approach the issue in a rigid and dogmatic fashion. Equity is dynamic. A great attribute, thus an advantage, of equity, is its flexibility to achieve the ends of justice. Constructive notice is a concept of equity and whether constructive notice should lead the court to intervene must necessarily depend on the presence of other factors which could invoke the conscience of the court, such as 'sharp practice' or 'unconscionable conduct.' Negligence per se, on the other hand, should not be sufficient to invoke equity. Parties to a contract do not owe a duty of care to each other....

"The point is raised by the appellants as to the relevance of the negligence of the mistaken party. Clearly, more often than not, whenever a mistake has occurred, there would have been carelessness, though the degree may vary from case to case. This will be a factor which the court should take into account to determine where equity lies. All we would add is that carelessness on the part of the mistaken party does not, ipso facto, disentitle that party to relief....

"In respect of each of the appellants, the judge found that each knew that there was a mistake as to the pricing on the websites, or at least that each had constructive knowledge of the same. This finding as to actual knowledge is a finding of fact. It was clearly based on the credibility of the parties and such a finding should not be lightly disturbed by an appellate court unless it is shown to be plainly wrong.

"The appellants did not deny that each of them was opportunistic and seeking profit. This was expressly admitted by them. But they contended that this was not a matter that was truly relevant. While we agree that being opportunistic and profit-seeking does not necessarily suggest knowledge, such motives are nevertheless factors which a court is entitled to take into account, together with other circumstances, in determining whether there was, in fact, knowledge of the mistake or that the appellants had reasons to suspect there could be a mistake.

"As mentioned before, knowledge, apart from an express admission or irrefutable evidence, has to be inferred from all the surrounding circumstances. This was what the trial judge did....

"It is trite law that an appellate court will be slow to overturn a finding of fact by the trial judge who had the benefit of hearing the witnesses and assessing their credibility. In this case the judge had assessed each appellant's credibility. The appellate court should only interfere where it is of the opinion that the finding is plainly against the weight of the evidence.....

"Finally, the appellants contended that the court below erred in awarding the respondent the full costs of the trial notwithstanding that it failed on all the defences raised except on the issue of unilateral mistake. A considerable portion of the trial was spent on the issues on which the respondent did not succeed, e.g., there were no effective contracts and the contracts were 'subject to stock availability.'... While the respondent had ultimately succeeded in defending the action, and for that the costs properly incurred should go to the respondent, we are unable to see why costs which had been incurred on issues which the respondent had unsuccessfully raised should be borne by the appellants.... Accordingly, while we appreciate that a court's decision on costs is a matter of discretion, the present order on costs ought to be set aside. Taking a broad view of things, we would substitute in its place an order that the appellants shall bear two-thirds of the taxed costs of the trial....

"In the result, the appeal is dismissed, except in relation to the order on costs of the trial as indicated above. As for the costs of this appeal, because the appellants have substantially failed, they will bear 90% of the costs based on the issues raised in the Appellants' Case. Should there be any dispute among the appellants as to the first appellant's share of the costs of this appeal, they shall be at liberty to apply for further directions." …

OLEFINS TRADING, INC. v. HAN YANG CHEMICAL CORP.
9 F.3d 282 (3rd Cir. 1993)

BACKGROUND: Olefins, a Connecticut company, buys and sells bulk chemicals and chemical products. Han Yang, a South Korean company, manufactures petrochemical products. On March 13, 1991, Y.I. Han of Olefins and Shin Lee of Han Yang entered into an oral contract for the purchase by Han Yang of 4500 metric tons (m.t.) of bulk ethylene (+5% at Olefins' option), at $915 per m.t. The parties exchanged written confirmations of the contract. Olefins would deliver the ethylene one month later, to Han Yang's facility at Yeosu, South Korea. Payment was to be by a letter of credit for $4,117,500. As later proved in the trial, arrangements for this letter of credit were to be made by March 15. Olefins would buy the ethylene from its supplier, Repsol Petroleum, who would ship it directly from a plant in Saragossa, Spain to Han Yang in South Korea. Olefins made a contract with Repsol, at a price of $890 per m.t.

By early April, the international market price had dropped to $600 per m.t. As of April 2, Han Yang still had not arranged for the letter of credit under its contract with Olefins. On April 4, those two parties agreed to reduce the quantity Han Yang was buying to 4200 m.t., and to reduce the price to $900 per m.t. Olefins claimed that they also agreed that Han Yang would issue Olefins a "commercial credit" in the amount of $238,125, to be paid with the next Han Yang purchase from Olefins. Han Yang disputes this. It sent a written confirmation of the oral modification of quantity and price, but did not mention the commercial credit. Olefins answered by insisting that Han Yang confirm the credit, "as per agreed on the phone." On April 8, Olefins sent a letter demanding that Han Yang immediately arrange for the letter of credit and that it also confirm the commercial settlement for $238,125. Han Yang did send a letter of credit for the modified total price of $3,780,000, but did nothing about the $238,125. Olefins then sued for its actual damages from the original contract, in the amount of $195,245.55. The jury decided for Olefins, but the trial judge said UCC 2-207 required a judgment for Han Yang. Olefins appealed to the U.S. Third Circuit Court of Appeals.

JUDGE MANSMANN:

"In returning a verdict in favor of Olefins, the jury specifically found that Han Yang had expressly agreed to issue the commercial credit to Olefins....

"Han Yang argues that ... UCC 2-207 prevents the commercial credit term from becoming a part of the Olefins-Han Yang contract. We disagree. We hold—consistent the jury verdict—that because the commercial credit term was specifically agreed upon over the telephone before the parties exchanged confirmatory memoranda, UCC 2-207 may not be used to exclude that term from the contract.

"Section 2-207 of the UCC is designed to prescribe by law, what non-negotiated terms are to be considered a part of the contract—not to exclude those terms specifically negotiated and agreed upon. One of the main purposes of UCC 2-207 is to facilitate oral contracts that are usually negotiated over the telephone and only later reduced to writing. In particular, UCC 2-207 is designed to serve as a way of dealing with conflicting or additional terms that were never part of the bargaining process.... In other words, terms governed by UCC 2-207 are those terms that were never expressly agreed upon; rather, they appear only later as nonnegotiated terms in confirmatory memoranda or other types of business forms purporting to 'confirm' what was previously discussed orally....

"This is not the situation before us. Here, Olefins and Han Yang expressly agreed to the commercial credit term. It is that agreement which must control....

"[W]e find that the district court erred by granting Han Yang's ... motion for judgment as a matter of law."

FILANTO, S.p.A. v. CHILEWICH INTERNATIONAL CORP.
789 F.Supp. 1229 (S.D. NY 1992)

BACKGROUND: Chilewich, a New York import-export company, sold shoes and boots to Razno Export, a Soviet Government foreign trade agency. This "Russian Contract" provided that any contract disputes would be arbitrated by the Moscow Chamber of Commerce and Industry. Chilewich then made a contract to buy the goods from Filanto, the largest Italian manufacturer of footwear. The parties do not agree as to when this Filanto contract was made, and as to its contents. Chilewich says that the March 13, 1990 "Memorandum Agreement" sent to Filanto contains the essential terms—specifically that the Russian Contract's terms were "incorporated ... as far as practicable," and that any arbitration should be handled the same way as under the Russian Contract. Filanto did sign and return a copy of the Memorandum Agreement, but included a cover letter in which it objected to most of the terms in the Russian Contract. Filanto thus argues that its response was a counteroffer, that the only contract was formed later—by the parties' conduct, and that such an implied contract would not contain an arbitration clause.

When Chilewich rejected a shipment of 90,000 boots, and Filanto sustained a loss as a result, Filanto brought this lawsuit in New York. Chilewich filed a motion with the court to halt further proceedings, pending a Moscow arbitration. Filanto asked the court to enjoin any attempt to arbitrate in Moscow.

CHIEF JUDGE BRIEANT:

"This Court concludes that the question of whether these parties agreed to arbitrate their disputes is governed by the Arbitration Convention and its implementing legislation. That Convention, as a treaty, is the supreme law of the land....

"Courts interpreting this 'agreement in writing' requirement have generally started their analysis with the plain language of the Convention, which requires 'an arbitral clause in a contract or an arbitration agreement, signed by the parties or contained in an exchange of letters or telegrams.'...

"[B]oth parties seem to have lost sight of the narrow scope of the inquiry required by the Arbitration Convention.... All that this Court need do is to determine if a sufficient 'agreement in writing' to arbitrate exists between these parties.... Although that inquiry is informed by the provisions of the [U.N.] Sale of Goods Convention, the Court lacks the authority on this motion to resolve all the outstanding issues between the parties. Indeed, contracts and the arbitration clauses included there are considered to be 'severable,' a rule that the Sale of Goods Convention itself adopts with respect to the avoidance of contracts generally.... There is therefore authority for the proposition that issues relating to the existence of the contract, as opposed to the existence of the arbitration clause, are issues for the arbitrators....

"The court is satisfied on this record that there was indeed an agreement to arbitrate between these parties."

MCC-MARBLE CERAMIC v. CERAMICA NUOVO D'AGOSTINO, S.p.A.
144 F.3d 1384 (11th Cir. 1998)

BACKGROUND: MCC-Marble, a Florida corporation that retails ceramic tiles, signed a contract to buy tiles from Ceramica, an Italian tile manufacturer. Juan Carlos Monzon, MCC's president, attended a trade fair in Bologna, Italy, and signed the contract there. Monzon did not read or speak Italian, but after negotiating with Gianni Silingardi (Ceramica's commercial director) using another Ceramica employee (Gianfranco Copelli) as translator, he nevertheless signed a contract pre-printed in Italian. One of the terms on the back of the form gave Ceramica the right to suspend or cancel the contract if the buyer defaulted in paying for goods delivered. However, the three men evidently agreed orally that the terms on the back of the form would not be part of the contract.

When MCC sued for failure to deliver goods, Ceramica cited the cancellation clause. MCC claimed that it had no intent to be bound by the terms on the back of the form, and introduced affidavits to that effect from Monzon, Silingardi, and Copelli. Ceramica was granted summary judgment by the U.S. District Court, since the USA's UCC does not permit alleged oral statements to contradict the provisions of a complete, signed written document. MCC appealed to the U.S. Eleventh Circuit Court of Appeals.

JUDGE BIRCH:

"Contrary to what is familiar practice in United States courts, the CISG appears to permit a substantial inquiry into the parties' subjective intent, even if the parties did not engage in any objectively ascertainable means of registering this intent.... The plain language of the Convention ... requires an inquiry into a party's subjective intent as long as the other party to the contract was aware of that intent....

"Given our determination that the magistrate judge and the district court should have considered MCC's affidavits regarding the parties' subjective intentions, we must address a question of first impression in this circuit: whether the parol evidence rule ... plays any role in cases involving the CISG....

"The CISG itself contains no express statement on the role of parol evidence.... It is clear, however, that the drafters of the CISG were comfortable with the concept of permitting parties to rely on oral contracts because they eschewed any statute[] of fraud[s] provision and expressly provided for the enforcement of oral contracts.... Given article 8(1)'s directive to use the intent of the parties to interpret their statements and conduct, article 8(3) is a clear instruction to admit and consider parol evidence regarding the negotiations to the extent they reveal the parties' subjective intent….

"Our reading of article 8(3) as a rejection of the parol evidence rule … is in accordance with the great weight of academic commentary on the issue….

"[MCC's] affidavits raise an issue of material fact regarding the parties' intent to incorporate the provisions on the reverse of the form contract. If the finder of fact determines that the parties did not intend to rely on those provisions, then the more general provisions of the CISG will govern the outcome of the dispute….

"[W]e conclude that the CISG … precludes summary judgment in this case because MCC has raised an issue of material fact concerning the parties' subjective intent to be bound by the terms on the reverse of the pre-printed contract. The CISG also precludes the application of the parol evidence rule…. Accordingly, we REVERSE the district court's grant of summary judgment and REMAND this case for further proceedings consistent with this opinion."

FEINBACKEREI OTTEN GmbH Kg v. RHUMVELD WINTER & KONIJN B.V.
Case No. 200.127.516-01 (Appellate Court The Hague [Netherlands] 2014)

BACKGROUND: R.W.&K. (Seller)—a Dutch company, seated in the Netherlands—deals in nuts, dried fruits, and seeds. F.O. GmbH (Buyer) is a producer of chocolate products, seated in Germany. In February 2011, Seller and Buyer entered into an agreement, on the basis of which Seller was bound to deliver 12,000 apple rings to Buyer. The law applicable to the agreement is the Vienna Convention on the International Sale of Goods ("CISG"). On September 5, 2011, Buyer complained to Seller that part of the apple rings delivered contained germs of mites, making them unsuitable for human consumption.

The parties had previously entered into seven similar agreements, and in all seven the Seller had referred to the applicable conditions of the Netherlands Association for the Trade in Dried Fruit, Spices and Allied Products. These references said: "Conditions According to the conditions of the [Association] registered at the Chamber of Commerce Haaglanden under number 40341013. The conditions are available for perusal in our office and upon request will be sent to you free of charge." The conditions included a clause specifying arbitration of any contract disputes.

Buyer sued for E250,000—the deductible amount on his insurance policy—plus interest.

Buyer's Insurance Company sued for the E107,440.65 it had paid Buyer, plus interest. Seller argued that the German courts could not hear these claims, because of the arbitration clause. The District Court agreed with the Seller and dismissed the case. The Plaintiffs appealed.

THE COURT:

"... The core of Buyer's complaint is that the District Court has assumed that the NZV-conditions (and the arbitration clause therein) became applicable to the agreement. Buyer and Buyer's Insurer contend that the District Court failed to appreciate the fact that Seller had not given Buyer a reasonable opportunity to take notice of the content of the NZV-conditions, which is necessary for the applicability of the conditions.

"... If the CISG is the applicable law to an agreement, the question whether or not a party has validly entered into that sales agreement and the standard terms that make part of that agreement shall be governed by the CISG.... The Court of Appeal argues that the answer to the question whether or not standard terms are applicable can be found in some of the articles of the CISG and that the Court should interpret these with observance to art. 7, para. 1 CISG. Currently, this is the prevalent approach taken by courts ... and this point of view has also been adopted by the CISG Advisory Council....

"... Art. 7, para. 1 CISG states that in the interpretation of the Convention, regard is to be had to its international character and to the need to promote conformity in its application. Given the lack of a supranational court that can guarantee the uniformity of law within its sphere, the judge that has to interpret the CISG should take into consideration decisions of courts and arbitral tribunals in other countries, as far as these rulings have *persuasive authority*. To facilitate that – besides the numerous initiatives to increase the accessibility of these rulings – the so-called CISG Advisory Council was set up in 2001. This Advisory Council, which has been created by a private initiative and is comprised of leading experts in the field of international commercial law, sets its purpose to promote the uniform interpretation of the CISG. In that respect, the Advisory Council provides ... authoritative opinions on the uniform application and interpretation of the treaty. On 20 January 2013, the Advisory Council adopted the 'CISG-AC Opinion No. 13 Inclusion of Standard Terms under the CISG', which deals with the applicability of the validity of standard terms.... The Court of Appeal will base its decision on this Opinion.

"... The position of Buyer and Buyer's Insurer finds its most authoritative source in a decision of the German Bundesgerichtshof.... In this case, the Bundesgerichtshof held that it may be expected under the uniform sales law that the provider of standard terms directly transmit or otherwise makes available the content of these conditions to the other party to whom he addresses his proposal to conclude the contract.

"... However, Seller argues that (in the current case) the requirement of 'directly transmitting or otherwise making available' is not fixed. In this regard, Seller relies on jurisprudence of the Oberster Gerichtshof of Austria (6 February 1006 and 17 December 2003), the Belgian Tribunal Commercial Nivelles (19 September 1995) and the Appellate Court of Gent (4 October 2004), in which, according to Seller, the requirement given above for the applicability of general terms and conditions by the German Bundesgerichtshof is not fixed. Moreover, both parties have further substantiated their cases by referring to doctrine and Dutch case law, in which one or more of the aforementioned jurisprudence has been mentioned....

"... Whether or not standard terms have become part of the agreement will be determined within the scope of the CISG, following the rules that determine the formation and interpretation of contracts. Besides which is determined in articles 8 and 9 concerning statements and usages, the provisions of Part II (Formation of the contract) are relevant in this respect, of which the core is formed by articles 14 (offer) and 18 (acceptance).... [I]t follows from this interplay of rules that standard terms will be part of the agreement if the parties at the time of the formation of the contract expressly or implicitly agreed to the incorporation of those standard terms into the agreement and the other party has had a reasonable opportunity to take notice of these standard terms....

"... First, the other party to the contract can usually not oversee what text it agrees to in a specific situation for there are significant differences between domestic legal systems and practices, while revising the content of the standard terms is not always guaranteed under the relevant domestic law. Second, seeking information from the provider of the standard terms by the other party may result in a delay in the formation of the contract, which is not in the interest of either party. Finally, it is relatively easy for the provider of standard terms, which are generally beneficial to that party, to add them to the offer. Therefore, it would be ... contrary to the principle of good faith in international trade (art. 7, para. 1 CISG) and to the general obligation of co-operation and providing information of the parties to impose upon the other party a duty to inquire with respect to the clauses that were not sent and to burden that other party with the risk and disadvantages of the unknown standard terms.

"... Next, the question is when the requirement of the reasonable opportunity to take notice of the standard term was met. The requirement postulated by some lower courts in Germany and the Netherlands, that general terms and conditions should be directly transmitted or sent to the other party at the time parties enter into the agreement is, according to the Advisory Council, based upon a too strict interpretation of the decision of the Bundesgerichtshof. The Advisory Council summarizes a (non-exhaustive) list of circumstances in which a party may have been considered to have had a reasonable opportunity to take notice of the standard terms:

3.1 Where the terms are attached to a document used in connection with the formation of the contract or printed on the reverse side of that document; 3.2 Where the terms are available to the parties in the presence of each other at the time of negotiating the contract;
3.3 Where, in electronic communications, the terms are made available to and retrievable electronically by that party and are accessible to that party at the time of negotiating the contract; 3.4 Where the parties have had prior agreements subject to the same standard terms.

"... That entails the following for the present case:

"... Seller has not contested (sufficiently supported by reasons) that it never sent the standard terms to Buyer. The sole possibility for Buyer to take notice of the standard terms which Seller mentions in its documents, is that they were on the internet, on the website of NZV, and Buyer could have consulted them there. However, this is – in the light of the foregoing – as there was no clear reference to such a possibility to take notice of the standard terms, insufficient to assume that these standard terms and conditions became part of the agreement.

"... The fact that, as Seller pointed out, the parties had already entered into seven prior agreements, on which occasions Seller always referred to the NZV-terms and conditions on its confirmations as well as on its invoices, also does not help it, as it has not stated nor proved that Buyer actually had a reasonable opportunity to take notice of the standard terms and conditions on those prior occasions and it can thus not be assumed that the standard terms were in fact applicable to these prior agreements. Moreover, the fact that Buyer on those prior occasions never felt the need to ask Seller to clarify the meaning of the reference, did not – under the CISG – give rise to a legitimate expectation that it agreed to the applicability of the NZV-conditions.

"... Also the fact that Buyer knew or should have been aware that the NZV-conditions contained an arbitration clause, does not change the above, as this does not affect the requirement of a reasonable opportunity to take notice.

"... Seller has not presented any submissions that–if proven–might lead to a different decision. Unlike Seller seems to believe, the obligation to furnish facts and the burden of proof with respect to the facts of which yield legal effect (lack of jurisdiction of the civil court) is not on Buyer or Buyer's Insurer, but on Seller.

"... The abovementioned leads to the conclusion that an agreement to arbitrate has not come into existence between the parties and that the District Court has wrongly declared itself incompetent. This implies that the Appellate Court should set aside the decision on the procedural issue, to which this appeal serves and ... refer the case back to the District Court, so that litigation can proceed in the main proceedings. Being the party against whom judgment was given in the procedural issue, Seller should bear the costs of the procedural issue in both instances. The fixed court fee that Buyer paid in first instance is not part of the costs, as these will be part of the decision on costs in the main proceedings."

[THE JUDGMENT

The Appellate Court: sets aside the ruling of the District Court whereof appeal and in a new judgment: dismisses the motion contesting jurisdiction; refers the case back to the District Court of Rotterdam for further proceedings, where Buyer and Buyer's Insurer should initiate proceedings on the merits in which the Seller should lodge a statement of defence; orders Seller to refund Buyer and Buyer's Insurer for all amounts that Buyer and Buyer's Insurer have already paid in performance of the contested decision, to be increased with the statutory interest beginning the day of payment; orders Seller to pay the costs of the proceedings of the procedural issue in first instance, which will be on the side of Buyer and Buyer's Insurer until the decision of 20 March 2013 estimated at € 452,—for attorney fees; orders Seller to pay the costs of the proceedings on appeal, which will be on the side of Buyer and Buyer's Insurer until the day of this decision estimated at € 775,82 in advances and € 894,—for attorney fees; declares the judgment to have immediate effect.]

RHEINBERG-KELLEREI G.m.b.H. v. VINEYARD WINE COMPANY, INC.
281 S.E.2d 425 (N.C. 1981)

BACKGROUND: Rheinberg-Kellerei is a German wine producer and exporter; it employed Sutton as its sales agent in the USA; Sutton in turn employed Switzer to make sales in North Carolina. Vineyard ordered 620 cases of wine, through Sutton and Switzer. The terms of the order included: "Insurance to be covered by customer"; "Send a 'Notice of Arrival' to both the customer and to Frank Sutton & Company"; and "Payment may be deferred until the merchandise has arrived at the port of entry." Rheinberg was to send the bill of lading and the invoice, through its bank, to Vineyard's bank (Wachovia) in North Carolina. When the goods arrived, Vineyard would go to its bank, pay the invoice, get the bill of lading, and pick up its wine.

Rheinberg gave the wine to a shipping company, and notified Sutton of the date of shipment, port of origin, name of ship, and port of arrival. Sutton sent no notice to Switzer or to Vineyard. The wine was loaded onto the *M.S. Munchen* at Rotterdam, and the ship left port in early December. The ship was lost at sea, with all hands and cargo, sometime between December 12 and 22, 1978. Vineyard first learned that the shipment had been made on January

24, 1979. When Vineyard refused to pay for the lost shipment, Rheinberg sued. The trial court dismissed the case, and Rheinberg appealed to the North Carolina Supreme Court.

JUDGE WELLS:

"All parties agree that the contract was a 'shipment' contract, i.e., one not requiring delivery of the wine at any particular destination.... The Uniform Commercial Code, as adopted in North Carolina, dictates when the transfer of risk of loss occurs in this situation.... '[T]he risk of loss passes to the buyer when the goods are duly delivered to the carrier....' Before a seller will be deemed to have 'duly delivered' the goods to the carrier, however, he must fulfill certain duties to the buyer. In the absence of any agreement to the contrary, these responsibilities [are] set out in [UCC] 2-504....

"The trial court concluded that the plaintiff's failure to notify the defendant of the shipment until after the sailing of the ship and the ensuing loss, was not 'prompt notice' within the meaning of ... 2-504, and therefore the risk of loss did not pass to defendant upon the delivery of the wine to the carrier pursuant to the provisions of ... 2-509(1)(a). We hold that the conclusions of the trial court were correct. The seller is burdened with special responsibilities under a shipment contract because of the nature of the risk of loss being transferred.... Where the buyer, upon shipment by seller, assumes the perils involved in carriage, he must have a reasonable opportunity to guard against these risks by independent arrangements with the carrier. The requirement of prompt notification by the seller ... must be construed as taking into consideration the need of a buyer to be informed of the shipment in sufficient time for him to take action to protect himself from the risk of damage to or loss of the goods while in transit.... It would not be practicable or desirable, however, for the courts to attempt to engraft onto ... 2-504 of the U.C.C. a rigid definition of prompt notice. Given the myriad factual situations which arise in business dealings, and keeping in mind the commercial realities, whether notification has been 'prompt' within the meaning of the U.C.C. will have to be determined on a case-by-case basis, under all the circumstances....

"In the case at hand, the shipment of wine was lost at sea sometime between 12 December and 22 December 1978. Although plaintiff did notify its agent, Frank Sutton, regarding the details of the shipment on or about November 27, 1978, this information was not passed along to defendant. The shipping documents were not received by defendant's bank for forwarding to defendant until December 27, 1978, days after the loss had already been incurred. Since defendant was never notified directly or by the forwarding of shipping documents within the time in which its interest could have been protected by insurance or otherwise, defendant was entitled to reject the shipment pursuant to ... 2-504."

RHEINBERG-KELLEREI G.m.b.H. v.
BROOKSFIELD NATIONAL BANK OF COMMERCE BANK
901 F.2d 481 (5th Cir. 1990)

BACKGROUND: In January 1986, Rheinberg-Kellerei GmbH (a German firm represented by a U.S. importer, Frank Sutton & Co.) sold a shipment of wine to J & J Wine in Texas, USA. Payment was to be made with an international letter of collection handled for the seller by Edekabank in Germany and for the buyer by Brooksfield National Bank of Commerce Bank in San Antonio ("NBC Bank"). The letter-of-collection process is used to make sure that the Seller gets paid and that the Buyer gets the goods: Seller's bank sends the letter to Buyer's bank, which collects the contract price from the Buyer (its customer), and then forwards the funds to the Seller's bank; Buyer's bank also receives the shipping documents, which the Buyer is not to receive without paying the contract price. On March 27, NBC Bank received the letter of collection, bill of lading, and invoices from Edeka. The letter of collection noted that payment was due "on arrival of goods in Houston harbor," and required NBC Bank to notify Sutton "in case of any difficulty or lack of payment." The invoices noted an estimated time of arrival: April 2, 1986. NBC Bank presented the documents to J & J Wine on March 27.

J & J Wine did not pay the amount due, and instead asked NBC Bank to hold the letter for a time while J & J Wine worked to raise the money for payment. NBC Bank did not notify Edeka or Sutton of J & J Wine's failure to pay on presentment. In fact, NBC Bank did nothing further until early May, when Sutton informed them that the wine was still at the Houston port and NBC Bank cabled Edeka for further instructions.

The wine arrived in Houston on March 31, but NBC Bank had no notice of that. Because J & J Wine did not take delivery of it, the wine sat—exposed—at Houston harbor in metal containers until it had deteriorated completely. U.S. Customs eventually sold it at auction—at a loss. J & J Wine went out of business, and Rheinberg was not paid for the wine. When Rheinberg sued, the U.S. District Court entered a judgment for NBC Bank. Rheinberg appealed to the U.S. Fifth Circuit Court of Appeals.

JUDGE GARZA:

"... Rheinberg Kellerei argues that, regardless of whether NBC Bank knew when the wine had arrived, once NBC Bank presented the documents, it had a duty to inform Edeka of any problem in collecting J & J Wine's payment. We agree. That duty arises both from the [international] Rules and the collection letter itself....

"The letter, which is the primary source of responsibility in this case, instructs NBC Bank to notify Sutton 'in case of any difficulty or lack of payment.' The district court found that section demanded notice only if there were a 'lack of payment or failure to pay.' Likewise, NBC Bank emphasizes that the trigger for notice is a lack of payment.

"What the court below and NBC Bank ignore is the word 'difficulty.' The letter did not instruct NBC Bank to notify Sutton only if there were a default, or a failure to pay, or a lack of payment. Rather, NBC Bank was called on to act also if there were any difficulty in collecting payment. And the request that NBC Bank hold the letter while J & J Wine sought financing certainly posed a difficulty in collection. Once NBC Bank knew that J & J Wine had asked for time to come up with the money, it should have notified Sutton in accordance with the letter's instructions....

"If [UCC] section 4.502 were applied to our case, NBC Bank would have a duty to notify Edeka of J & J Wine's failure to pay the letter of collection when it was presented on March 27, even though the goods were not yet in Houston harbor and the payment was not yet due. This is not to say the J & J Wine was in default at that time or had dishonored the letter. Rather, the notice is an act of prudence, an exercise in due care. And, as the aims of the Rules and the U.C.C. are more than consistent, and both demand the exercise of due care, we find that the Rules impose the same duty. NBC Bank should have notified Edeka of J & J Wine's failure to pay at presentment, as that failure constituted a 'non-payment.'...

"NBC Bank and the court below rely heavily on the fact that NBC Bank had no actual knowledge of the wine's arrival in Houston, and had no duty to inquire further. We agree with those premises, but do not feel they affect NBC Bank's duty to notify. That duty arose—under both the Rules and the letter itself—when J & J Wine failed to pay on presentment and asked for time. Arrival of the wine did not trigger it. And NBC Bank cannot avoid liability by hiding from knowledge of arrival and claiming that ignorance as a defense....

"NBC Bank is entitled to a credit for the net proceeds of any resale of the damaged wine.... Customs agents sold the wine at auction, but we have no evidence before us of the price paid or the net amount remaining after customs fees, wharfage, and the costs of the auction were paid. For that reason, we remand this case to the district court for the limited purpose of calculating that net amount. After finding that net amount, the district court should enter judgment for Rheinberg Kellerei for the contract price plus freight charges, less the net proceeds of the customs auction."

ST. PAUL GUARDIAN INS. v. NEUROMED MEDICAL SYSTEMS G.m.b.H
2002 U.S. Dist. LEXIS 5096 (S.D. NY 2002)

BACKGROUND: Neuromed—a German company—sold a Siemens mobile magnetic resonance imaging machine ("MRI machine") to Shared Imaging—a USA corporation. The shipment would be made "CIF New York Seaport." Ten percent of the $930,000 contract price was to be paid at once, and another 80 percent before shipment. The final 10 percent would be paid only after acceptance by the buyer—but within three business days after the MRI machine arrived in Calumet City, Illinois, USA. Title to the MRI machine remained with Neuromed until the price was paid in full. A handwritten note, allegedly initialed for Shared Imaging by Raymond Stachowiak, stated: "Acceptance subject to Inspection." The MRI machine— undamaged and in good working order when it was loaded onto the ship *Atlantic Carrier* at Antwerp, Belgium—was badly damaged (evidently due to cold weather) by the time it arrived in Illinois. St. Paul and Travelers (the insurance companies that had reimbursed Shared Imaging for $285,000 worth of repairs to the MRI machine) sued Neuromed in U.S. District Court. Neuromed asked the court to dismiss the complaint, since international shipping rules ("Incoterms") placed the risk of loss with the buyer.

JUDGE STEIN:

"INCOTERMS define 'CIF' (named port of destination) to mean the seller delivers when the goods pass 'the ship's rail in the port of shipment.'… The seller is responsible for paying the cost, freight and insurance necessary to bring the goods to the named port of destination, but the risk of loss or damage to the goods passes from seller to buyer upon delivery to the port of shipment.…

"Plaintiffs argue that Neuromed's explicit retention of title in the contract to the MRI machine modified the 'CIF' term, such that Neuromed retained title and assumed the risk of loss. INCOTERMS, however, only address passage of risk, not transfer of title…. Under the CISG, the passage of risk is likewise independent of the transfer of title….

"Moreover, according to Article 67(1) [of the CISG], the passage of risk and the transfer of title need not occur at the same time, as the seller's retention of 'documents controlling the disposition of the goods does not affect the passage of risk.'…

"German law also recognizes passage of risk and transfer of title as two independent legal acts….

"Plaintiffs next contend that … the other terms in the contract are that the parties' intention [was] to supersede and replace the 'CIF' term such that Neuromed retained title and the risk of loss. That is incorrect....

"The 'CIF' term as defined by INCOTERMS only requires the seller to 'clear the goods for export' and is silent as to which party bears the obligation to arrange for customs clearance.... The parties are therefore left to negotiate these obligations. As such, a clause defining the terms of customs clearance neither alters nor affects the 'CIF' clause in the contract....

"INCOTERMS do not mandate a payment structure, but rather simply establish that the buyer bears an obligation to 'pay the price as provided in the contract of sale.'... Inclusion of the terms of payment in the contract does not modify the 'CIF' clause....

"Finally, plaintiffs emphasize the handwritten note, 'Acceptance upon inspection.'... [D]espite plaintiffs' arguments to the contrary, the handwritten note does not modify the 'CIF' clause; it instead serves to qualify the terms of the transfer of title....

"For the foregoing reasons, Neuromed's motion to dismiss for failure to state a cause of action is granted and the complaint is dismissed."

KUNSTSAMMLUNGEN ZU WEIMAR v. ELICOFON
678 F.2d 1150 (2nd Cir. 1982)

BACKGROUND: In 1946, Edward Elicofon bought two small paintings for $450 from a young soldier returning from overseas service in Germany. Elicofon hung the paintings on the wall in his home in New York, along with his many other art objects. Over the years, he held numerous charity functions in his home, and his art collection was viewed by many people, including some who were knowledgeable about art. In 1966, Elicofon learned for the first time that these two small paintings were works of Albrecht Duerer and had been stolen from the Weimar art collection sometime between July 12 and 19, 1945—about the same time that Russian occupation troops had replaced American forces in that area of Germany. The paintings' current value was estimated at several million dollars each. KZW (the Weimar art museum) demanded return of the paintings in September 1966; Elicofon refused the demand. Since the USA did not then officially recognize the German Democratic Republic ("East Germany"), the Federal Republic of Germany ("West Germany"—"FRG") filed a lawsuit on behalf of KZW in U.S. District Court in January 1969. When the USA did recognize East Germany in 1974, the FRG withdrew as plaintiff, and KZW was allowed to sue in its own name. Meanwhile, the

Grand Duchess of Saxony-Weimar joined the lawsuit as a plaintiff, claiming that the Weimar art collection had been the private property of her late husband, not state property of Weimar. In 1978, the District Court dismissed the Grand Duchess' claim, and awarded ownership of the Duerer paintings to KZW in 1981. Elicofon and the Grand Duchess appealed to the U.S. Second Circuit Court of Appeals.

JUDGE MANSFIELD:

"Judge Mishler's holding that the State's ownership of the paintings was established by the 1927 [arbitration] Agreement is fully supported and indeed strengthened by the earlier occurrences, including the 1918 abdication [of the Grand Duke] and the 1921 [arbitration] Agreement, which unequivocally rebut the erroneous assumption underlying the Grand Duchess' interpretation of the 1927 Agreement…. Moreover, it is undisputed that the 1913 [KZW] Museum Catalogue, which clearly designates those objects owned privately by the Grand Duke, failed to designate the Duerer paintings as privately owned….

"Elicofon … contends that the GDR is not a successor in interest entitled to possession of the paintings. Judge Mishler held that the GDR did succeed to the paintings as property of the Land of Thuringia, either directly by an act of the GDR in 1952 or indirectly as a successor within its territorial jurisdiction to the rights of the Third Reich, to whom the Land's property rights passed. Second, Elicofon argues that subsequent to his purchase he acquired title under the German doctrine of Ersitzung, which awards title to the holder upon 10 years uninterrupted good faith possession. Judge Mishler held that New York's interest in regulating the transfers of any property located within its border (in this case for over 30 years) overrides any interest the GDR may have in applying the policy of Ersitzung to extraterritorial transactions…. Thus applying New York's choice of law rules, Ersitzung is inapplicable and New York law governs, under which a purchaser cannot acquire good title from a thief. We affirm both rulings….

"Elicofon's third argument is that KZW is barred by New York's statute of limitations from suing to recover the paintings. The essential facts are that in October 1966 Elicofon refused to comply with KZW's demand for the return of the paintings and in April 1969 KZW moved to intervene in this action, which was begun by FRG, thereby commencing KZW's action…. The applicable New York statute provides a three (3) year limitation period…. The question is when the limitation period began to run, or, in other words, when KZW's claim against Elicofon accrued…. Judge Mishler held that under New York law KZW's claim accrued in 1966 and that, even if it accrued earlier in 1946, the then-applicable limitation period of six years was tolled under New York's judicially-created 'non-recognition' toll because the United States did not recognize GDR until 1974, which precluded the KZW from intervening until then. We agree with both conclusions….

"Accordingly, we affirm the district court's holding that KZW is entitled to possession of the paintings, and order that the judgment entered below be enforced."

WILLIAMS DENTAL CO. v. AIR EXPRESS INTERNATIONAL
824 F.Supp. 435 (S.D. NY 1993)

BACKGROUND: Williams Dental (a supplier) shipped 50 ounces of dental gold and other dental equipment from New York to Sweden, via Air Express. The shipment was packed and put on board a plane. When the shipment was delivered in Sweden, the seals on the gold packaging were broken and the gold was missing. Williams sued, and filed for a summary judgment for the value of the shipment—$23,474.50. Air Express moved to dismiss the complaint, since its posted tariff prohibited shipment of gold; or alternatively, to limit its liability to $1,262.93, as per the Warsaw Convention limitation of $9.07 per pound for goods shipped via air freight.

JUDGE MUKASEY:

"[I]f plaintiff had not declared a special value for the entire shipment, defendant's liability would have been limited to $9.07 per pound.

"However, plaintiff chose not to be bound by this limit. Instead, plaintiff declared a special value for the entire shipment of $23,470.50…. Plaintiff claims that it declared separately a value for customs of $21,680.00 for the pail of 'Will Ceram Y' [the dental gold]….

"The cases support plaintiff's expectation that in the event of loss it would receive the declared value of the lost shipment, not the Warsaw Convention value….

"Holding defendant liable for the declared value of the gold is consistent with the goal of the Warsaw Convention to regulate uniformly the liability of international air carriers. The Second Circuit already has held that one who ships goods at a declared value substantially *below* their actual net worth in order to receive a recued freight rate 'is gambling that the goods will not be lost [and if] such loss occurs, the shipper … should not be entitled to recover the full value of the goods….' *Perera* v. *Varig Brazilian Airlines*….

"This case presents the converse of *Perera*—plaintiff shipped goods at a declared value substantially *above* the Warsaw Convention's liability limit and paid an increased freight rate. If a shipper who specifically declares a value less than the full value and pays the corresponding lower rate may recover only the declared value, then a shipper, such as the plaintiff, who declares a greater value (up to the actual value of the goods) and pays a corresponding greater rate also should recover the declared value. Such a rule applies uniformly to those shippers who declare a special value and pay the corresponding freight rate—all would recover the declared value....

"In sum, there is no genuine issue of fact that plaintiff told defendant the shipment contained one pail and two boxes of dental supplies worth almost $25,000.... Defendant accepted an additional rate to ship the package, based on its additional declared value. Thus, plaintiff provided information sufficient to notify defendant that the shipment contained gold. It was then up to defendant, a commercially sophisticated carrier, either to enforce its own tariff or to assume the additional risk associated with the increased shipping rate. In other words, because plaintiff declared that the shipment was worth far more than the Warsaw Convention limitation of $9.07 per pound, provided enough information to indicate that the shipment contained an item prohibited by defendant's tariff, and has not been [shown] to have been actually aware that the defendant prohibited the shipment, defendant is liable notwithstanding the existence of the tariff....

"Nevertheless, defendant is correct that plaintiff may recover only for that portion of the shipment which was actually lost. Although the [Shipper's Letter of Instruction] stated that the pail weighed 1.56 kilograms, or 55.03 ounces, the pail contained only 50 ounces of gold. Moreover, only the gold was lost, not the pail or other dental equipment.... Under ... the Warsaw Convention, a shipper may not declare a value for a shipment greater than its market value and then recover that amount if the shipment is lost. Therefore, the maximum plaintiff may recover for the lost gold is its market value. The amount listed on plaintiff's invoice—$21,680—is consistent with the market price of gold on August 21, 1990. The additional declared amount—$1794.50—relates to the other dental equipment, which was not lost and for which plaintiff may not recover.

VIMAR SEGUROS Y REASEGUROS, S.A. v. *M/V SKY REEFER*
515 U.S. 528 (1995)

BACKGROUND: Bacchus Associates, a New York partnership wholesaling fruit, bought a shipload of Moroccan oranges and lemons from Galaxie Negoce, S.A., a Moroccan supplier. Bacchus chartered the *M/V Sky Reefer* (a refrigerated cargo ship) to transport the fruit from Morocco to Massachusetts. The ship was owned by M.H. Maritima, S.A., a Panamanian company, and was "time-chartered" to Nichiro Gyogyo Kaisha, Ltd., a Japanese company. Galaxie hired a crew of stevedores to load the fruit onto the *Sky Reefer*. Nichiro, as the freight carrier, issued a bill of lading to Galaxie, the shipper; the bill of lading contained an arbitration clause specifying that any disputes must be submitted to arbitration in Tokyo. When the Sky Reefer arrived in the USA, Bacchus discovered that thousands of boxes of oranges had shifted during the voyage, causing over $1,000,000 in damage. Bacchus' marine insurer—Vimar Seguros—paid Bacchus $733,442.90. Vimar Seguros and Bacchus then sued the ship and its owners for damages, in the U.S. District Court in Massachusetts. The District Court enforced the "arbitration-in-Japan" clause, and that decision was affirmed by the U.S. Court of Appeals for the First Circuit. Vimar Seguros asked for U.S. Supreme Court review.

JUSTICE KENNEDY:

"The question is whether a foreign arbitration clause in a bill of lading is invalid under COGSA [the USA's Carriage of Goods by Sea Act] because it lessens liability in the sense that COGSA prohibits....

"The liability that may not be lessened is 'liability for loss or damage ... arising from negligence, fault, or failure in the duties and obligations provided in this section.' The statute thus addresses the lessening of the specific liability imposed by the Act, without addressing the separate question of the means and costs of enforcing that liability. The difference is that between explicit statutory guarantees and the procedure for enforcing them, between applicable liability principles and the forum in which they are vindicated. The liability imposed on carriers under COGSA s.3 is defined by explicit standards of conduct, and it is designed to correct specific abuses by carriers. In the 19th century it was a prevalent practice for common carriers to insert clauses in bills of lading exempting themselves from liability for damage or loss, limiting the period in which plaintiffs had to present their claim or bring suit, and capping any damages awards per package.... Thus, s.3, entitled 'Responsibilities and liabilities of carrier and ship,' requires that the carrier 'exercise due diligence to ... make the ship seaworthy' and 'properly man, equip, and supply the ship' before and at the beginning of the voyage, s.3(1), 'properly and carefully load, handle, stow, carry, keep, care for, and discharge the goods carried,' s.3(2), and issue a bill of lading with specified contents, s.3(3).… Section 3(6) allows the cargo owner to provide notice of loss or damage within three days and to bring suit within one year. These are the substantive obligations and particular procedures that s.3(8) prohibits a carrier from altering to its advantage in a bill of lading. Nothing in this section, however, suggests that the statute prevents the parties from agreeing to enforce these obligations in a particular forum. By its terms, it establishes certain duties and obligations, separate and apart from the mechanisms for their enforcement.…

"If the question whether a provision lessens liability were answered by reference to the costs and inconvenience to the cargo owner, there would be no principled basis for distinguishing national from foreign arbitration clauses. Even if it were reasonable to read s.3(8) to make a distinction based on travel time, airfare, and hotels [sic] bills, these factors are not susceptible of a simple and enforceable distinction between domestic and foreign forums. Requiring a Seattle cargo owner to arbitrate in New York likely imposes more costs and burdens than a foreign arbitration clause requiring it to arbitrate in Vancouver. It would be unwieldy and unsupported by the terms of policy or statute to require courts to proceed case by case to tally the costs and burdens to particular plaintiffs in light of their means, the size of their claims, and the relative burden on the carrier.…

"It would also be out of keeping with the objects of the [Arbitration] Convention for the courts of this country to interpret COGSA to disparage the authority or competence of international forums for dispute resolution. [Vimar Seguros'] skepticism over the ability of foreign arbitrators to apply COGSA or the Hague Rules, and its reliance on this aspect of *Indussa Corp. v. S.S. Ranborg* … must give way to contemporary principles of international comity and commercial practice. As the [U.S. Supreme] Court observed in *The Bremen v. Zapata Off-Shore Co.* … when it enforced a foreign forum selection clause, the historical judicial resistance to foreign forum selection clauses 'has little place in an era when … businesses once essentially local now operate in world markets.'… 'The expansion of American business and industry will hardly be encouraged,' we explained, 'if, notwithstanding solemn contracts, we insist on a parochial concept that all disputes must be resolved under our laws and in our courts.'…

"Whatever the merits of [Vimar Seguros'] comparative reading of COGSA and its Japanese counterpart, its claim is premature. At this … stage it is not established what law the arbitrators will apply to [the] claims or that [Vimar Seguros] will receive diminished protection as a result. The arbitrators may conclude that COGSA applies of its own force or that Japanese law does not apply so that, under another clause of the bill of lading, COGSA controls. [Defendants] seek only to enforce the arbitration agreement. The District Court has retained jurisdiction over the case and 'will have the opportunity at the award-enforcement stage to ensure that the legitimate interest in the enforcement of the … laws has been addressed.'…

"Because we hold that foreign arbitration clauses in bills of lading are not invalid under COGSA in all circumstances, both the FAA [USA's Federal Arbitration Act] and COGSA may be given full effect. The judgment of the Court of Appeals is affirmed, and the case is remanded for further proceedings consistent with this opinion."

ALAFOSS, h.f. v. PREMIUM CORPORATION OF AMERICA, INC.
448 F.Supp. 95 (D. MN 1978)

BACKGROUND: Alafoss is incorporated in Iceland and has its offices and principal place of business there. It engages in the business of export and sale of garments and other products made of the wool of Icelandic sheep. Icelandic Imports, Inc. is a corporation located in New York City and serving as agent for Alafoss. Premium Corporation of America ("PCA") is a Minnesota corporation in the business of direct mail marketing. From October 1971 through January 1974, PCA bought a variety of women's coats from Alafoss directly or through Icelandic Imports. PCA marketed many of these coats to American Express credit card holders.

In 1972, a PCA designer worked with Alafoss personnel to develop a woman's full-collared, wrap-around fur coat for sale through American Express. The body of the coat was to be all white wool, with a detachable white fur collar made from the fur of Icelandic sheep. Alafoss sent samples of the special coats to PCA for inspection and for photographing for a sales brochure. In 1973, PCA ordered 8,225 of the special coats, at $88.11 per coat (landed at PCA's warehouse in Chicago) and sent a mailing with the brochure to 3.4 million American Express cardholders. The coats were offered to customers at $199.90 plus $3.95 shipping and handling.

In October 1973, after some orders had been filled, PCA discovered that a large number of the fur collars had a significant yellow discoloration, including the 4,350 coats remaining in PCA's inventory. About 1,400 coats also had loosely sewn pockets. Some of the collars were sent to Mademoiselle Furs in New York for treatment at $5.55 per collar. PCA paid $24,186.90 for the collar treatments and another $2,800 to re-sew the loose pockets. The treatments did not solve the discoloration problem, so, after notifying Alafoss, PCA resold 3,736 coats to Alden's for about $20 each. When Alafoss sued for $132,470 still due on the purchase price, PCA counter-claimed for damages due to breach of warranty.

JUDGE MacLAUGHLIN:

"[T]he samples of the wrap coats were made part of the basis of the bargain and created an express warranty that the whole of the goods would conform to the sample or model.

"At the time of the contract Alafoss was aware that PCA was relying on Alafoss to select and furnish goods which would conform to the sample and which would be fit for PCA's particular purpose. In addition to a warranty of sample, an implied and express warranty of fitness for a particular purpose and use was created….

"PCA has sustained damages in the amount of $238,758.96 as a result of Alafoss' breach of warranties. Further, PCA has incurred incidental damages in the amount of $26,986.90 in its attempt to remedy the nonconformities, for a total amount of $265,745.86.

"PCA is liable to Alafoss in the sum of $132,470.00 for unpaid merchandise.

"PCA is entitled to a net judgment against Alafoss in the sum of $133,275.86 together with interest and costs."

MESMAN v. CRANE PRO SERVICES, a division of KONECRANES, INC.
409 F.3d 846 (7th Cir. 2005)

BACKGROUND: John Mesman, employed in Indiana by Infra-Metals, a manufacturer of steel products, lost one leg and suffered a serious injury to the other when a load of steel sheets that he was unloading from a boxcar fell on him from the crane that was lifting the sheets out of the boxcar. He and his wife filed a products liability suit in Indiana state court against the firm that had rebuilt the crane, Konecranes, which had the case removed to U.S. District Court. The jury's large damage award was set aside by the trial judge, who entered judgment for the defendant, ruling further that if this was wrong the defendant was entitled to a new trial because the jury had been confused by irrelevant evidence and had ignored critical instructions.

Infra-Metals wanted to renovate the very old crane built into the plant so that steel sheets could be unloaded from the rail siding that ran into the plant. Konecranes engineers visited the plant and watched the crane in operation. The most questionable feature they noticed was that when a boxcar was being unloaded underneath the section of the bridge to which the cab was attached, there was only a foot or two of clearance between the rim of the boxcar and the cab overhead. And if while being lifted by the hoist the beam above struck the cab, the load might be jarred loose and fall, hitting anyone standing beneath it.

Konecranes' renovation did not involve changing the physical structure. The main alteration was to substitute for the controls in the operator's cab a hand-held remote-control device with which the operator would operate the crane from ground level. To raise the load he would press the up button on the device, and to lower it he would press the down button. With the cab no longer being used for anything, it could have been removed to eliminate the danger of its being struck by the "spreader" beam. Konecranes did not remove the cab; instead it installed alongside the up and down buttons on the remote-control device an emergency-stop button, so that if the operator sensed an impending collision between the load and the cab he could bring the spreader beam to an immediate dead stop by pressing that button. Alternatively, by pressing the down button he could reverse the direction of the hoist; but because the up and down control had a deceleration feature to reduce wear and tear on the crane, the spreader beam would continue to rise for three seconds after the down button was pressed, traversing in that period about a foot, until it stopped and began its reverse motion. Thus, pressing the down button would not arrest the upward motion of the spreader beam and load as fast as pressing the emergency-stop button would.

On the day of the accident, the crane operator, Van Til, was standing about 20 feet away from a boxcar that was underneath the abandoned cab. Mesman, standing in the boxcar, fastened a load of steel sheets to the scoops beneath the spreader beam and Van Til pressed the up button, and the beam and load rose. As they rose, Van Til saw that the spreader beam was going to hit the cab; but instead of pressing the emergency-stop button, as he should have done to bring the rising load to a dead stop, he pressed the down button. Because of the deceleration feature—of which Van Til was aware—and the narrow clearance between the cab and the rim of the boxcar, the beam continued to rise for three seconds, hitting the cab and causing the load to fall on Mesman.

JUDGE POSNER:

"The case, filed five years ago, is actually quite simple. It has been badly handled by all concerned. There was no basis for the entry of judgment for the defendant; but with reluctance in light of the age of the case, we must sustain the judge's alternative ruling granting the defendant a new trial....

"Van Til's mistake was the principal cause of the accident, as the jury recognized in assigning two-thirds of the responsibility for the accident to Infra-Metals, the employer of Van Til (as of Mesman) and only one-third to Konecranes. The design of the renovated crane also contributed to the accident, however; for had Konecranes removed the cab, eliminated the deceleration feature, or modified the limit switch so that the limit could be lowered when a load was being unloaded beneath the cab, the accident would have been avoided: with certainty in the case of either of the first two modifications, less certainly in the case of the third, an adjustable limit switch, since Van Til might have forgotten to adjust it.

"Under Indiana's products liability law, a design defect can be made the basis of a tort suit only if the defect was a result of negligence in the design … that is, only if the product could have been redesigned at a reasonable cost to avoid the risk of injury…. *Expressly* requiring proof of negligence in a design-defect case, as Indiana law does, though unusual really isn't much of a legal innovation, since 'defect' always implied something that should not have been allowed into the product—something, in other words, that could have been removed at a reasonable cost in light of the risk that it created….

"The risk of a heavy load falling on a worker if the spreader beam struck the disused cab was substantial because of the narrow clearance under the section of the bridge to which the crane was attached; and if the load did fall on someone it would be likely to kill or seriously injure him. Loads did fall, especially in very cold weather; the cold made the steel sheets slippery and therefore more likely to slide out of the scoops fastened to the chains of the spreader beam. The part of the plant where the sheets were unloaded from rail cars was open to the elements, and the accident to Mesman occurred on a very cold winter day. The renovated crane had been in operation for only ten days when the accident occurred, and so the fact that no one else had been injured was not compelling evidence that the risk of such an injury was slight—indeed, one or two loads had already fallen that very day, though no one had been hurt. A reasonable jury could find that the risk of serious injury was not slight.

"In a negligence or 'defect' case, the risk of injury has to be weighed against the cost of averting it. In Learned Hand's influential negligence formula … failure to take a precaution is negligent only if the cost of the precaution (what he called the 'burden' of avoiding the accident) is less than the probability of the accident that the precaution would have prevented multiplied by the loss that the accident if it occurred would cause…. The cheaper the precaution, the greater the risk of accident, and the greater the harm caused by the accident, the likelier it is that the failure to take the precaution was negligent.

"In this case the risk, which we said was substantial, of an injury that would be likely to be serious could have been eliminated at little cost simply by removing the cab. The cab no longer had any function. It was just a dangerous eyesore. An alternative precaution, also cheap but, as we noted earlier, less fail-safe, would have been an adjustable limit switch, which Van Til could have set to prevent the spreader beam from hitting the cab when it was underneath it. Another alternative would have been to eliminate the deceleration feature, so that pressing the down button while the spreader beam was rising would have brought the beam to an immediate stop.

This would not have been an ideal solution, however, because without the feature the crane would wear out sooner. The same drawback would attend another alternative safety precaution—reducing the period of deceleration from three seconds to one, which would have stopped the spreader beam within four inches after the down button was pressed rather than twelve. Still another possibility would have been an additional automatic limit switch, one operative only when the unloading was taking place under the disused cab.

"The only really contestable issue in the case was whether any of these precautions was necessary given the emergency-stop button. Had Van Til pressed it instead of the down button the accident would not have occurred. By pressing the down button, Konecranes argues, Van Til exposed Mesman to a danger that was 'open and obvious' to Van Til … though not to Mesman; but as Van Til was the operator of the allegedly defective machine, it was the appearance of danger to him that is legally relevant to the apportionment of liability between Infra-Metals, Van Til's employer, and Konecranes…. The open and obvious danger would have been the danger that the rising spreader beam would not stop in time to avoid hitting the cab and dislodging the beam's load unless the emergency-stop button was pushed instead of the down button. Konecranes argues that it had no legal obligation to protect against such a danger.

"It used to be the law that manufacturers had indeed no obligation to protect against 'open and obvious' dangers in a negligence or 'defect' case…. But when the Indiana legislature decided to codify the state's products liability law, it omitted the 'open and obvious' defense, replacing it with a defense (usually referred to as 'incurred risk') that requires proof that the user of the product was actually 'aware of the danger in the product.'… The defendant has not pleaded or argued the defense. But the fact that a risk is open and obvious remains relevant to liability. It is circumstantial evidence that the user of the product knew of the danger (and thus 'incurred' the risk) … and it also bears on the question whether the risk was great enough to warrant protective measures beyond what the user himself would take…. It just is not conclusive evidence.

"Konecranes argues that the 'open and obvious' defense was abolished only with respect to defects in manufacture, as distinct from defects in the design of the manufactured product. There is no basis in the statutory text or logic for such a distinction…. What is true is that the initial codification of Indiana products liability law was limited to products liability claims based on a theory of strict liability, leaving design-defect claims, which as we said are essentially negligence claims, to be governed by common law, including the common law defense of open and obvious danger…. But that distinction was wiped out by a subsequent amendment….

"And rightly so. Suppose a machine is designed without a shield over its moving parts. It is obvious to the operator that if he sticks his hand into the machine while the machine is operating,

200

the hand will be mangled. In the old days that would have been a complete defense. But the new law recognizes that because of inadvertence or other human error, or because of debris or a slippery surface that might cause a worker to trip, or even because of a distracting noise or a sudden seizure, open and obvious hazards do on occasion result in accidents.... If those accidents can be avoided by a design modification at very little cost, then even if the risk is slight, the modification may be cost-justified.... The analogy to the doctrine of last clear chance, which imposes a duty of care on a potential injurer even when the potential victim has carelessly or even recklessly exposed himself to danger, is apparent.

"We are mindful that the Indiana Appellate Court ruled ... that 'to be unreasonably dangerous, a defective condition must be hidden or concealed,' so that 'whether a danger is open and obvious and whether the danger is hidden are two sides of the same coin'; 'evidence of the open and obvious nature of the danger serves . . . to negate a necessary element of the plaintiff's prima facie case that the defect was hidden.'... But we do not believe that the Indiana Supreme Court would follow these decisions of the state's intermediate appellate court when the products liability statute no longer distinguishes between actions based on strict liability and actions based on negligence.

"The specific question in the present case is whether there was a sufficient likelihood that the operator of the rebuilt crane would fail to press the emergency-stop button when he saw the spreader beam about to hit the cab that Konecranes should have modified the control. This is the question that the jury should have been instructed to focus on. The answer would depend on the likelihood of the kind of mistake that Van Til made and the cost and efficacy of additional precautions, such as removing the cab. It is easy enough to push the wrong button in an emergency or to forget that pushing the down button isn't as effective as pushing the emergency-stop button because of the deceleration feature. This argues for an automatic protective device, of which the cheapest would have been simply to remove the cab, made empty and useless by the removal from it of the crane controls. A jury that concluded that, all things considered, the failure to design the renovated crane in such a way as to protect Mesman against the kind of error that Van Til made was negligent could not be thought unreasonable.... The entry of judgment for Konecranes was therefore error.

"But we do not think the judge can be said to have abused her discretion when she ruled in the alternative that Konecranes was entitled to a new trial. The plaintiffs failed to put before the jury a clear picture of the cause of the accident and how it might have been prevented. Their principal expert witness, an engineer, did not visit the plant. He was turned away when he tried to visit, but that is no excuse, since the plaintiffs could easily have obtained an order directing Konecranes to allow the visit.... The evidence regarding the clearance between the boxcar and the cab was hazy, even though the meagerness of the clearance was the key fact in the case; so a visit would have been helpful. A 'human factors' analyst wasted the jury's time trying to show that the remote-control device should have been made to operate by means of a joystick rather than push-buttons, though the joystick wouldn't have altered the deceleration feature or made it more likely for Van Til to press the emergency-stop button rather than move the joystick from the up to the down position. Van Til gave implausible testimony that though aware of the deceleration feature he thought that pushing the down button would cause the hoist to reverse immediately, even though it could not go into reverse without stopping and it would take three seconds for it to stop.

"Konecranes contributed to the jury's confusion by presenting evidence that the renovated crane, including its three-second deceleration feature, complied with industry safety standards. Such evidence ordinarily would be relevant though not conclusive…. But it was irrelevant in this case because the danger arose from site-specific conditions that the industry standards don't address. The plaintiffs responded by criticizing the standards, but this simply distracted the jury from those conditions—specifically the narrow clearance between boxcar and spreading beam in the vicinity of the abandoned but not removed cab—on which resolution of the issue of negligence should have depended.

"In the new trial that we are constrained to order, the judge must take firm control and focus the lawyers, the witnesses, and the jury on the facts identified in this opinion as being critical to the issue of the defendant's negligence.

"AFFIRMED IN PART, REVERSED IN PART, AND REMANDED WITH DIRECTIONS."

BP OIL INT'L, LTD. v. EMPRESA ESTATAL PETROLEOS DE ECUADOR
332 F.3d 333 (5th Cir. 2003)

BACKGROUND: E.E.P.deE. (PetroEcuador) bought 140,000 barrels of gasoline from BP Oil. The contract specified that the gasoline would be shipped "CFR La Libertad-Ecuador," that it would have a gum content of less than 3 milligrams per 100 milliliters—to be determined at the port of shipment, and that Ecuadorian law applied. PetroEcuador hired Saybolt, Inc. to test for gum content. BP bought the gasoline from Shell Oil, and the gasoline was tested and approved by Saybolt, then loaded on board the *M/T Tiber* at Shell's Deer Park, Texas refinery. PetroEcuador refused to accept delivery of the gasoline when it arrived at La Libertad, claiming that it had excessive gum content. BP resold the gasoline at a loss, and then sued PetroEcuador and Saybolt for damages. The U.S. District Court in Texas applied Ecuador's own civil code rather than the CISG, and granted summary judgment for both defendants. BP Oil appealed to the U.S. Fifth Circuit Court of Appeals.

JUDGE SMITH:

"A signatory's assent to the CISG necessarily incorporates the treaty as part of that nation's domestic law…. Given that the CISG is Ecuadorian law, a choice of law provision designating Ecuadorian law merely confirms that the treaty governs the transaction….

"PetroEcuador's invitation to bid for the procurement of 140,000 barrels of gasoline proposed 'CFR' delivery. The final agreement, drafted by PetroEcuador, again specified that the gasoline be sent 'CFR La Libertad-Ecuador' and that the cargo's gum content be tested pre-shipment. Shipments designated 'CFR' require the seller to pay costs and freight to transport the goods to the delivery port, but pass title and risk of loss to the buyer once the goods 'pass the ship's rail' at the port of shipment. The goods should be tested for conformity before the risk of loss passes to the buyer…. In the event of subsequent damage of loss, the buyer must generally seek a remedy against the carrier or insurer….

"In light of the parties' unambiguous use of the 'CFR,' BP fulfilled its contractual obligations if the gasoline met the contract's qualitative specifications when it passed the ship's rail and risk passed to PetroEcuador…. Indeed, Saybolt's testing confirmed that the gasoline's gum content was adequate before departure from Texas. Nevertheless, in its opposition to BP's motion for summary judgment, PetroEcuador contends that BP purchased the gasoline from Shell on an 'as is' basis and therefore failed to add sufficient gum inhibitor as a way to cut corners. In other words, the cargo contained a hidden defect.

"Having appointed Saybolt to test the gasoline, PetroEcuador 'ought to have discovered' the defect before the cargo left Texas…. Permitting PetroEcuador now to distance itself from Saybolt's test would negate the parties' selection of CFR delivery and would undermine the key role that reliance plays in international sales agreements. Nevertheless, BP could have breached the agreement if it provided goods that it 'knew or could not have been unaware' were defective when they 'passed over the ship's rail' and risk shifted to PetroEcuador.

"Therefore, there is a fact issue as to whether BP provided defective gasoline by failing to add sufficient gum inhibitor. The district court should permit the parties to conduct discovery as to this issue only….

"If PetroEcuador improperly refused CFR delivery, it is liable to BP for any consequential damages…. If Saybolt negligently misrepresented the gasoline's gum content, PetroEcuador (not BP) becomes the party with a potential claim [against Saybolt]….

"The judgment dismissing PetroEcuador is REVERSED and REMANDED for proceedings consistent with this opinion. The judgment dismissing Saybolt is AFFIRMED."

In Re L.M.S. ASSOCIATES, INC. (ROEMELMEYER v. CAPITAL BANK)
18 B.R. 425 (S.D. FL 1982)

BACKGROUND: William Roemelmeyer (the bankruptcy trustee) asked the U.S. Bankruptcy Court to determine the priority of his lien as against Capital Bank, a secured creditor of the debtor—L.M.S. Capital Bank counter-claimed for modification of the (statutory) automatic stay against its collection efforts outside the bankruptcy proceeding. The trustee agreed to a lifting of the automatic stay if the court found that he did not have priority over Capital.

L.M.S. is a Florida corporation, headquartered there. It operates gift shops aboard cruise ships which sail in the Caribbean and Mediterranean Seas, and stop at ports in several countries. The ships are all of non-U.S. registry, so the L.M.S. goods on these ships are both physically and legally "outside" the USA (legally, in the nation in which the ship is registered).

Capital Bank loaned L.M.S. $140,000 on August 2, 1979 and $40,000 on November 23, 1979. The notes were renewed, and the current balance is $125,734.10. On August 2, 1979, L.M.S. and Capital had executed a security agreement covering the inventories of the various ship gift shops, including after-acquired property. In conformity with Article 9 of Florida's UCC, Capital had filed financing statements on August 7 with Florida's Secretary of State and with the Dade County (Florida) Clerk of Court.

L.M.S. obtained goods and air-shipped them to the various cruise ships. Most, but not all, of the goods were in Florida at some point. They were never sent to or kept in any foreign cities, but would be held by national customs agents in a given port only for delivery onto a vessel when it arrived in port. Goods were sent this way until four or five weeks prior to bankruptcy. About a week prior to the filing of the petition in bankruptcy, goods were removed from the *S.S. Victoria*, *S.S. Britannus*, and *S.S. Vera Cruz* and placed in a sealed, bonded warehouse in San Juan, Puerto Rico. It is these warehoused goods, worth about $75,000-$80,000, as to which the trustee seeks priority.

JUDGE GASSEN:

"In the present case, the financing statement had been filed prior to acquisition by the debtor of the collateral in question. Therefore, under UCC substantive law, the 'last event ... on which is based the assertion that the security interest is perfected' would be acquisition by L.M.S., UCC 9-303.... In some cases the goods were located in Florida when they were acquired by L.M.S. but not in all cases. The trustee has also asserted that the security interests became unperfected by being removed from Florida for more than four months. However, he relies on [UCC 9.103(1)(d)], which leads to the disperfection of security interests brought to Florida, but not the reverse. Since there is no other event which leads to an assertion of perfection or unperfection, under Florida law (and UCC) choice of law provisions, this court should look to the substantive law of the respective jurisdictions where each part of the collateral was located when L.M.S. acquired it....

"It is not ... easy to reach the conclusion that Florida and federal conflicts law would be the same in the case before this court. First of all, most of the jurisdictions where the collateral was located at various times were non-UCC jurisdictions and this court cannot assume that their law would be the same as that of Florida.

"[T]here was a printed choice of law provision in the security agreement executed August 2, 1979.... 'Paragraph 16: This agreement has been delivered in the State of Florida and shall be construed in accordance with the laws of Florida.' However, the UCC conflicts provision here is not 1-105(1), which authorizes the parties to designate the applicable law, but 9-103(1)(b) which does not.

"The difference between 1-105 and 9-103 is appropriate, because the issue at 9-103 is not one of general commercial law, but specifically of perfection of security interests. *Perfection* does not affect the rights and obligations between a debtor and his secured creditor, but relates to rights among competing creditors or others with interests in the collateral. It defines what notice is necessary to 'the world,' and without which the secured creditor may not assert his priority interest in the collateral. The concept is inherently connected with the location of the collateral because third parties who are interested in the collateral will most naturally look to the jurisdiction where the collateral is located for notice of prior interest. There will always be problems, of course, when collateral is moved from one jurisdiction to another. In 9-103 the Uniform Commercial Code has created an intricate framework of choice of law rules to cover situations where various types of collateral are moved for various purposes, to provide the best combination of efficiency in protecting security interests and fair notice to third parties. Since the framework depends on the reciprocal uniform provisions of other UCC jurisdictions, however, it collapses when the collateral is removed to a non-UCC jurisdiction, and may lead to an unfair result....

"The importance of the physical location of property is also demonstrated by the comment: 'In any event, the tendency of the courts is to treat the law of the situs of property at the commencement of the case as governing to the extent that Section 544(a) refers to non-bankruptcy laws.'...

"None of these rules seems effective to carry out the intent of the perfection provisions of secured transactions law on the facts of this case, however. At the time of perfection, the various items of collateral were either in Florida or in another jurisdiction where they were acquired by the debtor. In either case, they were immediately transported to ships of some other registry, and operated by corporations of yet another jurisdiction. On the high seas the collateral would be deemed to be constructively within the territory and therefore within the jurisdiction of a given ship's registry. It would probably continue to be subject to that jurisdiction although a ship would be in port in several additional jurisdictions.... Finally, at the commencement of the case the collateral was located in Puerto Rico, placed there only for the purpose of liquidation. Throughout it all the secured creditor and the debtor operated their businesses in Florida and their contracts were executed and performed in Florida.

"On these facts and because there is no binding authority on this court against the exercise of its independent judgment as to choice of law, this court concludes that the internal (substantive) law of Florida as to the method of perfection of security interests will be applied. The only other possibly appropriate internal law would be the law of the nation to which each vessel was registered. The physical location of the property is not of major significance here, however, because of the unique nature of its location on a (comparatively speaking) small and moving ship, and the fact that the physical location is not connected with the physical location of the jurisdiction. Normal commercial relations would not relate to the physical location of the goods. The primary 'local' persons who would be interested in property would be retail customers, and their rights are protected under Florida law. In this instance, the most logical place to search for prior liens would be Florida, not the location of the property. Similarly, it would not be logical, and it would be difficult to ascertain arid search the jurisdictions where the goods were located when acquired, if other than Florida (as would be required by application of UCC 9-103[1][b].)

"In concluding that the substantive law of Florida should be applied the court discounts the bank's argument of convenience to the secured party. It would not be unduly burdensome for the secured party to additionally perfect its security interest in the jurisdiction of a ship's registry, and convenience to secured parties is not the overriding factor in a policy determination.

The same is true of the bank's argument that it cannot have been required to perfect in Puerto Rico because it did not know the collateral was there. Difficult as it often is, secured party by taking collateral assumes the burden of keeping track of it.

"Applying the internal law of Florida, the secured party filed its financing statements as required under [UCC] 9.302 and [UCC] 9.401 ... to perfect this security interest in the goods It has priority over the trustee, [UCC] 9.312(5).... Therefore, the automatic stay will be modified to permit the bank to foreclose on its collateral."

In the Matter of CONDOR INSURANCE LIMITED
(FOGERTY and TACON v. PETROQUEST RESOURCES INC., et al.)
601 F.3d 319 (5th Cir. 2010)

BACKGROUND: Condor Insurance Ltd., a Nevis (small island nation in the Caribbean) corporation, was in the insurance and surety bond business. On November 27, 2006, a creditor filed a winding up petition in Nevis, much like a Chapter 7 proceeding under United States law. The petition was granted, and Richard Fogerty and William Tacon were appointed Joint Official Liquidators.

Fogerty and Tacon, as foreign representatives, filed a Chapter 15 bankruptcy proceeding in Mississippi contending that Condor Insurance fraudulently transferred over $313 million in assets to Condor Guaranty, Inc. to put them out of the reach of creditors during the Nevis proceeding. Chapter 15 permits foreign representatives of a foreign insolvency proceeding to seek assistance from U.S. courts in an ancillary proceeding once the foreign proceeding is recognized by the bankruptcy court as a foreign main or non-main proceeding under the Chapter. The bankruptcy court recognized the Nevis winding up proceeding as a foreign main proceeding and the foreign representatives filed an adversary proceeding alleging Nevis law claims against Condor Guaranty to recover the assets.

Condor Guaranty moved to dismiss the proceeding pursuant to Rule 12(b)(1) or alternatively Rule 12(b)(6) as avoidance actions only available through a Chapter 7 or 11 proceeding. As Condor Insurance is classified as a foreign insurance company, it is prohibited from filing a Chapter 7 or 11 case. The bankruptcy court dismissed the proceeding and the district court affirmed. The foreign representatives now appeal.

JUDGE HIGGINBOTHAM:

"This appeal concerns the jurisdiction of a bankruptcy court to offer avoidance relief under foreign law in a Chapter 15 bankruptcy proceeding. We hold that the bankruptcy court has that authority and reverse the judgment of the district court dismissing for want of jurisdiction....

"... There is no question that the bankruptcy court has jurisdiction to recognize the Nevis proceeding as a foreign main proceeding. Our question is whether the exceptions listed in section 1521(a)(7) to the relief available in the ancillary proceeding exclude not only avoidance actions under U.S. law but also exclude reliance upon domestic law of the foreign main proceeding....

"Our interpretive task in part guided by the circumstance that Chapter 15 implements the United Nations Commission on International Trade Law (UNCITRAL) Model Law on Cross-Border Insolvency. Chapter 15 directs courts to 'consider its international origin, and the need to promote an application of th[e] chapter that is consistent with the application of similar statutes adopted by foreign jurisdictions' in interpreting its provisions....

"Chapter 15 provides for the 'recognition' of a 'foreign proceeding' and an ancillary proceeding to assist the foreign proceedings. To be recognized, the foreign proceeding must either fall within the definition of a 'foreign main proceeding' ... or 'foreign nonmain proceeding.'... With recognition, the foreign representative may access federal courts with its claims under Chapter 15....

"The foreign representatives seek relief under section 1521(a) of Chapter 15. Section 1521(a) provides that the bankruptcy court may grant 'any appropriate relief,' including staying various aspects of the proceedings, suspending rights of transfer, providing for discovery, granting administrative powers to the foreign representatives and 'granting any additional relief that may be available to a trustee, except for relief available under sections 522, 544, 545, 547, 548, 550, and 724(a).'... This exception does not exist in the Model Law.... While it is plain that relief under the listed sections is excluded, the statute is silent regarding proceedings that apply foreign law, including any rights of avoidance such law may offer....

"The sections explicitly excepted from (a)(7) are often referred to as 'avoidance powers'—a trustee's powers to avoid the transfer of debtor property that would deplete the debtor's estate at the expense of creditors. Such powers, generally described, include those addressing exempt property (§ 522), the 'strong arm' power, which permits the trustee to act as a judicial lien creditor (§ 544), the power to avoid statutory liens (§ 545), the power to avoid transactions as 'preferences' (§ 547), the power to avoid fraudulent transfers (§ 548), and the power to avoid liens that secure claims for compensatory fine, penalty, or forfeiture, or punitive damages (§

724(a)). Section 550 contains the rules that govern the mechanics of avoidance actions.

"Where avoidance actions under U.S. law are excluded from a Chapter 15 ancillary proceeding, section 1523(a) ensures they may be brought in a full bankruptcy proceeding. And to ensure that a foreign representative enjoys the status of a trustee under those provisions, section 1523(a) grants standing to a foreign representative wishing to pursue an avoidance action not under its domestic law but under U.S. bankruptcy law in a Chapter 7 or 11 proceeding—a power generally reserved to the trustee or specific creditors…. This language roughly tracks that of the Model Law…. To be sure, section 1523(a) grants no substantive right of avoidance. Rather it lifts a potential standing roadblock for resort to Chapters 7 or 11….

"Generally where there are enumerated exceptions 'additional exceptions are not to be implied, in the absence of a contrary legislative intent.'… The statute provides for 'any relief' and excepts only actions under sections 522, 544, 545, 547, 548, 550, and 724(a) of the Code and includes no other language suggesting that other relief might be excepted. While the statute denies the foreign representative the powers of avoidance created by the U.S. Code absent a filing under Chapter 7 or 11 of the Bankruptcy Code, it does not necessarily follow that Congress intended to deny the foreign representative powers of avoidance supplied by applicable foreign law. If Congress wished to bar all avoidance actions whatever their source, it could have stated so; it did not….

"The stated purpose and overall structure of Chapter 15 reflects its international origin and strongly suggests the answer—section 1521(a)(7) does not exclude avoidance actions under foreign law. Section 1501 states the purpose of the Chapter is to further cooperation between the U.S. courts, parties in U.S. bankruptcy proceedings and foreign insolvency courts and authorities, as well as promote 'greater legal certainty,' 'fair and efficient administration of cross-border insolvencies that protects the interests of all creditors,' 'protection and maximization of the value of the debtor's assets,' and 'facilitation of the rescue of financially troubled businesses.'… Whatever its full reach, Chapter 15 does not constrain the federal court's exercise of the powers of foreign law it is to apply….

"The structure of Chapter 15 provides authority to the district court to assist foreign representatives once a foreign proceeding has been recognized by the district court. Neither text nor structure suggests additional exceptions to available relief. Though the language does not explicitly address the use of foreign avoidance law, it suggests a broad reading of the powers granted to the district court in order to advance the goals of comity to foreign jurisdictions. And this silence is loud given the history of the statute including the efforts of the United States to create processes for transnational businesses in extremis.

"The district court found and appellees now argue that Congress intended to relegate avoidance actions of all types to a full bankruptcy proceeding under Chapters 7 and 11. They argue that permitting the application of foreign avoidance law in a Chapter 15 case would allow the foreign representatives to section shop, bringing a Chapter 15 ancillary proceeding when they seek to use foreign law and a Chapter 7 or 11 proceeding when they seek to use U.S. law. While concern over choice of law difficulties is not without some force, we are not persuaded that it counsels a finding that foreign law is excluded....

"Conflict of laws issues arise when multiple jurisdictions seek to apply different bankruptcy law to the same estate.... When courts mix and match different aspects of bankruptcy law, the goals of any particular bankruptcy regime may be thwarted and the end result may be that the final distribution is contrary to the result that either system applied alone would have reached. These concerns were clearly articulated during the negotiations over the Model Law....

"... [T]he Model Law permitted the recognizing court to grant any appropriate relief and granted standing to the foreign representatives to bring avoidance actions under the law of the recognizing state.... This purposefully left open the question of which law the court should apply—in deference to the choice of law concerns raised by the United States....

"The drafters of Chapter 15, responsive to the concerns raised at the UNCITRAL debates, confined actions based on U.S. avoidance law to full Chapter 7 and 11 bankruptcy proceedings —where the court would also decide the law to be applied to the distribution of the estate.... The application of foreign avoidance law in a Chapter 15 ancillary proceeding raises fewer choice of law concerns as the court is not required to create a separate bankruptcy estate.... It accepts the helpful marriage of avoidance and distribution whether the proceeding is ancillary applying foreign law or a full proceeding applying domestic law—a marriage that avoids the more difficult ... rules of conflict law presented by avoidance and distribution decisions governed by different sources of law....

"It is no happenstance that this solution also addresses the concern that foreign representatives would bring an ancillary action simply to gain access to avoidance powers not provided by the law of the foreign proceeding. Access to foreign law offers no opportunity to gain the powers of avoidance provided by the U.S. Bankruptcy Code when there is no such power offered by the foreign state—at least not without filing a full bankruptcy case under the Code—and deference to comity does not invite forum shopping.

"This case is illustrative of Chapter 15's response to concerns of the UNCITRAL delegation. The foreign representatives are not seeking to mix and match foreign and U.S. law—they only seek the application of Nevis law. The foreign representatives gain no powers not contemplated by the laws of Nevis through filing suit in the United States and the distribution regime established by Nevis law is not threatened by the potential application of conflicting avoidance rules.

"Congress did not intend to restrict the powers of the U.S. court to apply the law of the country where the main proceeding pends. Refusing to do so would lend a measure of protection to debtors to hide assets in the United States out of the reach of the foreign jurisdiction, forcing foreign representatives to initiate much more expansive proceedings to recover assets fraudulently conveyed, the scenario Chapter 15 was designed to prevent. We are not persuaded that Congress has unwittingly facilitated such tactics—with foreign insurance companies, access to Chapters 7 and 11 is otherwise denied. Nor is the suggestion that the representatives need only render their claim in Nevis an answer. Not all defendants are necessarily within the jurisdictional reach of the Nevis court.

"Our interpretation is also supported by courts' interpretation of section 304, the predecessor of Chapter 15. Congress intended that case law under section 304 apply unless contradicted by Chapter 15.... Though section 304 was more limited in scope than Chapter 15, it provided significant discretionary relief: a court could enjoin actions or judgments against the debtor or debtor's property, order the turnover of the property to a foreign representative, or 'order other appropriate relief.'... The statute also provided that the courts should exercise discretion in the spirit of comity and in the interests of the parties.... This court summed up the function of section 304: 'The filing of a 304 petition does not create a bankruptcy "estate" that must be administered by a court in the United States, but it does allow the foreign debtor to prevent piecemeal distribution of its assets in the United States while its plan is being structured in the foreign jurisdiction.'...

"Lastly, the application of foreign law under Chapter 15 of the Bankruptcy Code implicates none of the salient concerns driving reliance by United States Courts upon the law of foreign nations in defining domestic norms. Providing access to domestic federal courts to proceedings ancillary to foreign main proceedings springs from distinct impulses of providing protection to domestic business and its creditors as they develop foreign markets. Settled expectations of the rules that will govern their efforts on distant shores is an important ingredient to the risk calculations of lenders and corporate management. In short, Chapter 15 is a congressional implementation of efforts to achieve the cooperative relationships with other countries essential to this objective. The hubris attending growth of the country's share of international commerce rests on a nourishing of its exceptionalism not its diminishment....

"As Chapter 15 was intended to facilitate cooperation between U.S. courts and foreign bankruptcy proceedings, we read section 1521(a)(7) in that light and hold that a court has authority to permit relief under foreign avoidance law under the section. We reverse the judgment of the district court dismissing for want of jurisdiction and remand for further proceedings consistent with this opinion."

CHAPTER IV

International Business Operations—Employment, Intellectual Property, and Investment

OVERVIEW:

Rebuilding the Global Economy. By the time World War II (the "War") ended in 1945, much of the world lay in ruins, millions had been killed, millions more seriously injured, and still more millions were homeless or starving—or both. (*See*, Keith Lowe, *Savage Continent*, New York: St. Martin's Press, 2012; *see also*, Chapter 26, "The Other Horror," in Richard J. Evans, *The Third Reich in History and Memory*, New York: Oxford University Press, 2015.) The economies of many nations were essentially nonexistent. The defeated "Axis" powers—Germany, Italy and Japan—had been subjected to extensive bombing and shelling, but so had much of Europe, China, and Southeast Asia. Even more devastating than the destruction of factories, farms, homes and infrastructure was the loss of a large proportion of the young adult population—especially the young men who had died in combat, or as prisoners. A disproportionate share of the reconstruction effort would have to be borne by women and children, and by men too old for combat (or otherwise exempt).

The nations of the Americas had largely escaped the War's physical ravages, although German submarines had sunk numbers of cargo ships off their Atlantic coasts in the early years, and the Hawaiian island of Oahu had suffered the devastating Pearl Harbor attack in 1941. (The hostilities came close to South America when the German battleship *Graf Spee* was scuttled in the harbor of Montevideo, Uruguay after being forced to stop there to repair damages inflicted by British naval units.) The members of the then British Commonwealth of Nations, who had been mobilized as part of the allied coalition—Australia, New Zealand, India, South Africa, et al.—were also generally far enough removed from the scope of Axis military activity to avoid extensive physical damages from bombing and shelling. Aside from the back-and-forth army movements along its northern coasts in the early 1940's, the African continent had also largely escaped the "total war" experience.

Given the comparative levels of development of the largely "undamaged" nations at the end of the War, the net result was that the USA was the only major industrial/commercial nation left. The USSR and China had both suffered extensive losses of population and physical assets, and Britain was virtually bankrupt. France had been ground up when it was conquered in 1940 and also when it was liberated in 1944/45, and had been badly divided internally. What was left of the Western Alliance feared that most of Western Europe would "go Communist." China, of course, did do exactly that in 1949, as its "Nationalist" government collapsed, and the Chinese Communist Party assumed power. (For an alternative perspective on that process, *see* James Bradley, *The China Mirage*, New York: Little, Brown and Company, 2015.) The USA's response was the "Marshall Plan" (named after the then Secretary of State, George C. Marshall, who had been the U.S. Army's Chief of Staff during the War—responsible for developing overall strategy and selecting commanders to implement it). The Marshall Plan was to provide assistance—material and human—to help the economic and political recovery of the nations of Europe. It was one of the most successful such "nation-building" programs ever undertaken. For his work in resuscitating Europe economically and politically, Marshall received the Nobel Peace Prize in 1953. However, at least from the USA's perspective, the "Policy for Asia" rebuilding effort had mixed results: China was still "lost" to the Communists, as noted above.

Japan's political and economic transformation during the immediate post-War period (1945-1952) was more successful. A new constitution established popular sovereignty, parliamentary supremacy, and civil rights—including women's right to vote. Land reform was enacted, and the *zaibatsu* (the huge business conglomerates) were dismembered. Japan was also in a strategic position to benefit from the USA's massive re-militarization after the outbreak of the Korean War. By 1967, the World Bank Group listed Japan as the second largest economy in the world (although they evidently did not list "Germany"—divided between East and West—until 1971, when it was ranked second and Japan third). Japan was # 2 again in 1972, and "Germany" dropped to third place. The USA-Japan-Germany trio remained as the top three GDPs until 2007, when China moved to # 3, and then moved up to # 2 in 2010.

The economic "miracles" in Germany and Japan and the dramatic economic expansion in China are, of course, only part of the story of the last seven decades of globalization. The many separate national economies are now interconnected to a degree unimaginable throughout most of human history. Large sectors of manufacturing have moved across national boundaries, in search of lower production costs—specifically, in many cases, lower wage costs—and new businesses have sprouted up to take advantage of new resources and new markets. The development of the Internet meant that many service functions could rather easily be out-sourced to lower wage locations and/or to independent contractors. Various technological innovations have facilitated the "off-shoring" of organizations, with dramatic lowering of tax liabilities—and perhaps also regulatory burdens. The vast range of location options now available to businesses has meant increased nation-v-nation competition *for* business investment, as well as increased business-v-business competition. Needless to say, these location and re-location decisions are generally quite complex—and difficult—and, quite often in relocation situations especially, painful.

Much of the "pain" resulting from business relocations has fallen on the employees and the local communities left behind by the footloose businesses. No nation has been completely immune to these economic stresses. Even the USA—the world's largest economy for most of the Twentieth Century and now into the new millennium—has experienced some of the downside of globalization. In fact, due to its federal system, in which the individual States retain a significant measure of governmental power, the USA has gone through its own internal relocation—State to State—as a kind of prelude to the worldwide process. Early on, textile manufacturing was concentrated in New England; iron and steel operations clustered around Chicago, Pittsburgh and Youngstown; automotive production was centered in Detroit/Flint; and tires came from Akron. Even before the moves to Mexico, various Caribbean nations and Asia, businesses were leaving the unionized northern States, in favor of the "sunny (and largely non-unionized) South"—Alabama, South Carolina, Tennessee, et al. Upgraded technology—and more flexible work rules—in the new plants equaled higher productivity: more units of product with fewer workers. High-pay, low-tech factory jobs got scarcer and scarcer. Access to and maintenance in the USA's "middle class" became considerably more difficult. And then came the double-barreled "overseas" challenge: relocations of USA companies' operations to other countries, and imports to the USA of competing products from foreign manufacturers—clothes, steel, cars, tires—and lots more.

International Employment. As a result of the increasingly multi-national reality of business operations, international employment relations have taken on a heightened significance. Of course, much international commerce is carried on via electronic and other non-physical-contact interchanges. But much also involves "boots on the ground"—your own personnel in another nation's territory. Whether a firm chooses to send home-nation persons to the other country, or to hire local personnel to carry out its business there, legal issues can arise. The employment relationship tends to be heavily regulated, but with very wide variances from nation to nation—both as to the substance of the regulations and as to their administration and enforcement. Which nation's regulations are applicable often becomes a difficult question. Generally, the nation where the work is actually being performed has a strong argument for enforcement of its employment laws, but the nation where the representative was originally hired also has a significant interest in the relationship. It may very well be that some such employments are subject to both sets of requirements.

Employment aboard ships or planes operating internationally also poses some special problems, since the general international-law rule is that the ship or plane is the "territory" of the nation where it is registered. Presumably, then, the employment regulations applicable aboard ship or plane would be those of the nation "under whose flag" she was operating. That rule raises some interesting questions as these vehicles move into and out of the geographical area of various countries. Trucks, buses, and other land vehicles are not subject to this same rule, and would generally be subject to the employment regulations of the country in which they were being operated.

Disputes arising from such actual or potential "double-coverage" may occur in a variety of situations. Laws/regulations of the place where the employment services are being performed generally determine what is permitted and what is prohibited, regardless of the nationalities of the employer and the employee. For example, USA regulations will generally apply to employment within the USA—even if the employer company, the employee, or both are non-USA persons. There are two major areas where USA law makes some adjustment for "cross-border" employment. If a nation has a Friendship, Commerce and Navigation Treaty (or Bilateral Investment Treaty) with the USA, that treaty may include a provision which permits companies of the other nation operating in the USA to employ certain executive and professional personnel "of their own choosing." These treaty provisions are generally interpreted as permitting some preferential treatment of citizens of the other nation, despite the provisions of the USA's statutes prohibiting many forms of discrimination. (Citizenship is not equated to "national origin.") The other overlap occurs from the 1991 amendments to the USA's major anti-discrimination statutes. They now apply so as to prohibit discrimination against USA citizens employed outside the USA by USA companies, or by non-USA companies "dominated" by USA persons.

Questions may also arise as to the respective liabilities of employer and employee for the employee's acts which affect third parties. Generally, the nation where the act occurred has the strongest argument for application of its law. Just as the operator of a motor vehicle must obey the rules of the road in the location where the vehicle is being operated, a person making contracts is subject to the rules of the place where the contract negotiations are being conducted. (*See* the *Finnish Fur* case in Chapter II.)

Similarly, there is a strong argument for applying the law of the nation where an alleged tortious act occurred, both to determine whether the act was in fact tortious and to determine appropriate remedies/penalties. A potentially very troublesome offshoot of this tort liability issue has its origins in legislation passed by the very first Congress of the United States and signed by our first President, George Washington—the Judiciary Act of 1789. One section of that statute provided for lawsuits in U.S. national courts by alien (i.e., non-U.S.) plaintiffs for torts that involved violations of U.S. treaties or of international law. (*See* the *Kiobel* case in Chapter I.)

For a number of reasons—availability of lawyers paid by "contingent fees" (i.e., no fee unless money damages won, then a percentage goes to the successful attorney); a losing plaintiff generally does not have to pay the winning defendant's lawyer bills; a liberal system of pre-trial discovery of evidence in the possession of the other party; jury trials, with the jury deciding damages, including possible punitive damages—overseas plaintiffs like to bring their cases to U.S. courts. The perceived advantages are so great that they are willing to travel thousands of miles to sue in the USA. Courts (here, and [hopefully] elsewhere) do have the discretion to decline to hear a case that they have the power to hear, under the doctrine called *forum non conveniens* ("inconvenient" forum—there is another location that is more appropriate for this trial). There are examples of this doctrine in Chapter II.

Employment Regulations. Nearly all government regulations of employment can be categorized as one of three types—labor standards, labor relations, or anti-discrimination. Regulation of "labor standards" would include all the government requirements for the terms of the employment contract: minimum wages, maximum hours, required vacation/personal/illness days, required notice period and/or procedures prior to termination, and the like. "Labor relations" regulations, of course, have to do with requirements for dealing with labor organizations as representatives of the workers—"bargaining" with those organizations with regard to wages, hours, and terms and conditions of employment. Most recently, USA-style "anti-discrimination" rules have been adopted in other nations as well, prohibiting adverse employment decisions on the basis of personal characteristics such as race, religion, gender, and age. As this anti-discrimination category is still in its early developmental stage (or even nonexistent) in many nations, there tends to be much wider variance from nation to nation. (It is hard to imagine a wider gap than that shown between India and Uganda in the *National Legal Services* and *Oloko-Onyango* cases, excerpted below.) Eight of our ten employment cases therefore deal with these discrimination issues.

In contrast, governmental regulation of employment contract terms has had a much longer period of development, and seems well established in many nations—although again, with variations. The USA, for example, seems to be somewhat of an outlier with its rather strict interpretation/application of the "employment-at-will" doctrine: unless otherwise specifically agreed, either party is legally free to end the employment relationship at any time, for any reason, or for no reason at all (but still subject to the anti-discrimination rules). Most nations seem to require at least some minimal notification period (especially if the employer is doing the terminating), and/or some minimal procedural formalities.

Using the USA's regulations as an example of the types of employment events that may be subject to government regulation, major national statutes include:

- the Social Security Act of 1935 ("SSA");
- the National Labor Relations Act of 1935 ("NLRA");
- the Fair Labor Standards Act of 1938 ("FLSA");
- Title VII of the Civil Rights Act of 1964 ("Title VII");
- the Age Discrimination in Employment Act of 1967 ("ADEA");
- the Occupational Safety and Health Act of 1970 ("OSHA");
- the Employment Retirement Income Security Act of 1974 ("ERISA");
- the Worker Adjustment & Retraining Notification Act of 1988 ("WARNA"); and
- the Americans with Disabilities Act of 1990 ("AwDA").

The original Acts are, of course, subject to future amendments to modify coverage and/or remedies. The NLRA had important modifications in 1947 and 1959; prohibition of gender-based wage differentials was added to the FLSA in 1963; "pregnancy" was added to Title VII as a prohibited basis for employment discrimination in 1978 and time-limits for filing claims were redefined in 2009. More directly relevant to our concerns here, the scope of both Title VII and AwDA was enlarged by the Civil Rights Act of 1991 to include some cases of employment discrimination against U.S. citizens *working in other nations*. In addition to the specifics contained in the original statutes, administrative agencies may have been given power to interpret the statute by adopting legally-binding regulations. The National Labor Relations Board has such authority under the NLRA; the OSH Administration, under its 1970 Act; the Department of Labor, under the FLSA. The Equal Employment Opportunity Commission has somewhat lesser powers under Title VII and the AwDA.

The 50 State governments in the USA may have their own versions of some of these national laws, with their own administrative boards or commissions. In addition, the States provide "workers' compensation" coverage for on-the-job injuries. Depending on the State, injured employees may have the right to collect periodic disability payments, medical expenses, economic losses, and (their families) death benefits. Employers are required to provide insurance to guarantee such payments will be made if awarded. The States and the National Government co-administer a program of unemployment compensation—to make periodic payments for a limited period of time to workers who have lost their jobs through no fault of their own. Here again, there are some differences from State to State.

Presumably, when employers decide whether or not to establish operations in another nation—and if so, where—the cost of compliance with these sorts of employment regulations needs to be factored in.

INTELLECTUAL PROPERTY AND OTHER INVESTMENTS. International recognition of intellectual property rights is generally subject to a nation-by-nation approach. Protection needs to be attained under each location's national laws. However, there are numerous treaties promising cross-border recognition, as well as attempts to develop single-filing registration systems for groups of nations (such as the EU—discussed below, and in the *Kingdom of Spain* case). These developments will presumably continue as the international community becomes more tightly connected by electronic networks. Until a fully international system is developed, nation-to-nation conflicts will continue to produce litigations.

Types of Intellectual Property. Four major types of intellectual property need to be considered—*trademark*, *copyright*, *patent*, and *trade secret*. A fifth category—"know-how"—is added by some commentators, and will also be discussed, though a bit more briefly.

A **trademark** is a product (or service—"service mark") identifier: a word or words, a symbol, a sound, a color—or some combination thereof—that indicates the product's origin. The gold-colored capital "M" = McDonald's fast-food restaurants. The "three diamonds" logo on a motor vehicle = Mitsubishi Motors. The image of an apple with a bite missing = the computer and electronics company Apple Inc. The underlying theory for the need to protect against the unauthorized use of a trademark by others is that potential customers are using the trademark—and its positive connotations for product or service qualities—as part of the basis for making their buying decisions. Competitors should not be able to misappropriate the customer good-will that the trademark owner has established for its product or service, by "passing off" the competing wares as the (properly trademarked) original.

Whether or not they have a system for officially registering them, most nations do protect the holder's rights in a trademark. Of course, there is again considerable variation from nation to nation in the protections available, the penalties provided, and the diligence with which enforcement occurs. In the USA, marks are categorized as "arbitrary"/"fanciful," "suggestive," "descriptive," or "generic." Marks in the first two categories are inherently distinctive, and thus generally protectable. An arbitrary or fanciful mark is a word or symbol that has no independent meaning—a "nonsense" term—made up by the business for use as its product or service identifier: "Polaroid," for example. "Tundra" as the model name for a Toyota SUV might be characterized as a "suggestive" trademark—suggesting a rugged motor vehicle, suitable for travelling a rugged country (the Russian word "tundra" meaning "treeless mountain area" or "uplands"). A descriptive mark—providing data about the product or its characteristics—cannot be registered (and thus not protected) unless it has acquired a "secondary meaning." The U.S. Supreme Court decided that the color of a product could be trademarked where it had become thus identified with a specific producer's goods in the minds of the customers. (*Qualitex Co. v. Jacobson Co.*, 514 U.S. 159 [1995].) Generic marks—the names of product categories—are not protectable. The danger for the trademark owner is that the popularity of its product leads consumers to so label the entire product category, and thus lose exclusive use of the word—"cellophane" is an example. Xerox Corporation reminds us that "'Xerox' is not a verb!" (i.e., one does not "xerox" a document; one photocopies the document, using [perhaps] a Xerox-brand photocopier).

Copyright, as the word itself indicates, is literally "the right to copy"—to produce additional units of a written work, or picture, or song recording—for sale/distribution/enjoyment. Generally, any original work expressed in a tangible form is potentially copyrightable, depending on the specific rules in each nation. In the USA, this exclusive right to reproduce the work exists from the time of its creation to 70 years after the author's death. Where an employee creates a "work for hire" (in one of the categories specified in the 1976 Copyright Act), and the parties sign a writing to that effect, protection is given for 95 years from first publication or for 120 years from creation—whichever occurs sooner.

The copyright on the original work also covers so-called "derivative works," e.g., the movie *Rear Window*—based on the magazine story *It Had to Be Murder* (litigated in *Stewart v. Abend,* 495 U.S. 207 [1990]). According to section 101 of the U.S. Copyright Act of 1976, the later, "derivative" work is one "based upon one or more preexisting works," whereby the original has been "recast" in another form. Duplication of the derivative work must be authorized by the holder of the copyright on the original work.

One important, and therefore frequently litigated, limitation on the grant of exclusivity is the concept of "fair use." Since—in the USA—the constitutionally-stated purpose of both copyright and patent is "To promote the Progress of Science and useful Arts" (Article I, Section 8[8]), writers and researchers ought to be able to utilize limited pieces of existing knowledge in developing their own works. As stated by Justice Story, in *Emerson* v. *Davies*, 8 F.Cas. 615, 619 (CCD Mass. 1845), "in truth—in literature, in science and in art, there are, and can be, few, if any, things, which in an abstract sense, are strictly new and original throughout." Rudyard Kipling expressed the same idea in verse: "When 'Omer smote 'is bloomin' lyre, He'd 'eard men sing on land an' sea; An' what he thought 'e might require, 'E went an' took - the same as me!" (Presumably, my use here of Story's and Kipling's words is permissible under the "fair use" doctrine. I'm surely not trying to "pass off" this paragraph as their original work; nor does it seem likely that this document would steal any sales from either original.)

In the USA, the fair use doctrine is now codified as Section 107 of the 1976 Copyright Act. The courts are to consider four factors—in combination—in deciding whether a particular use by another is permitted: the purpose and character of the use, including whether it is commercial or for nonprofit educational use; the nature of the copyrighted work; the amount and substantiality of the portion used in relation to the whole original work; and the effect of the use on the potential market for or the value of the original. Cases and commentaries seem to indicate that the greater the added creativity from the secondary user, the greater the chances that the court will permit the use as "fair."

The U.S. Supreme Court has decided that USA copyright protection ends (as to specific goods containing the copyrighted material) once the goods are lawfully sold. As the new owner of the goods, a buyer lawfully acquiring them outside the USA is free to bring them to the USA if it wishes, and to re-sell or otherwise dispose of them here on whatever terms are agreed to with the new transferee. The *Kirtsaeng* decision, excerpted below, illustrates this point.

A **patent** gives the inventor (or her transferee) the same sort of exclusive protection—to make and market the patented item or process within the nation granting the patent, for the specified period. To qualify for a "utility" (product or process) patent, the invention must be new, useful, and non-obvious. "New" is generally interpreted as meaning previously unknown, undisclosed, and unpatented. The invention must also be "useful," in the sense of producing some significant benefit or positive result. "Non-obvious" implies a requirement that there be some element of creativity involved; that the item proposed for patenting be something more than just a statement of what is apparent to anyone familiar with the industry or technology involved. A utility patent is valid for a period of 20 years from the date the application was filed. Because drug and other medical inventions must also fulfill added regulatory requirements, patent approval may be significantly delayed. The duration of such patents may be extended, to account for the extra regulatory review period.

The USA also recognizes design patents and plant patents. The patent process for new plants is administered through the Department of Agriculture, and the duration of these patents is also 20 years. For a design patent, the applicant must show that the design is "ornamental," rather than useful; but it must also be "new" and "non-obvious." The design patent is valid for 14 years from the date of *issue*, not the date of application.

A patent's limited duration is one obvious downside to this form of IP protection. To take just one rather simple consumer-product patent: the Lipton "flo-thru" tea-bag. Lipton patented a tea-bag design that had tea leaves distributed in a loop, stapled to the control string at the top; thus when the bag was inserted into hot water it was brewing on four sides, rather than just two sides. Presumably, this speeded up the brewing process—or at least that's what we were to infer. Now that the patent has (evidently) expired, everybody's tea-bags seem to "flo-thru"—but Lipton still has trademark protection for that specific hyphenated misspelling.

The other possible downside is inherent in the patenting process itself. Since the applicant must publicly disclose what the patented item is and what it does—with some rather detailed specificity, the way is open for a competitor to devise alternative ways of producing the same beneficial result. Such alternative "solutions" do not violate the existing patent. The patented dispenser box for Kleenex facial tissues may be an example here—it seems as if there are many tissue boxes that do the "pop-up" trick.

A third possible downside is neither legal nor ethical—but still very much part of the choice process. A competitor, seeing the significant value of the patented product or process, simply starts producing the product or using the process—and challenges the patent-holder to take legal action to protect its intellectual property! Such lawsuits may take years to decide, all the while siphoning off funds and effort from the patent-holder's business. Meanwhile, the IP thief is using the patent without paying royalties, deriving ill-gotten profits, and fighting a delaying-action in court. The court process may or may not produce proper results at the end of the ordeal.

For these—and perhaps other—reasons, a business may prefer protection of its "inside info" as a **trade secret**. Rather than making a public disclosure in exchange for a time-limited grant of exclusive production rights, the business attempts to keep its secret advantage to itself. It retains its advantage as long as it is successful in keeping the secret. Coca-Cola has apparently been successful in keeping its soft-drink formula secret for nearly 130 years, despite numerous attempts by others to reverse-engineer it or to uncover copies of it. Over a shorter (but still significant) period of time, Kentucky Fried Chicken has also been able to maintain secrecy on the "eleven secret herbs and spices" in its fried-chicken recipe. The trade-secret form of protection would of course not be available for publicly-distributed products whose physical features were the improvements or "advantages." Lipton's "flo-thru" tea bag, for example, would simply have been copied as soon as a competitor recognized that feature as an advantage.

The owner of the trade secret must rely on general rules of tort, contract, and property law for protection of its ownership rights. These general areas of civil law may be supplemented, as they are in many States in the USA, by special civil and/or criminal statutes providing additional remedies for wrongful disclosure or use of another company's trade secrets. Where criminal sanctions are provided, they may in fact be the most effective deterrents against such wrongdoing. (*See, e.g.,* Robyn Meredith, "VW Agrees to Pay G.M. $100 Million in Espionage Suit," *New York Times*, Business Day [January 10, 1997]: four of the eight GM executives who moved to VW in 1992 were later indicted in Germany for alleged theft of GM's trade secrets. The lead defendant, Lopez de Arriortua, was also indicted in 1999 by a Detroit, Michigan, USA grand jury. The USA's requested extradition from Spain, where he was then living, was refused by the Spanish High Court in 2001. *See,* Emma Daly, "Spain Court Refuses to Extradite Man G.M. Says Took Its Secrets," *New York Times*, Business Day [June 20, 2001].)

"**Know-how**" is a more elusive concept. In a business setting, it signifies an ability to perform a function or process smoothly and efficiently—"to do a good job." In a broad sense, know-how may include some information/knowledge that could qualify as a trade secret, or even be patented—since "processes" are patentable subject-matter. At an individual level, know-how might just signify personal skill or ability to utilize available tools and processes in the most productive manner. (That sort of personal characteristic may not be readily transferable to others, and thus not as easily converted into a stream of royalty payments from licensees using the "know-how.") Another complexity that needs to be considered is the "ownership" of the "know-how" as between employer and employee. When an employee moves to a new company, s/he takes along any accumulated skill, expertise, and experience—but *not* (generally) any trade secrets. If any disputes arise over who owns what, the differential definitions will have to be determined with more precision than is available in this paragraph.

Internationalization of Intellectual Property. As noted above, there are a number of multi-nation treaties dealing with the various international aspects of intellectual property. At the very minimum, one would imagine that there should be widespread agreement on the need for each nation to prevent theft and misuse of Intellectual Property ("IP") assets within its borders. There does indeed seem to be such agreement, although illegal IP activity has by no means been eliminated. From a more positive perspective, there have been ongoing efforts to facilitate the acquisition of IP protection across national borders. While the nation-by-nation registration/recognition approach still seems to be the dominant format, significant progress has been made toward truly "international" protection, most notably by the European Union.

Significant international agreements dealing with trademarks include the 1883 Convention of the Union of Paris (as revised/amended several times), the 1891 Madrid Agreement, the 1957 Arrangement of Nice, and the 1973 Vienna Trademark Registration Treaty. For copyrights, the two most important treaties are the 1886 Berne Convention and the 1952 Universal Copyright Convention. Patents are covered by the 1883 Convention of the Union of Paris and the 1970 Patent Cooperation Treaty. Most of these mechanisms are now administered through the World Intellectual Property Office ("WIPO") in Geneva—"WIPO Madrid" for international trademarks; "WIPO PCT" for international patents; and "WIPO Hague" for international designs. European patents are also subject to two separate arrangements—the 1973 European Patent Convention and the 2012 European Union Patent Convention, administered through the European Patent Office.

The Paris Convention requires the 176 members to provide "national treatment" (i.e., the same protection they give to IP property owned by their own citizens) within their separate nations to the holders of trademarks—or patents—from other members. Through the Madrid procedure, one can obtain a trademark that is valid in any or all of the (currently) 55 member-nations by filing one application (in English, French or Spanish) and designating the places where protection for the mark is desired. The Nice Arrangement provides a classification system for goods and services on which marks may be registered, and the Vienna Trademark Registration Treaty adds a classification system for the "figurative elements" of trademarks.

The Berne Convention, like the Paris Convention, requires its 168 members to provide "national treatment," within their respective nations, to holders of copyrights originating in other member-nations. Minimum standards for "national treatment" (subject to certain exceptions) include recognition of the rights to translate, to make adaptions, to perform or recite in public, to broadcast or communicate to the public, and to make reproductions. WIPO's website also indicates that the Convention "provides for 'moral rights', that is, the right to claim authorship of the work and the right to object to the mutilation, deformation or other modification of, or other derogatory action in relation to, the work that would be prejudicial to the author's honor or reputation." This required national treatment is to occur automatically, as a result of accession to the Berne Convention, without requiring additional registration or verification. Further, if the author of the work is not a citizen of the "country of origin" of the literary work, s/he shall enjoy "national treatment" in the country of origin. Also noted on the WIPO website is the fact that the "TRIPS" (Trade Related Intellectual Property) Annex to the 1994 World Trade Organization agreement requires *all* WTO members, including those who have not signed the Berne Convention, to comply with Berne's substantive rules—except for the "moral rights" clause.

In the immediate aftermath of World War II, there were two competing and somewhat conflicting international copyright systems—Berne, and a "Pan-American" system (largely based on the USA copyright approach). The USA, for instance, had full copyright reciprocity with some 50 nations; but USA-originated works had only partial protection, or none at all, in many other countries. In an effort to further strengthen the economies of what was then called the "Free World," the Universal Copyright Convention was developed under UNESCO (the United Nations Economic, Scientific and Cultural Organization) sponsorship, and opened for nations' adoption in 1952. As explained by an early commentator, this UNESCO UCC ("UUCC") "creates no new law of copyright, but [harmonizes] existing national systems"; it "shall not, in any way, affect Berne." (*See*, Joseph S. Dubin, "The Universal Copyright Convention," 42 *Cal. L.Rev.* 89 [1954], at 89 & 114. Dubin was chief studio counsel for Universal Pictures, and—in 1952—Chairman of the American Bar Association's Committee on Copyright Revision.)

The UUCC therefore contains most of the main principles of the Berne Convention—national treatment, minimum standards, and the like. There are provisions for "harmonizing" the national differences as to time-periods for copyright protection and similar variances. One obvious remaining difference from Berne has to do with authors' "moral rights": they are not protected under the UUCC (as they were not made mandatory under the more recent TRIPS

Agreement Annex to the WTO). Some 100 nations have agreed to the UUCC, many of them obviously also now members of the Berne system.

As noted above, the 1883 Paris Convention required member-states to extend "national treatment" to owners of patents from other member-states. That was an important advance, but only a first-level improvement. The 1970 Patent Cooperation Treaty allows the filing of one "international application" which will then automatically provide patent coverage in all the 148 member-nations if the patent is granted. (Non-members include a few nations each in South America, Africa, and South and Southeast Asia; protection in any of those nations will require a separate application and processing.)

Europe has clearly come closest to creating a truly international patent system. The European Patent Convention ("EPC"—signed in 1973, effective in 1977) took a large step forward, by providing a central filing system for the 38 member-nations (28 members of the EU, plus ten other European countries). Rather than separate application filing and processing in each of the 38, and the required language-translation expenses, the EPC permits a single filing with its EP Office—in one language. The translation costs are deferred until the patent is actually granted, at which point it morphs into "a group of essentially independent nationally-enforceable, nationally-revocable patents." On December 17, 2012, the European Council and the European Parliament made the ultimate internationalizing commitment for the EU patent law, by adopting regulations which created a "unified patent" system: *one EU* patent, granted through the EPO, valid throughout the EU, and enforced by an EU "Unified Patent Court." Spain, Italy and Croatia have refused to participate in this new system; and Spain and Italy filed lawsuits challenging its legal validity under the EU's treaty provisions. The recent decision by the EU Court of Justice on Spain's lawsuit is excerpted below.

International Investment. For international law purposes, corporations are generally recognized as separate persons, with their "citizenship" (nationality) determined by their nation of formation, rather than by the nationality of their shareholders. (*See* the *Sumitomo* and *Barcelona Traction* cases, excerpted below.) The legality and effects of business investments are generally determined by the law of the place where the investment is made. (*See* the *Elliott Associates* and *Nationwide Management* cases, excerpted below.) Sales of securities may be regulated by the place where the sale occurs and/or by the place where the securities are listed on an exchange. (*See* the *Morrison* case, excerpted below.)

Establishment of a physical business presence in the territory of another nation would almost certainly subject a firm to the legal authority of that other country—at least as to lawsuits arising out of that operation, and to appropriate forms of taxation on and regulation of those operations. If the only connections with the other nations are electronic ones, the jurisdiction questions become somewhat more complicated. There may be various permutations and combinations of rules, depending on whether we are distributing goods, performing services, or financing transactions for others. Licensing of the various forms of IP to other firms in other nations is likewise a bit complex as to jurisdiction over the IP owner for litigation, taxation, and regulation purposes. Our cases here (and in the next Chapter) are only intended to suggest some of these issues.

EXAMPLE CASES PREVIEW:

DEFRENNE: The anti-discrimination-in-employment provisions of the 1957 Treaty of Rome (which created the original European "Common Market") became part of each nation's internal law when each member-nation ratified the Treaty. Further national legislation was not required to make the Treaty provisions legally enforceable. Ms. Defrenne was protected against adverse differential treatment on the basis of gender.

SUMITOMO: This is a leading USA precedent case on the application of "Friendship, Commerce, & Navigation" treaties. The limited permission for favoritism is granted to companies of each treaty partner—meaning companies organized in the partner nation. What counts is the "citizenship" of the firm, not the citizenship of its owners. A USA-chartered wholly-owned subsidiary of a Japanese parent company was not a "company of Japan," and its USA employees were therefore protected by the USA's anti-discrimination laws.

DOW CHEMICAL: Texas courts would hear cases involving claims for employee on-the-job injuries occurring in other nations, where the other nation's laws did not provide an "adequate" remedy. To convince a court to decline to exercise its jurisdiction in favor of another court, the requesting party must convince the court that the proposed alternative location does provide adequate remedies.

SAUDI ARABIA: A citizen of one nation employed by the government of another nation may face additional problems in trying to enforce employment rights. Governments generally enjoy "immunity" from lawsuits—they cannot be sued without their consent. Some nations (including the USA) recognize an exception to this rule where the government is engaging in a "commercial" function—the sort of activity normally conducted by private businesses. Nelson was complaining about mistreatment by Saudi police—clearly a "governmental" function, and therefore not subject to the USA's exception.

MAHONEY: A Delaware corporation, operating a radio station in Germany for the USA government, had a collective bargaining agreement covering its workers in Germany. The agreement required that employees retire at age 65. Age discrimination in employment is prohibited under USA law, which applies to USA citizens employed overseas by USA firms—subject to an exception if compliance with USA law would "violate the laws" of the host country. The question is whether that exception applies here.

ECKHARD KALANKE: Kalanke claims gender discrimination, in violation of German national law and the European Economic Community's Equal Treatment Directive. The "equally qualified" female candidate received the promotion, as required by the Bremen law if women are under-represented in the relevant sector. The German national courts found no violation, and Kalanke has asked for review by the European Court of Justice.

HOCSMAN: Another EU employment discrimination case—this one more recent and interpreting the EU's attempt to facilitate cross-border employment among its member-nations. Dr. Hocsman has the right to have his credentials from one nation recognized by the other nations; but the nation of his proposed new location has the right to review his credentials to assure their comparability.

JIVRAJ: The issue here is a bit different—whether the EU's prohibition against religious discrimination in "employment" applies to the parties' arbitration agreement, which did specify a religious qualification for the arbitrators to be chosen.

NATIONAL LEGAL SERVICES: National Legal Services ("NLS") is seeking a declaration by the Supreme Court of India that members of the "Transgender Community" have status as a third gender, other than male or female. The claim is that non-recognition of such status amounts to violation of Articles 14 and 21 of the Constitution of India. (The obvious relevance of this issue would be the application of employment non-discrimination rules to staff working in India, whether Indian nationals or "ex-pats" working there.) While the idea of a "third gender" may sound revolutionary to some, it should be noted that the German sexologist Magnus Hirschfeld used similar language to describe homosexual men nearly 100 years ago. (*See* Richard J. Evans, *The Third Reich in History and Memory*, New York: Oxford University Press, 2015, p. 77 & fn. 34.) Elizabeth Pisani takes note of Indonesia's "third gender" (the *waria*) in Chapter 2, "The Ties That Bind," *Indonesia, Etc.,* New York: W.W. Norton & Company, 2014. (*Cf.,* Irfan Kortschak, "Defining waria," *Inside Indonesia*, www.insideindonesia.org/defining-waria.)

OLOKA-ONYANGO: The contrast between the potentially applicable legal rules in this case and the previous one could hardly be greater. At issue here is the legality, under the Ugandan

Constitution, of a national statute criminalizing—and providing severe penalties for (although not the death penalty included in the first draft)—homosexual conduct. The Constitutional Court of Uganda decides the case on a narrow procedural point, rather than deciding the many other claims of discrimination raised by the petitioners. How that Court might rule on those other issues is an open question. (Here again, the business relevance of this issue is its impact on alleged employment discrimination.)

CELANESE: This case serves as a "red alert" for the need to be aware of judicial (***and*** non-judicial) procedures in nations where one is doing business. The idea of a "no-notice, no-knock" search and seizure of business records sounds like a 20th-century horror story; but the process is recognized in the U.K.—which also generated the *Magna Carta*, one of the most important human-rights statements of all time. This drastic procedure is subject to safeguards (or is supposed to be), and extreme sanctions may be imposed by the courts for violations of the prescribed safeguards (as they were in this case).

FIRST FLIGHT: This dispute arose from an international IP licensing agreement. Questions arose about revenues derived from sub-licensing within the second nation, and about the need for reimbursement from the licensee for perfecting protection of the IP rights in the second nation.

RAYMOND DAYAN: Dayan claimed that he had been improperly terminated as a McDonald's franchisee operating in Paris, France. Reading the facts of the case, it seems amazing that he had not been terminated much earlier. His franchised locations could hardly have been less appealing if he had intentionally sabotaged them. He lost his lawsuit.

K-MART: The issue here is the legality of importing into the USA goods made outside the USA but bearing a USA-registered trademark. The USA Trademark Act of 1930 prohibits such importation without the consent of the trademark owner, but a regulation of the USA Customs Services permits importation if the USA owner of the trademark has licensed the overseas manufacture, even if the license prohibited the subsequent importation of the goods into the USA. By a 5-to-4 vote the U.S. Supreme Court said that this regulation violated the intent of the 1930 Act. Subsequent such importations are prohibited.

WINEWORTHS: This case illustrates the national basis for recognition of IP claims, using the long-standing dispute over the protectability of the word "champagne." The word is, of course, still firmly protected in France (its point of origin). Other nations are split, as illustrated by this dispute between uses of the term in New Zealand and in Australia.

THE GAP: A Delaware corporation was refused registration of its claimed trademark—a line/outline/diagram of a T-shirt—by the Korean authorities. The Korean Patent Court affirmed the refusal, and The Gap, Inc. requested review the by the Korean Supreme Court.

228

WALT DISNEY: This is another sub-licensing dispute, involving a licensee in another nation. (Even this random re-occurrence suggests that the sub-licensing arrangements in an IP license need particularly close attention.) Disney had included a specific prohibition against sub-licensing, but it was either misunderstood or intentionally disregarded. That such confusion can arise even with specific language suggests the need for careful "due diligence" in the selection of international IP licensees, *and* continual monitoring of the IP usage.

INTERNATIONAL BANCORP: This is a dispute over the USA trademark rights to "Casino de Monte Carlo." The mark was registered in Monaco to the original Monaco casino, but was not so registered in the USA. Five internet-gambling companies owned by a French citizen were using similar phrases in their USA advertising. The question is whether the Monaco casino's 18 years of USA promotion activities entitle the casino to protection of its mark in the USA, under the USA's Lanham Trademark Act.

MONSANTO TECHNOLOGY: Monsanto held a European patent on a certain herbicide used in soybean production. The defendants shipped soybean meal produced in Argentina (where the patent does not apply) to the Netherlands (where it does apply). Acting on a complaint by Monsanto, authorities in the Netherlands seized these shipments when they arrived. The question is whether the imports violate the European patent.

KIRTSAENG: A college student in the USA (Kirtsaeng) had his USA relatives traveling abroad buy "overseas" editions of college textbooks (with content identical to the USA editions, but at much lower prices) and send them to him in the USA, where he resold them at a profit. Publisher John Wiley tried to argue that these imports were unauthorized, because the "first sale" rule applied only to goods made in the USA. That argument was rejected by the U.S. Supreme Court.

GOOGLE SPAIN: A citizen of Spain is suing there to force Google to remove or conceal from its search mechanism a true story about him which was published years before in a Spanish newspaper. His claim is that such publication of personal information violates his right to privacy ("the right to be forgotten"), under EU Directive 95/46. Here again, the implications for internet operators and users are staggering.

DALLAS BUYERS CLUB: USA film owners asked the Australian Federal Court for an order forcing six Australian internet service providers to provide them with information on 4,726 Internet Service Provider ("ISP") customers who have allegedly been violating copyrights on the film. On May 7, 2015, the Court modified its previous decision (excerpted below), by requiring the six ISPs to pay 75% of the court costs assessed in the case. That modification obviously changes the dynamics of the enforcement-lawsuit process—significantly!

KINGDOM OF SPAIN: Spain objected to the adoption by the EU of a "unified patent" option for its member-nations. Any of the 28 EU nations that so agreed could have a single patent—filed with the EU patent office—effective in all of them, with the patent-holder no longer having to have separate patents issued by each nation in which it desired patent protection. Spain, Italy and Croatia have specifically rejected this idea, perhaps because translations of each patent into each national language are no longer required for unitary patents; official filings can occur in English, French, or German. The other 25 EU members have agreed to participate in the alternate system. Spain filed a lawsuit with the EU Court of Justice, challenging the legality of the EU's adoption of the "unified patent."

BARCELONA TRACTION: Belgium, purporting to represent Belgian stockholders in a Canadian corporation, filed a claim against Spain with the International Court of Justice. The ICJ rejected the claim, since whatever wrong/s Spain had committed were wrongs against the Canadian corporation (a separate legal person—"protectable" by Canada, *not* Belgium).

ELLIOTT ASSOCIATES: A New York statute prohibits the purchasing of an interest in a claim for the purpose of filing a lawsuit. Elliott Associates bought $28.75 million worth of Peruvian government "distressed" debt for $17.5 million—with knowledge that there had been payment defaults on the debt, but apparently believing that it was still worth more than the current value assigned to it by the sovereign debt market. The issue here is whether that sort of speculative investment in another nation's debt violates the state statute.

NATIONWIDE MANAGEMENT: Buyers of separate real estate units were not making an "investment" for purposes of the Australian securities law. The real estate sellers were therefore not required to comply with the securities law, and their failure to do so did not make the purchase contract voidable by the buyers. The buyers had to pay for their purchases.

MORRISON: The USA's securities laws did not apply to outside-the-USA purchases of shares which were not listed on USA exchanges. The communication of some allegedly misleading information in the USA was not, by itself, a sufficient basis for applying USA rules to foreign purchases of foreign shares.

CASE EXAMPLES:

DEFRENNE v.
SOCIETE ANONYME BELGE DE NAVIGATION ARIENNE (S.A.Be.N.A.)
[1976] E.C.R. 455; 2 C.M.L.R. 98 [1976]

BACKGROUND: Article 119 of the Treaty of Rome requires equal pay for equal work within what was then the EEC (now the EU). In 1951, the Belgian airline SABENA hired Gabrielle Defrenne as a "trainee air hostess." SABENA promoted her to "Cabin Steward and Air Hostess—Principal Cabin Attendant" in 1963. To comply with a collective bargaining agreement which required termination of female cabin staff at age forty, SABENA fired Defrenne in 1968. She sued SABENA for the differential between her wages from 1963 to 1968 and the amount a similarly-situated man would have received, as well as for severance pay and lost pension rights.

The Brussels *Tribunal du Travail* dismissed all these claims. When Defrenne appealed to the *Cour du Travail*, it affirmed dismissal as to severance pay and pension rights, but referred the equal pay issue to the European Court of Justice.

THE COURT:

"The question of the direct effect of Article 119 must be considered in the light of the nature of the principle of equal pay, the aim of this provision and its place in the scheme of the Treaty. Article 119 pursues a double aim. First, in the light of the different stages of the development of social legislation in the various member-States, the aim of Article 119 is to avoid a situation in which undertakings established in States which have actually implemented the principle of equal pay suffer a competitive disadvantage in intra-Community competition as compared with undertakings established in States which have not yet eliminated discrimination against women workers as regards pay. Secondly, this provision forms part of the social objectives of the Community, which is not merely an economic union but is at the same time intended, by common action, to ensure social progress and seek the constant improvement of the living and working conditions of their peoples, as is emphasized by the Preamble to the Treaty. This aim is accentuated by the insertion of Article 119 into the body of a chapter devoted to social policy whose preliminary provisions, Article 117, marks 'the need to promote improved working conditions and an improved standard of living for workers, so as to make possible their harmonisation while the improvement is being maintained.' This double aim, which is at once economic and social, shows that the principle of equal pay forms part of the foundations of the Community. Furthermore, this explains why the treaty has provided for the complete implementation of this principle by the end of the first stage of the transitional period. Therefore, in interpreting this provision, it is impossible to base any argument on the dilatoriness and resistance which have delayed the actual implementation of this basic principle in certain member-States. In particular, since Article 119 appears in the context of the harmonisation of working conditions while the improvement is being maintained, the objection that the terms of this Article may be observed in other ways than by raising the lowest salaries may be set aside.

"Under the terms of the first paragraph of Article 119, the member-States are bound to ensure and maintain 'the application of the principle that men and women should receive equal pay for equal work.'…

"The second question asks whether Article 119 has become 'applicable internal law of the member-States by virtue of measures adopted by the authorities of the European Economic Community' or whether the national legislature must 'be regarded as alone competent in this matter.'…

"Article 119 itself provides that the application of the principle of equal pay was to be uniformly ensured by the end of the first stage of the transitional period at the latest.…

"The reply to the second question should therefore be that the application of Article 119 was to have been fully secured by the original member-States as from 1 January 1962, the beginning of the second stage of the transitional period.…

"The Governments of Ireland and the United Kingdom have drawn the Court's attention to the possible economic consequences of attributing direct effect to the provisions of Article 119, on the ground that such a decision might, in many branches of economic life, result in the introduction of claims dating back to the time at which such effect came into existence.… Therefore, the direct effect of Article 119 cannot be relied on in order to support claims concerning pay periods prior to the date of this judgment, except as regards those workers who have already brought legal proceedings or made an equivalent claim."

SUMITOMO SHOJI AMERICA, INC. v. AVAGLIANO
457 U.S. 176 (1982)

BACKGROUND: Sumitomo Shoji America ("SSA") is a New York corporation that is a wholly owned subsidiary of Sumitomo Shoji Kabushiki Kaisha, a large Japanese "trading company." Ms. Avagliano and other past and present female SSA secretarial employees filed a class action, claiming race and gender employment discrimination. The plaintiffs were U.S. citizens, except for one—who was a Japanese citizen living in the USA. They claimed that SSA hired only male Japanese nationals for executive, managerial and sales positions, in violation of Title VII of the USA's 1964 Civil Rights Act. SSA claimed that it was exempt from Title VII and other USA employment laws because the "Friendship, Commerce & Navigation" treaty between the USA and Japan permitted the companies of each nation to follow their own nation's employment practices. SSA asked the U.S. District Court to dismiss the complaint. It refused to do so, but the U.S. Court of Appeals granted the dismissal. SSA asked for U.S. Supreme Court review.

CHIEF JUSTICE BURGER:

"Interpretation of the Friendship, Commerce and Navigation Treaty between Japan and the United States must, of course, begin with the language of the Treaty itself. The clear import of treaty language controls unless 'application of the words of the treaty according to their obvious meaning effects a result inconsistent with the intent or expectations of its signatories.'

"Article VIII(1) of the Treaty provides in pertinent part: '*[Companies] of either Party* shall be permitted to engage, within the territories of the other Party, accountants and other technical experts, executive personnel, attorneys, agents and other specialists of their choice.' (Emphasis added [by the Court].)

"Clearly Article VIII(1) only applies to companies of one of the Treaty countries operating in the other country. Sumitomo contends that it is a company of Japan, and that Article VIII(1) of the Treaty grants it very broad discretion to fill its executive, managerial, and sales positions with male Japanese citizens….

"Article VIII(1) does not define any of its terms; the definitional section of the Treaty is contained in Article XXII. Article XXII(3) provides: 'As used in the present Treaty, the term "companies" means corporations, partnerships, companies and other associations, whether or not with limited liability and whether or not for pecuniary profit. Companies constituted under the applicable laws and regulations within the territories of either party *shall be deemed companies thereof* and shall have their juridical status recognized within the territories of the other party.' (Emphasis added [by the Court].)

"Sumitomo [SSA] is 'constituted under the applicable laws and regulations' of New York; based on Article XXII(3), it is a company of the United States, not a company of Japan. As a company of the United States operating in the United States, under the literal language of the Article XXII(3) of the Treaty, Sumitomo cannot invoke the rights provided in Article VIII(1), which are available only to companies of Japan operating in the United States and to companies of the

United States operating in Japan.

"The Governments of Japan and the United States support this interpretation of the Treaty. Both the Ministry of Foreign Affairs of Japan and the United States Department of State agree that a United States corporation, even when wholly owned by a Japanese company, is not a company of Japan under the Treaty and is therefore not covered by Article VIII(1)...

"Sumitomo [SSA] maintains that although the literal language of the Treaty supports the contrary interpretation, the intent of Japan and the United States was to cover subsidiaries regardless of their place of incorporation. We disagree....

"Nor can we agree with the Court of Appeals view that literal interpretation of the Treaty would create a 'crazy-quilt pattern' in which the rights of branches of Japanese companies operating directly in the United States would be greatly superior to the right[s] of locally incorporated subsidiaries of Japanese companies.... The Court of Appeals maintained that if such subsidiaries were not companies of Japan under the Treaty, they, unlike branch offices of Japanese corporations, would be denied access to the legal system, would be left unprotected against unlawful entry and molestation, and would be unable to dispose of property, obtain patents, engage in importation and exportation, or make payments, remittances, and transfers of funds.... That this is not the case is obvious; the subsidiaries, as companies of the United States, would enjoy all of those rights and more. The only significant advantage branches may have over subsidiaries is that conferred by Article VIII(1).

"We are persuaded, as both signatories agree, that under the literal language of Article XXII(3) of the Treaty, Sumitomo [SSA] is a company of the United States; we discern no reason to depart from the plain meaning of the Treaty language. Accordingly, we hold that Sumitomo is not a company of Japan and thus is not covered by Article VIII(1) of the Treaty. The judgment of the Court of Appeals is vacated, and the case is remanded for further proceedings consistent with this opinion."

DOW CHEMICAL CO. v. CASTRO ALFARO
   786 S.W. 2d 674 (Tex. 1990)

BACKGROUND: Both defendants (Dow Chemical and Shell Oil) were Delaware corporations. Shell's world headquarters was in Houston, Texas. Dow operated what was then the largest chemical plant in the United States in Freeport, Texas, about sixty miles from Houston. Domingo Castro Alfaro and 81 other employees of Standard Fruit Company claim that they suffered personal injuries, including sterility, by being exposed to a pesticide which was manufactured by Dow and by Shell Oil, and then sold by those companies to Standard Fruit. The pesticide was used on Standard Fruit's banana plantation in Costa Rica, where Castro Alfaro and the others worked. The pesticide at issue, dibromachloropropane (DBCP), was banned from use in the United States in 1977. Dow and Shell, both before and after the U.S. ban, shipped hundreds of thousands of gallons of DBCP to Standard Fruit in Costa Rica, for use there. The employees and their wives filed a lawsuit against Dow and Shell in Houston, Texas, in state court.

Dow and Shell asked the Texas court to dismiss the case as being brought in an "inconvenient" location, since the injuries occurred in Costa Rica, to Costa Rica citizens. A Texas statute says that personal injury actions "may be enforced" in Texas courts even though the injury occurred in another country. In Costa Rica, $1,080 would be the estimated maximum recovery per worker for the claimed injuries.

The Texas trial court dismissed the case, based on *forum non conveniens*. The Texas Court of Appeals reversed, and sent the case back to the trial court for a trial on the merits of the plaintiffs' claims. Dow and Shell then asked for review by the Texas Supreme Court.

JUSTICE RAY:

"The doctrine of *forum non conveniens* arose from [a similar rule] in Scottish cases.... The Scottish courts recognized that the [rule] applied when to hear the case was not expedient for the administration of justice.... By the end of the nineteenth century, English courts had 'accepted the doctrine.'...

"Texas courts applied the doctrine ... in several cases prior to the enactment of article 4678 in 1913 [the section on which the current Texas statute was based]....

"Our interpretation of the [current statute] is controlled by ... *Allen* v. *Bass*.... In *Allen* the court of civil appeals conferred an absolute right to maintain a properly brought suit in Texas courts....

"We conclude that the legislature has statutorily abolished the doctrine of *forum non conveniens* in suits brought under [this statute]."

[Judgment of the Texas Court of Appeals is affirmed.]

CONCURRING OPINION by *Justice DOGGETT*:

"The [dissenting judges] are insistent that a jury of Texans be denied the opportunity to evaluate the conduct of a Texas corporation concerning decisions it made in Texas because the only ones allegedly hurt are foreigners. Fortunately, Texans are not so provincial and narrow-minded as these dissenters presume. Our citizenry recognizes that a wrong does not fade away because its immediate consequences are first felt far away rather than close to home. Never have we been required to forfeit our membership in the human race in order to maintain our proud heritage as citizens of Texas.

"The dissenters argue that it is *inconvenient* and *unfair* for farmworkers allegedly suffering permanent physical and mental injuries, including irreversible sterility, to seek redress by suing a multinational corporation in a court three blocks away from its world headquarters and another corporation, which operates in Texas this country's largest chemical plant.... [T]he 'doctrine' they advocate has nothing to do with fairness and convenience and everything to do with immunizing multinational corporations from accountability for their alleged torts causing injury abroad....

"The banana plantation workers allegedly injured by DBCP were employed by an American company on American-owned land and grew Dole bananas for export solely to American tables. The chemical allegedly rendering the workers sterile was researched, formulated, tested, manufactured, labeled and shipped by an American company in the United States to another American company. The decision to manufacture DBCP for distribution and use in the third world was made by these two American companies in their corporate offices in the United States. Yet now Shell and Dow argue that the one part of this equation that should not be American is the legal consequences of their actions....

"A *forum non conveniens* dismissal is often, in reality, a complete victory for the defendant.... 'In some instances ... invocation of the doctrine will send the case to a jurisdiction which has imposed such severe monetary limitations on recovery as to eliminate the likelihood that the case will be tried. When it is obvious that this will occur, discussion of the convenience of witnesses takes on a Kafkesque quality—everyone knows that no witnesses ever will be called to testify.'... Empirical data available demonstrate that less than four percent of cases dismissed under the doctrine ... ever reach trial in a foreign court....

"The abolition of *forum non conveniens* will further important public policy considerations by providing a check on the conduct of multinational corporations.... The misconduct of even a few multinational corporations can affect untold millions around the world. For example, after the United States imposed a domestic ban on the sale of cancer-producing ... children's sleepwear, American companies exported approximately 2.4 million pieces to Africa, Asia and South America. A similar pattern occurred when a ban was proposed for baby pacifiers that had been linked to choking deaths in infants.... These examples of indifference by some corporations towards children abroad are not unusual.

"The allegations against Shell and Dow, if proven true, would not be unique, since production of many chemicals banned for domestic use has thereafter continued for foreign marketing."

SAUDI ARABIA v. NELSON
507 U.S. 349 (1993)

BACKGROUND: Scott Nelson answered an ad in a trade periodical, placed by a recruiting agency for the King Faisal Specialist Hospital in Saudi Arabia. He was interviewed in Saudi Arabia, and then came back to the USA, where he signed an employment contract. He was employed as a safety monitor at the Hospital, but was imprisoned for 39 days after reporting certain safety violations. He was finally released and allowed to go home to the USA.

Scott and his wife Vivian sued the Kingdom of Saudi Arabia, the King Faisal Specialist Hospital, and Royspec—the hospital's U.S. purchasing agent. Plaintiffs alleged that Scott suffered personal injuries as a result of the Saudi Government's detention and torture of him, and the hospital's negligent failure to warn him of the possibility of severe retaliatory action if he attempted to report on-the-job hazards. The USA's "Foreign Sovereign Immunity Act" ("FSIA") gives U.S. courts jurisdiction where a lawsuit is "based upon a commercial activity carried on in the United States by the foreign state."

The U.S. District Court dismissed the complaint, but the Court of Appeals reversed. Saudi Arabia asked the Supreme Court for review.

JUSTICE SOUTER:

"The Foreign Sovereign Immunities Act 'provides the sole basis for obtaining jurisdiction over a foreign state in the courts of this country.'... Under the Act, a foreign state is presumptively immune from the jurisdiction of United States courts; unless a specified exception applies, a federal court lacks subject-matter jurisdiction over a claim against a foreign state....

"Only one such exception is said to apply here. The first clause of S.1605(a)(2) of the Act provides that foreign state shall not be immune from the jurisdiction of United State courts in any case 'in which the action is based upon a commercial activity carried on in the United States by the foreign state.' The Act defines such action as 'commercial activity carried on by such state and having substantial contact with the United States,' ... and provides that a commercial activity may be 'either a regular course of commercial conduct or a particular commercial transaction or act,' the 'commercial character of [which] shall be determined by reference to' its 'nature,' rather than its 'purpose.'...

"Under the restrictive, as opposed to the 'absolute,' theory of foreign sovereign immunity, a state is immune from the jurisdiction of foreign courts as to its sovereign or public acts (*jure imperii*), but not as to those that are private or commercial in character (*jure gestionis*)....

"[W]hether a state acts 'in the manner of' a private party is a question of behavior, not motivation: '[B]ecause the Act provides that the commercial character of an act is to be determined by reference to its "nature" rather than its "purpose," the question is not whether the foreign government is acting with a profit motive or instead with the aim of fulfilling uniquely sovereign objectives. Rather, the issue is whether the particular actions that the foreign state performs (whatever the motive behind them) are the *type* of actions by which a private party engages in "trade and traffic or commerce"....'

"[T]he intentional conduct alleged here (the Saudi Government's wrongful arrest, imprisonment, and torture of Nelson) could not qualify as commercial under the restrictive theory. The conduct boils down to abuse of the power of its police by the Saudi Government, and however monstrous such abuse undoubtedly may be, a foreign state's exercise of the power of its police has long been understood for purposes of the restrictive theory as peculiarly sovereign in nature."

MAHONEY et al. v. RFE/RL, INC.
47 F.3d 447 (DC Cir. 1995)

BACKGROUND: RFE/RL, Inc. is a Delaware non-profit corporation, funded but not controlled by the U.S. government. It provides broadcast services—Radio Free Europe and Radio Liberty. Its principal place of business is Munich, Germany. In 1982, the company entered into a collective bargaining agreement with unions representing its employees in Munich. One of the provisions of the labor contract, modeled after a nation-wide agreement in the German broadcast industry, required employees to retire at age sixty-five. In 1982, the USA Age Discrimination in Employment Act had no extraterritorial reach, and this portion of the RFE/RL collective bargaining agreement was presumably lawful.

Congress amended the Act in 1984 to cover USA citizens working for USA corporations overseas. RFE/RL applied to the "Works Council" for limited exemptions from its contractual obligation. Works Councils (*Betriebsrte*) exist in all German firms with twenty or more workers. They are bodies elected by both unionized and nonunionized employees. Their duties include insuring that management adheres to all provisions of union contracts. The Works

Council determined that allowing only those employees who were American citizens to work past the age of sixty-five would violate not only the mandatory retirement provision, but also the collective bargaining agreement's provision forbidding discrimination on the basis of nationality.

RFE/RL appealed the Works Council's decisions to the Munich Labor Court and lost. RFE/RL negotiated with the unions to delete the mandatory retirement provision from the collective bargaining agreement, but to no avail. Plaintiffs were discharged pursuant to the labor contract because they had reached the age of sixty-five. The parties agree that RFE/RL thereby violated the Age Discrimination in Employment Act unless the "foreign laws" exception applied. The USA District Court found that company liable for violating the Act, ruling that the "foreign laws" exception did not apply to breaches of collective bargaining agreements. RFE/RL appealed the judgment establishing its liability and the award of damages for violating the Act. Plaintiffs cross-appealed the judgment setting the amount of their damages.

JUDGE RANDOLPH:

"If an American corporation operating in a foreign country would have to 'violate the laws' of that country in order to comply with the Age Discrimination in Employment Act … the company need not comply with the Act. The question here is whether this 'foreign laws' exception in § 623(f)(1) applies when the overseas company, in order to comply with the Act, would have to breach a collective bargaining agreement with foreign unions….

"The 'foreign laws' exception to the Act states: 'It shall not be unlawful for an employer, employment agency, or labor organization—(1) to take any action otherwise prohibited under subsections (a), (b), (c), or (e) of this section where ... such practices involve an employee in a workplace in a foreign country, and compliance with such subsections would cause such employer, or a corporation controlled by such employer, to violate the laws of the country in which such workplace is located….'

"The district court held § 623(f)(1) inapplicable because the mandatory retirement provision 'is part of a contract between an employer and unions—both private entities—and has not in any way been mandated by the German government. Second, the provision does not have general application, as laws normally do, but binds only the parties to the contract.'… Although 'the mandatory retirement provision in the union contract had "legal" force in Germany in the sense that it was legally binding,' the court found this to be 'precisely the sense in which such contracts in this country may be said to have "legal" force; yet they are not ordinarily thought of as "laws".'…

"The decision of the Supreme Court in Norfolk & Western Railway v. American Train Dispatchers Ass'n, 499 U.S. 117 … (1991), stands firmly against the district court's interpretation. But the parties unaccountably failed to mention the case to the district court, and failed again even to cite the decision on appeal. If *Norfolk & Western* had been brought to the district court's attention, we have no doubt that it would have ruled the other way....

"The point of *Norfolk & Western* is that when a company fails to comply with a labor contract it violates 'law'.... If RFE/RL had not complied with the collective bargaining agreement in this case, if it had retained plaintiffs despite the mandatory retirement provision, the company would have violated the German laws standing behind such contracts, as well as the decisions of the Munich Labor Court. In the words of § 623(f)(1), RFE/RL's 'compliance with [the Act] would cause such employer ... to violate the laws of the country in which such workplace is located.' Domestic employers of course would never face a comparable situation; the Supremacy Clause of the Constitution would force any applicable state laws to give way ... and provisions in collective bargaining agreements contrary to the Act would be superseded. Congressional legislation cannot, however, set aside the laws of foreign countries. When an overseas employer's obligations under foreign law collide with its obligations under the Age Discrimination in Employment Act, § 623(f)(1) quite sensibly solves the dilemma by relieving the employer of liability under the Act....

"... [C]onstruing the foreign laws exception in the Age Discrimination in Employment Act consistently with *Norfolk & Western* would not render the Act senseless. Just the opposite. That construction agrees with § 623(f)(1)'s evident purpose—to avoid placing overseas employers in the impossible position of having to conform to two inconsistent legal regimes, one imposed from the United States and the other imposed by the country in which the company operates.... We recognize that RFE/RL's collective bargaining agreement is legally enforceable, which necessarily means that breaching the agreement in order to comply with the Act would, in the language of § 623(f)(1), 'cause' RFE/RL 'to violate the laws of' Germany.

"Plaintiffs complain that RFE/RL could have bargained harder for a change in the labor contract. But application of § 623(f)(1) does not depend on such considerations. The collective bargaining agreement here was valid and enforceable at the time of plaintiffs' terminations, and RFE/RL had a legal duty to comply with it. There is not, nor could there be, any suggestion that RFE/RL agreed to the mandatory retirement provision in order to evade the Age Discrimination in Employment Act. Such provisions are, the evidence showed, common throughout the Federal Republic of Germany, and RFE/RL entered into this particular agreement before Congress extended the Act beyond our borders....

"*Reversed*."

ECKHARD KALANKE v. FREIE HANSESTADT BREMEN
(Case C-450/93, Eur.Ct.repts.1995 Page I-03051, European Court of Justice, 1995)

BACKGROUND: Paragraph 4 of the Landesgleichstellungsgesetz of November 20, 1990 (Bremen Law on Equal Treatment for Men and Women in the Public Service, Bremisches Gesetzblatt, p. 433, ["the LGG"]) provides: "Appointment, assignment to an official post and promotion (1) In the case of an appointment (including establishment as a civil servant or judge) which is not made for training purposes, women who have the same qualifications as men applying for the same post are to be given priority in sectors where they are under-represented. (2) In the case of an assignment to a position in a higher pay, remuneration and salary bracket, women who have the same qualifications as men applying for the same post are to be given priority if they are under-represented. This also applies in the case of assignment to a different official post and promotion. (3) ... (4) Qualifications are to be evaluated exclusively in accordance with the requirements of the occupation, post to be filled or career bracket. Specific experience and capabilities, such as those acquired as a result of family work, social commitment or unpaid activity, are part of the qualifications within the meaning of subparagraphs (1) and (2) if they are of use in performing the duties of the position in question. (5) There is under-representation if women do not make up at least half of the staff in the individual pay, remuneration and salary brackets in the relevant personnel group within a department. This also applies to the function levels provided for in the organization chart."

At the final stage of recruitment to a post of Section Manager in the Bremen Parks Department, two candidates, both in pay bracket III, were shortlisted: Mr. Kalanke, the plaintiff in the main proceedings, holder of a diploma in horticulture and landscape gardening, who had worked since 1973 as a horticultural employee in the Parks Department and acted as permanent assistant to the Section Manager; and Ms. Glissmann, holder of a diploma in landscape gardening since 1983 and also employed, since 1975, as a horticultural employee in the Parks Department. The Staff Committee refused to give its consent to Mr. Kalanke's promotion proposed by the Parks Department management. Reference to arbitration resulted in a recommendation in favor of Mr. Kalanke. The Staff Committee then stated that the arbitration had failed, and appealed to the conciliation board which, in a decision binding on the employer, considered that the two candidates were equally qualified and that priority should therefore be given, in accordance with the LGG, to the woman.

Before the Arbeitsgericht (Labour Court), Mr. Kalanke claimed that he was better qualified than Ms. Glissmann; a fact which the conciliation board had failed to recognize. He argued that, by reason of its quota system, the LGG was incompatible with the Bremen Constitution, with the Grundgesetz (German Basic Law) and with Paragraph 611a of the BGB (German Civil Code). His application was dismissed, however, by the Arbeitsgericht and again, on appeal, by the Landesarbeitsgericht (Regional Labour Court). The First Chamber of the Bundesarbeitsgericht, hearing the plaintiff's application for review on a point of law, considers that resolution of the dispute depends essentially on the applicability of the LGG. It accepts the Landesarbeitsgericht's finding that the two applicants were equally qualified for the post. Considering itself bound also by that court's finding that women are under-represented in the Parks Department, it holds that the conciliation board was obliged, under Paragraph 4(2) of the LGG, to refuse to agree to the plaintiff's appointment to the vacant post. It considers that the quota system is compatible with the German constitutional and statutory provisions referred to above. It notes a number of factors suggesting that such a system is not incompatible with the Directive. Since doubts remain in that regard, the Bundesarbeitsgericht has stayed the proceedings and sought a preliminary ruling from the ECJ.

THE COURT:

"The [German] national court asks, essentially, whether Article 2(1) and (4) of the Directive precludes national rules such as those in the present case....

"The purpose of the Directive is, as stated in Article 1(1), to put into effect in the Member States the principle of equal treatment for men and women as regards, inter alia, access to employment, including promotion. Article 2(1) states that the principle of equal treatment means that 'there shall be no discrimination whatsoever on grounds of sex either directly or indirectly'. A national rule that, where men and women who are candidates for the same promotion are equally qualified, women are automatically to be given priority in sectors where they are under-represented, involves discrimination on grounds of sex.

"It must, however, be considered whether such a national rule is permissible under Article 2(4), which provides that the Directive 'shall be without prejudice to measures to promote equal opportunity for men and women, in particular by removing existing inequalities which affect women's opportunities'. That provision is specifically and exclusively designed to allow measures which, although discriminatory in appearance, are in fact intended to eliminate or reduce actual instances of inequality which may exist in the reality of social life.... It thus permits national measures relating to access to employment, including promotion, which give a specific advantage to women with a view to improving their ability to compete on the labour market and to pursue a career on an equal footing with men....

"National rules which guarantee women absolute and unconditional priority for appointment or promotion go beyond promoting equal opportunities and overstep the limits of the exception in Article 2(4) of the Directive. Furthermore, in so far as it seeks to achieve equal representation of men and women in all grades and levels within a department, such a system substitutes for equality of opportunity as envisaged in Article 2(4) the result which is only to be arrived at by providing such equality of opportunity.

OPERATIVE PART

"On those grounds,
THE COURT,
In answer to the questions referred to it by the Bundesarbeitsgericht by order of 22 June 1993, hereby rules: Article 2(1) and (4) of Council Directive 76/207/EEC of 9 February 1976 on the implementation of the principle of equal treatment for men and women as regards access to employment, vocational training and promotion, and working conditions precludes national rules such as those in the present case which, where candidates of different sexes shortlisted for promotion are equally qualified, automatically give priority to women in sectors where they are under-represented, under-representation being deemed to exist when women do not make up at least half of the staff in the individual pay brackets in the relevant personnel group or in the function levels provided for in the organization chart."

HOCSMAN v. MINISTRE DE L'EMPLOI ET DE LA SOLIDARITE
2000 ECR I-6623 (Court of Justice of the European Communities 1999)

BACKGROUND: Dr. Hugo Fernando Hocsman received his medical diploma from the University of Buenos Aires, Argentina, in 1977. In 1980, his diploma was recognized by the Spanish Ministry of Universities and Research as being equivalent for academic and professional purposes to the Spanish basic medical qualification of Licenciado en Medicina y Cirurgia, and he was authorized to practice medicine in Spain on the same terms as a holder of the Spanish qualification. He has been registered as a member of the Barcelona Medical Association since 1981. He became a Spanish citizen in 1986, and acquired French citizenship in 1998, after commencement of these court proceedings in France. In 1982 he was awarded a qualification as specialist in urology by the Spanish Ministry, and a specialist diploma in urology by the University of Barcelona. He was employed in France as a hospital doctor under rules which allowed public establishments to do so where the employee held medical qualifications obtained outside the European Community, but was working under supervision. When those rules were repealed in 1995, Dr. Hocsman's contract could not be renewed, and he has been unemployed since late 1997. When he applied in 1996 for membership in the French medical association, he was rejected. He then applied to the French Minister of Health for individual authorization to practice his urology specialty, and was again rejected when his request was referred to the

Ministry of Employment and Solidarity. Dr. Hocsman appealed to the Tribunal Administratif, which held that the M.E.&S. ruling was correct, but did refer the question to the European Court of Justice for further review.

JUDGE JACOBS:

"Under Article 52 of the EC Treaty (now, after amendment, Article 43 EC) ... restrictions on the freedom of establishment of nationals of a Member State in the territory of another Member State shall be abolished ... (...'prohibited' in the amended version).

"Article 57 of the EC Treaty (now, after amendment, Article 47 EC) provides for the adoption of Council directives regarding the mutual recognition of qualifications and the coordination of national requirements for the taking-up and pursuit of self-employed activities in general. It goes on to specify: '3. In the case of the medical ... professions, the progressive abolition of restrictions shall be dependent upon coordination of the conditions for their exercise in the various Member States.'

"In the field of mutual recognition of medical diplomas and the coordination of laws relating to the practice of medicine, various [EC] Council directives have been in force since 1975. The legislation currently in force is Directive 93/16 (the Directive).

"Pursuant to Article 2 of the Directive, each Member State shall recognize the diplomas, certificates and other evidence of formal qualifications awarded to nationals of Member States by other Member States in accordance with Article 23 and which are listed in Article 3, by giving such qualifications, as far as the right to take up and pursue the activities of a doctor is concerned, the same effect in its territory as those which the member State itself awards.

"The list in Article 3 includes the Spanish Titulo de Licenciado en Medicina y Cirurgia. Article 23 provides that Member States are to require persons wishing to take up and pursue a medical profession to hold one of the qualifications in medicine referred to in Article 3 and lays down certain minimum criteria for the training to which that qualification attests; in particular, the course must comprise at least six years or 5500 hours of theoretical and practical instruction....

"Thus, under ... provisions of the Directive, one Member State must recognise a basic medical qualification awarded in another Member State provided that it meets certain minimum standards. The same holds for specialist qualifications meeting certain minimum standards, provided that the basic training stipulated by the Directive itself has been completed....

"I therefore take the view that, where a person holds a basic medical qualification from outside the Community and a specialist qualification granted by a Member State on the basis of its voluntary recognition of that basic qualification, other Member States are not required under the Directive to recognise either of those qualifications. I therefore now turn to consider the Treaty provisions….

"The Treaty itself already prohibits restrictions on freedom of establishment for Community nationals. The role of directives is to create a framework of common minimum standards within which mutual recognition of professional qualifications obtained within the Community becomes not only possible, but even compulsory. Thus the purpose of Article 57(3) of the EC Treaty is not to permit freedom of establishment for the medical professions in the first instance, but simply to ensure that systematic mutual recognition of qualifications does not take place without coordination of provisions governing the exercise of those professions. It does not supplant the basic right of freedom of establishment provided by Article 52 of the EC Treaty for all professions, whether medical or otherwise….

"Furthermore, a basic right under the Treaty does not lapse simply because a directive has been adopted in a particular professional area. As the Commission notes in its observations, it would be paradoxical if a directive could restrict freedom of establishment by taking away a right that certainly would have existed under the Treaty in the absence of that directive….

"[The] examination procedure must enable the authorities of the host Member State to assure themselves, on an objective basis, that the foreign diploma certifies that is holder has knowledge and qualifications which are, if not identical, at least equivalent to those certified by the national diploma. That assessment of the equivalence of the foreign diploma must be carried out exclusively in the light of the level of knowledge and qualifications which its holder can be assumed to possess in the light of that diploma, having regard to the nature and duration of the studies and practical training to which the diploma relates….

"If that examination of diplomas results in the finding that the knowledge and qualifications certified by the foreign diploma correspond to those required by the national provisions, the Member State must recognise that diploma as fulfilling the requirements laid down by its national provisions. If, on the other hand, the comparison reveals that the knowledge and qualifications certified by the foreign diploma and those required by the national provisions correspond only partially, the host Member State is entitled to require the person concerned to show that he has acquired the knowledge and qualifications which are lacking.

"In this regards, the competent national authorities must assess whether the knowledge acquired in the host Member State, either during a course of study or by way of practical experience, is sufficient in order to prove possession of the knowledge which is lacking….

"The Treaty rules on freedom of establishment apply to a person in Dr. Hocsman's position by virtue of his being, at the material time, a national of one Member State seeking to pursue his profession, for which he possesses qualifications, in another member State. Those rules require there be no restriction on such a person's freedom of establishment....

"It is clear, furthermore, that the Treaty provisions are intended to eliminate not only discrimination on grounds of nationality, but also obstacles to freedom of movement which may derive from differences in national requirements concerning qualifications....

"In view of all the above considerations, I am of the opinion that the question referred by the Tribunal Administratif, Chalons en Champagne, should be answered as follows: Where a Community national who possesses qualifications which give entitlement to practise medicine in one Member State moves to a second Member State and seeks authorisation to practise there, but recognition of those qualifications by the authorities of the second Member States is not compulsory under the relevant Community legislation, those authorities are required in accordance with Article 52 of the EC Treaty (now Article 43 EC) to take account of all of that person's relevant qualifications and experience when assessing whether such authorisation is to be granted. If such qualifications and experience do not correspond fully to the national requirements, the authorities of the second Member State should give the person concerned the opportunity to prove that he possesses the knowledge and qualifications lacking but may not impose any tests which are not proportionate for that purpose. If, on the basis of the assessment made, authorisation is refused, that refusal must be in a form which clearly indicates the reasons on which it is based and is capable of being made the subject of judicial proceedings in which its legality under Community law can be reviewed."

JIVRAJ v. HASHWAMI
[2011] UKSC 40 (United Kingdom Supreme Court 2011)

FACTS: In January 1981 Jivraj and Hashwami signed a joint venture agreement ("JVA") establishing a world-wide real estate business. The JVA included an arbitration clause that required the arbitrators chosen to be members of the Ismaili religious community, of which both parties were members and which had its own conciliation and arbitration organization. Over the next several years, the business acquired substantial holdings in Canada, Pakistan, the UK, and the USA. When the parties agreed to end their JVA in 1988, they appointed a three-man conciliation panel to supervise the division of the JVA's assets. The three panel members were all from the Ismaili community, but by February 1990, were unable to resolve all of the differences between the parties. They then agreed to submit the remaining issues to a single

Ismaili, Zaher Ahamed. He provided a determination in December 1993, but disputes still remained when he resigned in 1995. Hashwami claimed there was still a balance due him, and Jivraj claimed that Hashwami had failed to declare some tax liabilities, for which Jivraj might be liable.

On July 31, 2008, Hashwami's lawyers wrote to Jivraj, asserting a claim for $1,412,494—plus interest compounded since 1994—totaling $4,403,817. The letter said that Hashwami had appointed Sir Anthony Coleman as his arbitrator pursuant to the original JVA arbitration clause, and that if Jivraj failed to appoint his arbitrator within seven days, the UK's 1996 Arbitration Act specified that Coleman would be the sole arbitrator of their dispute. Although Coleman was not a member of the Ismaili community, Hashwami claimed that that requirement in the JVA had been rendered void when the UK adopted its 1998 Human Rights Act ("HRA"), prohibiting religious discrimination in employment. Jivrai responded by filing an action in the Commercial Court, asking that the appointment of Coleman be declared invalid. Hashwami requested an order declaring Coleman as the sole arbitrator. Finding that the 1998 HRA did not apply, the trial judge ruled for Jivrai. The three-judge panel of the Court of Appeal reversed that decision. Jivrai appealed.

JUDGMENT by *LORD CLARKE, with whom LORD PHILLIPS, LORD WALKER and LORD DYSON agree*:

"It is common ground, at any rate in this class of case, that there is a contract between the parties and the arbitrator or arbitrators appointed under a contract and that his or their services are rendered pursuant to that contract. It is not suggested that such a contract provides for 'employment under a contract of service or of apprenticeship'. The question is whether it provides for 'employment under a contract personally to do any work'. There is in my opinion some significance in the fact that the definition does not simply refer to a contract to do work but to 'employment under' such a contract. I would answer the question in the negative on the ground that the role of an arbitrator is not naturally described as employment under a contract personally to do work. That is because his role is not naturally described as one of employment at all. I appreciate that there is an element of circularity in that approach but the definition is of 'employment' and this approach is consistent with the decided cases.

"Given the provenance of the Regulations, it is appropriate to consider first the decisions of the Court of Justice. The most important of these is perhaps *Allonby v Accrington and Rossendale College* (Case C-256/01) [2004] ICR 1328....

"In *Allonby* the court addressed an equal pay claim by a college lecturer who had been dismissed by the college and then re-engaged, ostensibly as a self-employed sub-contractor supplied by an agency. For the purposes of article 141(1) of the EC Treaty, the court drew a clear distinction between 'workers' and 'independent suppliers of services'. It discussed the concept of worker within the meaning of article 141(1) between paras 62 and 72, which included the following:

'62. The criterion on which article 141(1) EC is based is the comparability of the work done by workers of each sex: see, to that effect, Defrenne v Sabena (No 2) [1978] ECR 1365.... Accordingly, for the purpose of the comparison provided for by article 141(1) EC, only women and men who are workers within the meaning of that article can be taken into consideration.

63. In that connection, it must be pointed out that there is no single definition of worker in Community law: it varies according to the area in which the definition is to be applied....

64. The term "worker" within the meaning of article 141(1) EC is not expressly defined in the EC Treaty. It is therefore necessary, in order to determine its meaning, to apply the generally recognised principles of interpretation, having regard to its context and to the objectives of the Treaty....

66. Accordingly, the term "worker" used in article 141(1) EC cannot be defined by reference to the legislation of the member states but has a Community meaning. Moreover, it cannot be interpreted restrictively.

67. For the purposes of that provision, there must be considered as a worker a person who, for a certain period of time, performs services for and under the direction of another person in return for which he receives remuneration....

68. Pursuant to the first paragraph of article 141(2) EC, for the purpose of that article, 'pay' means the ordinary basic or minimum wage or salary and any other consideration, whether in cash or in kind, which the worker receives directly or indirectly, in respect of his employment, from his employer. It is clear from that definition that the authors of the Treaty did not intend that the term 'worker', within the meaning of article 141(1) EC, should include independent providers of services who are not in a relationship of subordination with the person who receives the services....

69. The question whether such a relationship exists must be answered in each particular case having regard to all the factors and circumstances by which the relationship between the parties is characterised.

70. Provided that a person is a worker within the meaning of article 141(1) EC, the nature of his legal relationship with the other party to the employment relationship is of

no consequence in regard to the application of that article….

71. The formal classification of a self-employed person under national law does not exclude the possibility that a person must be classified as a worker within the meaning of article 141(1) EC if his independence is merely notional, thereby disguising an employment relationship within the meaning of that article.'

"On the basis of those materials I would accept Mr. Davies' submission that the Court of Justice draws a clear distinction between those who are, in substance, employed and those who are 'independent providers of services who are not in a relationship of subordination with the person who receives the services'. I see no reason why the same distinction should not be drawn for the purposes of the Regulations between those who are employed and those who are not notionally but genuinely self-employed. In the light of *Allonby,* there can be no doubt that that would be the correct approach to the near identical definition in section 1(6) of the Equal Pay Act 1970 and must remain the correct approach to the definition of employment in section 83(2) of the EA…. That definition is almost identical to the definition in regulation 2(3) of the Regulations and, since it applies to equal pay issues by virtue of sections 83(4), 80(2) and 64 of the EA, it must equally apply to the Regulations.

"In my opinion there is nothing in the domestic authorities which requires the court to come to any different conclusion….

"If the approach in *Allonby* is applied to a contract between the parties to an arbitration and the arbitrator (or arbitrators), it is in my opinion plain that the arbitrators' role is not one of employment under a contract personally to do work. Although an arbitrator may be providing services for the purposes of VAT and he of course receives fees for his work, and although he renders personal services which he cannot delegate, he does not perform those services or earn his fees for and under the direction of the parties as contemplated in para 67 of *Allonby*. He is rather in the category of an independent provider of services who is not in a relationship of subordination with the parties who receive his services, as described in para 68.

"The arbitrator is in critical respects independent of the parties. His functions and duties require him to rise above the partisan interests of the parties and not to act in, or so as to further, the particular interests of either party. As the International Chamber of Commerce … puts it, he must determine how to resolve their competing interests. He is in no sense in a position of subordination to the parties; rather the contrary. He is in effect a 'quasi-judicial adjudicator.'…

"In England his role is spelled out in the 1996 Act. By section 33, he has a duty to act fairly and impartially as between the parties and to adopt procedures suitable to the circumstances of the particular case so as to provide a fair means of determination of the issues between the parties.

Section 34 provides that, subject to the right of the parties to agree any matter, it is for the arbitrator to decide all procedural matters.... Section 40 provides that the parties shall do all things necessary for the proper and expeditious conduct of the arbitration, which includes complying with any order of the arbitrator, whether procedural or otherwise. Once an arbitrator has been appointed, at any rate in the absence of agreement between them, the parties effectively have no control over him. Unless the parties agree, an arbitrator may only be removed in exceptional circumstances: *see* sections 23 and 24. The court was referred to many other statutory provisions in other parts of the world and indeed many other international codes, including the UNCITRAL (United Nations Commission on International Trade Law) Model Law on International Commercial Arbitration 1985, the ICC Rules and the London Court of International Arbitration ... Rules to similar effect.

"The Regulations themselves include provisions which would be wholly inappropriate as between the parties and the arbitrator or arbitrators. For example, regulation 22(1) provides: 'Anything done by a person in the course of his employment shall be treated for the purposes of these Regulations as done by his employer as well as by him, whether or not it was done with the employer's knowledge or approval.' It is evident that such a provision could not apply to an arbitrator....

"For these reasons I prefer the conclusion of the judge to that of the Court of Appeal. I agree with the judge that the Regulations are not applicable to the selection, engagement or appointment of arbitrators. It follows that I would hold that no part of clause 8 of the JVA is invalid by reason of the Regulations and would allow the appeal on this ground.

"*Genuine occupational requirement*

"If the above conclusion is correct, this point does not arise but it was fully argued and I will briefly consider it. The question considered by the judge was whether, if regulation 6(1)(a) or (c) would otherwise apply, it is prevented from applying by regulation 7(1) and (3). It will be recalled that, by regulation 7(1), regulations 6(1)(a) and (c) do not apply where regulation 7(3) applies....

"Those provisions were made in accordance with the exceptions in relation to occupational requirements made by article 4 of the Directive, which provides:
    '1. Notwithstanding article 2(1) and (2), member states may provide that a difference of treatment which is based on a characteristic related to any of the grounds referred to in article 1 shall not constitute discrimination where, by reason of the nature of the particular occupational activities concerned or of the context in which they are carried out, such a characteristic constitutes a genuine and determining occupational

requirement, provided that the objective is legitimate and the requirement is proportionate.'…

"In my opinion the judge was justified in concluding that the requirement of an Ismaili arbitrator can be regarded as a genuine occupational requirement on the basis that it was not only genuine but both legitimate and justified, so that requirement (2) was satisfied. As to requirement (3), the judge said .. that, had proportionality been a live issue, having regard to the parties' freedom in section 1 of the 1996 Act … he would have held that article 8 of the JVA was proportionate.

"I prefer the approach of the judge. For the reasons given earlier, I am not persuaded that the test is one of necessity. The question is whether, in all the circumstances the provision that all the arbitrators should be respected members of the Ismaili community was legitimate and justified. In my opinion it was. The approach of the Court of Appeal seems to me to be too legalistic and technical. The parties could properly regard arbitration before three Ismailis as likely to involve a procedure in which the parties could have confidence and as likely to lead to conclusions of fact in which they could have particular confidence.

"For these reasons I would, if necessary, have allowed the appeal on the basis that article 8 was a GOR within regulation 7(3). This conclusion makes it unnecessary to consider whether it also satisfied regulation 7(2)….

"*CONCLUSION*

"I would allow the appeal."

NATIONAL LEGAL SERVICES AUTH. v. UNION OF INDIA & ORS.
Writ Petition (Civil) NO.400 of 2012 (Supreme Court of India)

BACKGROUND: This case is concerned with the grievances of members of the Transgender Community, who seek a legal declaration of their gender identity other than the one assigned to them, male or female, at the time of birth. Their claim is that non-recognition of their gender identity violates Articles 14 and 21 of the Constitution of India. Hijras/Eunuchs, who also fall in that group, claim legal status as a third gender with all legal and constitutional protection. The National Legal Services Authority, constituted under the Legal Services Authority Act, 1997, to provide free legal services to the weaker and other marginalized sections of society, has come forward to advocate their cause, by filing Writ Petition No. 400 of 2012—directly with the Supreme Court. Poojaya Mata Nasib Kaur Ji Women Welfare Society, a registered association, has also preferred Writ Petition No. 604 of 2013, seeking similar reliefs in respect of the Kinnar ("TG") community. Counsel traced the historical background of the third gender identity in India and the position accorded to them in Hindu Mythology, Vedic and Puranic literatures, and the prominent role played by them in the royal courts of the Islamic world, etc. Reference was also made to the repealed 1871 Criminal Tribes Act and the inhuman manner by which TGs were treated at the time of the British Colonial rule. Counsel also submitted that various International Forums and U.N. bodies have recognized their gender identity, and referred to the Yogyakarta Principles, pointing out that those principles have been recognized by various countries around the world. Reference was also made to a few legislations giving recognition to trans-sexual persons in other countries. Counsel also argued that non-recognition of gender identity of the TG community violates the fundamental rights guaranteed to them as citizens of India.

JUSTICE K.S.RADHAKRISHNAN:

"Seldom, our society realizes or cares to realize the trauma, agony and pain which the members of Transgender community undergo, nor appreciates the innate feelings of the members of the Transgender community, especially of those whose mind and body disown their biological sex. Our society often ridicules and abuses the Transgender community and in public places like railway stations, bus stands, schools, workplaces, malls, theatres, hospitals, they are sidelined and treated as untouchables, forgetting the fact that the moral failure lies in the society's unwillingness to contain or embrace different gender identities and expressions, a mindset which we have to change….

"Transgender is generally described as an umbrella term for persons whose gender identity, gender expression or behavior does not conform to their biological sex. TG may also takes in persons who do not identify with their sex assigned at birth, which include Hijras/Eunuchs who, in this writ petition, describe themselves as 'third gender' and they do not identify as either male or female…. TG also includes persons who intend to undergo Sex Re-Assignment Surgery (*SRS*) or have undergone *SRS* to align their biological sex with their gender identity in order to become male or female. They are generally called transsexual persons. Further, there are persons who like to cross-dress in clothing of opposite gender, i.e. transvestites. Resultantly, the term 'transgender', in contemporary usage, has become an umbrella term that is used to describe a wide range of identities and experiences, including but not limited to pre-operative, post-operative and non-operative transsexual people, who strongly identify with the gender opposite to their biological sex; male and female….

"Gender identity is one of the most-fundamental aspects of life which refers to a person's intrinsic sense of being male, female or transgender or transsexual person. A person's sex is usually assigned at birth, but a relatively small group of persons may born with bodies which incorporate both or certain aspects of both male and female physiology. At times, genital anatomy problems may arise in certain persons, their innate perception of themselves, is not in conformity with the sex assigned to them at birth and may include pre and post-operative transsexual persons and also persons who do not choose to undergo or do not have access to operation and also include persons who cannot undergo successful operation. Countries, all over the world, including India, are grappled with the question of attribution of gender to persons who believe that they belong to the opposite sex. Few persons undertake surgical and other procedures to alter their bodies and physical appearance to acquire gender characteristics of the sex which conform to their perception of gender, leading to legal and social complications since official record of their gender at birth is found to be at variance with the assumed gender identity. Gender identity refers to each person's deeply felt internal and individual experience of gender, which may or may not correspond with the sex assigned at birth, including the personal sense of the body which may involve a freely chosen, modification of bodily appearance or functions by medical, surgical or other means and other expressions of gender, including dress, speech and mannerisms. Gender identity, therefore, refers to an individual's self-identification as a man, woman, transgender or other identified category.

"Sexual orientation refers to an individual's enduring physical, romantic and/or emotional attraction to another person. Sexual orientation includes transgender and gender-variant people with heavy sexual orientation and their sexual orientation may or may not change during or after gender transmission, which also includes homo-sexuals, bysexuals, heterosexuals, asexual etc. Gender identity and sexual orientation, as already indicated, are different concepts. Each person's self-defined sexual orientation and gender identity is integral to their personality and is one of the most basic aspects of self-determination, dignity and freedom and no one shall be forced to undergo medical procedures, including *SRS*, sterilization or hormonal therapy, as a requirement for legal recognition of their gender identity….

"[The] United Nations has been instrumental in advocating the protection and promotion of rights of sexual minorities, including transgender persons. Article 6 of the Universal Declaration of Human Rights, 1948 and Article 16 of the International Covenant on Civil and Political Rights, 1966 (ICCPR) recognize that every human being has the inherent right to live and this right shall be protected by law and that no one shall be arbitrarily denied of that right. Everyone shall have a right to recognition, everywhere as a person before the law. Article 17 of the ICCPR states that no one shall be subjected to arbitrary or unlawful interference with his privacy, family, home or correspondence, nor to unlawful attacks on his honour and reputation and that everyone has the right to protection of law against such interference or attacks. [The] International Commission of Jurists and the International Service for Human Rights on behalf of a coalition of human rights organizations, took a project to develop a set of international legal principles on the application of international law to human rights violations based on sexual orientation and sexual identity to bring greater clarity and coherence to State's human rights obligations. A distinguished group of human rights experts has drafted, developed, discussed and reformed the principles in a meeting held at Gadjah Mada University in Yogyakarta, Indonesia from 6 to 9 November, 2006, which [] unanimously adopted the Yogyakarta Principles on the application of International Human Rights Law in relation to Sexual Orientation and Gender Identity. Yogyakarta Principles address a broad range of human rights standards and their application to issues of sexual orientation gender identity.... UN bodies, Regional Human Rights Bodies, National Courts, Government Commissions and the Commissions for Human Rights, Council of Europe, etc. have endorsed the Yogyakarta Principles and have considered them as an important tool for identifying the obligations of States to respect, protect and fulfill the human rights of all persons, regardless of their gender identity....

"We have referred exhaustively to the various judicial pronouncements and legislations on the international arena to highlight the fact that the recognition of 'sex identity gender' of persons, and 'guarantee to equality and non-discrimination' on the ground of gender identity or expression is increasing and gaining acceptance in international law and [should], therefore, be applied in India as well....

"Transgender people, as a whole, face multiple forms of oppression in this country. Discrimination is so large and pronounced, especially in the field of health care, employment, education, leave aside social exclusion.... Social exclusion and discrimination on the ground of gender stating that one does not conform to the binary gender (male/female) does prevail in India....

"Above-mentioned International Human Rights instruments which are being followed by various countries in the world are aimed to protect the human rights of transgender people since it has been noticed that transgenders/transsexuals often face serious human rights violations, such as harassment in work place, hospitals, places of public conveniences, market places, theaters, railway stations, bus stands, and so on.

"Indian Law, on the whole, only recognizes the paradigm of binary genders of male and female, based on a person's sex assigned by birth, which permits gender system, including the law relating to marriage, adoption, inheritance, succession and taxation and welfare legislations.... Unfortunately we have no legislation in this country dealing with the rights of transgender community. Due to the absence of suitable legislation protecting the rights of the members of the transgender community, they are facing discrimination in various areas and hence the necessity to follow the International Conventions to which India is a party and to give due respect to other non-binding International Conventions and principles.... Courts in India would apply the rules of International law according to the principles of comity of Nations, unless they are overridden by clear rules of domestic law…. India has ratified the above mentioned covenants, hence, those covenants can be used by the municipal courts as an aid to the Interpretation of Statutes by applying the Doctrine of Harmonization. But, certainly, if the Indian law is not in conflict with the International covenants, particularly pertaining to human rights, to which India is a party, the domestic court can apply those principles in the Indian conditions. The Interpretation of International Conventions is governed by Articles 31 and 32 of the Vienna Convention on the Law of Treaties of 1969….

"Article 14 of the Constitution of India states that the State shall not deny to 'any person' equality before the law or the equal protection of the laws within the territory of India. Equality includes the full and equal enjoyment of all rights and freedom. Right to equality has been declared as the basic feature of the Constitution and treatment of equals as unequals or unequals as equals will be violative of the basic structure of the Constitution. Article 14 of the Constitution also ensures equal protection and hence a positive obligation on the State to ensure equal protection of laws by bringing in necessary social and economic changes, so that everyone including TGs may enjoy equal protection of laws and nobody is denied such protection. Article 14 does not restrict the word 'person' and its application only to male or female. Hijras/transgender persons who are neither male/female fall within the expression 'person' and, hence, entitled to legal protection of laws in all spheres of State activity, including employment, healthcare, education as well as equal civil and citizenship rights, as enjoyed by any other citizen of this country….

"Article 19(1) of the Constitution guarantees certain fundamental rights, subject to the power of the State to impose restrictions from exercise of those rights. The rights conferred by Article 19 are not available to any person who is not a citizen of India. Article 19(1) guarantees those great basic rights which are recognized and guaranteed as the natural rights inherent in the status of the citizen of a free country….

"Principles referred to above clearly indicate that the freedom of expression guaranteed under Article 19(1)(a) includes the freedom to express one's chosen gender identity through varied ways and means by way of expression, speech, mannerism, clothing etc….

"We, therefore, hold that values of privacy, self-identity, autonomy and personal integrity are fundamental rights guaranteed to members of the transgender community under Article 19(1)(a) of the Constitution of India and the State is bound to protect and recognize those rights….

"We, therefore, conclude that discrimination on the basis of sexual orientation or gender identity includes any discrimination, exclusion, restriction or preference which has the effect of nullifying or transposing equality by the law or the equal protection of laws guaranteed under our

Constitution, and hence we are inclined to give various directions to safeguard the constitutional rights of the members of the TG community."

CONCURRING OPINION by JUSTICE A.K. SIKRI:

"I have carefully, and with lot of interest, gone through the perspicuous opinion of brother Radhakrishnan, J. I am entirely in agreement with the discussion contained in the said judgment on all the cardinal issues that have arisen for consideration in these proceedings. At the same time, having regard to the fact that the issues my involved are of seminal importance, I am also inclined to pen down my thoughts....

"Indubitably, the issue of choice of gender identify has all the trappings of a human rights. That apart, as it becomes clear from the reading of the judgment of my esteemed Brother Radhakrishnan, J., the issue is not limited to the exercise of choice of gender/sex. Many rights which flow from this choice also come into play, inasmuch not giving them the status of a third gender results in depriving the community of TGs of many of their valuable rights and privileges which other persons enjoy as citizens of this Country. There is also deprivation of social and cultural participation which results into eclipsing their access to education and health services. Radhakrishnan, J. has exhaustively described the term 'Transgender' as an umbrella term which embraces within itself a wide range of identities and experiences including but not limited to pre-operative/post-operative trans sexual people who strongly identify with the gender opposite to their biological sex i.e. male/female. Therein, the history of transgenders in India is also traced and while doing so, there is mention of upon the draconian legislation enacted during the British Rule, known as Criminal Tribes Act, 1871 which treated, per se, the entire community of Hizra persons as innately 'criminals', 'addicted to the systematic commission of non-bailable offences'.

"With these introductory remarks, I revert to the two facets of pivotal importance mentioned above. Before embarking on the discussion, I may clarify that my endeavour would be not to repeat the discussion contained in the judgment of my Brother Radhakrishnan, J., as I agree with every word written therein. However, at times, if some of the observations are re-narrated, that would be only with a view to bring continuity in the thought process....

"There is thus a universal recognition that human rights are rights that 'belong' to every person, and do not depend on the specifics of the individual or the relationship between the right-holder and the right-grantor. Moreover, human rights exist irrespective of the question whether they are granted or recognized by the legal and social system within which we live. They are devices to evaluate these existing arrangements: ideally, these arrangements should not violate human rights. In other words, human rights are moral, pre-legal rights. They are not granted by people nor can they be taken away by them....

"The basic spirit of our Constitution is to provide each and every person of the nation equal opportunity to grow as a human being, irrespective of race, caste, religion, community and social status…. The Constitution, although drafted by the Constituent Assembly, was meant for the people of India and that is why it is given by the people to themselves as expressed in the opening words 'We the People'. What is the most people important gift to the common person given by this Constitution is 'fundamental rights' which may be called Human Rights as well.

"The concept of equality in Article 14 so also the meaning of the words 'life', 'liberty' and 'law' in Article 21 have been considerably enlarged by judicial decisions. Anything which is not 'reasonable, just and fair' is not treated to be equal and is, therefore, violative of Article 14….

"A most remarkable feature of this expansion of Art.21 is that many of the non-justiciable Directive Principles embodied in Part IV of the Constitution have now been resurrected as enforceable fundamental rights by the magic wand of judicial activism, playing on Art.21….

"A corollary of this development is that while so long the negative language of Art.21 and use of the word 'deprived' was supposed to impose upon the State the negative duty not to interfere with the life or liberty of an individual without the sanction of law, the width and amplitude of this provision has now imposed a positive obligation … upon the State to take steps for ensuring to the individual a better enjoyment of his life and dignity….

"The common golden thread which passes through all these pronouncements is that Art.21 guarantees enjoyment of life by all citizens of this country with dignity, viewing th[ese] human rights in terms of human development….

"In fact, the recognition that every individual has [a] fundamental right to achieve the fullest potential is founded on the principle that all round growth of an individual leads to common public good…. A person who is born with a particular sex and [is] forced to grow up identifying with that sex, and not a sex that his/her psychological behavior identifies with, faces innumerable obstacles in growing up….

"For these reasons, we are of the opinion that even in the absence of any statutory regime in this country, a person has a constitutional right to get the recognition as male or female after SRS, which was not only his/her gender characteristic but has become his/her physical form as well….

"We are of the firm opinion that by recognizing such TGs as third gender, they would be able to enjoy their human rights, to which they are largely deprived of for want of this recognition….

"By recognizing TGs as third gender, this Court is not only upholding the rule of law but also advancing justice to the class, so far deprived of their legitimate natural and constitutional rights.

It is, therefore, the only just solution which ensures justice not only to TGs but to the society as well....

"We, therefore, declare (1) Hijras, Eunuchs, apart from binary gender, be treated as 'third gender' for the purpose of safeguarding their rights under Part III of our Constitution and the laws made by the Parliament and the State Legislature. (2) Transgender persons' right to decide their self-identified gender is also upheld and the Centre and State Governments are directed to grant legal recognition of their gender identity such as male, female or as third gender. (3) We direct the Centre and the State Governments to take steps to treat them as socially and educationally backward classes of citizens and extend all kinds of reservation in cases of admission in educational institutions and for public appointments. (4) Centre and State Governments are directed to operate separate HIV Sero-survellance Centres since Hijras/Transgenders face several sexual health issues. (5) Centre and State Governments should seriously address the problems being faced by Hijras/Transgenders such as fear, shame, gender dysphoria, social pressure, depression, suicidal tendencies, social stigma, etc. and any insistence for SRS for declaring one's gender is immoral and illegal. (6) Centre and State Governments should take proper measures to provide medical care to TGs in the hospitals and also provide them separate public toilets and other facilities. (7) Centre and State Governments should also take steps for framing various social welfare schemes for their betterment. (8) Centre and State Governments should take steps to create public awareness so that TGs will feel that they are also part and parcel of the social life and be not treated as untouchables. (9) Centre and the State Governments should also take measures to regain their respect and place in the society which once they enjoyed in our cultural and social life.

"We are informed an Expert Committee has already been constituted to make an in-depth study of the problems faced by the Transgender community and suggest measures that can be taken by the Government to ameliorate their problems and to submit its report with recommendations within three months of its constitution. Let the recommendations be examined based on the legal declaration made in this Judgment and implemented within six months.

"Writ Petitions are, accordingly, allowed, as above."

OLOKA-ONYANGO & 9 ORS. v. ATTORNEY GENERAL
Constitutional Petition No. 08 OF 2014 (Constitutional Court of Uganda, 2014)

BACKGROUND: Professor Oloka-Onyango, seven other individuals, the Human Rights Awareness and Promotion Forum, and the Centre for Health Human Rights & Development filed this petition, alleging that the Anti-Homosexuality Act of 2014 violated the Ugandan Constitution in 14 specific ways:

(a) That the enactment of the Anti-Homosexuality Act 2014 by the 9th Parliament on 20th December 2013, without quorum in the house was in contravention of Articles 2, 88 and 94 and Rule 23 of the Parliamentary Rules of Procedure; (b) That the Act, in criminalising consensual same sex/gender sexual activity among adults in private, is in contravention of the right to equality before the law guaranteed under Articles 2, 21 and 27; (c) That the Act, in criminalising touching by persons of the same sex creates an offence that is overly broad and is in contravention of the principle of legality under Articles 2, 28, 42 and 44; (d) That the Act, in imposing a maximum life sentence for Homosexuality provides for a disproportionate punishment for the offence in contravention of the right to equality and freedom from cruel, inhuman and degrading punishment guaranteed under Articles 2, 24 and 44; (e) That the Act, in criminalising consensual same sex/gender sexual activity among adults in which one is a person living with HIV is in contravention of the freedom from discrimination guaranteed under Articles 2 and 21; (f) That the Act, in criminalising consensual same sex/gender sexual activity among adults in which one is a person with disability is in contravention of the freedom from discrimination and the right to dignity of persons with disabilities guaranteed under Articles 2, 21 and 35; (g) That the Act, in subjecting persons charged with aggravated homosexuality to a compulsory HIV test, is in contravention of the freedom from discrimination, the right to privacy, freedom from cruel, inhuman and degrading treatment and the right to the presumption of innocence guaranteed under Articles 2, 21, 24, 27, 28, 44 and 45; (h) That the Act, in imposing a maximum life sentence for attempted aggravated homosexuality, provides for a disproportionate punishment for the offence in contravention of the right to equality, and the freedom from cruel, inhuman and degrading punishment guaranteed under Articles 2, 21, 24 and 44; (i) That the Act, in criminalising aiding, abetting, counseling, procuring and promotion of homosexuality, create offences that are overly broad, penalise, legitimate debate, professional counsel, HIV-related service provision and access to health services, in contravention of the principle of legality, the freedoms of expression, thought, assembly and association, and the right to civic participation guaranteed under Principle XIV of the National Objectives and Directive Principles of State Policy, and Articles 2, 8A, 28(1), (3b), & 12, 29(1), 36, 38(2), 42 and 44(c) of the Constitution; (j) That Section 8 of the Anti-Homosexuality Act 2014, criminalising conspiracy by any means of false pretence or other fraudulent means, is vague, uncertain and ambiguous and in contravention of the principal of legality under Articles 2, 28, 42, 44; (k) That the Act, in classifying houses or rooms as brothels merely on the basis of occupation by homosexuals, creates an offence that is overly broad and in contravention of the principle of legality guaranteed under Article 28; and is further in contravention of the rights to property and privacy guaranteed under Articles 2, 21, 26, 27 and 28 of the Constitution; (l) That the spirit of the Act, by promoting and encouraging homophobia, amounts to institutionalised promotion of a culture of hatred and constitutes a contravention of the right to dignity and is inconsistent with and in contravention of the National Objectives and Directive Principles of State Policy and Articles 2, 8A, 24 and 44; (m) That the Act, by encouraging homophobia and stigmatisation, is in contravention of the duty of the government to respect, protect and promote the rights and freedoms of persons likely to be affected by the Act as stipulated under Articles 2, 20, 21, 32; (n)That the Act, in criminalising consensual same sex/gender sexual activity among adults, is in contravention of obligations with regards to the rights guaranteed under international Human Rights instruments ratified or acceded by Uganda, including the African Charter on Human and People's Rights, the Protocol to the African Charter on Human and Peoples' Rights, the Rights of Women in Africa, the UN Covenant on Civil and Political Rights; and the UN Covenant on Economic, Social and Cultural Rights; and in contravention of the National Objectives and Directive Principles of State Policy, and Articles 2, 8A, 20, 45 and 287 of the Constitution.

Eleven issues were framed to be resolved by the Court. However, at the commencement of the hearing, counsel for both parties agreed with Court that it should first hear their arguments on the first issue—which could dispose of the whole petition, namely; "Whether the Anti-Homosexuality Act 2014, was enacted without quorum in the House in a manner that is inconsistent with and in contravention of Articles 2(1) & (2) and 88 of the Constitution of the Republic of Uganda 1995 and Rule 23 of the Parliamentary Rules of Procedure."

THE COURT:

"We have heard and considered the useful submissions made by both counsel and we are highly indebted to them. Though much has been said, two simple questions emerge for our answer on issue one: 1. Was the Anti Homosexuality Act passed in accordance with the law? 2. Whether the petitioners had proved that during the enacting process of the Anti Homosexuality Act, the Rt. Hon Speaker ignored to invoke Rule 23 when the Prime Minister and Hon. Betty Aol raised an objection that there was no quorum at the time the Bill was put to vote at the 2nd and 3rd reading as alleged?

"Answer to question one

"The petitioners in their petition and evidence allege that the Anti-Homosexuality Act was not passed in accordance with the Law. On the other hand, the respondent states that there is no evidence to prove that there was no Coram [quorum] and that the burden to prove that fact rested with the Petitioners.

"We agree with learned counsel Mutesi Patricia that the burden of proof of that fact rested with the Petitioners who alleged the violation of the various provisions of the Constitution and Rule 23 of the Rules of Procedure of Parliament.

"An exception to the above Rule is that where one has alleged a fact and the person against whom the fact is alleged, does not deny, he is presumed to have accepted that fact. The respondent was served with the Petition and the accompanying affidavits of Hon. Fox Odoi and Professor Ogenga Latigo, among others, alleging violation of the Constitution and Rules of Procedure in the process of passing of the Anti-Homosexuality Act.

"In his reply, and the accompanying affidavit of Mr. Bireije, Commissioner for Civil Litigation, the respondent did not specifically deny the said allegations of violation and lack of Coram.

"The law applicable to determine what happens when there is no specific denial is the Civil Procedure Act … and the Civil Procedure Rule …. Rule 23 of the Constitutional Court (Petitions and References) Rules … empowers this court to apply the Civil Procedure Act and Rules thereunder to regulate the practice and procedure in Petitions and References with such modifications as the Court may consider necessary in the interest of Justice.

"Order VIII Rule 3 of the Civil procedure rules provides: 'Every allegation of fact in the plaint, if not denied specifically or by necessary implication or stated to be not admitted in the pleading of the opposite party, shall be taken to be admitted except as against a person under disability but the court may in its discretion require any facts so admitted to be proved otherwise than by that admission'.

"In view of the above Rule and in the absence of a specific denial by the respondent in his pleadings with regard to issue one, we are unable to accept the submission of learned counsel Patricia Mutesi that the petitioners had a burden to do more than what they did. The evidence contained in the affidavit (including the annexure of the Hansard), of Hon. Fox Odoi stood strong and unchallenged. In the case of H.G. Gandesha & Another vs G.J Lutaya … [the] Court observed that where facts are sworn to an affidavit, the burden to deny them is on the other party. Failure to do that, [and] they are presumed to have been accepted.

"It is clear from that evidence, that at least three Members of Parliament including the Prime Minister expressed concern about the issue of lack of Coram.

"[The] Court is enjoined under Section 56 of the Evidence Act to take judicial notice of the following fact ... 'c. The course of Proceeding of Parliament and of councils or other authorities for the purpose of making laws and Regulations published under any law for the time being relating thereto.... f. The accession to office, names, titles, functions and signatures of the persons filling for the time being of any public office in any part of Uganda if the fact the their appointment to that office is notified in the gazette'....

"Coram is defined in the Rules of Procedure of Parliament to mean at least a third of all the members entitled to vote. As indicated above, Court may take judicial notice of the Uganda Gazette where Members of Parliament representing different Constituencies are published and Court may easily ascertain what a third of the eligible voting members is equal to.

"It is our decision that the respondent having been presumed to have admitted the allegations of the Petitioners in the petition that there was no Coram, we find that on the balance of probabilities, the Petitioners have proved that at the time the Prime Minister (twice) and Hon. Betty Aol, raised the objection that there was no Coram and Coram was never established, and that was in contravention of the Constitution and the Rules.

"Answer to question 2

"We find that the respondent in his pleadings and submissions did not even attempt to suggest that the Rt. Hon. Speaker responded in any way to the objection raised that there was no Coram.

"Rule 23 of the Parliamentary Rules of Procedure require the Speaker, even without prompting by any Member of Parliament to ensure that Coram exists before a law is passed. We note that the Speaker was prompted three times by Hon. Mbabazi and Hon. Aol to the effect that there was no Coram in the house. The speaker was obliged to ensure compliance with the provisions of Rule 23 of the Rules of Procedure of Parliament. She did not.

"Parliament as a law making body should set standards for compliance with the Constitutional provisions and with its own Rules. The Speaker ignored the Law and proceeded with the passing of the Act. We agree with Counsel Opiyo that the enactment of the law is a process, and if any of the stages therein is flawed, that vitiates the entire process and the law that is enacted as a result of it.

"We have therefore no hesitation in holding that there was no Coram in Parliament when the Act was passed, [and] that the Speaker acted illegally in neglecting to address the issue of lack of Coram.

"We come to the conclusion that she acted illegally. Following the decision of Makula International vs. Cardinal Emmanuel Nsubuga, ... failure to obey the Law (Rules) rendered the whole enacting process a nullity. It is an illegality that this Court cannot sanction.

"In the result, we uphold issue one in favour of the petitioners and grant them the following declarations under prayer (e): i. That the act of the 9th Parliament in enacting the Anti-Homosexuality Act 2014 on 20 December 2013 without quorum in the House is inconsistent with and in contravention of Articles 2 … and 88 of the Constitution … and Rule 23 of the Parliamentary Rules of Procedure and thus null and void. ii. That the act of the Rt. Hon. Speaker of not entertaining the objection that there was no Coram was an illegality under Rule 23 of the Rules of Procedure which tainted the enacting process and rendered it a nullity. The Act itself so enacted by this reason is unconstitutional. The issue therefore ... disposes of the whole petition.

"Having found in the affirmative on Issue 1, we find that that has the effect of resolving the entire Petition. The Petition is, therefore, hereby allowed.

"We award the petitioners 50% of the taxed costs.

"That aside, in the course of the hearing, the respondent was aggrieved by our decision not to grant counsel for the respondent adjournment to enable her to correct further evidence. She indicated that the respondent intended to appeal against our decision and sought stay of the hearing under Rule 2(2) of the Rules of this Court pending the said intended appeal.

"We declined to give the said stay and he promised to give our reasons in this judgment. The above Rule talks of inherent powers of this court. In the absence of evidence that the appeal process had been commenced, we refused to invoke the said inherent powers.

"Dated at Kampala this...01st ....day of...August....2014."

CELANESE CANADA INC. v. MURRAY DEMOLITION CORP.
[2006] 2 SCR 189 (Supreme Court of Canada 2006)

BACKGROUND: Celanese sued Canadian Bearings for alleged industrial espionage (trying to steal trade secrets and other confidential business information). Following an *ex parte* application and hearing (only the Plaintiff appears before the judge), a judge granted Celanese an *Anton Piller* order (so named for the case in which the process originated) against Canadian Bearings. It was executed by an accounting firm. The search was overseen by an independent supervising solicitor (lawyer). The solicitors for Canadian Bearings—Borden Ladner Gervais ("BLG")—were present at the search, but later complained that they were not given adequate time to review the material, due to the large volume of electronic material and the fast pace of the search. Frequently, entire folders would be copied electronically without examination of individual documents. However, material that could be identified as potentially privileged was segregated into an electronic folder labelled "Borden Ladner Gervais." In all, about 1400 electronic documents thought relevant, but not then screened for potential solicitor-client privilege claims, were downloaded by the accounting firm onto a portable hard drive and copied onto CD-ROMs. These were placed in a plastic envelope, sealed, initialed by a BLG solicitor and the supervising solicitor, and given to the accounting firm. Contrary to the court's order, no list of the seized documents was made prior to their removal from the searched premises. A lawyer from the firm representing Celanese, Cassels Brock Blackwell ("CBB"), later directed the accounting firm to copy the envelope's contents. The seal was broken without the consent of Canadian Bearings or its law firm BLG, and the contents copied onto CBB's computer. A copy was also sent to Celanese's USA counsel, Kasowitz Benson Torres & Friedman ("KBTF"). When BLG learned that privileged documents had been transferred to CBB and KTBF, BLG demanded immediate return of the documents. Rather than doing so, CBB and KTBF advised BLG that they had deleted the documents claimed to be privileged. Canadian Bearings then moved to have both law firms disqualified from continuing to represent Celanese. The motion was initially denied, but on appeal the Divisional Court reversed that ruling. The Court of Appeal for Ontario set aside that decision, holding that Canadian Bearings had to prove a "real risk" of prejudicial use of the privileged information by the defendant's lawyers. Canadian Bearings then appealed to the Canadian Supreme Court. (It is not clear from the case why it is indexed under "Murray Demolition"—possibly a d.b.a. ["doing business as"] is involved somewhere.)

JUSTICE BINNIE:

"An *Anton Piller* order bears an uncomfortable resemblance to a private search warrant. No notice is given to the party against whom it is issued. Indeed, defendants usually first learn of them when they are served and executed, without having had an opportunity to challenge them or the evidence on which they were granted. The defendant may have no idea a claim is even pending. The order is not placed in the hands of a public authority for execution, but authorizes a private party to insist on entrance to the premises of its opponent to conduct a surprise search, the purpose of which is to seize and preserve evidence to further its claim in a private dispute. The only justification for such an extraordinary remedy is that the plaintiff has a strong *prima facie* case and can demonstrate that on the facts, absent such an order, there is a real possibility relevant evidence will be destroyed or otherwise made to disappear. The protection of the party against whom an *Anton Piller* order is issued ought to be threefold: a carefully drawn order which identifies the material to be seized and sets out safeguards to deal, amongst other things, with privileged documents; a vigilant court-appointed supervising solicitor who is independent of the parties; and a sense of responsible self-restraint on the part of those executing the order. In this case, unfortunately, none of those protections proved to be adequate to protect against the disclosure of relevant solicitor-client confidences. Inadequate protections had been written into the order. Those which had been were not properly respected. The vigilance of the supervising solicitor appears to have fallen short. Celanese's solicitors in the aftermath of the search seem to have lost sight of the fact that the limited purpose of the order was to *preserve* evidence not to rush to exploit it….

"This appeal thus presents a clash between two competing values—solicitor-client privilege and the right to select counsel of one's choice. The conflict must be resolved, it seems to me, on the basis that no one has the right to be represented by counsel who has had access to relevant solicitor-client confidences in circumstances where such access ought to have been anticipated and, without great difficulty, avoided and where such counsel has failed to rebut the presumption of a resulting risk of prejudice to the party against whom the *Anton Piller* order was made.

"This Court's decision in *MacDonald Estate* … makes it clear that prejudice will be presumed to flow from an opponent's access to relevant solicitor-client confidences…. Thus Spinka J. wrote that 'once it is shown by the client that there existed a previous relationship which is sufficiently related to the retainer from which it is sought to remove the solicitor, the court should infer that confidential information was imparted unless the solicitor satisfies the court that no information was imparted which could be relevant. This will be a difficult burden to discharge.'…

"The *Anton Piller* situation is somewhat different because the searching solicitors ought to have a record of exactly what was seized and what material, for which confidentiality is claimed, they subsequently looked at. Here again, rebuttal should be permitted, but rebuttable evidence should require the party who obtained access to disclose to the court what has been learned and the measures taken to avoid the presumed resulting prejudice. While all solicitor confidences are not of the same order of importance, the party who obtained the wrongful access is not entitled to have the court assume in its favour that such disclosure carried no risk of prejudice to its opponent, and therefore does not justify the removal of the solicitors. … I conclude, contrary to the view taken by the Court of Appeal, with respect, that Celanese and its lawyers *did* have the onus to rebut the presumption of a risk of prejudice and they failed to do so. Accordingly, the appeal is allowed, the order of the Ontario Court of Appeal is set aside and the order of the Divisional Court is restored removing Cassels Brock as solicitors for Celanese and precluding the latter from continuing to seek the advice of Kasowitz, in connection with any Canadian litigation arising out of the facts alleged in the amended statement of claim."

FIRST FLIGHT ASSOCIATES, INC. v. PROFESSIONAL GOLF COMPANY
527 F.2d 931 (6th Cir. 1975)

BACKGROUND: Pro Golf is a USA company engaged in the manufacture and sale of golf equipment (golf balls and clubs), under the trademark "First Flight." In 1961, Robert Wynn became its Far East sales representative and formed First Flight Associates ("FFA"), a Japanese company, to carry on that business. Pro Golf and FFA had no formal contract; but a 1970 letter indicated that Wynn/FFA had exclusive sales rights in Japan so long as he "did a satisfactory business." In 1966/67, Wynn/FFA had also been given the right to use the trademark on golf "soft goods" (bags, clothing items, and the like). In 1972, FFA granted a sub-license to Teito Company to use the trademark on golf "soft goods." When a dispute arose between Pro Golf and FFA, it was discovered that Pro Golf had not finalized its registration of the "First Flight" trademark in Japan for use on soft goods. These difficulties led to the termination of Wynn/FFA as Pro Golf's representative. FFA sued for unpaid commissions and various claimed breaches of contract; Pro Golf counter-claimed for the commissions received from Teito and its expenses relating to the Japanese trademark registration. The U.S. District Court awarded FFA its sales commissions and dismissed all other claims.

CHIEF JUDGE MARKEY:

"We agree with the district court's view that FFA was entitled to commissions on orders placed, but not shipped, prior to contract termination…. Pro Golf argues here, as it did below, that by course of conduct and custom, payment of commissions was required only upon shipment of the order and that its termination of the sales representation contract prior to shipment extinguished FFA's right to the commissions. We cannot agree.

"Pro Golf's only evidence of its commission 'custom' is the testimony of one of its directors, Louis W. Oehmig. The testimony indicated that commissions had been 'credited' when an order was shipped and that commissions on orders shipped after a salesman's discharge were not paid. There is no indication that the alleged custom was known or agreed to by Wynn/FFA, or that it was uniformly applied, or that it had been in continuance for any particular time period….

"That enjoyment of some earned commissions of some salesmen may have been postponed until an order was shipped, cannot entitle Pro Golf, by its unilateral act of termination, to deprive FFA of its earned commissions….

"As to the initial 1961 contract for Japanese sales representation on clubs and balls, we agree with the district court that Pro Golf effectively and lawfully terminated FFA as its sales representative…. That termination did not breach to contract…. The contract was … clearly one for an indefinite period of time….

"FFA alleges that the … communications with Teito, advising it of trademark ownership deficiencies and Wynn's lack of authority to contractually bind Pro Golf, constitute trade libel or defamation, as well as an attempt to procure a breach of Teito's contract with FFA. On both of those issues the court below found the evidence insufficient to sustain FFA's allegations. FFA has failed to demonstrate error in that finding and we can detect none. No evidence indicates that the communications were untrue or were made in bad faith or with malice. Indeed, an objective view of all the relevant evidence favors the impression that the contacts with Teito were, in major part, an attempt to clarify the extent of Pro Golf's rights and activities in Japan. That such contacts may have been in the interests of Pro Golf is neither unexpected nor fatal to the conclusion that they were truthful and privileged efforts to protect a business interest and not trade libel or defamation.

"Nor do we find error in the trial court's interpretation of the evidence as failing to disclose an unlawful interference with, or an inducement to breach, a contract…. Because the [Tennessee] statute provides for treble damages, a penal aspect, it is strictly construed…. Communication of Pro Golf's concern about its trademark rights in Japan to Teito, which may have had a business interest in the trademark was not a violation of [the statute]….

"Pro Golf contends that royalties paid to FFA by Teito should have been passed through to Pro Golf. That contention is based on Pro Golf's fundamentally unsound characterization of FFA as its agent in entering into the Teito contract…. Nothing in FFA's trademark license contract with Pro Golf prohibited FFA from granting sub-licenses to others or required FFA to pass along to Pro Golf any royalties FFA might receive from such sub-licensees.

"Pro Golf also counterclaimed for damages equal to its expenditures incurred in attempting to perfect its Japanese rights in FIRST FLIGHT as applied to certain golf 'soft goods.' Pro Golf's difficulties stemmed from its own failure to obtain complete registration in Japan of FIRST FLIGHT in all relevant classes of goods. Under Japanese trademark law, rights are acquired through registration and not through use in commerce as in the United States…. We fully agree with the district court that FFA is not liable for expenditures 'incurred by reason of Pro Golf's own failure to properly register its trademark in Japan.'

"Accordingly, the decision of the district court is in all respects affirmed."

RAYMOND DAYAN v. McDONALD'S CORPORATION
466 N.E.2d 958 (IL App. 1984)

BACKGROUND: Dayan originally sued McDonald's in 1970, alleging breach of an agreement to grant him a license to operate restaurants in Paris, France. After extensive negotiations, a 1971 settlement of that case resulted in a master licensing agreement ("MLA") which differed significantly from McDonald's standard license contract. Despite the urging of McDonald's managers, Dayan insisted on doing all his own development work—in exchange for a lower franchise fee. The MLA did obligate Dayan to maintain McDonald's quality, service and cleanliness ("QSC") standards, give McDonald's the right to terminate the license after 60 days' notice for any breach of the terms, and provide that French and Illinois courts had concurrent jurisdiction over any disputes. Despite extensive help and support from McDonald's, Dayan's restaurants were "filthy," without many necessary items of equipment, staffed by poorly-trained personnel, and subject to numerous customer complaints. After "five years of indulgence," Dayan was notified that he had six months to clean up the operations, after which he would be subject to a formal inspection. The inspection was followed by a letter giving him another six months to correct the problems. Finally, McDonald's sued in France to terminate the license. The French courts use *"huissers de audiencer"* to find the facts and report to the court; they may be assigned by the court itself or at the request of a private party. Five such persons were appointed by the French court; their reports confirmed the existence of serious QSC problems. Meanwhile, Dayan sued in Illinois for an injunction to prevent McDonald's from terminating him as a licensee. The Illinois trial court held for McDonald's, and Dayan appeals.

JUSTICE BUCKLEY:

"Our review of the evidence admits of no doubt; the trial court correctly resolved this issue in favor of McDonald's. To characterize the condition of Dayan's restaurants as being in substantial noncompliance with McDonald's QSC standards is to engage in profound understatement. Throughout trial the various witnesses struggled to find the appropriate words to describe the unsanitary conditions observed in these restaurants, as did the trial court in its memorandum opinion. Terms describing the uncleanliness—such as 'indescribable,' 'extremely defective sanitary conditions,' 'filthy, grimy, cruddy,' 'deplorable,' 'significantly unsanitary,' 'contaminated,' 'insanitary,' 'very dirty,' 'very, very dirty,' 'disgusting,' 'abundance of filth,' 'pig pens'—tell only part of the story. The accuracy of these epithets is supported by voluminous, detailed testimonial evidence which consumed many weeks of trial and thousands of pages of transcript and is also corroborated by over 1000 photographs admitted in evidence at trial. The trial court described this evidence as a 'staggering number of minute facts.'… Suffice it to say, we find more than ample evidence of record to support the trial court's finding of substantial noncompliance with McDonald's QSC standards…. Accordingly, we find no error with respect to the trial court's determination that McDonald's terminated the franchise agreement for good cause and in good faith.

"Dayan also argues that McDonald's was obligated to provide him with the operational assistance necessary to enable him to meet the QSC standards. He further contends that McDonald's failed to fulfill his request for assistance and that the trial court's findings to the contrary were against the manifest weight of the evidence.…

"[T]he extent of McDonald's service obligation to Dayan was expressly addressed in … the MLA. Dayan was to pay a 1% royalty on gross receipts and receive no service unless he first requested it in writing, McDonald's overseas personnel were available to render service, and Dayan paid for the service.… Our analysis of plaintiff's contention will therefore require us to determine only whether the evidence adduced at trial supports the trial court's finding that McDonald's fulfilled any request for assistance made by Dayan.

"During the first five years of the MLA Dayan consistently refused to request any operational assistance even though several McDonald's employees testified that they urged him to do so after observing the disgraceful condition of his restaurants. Following the inspection of Allin and Sollars [McDonald's employees] in February 1977 and after being advised by Barnes [president of McDonald's international division] that McDonald's would no longer tolerate his substandard operation, Dayan verbally asked Sollars for a French-speaking operations person to work in the market for six months. Sollars testified that he told Dayan it would be difficult to find someone with the appropriate background who spoke French but that McDonald's could immediately send him an English-speaking operations man. Sollars further testified that this idea was summarily rejected by Dayan as unworkable even though he had informed Dayan that sending operations personnel who did not speak the language to a foreign country was very common and very successful in McDonald's international system. Nonetheless, Sollars agreed to attempt to locate a qualified person with the requisite language skills for Dayan.…

"Through Sollars' efforts, Dayan was put in contact with Michael Maycock, a person with McDonald's managerial and operational experience who spoke French. Dayan testified that he hired Maycock sometime in October 1977 and placed him in charge of training, operations, quality control, and equipment. Dayan further testified that Maycock continued in his employ at the time of trial, more than four years after being hired.…

"Clearly, Maycock satisfied Dayan's request for a French-speaking operations man to run his training program. This is evidenced by Maycock's continuing employment in this capacity.… The finding that Dayan refused non-French-speaking operational assistance and that McDonald's fulfilled Dayan's limited request for a French-speaking operational employee is well supported by the record.... Accordingly, we find McDonald's fulfilled its contractual obligation to provide requested operational assistance to Dayan....

"In view of the foregoing reasons, the judgment of the trial court denying plaintiff's request for a permanent injunction and finding that McDonald's properly terminated the franchise agreement is affirmed."

K MART CORP. v. CARTIER, INC., et al.
486 U.S. 281 (1988)

BACKGROUND: The 1930 U.S. Trademark Act prohibits importation into the USA of foreign-made goods bearing a USA-registered trademark unless the trademark owner gives consent. This case involves the importation of so-called "gray-market" goods. Goods are legally manufactured in one country, but then imported into another country and sold there in competition with goods made in that second country by a second firm which has the right to use the same trademark there. Regulations adopted by the U.S. Customs Service permitted importation in three situations. In Case 1, a foreign company owns the trademark and has licensed a USA company to use it there. Trademarked goods are then imported into the USA, either by the trademark owner itself or by someone who has bought them from the trademark owner. In Case 2, the USA and foreign companies are linked together as subsidiary and parent (either way). Case 3 is essentially the reverse of Case 1: the USA firm is the trademark owner and has licensed a foreign firm to use it in a particular nation; goods made overseas are then imported into the USA by the licensee firm itself or by one of its buyers. An association of U.S. trademark owners (Cartier and others) filed a lawsuit challenging the validity of the Customs Service regulations. The U.S. District Court upheld the regulations, but the Court of Appeals reversed that decision. Certain importers (K-Mart and others) and the U.S. Government filed for U.S. Supreme Court review. Four Justices said all three rules were valid, and thus importations could continue in all three cases. Four other Justices said all three were invalid, so importation would be prohibited in all three situations. Justice Kennedy provided the fifth vote to validate parts 1 and 2, but to overturn part 3 (which permits importation in Case 3 as well—even where the USA owner of the USA-registered mark is objecting to the importation!).

JUSTICE KENNEDY:

"Until 1922, the Federal Government did not regulate the importation of gray market goods, not even to protect the investment of an independent purchaser of a foreign trademark, and not even in the extreme case where the independent foreign manufacturer breached its agreement to refrain from direct competition with the purchaser. That year, however, Congress was spurred to action by a Court of Appeals decision declining to enjoin the parallel importation of goods bearing a trademark that (as in case 1) a domestic company had purchased from an independent foreign manufacturer at a premium….

"In an immediate response … Congress enacted S.526 of the Tariff Act of 1922…. That provision [was] later reenacted in identical form as S.526 of the 1930 Tariff Act….

"The regulations implementing S.526 for the past 50 years have not applied the prohibition to all gray-market goods. The Customs Service regulation now in force provides generally that 'foreign-made articles bearing a trademark identical with one owned and recorded by a citizen of the United States or a corporation or association created or organized within the United States are subject to seizure and forfeiture as prohibited importations.'… But the regulation furnishes a 'common-control' exception from the ban, permitting the entry of gray-market goods manufactured abroad by the trademark owner or its affiliate [in cases 1 & 2].

"The Customs Service regulation further provides an 'authorized use' exception, which permits importation of gray-market goods where '(3) the articles of foreign manufacture bear a recorded trademark or trade name applied under authorization of the U.S. owner.'…

"Subsection (c)(3) … of the regulation … cannot stand. The ambiguous statutory phrases that we have already discussed, 'owned by' and 'merchandise of foreign manufacture,' are irrelevant to the proscription contained in subsection (3) of the regulation. This subsection of the regulation denies a domestic trademark holder the power to prohibit the importation of goods made by an independent foreign manufacturer where the domestic trademark holder has authorized the foreign manufacturer to use the trademark. Under no reasonable construction of the statutory language can goods made in a foreign country by an independent foreign manufacturer be removed from the purview of the statute.

"The design of the regulation is such that the subsection of the regulation dealing with case 3 … is severable…. The severance and invalidation of this subsection will not impair the function of the statute as a whole, and there is no indication that the regulation would not have been passed but for its inclusion. Accordingly, subsection (c)(3) of S.133.21 must be invalidated for its conflict with the unequivocal language of the statute.

"We hold that the Customs Service regulation is consistent with S.526 insofar as it exempts from the importation ban goods that are manufactured abroad by the 'same person' who holds the United States trademark … or by a person who is 'subject to common … control' with the United States trademark holder…. Because the authorized-use exception of the regulation … is in conflict with the plain language of the statute, that provision cannot stand. The judgment of the

Court of Appeals is therefore reversed insofar as it invalidated SS.133.21(c)(1) and (c)(2), but affirmed as to S.133.21(c)(3)."

WINEWORTHS GROUP LTD. v.
COMITE INTERPROFESSIONEL DU VIN DE CHAMPAGNE
2 NZLR 327 (Court of Appeal Wellington 1992)

BACKGROUND: Comite Interprofessional du Vin de Champagne ("CIVC") is a semi-official body created under French law to protect the product name "champagne" from use by wine-sellers on wines other than the sparkling wine produced in the Champagne district in France, from grapes grown in that district. In 1987, Wineworths entered into a contract with an Australian wine producer to import a product labeled "Australian Champagne" into New Zealand. CIVC and three leading French champagne producers sued for an injunction in the New Zealand courts, claiming that Wineworths was "passing off" its product as genuine champagne, and that Wineworths had violated section 9 of New Zealand's Fair Trading Act of 1986 by misleading consumers into believing they were buying genuine champagne. Wineworths claimed that "champagne" had become a generic term for any white sparkling wine in New Zealand, as it had in Australia and Canada. The High Court Wellington held for the plaintiffs on the "passing off" claim, but dismissed the Fair Trading Act claim because there had been no prior official determination that "champagne" was or was not a generic term. Wineworths appealed the "passing off" part of the High Court's decision, and CIVC appealed the Fair Trading part of the decision.

JUDGE COOKE:

"In New Zealand as in many other countries Champagne has long been par excellence the wine for occasions of special celebration. It has been known here from the early days of European settlement. Newspaper advertisements from 1845 … are in evidence and it is of interest that the history of Levin & Co., the old established merchants, lists among its principal agencies in 1896 Moet et Chandon's Champagne, GH Mumm's Champagne, Irroy Champagne and Heidsieck's Champagne…. [A]t least by the end of the 19th century and probably much earlier the name Champagne had become distinctive in this country. That is to say, the producers of genuine Champagne had acquired in New Zealand a class goodwill of the kind recognized as entitled to protection….

"The Australian history is different. Sparkling wines called champagne have been produced there from the mid-19th century, initially by settlers but commercial production was established before the end of the century. In Australia champagne has apparently come to mean any sparkling white wine, including any produced by a method of transferring the wine after initial bottle fermentation to bulk tanks, a method inferior to the secondary bottle fermentation insisted upon in France, on the evidence, for true Champagne. In Australia all sorts of grapes are used, by no means confined to pinot noir, pinot meunier and chardonnay as true Champagne is supposed to be. Indeed, as I understand it, Australian 'champagne' need not use any of those grapes…. No judicial decision on the subject was drawn to our attention, but it seems that the word is given a generic sense in Australia. If so, although some Australian sparkling wines described there as champagne are of good quality, it is accurate to say that the meaning of the word has become debased….

"[I]t is clear that there could be no question of concurrent rights when the second class of entrants into the New Zealand market did not enter that market for more than 100 years after the first. The same must apply to any claim or suggestion that the second class of entrants, by passing off their products as those of the first class, have contrived to render the latter's name no longer distinctive….

"Distinctiveness could be lost, though, by acquiescence through unreasonable delay in taking steps to protect a threatened distinctiveness and the consequent goodwill. As regards Champagne, that has occurred not only in Australia but also in Canada…. In those countries the true Champagne makers of France were not sufficiently diligent in protecting their rights. The word has gone the way of sherry, port, burgundy, chablis (at least in this country, I think) etc. A defence that the same has happened in New Zealand to Champagne was presented to Jeffries, J but rejected by him for reasons he gave—principally the virtually minimal quantities of 'Australian champagne' imported into New Zealand before 1986. It is noteworthy that in this Court that defence was expressly abandoned….

"Once acquiescence is out of the way, it is apparent in the light of the different histories that the Australian generic usage cannot be permitted in New Zealand to defeat the New Zealand specific usage. This Court has been and is sympathetic to progress in integrating the general market in the two countries as far as reasonably practicable, and has been willing therefore to develop the law to protect the legitimate interest of Australian traders…. The protection of illegitimate interests is different matter. It seems to me that the very small importations of 'Australian champagne' between 1958 and 1986 and the subsequent major incursions about to be described have alike been in violation of the common law goodwill rights in this country of the producers of true Champagne….

"… I agree in all material respects with the findings of fact, inferences of fact and conclusions of Jeffries, J as to passing off. In particular I accept his assessment that the word 'champagne' in

New Zealand is not used generically to describe sparking white wine.... Some people in this country do speak of 'champagne' in the generic sense, though probably many of them are conscious of speaking loosely and know that Australian or New Zealand 'champagne' is not the real thing. For reasons of pretension or tact of the constraints of one's purse it is sometimes convenient to depart knowingly from Accuracy. To speak of Australian or New Zealand champagne can be to indulge in a white lie....

"Last it is necessary to turn to the cause of action under the Fair Trading Act. Section 9 provides simply that no person shall, in trade, engage in conduct that is misleading or deceptive or is likely to mislead or deceive. A rival trader can succeed in an action under s.9 without showing damage to goodwill. The ordinary words of s.9 are to be applied to the particular facts and are not to be superseded by judicial exegesis....

"For these reasons I would dismiss the appeal and allow the cross-appeal, although the success of the latter would not in the particular circumstances necessitate any change in the wording of the injunction.... The Court being unanimous, there will be orders accordingly."

THE GAP, INC. v. KOREAN INTELLECTUAL PROPERTY OFFICE
Decision 2010Hu2339 (Korea Supreme Court 2012)

BACKGROUND: Gap (a Delaware corporation) applied to register a diagram/drawing as a trademark but was refused by the Korean Intellectual Property Office examiner. The refusal was confirmed by the Patent Court of Korea in a 2010 decision, and Gap sought review by the Korean Supreme Court.

THE COURT:

"The judgment below is reversed, and the case is remanded to the Patent Court of Korea.

"REASONING:

"... The provision regarding the definition of trademark was amended multiple times since its legislation as Article 1 (1) of the Trademark Act (Act No. 71) on Nov. 28, 1949, to Article 2 (1)-1 of the previous Trademark Act (amended by Act No. 11113 on Dec. 2, 2011), which applies to the applied trademark of this case. However, all versions include the understanding that a trademark is 'any sign, any letter, any figure or the combination thereof used for the purpose of distinguishing his/her service business from those of others.' Thus, these definition provisions regarding trademark include every shape of mark that can be visually recognized through the combination of any sign, any letter, or any figure. Therefore according to the provision, 'a mark which is a consistent image or shape formed by an individual sign, letter, figure or the combination thereof; and by being attached to a certain location of the designated product, distinguishes it from another product' can also be acknowledged as a trademark (henceforth, such marks are referred to as 'position mark'). In order to explain a specific position where an image or shape is attached to the designated product, a position mark needs a portion that labels the image of the designated product. As long as it is obvious that the overall composition of the mark, the types of lines used on each portion of the mark, and the type and characteristics of the designated product indicate that the trademark applicant simply intended to prescribe the aforementioned explanation to the expression of the designated product, the aforementioned portion should not be perceived as a figure forming the outline of the mark itself. Additionally, circumstances such as the applicant having expressed his/her aforementioned intention to the patent examiner via a written opinion following a notification for opinion submission, should also be considered. Meanwhile, the reasoning that the current trademark application and examination process of Korea has no procedure of submitting a trademark description distinctively explaining that the applicant's intended the trademark as a position mark, or a procedure for writing a disclaimer clarifying in advance that the shape marked on the aforementioned designated product is a portion where copyright will not be exercised, does not obstruct the acknowledgment of the aforementioned position mark. And even when a position mark lacks distinctiveness in its consistent image or shape; as long as the position mark's attachment to a specific location of the designated product was successful in enabling traders and consumers to recognize the product as that of a specific trademark owner, it may be registered as a trademark since distinctiveness was acquired through the aforementioned use of the position mark.

"Therefore, Supreme Court Decisions 90Hu168 (decided Sept. 25, 1990), 2003Hu1970 (decided July 8, 2003), and 2003Hu1987 (decided July 8, 2004) will be overruled to the extent they are inconsistent with this court's opinion, since they perceived that the shape portion of the designated product was a figure which forms the outline of the trademark itself—without examining the specific meaning of the portion—and ruled that a trademark including the portion conforms to a trademark that marks the shape of the product in the commonly used method….

"According to the court below: as depicted in [the proposed] image, the applied trademark of this case (application No. 2007-31449) is a top composed not of simple lines, but alternated long and short dash lines, with three thick lines running from the side down to the waist; to summarize, the outlines of the top and the three thick lines are clearly distinguished from each other. Additionally, the designated products were sports shirts, sports jackets, and pullover sweaters—all of which were tops, and thus a consistent image or shape, such as the aforementioned thick line running from the side down to the waist, can be attached. In light of the overall composition of the mark, the types of lines used on each portion of the mark, and the type and characteristics of the designated product; it is obvious that the plaintiff (who submitted the applied trademark of this case) simply intended to show where the three thick lines were positioned using the above illustration. Furthermore, according to records, it appears the plaintiff did clarify its intention during the examination process of the applied trademark of this case, stating that the dotted lines (the plaintiff describes the long and short dash lines as 'dotted lines') which outline the shape was used to show precisely where the three thick lines are marked. Thus, the applied trademark of this case is in fact a position mark which distinguishes the designated product by the above thick lines that run down from the side to the waist; and there is sufficient reason to perceive that the above long and short dash line portion is not the figure forming the outline of the applied trademark itself.

"The court below perceived that the applied trademark of this case is a figure trademark in the shape of a sports top outlined in dotted lines (the court below describes the long and short dash lines as 'dotted lines') with three thick lines running down from the side to the waist; and determined that the applied trademark of this case conforms to a descriptive mark as provided by Article 6 (1)-3 of the Trademark Act, and also other marks lacking in distinctiveness, as provided by Article 6 (1)-7 of the same Act on grounds that it lacks distinctiveness because: since the sports top outlined in dotted lines merely shows the general image of the designated product; and the 'three thick lines running down from the side to the waist' portion is more of a decorative pattern than an independently recognizable figure in itself. Therefore, the court below determined on the distinctiveness of the applied trademark of this case, and its acquired distinctiveness through use based on the wrong assumption that the sportswear top portion of the applied trademark was a figure composing the outline of the mark itself. This measure was erroneous for misapprehending the legal principles regarding determination on the distinctiveness of trademarks, and allowing it to affect the judgment. The ground of appeal which identifies this issue is with merit.

"… Thus the judgment of the court below is reversed; any judgment on the remaining grounds of appeal are [sic] omitted; and the case is remanded to the court below for a new trial and determination. It is thus decided per Disposition by the assent of all participating judges."

WALT DISNEY COMPANY v. BEIJING PUBLISHING PRESS et al.
Zhongjing Zhichu No. 141 (Beijing First Intermediate Court 1994)

BACKGROUND: Disney licensed Maxwell Company to publish and sell in China Chinese-language publications based on Disney's cartoon characters. The license specified that it "may not be assigned by the Licensee to any third party in any manner or by means of any legal procedure." Disregarding this prohibition, Maxwell Company assigned its exclusive right to Beijing Children's Publishing Press, an affiliate of Beijing Publishing Press. Children's Press also signed an agreement with Maxworld (a joint venture between Maxwell and Children's Press) that obligated Maxworld to finalize the details of the assignment and prepare the printing plates for the Chinese publications. When Children's Press presented the assignment contract to the Beijing Municipal Copyright Authority for examination and approval, it was denied, because there was no authorization from Disney. Nonetheless, Beijing Publishing and the Beijing Distribution Office signed an agreement for distribution of foreign books, which did provide that the publishing press was liable "for any disputes that may arise" from the selling of foreign copyrighted materials. On March 17, 1992, the USA and the People's Republic of China signed the Sino-American Memorandum of Understanding, protecting copyrights of nationals of the parties. Beijing Publishing's production and sale of *Collection of Disney Moral Tales* resulted in this lawsuit.

CHIEF JUDGE SU CHI: *(translated sections)*

This Court decides that properties of U.S. persons have been protected by Chinese law since the Sino-U.S. Memorandum of Understanding became effective 17 March 1992. Therefore, Disney Company's cartoon likenesses involved here do have copyright protection. Unless authorized by Disney, commercial use of these cartoon likenesses in China constitutes infringement.

Disney did authorize the Maxwell Company to publish an album of cartoon likenesses here, but it never authorized them to assign such publishing rights to third parties. Therefore, the purported assignment by Maxwell of its rights in these products to the Children's Press is both an infringement of Disney's rights and also a fraud on the Children's Press. The Contract by which this assignment was said to be made is void as a matter of law.

Legally, Maxwell's fraud was the main cause of this infringement of rights. But because the Maxwell Company became bankrupt in July 1993, we will not discuss their liability here.

The Children's Press was extremely reckless in signing a publication agreement with Maxwell without having first investigated whether they had any right to assign such publication rights. The State Copyright Administration requires that: "Effective 1 March 1988, any unit or individual entering into a publishing trading contract with Taiwan, Hong Kong or Macao, and regardless of whether it provides for licensing out of copyrights or for authorizing use or for taking assignment of authorizations, shall submit it to the Copyright Administration Authority for review and registration. Where a contract has not been reviewed and registered, it shall, prior to 1 March 1990, be submitted to the review and registration authority in accordance with procedures. Contracts not reviewed and registered shall be void."

Children's Press was refused permission by the relevant department of the State Copyright Administration to register this contract on the ground that it could show no legal proof of copyright, but still did not conduct any inquiry or implement required registration procedures. It nevertheless proceeded to publish picture albums containing likenesses of Disney cartoon characters. That it was aware that it was at fault in so doing is clear. Since the Children's Press is not an independent legal entity, its liability shall be borne by the Beijing Publishing Press.

Beijing Distribution Office participated in marketing the publications by the Beijing Publishing Press. In accordance with "Implementing Regulations of the People's Republic of China on the Law of Authorship Rights", marketing—regardless of whether it takes the form of "consignment sales" or "distribution"—is a form of publishing. A publisher has a legal responsibility to know whether or not the publications it handles are legally defective. Beijing Distribution Office, at the time it signed the agreement with Beijing Publishing Press, took notice of the relevant regulations, but did not implement them. Beijing Distribution Office was aware of its fault in this regard and should accept responsibility for publishing the infringing books.

[T]he amount payable to the plaintiff as compensation should be [sales income minus reasonable costs of production] plus reasonable bank interest and reasonable fees it incurred in prosecuting this lawsuit.

With regard to plaintiff's request for an order "that the defendants guarantee in writing that they will never again infringe the copyrights of the plaintiff," this is not a usually available civil remedy, and therefore cannot be ordered by this court.

INTERNATIONAL BANCORP LLC, et al. v.
SOCIETE DES BAINS DE MER ET DU CERCLE DES ETRANGERS A MONACO
329 F.3d 359 (4th Cir. 2003)

BACKGROUND: Appellee, Societe des Bains de Mer et du Cercle des Etrangers a Monaco ("SBM"), owns and operates historic properties in Monte Carlo, Monaco, including resort and casino facilities. One of its properties, a casino, has operated under the "Casino de Monte Carlo" trademark since 1863. The mark is registered in Monaco, but not in the United States. SBM promotes this casino, along with its other properties, around the world. For 18 years, SBM has promoted its properties from a New York office staffed with four employees. SBM's promotions within the United States, funded with $1 million annually, include trade show participation, advertising campaigns, charity partnerships, direct mail solicitation, telephone marketing, and solicitation of media coverage.

The five plaintiff companies are controlled by a French national, and operate more than 150 web sites devoted to online gambling. Included in this roster are 53 websites whose domain addresses incorporate some portion of the term "Casino de Monte Carlo." These websites, along with the gambling software they employ, also exhibit pictures of the Casino de Monte Carlo's exterior and interior, contain renderings that are strikingly similar to the Casino de Monte Carlo's interior, and make allusion to the geographic location of Monte Carlo, implying that they offer online gambling as an alternative to *their* Monaco-based casino, though they operate no such facility.

When SBM learned of the plaintiff companies' websites and their uses of the "Casino de Monte Carlo" mark, it challenged them in the World Intellectual Property Organization ("WIPO"). A WIPO panel ruled against the plaintiff companies and ordered the transfer of the 53 domain addresses to SBM. To escape this judgment, the plaintiff companies brought suit in federal court against SBM seeking declaratory judgment that they are entitled to the disputed domain names. SBM counterclaimed under the Lanham Act for trademark infringement under section 1125(a); trademark dilution under section 1125(c); cybersquatting under section 1125(d)(1); and unfair competition in violation of section 1126(h). The district court ruled against SBM on its section 1125(c) trademark dilution claim, because SBM had not shown actual economic harm, and on its section 1126(h) unfair competition claim. But the court ruled in favor of SBM on its trademark infringement claim and on its cybersquatting claim, awarding SBM $51,000 in statutory damages and transfer of 43 of the 53 contested domain addresses. The plaintiff companies now appeal from that adverse judgment.

JUDGE LUTTIG:

"Plaintiff companies appeal from the district court's summary judgment that their registration and use of forty-three domain addresses infringe a foreign corporation's rights under the Lanham Act and violate the Anticybersquatting Act, where the foreign corporation advertised its trademark domestically, but only rendered services under it abroad. We conclude that the district court's judgment, although not its reasoning, was correct, and therefore affirm....

"The plaintiff companies first challenge the district court's determination that their use of 43 domain addresses violated 15 U.S.C. § 1125(a) of the Lanham Act, infringing on SBM's trademark. Central to their challenge is the claim that SBM did not have a protectable interest in the 'Casino de Monte Carlo' mark, a prerequisite to SBM's ability to claim against the plaintiff companies under the Act....

"This circuit requires that an *unregistered* trademark satisfy two requirements if its owner is to have a protectable interest in the trademark: The mark must be used in commerce ... and it must be distinctive.... The plaintiff companies argue that the district court erred in concluding that SBM met these two requirements. We address both arguments in turn.

"Both parties have agreed, in their briefs and at oral argument, that the critical question in assessing whether SBM 'used its mark in commerce' is whether the *services* SBM provided under the 'Casino de Monte Carlo' mark were *rendered in commerce*. As shown below, the Lanham Act's plain language makes this conclusion unavoidable and the parties' agreement unsurprising.

"We must first contend with a threshold matter, however. This circuit has never directly addressed the scope of the term 'commerce' within the Lanham Act. Because of the clarity of the Act's own definition of the term ... we now hold that 'commerce' under the Act is coterminous with that commerce that Congress may regulate under the Commerce Clause of the United States Constitution. The other circuits to address this question have concluded the same.... Consequently, 'commerce' under the Lanham Act necessarily includes all the explicitly identified variants of interstate commerce, foreign trade, and Indian commerce.

"Understanding commerce under the Act to be coterminous with that commerce Congress may regulate under the Commerce Clause, we turn next to the determination of what constitutes '*use in* commerce' under the Act. Again we rely on section 1127, which provides, of particular relevance here, a specific definition of that term as it relates to servicemarks, which the 'Casino de Monte Carlo' mark unquestionably is:

> The term 'use in commerce' means the *bona fide use of a mark in the ordinary course of trade, and not made merely to reserve a right in a mark*. For purposes of this chapter, a mark shall be deemed to be used in commerce ...
> (2) *on services* when it is used or displayed in the sale or advertising of services *and the services are rendered in commerce*, or the services are rendered in more than one State or in the United States and a foreign country and the person rendering the services is engaged in commerce in connection with the services....

"Consistent with this definition of the statutory 'use in commerce' requirement, the Supreme Court has said that 'there is no such thing as property in a trade-mark except as a right appurtenant to an established business or trade in connection with which the mark is employed. . . . The right to a particular mark grows out of its use, not its mere adoption.'... Because a mark is used in commerce only if it accompanies services rendered in commerce, *i.e.*, it is employed appurtenant to an established business or trade that is in commerce, 'mere advertising' of that mark does not establish its protectibility, though advertising is itself commerce that Congress may regulate.

"With these principles in clear view, we proceed to address whether the 'Casino de Monte Carlo' mark was used in commerce. In their briefs and before the court below, the parties debate principally whether the activities of SBM's New York office conducted under the 'Casino de Monte Carlo' mark constitute services rendered in interstate commerce. SBM, for its part, contends that the office's booking of reservations is a rendered service, and that its maintenance of the office, its advertising in this country, and its promotional web page attach the 'Casino de Monte Carlo' mark for sales and advertising purposes to this interstate service, thereby satisfying the 'use in commerce' requirement. The plaintiff companies argue, to the contrary, that there is no evidence in the record that the New York office books reservations to the casino, and that, as a result, the office engages in no activity beyond 'mere advertising.' They argue further that the casino gambling services are the only established business to which the trademark applies, and that *that* service, being rendered in Monaco, is not rendered in commerce that Congress may regulate. The district court accept[ed] SBM's arguments....

"SBM's argument and the district court's reasoning are in error because the New York-office bookings on which they rely do not relate to the casino in question, but, rather, to SBM's resort facilities. As became evident at oral argument and upon our review of the record, SBM's assertion that the record contains evidence that its New York office booked reservations to the casino is unsubstantiated. The plaintiff companies correctly point out that since the 'Casino de Monte Carlo' mark only pertains to the casino and its gambling services, any guest reservations SBM's New York office and web site book for SBM's various resorts, which reservation services the record does disclose, are irrelevant to the analysis. And the other operations of SBM's New York office, at least as they appear in the record, are merely promotional in nature. The Lanham Act and the Supreme Court, as shown above, make clear that a mark's protection may not be based on 'mere advertising.'

"Because SBM presented no record evidence that the New York office did anything other than advertise the 'Casino de Monte Carlo' mark, if its case rested on this alone, the plaintiff companies would have the better of the argument. When they appeared before the court, however, we asked the parties to address themselves to the question of whether the casino services at issue were rendered in foreign trade, and the plaintiff companies conceded that the record contained evidence that United States citizens went to and gambled at the casino. This concession, when taken together with the undisputed fact that the Casino de Monte Carlo is a subject of a foreign nation, makes unavoidable the legal conclusion that foreign trade was present here, and that as such, so also was 'commerce' under the Lanham Act.

"Since the nineteenth century, it has been well established that the Commerce Clause reaches to foreign trade. And, for the same length of time, the Supreme Court has defined foreign trade as trade between subjects of the United States and subjects of a foreign nation....

"At oral argument, the plaintiff companies ... argued first that any trade that United States citizens engaged in at the casino was not subject to regulation by Congress since it did not occur in the United States.... In the alternative, they argued that even if Congress could regulate transactions between United States citizens and foreign subjects that occur abroad, the particular transactions at issue here should not be considered foreign trade because the Casino de Monte Carlo was a 'playground for the very, very rich' ... and thus did not have a substantial effect on foreign trade. Both arguments are unavailing.

"The plaintiff companies' first argument fails because the *locality* in which foreign commercial intercourse occurs is of no concern to Congress' power under the Constitution to regulate such commerce.... The subject of foreign trade ... is defined not by where the trade occurs, but by the characteristics of the parties who engage in the trade....

"The plaintiff companies' second argument, that the purchase of gambling services by United States citizens at the Casino de Monte Carlo is not commerce because it does not have a substantial effect on the foreign commerce of the United States, also fails. The substantial effects test is not implicated here at all....

"The Supreme Court has articulated the substantial effects test to ensure that Congress does not exceed its constitutional authority to regulate interstate commerce by enacting legislation that, rather than regulating interstate commerce, trammels on the rights of states to regulate purely intra-state activity for themselves pursuant to their police power. But while 'Congress' power to regulate interstate commerce may be restricted by considerations of federalism and state sovereignty[,] it has never been suggested that Congress' power to regulate foreign commerce could be so limited.'... The rationale that underlies application of the substantial effects test in the analysis of congressional legislation purporting to regulate interstate commerce is therefore absent from analysis of congressional legislation purporting to regulate foreign commerce.

"Furthermore, the substantial effects test only limits Congress' authoritative reach with respect to one of the three broad categories of activity that Congress may regulate under the Commerce Clause.... Consequently, the substantial effects test does not limit Congress' regulation of activity that is itself commercial intercourse occurring interstate; it governs only Congress' regulation of non-commercial intercourse activity that effects interstate commerce....

"The use of an unregistered mark in foreign trade does not in any way assure its owner that the mark will merit Lanham Act protection; it only makes such protection possible. For an unregistered mark that is used in foreign trade to merit Lanham Act protection, that mark must be distinctive among United States consumers. The plaintiff companies argue that even if the 'Casino de Monte Carlo' mark is used in commerce, it is not distinctive because it is merely geographically descriptive, and that since it is not distinctive, it is not protectible.

"Though the plaintiff companies correctly argue that the mark is geographically descriptive (*i.e.*, it geographically describes where the casino is located and nothing more), this objection does not foreclose the mark's distinctiveness. Descriptive marks will be deemed distinctive if they achieve secondary meaning.... Thus, the relevant question here is whether the district court correctly found that the mark possessed secondary meaning....

"The district court, finding that SBM provided proof of substantial advertising expenditures; significant sales success within the United States; substantial unsolicited media coverage of the casino; frequent attempts by others to plagiarize the mark; and a long history of continuous, if not exclusive, use of the mark; concluded that SBM had met its burden.... Upon our review of the record, we conclude that the court's conclusion as to these points is not clear error....

"Because the district court properly concluded, though for the wrong reasons, that the 'Casino de Monte Carlo' mark was used in commerce, and because its conclusion that the mark had secondary meaning was not clearly erroneous, the court's determination that the mark was protectible was proper, and it did not err by proceeding to assess whether the plaintiff companies' use of the mark constituted trademark infringement....

"This case presents a record replete with demonstrations of SBM's singularly impressive commitment to building brand identity in the United States. These efforts constitute ... a 'use or display in the sale or advertising' of the services that we elsewhere determined were *also* rendered in commerce. It cannot but be concluded that *this* use of the mark—that is the building of brand identity among United States consumers—very much occurred in the United States, and indisputably so.

"On our understanding of the statutory language it does not follow that since the mark has not been *rendered in commerce* in the United States it is equally fair to say that the mark has not been *used in the United States*, when in fact it has been widely used in the United States for advertising and marketing purposes. Unless one conflates these two elements then, one cannot fairly criticize our holding today as protecting a mark 'exclusively' used in Mon[]aco. At most one can criticize us for providing protection to a mark used in *both* Monaco and the United

283

States....

"... [T]he proper inquiry in such circumstances is to evaluate first whether the commerce to which both parties claim their mark is attached may be regulated by Congress, and then to evaluate at what point in time the mark owners began to use or display the mark in the advertising and sale of *those* qualifying services *to the qualifying consumers*.... [O]ur circuit's law will be better served if we hew to the language of the statute and apply the Lanham Act with a careful eye toward, and an appreciation of, the two distinct elements of the 'use in commerce' requirement.

"Indeed, that it is not enough for a mark owner to engage in qualifying commerce to create rights in his mark, and that it is not enough for a mark owner to use or display the mark in the advertising or sale of services to create rights in his mark, is critical. This point cannot be missed else the holding we reach today will indeed be distorted.... Rather, a mark owner must both engage in qualifying commerce and use or display its mark in the sale or advertising of these services to the consumers that engage in that qualifying commerce....

"Having determined that the district court properly ruled that SBM's mark was protectible under the Lanham Act, we turn next to review its conclusion that its mark was infringed by the plaintiff companies' activity.

"To prove infringement of a protectible trademark, a trademark owner must demonstrate that the infringer's use of the mark is likely to cause consumer confusion.... On the record before us we cannot conclude that the district court committed clear error in determining that the plaintiff companies' use of the mark would cause consumer confusion. The domain addresses in question, their use of pictures and renderings of the actual Casino de Monte Carlo, and the web sites implying that they provided online gambling as an alternative to their non-existent Monte Carlo-based casino all support the conclusion that ordinary consumers would be confused. The district court's grant of summary judgment to SBM for trademark infringement under § 1125(a) was therefore justified....

"The plaintiff companies lastly argue that the district court's injunctive remedy, ordering transfer of 43 domain names to SBM, was overbroad and vague, and that less burdensome remedies were available. But the injunctive order was proper under § 1125(d)(1), the anticybersquatting provision that the court concluded the plaintiff companies had violated, since that provision expressly provides domain name transfer as remedy. The plaintiff companies do not challenge the district court's determination under § 1125(d)(1), other than by their objection that the 'Casino de Monte Carlo mark is not protectable, which contention we reject above. In light of SBM's protectable interest in the mark, and the plaintiff companies' failure to challenge the judgment under § 1125(d)(1) on other grounds, we conclude that the court's provision of injunctive remedy was proper....

"For the reasons provided herein, the judgment of the district court is affirmed."

MONSANTO TECHNOLOGY LLC v. CEFETRA BV, et al.
Case C-428/08 (European Court of Justice 2010)

BACKGROUND: Article 27 of the Agreement on Trade-Related Aspects of Intellectual Property Rights ("TRIPS"), as regards matters within its competence, provides essentially as follows under the heading "Patentable subject-matter": "[P]atents are to be available for any inventions, whether products or processes, in all fields of technology, provided that they are new, involve an inventive step and are capable of industrial application; patents are to be available and patent rights enjoyable without discrimination as to the place of invention, the field of technology and whether products are imported or locally produced." Article 30 of the same agreement, entitled "Exceptions to Rights Conferred" states that members may provide limited exceptions to the exclusive rights conferred by a patent, provided that such exceptions do not unreasonably conflict with a normal exploitation of the patent and do not unreasonably prejudice the legitimate interests of the patent owner, taking account of the legitimate interests of third parties.

Article 1 of the E.U. Directive provides that Member States are to protect biotechnological inventions under national patent law and that, if necessary, they are to adjust the latter to take account of the provisions of that directive. It adds that the Directive is to be without prejudice to the obligations of the Member States pursuant, inter alia, to the TRIPs Agreement. Article 5(3) of the Directive, contained in Chapter I, entitled "Patentability," requires that the industrial application of a sequence or a partial sequence of a gene be disclosed in the patent application. Article 9, entitled "Scope of protection," provides: "The protection conferred by a patent on a product containing or consisting of genetic information shall extend to all material … in which the product is incorporated and in which the genetic information is contained and performs its function."

Article 53 of the 1995 Netherlands Law on patents provides: "… A patent shall give the patent holder … the exclusive right (a) to manufacture the patented product in or for its business, to use it, to bring it into circulation or to sell it on, to hire it out, to deliver it or otherwise trade in it, or to offer it, to import it or to have it in stock for any of those purposes; (b) to apply the patented process in or for its business, or to use, to bring into circulation or to sell on, to hire out or deliver the product derived directly from the application of that process, or otherwise to trade in that product, or to offer it, to import it or have it in stock for any of those purposes." Article 53a[3] of that law reads as follows: "In respect of a patent on a product containing or consisting of genetic information, the exclusive right shall extend to all material in which the product is incorporated and in which the genetic information is contained and performs its function. ..."

Monsanto is the holder of European patent EP 0 546 090 granted on June 19, 1996, relating to "Glyphosate tolerant 5-enolpyruvylshikimate-3-phosphate synthases." The European patent is valid, inter alia, in the Netherlands. Glyphosate is a non-selective herbicide. In a plant, it works by inhibiting the Class I enzyme 5-enol-pyruvylshikimate-3-phosphate synthase (also called "EPSPS"), which plays an important role in the growth of the plant. The effect of glyphosate is that the plant dies. The European patent describes a class of EPSPS enzymes which are not sensitive to glyphosate. Plants containing such enzymes survive the use of glyphosate, whilst weeds are destroyed. The genes encoding these Class II enzymes have been isolated from three different bacteria. Monsanto has inserted those genes into the DNA of a soy plant it has called RR (Roundup Ready) soybean plant. As a result, the RR soybean plant produces a Class II EPSPS enzyme called CP4-EPSPS, which is glyphosate-resistant. It thus becomes resistant to the herbicide "Roundup."

The RR soybean is cultivated on a large scale in Argentina, where there is no patent protection for the Monsanto invention. Cefetra and Toepfer trade in soy meal. Three cargoes of soy meal from Argentina arrived in the port of Amsterdam on June 16, 2005, and March 21 and May 11, 2006. Vopak made a customs declaration for one of the cargoes. The three consignments were detained by the customs authorities pursuant to Council Regulation (EC) No 1383/2003 concerning customs action against goods suspected of infringing certain intellectual property rights and the measures to be taken against goods found to have infringed such rights. The consignments were released after Monsanto had taken samples. Monsanto tested the samples to determine whether they originated from RR soybeans. Following the tests, which revealed the presence of CP4-EPSPS in the soy meal and the DNA sequence encoding it, Monsanto applied for injunctions against Cefetra, Vopak and Toepfler before the Rechtbank's-Gravenhage, and for a prohibition of infringement of the European patent in all countries in which the patent is valid. The Argentine State intervened in support of the forms of order sought by Cefetra.

The Rechtbank's-Gravenhage considers that Monsanto has established the presence, in one of the disputed cargoes, of the DNA sequence protected by its European patent. It is nevertheless unsure as to whether that presence alone is sufficient to constitute infringement of Monsanto's European patent when the soy meal is marketed in the Community. It concludes that the DNA cannot perform its function in soy meal, which is dead material. In that context, the Rechtbank's-Gravenhage decided to stay the proceedings and to refer four questions to the Court of Justice for a preliminary ruling.

THE COURT:

"... By its first question, the national court asks, essentially, whether Article 9 of the Directive is to be interpreted as conferring patent right protection in circumstances such as those of the case in the main proceedings, in which the patented product is contained in the soy meal, where it does not perform the function for which it was patented, but did perform that function previously in the soy plant, of which the meal is a processed product, or would possibly again be able to perform its function after it has been extracted from the soy meal and inserted into the cell of a living organism.

"... In that regard, it must be noted that Article 9 of the Directive makes the protection for which it provides subject to the condition that the genetic information contained in the patented product or constituting that product 'performs' its function in the 'material ... in which' that information is contained. ... The usual meaning of the present tense used by the Community legislature and of the phrase 'material ... in which' implies that the function is being performed at the present time and in the actual material in which the DNA sequence containing the genetic information is found. ... In the case of genetic information such as that at issue in the main proceedings, the function of the invention is performed when the genetic information protects the biological material in which it is incorporated against the effect, or the foreseeable possibility of the effect, of a product which can cause that material to die. ... The use of a herbicide on soy meal is not, however, foreseeable, or even normally conceivable. Moreover, even if it was used in that way, a patented product intended to protect the life of biological material containing it could not perform its function, since the genetic information can be found only in a residual state in the soy meal, which is a dead material obtained after the soy has undergone several treatment processes.

"... It follows from the foregoing that the protection provided for in Article 9 of the Directive is not available when the genetic information has ceased to perform the function it performed in the initial material from which the material in question is derived. ... It also follows that that protection cannot be relied on in relation to the material in question on the sole ground that the DNA sequence containing the genetic information could be extracted from it and perform its function in a cell of a living organism into which it has been transferred. In such a scenario, the function would be performed in a material which is both different and biological. It could therefore give rise to a right to protection only in relation to that material. ... To allow protection under Article 9 of the Directive on the ground that the genetic information performed its function previously in the material containing it or that it could possibly perform that function again in another material would amount to depriving the provision interpreted of its effectiveness, since one or other of those situations could, in principle, always be relied on. ...

"... [I]t should be borne in mind that recital 23 in the preamble to the Directive states that 'a mere DNA sequence without indication of a function does not contain any technical information and is therefore not a patentable invention.'... Since the Directive thus makes the patentability of a DNA sequence subject to indication of the function it performs, it must be regarded as not according any protection to a patented DNA sequence which is not able to perform the specific function for which it was patented. ...

"... By its second question, the national court asks, essentially, whether Article 9 of the Directive effects an exhaustive harmonisation of the protection it confers, with the result that it precludes national patent legislation from offering absolute protection to the patented product as such, regardless of whether it performs its function in the material containing it. ... That question is based on the premise, referred to in the order for reference, that a national provision such as Article 53 of the 1995 Law does in fact accord absolute protection to the patented product. ... It follows from those statements that the Community legislature intended to effect a harmonisation which was limited in its substantive scope, but suitable for remedying the existing differences and preventing future differences between Member States in the field of protection of biotechnological inventions. ... It follows that the harmonisation effected by Article 9 of the Directive must be regarded as exhaustive. ... The answer to the second question is therefore that Article 9 of the Directive effects an exhaustive harmonisation of the protection it confers, with the result that it precludes the national patent legislation from offering absolute protection to the patented product as such, regardless of whether it performs its function in the material containing it. ...

"... By its third question, the national court asks, essentially, whether Article 9 of the Directive precludes the holder of a patent issued prior to the adoption of that directive from relying on the absolute protection for the patented product accorded to it under the national legislation then applicable. ... The Directive does not provide for any derogation from that principle.... The answer to the third question is therefore that Article 9 of the Directive precludes the holder of a patent issued prior to the adoption of that directive from relying on the absolute protection for the patented product accorded to it under the national legislation then applicable. ...

"... By its fourth question, the national court asks, essentially, whether Articles 27 and 30 of the TRIPS Agreement affect the interpretation given of Article 9 of the Directive. ... In that regard, it should be borne in mind that the provisions of the TRIPS Agreement are not such as to create rights upon which individuals may rely directly before the courts by virtue of European Union law.... Article 9 of the Directive governs the scope of the protection conferred by a patent on its holder, whilst Articles 27 and 30 of the TRIPS Agreement concern, respectively, patentability and the exceptions to the rights conferred by a patent. ... The answer to the fourth question is therefore that Articles 27 and 30 of the TRIPS Agreement do not affect the interpretation given of Article 9 of the Directive. ...

"On those grounds, the Court (Grand Chamber) hereby rules:

1.   Article 9 of Directive 98/44/EC ... is to be interpreted as not conferring patent right protection in circumstances such as those of the case in the main proceedings....

2.   Article 9 of the Directive effects an exhaustive harmonisation of the protection it confers, with the result that it precludes the national patent legislation from offering absolute protection to the patented product as such, regardless of whether it performs its function in the material containing it.

3.   Article 9 of the Directive precludes the holder of a patent issued prior to the adoption of that directive from relying on the absolute protection for the patented product accorded to it under the national legislation then applicable.

4.   Articles 27 and 30 of the Agreement on Trade-Related Aspects of Intellectual Property Rights ... do not affect the interpretation given of Article 9 of the Directive."

KIRTSAENG v. JOHN WILEY & SONS, INC.
133 S.Ct. 1353 (2013)

BACKGROUND: John Wiley sued Kirtsaeng, claiming unauthorized importation and resale of its textbooks in the USA—in violation of the USA's Copyright Act. The U.S. District Court held that the Act's "first sale doctrine" did not apply to copies of U.S. copyrighted works manufactured abroad, and a jury found willful infringement. The U.S. Court of Appeals for the Second Circuit affirmed. Kirtsaeng's petition for certiorari was granted by the U.S. Supreme Court.

The copies of the textbooks were lawfully manufactured abroad. When Kirtsaeng moved from Thailand to the U.S. to study, he asked friends and family to buy foreign edition English-language textbooks in Thai book shops, where they sold at low prices, and mail them to him in the U.S. He then sold over 600 of these books, reimbursed his family and friends, and kept the profit.

JUSTICE BREYER:

"Section 106 of the Copyright Act grants 'the owner of copyright under this title' certain 'exclusive rights,' including the right 'to distribute copies . . . of the copyrighted work to the public by sale or other transfer of ownership.'... These rights are qualified, however, by the application of various limitations set forth in the next several sections of the Act, §§107 through 122. Those sections, typically entitled 'Limitations on exclusive rights,' include, for example, the principle of 'fair use' (§107), permission for limited library archival reproduction, (§108), and the doctrine at issue here, the 'first sale' doctrine (§109).

"Section 109(a) sets forth the 'first sale' doctrine as follows:
> 'Notwithstanding the provisions of section 106(3) [the section that grants the owner exclusive distribution rights], the owner of a particular copy or phonorecord lawfully made under this title . . . is entitled, without the authority of the copyright owner, to sell or otherwise dispose of the possession of that copy or phonorecord.'...

Thus, even though §106(3) forbids distribution of a copy of, say, the copyrighted novel *Herzog* without the copyright owner's permission, §109(a) adds that, once a copy of *Herzog* has been lawfully sold (or its ownership otherwise lawfully transferred), the buyer of *that copy* and subsequent owners are free to dispose of it as they wish. In copyright jargon, the 'first sale' has 'exhausted' the copyright owner's §106(3) exclusive distribution right.

"What, however, if the copy of *Herzog* was printed abroad and then initially sold with the copyright owner's permission? Does the 'first sale' doctrine still apply? Is the buyer, like the buyer of a domestically manufactured copy, free to bring the copy into the United States and dispose of it as he or she wishes?

"To put the matter technically, an 'importation' provision, §602(a)(1), says that
> 'Importation into the United States, without the authority of the owner of copyright under this title, of copies ... of a work that have been acquired outside the United States is an infringement of the exclusive right to distribute copies ... under section 106.'...

Thus §602(a)(1) makes clear that importing a copy without permission violates the owner's exclusive distribution right. But in doing so, §602(a)(1) refers explicitly to the *§106(3)* exclusive distribution right. As we have just said, §106 is by its terms '[s]ubject to' the various doctrines and principles contained in §§107 through 122, including §109(a)'s 'first sale' limitation. Do those same modifications apply—in particular, does the 'first sale' modification apply—when considering whether §602(a)(1) prohibits importing a copy?

"In *Quality King Distribs. v. L'anza Research Int'l* ... (1998), we held that §602(a)(1)'s reference to §106(3)'s exclusive distribution right incorporates the later subsections' limitations, including, in particular, the 'first sale' doctrine of §109. Thus, it might seem that, §602(a)(1) notwithstanding, one who buys a copy abroad can freely import that copy into the United States and dispose of it, just as he could had he bought the copy in the United States.

"But *Quality King* considered an instance in which the copy, though purchased abroad, was initially manufactured in the United States (and then sent abroad and sold). This case is like *Quality King* but for one important fact. The copies at issue here were manufactured abroad. That fact is important because §109(a) says that the 'first sale' doctrine applies to 'a particular copy or phonorecord *lawfully made under this title*.' And we must decide here whether the five words, 'lawfully made under this title,' make a critical legal difference.

"Putting section numbers to the side, we ask whether the 'first sale' doctrine applies to protect a buyer or other lawful owner of a copy (of a copyrighted work) lawfully manufactured abroad. Can that buyer bring that copy into the United States (and sell it or give it away) without obtaining permission to do so from the copyright owner? Can, for example, someone who purchases, say at a used bookstore, a book printed abroad subsequently resell it without the copyright owner's permission?

"In our view, the answers to these questions are, yes. We hold that the 'first sale' doctrine applies to copies of a copyrighted work lawfully made abroad....

"Respondent, John Wiley & Sons, Inc., publishes academic textbooks.... Each copy of a Wiley Asia foreign edition will likely contain language making clear that the copy is to be sold only in a particular country or geographical region outside the United States....

"The upshot is that there are two essentially equivalent versions of a Wiley textbook ... each version manufactured and sold with Wiley's permission: (1) an American version printed and sold in the United States, and (2) a foreign version manufactured and sold abroad. And Wiley makes certain that copies of the second version state that they are not to be taken (without permission) into the United States....

"We must decide whether the words 'lawfully made under this title' restrict the scope of §109(a)'s 'first sale' doctrine geographically. The Second Circuit, the Ninth Circuit, Wiley, and the Solicitor General (as *amicus*) all read those words as imposing a form of *geographical* limitation....

"Under any of these geographical interpretations, §109(a)'s 'first sale' doctrine would not apply to the Wiley Asia books at issue here. And, despite an American copyright owner's permission to *make* copies abroad, one who *buys* a copy of any such book or other copyrighted work— whether at a retail store, over the Internet, or at a library sale—could not resell (or otherwise dispose of) that particular copy without further permission.

"Kirtsaeng, however, reads the words 'lawfully made under this title' as imposing a *non-geographical limitation. He says that they mean made 'in accordance with' or 'in compliance with' the Copyright Act…. In that case, §109(a)'s 'first sale' doctrine would apply to copyrighted works as long as their manufacture met the requirements of American copyright law. In particular, the doctrine would apply where, as here, copies are manufactured abroad with the permission of the copyright owner….

"In our view, §109(a)'s language, its context, and the common-law history of the 'first sale' doctrine, taken together, favor a *non*-geographical interpretation. We also doubt that Congress would have intended to create the practical copyright-related harms with which a geographical interpretation would threaten ordinary scholarly, artistic, commercial, and consumer activities. We consequently conclude that Kirtsaeng's nongeographical reading is the better reading of the Act.

"The language of §109(a) read literally favors Kirtsaeng's nongeographical interpretation, namely, that 'lawfully made under this title' means made 'in accordance with' or 'in compliance with' the Copyright Act. The language of §109(a) says nothing about geography…. And a nongeographical interpretation provides each word of the five-word phrase with a distinct purpose. The first two words of the phrase, 'lawfully made,' suggest an effort to distinguish those copies that were made lawfully from those that were not, and the last three words, 'under this title,' set forth the standard of 'lawful[ness].' Thus, the nongeographical reading is simple, it promotes a traditional copyright objective (combatting piracy), and it makes word-by-word linguistic sense.

"The geographical interpretation, however, bristles with linguistic difficulties. It gives the word 'lawfully' little, if any, linguistic work to do. (How could a book be *un*lawfully 'made under this title'?) It imports geography into a statutory provision that says nothing explicitly about it. And it is far more complex than may at first appear.

"To read the clause geographically, Wiley, like the Second Circuit and the Solicitor General, must first emphasize the word 'under.' Indeed, Wiley reads 'under this title' to mean 'in conformance with the Copyright Act *where the Copyright Act is applicable*.'… Wiley must then take a second step, arguing that the Act 'is applicable' only in the United States…. One difficulty is that neither 'under' nor any other word in the phrase means 'where.'…

"A far more serious difficulty arises out of the uncertainty and complexity surrounding the second step's effort to read the necessary geographical limitation into the word 'applicable' (or the equivalent). Where, precisely, is the Copyright Act 'applicable'? The Act does not instantly *protect* an American copyright holder from unauthorized piracy taking place abroad. But that fact does not mean the Act is *inapplicable* to copies made abroad. As a matter of ordinary English, one can say that a statute imposing, say, a tariff upon 'any rhododendron grown in

Nepal' applies to *all* Nepalese rhododendrons. And, similarly, one can say that the American Copyright Act is *applicable* to *all* pirated copies, including those printed overseas. Indeed, the Act itself makes clear that (in the Solicitor General's language) foreign-printed pirated copies are 'subject to' the Act....

"The appropriateness of this linguistic usage is underscored by the fact that § 104 of the Act itself says that works '*subject to protection under this title*' include unpublished works 'without regard to the nationality or domicile of the author,' and works 'first published' in any one of the nearly 180 nations that have signed a copyright treaty with the United States.... Thus, ordinary English permits us to say that the Act 'applies' to an Irish manuscript lying in its author's Dublin desk drawer as well as to an original recording of a ballet performance first made in Japan and now on display in a Kyoto art gallery....

"In sum, we believe that geographical interpretations create more linguistic problems than they resolve. And considerations of simplicity and coherence tip the purely linguistic balance in Kirtsaeng's, nongeographical, favor.

"Both historical and contemporary statutory context indicate that Congress, when writing the present version of §109(a), did not have geography in mind....

"The 'first sale' doctrine is a common-law doctrine with an impeccable historic pedigree. In the early 17th century Lord Coke explained the common law's refusal to permit restraints on the alienation of chattels. Referring to Littleton, who wrote in the 15th century, ... Lord Coke wrote:

> '[If] a man be possessed of . . . a horse, or of any other chattel . . . and give or sell his whole interest . . . therein upon condition that the Donee or Vendee shall not alien[ate] the same, the [condition] is voi[d], because his whole interest . . . is out of him, so as he hath no possibilit[y] of a Reverter, and it is against Trade and Traffi[c], and bargaining and contracting betwee[n] man and man: and it is within the reason of our Author that it should ouster him of all power given to him.'

A law that permits a copyright holder to control the resale or other disposition of a chattel once sold is similarly 'against Trade and Traffi[c], and bargaining and contracting.'...

"With these last few words, Coke emphasizes the importance of leaving buyers of goods free to compete with each other when reselling or otherwise disposing of those goods. American law too has generally thought that competition, including freedom to resell, can work to the advantage of the consumer....

"The 'first sale' doctrine also frees courts from the administrative burden of trying to enforce restrictions upon difficult-to-trace, readily movable goods. And it avoids the selective enforcement inherent in any such effort. Thus, it is not surprising that for at least a century the 'first sale' doctrine has played an important role in American copyright law....

"The common-law doctrine makes no geographical distinctions; nor can we find any in *Bobbs-Merrill* (where this Court first applied the 'first sale' doctrine) or in §109(a)'s predecessor provision, which Congress enacted a year later.... And we can find no language, context, purpose, or history that would rebut a 'straightforward application' of that doctrine here....

"For these reasons we conclude that the considerations supporting Kirtsaeng's nongeographical interpretation of the words 'lawfully made under this title' are the more persuasive. The judgment of the Court of Appeals is reversed, and the case is remanded for further proceedings consistent with this opinion.

"It is so ordered."

GOOGLE SPAIN SL & GOOGLE INC. v.
AGENCIA ESPANOLADE PROTECCION DE DATOS & COSTEJA GONZALEZ
Case C-131/12 (Audencia Nacional-Grand Chamber [Spain] 2014)

BACKGROUND: EU Directive 95/46 which, according to Article 1, has the object of protecting the fundamental rights and freedoms of natural persons, and in particular their right to privacy with respect to the processing of personal data, and of removing obstacles to the free flow of such data, states in recitals 2, 10, 18 to 20 and 25 in its preamble:

"(2) ... data-processing systems are designed to serve man; ... they must, whatever the nationality or residence of natural persons, respect their fundamental rights and freedoms, notably the right to privacy, and contribute to ... the well-being of individuals ...

(10) ... the object of the national laws on the processing of personal data is to protect fundamental rights and freedoms, notably the right to privacy, which is recognised both in Article 8 of the European Convention for the Protection of Human Rights and Fundamental Freedoms [, signed in Rome on 4 November 1950,] and in the general principles of Community law; ... for that reason, the approximation of those laws must not result in any lessening of the protection they afford but must, on the contrary, seek to ensure a high level of protection in the Community ...

(18) ... in order to ensure that individuals are not deprived of the protection to which they are

entitled under this Directive, any processing of personal data in the Community must be carried out in accordance with the law of one of the Member States; … in this connection, processing carried out under the responsibility of a controller who is established in a Member State should be governed by the law of that State …

(19)   … establishment on the territory of a Member State implies the effective and real exercise of activity through stable arrangements; … the legal form of such an establishment, whether simply [a] branch or a subsidiary with a legal personality, is not the determining factor in this respect; … when a single controller is established on the territory of several Member States, particularly by means of subsidiaries, he must ensure, in order to avoid any circumvention of national rules, that each of the establishments fulfils the obligations imposed by the national law applicable to its activities;

(20)   … the fact that the processing of data is carried out by a person established in a third country must not stand in the way of the protection of individuals provided for in this Directive; … in these cases, the processing should be governed by the law of the Member State in which the means used are located, and there should be guarantees to ensure that the rights and obligations provided for in this Directive are respected in practice …

(25)   … the principles of protection must be reflected, on the one hand, in the obligations imposed on persons … responsible for processing, in particular regarding data quality, technical security, notification to the supervisory authority, and the circumstances under which processing can be carried out, and, on the other hand, in the right conferred on individuals, the data on whom are the subject of processing, to be informed that processing is taking place, to consult the data, to request corrections and even to object to processing in certain circumstances."

Directive 95/46 was transposed into Spanish Law by Organic Law No 15/1999 of 13 December 1999 on the protection of personal data (BOE No 298 of 14 December 1999, p. 43088).

On March 5, 2010, Mr. Costeja González, a Spanish national resident in Spain, lodged with the Agencia Espanola de Proteccion de Datos ("AEPD") a complaint against La Vanguardia Ediciones SL, which publishes a daily newspaper with a large circulation, in particular in Catalonia (Spain) ("La Vanguardia"), and against Google Spain and Google Inc. The complaint was based on the fact that, when an internet user entered Costeja González's name in the search engine of the Google group ("Google Search"), he would obtain links to two pages of La Vanguardia's newspaper, of January 19 and March 9, 1998 respectively, on which an announcement mentioning Costeja González's name appeared for a real-estate auction connected with attachment proceedings for the recovery of social security debts. By that complaint,

Costeja González requested, first, that La Vanguardia be required either to remove or alter those pages so that the personal data relating to him no longer appeared or to use certain tools made available by search engines in order to protect the data. Second, he requested that Google Spain or Google Inc. be required to remove or conceal the personal data relating to him so that they ceased to be included in the search results and no longer appeared in the links to La Vanguardia. Costeja González stated in this context that the attachment proceedings concerning him had been fully resolved for a number of years and that reference to them was now entirely irrelevant. By decision of July 30, 2010, the AEPD rejected the complaint in so far as it related to La Vanguardia, taking the view that the publication by it of the information in question was legally justified as it took place upon order of the Ministry of Labour and Social Affairs and was intended to give maximum publicity to the auction in order to secure as many bidders as possible. On the other hand, the complaint was upheld in so far as it was directed against Google Spain and Google Inc. The AEPD considered in this regard that operators of search engines are subject to data protection legislation given that they carry out data processing for which they are responsible and act as intermediaries in the information society. The AEPD took the view that it has the power to require the withdrawal of data and the prohibition of access to certain data by the operators of search engines when it considers that the locating and dissemination of the data are liable to compromise the fundamental right to data protection and the dignity of persons in the broad sense, and this would also encompass the mere wish of the person concerned that such data not be known to third parties. The AEPD considered that that obligation may be owed directly by operators of search engines, without it being necessary to erase the data or information from the website where they appear, including when retention of the information on that site is justified by a statutory provision.

Google Spain and Google Inc. brought separate actions against that decision before the Audencia Nacional (National High Court). The Audencia Nacional considered the two actions together.

THE COURT:

"[T]he actions raise the question of what obligations are owed by operators of search engines to protect personal data of persons concerned who do not wish that certain information, which is published on third parties' websites and contains personal data relating to them that enable that information to be linked to them, be located, indexed and made available to internet users indefinitely. The answer to that question depends on the way in which Directive 95/46 must be interpreted in the context of these technologies, which appeared after the directive's publication....

"1.   With regard to the territorial application of Directive [95/46] and, consequently, of the

Spanish data protection legislation:

(a)   must it be considered that an 'establishment', within the meaning of Article 4(1)(a) of Directive 95/46, exists when any one or more of the following circumstances arise: –when the undertaking providing the search engine sets up in a Member State an office or subsidiary for the purpose of promoting and selling advertising space on the search engine, which orientates its activity towards the inhabitants of that State, or –when the parent company designates a subsidiary located in that Member State as its representative and controller for two specific filing systems which relate to the data of customers who have contracted for advertising with that undertaking, or –when the office or subsidiary established in a Member State forwards to the parent company, located outside the European Union, requests and requirements addressed to it both by data subjects and by the authorities with responsibility for ensuring observation of the right to data protection, even where such collaboration is engaged in voluntarily?

(b)   Must Article 4(1)(c) of Directive 95/46 be interpreted as meaning that there is 'use of equipment … situated on the territory of the said Member State': –when a search engine uses crawlers or robots to locate and index information contained in web pages located on servers in that Member State, or –when it uses a domain name pertaining to a Member State and arranges for searches and the results thereof to be based on the language of that Member State?

(c)   Is it possible to regard as a use of equipment, in the terms of Article 4(1)(c) of Directive 95/46, the temporary storage of the information indexed by internet search engines? If the answer to that question is affirmative, can it be considered that that connecting factor is present when the undertaking refuses to disclose the place where it stores those indexes, invoking reasons of competition?

(d)   Regardless of the answers to the foregoing questions and particularly in the event that the Court … considers that the connecting factors referred to in Article 4 of [Directive 95/46] are not present: must Directive 95/46 … be applied, in the light of Article 8 of the [Charter], in the Member State where the centre of gravity of the conflict is located and more effective protection of the rights of … Union citizens is possible?

"2.   As regards the activity of search engines as providers of content in relation to Directive 95/46 …:

(a)   in relation to the activity of [Google Search], as a provider of content, consisting in locating information published or included on the net by third parties, indexing it automatically, storing it temporarily and finally making it available to internet users according to a particular order of preference, when that information contains personal data of third parties: must an activity like the one described be interpreted as falling within the concept of "processing of … data" used in Article 2(b) of Directive 95/46?

(b)   If the answer to the foregoing question is affirmative, and once again in relation to an activity like the one described: must Article 2(d) of Directive 95/46 be interpreted as meaning that the undertaking managing [Google Search] is to be regarded as the "controller" of the personal data contained in the web pages that it indexes?

(c)   In the event that the answer to the foregoing question is affirmative: may the [AEPD], protecting the rights embodied in [Article] 12(b) and [subparagraph (a) of the first paragraph of Article 14] of Directive 95/46, directly impose on [Google Search] a requirement that it withdraw from its indexes an item of information published by third parties, without addressing itself in advance or simultaneously to the owner of the web page on which that information is located?

(d)   In the event that the answer to the foregoing question is affirmative: would the obligation of search engines to protect those rights be excluded when the information that contains the personal data has been lawfully published by third parties and is kept on the web page from which it originates?

"3.   Regarding the scope of the right of erasure and/or the right to object, in relation to the 'derecho al olvido' (the 'right to be forgotten'), the following question is asked: must it be considered that the rights to erasure and blocking of data, provided for in Article 12(b), and the right to object, provided for by [subparagraph (a) of the first paragraph of Article 14] of Directive 95/46, extend to enabling the data subject to address himself to search engines in order to prevent indexing of the information relating to him personally, published on third parties' web pages, invoking his wish that such information should not be known to internet users when he considers that it might be prejudicial to him or he wishes it to be consigned to oblivion, even though the information in question has been lawfully published by third parties?'

"Consideration of the questions referred ...

"By Question 2(a) and (b), which it is appropriate to examine first, the referring court asks, in essence, whether Article 2(b) of Directive 95/46 is to be interpreted as meaning that the activity of a search engine as a provider of content which consists in finding information published or placed on the internet by third parties, indexing it automatically, storing it temporarily and, finally, making it available to internet users according to a particular order of preference must be classified as 'processing of personal data' within the meaning of that provision when that information contains personal data. If the answer is in the affirmative, the referring court seeks to ascertain furthermore whether Article 2(d) of Directive 95/46 is to be interpreted as meaning that the operator of a search engine must be regarded as the 'controller' in respect of that processing of the personal data, within the meaning of that provision....

"Article 2(b) of Directive 95/46 defines 'processing of personal data' as 'any operation or set of operations which is performed upon personal data, whether or not by automatic means, such as collection, recording, organisation, storage, adaptation or alteration, retrieval, consultation, use, disclosure by transmission, dissemination or otherwise making available, alignment or combination, blocking, erasure or destruction'…. So far as concerns the activity at issue in the main proceedings, it is not contested that the data found, indexed and stored by search engines and made available to their users include information relating to identified or identifiable natural persons and thus 'personal data' within the meaning of Article 2(a) of that directive.

"Therefore, it must be found that, in exploring the internet automatically, constantly and systematically in search of the information which is published there, the operator of a search engine 'collects' such data which it subsequently 'retrieves', 'records' and 'organises' within the framework of its indexing programmes, 'stores' on its servers and, as the case may be, 'discloses' and 'makes available' to its users in the form of lists of search results. As those operations are referred to expressly and unconditionally in Article 2(b) of Directive 95/46, they must be classified as 'processing' within the meaning of that provision, regardless of the fact that the operator of the search engine also carries out the same operations in respect of other types of information and does not distinguish between the latter and the personal data. Nor is the foregoing finding affected by the fact that those data have already been published on the internet and are not altered by the search engine….

"As to the question whether the operator of a search engine must be regarded as the 'controller' in respect of the processing of personal data that is carried out by that engine in the context of an activity such as that at issue in the main proceedings, it should be recalled that Article 2(d) of Directive 95/46 defines 'controller' as 'the natural or legal person, public authority, agency or any other body which alone or jointly with others determines the purposes and means of the processing of personal data'…. Moreover, it is undisputed that that activity of search engines plays a decisive role in the overall dissemination of those data in that it renders the latter accessible to any internet user making a search on the basis of the data subject's name, including to internet users who otherwise would not have found the web page on which those data are published. Also, the organisation and aggregation of information published on the internet that are effected by search engines with the aim of facilitating their users' access to that information may, when users carry out their search on the basis of an individual's name, result in them obtaining through the list of results a structured overview of the information relating to that individual that can be found on the internet enabling them to establish a more or less detailed profile of the data subject. Inasmuch as the activity of a search engine is therefore liable to affect significantly, and additionally compared with that of the publishers of websites, the fundamental rights to privacy and to the protection of personal data, the operator of the search engine as the person determining the purposes and means of that activity must ensure, within the framework of its responsibilities, powers and capabilities, that the activity meets the requirements of Directive 95/46 in order that the guarantees laid down by the directive may have full effect and that effective and complete protection of data subjects, in particular of their right to privacy, may actually be achieved….

"Question 1(a) to (d), concerning the territorial scope of Directive 95/46 …

"… [I]t cannot be accepted that the processing of personal data carried out for the purposes of the operation of the search engine should escape the obligations and guarantees laid down by Directive 95/46, which would compromise the directive's effectiveness and the effective and complete protection of the fundamental rights and freedoms of natural persons which the directive seeks to ensure … in particular their right to privacy, with respect to the processing of personal data, a right to which the directive accords special importance as is confirmed in particular by Article 1(1) thereof and recitals 2 and 10 in its preamble….

"It follows … that the answer to Question 1(a) is that Article 4(1)(a) of Directive 95/46 is to be interpreted as meaning that processing of personal data is carried out in the context of the activities of an establishment of the controller on the territory of a Member State, within the meaning of that provision, when the operator of a search engine sets up in a Member State a branch or subsidiary which is intended to promote and sell advertising space offered by that engine and which orientates its activity towards the inhabitants of that Member State….

"In view of the answer given to Question 1(a), there is no need to answer Question 1(b) to (d).

"Question 2(c) and (d), concerning the extent of the responsibility of the operator of a search engine under Directive 95/46

"By Question 2(c) and (d), the referring court asks, in essence, whether Article 12(b) and subparagraph (a) of the first paragraph of Article 14 of Directive 95/46 are to be interpreted as meaning that, in order to comply with the rights laid down in those provisions, the operator of a search engine is obliged to remove from the list of results displayed following a search made on the basis of a person's name links to web pages, published by third parties and containing information relating to that person, also in a case where that name or information is not erased beforehand or simultaneously from those web pages, and even, as the case may be, when its publication in itself on those pages is lawful….

"Article 7 of the Charter guarantees the right to respect for private life, whilst Article 8 of the Charter expressly proclaims the right to the protection of personal data. Article 8(2) and (3) specify that such data must be processed fairly for specified purposes and on the basis of the consent of the person concerned or some other legitimate basis laid down by law, that everyone has the right of access to data which have been collected concerning him or her and the right to have the data rectified, and that compliance with these rules is to be subject to control by an independent authority. Those requirements are implemented inter alia by Articles 6, 7, 12, 14 and 28 of Directive 95/46....

"... [I]t is to be noted that it is clear from Article 28(3) and (4) of Directive 95/46 that each supervisory authority is to hear claims lodged by any person concerning the protection of his rights and freedoms in regard to the processing of personal data and that it has investigative powers and effective powers of intervention enabling it to order in particular the blocking, erasure or destruction of data or to impose a temporary or definitive ban on such processing....

"Following the appraisal of the conditions for the application of Article 12(b) and subparagraph (a) of the first paragraph of Article 14 of Directive 95/46 which is to be carried out when a request such as that at issue in the main proceedings is lodged with it, the supervisory authority or judicial authority may order the operator of the search engine to remove from the list of results displayed following a search made on the basis of a person's name links to web pages published by third parties containing information relating to that person, without an order to that effect presupposing the previous or simultaneous removal of that name and information—of the publisher's own accord or following an order of one of those authorities—from the web page on which they were published.

"In the light of all the foregoing considerations, the answer to Question 2(c) and (d) is that Article 12(b) and subparagraph (a) of the first paragraph of Article 14 of Directive 95/46 are to be interpreted as meaning that, in order to comply with the rights laid down in those provisions and in so far as the conditions laid down by those provisions are in fact satisfied, the operator of a search engine is obliged to remove from the list of results displayed following a search made on the basis of a person's name links to web pages, published by third parties and containing information relating to that person, also in a case where that name or information is not erased beforehand or simultaneously from those web pages, and even, as the case may be, when its publication in itself on those pages is lawful.

"Question 3, concerning the scope of the data subject's rights guaranteed by Directive 95/46

"By Question 3, the referring court asks, in essence, whether Article 12(b) and subparagraph (a) of the first paragraph of Article 14 of Directive 95/46 are to be interpreted as enabling the data subject to require the operator of a search engine to remove from the list of results displayed following a search made on the basis of his name links to web pages published lawfully by third parties and containing true information relating to him, on the ground that that information may be prejudicial to him or that he wishes it to be 'forgotten' after a certain time....

"... In this connection, it must be pointed out that it is not necessary in order to find such a right that the inclusion of the information in question in the list of results causes prejudice to the data subject....

"As regards a situation such as that at issue in the main proceedings, which concerns the display, in the list of results that the internet user obtains by making a search by means of Google Search on the basis of the data subject's name, of links to pages of the on-line archives of a daily newspaper that contain announcements mentioning the data subject's name and relating to a real-estate auction connected with attachment proceedings for the recovery of social security debts, it should be held that, having regard to the sensitivity for the data subject's private life of the information contained in those announcements and to the fact that its initial publication had taken place 16 years earlier, the data subject establishes a right that that information should no longer be linked to his name by means of such a list. Accordingly, since in the case in point there do not appear to be particular reasons substantiating a preponderant interest of the public in having, in the context of such a search, access to that information, a matter which is, however, for the referring court to establish, the data subject may, by virtue of Article 12(b) and subparagraph (a) of the first paragraph of Article 14 of Directive 95/46, require those links to be removed from the list of results....

"On those grounds, the Court (Grand Chamber) hereby rules:

1.   Article 2(b) and (d) of Directive 95/46/EC of the European Parliament and of the Council of 24 October 1995 on the protection of individuals with regard to the processing of personal data and on the free movement of such data are to be interpreted as meaning that, first, the activity of a search engine consisting in finding information published or placed on the internet by third parties, indexing it automatically, storing it temporarily and, finally, making it available to internet users according to a particular order of preference must be classified as 'processing of personal data' within the meaning of Article 2(b) when that information contains personal data and, second, the operator of the search engine must be regarded as the 'controller' in respect of that processing, within the meaning of Article 2(d).

2.   Article 4(1)(a) of Directive 95/46 is to be interpreted as meaning that processing of personal data is carried out in the context of the activities of an establishment of the controller on the territory of a Member State, within the meaning of that provision, when the operator of a search engine sets up in a Member State a branch or subsidiary which is intended to promote and sell advertising space offered by that engine and which orientates its activity towards the inhabitants of that Member State.

3.   Article 12(b) and subparagraph (a) of the first paragraph of Article 14 of Directive 95/46 are to be interpreted as meaning that, in order to comply with the rights laid down in those provisions and in so far as the conditions laid down by those provisions are in fact satisfied, the

operator of a search engine is obliged to remove from the list of results displayed following a search made on the basis of a person's name links to web pages, published by third parties and containing information relating to that person, also in a case where that name or information is not erased beforehand or simultaneously from those web pages, and even, as the case may be, when its publication in itself on those pages is lawful.

4.   Article 12(b) and subparagraph (a) of the first paragraph of Article 14 of Directive 95/46 are to be interpreted as meaning that, when appraising the conditions for the application of those provisions, it should inter alia be examined whether the data subject has a right that the information in question relating to him personally should, at this point in time, no longer be linked to his name by a list of results displayed following a search made on the basis of his name, without it being necessary in order to find such a right that the inclusion of the information in question in that list causes prejudice to the data subject. As the data subject may, in the light of his fundamental rights under Articles 7 and 8 of the Charter, request that the information in question no longer be made available to the general public on account of its inclusion in such a list of results, those rights override, as a rule, not only the economic interest of the operator of the search engine but also the interest of the general public in having access to that information upon a search relating to the data subject's name. However, that would not be the case if it appeared, for particular reasons, such as the role played by the data subject in public life, that the interference with his fundamental rights is justified by the preponderant interest of the general public in having, on account of its inclusion in the list of results, access to the information in question."

DALLAS BUYERS CLUB LLC v. iiNET LIMITED
   [2015] FCA 317 (Federal Court of Australia, 2015)

BACKGROUND: Dallas Buyers Club LLC, a USA entity claiming to own the copyright on the 2012 film, *Dallas Buyers Club*, and its parent company—Voltage Pictures LLC—asked the court for a discovery order against six Australian internet service providers ("ISPs"). The applicants say that they have identified 4,726 unique IP addresses from which their film was shared online using BitTorrent, a peer-to-peer file sharing network, and that this occurred without their permission, thus infringing their copyright contrary to the 1968 Australian Copyright Act. The applicants do not know the identity of the 4,726 individuals involved in this activity, but they do have evidence that each of the IP addresses from which the sharing occurred was supplied by the respondent ISPs and they believe that the ISPs can identify the relevant account holder associated with each IP address.

REASONS FOR JUDGMENT:

"The ISPs resist the application on many bases. They say that the evidence which the applicants have put forward to identify the infringing IP addresses is not sufficient to do so, that the claim against any putative respondent is speculative and that the pre-conditions which must exist before this Court is permitted to order preliminary discovery have not been satisfied. In that context, the ISPs also deny that the applicants have proven that either of them is the owner of the copyright in the film. If all of those contentions are rejected they submit that the Court should not, as a matter of discretion, order them to divulge their customers' personal and private information. The reasons for this were various. The monetary claims which the applicants had against each infringer were so small that it was plain that no such case could or would be maintained by the applicants. There was, on this view, no point in ordering the ISPs to divulge their customers' details because there was never going to be a court case against the customers which made any commercial sense. Allied to that point, the ISPs submitted that they were subject to statutory obligations of privacy which, given what they said was the paucity of the case against the customers, were not lightly to be cast aside by Court orders...

"My conclusions are these: I will order the ISPs to divulge the names and physical addresses of the customers associated in their records with each of the 4,726 IP addresses. I will impose upon the applicants a condition that this information only be used for the purposes of recovering compensation for the infringements and is not otherwise to be disclosed without the leave of this Court. I will also impose a condition on the applicants that they are to submit to me a draft of any letter they propose to send to account holders associated with the IP addresses which have been identified. The applicants will pay the costs of the proceedings...

"In this Court there are two kinds of preliminary discovery, one of which facilitates finding out whether a party has a case against another person and the other of which is to ascertain the identity of a putative respondent where that is not known. This case is concerned with the latter. It is governed by r 7.22 of the *Federal Court Rules 2011* (Cth) ('FCR 7.22')....

"To meet the requirements of FCR 7.22 it is therefore necessary for the applicants to satisfy the Court that they may have a right to obtain relief against a prospective respondent, that they cannot identify the prospective respondent and that the ISPs know or are likely to know the identity of that person or have a document which reveals it. In addition, the definition of 'prospective applicant' in r 7.21 of the *Federal Court Rules 2011* as a person who 'reasonably believes that there may be a right for the person to obtain relief against another person who is not presently a party to a proceeding in the Court' means that the applicants must possess such a belief and that belief must be reasonable. The ISPs submitted that this was significant because there was no evidence which the Court would accept that Dallas Buyers Club LLC believed that it might have such a right....

"In [these] circumstances, I conclude that the pre-conditions to the operation of FCR 7.22 have been met. The Court's power to order the ISPs to give preliminary discovery is enlivened. I turn then to the issue of discretion, that is, whether that power should be exercised.

"The ISPs advanced 8 reasons why the Court ought to decline to order preliminary discovery even if the power to do so under FCR 7.22 were enlivened. These were: (i) it was only shown that a single sliver of the film was shared from each IP address. Whatever infringement of the copyright was involved it was minor; (ii) given the trivial nature of the demonstrated infringements it was unlikely that any real case would be brought against the infringers. The value of each copy of the film was less than $10 and it was simply not plausible to think that the applicants would seek to recover such sums; (iii) there were no realistic chances of the applicants obtaining injunctive relief, either because all that was shown was the sharing of a sliver or because there was no demonstrated risk of repetition; (iv) the applicants had failed to do adequate monitoring which could have revealed serious infringers, i.e. persons involved in multiple downloads of multiple films; (v) there was evidence which suggested that the applicants were going to engage in the practice of speculative invoicing if they were given the information which they sought. What was meant by this was that the applicants would write to the account holders demanding a large sum of money and offering to settle for a smaller sum which was still very much in excess of what might actually be recovered in any actual suit. This was said, in effect, to be sharp practice; (vi) the ISPs were subject to privacy obligations with respect to their customers which should be respected; (vii) the Federal government had required the industry to formulate an industry code dealing with the issue of internet piracy and the Court should wait until that code was in place rather than granting the relief sought; and (viii) the FCR 7.22 process was being used as a tool of investigation rather than identification.

"I do not accept that these matters, either individually or cumulatively, would justify me in withholding relief to the applicants, although I do accept that some of them impact on the terms upon which discovery should be granted....

"As to ... (the trivial nature of each sharing incident): it is, I think, important to be clear about what is involved in an application under FCR 7.22. It is a procedure to identify putative respondents. It is not a procedure for working out how good those claims are, other than in the sense of eliminating plainly frivolous exercises. But it is very far from apparent that the current exercise is frivolous. It may be true that for single instances of infringement the damages are likely to be modest and quite possibly limited to the foregone licence fee that would have been paid had the film been lawfully downloaded, although *quaere* whether this is so where the film had been shared because it was not available in the Australian market at all.

"Regardless, I am not persuaded that a suit by the copyright owner naming individual BitTorrent users would be economically pointless. Further, in the case of multiple downloaders it must be considered at least plausible that a copyright owner may be able to obtain aggravated damages....

"Having regard to the likely identity of many account holders and their potential vulnerability to what may appear to be abusive practices I propose to impose conditions on the applicants that will prevent speculative invoicing. This course has been taken in other jurisdictions....

"As to ... (privacy concerns): this is indeed a relevant matter. Elaborate provision is made under Federal law for the protection of the privacy of individuals' telecommunications activity.... By s 280, nothing in Div 2 prevents disclosure required by law. Thus, regardless of its contents, nothing in Div 2 prevents this Court from ordering the ISPs to disclose the information in question....

"In situations where different rights clash it is usual for courts to try and accommodate both rights as best they can. Here that can be done by requiring the information to be provided but by imposing, by way of conditions, safeguards to ensure that the private information remains private....

"Further, I propose to constrain the use to which the information may be put to purposes relating only to the recovery of compensation for infringement. Those purposes would seem to be limited to three situations: (a) seeking to identify end-users using BitTorrent to download the film; (b) suing end-users for infringement; and (c) negotiating with end-users regarding their liability for infringement....

"The *Federal Court Rules 2011* (Cth) do not authorise the Court to order the production of email addresses and I do not propose to order that the operation of the rules be altered to achieve that outcome. In *Voltage Pictures LLC v John Doe* [2014] ... it was recognised that the Court should not generally order the production of email addresses.

"I will make orders in due course which: (a) provide for the preliminary discovery sought; (b) impose privacy obligations on the material produced; (c) require the applicants to submit to this Court for its approval a draft of the letter they propose to write to account holders; (d) require the applicants to pay the ISPs' costs of these proceedings as taxed or agreed; and (e) require the applicants to pay the ISPs' costs of giving preliminary discovery as taxed or agreed....

"The only order I will make [at this point] is that the matter be listed on 21 April 2015 for the making of orders."

KINGDOM OF SPAIN v.
EUROPEAN PARLIAMENT & COUNCIL OF THE EUROPEAN UNION
Case C-146/13 (E.U. Court of Justice, 5 May 2015)

BACKGROUND: The Kingdom of Spain requests the annulment of Regulation No 1257/2012 of the European Parliament and of the Council of December 17, 2012, implementing enhanced cooperation in the area of the creation of unitary patent protection. Article 2 of the European Patent Convention ("EPC") states: "(1) Patents granted under this Convention shall be called European patents; (2) The European patent shall, in each of the Contracting States for which it is granted, have the effect of and be subject to the same conditions as a national patent granted by that State, unless this Convention provides otherwise." Article 142 of the EPC, headed "Unitary patents," provides: "(1) Any group of Contracting States which has provided by a special agreement that a European patent granted for those States has a unitary character throughout their territories may provide that a European patent may only be granted jointly in respect of all those States; (2) Where any group of Contracting States has availed itself of the authorisation given in paragraph 1, the rules of this Part shall apply...."

"In support of its action, the Kingdom of Spain relies on seven pleas in law: (i) infringement of the values of the rule of law; (ii) a lack of legal basis; (iii) a misuse of powers; (iv) infringement of Article 291(2) TFEU [Treaty on the Functioning of the EU] and, in the alternative, of the principles laid down in the judgment in *Meroni* v *High Authority* ... ; (v) infringement of those principles owing to the delegation to the EPO [European Patent Office] of certain administrative tasks relating to the EPUE [European Patent with Unitary Effect], and (vi) and (vii) infringement of the principles of autonomy and uniform application of EU law."

JUDGMENT:

"The Kingdom of Spain claims that the contested regulation must be annulled on the ground that it disregards the values of the rule of law set out in Article 2 TEU [Treaty of the European Union]. It argues that the contested regulation provides for protection based on the European patent, although the administrative procedure preceding the grant of such a patent is not subject to judicial review to ensure the correct and uniform application of EU law and the protection of fundamental rights, which undermines the principle of effective judicial protection. The Kingdom of Spain adds that it is unacceptable that that regulation should 'incorporate' into the EU legal order measures emanating from an international body which is not subject to the aforementioned principles and that the EU legislature should incorporate within its legislation an international system in which compliance with the constitutional principles set out in the FEU

Treaty is not guaranteed. The Kingdom of Spain argues, in that context, first, that the Boards of Appeal and the Enlarged Board of Appeal of the European Patent Office are bodies established within that office which are not independent of it, and, second, that the decisions of those boards of appeal are not subject to any form of judicial review, since the European Patent Organisation enjoys immunity from legal proceedings and enforcement.

"The Parliament, after stating that the EPUE system is based on a rational choice made by the EU legislature, which is recognised to have broad discretion in such matters, contends that the level of protection of rights of individuals which is offered by the contested regulation and guaranteed by both the EPC and the Unified Patent Court is compatible with the principles of the rule of law. Administrative appeals may be brought before various bodies within the European Patent Office against administrative decisions of that office regarding the grant of an EPUE. The level of protection enjoyed by individuals under the EPC has been deemed acceptable by the Member States, which are all parties to that convention.

"The Council asserts that the first plea in law lacks clarity, contending, primarily, that the transfer of powers to an international organisation is compatible with the protection of human rights, provided that fundamental rights enjoy equivalent protection within the organisation concerned, as is the situation in the present case. In the alternative, according to the Council, Article 9(3) of the contested regulation obliges the Member States to ensure effective legal protection....

"It follows from the foregoing that the contested regulation is in no way intended to delimit, even partially, the conditions for granting European patents—which are exclusively governed by the EPC and not by EU law—and that it does not 'incorporate' the procedure for granting European patents laid down by the EPC into EU law.

"Instead, it necessarily follows from the characterisation of the contested regulation as 'a special agreement within the meaning of Article 142 of the EPC'—a characterisation which is not contested by the Kingdom of Spain—that that regulation merely (i) establishes the conditions under which a European patent previously granted by the EPO pursuant to the provisions of the EPC may, at the request of the patent proprietor, benefit from unitary effect and (ii) provides a definition of that unitary effect.

"It follows ... that the first plea in law, which is intended to contest the legality, in the light of EU law, of the administrative procedure preceding the grant of a European patent, is ineffective and must therefore be rejected....

"By its seventh plea in law, the Kingdom of Spain submits that the second subparagraph of Article 18(2) of the contested regulation gives the Member States the capacity to decide unilaterally whether that regulation is to apply to them. Thus, if a Member State were to decide not to ratify the UPC Agreement, the contested regulation would not be applicable to that Member State and the Unified Patent Court would not acquire exclusive jurisdiction over its territory to decide on EPUE cases, with the result that EPUEs would not have unitary effect as regards that Member State. Accordingly, that provision infringes the principles of autonomy and the uniform application of EU law.

"The Parliament observes, as a preliminary point, that the relationship between the contested regulation and the UPC Agreement is an essential prerequisite of the functioning of the EPUE and does not constitute a breach of EU law. The UPC Agreement fulfils the two essential conditions required to preserve the autonomy of the EU legal order given that, first, the essential character of the powers of the European Union and its institutions is not altered and, second, that agreement does not impose any particular interpretation of the EU legal provisions contained therein on the European Union or on its institutions in the exercise of their internal powers.

"Neither does the creation of the Unified Patent Court undermine any competence of the European Union. First of all, the power to create a unified patent court and to determine the scope of its powers continues to fall to the Member States and has not been entrusted exclusively to the European Union. Next, the contested regulation expressly requires Member States to grant the Unified Patent Court exclusive jurisdiction. That regulation, the legal basis of which is the first paragraph of Article 118 TFEU, explicitly allows the Member States to adopt provisions in respect of patents which provide for derogations from Regulation No 1215/2012. Furthermore, the EU legislature makes the entry into force of the UPC Agreement conditional upon the necessary changes being made by that legislator to Regulation No 1215/2012 as regards the relationship between that regulation and that agreement. Last, several provisions of the FEU Treaty make the entry into force of an act of secondary EU legislation conditional upon its approval by the Member States.

"The Parliament also contends that a Member State's refusal to ratify the UPC Agreement, which would mean that the contested regulation would not apply in its territory, would constitute a failure to fulfil its obligations under Article 4(3) TEU. According to that institution, even assuming that there is a risk to the uniform application of the contested regulation, such a risk is justified in view of the need to provide effective legal protection and to comply with the principle of legal certainty.

"The Council contends that the policy choice made by the EU legislature was to link the EPUE to the functioning of a distinct judicial body (the Unified Patent Court), thereby both ensuring consistency of case-law and providing legal certainty. There is no legal obstacle to the creation of a link between the EPUE and the Unified Patent Court, a link which is explained in recitals 24 and 25 of the contested regulation. Moreover, there are several examples in legislative practice of cases where the applicability of a Union act has been conditional upon the occurrence of an event outside the scope of that act. Concerning the matter of the number of ratifications necessary for the UPC Agreement to enter into force, the reason for setting that number at 13 was the desire of the Member States to ensure that the EPUE and the Unified Patent Court be established quickly.

"As a preliminary point, it should be stated that the first two parts of the sixth plea in law are intended to establish, first, that the provisions of the UPC Agreement are not compatible with EU law and, second, that ratification by the participating Member States of the UPC Agreement is impossible unless they disregard their obligations under EU law.

"However, it should be borne in mind that, in an action brought under Article 263 TFEU, the Court does not have jurisdiction to rule on the lawfulness of an international agreement concluded by Member States.

"Nor do the Courts of the European Union have jurisdiction in such an action to rule on the lawfulness of a measure adopted by a national authority....

"It follows that the first two parts of the sixth plea in law must be rejected as being inadmissible.

"Regarding the third part of that plea, it should be noted that the first subparagraph of Article 18(2) of the contested regulation provides that that regulation is to apply 'from 1 January 2014 or the date of entry into force of [the UPC Agreement], whichever is the later'....

"As regards the argument raised by the Kingdom of Spain in the seventh plea in law that the second subparagraph of Article 18(2) of the contested regulation gives the Member States the capacity to decide unilaterally whether that regulation is to apply to them, it is based on a false premiss, given that the provision in question allows for derogation only from Article 3(1) and (2) and Article 4(1) of the contested regulation, to the exclusion of all other provisions of that regulation. A partial and temporary derogation of that kind is moreover justified on the grounds set out ... above.

"It follows from the foregoing that the sixth and seventh pleas in law must be rejected. In the light of all the foregoing, the action, including the Kingdom of Spain's claim in the alternative for the partial annulment of the contested regulation, must be dismissed in its entirety....

"On those grounds, the Court (Grand Chamber) hereby:

1.   Dismisses the action;

2.   Orders the Kingdom of Spain to bear its own costs and to pay the costs incurred by the European Parliament and the Council of the European Union;

3.   Orders the Kingdom of Belgium, the Czech Republic, the Kingdom of Denmark, the Federal Republic of Germany, the French Republic, the Grand Duchy of Luxembourg, Hungary, the Kingdom of the Netherlands, the Kingdom of Sweden, the United Kingdom of Great Britain and Northern Ireland and the European Commission to bear their own costs."

[Signatures]

THE BARCELONA TRACTION, LIGHT AND POWER COMPANY, LIMITED (BELGIUM v. SPAIN)
I.C.J. Reports 1970, p. 3 (International Court of Justice 1970)

THE COURT ... *delivers the following Judgment*:

"1. In 1958 the Belgian Government filed with the International Court of Justice an Application against the Spanish Government seeking reparation for damage allegedly caused to the Barcelona Traction, Light and Power Company, Limited, on account of acts said to be contrary to international law committed by organs of the Spanish State. After the filing of the Belgian Memorial and the submission of preliminary objections by the Spanish Government, the Belgian Government gave notice of discontinuance of the proceedings, with a view to negotiations between the representatives of the private interests concerned. The case was removed from the Court's General List on 10 April 1961.

"2. On 19 June 1962, the negotiations having failed, the Belgian Government submitted to the Court a new Application, claiming reparation for the damage allegedly sustained by Belgian nationals, shareholders in the Barcelona Traction company, on account of acts said to be contrary to international law committed in respect of the company by organs of the Spanish State. On 15 March 1963 the Spanish Government raised ... preliminary objections to the Belgian Application....

"8. The Barcelona Traction, Light and Power Company, Limited, is a holding company incorporated in 1911 in Toronto (Canada), where it has its head office. For the purpose of creating and developing an electric power production and distribution system in Catalonia (Spain), it formed a number of operating, financing and concession-holding subsidiary companies. Three of these companies, whose shares it owned wholly or almost wholly, were

311

incorporated under Canadian law and had their registered offices in Canada (Ebro Irrigation and Power Company, Limited, Catalonian Land Company, Limited and International Utilities Finance Corporation, Limited); the others were incorporated under Spanish law and had their registered offices in Spain. At the time of the outbreak of the Spanish Civil War the group, through its operating subsidiaries, supplied the major part of Catalonia's electricity requirements....

"9. According to the Belgian Government, some years after the First World War Barcelona Traction's share capital came to be very largely held by Belgian nationals—natural or juristic persons—and a very high percentage of the shares has since then continuously belonged to Belgian nationals, particularly the Societe Internationale d'Energie Hydro-Electrique (Sidro), whose principal shareholder, the Societe Financiere de Transports et d'Entreprises Industrielles (Sofina), is itself a company in which Belgian interests are preponderant. The fact that large blocks of shares were for certain periods transferred to American nominees, to protect these securities in the event of invasion of Belgian territory during the Second World War, is not, according to the Belgian contention, of any relevance in this connection, as it was Belgian nationals, particularly Sidro, who continued to be the real owners. For a time the shares were vested in a trustee, but the Belgian Government maintains that the trust terminated in 1946. The Spanish Government contends, on the contrary, that the Belgian nationality of the shareholders is not proven and that the trustee or the nominees must be regarded as the true shareholders in the case of the shares concerned....

"10. Barcelona Traction issued several series of bonds, some in pesetas but principally in sterling. The issues were secured by trust deeds, with the National Trust Company, Limited, of Toronto as trustee of the sterling bonds, the security consisting essentially of a charge on bonds and shares of Ebro and other subsidiaries and of a mortgage executed by Ebro in favour of National Trust. The sterling bonds were serviced out of transfers to Barcelona Traction effected by the subsidiary companies operating in Spain.

"In 1936 the servicing of the Barcelona Traction bonds was suspended on account of the Spanish civil war. In 1940 payment of interest on the peseta bonds was resumed with the authorization of the Spanish exchange control authorities (required because the debt was owed by a foreign company), but authorization for the transfer of the foreign currency necessary for the servicing of the sterling bonds was refused and those interest payments were never resumed.

"11. In 1946 Barcelona Traction proposed a plan of compromise which provided for the reimbursement of the sterling debt. When the Spanish authorities refused to authorize the transfer of the necessary foreign currency, this plan was twice modified. In its final form, the plan provided ... for an advance redemption by Ebro of Barcelona Traction peseta bonds, for

312

which authorization was likewise required. Such authorization was refused by the Spanish authorities. Later, when the Belgian Government complained of the refusals to authorize foreign currency transfers, without which the debts on the bonds could not be honoured, the Spanish Government stated that the transfers could not be authorized unless it was shown that the foreign currency was to be used to repay debts arising from the genuine importation of foreign capital into Spain, and that this had not been established....

"33. When a State admits into its territory foreign investments or foreign nationals, whether natural or juristic persons, it is bound to extend to them the protection of the law and assumes obligations concerning the treatment to be afforded them. These obligations, however, are neither absolute nor unqualified. In particular, an essential distinction should be drawn between the obligations of a State towards the international community as a whole, and those arising vis-à-vis another State in the field of diplomatic protection. By their very nature the former are the concern of all States. In view of the importance of the rights involved, all States can be held to have a legal interest in their protection....

"35. Obligations the performance of which is the subject of diplomatic protection are not of the same category. It cannot be held, when one such obligation in particular is in question, in a specific case, that all States have a legal interest in its observance. In order to bring a claim in respect of the breach of such an obligation, a State must first establish its right to do so, for the rules on the subject rest on two suppositions: 'The first is that the defendant State has broken an obligation towards the national State in respect to its nationals. The second is that only the party to whom an international obligation is due can bring a claim in respect to its breach.' (... *I.C.J. Reports 1949*, pp. 181-182.) In the present case it is therefore essential to establish whether the losses allegedly suffered by Belgian shareholders in Barcelona Traction were the consequence of the violation of obligations of which they were the beneficiaries. In other words: has a right of Belgium been violated on account of its nationals having suffered infringement of their rights as shareholders in a company not of Belgian nationality? ...

"37. In seeking to determine the law applicable to this case, the Court has to bear in mind the continuous evolution of international law. Diplomatic protection deals with a very sensitive area of international relations, since the interest of a foreign State in the protection of its nationals confronts the rights of the territorial sovereign, a fact of which the general law on the subject has had to take cognizance in order to prevent abuses and friction. From its origins closely linked with international commerce, diplomatic protection has sustained a particular impact from the growth of international economic relations, and at the same time from the profound transformations which have taken place in the economic life of nations. These latter changes have given birth to municipal institutions, which have transcended frontiers and have begun to exercise considerable influence on international relations. One of these phenomena which has a particular bearing on the present case is the corporate entity.

"38. In this field international law is called upon to recognize institutions of municipal law that have an important and extensive role in the international field. This does not necessarily imply drawing any analogy between its own institutions and those of municipal law, nor does it amount to making rules of international law dependent upon categories of municipal law. All it means is that international law has had to recognize the corporate entity as an institution created by States in a domain essentially within their domestic jurisdiction. This in turn requires that, whenever legal issues arise concerning the rights of States with regard to the treatment of companies and shareholders, as to which rights international law has not established its own rules, it has to refer to the relevant rules of municipal law. Consequently, in view of the relevance to the present case of the rights of the corporate entity and its shareholders under municipal law, the Court must devote attention to the nature and interrelation of those rights....

"40. There is, however, no need to investigate the many different forms of legal entity provided for by the municipal laws of States, because the Court is concerned only with that exemplified by the company involved in the present case: Barcelona Traction—a limited liability company whose capital is represented by shares. There are, indeed, other associations, whatever the name attached to them by municipal legal systems, that do not enjoy independent corporate personality. The legal difference between the two kinds of entity is that for the limited liability company it is the overriding tie of legal personality which is determinant; for the other associations, the continuing autonomy of the several members....

"44. Notwithstanding the separate corporate personality, a wrong done to the company frequently causes prejudice to its shareholders. But the mere fact that damage is sustained by both company and shareholder does not imply that both are entitled to claim compensation. Thus no legal conclusion can be drawn from the fact that the same event caused damage simultaneously affecting several natural or juristic persons. Creditors do not have any right to claim compensation from a person who, by wronging their debtor, causes them loss. In such cases, no doubt, the interests of the aggrieved are affected, but not their rights. Thus whenever a shareholder's interests are harmed by an act done to the company, it is to the latter that he must look to institute appropriate action; for although two separate entities may have suffered from the same wrong, it is only one entity whose rights have been infringed....

"48. The Belgian Government claims that shareholders of Belgian nationality suffered damage in consequence of unlawful acts of the Spanish authorities and, in particular, that the Barcelona Traction shares, though they did not cease to exist, were emptied of all real economic content. It accordingly contends that the shareholders had an independent right to redress, notwithstanding the fact that the acts complained of were directed against the company as such. Thus the legal issue is reducible to the question of whether it is legitimate to identify an attack on company rights, resulting in damage to shareholders, with the violation of their direct rights....

"50. In turning now to the international legal aspects of the case, the Court must, as already indicated, start from the fact that the present case essentially involves factors derived from municipal law—the distinction and the community between the company and the shareholder—which the Parties, however widely their interpretations may differ, each take as the point of departure of their reasoning. If the Court were to decide the case in disregard of the relevant institutions of municipal law it would, without justification, invite serious legal difficulties. It would lose touch with reality, for there are no corresponding institutions of international law to which the Court could resort. Thus the Court has, as indicated, not only to take cognizance of municipal law but also to refer to it. It is to rules generally accepted by municipal legal systems which recognize the limited company whose capital is represented by shares, and not to the municipal law of a particular State, that international law refers. In referring to such rules, the Court cannot modify, still less deform them.

"51. On the international plane, the Belgian Government has advanced the proposition that it is inadmissible to deny the shareholders' national State a right of diplomatic protection merely on the ground that another State possesses a corresponding right in respect of the company itself. In strict logic and law this formulation of the Belgian claim to *jus standi* assumes the existence of the very right that requires demonstration. In fact the Belgian Government has repeatedly stressed that there exists no rule of international law which would deny the national State of the shareholders the right of diplomatic protection for the purpose of seeking redress pursuant to unlawful acts committed by another State against the company in which they hold shares. This, by emphasizing the absence of any express denial of the right, conversely implies the admission that there is no rule of international law which expressly confers such a right on the shareholders' national State.

"52. International law may not, in some fields, provide specific rules in particular cases. In the concrete situation, the company against which allegedly unlawful acts were directed is expressly vested with a right, whereas no such right is specifically provided for the shareholder in respect of those acts. Thus the position of the company rests on a positive rule of both municipal and international law. As to the shareholder, while he has certain rights expressly provided for him by municipal law … appeal can, in the circumstances of the present case, only be made to the silence of international law. Such silence scarcely admits of interpretation in favour of the shareholder.

"53. It is quite true, as was recalled in the course of oral argument in the present case, that concurrent claims are not excluded in the case of a person who, having entered the service of an international organization and retained his nationality, enjoys simultaneously the right to be protected by his national State and the right to be protected by the organization to which he belongs. This however is a case of one person in possession of two separate bases of protection, each of which is valid *(Reparation for Injuries Suffered in the Service of the United Nations, Advisory Opinion, I.C.J. Reports 1949,* p. 185). There is no analogy between such a situation and that of foreign shareholders in a company which has been the victim of a violation of international law which has caused them damage....

"55. The Court will now examine other grounds on which it is conceivable that the submission by the Belgian Government of a claim on behalf of shareholders in Barcelona Traction may be justified.

"56. For the same reasons as before, the Court must here refer to municipal law. Forms of incorporation and their legal personality have sometimes not been employed for the sole purposes they were originally intended to serve; sometimes the corporate entity has been unable to protect the rights of those who entrusted their financial resources to it; thus inevitably there have arisen dangers of abuse, as in the case of many other institutions of law. Here, then, as elsewhere, the law, confronted with economic realities, has had to provide protective measures and remedies in the interests of those within the corporate entity as well as of those outside who have dealings with it: the law has recognized that the independent existence of the legal entity cannot be treated as an absolute. It is in this context that the process of "lifting the corporate veil" or "disregarding the legal entity" has been found justified and equitable in certain circumstances or for certain purposes. The wealth of practice already accumulated on the subject in municipal law indicates that the veil is lifted, for instance, to prevent the misuse of the privileges of legal personality, as in certain cases of fraud or malfeasance, to protect third persons such as a creditor or purchaser, or to prevent the evasion of legal requirements or of obligations.

"Hence the lifting of the veil is more frequently employed from without, in the interest of those dealing with the corporate entity. However, it has also been operated from within, in the interest of—among others—the shareholders, but only in exceptional circumstances.

"57. In accordance with the principle expounded above, the process of lifting the veil, being an exceptional one admitted by municipal law in respect of an institution of its own making, is equally admissible to play a similar role in international law. It follows that on the international plane also there may in principle be special circumstances which justify the lifting of the veil in the interest of shareholders....

"64. The Court will now consider whether there might not be, in the present case, other special circumstances for which the general rule might not take effect. In this connection two particular situations must be studied: the case of the company having ceased to exist and the case of the company's national State lacking capacity to take action on its behalf....

"68. ... In brief, a manager was appointed in order to safeguard the company's rights; he has been in a position directly or indirectly to uphold them. Thus, even if the company is limited in its activity after being placed in receivership, there can be no doubt that it has retained its legal capacity and that the power to exercise it is vested in the manager appointed by the Canadian courts. The Court is thus not confronted with the first hypothesis contemplated in paragraph 64, and need not pronounce upon it.

"69. The Court will now turn to the second possibility, that of the lack of capacity of the company's national State to act on its behalf. The first question which must be asked here is whether Canada—the third apex of the triangular relationship—is, in law, the national State of Barcelona Traction.

"70. In allocating corporate entities to States for purposes of diplomatic protection, international law is based, but only to a limited extent, on an analogy with the rules governing the nationality of individuals. The traditional rule attributes the right of diplomatic protection of a corporate entity to the State under the laws of which it is incorporated and in whose territory it has its registered office. These two criteria have been confirmed by long practice and by numerous international instruments. This notwithstanding, further or different links are at times said to be required in order that a right of diplomatic protection should exist. Indeed, it has been the practice of some States to give a company incorporated under their law diplomatic protection solely when it has its seat *(siege social)* or management or centre of control in their territory, or when a majority or a substantial proportion of the shares has been owned by nationals of the State concerned. Only then, it has been held, does there exist between the corporation and the State in question a genuine connection of the kind familiar from other branches of international law. However, in the particular field of the diplomatic protection of corporate entities, no absolute test of the "genuine connection" has found general acceptance. Such tests as have been applied are of a relative nature, and sometimes links with one State have had to be weighed against those with another. In this connection reference has been made to the *Nottebohm* case. In fact the Parties made frequent reference to it in the course of the proceedings. However, given both the legal and factual aspects of protection in the present case the Court is of the opinion that there can be no analogy with the issues raised or the decision given in that case.

"71. In the present case, it is not disputed that the company was incorporated in Canada and has its registered office in that country. The incorporation of the company under the law of Canada was an act of free choice. Not only did the founders of the company seek its incorporation under Canadian law but it has remained under that law for a period of over *50* years. It has maintained in Canada its registered office, its accounts and its share registers. Board meetings were held there for many years; it has been listed in the records of the Canadian tax authorities. Thus a close and permanent connection has been established, fortified by the passage of over half a century. This connection is in no way weakened by the fact that the company engaged from the very outset in commercial activities outside Canada, for that was its declared object. Barcelona Traction's links with Canada are thus manifold....

"77. It is true that at a certain point the Canadian Government ceased to act on behalf of Barcelona Traction, for reasons which have not been fully revealed, though a statement made in a letter of 19 July 1955 by the Canadian Secretary of State for External Affairs suggests that it felt the matter should be settled by means of private negotiations. The Canadian Government has nonetheless retained its capacity to exercise diplomatic protection; no legal impediment has prevented it from doing so: no fact has arisen to render this protection impossible. It has discontinued its action of its own free will....

"92. Since the general rule on the subject does not entitle the Belgian Government to put forward a claim in this case, the question remains to be considered whether nonetheless, as the Belgian Government has contended during the proceedings, considerations of equity do not require that it be held to possess a right of protection. It is quite true that it has been maintained that, for reasons of equity, a State should be able, in certain cases, to take up the protection of its nationals, shareholders in a company which has been the victim of a violation of international law. Thus a theory has been developed to the effect that the State of the shareholders has a right of diplomatic protection when the State whose responsibility is invoked is the· national State of the company. Whatever the validity of this theory may be, it is certainly not applicable to the present case, since Spain is not the national State of Barcelona Traction.

"93. On the other hand, the Court considers that, in the field of diplomatic protection as in all other fields of international law, it is necessary that the law be applied reasonably. It has been suggested that if in a given case it is not possible to apply the general rule that the right of diplomatic protection of a company belongs to its national State, considerations of equity might call for the possibility of protection of the shareholders in question by their own national State. This hypothesis does not correspond to the circumstances of the present case....

"96. The Court considers that the adoption of the theory of diplomatic protection of shareholders as such, by opening the door to competing diplomatic claims, could create an atmosphere of confusion and insecurity in international economic relations. The danger would be all the greater inasmuch as the shares of companies whose activity is international are widely scattered and frequently change hands. It might perhaps be claimed that, if the right of protection belonging to the national States of the shareholders were considered as only secondary to that of the national

State of the company, there would be less danger of difficulties of the kind contemplated. However, the Court must state that the essence of a secondary right is that it only comes into existence at the time when the original right ceases to exist. As the right of protection vested in the national State of the company cannot be regarded as extinguished because it is not exercised, it is not possible to accept the proposition that in case of its non-exercise the national States of the shareholders have a right of protection secondary to that of the national State of the company....

"100. In the present case, it is clear from what has been said above that Barcelona Traction was never reduced to a position of impotence such that it could not have approached its national State, Canada, to ask for its diplomatic protection, and that, as far as appeared to the Court, there was nothing to prevent Canada from continuing to grant its diplomatic protection to Barcelona Traction if it had considered that it should do so.

"101. For the above reasons, the Court is not of the opinion that, in the particular circumstances of the present case, *jus standi* is conferred on the Belgian Government by considerations of equity....

"103. Accordingly,

THE COURT
rejects the Belgian Government's claim by fifteen votes to one, twelve votes of the majority being based on the reasons set out in the present Judgment.

"Done in French and in English, the French text being authoritative, at the Peace Palace, The Hague, this fifth day of February, one thousand nine hundred and seventy, in three copies, one of which will be placed in the Archives of the Court and the others transmitted to the Government of the Kingdom of Belgium and to the Government of the Spanish State, respectively.

(Signed) J.L. BUSTAMANTE y RIVERO, President.
(Signed) S. AQUARONE, Registrar."

ELLIOTT ASSOCIATES, L.P. v. BANCO DE LA NACION & REPUBLIC OF PERU
194 F.3d 363 (2nd Cir. 1999)

BACKGROUND: Elliott Associates, L.P. appeals from the amended final judgments entered by the United States District Court for the Southern District of New York. The District Court, after a bench trial, dismissed with prejudice Elliott's complaints seeking damages for the non-payment of certain debt by the Republic of Peru and Banco de la Nacion (together, the "Debtors") because it found that Elliott had purchased the debt in violation of Section 489 of the New York Judiciary Law....

Elliott is an investment fund with its principal offices located in New York City. Elliott was founded by Paul Singer in 1977, and he remains its sole general partner. One of the primary types of instruments that Elliott invests in is the securities of "distressed" debtors, that is, debtors that have defaulted on their payments to creditors. Singer testified that he invests in debt when he believes that the true or "fundamental" value of the debt is greater than the value accorded by the market. Elliott characterizes its approach to its investments as "activist." Thus, despite sometimes accepting the terms offered to other creditors, Elliott explains that it frequently engages in direct negotiations with the debtor and argues that, as a result, it has occasionally received a greater return than other creditors.

In August or September of 1995, Singer was approached by Jay Newman to discuss investing in distressed foreign sovereign debt. Newman, an independent consultant, had worked in the emerging market debt field at major brokerage houses Lehman Brothers, Dillon Read, and Morgan Stanley, as well as managing his own offshore fund, the Percheron Fund. The secondary market for such debt first developed in the early 1980s when the original lender banks began selling the non-performing debt of countries that had ceased servicing their external debt to other investors, including brokerage firms, in order to reduce the banks' exposure and to permit them to lend additional funds to developing countries. At Newman's recommendation, in October 1995, Elliott purchased approximately $28.75 million (principal amount) of Panamanian sovereign debt for approximately $17.5 million. In July 1996, Elliott brought suit against Panama seeking full payment of the debt. Elliott obtained a judgment and attachment order and, with interest included, ultimately received over $57 million in payment.

At the time of Elliott's purchase of Panamanian debt, Panama was finalizing its Brady Plan debt restructuring program. The term "Brady Plan" derives from a March 1989 speech by Nicholas Brady, then Secretary of the United States Treasury, urging commercial lenders to forgive some of the debt that they were owed by less developed countries, restructure what remained, and continue to grant those countries additional loans. In January 1996, Newman recommended that Elliott purchase Peruvian sovereign debt. Newman testified at trial that he believed that Peruvian sovereign debt was a good investment because of the sweeping economic reforms implemented by President Alberto Fujimori following his election in November 1990 in the wake of a severe six-year recession. Newman testified that he viewed Peru's Brady Plan, announced in October 1995, as undervaluing Peru's outstanding debt. In particular, Newman contended that the large commercial bank creditors that made up the Bank Advisory Committee had institutional incentives to accept reduced terms for the debt they held, such as the desire to make additional loans and to operate domestically within the country, and that he believed that the Bank Advisory Committee had not been privy to all material financial information, including Peru's rumored repurchase of a significant proportion of its debt.

Between January and March 1996, Elliott purchased from international banks ING Bank, N.V. and Swiss Bank Corporation approximately $20.7 million (in principal amount) of the working capital debt of Nacion and Banco Popular del Peru, a bankrupt Peruvian bank. The debt was sold under a series of twenty-three letter agreements (the "Letter Agreements"). Elliott paid approximately $11.4 million for these debt obligations, and all of the debt was guaranteed by Peru pursuant to a written guaranty dated May 31, 1983 (the "Guaranty"). Under their express terms, both the Letter Agreements and the Guaranty were governed by New York law. In connection with this transaction, Elliott executed two separate assignment agreements with ING and Swiss Bank, dated March 29, 1996, and April 19, 1996, respectively.

On June 25, 1996, after a continued impasse in the parties' discussions, Elliott formally requested repayment by sending the Debtors a notice of default. The Debtors pointed out at trial that this notice was sent during the voting period on the Term Sheet of Peru's Brady Plan. The Debtors also noted that, although the Brady Plan negotiations took place from January to June 1996, Elliott did not contact the Bank Advisory Committee to express its views. Ultimately, Peru's Brady Plan was agreed upon by 180 commercial lenders and suppliers, and entailed, *inter alia*, an Exchange Agreement under which old Peruvian commercial debt, including the 1983 Letter Agreements, would be exchanged for Brady bonds and cash.

On October 18, 1996, ten days before the Exchange Agreement was scheduled to be executed, Elliott filed suit against the Debtors in New York Supreme Court and sought an *ex parte* order of prejudgment attachment. The Debtors subsequently alleged at trial that the reason for Elliott filing suit at that time was that the collateral for the Brady bonds was United States Treasury bonds, which were held at the Federal Reserve Bank of New York, and thus made suitable assets for attachment. The Exchange Agreement was finally executed on November 8, 1996.

Elliott's suit was subsequently removed to federal district court pursuant to the Foreign Sovereign Immunities Act, where the district court denied Elliott's motion for prejudgment attachment and its motion for summary judgment. After discovery, the case was tried in a bench trial. On August 6, 1998, the district court issued its opinion dismissing Elliott's complaint on the ground that Elliott's purchase of the Peruvian debt violated Section 489 of the New York Judiciary Law. The District Court found as a fact that "Elliott purchased the Peruvian debt with the intent and purpose to sue."

JUDGE MICHEL:

"The pivotal issue upon which this appeal necessarily turns is whether, within the meaning of Section 489 of the New York Judiciary Law, Elliott's purchase of Peruvian sovereign debt was 'with the intent and for the purpose of bringing an action or proceeding thereon,' thereby rendering the purchase a violation of law....

"In interpreting Section 489, we are guided by the principle that we 'look first to the plain language of a statute and interpret it by its ordinary, common meaning.'... 'If the statutory terms are unambiguous, our review generally ends and the statute is construed according to the plain meaning of its words.'... 'Legislative history and other tools of interpretation may be relied upon only if the terms of the statute are ambiguous.' Indeed, 'where the language is ambiguous, we focus upon the broader context and primary purpose of the statute.'... At all times, we are cognizant of the Supreme Court's admonition that 'statutes should be interpreted to avoid untenable distinctions and unreasonable results whenever possible.'... Parsing the plain language of Section 489 offers little helpful guidance as to the intended scope of the provision. The statutory language simply provides that certain types of people or entities are prohibited from soliciting, buying or taking by assignment, particular types of debt instruments 'with the intent and for the purpose of bringing an action or proceeding thereon.' On its face, this statutory command might appear to be remarkably broad in scope, forbidding essentially all 'secondary' transactions in debt instruments where the purchaser had an intent to enforce the debt obligation through litigation. However, ambiguity resides in the term 'with the intent and for the purpose of bringing an action or proceeding thereon.' The nature of the proscribed intent and purpose is unclear. After reviewing the pertinent New York state decisions interpreting Section 489, we are convinced that, if the New York Court of Appeals, not us, were hearing this appeal, it would rule that the acquisition of a debt with intent to bring suit against the debtor is not a violation of the statute where, as here, the primary purpose of the suit is the collection of the debt acquired. Consequently we must reverse the judgment of the district court.

"The predecessor statute to Section 489 of the New York Judiciary Law was enacted at least as early as 1813. However, its origins are even more archaic. New York courts have recognized that '§ 489 [is] the statutory codification of the ancient doctrine of champerty.'... Commentators have traced the doctrine of champerty, and its doctrinal near-cousins of maintenance and barratry, back to Greek and Roman law, through the English law of the Middle Ages, and into the statutory or common law of many of the states…. As explained by the Supreme Court, 'put simply, maintenance is helping another prosecute a suit; champerty is maintaining a suit in return for a financial interest in the outcome; and barratry is a continuing practice of maintenance or champerty.'…

"While New York courts have not been unwilling to characterize Section 489 as a champerty statute, it is apparent that they have consistently interpreted the statute as proscribing something narrower than merely 'maintaining a suit in return for a financial interest in the outcome.' Indeed, far from prohibiting the taking of a financial interest in the outcome of a lawsuit, payment of attorneys by fees contingent upon the outcome of litigation is expressly permissible in New York by statute and court rule….

"The seminal New York Court of Appeals case of *Moses v. McDivitt*, 88 N.Y. 62 (1882), confirmed that the mischief Section 489 was intended to remedy did not include the acquisition of debt with the motive of collecting it, notwithstanding that litigation might be a necessary step in the process. 'Although decided [over] 100 years ago, [*Moses*] still remains good law.'…

"The continuing vitality of the distinction drawn in *Moses* between cases involving an impermissible 'primary' purpose of bringing suit and those where the intent to sue is merely 'secondary and contingent' is confirmed by the post-*Moses* case law….

"The cases, spread over more than a century, are not always entirely clear or plainly consistent. Thus the district court found some basis for its construction of the coverage of Section 489 to include Elliott's purchase of the Peruvian debt. We do not agree, however, with this interpretation. Furthermore, in light of the case law surveyed above, we do not agree with the district court that *Moses* in conjunction with later New York case law 'provides little guidance for construing the statute's proper scope.'… To the contrary, New York courts have stated that *Moses* 'undoubtedly correctly states the objects and limitations of the statute.'… We believe the district court misunderstood *Moses*. The *Moses* court made clear that where the debt instrument is acquired for the primary purpose of enforcing it, with intent to resort to litigation to the extent necessary to accomplish the enforcement, the intent to litigate is 'merely incidental and contingent' and does not violate the statute. Indeed, the *Moses* court made precisely this point when it explained that 'the object of the statute . . . was to prevent attorneys, etc., from purchasing things in action for the purpose of obtaining costs by the prosecution thereof, and it was not intended to prevent a purchase for the purpose of protecting some other right of the assignee.'… Elsewhere, the Court of Appeals in *Moses* specifically stated that conduct not prohibited by the statute included where 'the plaintiff bought the bond as an investment, but with the intention of collecting it by suit if compelled to resort to that means for obtaining payment.'…

While *Moses* does not set forth a complete taxonomy of conduct prohibited by Section 489 (and neither do we), it plainly sets forth certain conduct that is *not* made unlawful by Section 489.

"Even accepting as correct the facts as found by the district court, we see no meaningful distinction between Elliott's conduct and the conduct *Moses* expressly states to be outside of the scope of the statute. Here, the district court found that Elliott was the lawful assignee of Nacion's Letter Agreements, that Peru had guaranteed those Letter Agreements, and that both Peru and Nacion are liable to Elliott as a result of Nacion's failure to pay the amounts due and owing under the Letter Agreements…. Far from being a trivial claim that might serve, for example, as the illegitimate vehicle for the recovery of attorney fees, the district court expressly found that 'Elliott has suffered damages in excess of $7,000,000 as a result [of the breach].'…

"In purchasing the Peruvian debt the district court found that Elliott's principal aim was to obtain full payment. As it expressly found, 'Elliott's primary goal in investing in Peruvian debt was to be paid in full.'… We cannot agree with the district court's equating of Elliott's intent to be paid in full, if necessary by suing, with the primary intent to sue prohibited by Section 489 as delineated by *Moses* and the related case law….

"We hold that, in light of the pertinent New York precedent and compelling policy considerations, the district court erroneously interpreted Section 489 of the New York Judiciary Law. In particular, we hold that Section 489 is not violated when, as here, the accused party's 'primary goal' is found to be the satisfaction of a valid debt and its intent is only to sue absent full performance. Given that, notwithstanding the Section 489 issue, the district court found the Letter Agreements and Guaranty to have been breached by the Debtors, we remand only for the purpose of calculating damages more accurately than the approximate figures given in the district court's opinion and the possible resolution of other attendant damages-related issues.

"Accordingly, the judgments of the district court are reversed and the case is remanded."

NATIONWIDE MANAGEMENT PTY. LTD. v. BRIGHTFORD INVESTMENTS PTY. LTD.
BC 2000203473 (Supreme Court of Victoria, Australia 2002)

BACKGROUND: Nationwide is a property-management subsidiary of Advance Bank Australia Ltd. ("ABAL"), which was subsequently merged into St. George's Bank Ltd. One of ABAL's subsidiaries had loaned $18,000,000 to a builder for construction of a 13-story structure on Victoria Street, Melbourne. ABAL took possession of the building when the contractor defaulted on the loan. Having been advised that sale of the entire building as a unit would be difficult, ABAL decided to sell each of the 13 floors separately. Grey Winter Properties ("GWP") agreed to buy the top three (residential) floors itself, and to find buyers for the lower ten (commercial) floors. William Areson stated that he was part of "a syndicate" of ten or so Hong Kong investors, and that he was contacted by a GWP representative about buying the building for less than half of what it would cost to build—$9,000,000. ABAL agreed to loan $9,000,000 to purchasers of the lower ten floors, but specified that this would be distributed as ten separate loans—one for each floor, with each floor separately securing the loan to the buyer of that floor, and with each loan applicant to be separately evaluated and approved. Areson's company—Brightford—bought the tenth floor for $987,125, but later defaulted on its purchase loan. Nationwide repossessed and resold the tenth floor and sued for the balance still due—$317,444.52 plus interest and costs. Brightford then sent a Notice purporting to avoid its sale contract and the related transactions, on the basis that the sale was subject to the requirements of the Corporations Law, and that those had not been complied with by the sellers.

JUDGE HABERSBERGER:

"No doubt the reference in Mr. Areson's affidavit to a 'syndicate' of investors was intended to suggest that the sale of the Victoria Street Building to the 'syndicate' was a 'financial or business undertaking or scheme.' Counsel for [Nationwide] submitted, however, that for para(a) to be applicable there must be an acquisition of an interest in a 'financial or business undertaking or scheme' and that it is not sufficient for there to be an acquisition *from* a 'financial or business undertaking or scheme.'…

"Construing the agreements in the context in which they were made, we do not think that they give rise to any 'interest' in terms of para(a)…. The agreements do not give to a unit holder an interest in the agent's profit, nor his assets. Nor does he have any interest in the 'realisation' of any financial or business undertaking or scheme of the agent…. We agree with the conclusion of the learned trial judge that the ownership of a unit and a share in common property together with the possibility of associated services for management and maintenance of the building and the letting units do not answer the description of the phrase 'financial or business undertaking or scheme,' notwithstanding its wide import….

"The situation in the present case can be contrasted with that in Amadio Pty. Ltd.… [That] case involved a declaration that the contract of sale of [a building] was in contravention of … the Companies (Victoria) Code. A number of investors … formed a partnership to buy the building. The parties were inextricably linked to each other in terms of their expectation of some return, in the form of rent or capital gain, from their investment. The interest offered involved use by the partnership of the co-owned property interests in common for profit and also to obtain and secure the principal sum for which the partners were jointly and severally liable with rights of contribution as between all of the parties. No partner was free to deal with his, her or its interest because it was encumbered by that partner's obligations as partner and the inter-related rights of contribution.

"The full Federal Court in Amadio ... observed that: 'In cases such as Munna Beach or Brisbane Unit ... the owners of interests held the title to a specific apartment, as well as to a share in the common property. Thus, where separate interests in an investment are to be held by individuals and there are separate benefits and obligations on the part of the holder of each interest the separate and discrete interest offered to the participants may not be a prescribed interest. However, where investors hold title to an asset with no separate or discrete interest which they could use or employ for their own benefit and will be obliged to use and mortgage their interest in common with the other investors if they wish to make a profit from it, the interest held is more likely to have the requisite interaction of rights, benefits and obligations and therefore constitute a prescribed interest....'

"The Amadio ... case fell into the latter category, whereas, in my opinion, the present case is in the former category. There was no 'investment contract' within the meaning of ... the definition of 'participation interest' because Brightford's purchase was separate from the purchase of other floors in the Victoria Street Building and there was no mingling of income or sharing of profits between the various purchasers. Brightford's investment was separate to that of the other investors.

"I, therefore, conclude that the transaction involving the contract of sale of the property and the other associated contracts did not involve a prescribed interest. Thus, there was no contravention of the Corporations Law and the purported avoidance of those contracts by the s1073(2) notice dated 20 November 2000 was of no effect."

MORRISON v. NATIONAL AUSTRALIAN BANK LTD.
561 U.S. 247 (2010)

BACKGROUND: Robert Morrison (a U.S. citizen), and Russell Owen and Brian and Geraldine Silverlock (all Australian citizens) bought shares of National Australian Bank in 2000 and 2001, shortly before the assets of one of its recently-purchased subsidiaries (HomeSide Lending) were "written down" by some $2.2 billion. Claiming that HomeSide's financial models had been manipulated to make it appear to be a more valuable asset than it really was, plaintiffs sued the two companies, Frank Cicutto (the Bank's managing director), Kevin Race

(HomeSide's COO), and Hugh Harris (HomeSide's CEO). The lawsuit was filed in U.S. District Court for the Southern District of New York, on the basis that the communication of this false information violated sections 10(b) and 20(a) of the Securities and Exchange Act of 1934 and SEC Rule 10b-5. The District Court dismissed Morrison's claim because he failed to allege that he had sustained any damages, and dismissed the Australian plaintiffs' claims because they lacked subject-matter jurisdiction. (For some unexplained reason, the case continued to appear under Morrison's name.)

JUSTICE SCALIA:

"Before addressing the question presented, we must correct a threshold error in the Second Circuit's analysis. It considered the extraterritorial reach of S.10(b) to raise a question of subject-matter jurisdiction, wherefore it affirmed the District Court's dismissal....

"But to ask what conduct S.10(b) reaches is to ask what conduct S.10(b) prohibits, which is a merits question. Subject-matter jurisdiction, by contrast, 'refers to a tribunal's '"power to hear a case."'"... The District Court here had jurisdiction under 15 U.S.C. s.78aa to adjudicate the question whether S.10(b) applies to National's conduct....

"In view of this error, which the parties do not dispute, petitioners [plaintiffs] ask us to remand. We think that unnecessary.... [W]e proceed to address whether petitioners' allegations state a claim....

"It is a 'longstanding principle of American law that "legislation of Congress, unless a contrary intent appears, is meant to apply only within the territorial jurisdiction of the United States".'... It rests on the perception that Congress ordinarily legislates with respect to domestic, not foreign matters.... Thus, 'unless there is affirmative intention of the Congress clearly expressed' to give a statute extraterritorial effect, 'we must presume it is primarily concerned with domestic conditions.'... When a statute gives no clear indication of an extraterritorial application, it has none.

"Despite this principle of interpretation, long and often recited in our opinions, the Second Circuit believed that, because the Exchange Act is silent as to the extraterritorial application of S.10(b), it was left to the court to 'discern' whether Congress would have wanted the statute to apply.... This disregard of the presumption against extraterritoriality did not originate with the Court of Appeals in this case. It has been repeated over many decades by various courts of appeals in determining the application of the Exchange Act, and S. 10(b) in particular, to fraudulent schemes that involve conduct and effects abroad. That has produced a collection of tests for divining what Congress would have wanted, complex in formulation and unpredictable in application....

"As they developed, these tests were not easy to administer. The conduct test was held to apply differently depending on whether the harmed investors were Americans or foreigners: When the alleged damages consisted of losses to American investors abroad, it was enough that acts of 'material importance' performed in the United States 'significantly contributed' to that result; whereas those acts must have 'directly caused' the result when losses to foreigners abroad were at issue…. And 'merely preparatory activities in the United States' did not suffice 'to trigger application of the securities laws for injury to foreigners located abroad.'… This required the court to distinguish between mere preparation and using the United States as a 'base' for fraudulent activities in other countries…. But merely satisfying the conduct test was sometimes insufficient without '"some additional factor tipping the scales"' in favor of the application of American law…. District courts have noted the difficulty of applying such vague formulations…. There is no more damning indictment of the 'conduct' and 'effects' tests than the Second Circuit's own declaration that 'the presence or absence of any single factor which was considered significant in other cases … is not necessarily dispositive in future cases.'…

"Other Circuits embraced the Second Circuit's approach, though not its precise application….

"At least one Court of Appeals has criticized this line of cases and the interpretive assumption that underlies it….

"Commentators have criticized the unpredictable and inconsistent application of S.10(b) to transnational cases….

"The criticisms seem to us justified. The results of judicial-speculation-made-law—divining what Congress would have wanted if it had thought of the situation before the court—demonstrate the wisdom of the presumption against extraterritoriality. Rather than guess anew in each case, we apply the presumption in all cases, preserving a stable background against which Congress can legislate with predictable effects….

"Petitioners argue that the conclusion that S.10(b) does not apply extraterritorially does not resolve this case. They contend that they seek no more than domestic application anyway, since Florida is where HomeSide and its senior executives engaged in the deceptive conduct of manipulating HomeSide's financial models; their complaint also alleged that Race and Hughes made misleading public statements there. This is less an answer to the presumption against extraterritorial application than it is an assertion—a quite valid assertion—that that presumption here (as often) is not self-evidently dispositive, but its application requires further analysis. For it is a rare case of prohibited extraterritorial application that lacks *all* contact with the territory of the United States. But the presumption against extraterritorial application would be a craven watchdog indeed if it retreated to its kennel whenever *some* domestic activity is involved in the case. The concurrence seems to imagine just such a timid sentinel … but our cases are to the contrary….

"Applying the [*Aramco*] mode of analysis here, we think that the focus of the Exchange Act is not upon the place where the deception originated, but upon purchases and sales of securities in the United States. Section 10(b) does not punish deceptive conduct, but only deceptive conduct 'in connection with the purchase or sale of any security registered on a national securities exchange or any security not so registered.'… Those purchase-and-sale transactions are the objects of the statute's solicitude. It is those transactions that the statute seeks to 'regulate' … it is parties or prospective parties to those transactions that the statute seeks to 'protec[t].'… And it is in our view only transactions in securities listed on domestic exchanges, and domestic transactions in other securities, to which S.10(b) applies….

"Finally, we reject the notion that the Exchange Act reaches conduct in this country affecting exchanges or transactions abroad for the same reason that *Aramco* rejected overseas application of Title VII to all domestically concluded employment contracts or all employment contracts with American employers: The probability of incompatibility with the applicable laws of other countries is so obvious that if Congress intended such foreign application 'it would have addressed the subject of conflicts with foreign laws and procedures.'…

"Section 10(b) reaches the use of a manipulative or deceptive device or contrivance only in connection with the purchase or sale of a security listed on an American stock exchange, and the purchase or sale of any other security in the United States. This case involves no securities listed on a domestic exchange, and all aspects of the purchases complained of by those petitioners who still have live claims occurred outside the United States. Petitioners have therefore failed to state a claim on which relief can be granted. We affirm the dismissal of petitioners' complaint on this ground.

"It is so ordered."

CHAPTER V

International Trade and Taxation and Environmental Regulation

OVERVIEW:

INTERNATIONAL TRADE AND TAXATION. Taxation of international business operations presents problems of staggering complexity. With some 200 nations, plus thousands of local governmental units, and many different types of "taxable" events, the resulting permutations and combinations provide many opportunities for litigation. On a smaller scale, and with the U.S. Supreme Court as the ultimate "referee"—determining what forms of taxation comply with the "due process" requirement of the 14th Amendment to the USA's national Constitution—many of these same issues have been frequently litigated in the U.S. In general, to impose a tax, the taxing authority must demonstrate that there is a "nexus" (relationship/connection) between what the tax is designed to reach and the taxing State. A sales tax, for example, can be applied only to sales which occur within the taxing jurisdiction. A tax on tangible personal property can (generally) only be applied to property within the taxing State or nation. Thus, where property is being used in several States/nations (airplanes, for example), the full value cannot be taxed by a single location (other than the "home port," perhaps). Only a fairly "apportioned" part of the full value can be taxed by an "in-out" State/nation. If income is being earned by cross-border activities, the same apportionment requirement exists. Unfortunately, States or nations may not use the same apportionment factors, or the same formula for doing the allocations. Thus, many litigations result.

Taxation of income is a widely-adopted and seemingly straight-forward method of generating governmental revenues. Either or both individuals and business entities may be targeted as taxpayers. If both are required to pay, they may be subjected to different rates of tax and/or different allowable deductions from total received income and/or different systems of collection and enforcement. Considering for the moment just taxation of personal income,— which is what one would expect to be the least complicated of tax relationships: the *Wikipedia* entry for "International taxation" contains eight pages of colorful charts, showing the variances among 244 taxing entities, across a set of six "Yes/No"—tax/no-tax alternatives for individuals. (There is also a ten-plus-page chart with nation-by-nation comparisons of rates for four different taxes—corporate, individual income [minimum and maximum rates], payroll, and sales/value-added/goods-and-services.)

The 244 taxing authorities listed include 194 nations, plus "their 40 inhabited dependent territories (most of which have separate tax systems)"—and ten "countries with limited recognition." For each of the 244, the *Wikipedia* chart indicates whether the entity taxes the "local" income of "nonresident" individuals, "resident citizens," and "resident foreigners"; and whether it taxes the "foreign" income of "resident citizens," "resident foreigners," and "nonresident citizens." Some interesting differences are observable, but perhaps fewer than one might expect given the wide range of economic, political, social and cultural backgrounds represented in the 244 taxing units.

Not all of the theoretically possible "Yes/No" combinations are seen in the data. Only two nations—Eritrea and the USA—are listed with all six "Yes" answers, including in income category number six: the foreign income of nonresident citizens is subject to taxation in those two nations. Cuba is the only nation listed as not taxing the local income of nonresident individuals, or the foreign income of resident foreigners, or the foreign income of nonresident citizens. North Korea is the only nation listed as not taxing the local income of resident citizens, or the foreign income of resident citizens, or the foreign income of nonresident citizens. The Philippines and Saudi Arabia are the only two nations listed as taxing the local income of all three groups and the foreign income of resident citizens, but not the foreign income of resident foreigners or of nonresident citizens.

Nearly all of the 244 systems of individual income taxation are therefore characterized by one of just three "Yes/No" combinations. Twenty-three of the 244 taxing units (nearly ten percent) impose *no* personal income taxes—in any of the six income categories. Several of these units would be categorized as "inhabited dependent territories." Thirty-three units impose individual income tax on all three classes of taxpayers receiving local income, but do not tax anyone for foreign income. Obviously, the "local"-v-"foreign" categorization will be a key issue for income-earning individuals in those jurisdictions. The vast majority of taxing units (182 of 244) assess individual income taxes in the first five categories, but do not tax the foreign income of nonresident citizens.

This little data-set thus provides a nice example of the kind of taxation differences that may exist as we evaluate our international location choices for business operations. Of course, the data represents only the most basic and simplistic features of the 244 taxing systems—only the very small tip of a very large "iceberg." There are very likely to be significant differences from system to system on all sorts of details and definitions. Even something as seemingly clear-cut as "citizenship" may be contested—recall our *Nottebohm* case from Chapter I. If there are income categories which are not taxed at all, or are taxed at significantly lower rates, there will almost certainly be efforts by some taxpayers to shift income into lower-tax categories. Likewise, where related business units are performing complementary operations in nations having different taxing structures, there will be efforts to adjust intra-group relationships so as to maximize profits in the lowest-tax-liability country. (Hence, the "transfer-pricing" issue.)

In addition to the application of common sense and good faith in the administration and enforcement of national tax policies, there are at least two major processes at work that help minimize nation-v-nation conflicts. Nations engaged in significant ongoing commercial dealings with each other may negotiate a specific tax treaty to deal with recurring ambiguities. It's also conceivable that some of the Friendship, Commerce and Navigation ("FCN") or Bilateral Investment ("BIT") treaties mentioned in Chapter III might contain tax-treatment provisions. The "International taxation" webpage noted above indicates that the U.K., for example, has tax treaties with 110 nations. The website for the USA's Internal Revenue Service, in its "Publication 901—U.S. Tax Treaties," lists 57 nations with whom the USA has such agreements. In addition to "the usual suspects" (major trading partners), the list includes Bangladesh and Barbados, Cyprus and Egypt, Slovenia and Sri Lanka, and Tunisia and Venezuela. The IRS "Tax Treaty Overview" states: "The United States has income tax treaties with a number of foreign countries. Under these treaties, residents (not necessarily citizens) of foreign countries are taxed at a reduced rate, or are exempt from U.S. income taxes on certain items of income they receive from sources within the United States. These reduced rates and exemptions vary among countries and specific items of income." Whether or not a specific treaty contains its own dispute-resolution procedure, the mere fact of its existence would seem to facilitate the resolution of disputes, if only by providing a basic framework for discussion.

Evidence indicates that considerable effort is also being expended at the international level towards development of cooperation and common policies. As one significant example, the Organization for Economic Development and Cooperation ("OECD") has developed "comprehensive guidelines" for transfer pricing. Even if not universally accepted, the OECD's standards provide a much-needed benchmark—from a widely-respected source—against which variances can be measured and judged. There is also a "United Nations Practical Manual on Transfer Pricing for Developing Countries." Acting through its "Committee of Experts on International Cooperation in Tax Matters," the UN's Economic and Social Council has produced a number of studies and recommendations, including the "United Nations Model Double Taxation Convention between Developed and Developing Countries" and the "Manual for the Negotiation of Bilateral Tax Treaties between Developed and Developing Nations." Thus it does seem that important work is being done to coordinate and systematize international taxation.

INTERNATIONAL ENVIRONMENTAL REGULATION. Air and water pollution obviously do not recognize national boundaries. The environmental harm resulting from business operations may not be confined within one nation. Wind currents may carry airborne pollutants across boundaries; the pollutants in a river don't make a customs stop at the national border. Pollution generated in one nation crosses borders and produces bad effects in other nations. Conduct lawful in one nation may thus cause harm in another. Is there a remedy for this sort of injury? If so, where—and according to whose rules? While there have been numerous treaties and resolutions over the years, the international law in this area is still very much in the developmental stage.

One of the earliest examples of this sort of dispute is our *Trail Smelter* case. It arose from the environmental degradation caused in the State of Washington, USA, by a metal smelting operation located at Trail, British Columbia, Canada. A treaty was negotiated between the two nations, setting up an arbitration proceeding to determine the rights and wrongs as between them. The panel ultimately decided that Canada was liable under international law for the acts of its nationals which caused injury to the nationals of the USA. Relatively small amounts of damages were awarded in 1938 and 1941. (Both nations had much larger international concerns after September 1, 1939, and December 7, 1941.) We've given this case rather extensive coverage because of the importance of the liability principle it established. In that sense, it is an important milestone in establishing international environmental rules.

As it turns out, even the most preliminary of research efforts will uncover a sizeable mass of "international environmental law." The 58 pages of Chapter 15 (so titled) of Malcolm Shaw's sixth edition of *International Law* contain references to dozens of conventions, treaties, protocols, declarations, resolutions and cases, as well as numerous secondary sources—texts, law reviews, and articles. Anyone concerned about protecting the ecology of our fragile planet would surely be pleased that so much is being done. One feels a certain unease, however, about the seeming randomness of it all. There does not appear to be sufficient coordination or direction to these many, many efforts. It seems that international environmental law is just like "Topsy" in *Uncle Tom's Cabin*: "I 'spect I jest growed." There's nothing inherently wrong with healthy organic growth, of course, but there are problems if duplicative and overlapping efforts result in wasted resources—expertise, time, and funding. If no one is really in charge, there may be a lot of "re-inventing the wheel" and even possible working at cross-purposes.

So what can we present about international environmental regulation in these few pages that might be useful? One possibility for a little "value added" may be a listing of some of the major international agreements, grouped by the targeted environmental damage—air pollution, water pollution, species destruction, et al. With the name (and date) of a specific agreement, web access to the original document—and several commentaries on it—is generally available. (For example, one learns that the U.N. Convention to Combat Desertification ["UNCCD"] has been adopted by 195 nations and the European Union. There is thus nearly universal agreement that the environmental problem exists—or is pending—and at least some level of agreement that something needs to be done about it. The UNCCD's very existence would itself seem to be useful information for a business contemplating operations in a location where such "desert" conditions are present or threatened.) To the rather limited extent possible, some general observations will be attempted here.

What seems like a suitable starting point is Professor Shaw's statement on page 851: "The basic [environmental] duty upon states is not so to act as to injure the rights of other states." As support for this proposition, he cites the Permanent Court of International Justice's 1929 ruling in *International Commission on the River Oder*, our *Trail Smelter* example case (excerpted below), Article 192 of the 1992 Law of the Sea Convention, and Principle 21 of the 1972 Stockholm Declaration. It's a sort of "Golden Rule" of international environmental law: "Do unto others as you would have them do unto you!" Perhaps, if we were all reading from the same book, and acting in good faith, that would be all the "law" we needed. But because we are only flawed humans, operating human institutions, there is of course lots more "law."

One area of interest to all nations concerns the "common areas of mankind"—outer space, the moon, Antarctica, and the oceans. Not all of us have the same interests in these areas; only a very few individuals have flown in space or walked on the moon, and only a few more have been in Antarctica. Many of us use the oceans—for trade, for recreation, for resource exploration and exploitation. So there need to be some rules—for now, and for the future. There is a 1959 Antarctic Treaty (52 parties), and a 1967 Outer Space Treaty (129 parties and signers), and a 1979 Moon Treaty (only 16 signers). The 1972 Convention on International Liability for Damage Caused by Space Objects has been ratified by 89 nations, and "signed" by 22 more. (One estimate indicated that there were over 1000 operating space satellites as of early 2014— nearly half of them launched from the USA. The first collision between intact satellites—the USA's *Iridium* and Russia's *Kosmos 2251*—occurred in 2009. *See*, Elizabeth Wason, "Polluting the Heavens: The Problem of Space Junk," *LSA Magazine*, Spring 2014, pp. 42-44.)

There are a number of multi-party agreements dealing with use and protection of the oceans, and many other bilateral agreements as well (fishing rights and other common usage). Surely the most significant of these is the 1992 U.N. Convention on the Law of the Sea ("UNCLOS"): 202 pages in the web version, 320 Articles—plus 116 more in the nine "Annexes." It is a real attempt at comprehensive coverage, starting with the traditional sea-law concerns for control by shoreline nations and the navigation rights of others: "Territorial Sea and

Contiguous Zone," "Straits Used for International Navigation," "Archipelagic States," "Exclusive Economic Zone," "Continental Shelf," "High Seas," "Regime of Islands," "Enclosed and Semi-Enclosed Seas," "Right of Access of Land-Locked States," et al. These topics are covered in the first ten Parts of UNCLOS, and the control-and-usage rules stated there seem not to have generated too many objections.

Part XII of UNCLOS is a worthy effort at summarizing the rules for "Protection and Preservation of the Marine Environment." Section 5 states the rules for preventing or reducing pollution—from land-based sources, seabed activities under national jurisdiction, seabed activities in the "Area," dumping, vessels, and the atmosphere. Section 6 covers the various enforcement mechanisms for each of these potential pollution sources, and for vessels—the different possible enforcers. Prior agreements dealing with ocean dumping and oil pollution had been entered into in 1954, 1969 (two of them), 1971, 1972 (two of them), 1973, 1974, 1976 and 1978. Even with UNCLOS in effect, two additional agreements were negotiated in the 1990s: the 1990 International Convention on Oil Pollution Preparedness, Responsibility and Co-operation, and the 1996 International Convention on Civil Liability for Oil Pollution Damage. The relationship between UNCLOS and these two subsequent Conventions is not clear.

Part XI—"The Area"—some thirty pages in length—is the proverbial Joker-in-the-Deck, and has generated considerable controversy and opposition, much of it from the USA. Article I of UNCLOS defines "Area" as "the seabed and ocean floor and subsoil thereof, beyond the limits of national jurisdiction." UNCLOS creates an "International Seabed Authority" to regulate all "activities in the Area"—defined as meaning "all activities of exploration for, and exploitation of, the resources of the Area." Part XI (Article 133) then proceeds to define "resources" as "all solid, liquid or gaseous mineral resources *in situ* in the Area at or beneath the seabed, including polymetallic nodules." And further, "resources, when recovered from the Area, are referred to as 'minerals'." Article 136 then provides: "The Area and its resources are the common heritage of mankind." Just to make sure that everyone understands what is intended here, Article 137 explains in more detail: "1. No State shall claim or exercise sovereign rights over any part of the Area or its resources, nor shall any State or natural or juridical person appropriate any part thereof. No such claim or exercise of sovereignty or sovereign rights nor such appropriation shall be recognized. 2. All rights in the resources of the Area are vested in mankind as a whole, on whose behalf the Authority shall act. These resources are not subject to alienation. The minerals recovered from the Area, however, may only be alienated in accordance with this Part and the rules, regulations and procedures of the Authority. 3. No State or natural or juridical person shall claim, acquire or exercise rights with respect to the minerals recovered from the Area except in accordance with this Part. Otherwise, no such claim, acquisition or exercise of such rights shall be recognized." Section 2 of Article 140 is also worth noting: "The Authority shall provide for the equitable sharing of financial and other economic benefits derived from activities in the Area through any appropriate mechanism, on a non-discriminatory basis...."

The "Authority" will have a governing "Assembly," an executive "Council," a "Legal and Technical Commission," a "Secretariat—headed by a 'Secretary-General,'" and an "Enterprise"— a legal entity to "carry out activities in the Area directly," including "the transporting, processing and marketing of minerals recovered from the Area." UNCLOS (Annex VI) also establishes its own court—the "International Tribunal for the Law of the Sea," and provides for a special "Seabed Disputes Chamber" thereof, to hear cases involving the harvesting of the untold billions-worth of seabed polymetallic nodules. Just to make sure that legal processes don't get out of hand, however, Article 178 states: "The Authority, its property and assets, shall enjoy immunity from legal process except to the extent that the Authority expressly waives this immunity in a particular case." Further, Article 179 makes the Authority's property "immune from search, requisition, confiscation, expropriation or any other form of seizure by executive or legislative action," and Article 180 makes such property "exempt from restrictions, regulations, controls and moratoria of any nature." Section 1 of Article 181 states: "The archives of the Authority, wherever located, shall be inviolable."

Thus, while much of UNCLOS is devoted to restating customary international law of the sea, Part XI and Annex VI represent what appears to be the most significant international legislation of all time. Aside from the USA and a few other nations, UNCLOS has had world-wide adoption: 160+ UN members, plus the EU collectively. (The U.S. appears close to full formal ratification; Part XI remains the final sticking point.) UNCLOS now clearly represents the international law of the sea. Presumably, previous treaties would be superseded by the provisions of UNCLOS, at least to the extent of any inconsistencies. What is not clear, however, is the extent to which the more general rules in UNCLOS can themselves be superseded by later international agreements dealing with the same topics.

Since the UNCLOS environmental rules apply only to pollution of the oceans, they would not preempt rules dealing with other environmental concerns, whether those rules were contained in agreements effective before or after the adoption of UNCLOS. Covering pollution of inland waterways, for example, are the 1990 Code of Conduct on Accidental Pollution of Transboundary Inland Waters, the 1992 Convention on the Protection and Use of Transboundary Watercourses and Inland Lakes, the 1997 Convention on the Law of the Non-Navigation Uses of International Watercourses, and the 2003 Protocol on Civil Liability and Compensation for Damage Caused by Transboundary Effects of Industrial Accidents on Transboundary Waters. There are several agreements dealing with air pollution: the 1979 Geneva Convention on Long-Range Transboundary Air Pollution, the 1985 Vienna Convention for the Protection of the Ozone Layer, the 1991 Canada-United States Air Quality Agreement (the result of Her Majesty's 1990 lawsuit?), the 1992 Convention on the Transboundary Effects of Industrial Accidents (think Chernobyl?), and the 1997 Kyoto Protocol. Concern for the protection of plant and animal species has led to the 1946 International Convention for the Regulation of Whaling, the 1973 Convention on Trade in Endangered Species, the 1987 Montreal Protocol on Biodiversity, and the 1992 Convention on Biological Diversity.

Since the world at large was introduced to the "atomic age" via Hiroshima and Nagasaki, any private or public use of things atomic has raised concerns about potential harm to persons, property and the environment. Hence, there have been a number of international agreements on the handling and use of nuclear materials: the 1956 Statute of the International Atomic Energy Agency, the 1960 OECD Paris Convention on Third Party Liability for Nuclear Damage, the 1963 IAEA Vienna Convention on Liability for Nuclear Damage, the 1963 Treaty Banning Nuclear Weapons Tests in the Atmosphere, Outer Space and Under Water, the 1967 Treaty for the Prohibition of Nuclear Weapons in Latin America, the 1971 Treaty on the Prohibition of the Emplacement of Nuclear Weapons or Other Weapons of Mass Destruction on the Seabed, the 1985 South Pacific Nuclear Free Zone Treaty, the 1986 Vienna Convention on Early Notification of a Nuclear Accident, the 1989 Basle Convention on the Control of Transboundary Movement of Hazardous Wastes, the 1990 IAEA Code of Practice on the International Transboundary Movement of Radioactive Waste, and the 1994 Convention on Nuclear Safety.

The above recitation of specific environmental agreements is somewhat extensive, but it is by no means exhaustive. Perhaps it is time for an attempt at a comprehensive restatement of international environmental law, à la UNCLOS—but without a "Part XI." Meanwhile, we will just have to use the law that's here, and hope that the courts can do a reasonable job of putting the jigsaw puzzles together, case by case.

EXAMPLE CASES PREVIEW:

XEROX: The specially-designed-for-Latin-America machines held in a bonded U.S. government warehouse were not subject to personal property taxation by a Texas county.

NISSAN: Nissan could not use the machinery that it imported into the tax-free zone in the USA to produce car parts, and still exempt the machinery from taxation. That sort of use was not permitted under the "tax-free" rules.

BROTHER: For purposes of protection by the "anti-dumping" trade rules, Brother was a USA "manufacturer," even though most/all of its research and development work and technical development functions were being done outside the USA. It did in fact have a significant manufacturing operation in the USA.

U.S. v. IBM: The USA's constitutional prohibition of taxation on exports also included a prohibition on activities that were a closely-related part of the export process (including buying insurance on the exported goods).

FAG KUGELFISCHER: Manufacturers of antifriction bearings ("AFBs") were found to have "dumped" their products in the USA at unfairly-low prices. They are requesting further court review of the U.S. Department of Commerce determination of the "dumping margin"—the size of the variance. The U.S. Court of International Trade ("CIT") had already affirmed Commerce's methodology in a prior appeal, but the Federal Circuit Court of Appeals had sent the case back to Commerce, with instructions that it was to further explain its decision. The CIT had reaffirmed the revised decision by Commerce, and the manufacturers request a second review by the Federal Circuit.

JAPAN LINE: The shipping containers here were already fully taxed as personal property in Japan (their home port). Any added taxation by California would result in double taxation. In addition, the California tax would seem to violate the USA/Japan agreement on taxation of this type of property, and prevent the USA from "speaking with one voice" in international affairs.

MOBIL OIL: Vermont could impose its State income tax on Mobil Oil (which had some operations there), using a formula which apportioned Mobil's world-wide income, since the Vermont operations were part of an integrated, world-wide business.

ALLIED-SIGNAL: New Jersey could not subject to its State income tax the capital gain that Bendix (now part of Allied-Signal) had made when it resold its ASARCO shares, since that investment was not part of or connected to the operations Bendix had in New Jersey.

BARCLAY'S: California was permitted to levy its State income tax on an apportioned part of the income of a multi-national bank, even though the bank would be burdened by having to file the required income statements—due to currency-conversion problems and different accounting methods.

U.S. v. WILLIAMS: Here's a rather different case—an individual USA citizen being prosecuted *criminally* by the national government for failing to report ownership of overseas financial assets. The government's interest in such business transactions is the collection of income taxes on the overseas income/profits. The business implications are the potential added disincentives to foreign investment and/or repatriation of profits. (It has been widely reported that USA businesses are refusing to repatriate billions of dollars of earnings due to USA income taxes which would thus be incurred.)

TRAIL SMELTER: This arbitration between the USA and Canada stated the principle that one nation is responsible for the activities within its territory which cause environmental damage in another nation. That is a point that needs to be reaffirmed in future practice and decisions.

NUCLEAR TESTS: New Zealand asked the International Court of Justice to consider the legality under international law of France's nuclear-testing program in the South Pacific (near New Zealand). Do France's "assurances" seem sufficient to remove the source of the dispute?

HER MAJESTY: This time, it's USA activities that are allegedly causing environmental damage in Canada, and the Province of Ontario wants the U.S. Environmental Protection Agency ("EPA") to do something about it. The court did decide that the EPA's "no-action" letter was a decision that the court could review, but it then agreed with the EPA that no agency action could be taken until the agency had sufficient facts to determine which U.S. State was causing the acid rain.

E.D.F. v. MASSEY: The court decided that USA environmental law could be applied to the USA's activities in Antarctica, since there would be no conflict with another nation's rules, and since the ultimate policy decision on how to dispose of waste at the research station there had been made (or approved) in Washington, DC.

JUAN ANTONIO [OPOSA]: The interesting twist to this case is, of course, the addition of "future generations" as part of the class of plaintiffs bringing suit to protect the environment. A lawsuit on behalf of nonexistent persons certainly seems to raise some unusual legal (to say nothing of philosophical) questions.

CAMUOCO **CASE:** This is an early decision by the International Tribunal for the Law of the Sea ("ITLOS"), the new international court created by the UN Convention on the Law of the Sea. It's a classic kind of case—seizure of a foreign ship fishing in territorial waters without permission, thus violating the law. (Remember *La Jeune Eugenie* from Chapter I.) ITLOS applies the provisions of its treaty—UNCLOS—as an authoritative statement of international maritime law.

MASSACHUSETTS: By a 5-to-4 vote the U.S. Supreme Court decided that Massachusetts had enough interest (as a coastal State) to bring an action against the Environmental Protection Agency ("EPA"), challenging its decision not to regulate motor vehicle exhaust emissions. Further, on the merits of the case, it decided that the EPA had not provided an adequate explanation on why it had decided not to do so. There were strong dissents on both points.

WHALING IN THE ANTARCTIC: The continued killing (and merchandising) of significant numbers of whales, despite an international treaty prohibiting such activity, raises questions about our commitment to protection of endangered species. Concerned individuals have had mixed success, at best, in trying to use direct action to achieve such protection. "Government v. Government" litigation before the International Court of Justice is perhaps a better way to focus world attention on the problem, although international sanctions have also proved problematical in such situations. As another example of this ongoing "environmental" problem, *see* Peter Canby, "Elephant Watch," *The New Yorker*, (May 11, 2015), pp. 34-41.

CASE EXAMPLES:

XEROX CORP. v. COUNTY OF HARRIS TEXAS
459 U.S. 145 (1982)

BACKGROUND: Xerox operates globally, making and selling business machines. Some of its copying-machine parts were made in Colorado and New York, and then sent to Mexico City for assembly into copiers. Those copiers were intended for sale in Central and South America; and the operating instructions for the machines were either in Portuguese or Spanish. The machines could not use U.S. electrical current without modification and could not be certified for sale in the USA. From Mexico City, the finished copiers were brought back to Houston, Texas, where they were stored in the U.S. Customs Service Warehouse until purchase orders were received. Transportation from Mexico to Houston and from Houston to the eventual shipment port of Miami, Florida, was done by bonded carrier. Since the copiers were for sale outside the USA and were in the possession of U.S. Customs while they were in the USA, they were exempted from U.S. import duties when Xerox brought them back to Houston from Mexico City.

Harris County and Houston notified Xerox in 1977 that it owed local personal property taxes on the copiers it had been storing there. Xerox filed a lawsuit to prevent collection of these local taxes. Xerox won in the Texas trial court, but the Texas Appeals Court reversed that ruling, and the Texas Supreme Court refused to hear the case. Xerox petitioned the U.S. Supreme Court for further review.

CHIEF JUSTICE BURGER:

"Pursuant to its powers under the Commerce Clause, Congress established a comprehensive customs system which includes provisions for Government-supervised bonded warehouses where imports may be stored duty-free for prescribed periods. At any time during that period the goods may be withdrawn and re-exported without payment of duty. Only if the goods are withdrawn for domestic sale or stored beyond the prescribed period does any duty become due.... While the goods are in bonded warehouses they are in the joint custody of the United States Customs Service and the warehouse proprietor and under the continuous control and supervision of the local customs officers.... Detailed regulations control every aspect of the manner in which the warehouses are to be operated....

"In short, Congress created secure and duty-free enclaves under federal control in order to encourage merchants here and abroad to make use of American ports. The question is whether it would be compatible with the comprehensive scheme Congress enacted to effect these goals if the states were free to tax such goods while they were lodged temporarily in government-regulated bonded storage in this country....

"... First, Congress sought ... to benefit American industry by remitting duties otherwise due.... Here, the remission of duties benefited those shippers using American ports as transshipment centers. Second, the system of customs regulation is ... pervasive for the stored goods in the present case.... [T]he imported goods were segregated in warehouses under continual federal custody and supervision. Finally, the state tax was large enough in each case to offset substantially the very benefits Congress intended to confer by remitting the duty. In short, freedom from state taxation is ... necessary to the congressional scheme here....

"Accordingly, we hold that state property taxes on goods stored under bond in a customs warehouse are pre-empted by Congress' comprehensive regulation of customs duties....

"It is unnecessary for us to consider whether, absent congressional regulation, the taxes here would pass muster under the Import-Export Clause or the Commerce Clause.

"The judgment of the Texas Court of Civil Appeals is reversed, and the case is remanded for proceedings not inconsistent with this opinion."

NISSAN MOTOR MFG. CORP. v. UNITED STATES
884 F.2d 1375 (Fed.Cir. 1989)

BACKGROUND: The U.S. Foreign Trade Zones Act authorizes the establishment of foreign trade zones, where "merchandise" may be imported, duty-free, for sales-related purposes—including "stored, sold, broken up, repacked, assembled, distributed, sorted, graded, cleaned, mixed with foreign or domestic merchandise, or otherwise manipulated, or be manufactured except as otherwise provided in this chapter." A foreign trade subzone for Nissan was established at its plant in Smyrna, Tennessee. Nissan imported some $116 million worth of machinery which it was using to manufacture cars at the plant. The U.S. Customs Service assessed over $3,000,000 in import duties on this machinery. Nissan paid the tax under protest, and challenged its validity in court. The U.S. Court of International Trade upheld the assessment, and Nissan appealed.

JUDGE ARCHER:

"The activities performed by Nissan in the foreign trade zone with the imported equipment are not among those permitted by a plain reading of the statute.... The Act does not say that the imported equipment may be 'installed,' 'used,' 'operated' or 'consumed' in the zone, which are the kinds of operations Nissan performs in the zone with the subject equipment. Alternative operations of a different character should not be implied when Congress has made so exhaustive a list....

"Nissan relies upon the case of *Hawaiian Indep. Refinery v. United States* ... in support of its position. The merchandise there involved was crude oil which was entered into a foreign trade zone for manufacture into fuel oil products. This, of course, is an activity delineated by the Act and entry into the zone was exempted from Customs duties. Thereafter, a portion of the crude oil was consumed in the manufacturing process and Customs assessed duty on the theory that there had been a 'constructive' entry into the customs territory of the United States. In holding that the assessment was improper, the Court of International Trade did not have to deal with the question at issue here of whether the initial entry into the zone was exempt. Clearly, in that case the crude oil was exempt at the time of entry. Thus, the Court of International Trade properly concluded that th[at] case was not dispositive of this case.

"We are convinced that the Court of International Trade correctly determined that the importation by Nissan of the machinery and capital equipment at issue into the foreign trade zone was not for the purpose of being manipulated in one of the ways prescribed by the statute. Instead it was to be used (consumed) in the subzone for the production of motor vehicles. Under the plain language of the 1950 amendment to the Act and the legislative history of that amendment, and Customs' published decision interpreting the Act as amended, such a use does not entitle the equipment to exemption from Customs duties. Accordingly, the judgment of the Court of International Trade is affirmed."

BROTHER INDUSTRIES (USA) INC. v. UNITED STATES
801 F.Supp. 751 (U.S. Ct. Int'l Trade 1992)

BACKGROUND: BIUSA, a Delaware corporation, is a wholly owned subsidiary of Brother Industries, Ltd.—a Japanese corporation. BIUSA produces portable electronic typewriters ("PETs"), portable automatic typewriters ("PATs"), and portable word processors ("PWPs") at its factory in Bartlett, Tennessee. Its principal competitor in the USA is Smith Corona Corp., which manufactures typewriters in the USA and in Singapore. In 1980, Brother Industries—Japan was found to be dumping typewriters in the USA market, and sanctions were imposed. BIUSA was established in Bartlett in 1986. In 1991, Smith Corona alleged that Brother—Japan was using BIUSA to avoid the anti-dumping penalties. The U.S. International Trade Administration ("ITA") found in favor of Brother—Japan.

Meanwhile, BIUSA had filed its own petition with the ITA, alleging damage to a USA "domestic industry" resulting from below-cost sales in the USA from Smith Corona's Singapore plant. Smith Corona asked that the petition be dismissed, since BIUSA was only an assembler of PETs—not a manufacturer or producer—and therefore could not file on behalf of a domestic industry. The ITA did dismiss the petition, and BIUSA appealed.

JUDGE RESTANI:

"To determine whether BIUSA was an interested party with standing to file a petition, ITA considered 'the overall nature of [BIUSA's] production-related activities in the United States, including the following specific factors: (1) the extent and source of [its] ... capital investment; (2) the technical expertise involved in the production activity in the United States; (3) the value added to the product in the United States; (4) employment levels; (5) the quantity and types of parts sourced in the United States; and (6) any other costs and activities in the United States directly leading to production of the like product....' No single factor is determinative, nor is the list exhaustive....

"ITA found that the absolute levels of investment and employment were not instructive given the high output from the plant. It discounted both elements, finding that neither argues strongly for or against BIUSA's status as a domestic producer. After describing BIUSA's operations at Bartlett, ITA characterized the level of technical expertise as 'what could be expected in any large assembly operation.'... ITA then turned to value-added. It described value-added as 'perhaps not small ... [but] not significant,' and noted that this factor alone is not dispositive since 'one can envision cases in which a similar degree of domestic value is added by a firm determined to be a domestic producer.'... ITA found that the quantity and types of parts sourced in the United States were non-critical, and that the primary mechanical and electronic elements were imported.

"ITA then turned to the final factor—other costs and activities leading to production of the like product. This factor proved dispositive. ITA found:

> 'Brother's products have been developed, designed, and engineered outside the United States over several years. While this, due to the fact that the product is not new, means that such activities are no longer large quantitatively, they remain an important factor in determining Brother's status as a domestic producer, because design is an essential part of producing a manufactured product. Though some market research is done by Brother in the United States, this is to be expected in the course of selling any product, domestic or imported. It is however, much less critical to the manufacture of a product than is the research, development, design and engineering activity. This factor, when considered in combination with the nature of Brother's operation, the low number of domestic parts, and its domestic value-added, is one of the most compelling factors affecting our analysis.

> 'The nature of Brother's operation is qualitatively different from the type of operation characterized by design, engineering, and the actual manufacturing of some of the essential parts, to which Congress intended to afford a remedy.'...

"ITA concluded that BIUSA was not an interested party under the statute and lack[ed] standing to maintain the action....

"To have standing to file a petition, a party must be a 'manufacturer, producer, or wholesaler.'... These terms are not defined in the statute, but the legislative history states that the 'standing requirements [should] be administered to provide an opportunity for relief for an adversely affected industry and to prohibit petitions filed by person with no stake in the result of the investigation.'... Nothing suggests that a petitioner must make anything more than a threshold showing of injury. Thus, the legislative history calls for a liberal construction of the standing requirement....

"ITA's analysis, however, imposes burdens on a petitioner for which there is not support in the statute or legislative history. ITA elevates the situs of research, development, design and engineering to a primary position. As BIUSA notes, based on ITA's analysis, without research and development, a 'company is cast outside the pale of qualified antidumping petitioners.'... Thus, any company that is manufacturing a product that has been researched and developed outside the United States likely would be disqualified under ITA's analysis.... A company may be a U.S. manufacturer for purposes of standing requirements even though its product is designed abroad....

"In emphasizing the situs of design and engineering, ITA has given inadequate consideration to several other factors such as capital investment and employment levels, even though it characterized these factors as 'substantial' and 'not insignificant.' It also fails to note that BIUSA's U.S. value-added figures, even as calculate by ITA, compare favorably to at least one other case where ITA found the firm was part of domestic industry.... Moreover, ITA's disregard of the value-added, based on its belief that a determined firm could inflate its domestic value, is completely unsupported by the record. Finally, the fact that BIUSA imports critical component parts from Japan does not preclude a finding that BIUSA is an interested party....

"In short, ITA's analysis is not supported by the statute or legislative history.... Because ITA's determination that BIUSA is not a manufacturer is not supported by substantial evidence and is not in accordance in law, it cannot stand. Moreover, a fair application of the ITC factors to the facts of record demonstrated that BIUSA is a United States 'manufacturer' with a clear stake in the outcome of the antidumping investigation. The investment and employment levels at BIUSA, even as characterized by ITA, are not insignificant. The value-added is also significant, and at least as great as in other cases where a firm has been found to be part of the domestic industry.

"Based on the record before the court, and the test selected by ITA, the fact that BIUSA performs design and engineering abroad, or that major parts are imported does not preclude a finding that it is part of the domestic industry. BIUSA's operations at Bartlett can only be described as 'manufacturing.' Accordingly, ITA's determination is reversed, and the case is remanded for ITA to consider whether BIUSA has filed the petition 'on behalf of' the domestic industry, and if so, to proceed with an investigation under the antidumping laws."

UNITED STATES v. INTERNATIONAL BUSINESS MACHINES CORP.
517 U.S. 843 (1996)

BACKGROUND: The U.S. Constitution, Section 9, Clause 5 states: "No Tax or Duty shall be laid on Articles exported from any State." The U.S. levies a tax on insurance premiums paid to foreign insurance companies that are not subject to the U.S. income tax. International Business Machines Corp. ("IBM") ships its USA-made products to several foreign subsidiaries. Those subsidiaries often buy the insurance coverage for the shipments, using a foreign insurer—with both the foreign subsidiary and IBM named as beneficiaries. For years 1975 through 1984, the "foreign insurance" tax was not paid by IBM. The U.S. Internal Revenue Service claimed the back taxes were owed. IBM paid—under protest—then sued for a refund, claiming that the tax violated the Constitution's prohibition against taxes on exports. The U.S. Court of Federal

Claims and the Court of Appeals for the Federal Circuit agreed with IBM. The U.S. Government requested further review by the U.S. Supreme Court.

JUSTICE THOMAS:

"... We have had few occasions to interpret the language of the Export Clause, but our cases have broadly exempted from federal taxation not only export goods, but also services and activities closely related to the export process. At the same time, we have attempted to limit the term 'Articles exported' to permit federal taxation of pre-export goods and services....

"The Government contends that ... our traditional understanding of the Export Clause, which is based partly on an outmoded view of the Commerce Clause, can no longer be justified....

"Our rejection ... of much of our early dormant Commerce Clause jurisprudence did not, however, signal a similar rejection of our Export Clause cases. Our decades-long struggle over the meaning of the nontextual negative command of the dormant Commerce Clause does not lead to the conclusion that our interpretation of the textual command of the Export Clause is equally fluid....

"The Import-Export Clause, which is textually similar to the Export Clause, says in relevant part, 'No State shall ... lay any Imposts or Duties on Imports or Exports.'... Though minor textual differences exist and the Clauses are directed at different sovereigns, historically both have been treated as broad bans on taxation of exports, and in several cases the Court has interpreted the provisions of the two clauses in tandem....

"We are ... hesitant to adopt the Import-Export Clause's policy-based analysis without some indication that the Export Clause was intended to alleviate the same 'evils' to which the Import-Export Clause was directed. Unlike the Import-Export Clause, which was intended to protect federal supremacy in international commerce, to preserve federal revenue from import duties and imposts, and to prevent coastal States with ports from taking unfair advantage of inland states ... the Export Clause serves none of those goals. Indeed, textually, the Export Clause does quite the opposite. It specifically prohibits Congress from regulating international commerce through export taxes, disallows any attempt to raise federal revenue from exports, and has no direct effect on the way the States treat imports and exports....

"[W]e think the text of the constitutional provision provides a better decisional guide than that offered by the Government. The Government's policy argument—that the Framers intended the Export Clause to narrowly alleviate the fear of northern repression through taxation of southern exports by prohibiting only discriminatory taxes—cannot be squared with the broad language of the Clause. The better reading, that adopted by our earlier cases, is that the Framers sought to alleviate their concerns by completely denying to Congress the power to tax exports at all.

"We conclude that the Export Clause does not permit assessment of nondiscriminatory federal taxes on goods in export transit. Reexamination of the question whether a particular assessment on an activity or service is so closely connected to the goods as to amount to a tax on the goods themselves must await another day…. The judgment of the Court of Appeals for the Federal Circuit is affirmed.

"*It is so ordered.*"

FAG KUGELFISCHER GEORG SCHAFER AG, et al. v. UNITED STATES
332 F.3d 1370 (Fed.Cir. 2003)

BACKGROUND: FAG Kugelfischer Georg Schaefer AG, FAG Italia SpA, Barden Corporation (UK), FAG Bearings Corporation, and the Barden Corporation (collectively "FAG"), and SKF USA, Inc., SKF France S.A., SKF GmbH, SKF Industrie S.p.A., and SKF Sverige AB (collectively "SKF") appeal the judgments of the Court of International Trade affirming the Department of Commerce's Final Remand Determinations.

FAG and SKF produce antifriction bearings ("AFBs"), and import these products into the United States. In June 1998 and July 1999, Commerce published the final results of the eighth and ninth administrative reviews, respectively, of antidumping duty orders on AFBs, including FAG's and SKF's subject merchandise. FAG and SKF appealed Commerce's methodology for measuring the dumping margin with respect to the data used to represent "foreign like product" to calculate two specific variables: price, per 19 U.S.C. § 1677b(b)(1), and constructed value profit, per 19 U.S.C. § 1677b(e)(2)(A). The Court of International Trade affirmed Commerce's methodology. On appeal, the Federal Circuit Court consolidated the cases, and vacated and remanded, instructing Commerce to provide a reasonable explanation as to "why it uses different definitions of 'foreign like product' for price purposes and when calculating constructed value." Commerce issued the *Final Remand Determinations* on March 29, 2002. On appeal to the Court of International Trade, the court affirmed the remand determinations in their entirety. FAG and SKF appeal.

CHIEF JUDGE MAYER:

"We review the Court of International Trade's judgment, affirming or reversing the final results of an administrative review, *de novo*…. We apply anew the same standard used by the Court of

International Trade … and will uphold Commerce's determination unless it is 'unsupported by substantial evidence on the record, or otherwise not in accordance with law.'… We review issues of statutory interpretation without deference…. In this instance, we required that upon remand Commerce's explanation for its methodology be reasonable….

"'Foreign like product' is the merchandise offered for sale in the producing and exporting country that is most like, and may be reasonably compared to, the allegedly dumped subject merchandise here in the United States….

"In this proceeding, to calculate normal value, Commerce first looked to the data characterized in sections 1677(16)(A) and (B) above, sales of identical models or those from the same family of products. Commerce then eliminated sales not in the ordinary course of trade from the normal-value data pool. It disregarded sales made at below the cost of production and conducted a price-to-price comparison. And it rejected non-contemporaneous data, which did not occur 'at a time reasonably corresponding to the time' of the U.S. sale….

"Because insufficient data to determine normal value remained in the sections 1677(16)(A) and (B) data pools after these adjustments, Commerce resorted to constructing the normal value…. One component of constructed value ('CV') is profit made 'in connection with the production and sale of a foreign like product, in the ordinary course of trade.'… Commerce calculated CV profit here by utilizing section 1677(16)(C) data, aggregate data from all foreign like products, within the same level of trade and class or kind of merchandise, under consideration for normal value. It determined a single profit ratio for all sales. Commerce thereby applied different subparts of the definition of foreign like product within the same administrative proceeding. At issue here is whether Commerce reasonably justified such application in its remand determinations. We hold that it has.

"FAG and SKF do not challenge the use of sections 1677(16)(A) and (B) data to make price-to-price determinations (which eliminate below cost sales), but assert that Commerce did not reasonably justify its use of section 1677(16)(C) data to calculate CV profit. FAG and SKF contend that Commerce violated the rule of statutory construction that the same term, foreign like product, be given the same meaning throughout the statute, and that therefore, CV profit should have been calculated with sections 1677(16)(A) and (B) foreign like product categories.

"Section 1677(16), however, offers three alternative definitions for foreign like product, which increase in the scope of products that may be included…. The first available category of merchandise, with which differing determinations may be satisfactorily made, is to be applied…. There is no restriction that Commerce use just one subsection per proceeding…. Accordingly, we believe that Commerce reasonably explained that the determinations for the variables at issue require different sets of foreign like product data. The bearing market, with its wide disparity in products, necessitates that direct price comparisons be done on a model-by-model basis. Therefore, the use of price comparisons requires the identical model and product family data of sections 1677(16)(A) and (B). And CV profit may be based on a broader scope of products because use of aggregate data, as described in section 1677(16)(C), results in a practical measure of profit that can be applied consistently and with administrative ease over the range of included products.

"FAG and SKF argue that Commerce did not work its way through the hierarchy of definitions in section 1677(16), in contravention of Congress's direction, when it defined foreign like product to calculate CV profit. FAG and SKF suggest that if Commerce had started with sections 1677(16)(A) and (B) data it would not have eliminated below cost or non-contemporaneous data because the constructed value sections of the statute do not so require. This logic fails, however, because calculating constructed value under section 1677b(e)(2)(A) requires that the sales of foreign like product occur within the ordinary course of trade. And the definition of ordinary course of trade requires that the sales used must not be below cost, and must be contemporaneous to the exportation of the subject merchandise....

"Seeking to avoid the ordinary course of trade limitation in section 1677b(e)(2)(A), FAG and SKF argue that Commerce should have calculated constructed value under subsections 1677b(e)(2)(B)(i) or (iii). FAG and SKF assert that the scope of the data identified by Commerce as section 1677(16)(C) data was overbroad and should instead be characterized as the 'same general category of products' in subsections 1677b(e)(2)(B)(i) and (iii). Pursuant to our conclusion above, Commerce's use of aggregate sales within the same level of trade and class or kind of merchandise as foreign like product under section 1677(16)(C) was reasonable and not overbroad. And because section 1677b(e)(2)(A) is the preferred methodology to calculate CV profit ... its application by Commerce was reasonable....

"Accordingly, the judgment of the Court of International Trade is affirmed."

JAPAN LINE, LTD. v. COUNTY OF LOS ANGELES
441 U.S. 434 (1979)

BACKGROUND: Local political units in California, including Los Angeles County, impose "apportioned" taxes on tangible personal property, based on the amount of time the property is located in the various political units during the tax year. Japan Line and five other Japanese shipping corporations own large cargo-shipping containers, which have their home ports in Japan and are used exclusively in international commerce. All of these containers are taxed as property—at their full value—by Japan. Each container is in constant transit, except for repair time, loading and unloading. None of the containers is in California permanently; they are usually there less than three weeks, as part of international shipments of goods. Japan does not impose similar taxes on USA ships and containers that are in Japan temporarily as part of international commerce. The apportioned taxes being challenged totaled $550,000 for the three years at issue.

The Japanese companies claim these local taxes violate the U.S. Constitution, and the California trial court agreed. The California appeal court reversed that decision, and the California Supreme Court affirmed the reversal. The Japanese companies petitioned for U.S. Supreme Court review.

JUSTICE BLACKMUN:

"First, California's tax results in multiple taxation of the instrumentalities of foreign commerce. By stipulation, [the] containers are owned, based and registered in Japan; they are used exclusively in international commerce; and they remain outside Japan only so long as needed to complete their international missions. Under these circumstances, Japan has the right and the power to tax the containers in full. California's tax, however, creates more than the *risk* of multiple taxation; it produces multiple taxation in fact. [The] containers not only are 'subject to property tax … in Japan' … but, as the trial court found, 'are, in fact, taxed in Japan." Thus, if [the taxes] were sustained, [the companies] 'would be paying a double tax.'…

"Second, California's tax prevents this Nation from 'speaking with one voice' in regulating foreign trade. The desirability of uniform treatment of containers used exclusively in foreign commerce is evidenced by the Customs Convention on Containers, which the United States and Japan have signed…. Under this Convention, containers temporarily imported are admitted free of 'all duties and taxes whatsoever chargeable by reason of importation.'… The Convention reflects a national policy to remove impediments to the use of containers as 'instruments of international traffic.'… California's tax, however, will frustrate attainment of federal uniformity. It is stipulated that American-owned containers are not taxed in Japan…. California's tax thus creates asymmetry in international maritime taxation operating to Japan's disadvantage. The risk of retaliation by Japan, under these circumstances, is acute, and such retaliation of necessity would be felt by the Nation as a whole…. California, by its unilateral act, cannot be permitted to place these impediments before this Nation's conduct of its foreign relations and its foreign trade.

"Because California's … tax, as applied to [the] containers, results in multiple taxation of the instrumentalities of foreign commerce, and because it prevents the Federal Government from 'speaking with one voice' in international trade, the tax is inconsistent with Congress' power to 'regulate Commerce with foreign Nations.' We hold the tax, as applied, unconstitutional under the Commerce Clause....

"The judgment of the Supreme Court of California is reversed.

"*It is so ordered.*"

MOBIL OIL CORP. v. COMMISSIONER OF TAXES OF VERMONT
   445 U.S. 425 (1980)

BACKGROUND: Mobil Oil, a New York corporation, operates an integrated petroleum business, including exploration, production, refining, transportation, distribution, and sale of petroleum products. It does business in over 40 States (including Vermont), and in a number of foreign nations.

Mobil uses wholly or partly owned subsidiaries and affiliates to conduct significant parts of its non-USA operations. These companies are organized in other nations or in other U.S. States. They do not do business in Vermont, nor are Mobil's shares in them managed in Vermont. Mobil's Vermont operations consist of wholesaling and retailing petroleum and related products—only a small fraction of its total business. Mobil has no production or refining facilities in Vermont.

Every corporation doing business in Vermont is subject to the State's annual net income tax; "net income" is defined as the taxpayer's taxable income "under the laws of the United States"—i.e., the corporation's taxable income as reported for the national income tax. If a taxpayer corporation has done business both inside and outside Vermont, the State uses a three-part equation to determine the portion of the net income it can properly tax. The taxable portion is calculated by multiplying "net income" by a fraction representing the average of the ratios of sales, payroll, and property values in Vermont to those of the corporation as a whole. Vermont's Supreme Court held that Mobil was subject to the tax as calculated. Mobil specifically objected to having the dividend income it received from foreign subsidiaries included as part of its "net income," and petitioned for review by the U.S. Supreme Court.

JUSTICE BLACKMUN:

"In this case we are called upon to consider constitutional limits on a nondomiciliary State's taxation of the income received by a domestic corporation in the form of dividends from subsidiaries and affiliates doing business abroad....

"It has long been established that the income of a business operating in interstate commerce is not immune from fairly apportioned state taxation.... For a State to tax income generated in interstate commerce, the Due Process Clause of the Fourteenth Amendment imposes two requirements: a 'minimal connection' between the interstate activities and the taxing State, and a rational relationship between the income attributed to the State and the intrastate values of the enterprise.... The requisite 'nexus' is supplied if the corporation avails itself of the 'substantial privilege of carrying on business' within the State; and '[the] fact that a tax is contingent upon events brought to pass without a state does not destroy the nexus between such a tax and transactions within a state for which the tax is an exaction.'...

"... [T]he linchpin of apportionability in the field of state income taxation is the unitary-business principle. In accord with this principle, what [Mobil Oil] must show in order to establish that its dividend income is not subject to an apportioned tax in Vermont, is that the income was earned in the course of activities unrelated to the sale of petroleum products in that State.... [Mobil Oil] has made no effort to demonstrate that the foreign operations of its subsidiaries and affiliates are distinct in any business or economic sense from its petroleum sales activities in Vermont. Indeed, all indications in the record are to the contrary, since it appears that these foreign activities are part of [its] integrated petroleum enterprise. In the absence of any proof of discrete business enterprise, Vermont was entitled to conclude that the dividend income's foreign source did not destroy the requisite nexus with instate activities....

"The reasons for allocation to a single situs that often apply in the case of private taxation carry little force in the present context. Mobil no doubt enjoys privileges and protections conferred by New York law with respect to ownership of its stock holdings, and its activities in that State no doubt supply some nexus for jurisdiction to tax.... Since Vermont seeks to tax income, not ownership, we hold that its interest in taxing a proportionate share of [Mobil's] dividend income is not overridden by any interest of the State of commercial domicile....

"In sum, [Mobil] has failed to demonstrate any sound basis, under either the Due Process Clause or the Commerce Clause, for establishing a constitutional preference for allocation of its foreign-source dividend income to the State of commercial domicile. Because the issue has not been presented, we need not, and do not, decide what the constituent elements of a fair apportionment formula applicable to such income would be. We do hold, however, that Vermont is not precluded from taxing its proportionate share.

"The judgment of the Supreme Court of Vermont is affirmed."

ALLIED-SIGNAL, INC. v. DIRECTOR, DIVISION OF TAXATION
504 U.S. 768 (1992)

BACKGROUND: Bendix, a Delaware corporation, but with its headquarters in Michigan, did business in all 50 U.S. States and in 22 other nations—primarily manufacturing automotive and aerospace components. Allied-Signal ("ASARCO"), a New Jersey corporation with New York headquarters, was one of the world's largest producers of nonferrous metals. In the late 1970s, Bendix bought a 20.6 percent stock interest in ASARCO, but ASARCO continued to operate as a completely separate business. Bendix sold the stock in 1981, making a $211.5 million profit. New Jersey included this gain when calculating how much state income tax Bendix owed in New Jersey. Bendix paid the full amount New Jersey claimed, and then sued for a refund. The New Jersey courts held that the stock-sale profit was properly included as "income" for New Jersey state tax purposes. Allied-Signal (having bought Bendix) now claims the refund, and requested U.S. Supreme Court review of the New Jersey courts' decision.

JUSTICE KENNEDY:

"Among the limitations the Constitution sets on the power of a single State to tax the multi-state income of a nondomiciliary corporation are these: there must be 'a "minimal connection" between the interstate activities and the taxing state,'... and there must be a rational relation between the income attributed to the taxing State and the intrastate value of the corporate business. Under our precedents, a State need not attempt to isolate the intrastate income producing activities from the rest of the business; it may tax an apportioned sum if the corporation's multistate business is unitary.... A State may not tax a nondomiciliary corporation's income, however, if it is 'derive[d] from "unrelated business activity" which constitutes a "discrete business enterprise".'...

"The principle that a state may not tax value earned outside its borders rests on the fundamental requirement of both the Due Process and Commerce Clauses that there be 'some definite link, some minimum connection, between a state and the person, property or transaction it seeks to tax.'... The reason the Commerce Clause includes this limit is self-evident: in a Union of 50 States, to permit each State to tax activities outside its borders would have drastic consequences for the national economy, as businesses would be subject to severe multiple taxation. But the

353

Due Process Clause also underlies our decisions in this area. Although our modern due process jurisprudence rejects a rigid, formalistic definition of minimum connection..., we have not abandoned the requirement that, in the case of a tax on an activity, there must be a connection to the activity itself, rather than a connection only to the actor the State seeks to tax.... The present inquiry focuses on the guidelines necessary to circumscribe the reach of the State's legitimate power to tax. We are guided by the basic principle that the State's power to tax an individual's or corporation's activities is justified by the 'protection, opportunities and benefits' the State confers on those activities....

"Because of the complications and uncertainties in allocating the income of multistate business to the several States, we permit States to tax a corporation on an apportionable share of the multistate business carried on in part in the taxing State. That is the unitary business principle. It is not a novel construct, but one which we approved rather a short time after the passage of the Fourteenth Amendment's Due Process Clause....

"... [I]f anything would be unworkable in practice, it would be for us now to abandon our settled jurisprudence defining the limits of state power to tax under the unitary business principle. State legislatures have relied upon our precedents by enacting tax codes which allocate intangible nonbusiness income to the domiciliary State.... Were we to adopt New Jersey's theory, we would be required either to invalidate those statutes or authorize what would be certain double taxation. And, of course, we would defeat the reliance interest of those corporations which have structured their activities and paid their taxes based upon the well-established rules we here confirm. Difficult questions respecting the retroactive effect of our decision would also be presented.... New Jersey's proposal would disrupt settled expectations in an area of the law in which the demands of the national economy require stability....

"Application of the foregoing principles to the present case yields a clear result.... There is no serious contention that any of the three factors upon which we focused in [a prior case] were present. Functional integration and economies of scale could not exist because, as the parties have stipulated, 'Bendix and ASARCO were unrelated business enterprises each of whose activities had nothing to do with the other.'... Moreover, because Bendix owned only 20.6% of ASARCO's stock, it did not have the potential to operate ASARCO as an integrated division of a single unitary business, and of course, even potential control is not sufficient.... There was no centralization of management....

"Furthermore, contrary to the view expressed ... by the New Jersey Supreme Court..., the mere fact that an intangible asset was acquired pursuant to a long-term corporate strategy of acquisitions and dispositions does not convert an otherwise passive investment into an integral operational one. Indeed, in [a prior case] we noted the important distinction between a capital investment which serves an investment function and one which serves an operational function.... If that distinction is to retain its vitality, then ... the fact that a transaction was undertaken for a business purpose does not change its character.... [Other states have] argued that intangible income could be treated as earned in the course of a unitary business if the intangible property which produced the income is 'acquired, managed or disposed of for purposes relating or contributing to the taxpayer's business.'... In rejecting that argument we observed: 'This definition of unitary business would destroy the concept. The business of a corporation requires that it earn money to continue operations and to provide a return on its invested capital. Consequently all of its operations, including any investments made, in some sense can be said to be "for purposes relating to or contributing to the [corporation's] business." When pressed to its logical limit, this conception of the "unitary business" limitation becomes no limitation at all.'...

"Apart from semantics, we see no distinction between the 'purpose' test we [have already] rejected ... and the 'ingrained acquisition-divestiture policy' approach adopted by the New Jersey Supreme Court.... The hallmarks of an acquisition which is part of the taxpayer's unitary business continue to be functional integration, centralization of management, and economies of scale.... [T]hese essentials could respectively be shown by transactions not undertaken at arm's length..., a management role by the parent which is grounded in its own operational expertise and operational strategy..., and the fact that the corporations are engaged in the same line of business.... It is undisputed that none of these circumstances existed here....

"In sum, the agreed-upon facts make clear that under our precedents New Jersey was not permitted to include the gain realized on the sale of Bendix's ASARCO stock in the former's apportionable tax base.

"The judgment of the New Jersey Supreme Court is reversed, and the case is remanded for further proceedings not inconsistent with this opinion.

"*It is so ordered.*"

BARCLAYS BANK PLC v. FRANCHISE TAX BOARD OF CALIFORNIA
512 U.S. 298 (1994)

BACKGROUND: California levies a franchise tax on privilege of doing local business in the State. For multinational enterprises, the State uses an apportionment formula to allocate an appropriate part of worldwide income for purposes of its franchise tax. The income taxable by California is equal to the average of the proportions of worldwide payroll, property, and sales located in the State. Barclays Group is a multinational banking enterprise of over 220 companies doing business in some 60 nations. Barclays Bank PLC—a United Kingdom corporation—does local business in California. Barclays Bank paid the franchise tax under protest, and then sued in California state court for a refund. It won in the trial court and the California Court of Appeals, but the California Supreme Court held the tax was valid and remanded the case. The California Court of Appeals then denied the refund claim. Barclays petitioned for U.S. Supreme Court review.

JUSTICE GINSBURG:

"The [Commerce] Clause does not shield interstate (or foreign) commerce from 'its fair share of the state tax burden.'... Absent congressional approval, however, a state tax on such commerce will not survive Commerce Clause scrutiny if the taxpayer demonstrates that the tax (1) applies to an activity lacking a substantial nexus to the taxing State; (2) is not fairly apportioned; (3) discriminates against interstate commerce; or (4) is not fairly related to services provided by the State....

"A tax affecting foreign commerce ... raises two concerns in addition to the four delineated [above]. The first is prompted by 'the enhanced risk of multiple taxation.'... The second relates to the Federal Government's capacity to 'speak with one voice when regulating commercial relations with foreign governments.'...

"Barclays ... vigorously contends ... that California's worldwide combined reporting scheme violates the antidiscrimination component of the ... test. Barclays maintains that a foreign owner of a taxpayer filing a California tax return 'is forced to convert its diverse financial and accounting records from around the world into the language, currency, and accounting principles of the United States' at 'prohibitive' expense.... Domestic-owned taxpayers, by contrast, need not incur such expense because they 'already keep most of their records in English, in United States currency, and in accord with United States accounting principles.'...

"Compliance burdens, if disproportionately imposed on out-of-jurisdiction enterprises, may indeed be inconsistent with the Commerce Clause....

"California's regulations, however, also provide that the Tax Board 'shall consider the effort and expense required to obtain the necessary information,' and, in 'appropriate cases, such as when the necessary data cannot be developed from financial records maintained in the regular course of business,' may accept 'reasonable approximations.'...

"... [M]ultiple taxation was not the 'inevitable result' of the California tax; and ... the 'alternative reasonably available to the taxing State' ... 'could not eliminate the risk of double taxation' and might in some cases enhance that risk….

"We turn, finally, to the question ultimately and most energetically presented: Did California's worldwide combined reporting requirement … 'impair federal uniformity in an area where federal uniformity is essential' …; in particular, did the State's taxing scheme 'prevent the Federal Government from "speaking with one voice" in international trade'? ...

"[W]e discern no 'specific indication of congressional intent' to bar the state action here challenged. Our decision … in *Container Corp.* left the ball in Congress' court; had Congress … considered nationally uniform use of separate accounting 'essential,' … it could have enacted legislation prohibiting the States from taxing corporate income based on the worldwide combined reporting method. In the 11 years that have elapsed since our decision in *Container Corp.*, Congress has failed to enact such legislation….

"The Constitution does '"not make the judiciary the overseer of our government."'… Having determined that the taxpayers before us had an adequate nexus with the State, that worldwide combined reporting led to taxation which was fairly apportioned, nondiscriminatory, fairly related to the services provided by the State, and that its imposition did not result inevitably in multiple taxation, we leave it to Congress—whose voice, in this area, is the Nation's—to evaluate whether the national interest is best served by tax uniformity, or state autonomy. Accordingly, the judgments of the California Court of Appeal are *Affirmed*."

UNITED STATES OF AMERICA v. J. BRYAN WILLIAMS
489 Fed. Appx. 655 (4th Cir. 2012)

BACKGROUND: Federal law requires taxpayers to report annually to the Internal Revenue Service ("IRS") any financial interests they have in any bank, securities, or other financial accounts in a foreign country. The report is made by filing a completed form TD F 90-22.1 ("Foreign Bank Account Report"—"FBAR") with the Department of the Treasury. The FBAR must be filed on or before June 30 of each calendar year with respect to foreign financial accounts maintained during the previous calendar year, and the Secretary of the Treasury may impose a civil money penalty on any person who fails to timely file the report. Moreover, in cases where a person willfully fails to file the FBAR, the Secretary may impose an increased maximum penalty, up to $100,000 or fifty percent of the balance in the account at the time of the violation.

The Government brought this action seeking to enforce civil penalties assessed against J. Bryan Williams for his failure to report his interest in two foreign bank accounts for tax year 2000, in violation of 31 U.S.C. § 5314. In 1993, Williams opened two Swiss bank accounts in the name of ALQI Holdings, Ltd., a British Corporation (the "ALQI accounts"). From 1993 through 2000, Williams deposited more than $7,000,000 into the ALQI accounts, earning more than $800,000 in income on the deposits. However, for each of the tax years during that period, Williams did not report to the IRS the income from the ALQI accounts or his interest in the accounts, as he was required to do. By the fall of 2000, Swiss and Government authorities had become aware of the assets in the ALQI accounts. Williams retained counsel and on November 13, 2000, he met with Swiss authorities to discuss the accounts. The following day, at the request of the Government, the Swiss authorities froze the ALQI accounts.

Relevant to this appeal, Williams completed a "tax organizer" in January 2001, which had been provided to him by his accountant in connection with the preparation of his 2000 federal tax return. In response to the question in the tax organizer regarding whether Williams had "an interest in or a signature or other authority over a bank account, or other financial account in a foreign country," Williams answered "No." In addition, the 2000 Form 1040, line 7a in Part III of Schedule B asks: "At any time during 2000, did you have an interest in or a signature or other authority over a financial account in a foreign country, such as a bank account, securities account, or other financial account? See instructions for exceptions and filing requirements for Form TD F 90-22.1." On his 2000 federal tax return, Williams checked "No" in response to this question, and he did not file an FBAR by the June 30, 2001, deadline. Subsequently, upon the advice of his attorneys and accountants, Williams fully disclosed the ALQI accounts to an IRS agent in January 2002. In October 2002 he filed his 2001 federal tax return on which he acknowledged his interest in the ALQI accounts. Williams also disclosed the accounts to the IRS in February 2003 as part of his application to participate in the Offshore Voluntary Compliance Initiative. At that time he also filed amended returns for 1999 and 2000, which disclosed details about his ALQI accounts.

In June 2003, Williams pled guilty to a two-count superseding criminal information, which charged him with conspiracy to defraud the IRS and criminal tax evasion, in connection with the funds held in the ALQI accounts from 1993 through 2000. As part of the plea, Williams agreed to allocute to all of the essential elements of the charged crimes, including that he unlawfully, willfully, and knowingly evaded taxes by filing false and fraudulent tax returns on which he failed to disclose his interest in the ALQI accounts. In exchange for his allocution, Williams received a three-level reduction under the Sentencing Guidelines for acceptance of responsibility.

In his allocution, Williams admitted the following: "I knew that most of the funds deposited into the Alqi accounts and all the interest income were taxable income to me. However, the calendar year tax returns for '93 through 2000, I chose not to report the income to my—to the Internal Revenue Service in order to evade the substantial taxes owed thereon, until I filed my 2001 tax return. I also knew that I had the obligation to report to the IRS and/or the Department of the Treasury the existence of the Swiss accounts, but for the calendar year tax returns 1993 through 2000, I chose not to in order to assist in hiding my true income from the IRS and evade taxes thereon, until I filed my 2001 tax return.... I knew what I was doing was wrong and unlawful. I, therefore, believe that I am guilty of evading the payment of taxes for the tax years 1993 through 2000. I also believe that I acted in concert with others to create a mechanism, the Alqi accounts, which I intended to allow me to escape detection by the IRS. Therefore, I am—I believe that I'm guilty of conspiring with the people would (sic) whom I dealt regarding the Alqi accounts to defraud the United States of taxes which I owed."

In January 2007, Williams finally filed an FBAR for each tax year from 1993 through 2000. Thereafter, the IRS assessed two $100,000 civil penalties against him, for his failure to file an FBAR for tax year 2000. Williams failed to pay these penalties, and the Government brought this enforcement action to collect them. Following a bench trial, the district court entered judgment in favor of Williams, finding that the Government failed to establish that Williams willfully violated § 5314. The Government appealed.

JUDGE SHEDD:

"The parties agree that Williams violated § 5314 by failing to timely file an FBAR for tax year 2000. The only question is whether the violation was willful. The district court found that (1) Williams 'lacked any motivation to willfully conceal the accounts from authorities' because they were already aware of the accounts and (2) his failure to disclose the accounts 'was not an act undertaken intentionally or in deliberate disregard for the law, but instead constituted an understandable omission given the context in which it occurred.' Therefore, the district court found that Williams's violation of § 5314 was not willful.... In making its determination, the district court emphasized Williams's motivation rather than the relevant issue of his intent.... '[M]alice or improper motive is not necessary to establish willfulness.' To the extent the district court focused on motivation as proof of the lack of intent, it simply drew an unreasonable inference from the record. In November 2000, Swiss authorities met with Williams to discuss the ALQI accounts and thereafter froze them at the request of the United States Government. Although the Government knew of the existence of the accounts, nothing in the record indicates that, when the accounts were frozen, the Government knew the extent, control, or degree of Williams's interest in the accounts or the total funds held in the accounts. As Williams admitted in his allocution, his decision not to report the accounts was part of his tax evasion scheme that continued until he filed his 2001 tax return. Thus, his failure to disclose information about the

ALQI accounts on his 2000 tax return in May 2001 was motivated by his desire not to admit his interest in the accounts, even after authorities had been aware of them for over six months. Rarely does a person who knows he is under investigation by the Government immediately disclose his wrongdoing because he is not sure how much the Government knows about his role in that wrongdoing. Thus, without question, when Williams filed in May of 2001, he was clearly motivated not to admit his interest in the ALQI accounts.

"'Willfulness may be proven through inference from conduct meant to conceal or mislead sources of income or other financial information,' and it 'can be inferred from a conscious effort to avoid learning about reporting requirements.'... Similarly, 'willful blindness' may be inferred where 'a defendant was subjectively aware of a high probability of the existence of a tax liability, and purposefully avoided learning the facts point to such liability.'... Importantly, in cases 'where willfulness is a statutory condition of civil liability, [courts] have generally taken it to cover not only knowing violations of a standard, but reckless ones as well.'... Whether a person has willfully failed to comply with a tax reporting requirement is a question of fact....

"Here, the evidence as a whole leaves us with a definite and firm conviction that the district court clearly erred in finding that Williams did not willfully violate § 5314. Williams signed his 2000 federal tax return, thereby declaring under penalty of perjury that he had 'examined this return and accompanying schedules and statements' and that, to the best of his knowledge, the return was 'true, accurate, and complete.' 'A taxpayer who signs a tax return will not be heard to claim innocence for not having actually read the return, as he or she is charged with constructive knowledge of its contents.'... Williams's signature is prima facie evidence that he knew the contents of the return ... and at a minimum line 7a's directions to '[s]ee instructions for exceptions and filing requirements for Form TD F 90-22.1' put Williams on inquiry notice of the FBAR requirement.

"Nothing in the record indicates that Williams ever consulted Form TD F 90-22.1 or its instructions. In fact, Williams testified that he did not read line 7a and 'never paid any attention to any of the written words' on his federal tax return. Thus, Williams made a 'conscious effort to avoid learning about reporting requirements' ... and his false answers on both the tax organizer and his federal tax return evidence conduct that was 'meant to conceal or mislead sources of income or other financial information.'... 'It is reasonable to assume that a person who has foreign bank accounts would read the information specified by the government in tax forms. Evidence of acts to conceal income and financial information, combined with the defendant's failure to pursue knowledge of further reporting requirements as suggested on Schedule B, provide a sufficient basis to establish willfulness on the part of the defendant.'... This conduct constitutes willful blindness to the FBAR requirement....

"Williams's guilty plea allocution further confirms that his violation of § 5314 was willful. During that allocution, Williams acknowledged that he willfully failed to report the existence of the ALQI accounts to the IRS or Department of the Treasury as part of his larger scheme of tax evasion. This failure to report the ALQI accounts is an admission of violating § 5314. In light of his allocution, Williams cannot now claim that he was unaware of, inadvertently ignored, or otherwise lacked the motivation to willfully disregard the FBAR reporting requirement....

"Thus, we are convinced that, at a minimum, Williams's undisputed actions establish reckless conduct, which satisfies the proof requirement under § 5314.... Accordingly, we conclude that the district court clearly erred in finding that willfulness had not been established.

"For the foregoing reasons, we reverse the judgment of the district court and remand this case for proceedings consistent with this opinion."

TRAIL SMELTER ARBITRATION (UNITED STATES v. CANADA)
ARBITRATION AGREEMENT: Convention of Ottawa, April 15, 1935
AWARD: April 16, 1938, and March 11, 1941.

CONVENTION FOR SETTLEMENT OF DIFFICULTIES ARISING FROM OPERATION
OF SMELTER AT TRAIL, B.C.

Signed at Ottawa, April 15, 1935; ratifications exchanged Aug. 3, 1935

The President of the United States of America, and His Majesty the King of Great Britain, Ireland and the British dominions beyond the Seas, Emperor of India, in respect of the Dominion of Canada,
Considering that the Government of the United States has complained to the Government of Canada that fumes discharged from the smelter of the Consolidated Mining and Smelting Company at Trail, British Columbia, have been causing damage in the State of Washington, and Considering further that the International Joint Commission, established pursuant to the Boundary Waters Treaty of 1909, investigated problems arising from the operation of the smelter at Trail and rendered a report and recommendations thereon, dated February 28, 1931, and Recognizing the desirability and necessity of effecting a permanent settlement,
Have decided to conclude a convention for the purposes aforesaid, and to that end have named as their respective plenipotentiaries:

The President of the United States of America:

PIERRE DE L. BOAL, Charge d'Affaires ad interim of the United States of America at Ottawa;

His Majesty the King of Great Britain, Ireland and the British dominions beyond the Seas, Emperor of India, for the Dominion of Canada:

The Right Honorable RICHARD BEDFORD BENNETT, Prime Minister, President of the Privy Council and Secretary of State for External Affairs;

Who, after having communicated to each other their full powers, found in good and due form, have agreed upon the following Articles: ...

ARTICLE III.

The Tribunal shall finally decide the questions, hereinafter referred to as "the Questions", set forth hereunder, namely:
(1) Whether damage caused by the Trail Smelter in the State of Washington has occurred since the first day of January, 1932, and, if so, what indemnity should be paid therefor?
(2) In the event of the answer to the first part of the preceding Question being in the affirmative, whether the Trail Smelter should be required to refrain from causing damage in the State of Washington in the future and, if so, to what extent?
(3) In the light of the answer to the preceding Question, what measures or regime, if any, should be adopted or maintained by the Trail Smelter?
(4) What indemnity or compensation, if any, should be paid on account of any decision or decisions rendered by the Tribunal pursuant to the next two preceding Questions?

ARTICLE IV.

The Tribunal shall apply the law and practice followed in dealing with cognate questions in the United States of America as well as international law and practice, and shall give consideration to the desire of the high contracting parties to reach a solution just to all parties concerned. ...

ARTICLE XIII.

Each Government shall pay the expenses of the presentation and conduct of its case before the Tribunal and the expenses of its national member and scientific assistant.

All other expenses, which by their nature are a charge on both Governments, including the honorarium of the neutral member of the Tribunal, shall be borne by the two Governments in equal moieties....

TRAIL SMELTER ARBITRAL TRIBUNAL

DECISION
REPORTED ON APRIL 16, 1938, TO THE GOVERNMENT OF THE UNITED STATES
OF AMERICA AND TO THE GOVERNMENT OF THE DOMINION OF CANADA
UNDER THE CONVENTION SIGNED APRIL 15, 1935.

The Tribunal met in Washington, in the District of Columbia, on June 21, 22, 1937, for organization, adoption of rules of procedure and hearing of preliminary statements. From July 1 to July 6, it travelled over and inspected the area involved in the controversy in the northern part of Stevens County in the State of Washington and it also inspected the smelter plant of the Consolidated Mining and Smelting Company of Canada, Limited, at Trail in British Columbia. It held sessions for the reception and consideration of such evidence, oral and documentary, as was presented by the Governments or by interested parties, as provided in Article VIII, in Spokane in the State of Washington, from July 7 to July 29, 1937; in Washington, in the District of Columbia, on August 16, 17, 18, 19, 1937; in Ottawa, in the Province of Ontario, from August 23 to September 18, 1937; and it heard arguments of counsel in Ottawa from October 12 to October 19, 1937.

On January 2, 1938, the Agents of the two Governments jointly informed the Tribunal that they had nothing additional to present. Under the provisions of Article XI of the Convention, it then became the duty of the Tribunal "to report to the Governments its final decisions ... within a period of three months after the conclusion of the proceedings", *i.e.,* on April 2, 1938.

After long consideration of the voluminous typewritten and printed record and of the transcript of evidence presented at the hearings, the Tribunal formally notified the Agents of the two Governments that, in its opinion, unless the time limit should be extended, the Tribunal would be forced to give a permanent decision on April 2, 1938, on the basis of data which it considered inadequate and unsatisfactory. Acting on the recommendation of the Tribunal and under the provisions of Article XI authorizing such extension, the two Governments by agreement extended the time for the report of final decision of the Tribunal to three months from October 1, 1940.

The Tribunal is prepared now to decide finally Question No. 1, propounded to it in Article III of the Convention; and it hereby reports its final decision on Question No. 1, its temporary decision on Questions No. 2 and No. 3, and provides for a temporary regime thereunder and for a final decision on these questions and on Question No. 4, within three months from October 1, 1940....

The controversy is between two Governments involving damage occurring in the territory of one of them (the United States of America) and alleged to be due to an agency situated in the territory of the other (the Dominion of Canada). For which damage the latter has assumed by the Convention an international responsibility. In this controversy, the Tribunal is not sitting to pass upon claims presented by individuals or on behalf of one or more individuals by their Government, although individuals may come within the meaning of "parties concerned", in Article IV and of "interested parties", in Article VIII of the Convention and although the damage suffered by individuals may, in part, "afford a convenient scale for the calculation of the reparation due to the State."…

PART ONE.

By way of introduction to the Tribunal's decision, a brief statement, in general terms, of the topographic and climatic conditions and economic history of the locality involved in the controversy may be useful.…

The subject of fumigations and damage claimed to result from them was first taken up officially by the Government of the United States in June 1927, in a communication from the Consul General of the United States at Ottawa, addressed to the Government of the Dominion of Canada.…

PART TWO.

The first question under Article III of the Convention which the Tribunal is required to decide is as follows: (1) Whether damage caused by the Trail Smelter in the State of Washington has occurred since the first day of January, 1932, and, if so, what indemnity should be paid therefor.

In the determination of the first part of this question, the Tribunal has been obliged to consider three points, *viz.,* the existence of injury, the cause of the injury, and the damage due to the injury.…

In considering the second part of the question as to indemnity, the Tribunal has been mindful at all times of the principle of law which is set forth by the United States courts in dealing with cognate questions, particularly by the United States Supreme Court in Story Parchment Company *v.* Paterson Parchment Paper Company (1931) … "Where the tort itself is of such a nature as to preclude the ascertainment of the amount of damages with certainty, it would be a perversion of fundamental principles of justice to deny all relief to the injured person, and thereby relieve the wrongdoer from making any amend for his acts. In such case, while the damages may not be determined by mere speculation or guess, it will be enough if the evidence show the extent of the damages as a matter of just and reasonable inference, although the result be only approximate."…

The Tribunal has first considered the items of indemnity claimed by the United States in its Statement ... "on account of damage occurring since January 1, 1932, covering: (a) Damages in respect of cleared land and improvements thereon; (b) Damages in respect of uncleared land and improvements thereon; (c) Damages in respect of livestock; (d) Damages in respect of property in the town of Northport; (g) Damages in respect of business enterprises".

With respect to Item (a) and to Item (b) ... the Tribunal has reached the conclusion that damage due to fumigations has been proved to have occurred since January 1, 1932, and to the extent set forth hereafter....

It appears from a careful study and comparison of recorder data furnished by the two Governments, that on numerous occasions fumigations occur practically simultaneously at points down the valley many miles apart-this being especially the fact during the growing season from April to October. It also appears from the data furnished by the different recorders, that the rate of gas attenuation down the river does not show a constant trend, but is more rapid in the first few miles below the boundary and more gradual further down the river. The Tribunal finds it impossible satisfactorily to account for the above conditions, on the basis of the theory presented to it. The Tribunal finds it further difficult to explain the times and durations of the fumigations on the basis of any probable surface-wind conditions.

The Tribunal is of opinion that the gases emerging from the stacks of the Trail Smelter find their way into the upper air currents, and are carried by these currents in a fairly continuous stream down the valley so long as the prevailing wind at that level is in that direction....

With respect to damage to cleared land not used for crops and to all uncleared (other than uncleared land used for timber), the Tribunal has adopted as the measure of indemnity, the measure of damages applied by American courts, *viz.,* the amount of reduction in the value of the use or rental value of the land....

It is evident that for many years prior to January 1, 1932, much of the forests in the area included in the present Northport and Boundary Precincts had been in a poor condition.... It is uncontroverted that heavy fumigations from the Trail Smelter which destroyed and injured trees occurred in 1930 and 1931; and there were also serious fumigations in earlier years....

The Tribunal has adopted as the measure of indemnity, to be applied on account of damage in respect of uncleared land used for merchantable timber, the measure of damages applied by American courts, viz., that since the destruction of merchantable timber will generally impair the value of the land itself, the measure of damage should be the reduction in the value of the land itself due to such destruction of timber; but under the leading American decisions, however, the value of the merchantable timber destroyed is, in general, deemed to be substantially the equivalent of the reduction in the value of the land….

With regard to "damages in respect of livestock", claimed by the United States, the Tribunal is of opinion that the United States has failed to prove that the presence of fumes from the Trail Smelter has injured either the livestock or the milk or wool productivity of livestock since January 1, 1932, through impaired quality of crop or grazing. So far as the injury to livestock is due to reduced yield of crop or grazing, the injury is compensated for in the indemnity which is awarded herein for such reduction of yield….

With regard to "damages in respect of business enterprises", the counsel for the United States … stated: "The business men unquestionably have suffered loss of business and impairment of the value of good will because of the reduced economic status of the residents of the damaged area." The Tribunal is of opinion that damage of this nature "due to reduced economic status" of residents in the area is too indirect, remote, and uncertain to be appraised and not such for which an indemnity can be awarded. None of the cases cited by counsel … sustain the proposition that indemnity can be obtained for an injury to or reduction in a man's business due to inability of his customers or clients to buy, which inability or impoverishment is caused by a nuisance. Such damage, even if proved, is too indirect and remote to become the basis, in law, for an award of indemnity….

The United States in its Statement … itemizes under the claim of damage for "violation of sovereignty" [Item e] only money expended "for the investigation undertaken by the United States Government of the problems created in the United States by the operation of the Smelter at Trail". The Tribunal is of the opinion that it was not within the intention of the parties, as expressed in the words "damage caused by the Trail Smelter" in Article III of the Convention, to include such moneys expended….

With respect to (Item f), "damages in respect of interest on $350,000 eventually accepted in satisfaction of damage to January 1, 1932, but not paid until November 2, 1935", the Tribunal is of opinion that no payment of such interest was contemplated by the Convention"….

In conclusion, the Tribunal answers Question 1 in Article III, as follows: Damage caused by the Trail Smelter in the State of Washington has occurred since the first day of January, 1932, and up to October 1, 1937, and the indemnity to be paid therefor is seventy-eight thousand dollars ($78,000), and is to be complete and final indemnity and compensation for all damage which occurred between such dates. Interest at the rate of six per centum per year will be allowed on the above sum of seventy-eight thousand dollars ($78,000) from the date of the filing of this report and decision until date of payment. This decision is not subject to alteration or modification by the Tribunal hereafter.

The fact of existence of damage, if any, occurring after October 1, 1937, and the indemnity to be paid therefor, if any, the Tribunal will determine in its final decision.

PART THREE.

As to Question No. 2, in Article III of the Convention … the Tribunal decides that until the date of the final decision provided for in Part Four of this present decision, the Trail Smelter shall refrain from causing damage in the State of Washington in the future to the extent set forth in such Part Four until October 1, 1940, and thereafter to such extent as the Tribunal shall require in the final decision provided for in Part Four.

PART FOUR.

As to Question No. 3, in Article III of the Convention … the Tribunal is unable at the present time, with the information that has been placed before it, to determine upon a permanent regime, for the operation of the Trail Smelter….

To enable it to establish a permanent regime based on the more adequate and intensive study and knowledge above referred to, the Tribunal establishes [a] temporary regime….

Nothing in the above paragraphs of Part Four of this decision shall relieve the Dominion of Canada from any obligation now existing under the Convention with reference to indemnity or compensation, if any, which the Tribunal may find to be due for damage, if any, occurring during the period from October 1, 1937 (the date to which indemnity for damage is now awarded) to October 1, 1940, or to such earlier date at which the Tribunal may render its final decision.

(*Signed*) JAN HOSTIE
(*Signed*) CHARLES WARREN
(*Signed*) R. A. E. GREENSHIELDS

DECISION
REPORTED ON MARCH 11, 1941, TO THE GOVERNMENT OF THE UNITED STATES OF AMERICA AND TO THE GOVERNMENT OF THE DOMINIO OF CANADA, UNDER THE CONVENTION SIGNED APRIL 15, 1935.

The Tribunal herewith reports its final decisions….

PART TWO.

The first question under Article III of the Convention is: "(I) Whether damage caused by the Trail Smelter in the State of Washington has occurred since the first day of January, 1932, and, if so, what indemnity should be paid therefor."

This question has been answered by the Tribunal in its previous decision, as to the period from January 1, 1932 to October 1, 1937, as set forth above. Concerning this question, three claims are now propounded by the United States.

The Tribunal is requested to "reconsider its decision with respect to expenditures incurred by the United States during the period January 1, 1932, to June 30, 1936". It is claimed that "in this respect the United States is entitled to be indemnified in the sum of $89,655, with interest at the rate of five per centum per annum from the end of each fiscal year in which the several amounts were expended to the date of the Tribunal's final decision".

This claim was dealt with in the previous decision … and was disallowed….

There can be no doubt that the Tribunal intended to give a final answer to Question I for the period up to October 1, 1937. This is made abundantly clear by the passage quoted above, in particular by the words: "This decision is not subject to alteration or modification by the Tribunal hereafter."…

That the sanctity of res judicata attaches to a final decision of an international tribunal is an essential and settled rule of international law.

If it is true that international relations based on law and justice require arbitral or judicial adjudication of international disputes, it is equally true that such adjudication must, in principle, remain unchallenged, if it is to be effective to that end.

Numerous and important decisions of arbitral tribunals and of the Permanent Court of International Justice show that this is, in effect, a principle of international law….

In the absence of agreement between parties, the first question concerning a request tending to revision of a decision constituting *res judicata,* is: can such a request ever be granted in international law, unless special powers to do so have been expressly given to the tribunal?...

Arbitral decisions do not give to the question an unanimous answer….

The Tribunal, therefore, decides that, at this stage, at least, the Convention does not deny it the power to grant a revision….

The second question is whether revision should be granted; and this question subdivides itself into two separate parts: first, whether the petition for revision should be entertained, and second, if entertained, whether the previous decision should be revised in view of the considerations presented by the United States....

A mere error in law is no sufficient ground for a petition tending to revision....

For these reasons, the Tribunal is of opinion that the petition must be denied.

The Tribunal is requested to say that damage has occurred in the State of Washington since October 1, 1937, as a consequence of the emission of sulphur dioxide by the smelters of the Consolidated Mining and Smelting Company at Trail, B.C., and that an indemnity in the sum of $34,807 should be paid therefor....

The Tribunal has examined carefully the records of all fumigations specifically alleged by the United States as having caused or been likely to cause damage, as well as the records of all other fumigations which may be considered likely to have caused damage....

As a result, it has come to the conclusion that the United States has failed to prove that any fumigation between October 1, 1937, and October 1, 1940, has caused injury to crops, trees or otherwise.

The Tribunal is finally requested as to Question I to find with respect to expenditures incurred by the United States during the period July 1, 1936, to September 1, 1940, that the United States is entitled to be indemnified in the sum of $38,657.79 with interest at the rate of five per centum per annum from the end of each fiscal year in which the several amounts were expended to the date of the Tribunal's final decision....

There is a fundamental difference between expenditure incurred in mending the damageable consequences of an injury and monies spent in ascertaining the existence, the cause and the extent of the latter.

These are not part of the damage, any more than other costs involved in seeking and obtaining a judicial or arbitral remedy, such as the fees of counsel, the travelling expenses of witnesses, etc. In effect, it would be quite impossible to frame a logical distinction between the costs of preparing expert reports and the cost of preparing the statements and answers provided for in the procedure. Obviously, the fact that these expenditures may be incurred by different agencies of the same government does not constitute a basis for such a logical distinction....

The preamble states that the damage complained of is damage caused by fumes in the State of Washington and there is every reason to admit that this, and this alone, is what is meant by the same word when it is used again in the text of the Convention....

When a State espouses a private claim on behalf of one of its nationals, expenses which the latter may have incurred in prosecuting or endeavoring to establish his claim prior to the espousal are sometimes included and, under appropriate conditions, may legitimately be included in the claim. They are costs, incidental to damage, incurred by the national in seeking local remedy or redress, as it is, as a rule, his duty to do, if, on account of injury suffered abroad, he wants to avail himself of the diplomatic protection of his State. The Tribunal, however, has not been informed of any case in which a Government has sought before an international jurisdiction or been allowed by an international award or judgment indemnity for expenses by it in preparing the proof for presenting a national claim or private claims which it had espoused; and counsel for the United States, on being requested to cite any precedent for such an adjudication, have stated that they know of no precedent. Cases cited were instances in which expenses allowed had been incurred by the injured national, and all except one prior to the presentation of the claim by the Government.

In the absence of authority established by settled precedents, the Tribunal is of opinion that, where an arbitral tribunal is requested to award the expenses of a Government incurred in preparing proof to support its claim, particularly a claim for damage to the national territory, the intent to enable the Tribunal to do so should appear, either from the express language of the instrument which sets up the arbitral tribunal or as a necessary implication from its provision. Neither such express language nor implication is present in this case....

No damage caused by the Trail Smelter in the State of Washington has occurred since the first day of October, 1937, and prior to the first day of October, 1940, and hence no indemnity shall be paid therefor.

PART THREE.

The second question under Article III of the Convention is as follows: In the event of the answer to the first part of the preceding question being in the affirmative, whether the Trail Smelter should be required to refrain from causing damage in the State of Washington in the future and, if so, to what extent?

Damage has occurred since January 1, 1932, as fully set forth in the previous decision. To that extent, the first part of the preceding question has thus been answered in the affirmative....

The first problem which arises is whether the [second part of the] question should be answered on the basis of the law followed in the United States or on the basis of international law. The Tribunal, however, finds that this problem need not be solved here as the law followed in the

United States in dealing with the quasi-sovereign rights of the States of the Union, in the matter of air pollution, whilst more definite, is in conformity with the general rules of international law....

As Professor Eagleton puts [it] (*Responsibility of States in International Law,* 1928, p. 80): "A State owes at all times a duty to protect other States against injurious acts by individuals from within its jurisdiction." A great number of such general pronouncements by leading authorities concerning the duty of a State to respect other States and their territory have been presented to the Tribunal. These and many others have been carefully examined. International decisions, in various matters ... are based on the same general principle, and, indeed, this principle, as such, has not been questioned by Canada. But the real difficulty often arises rather when it comes to determine what ... is deemed to constitute an injurious act....

A case concerning, as the present one does, territorial relations, decided by the Federal Court of Switzerland between the Cantons of Soleure and Argovia, may serve to illustrate the relativity of the rule. Soleure brought a suit against her sister State to enjoin use of a shooting establishment which endangered her territory. The court, in granting the injunction, said: "This right (sovereignty) excludes ... not only the usurpation and exercise of sovereign rights (of another State) ... but also an actual encroachment which might prejudice the natural use of the territory and the free movement of its inhabitants."...

No case of air pollution dealt with by an international tribunal has been brought to the attention of the Tribunal nor does the Tribunal know of any such case. The nearest analogy is that of water pollution. But, here also, no decision of an international tribunal has been cited or has been found.

There are, however, as regards both air pollution and water pollution, certain decisions of the Supreme Court of the United States which may legitimately be taken as a guide in this field of international law, for it is reasonable to follow by analogy, in international cases, precedents established by that court in dealing with controversies between States of the Union or with other controversies concerning the quasi-sovereign rights of such States, where no contrary rule prevails in international law and no reason for rejecting such precedents can be adduced from the limitations of sovereignty inherent in the Constitution of the United States....

What the [U.S.] Supreme Court says ... of its power under the Constitution equally applies to the extraordinary power granted this Tribunal under the Convention. What is true between States of the Union is, at least, equally true concerning the relations between the United States and the Dominion of Canada....

Great progress in the control of fumes has been made by science in the last few years and this progress should be taken into account.

The Tribunal, therefore, finds that the above decisions, taken as a whole, constitute an adequate basis for its conclusions, namely, that, under the principles of international law, as well as of the law of the United States, no State has the right to use or permit the use of its territory in such a manner as to cause injury by fumes in or to the territory of another or the properties or persons therein, when the case is of serious consequence and the injury is established by clear and convincing evidence.

The decisions of the Supreme Court of the United States which are the basis of these conclusions are decisions in equity and a solution inspired by them, together with the regime hereinafter prescribed, will, in the opinion of the Tribunal, be "just to all parties concerned", as long, at least, as the present conditions in the Columbia River Valley continue to prevail.

Considering the circumstances of the case, the Tribunal holds that the Dominion of Canada is responsible in international law for the conduct of the Trail Smelter. Apart from the undertakings in the Convention, it is, therefore, the duty of the Government of the Dominion of Canada to see to it that this conduct should be in conformity with the obligation of the Dominion under international law as herein determined.

The Tribunal, therefore, answers Question No. 2 as follows: (2) So long as the present conditions in the Columbia River Valley prevail, the Trail Smelter shall be required to refrain from causing any damage through fumes in the State of Washington; the damage herein referred to and its extent being such as would be recoverable under the decisions of the courts of the United States in suits between private individuals. The indemnity for such damage should be fixed in such manner as the Governments, acting under Article XI of the Convention, should agree upon.

PART FOUR.

The third question under Article III of the Convention is as follows: "In the light of the answer to the preceding question, what measures or regime, if any, should be adopted and maintained by the Trail Smelter?"

Answering this question in the light of the preceding one, since the Tribunal has, in its previous decision, found that damage caused by the Trail Smelter has occurred in the State of Washington since January 1, 1932, and since the Tribunal is of opinion that damage may occur in the future unless the operations of the Smelter shall be subject to some control, in order to avoid damage occurring, the Tribunal now decides that a regime or measure of control shall be applied to the operations of the Smelter and shall remain in full force unless and until modified in accordance with the provisions hereinafter set forth in Section 3, Paragraph VI of the present part of this decision….

The Tribunal is of opinion that the regime should be given an uninterrupted test through at least two growing periods and one non-growing period. It is equally of opinion that thereafter opportunity should be given for amendment or suspension of the regime, if conditions should warrant or require….

The Tribunal has carefully considered the suggestions made by the United States for a regime by which a prefixed sum would be due whenever the concentrations recorded would exceed a certain intensity for a certain period of time or a certain greater intensity for any twenty minute period.

It has been unable to adopt this suggestion. In its opinion, and in that of its scientific advisers, such a regime would unduly and unnecessarily hamper the operations of the Trail Smelter and would not constitute a "solution fair to all parties concerned."…

While the Tribunal refrains from making the following suggestion a part of the regime prescribed, it is strongly of the opinion that it would be to the clear advantage of the Dominion of Canada, if during the interval between the date of filing of this Final Report and December 31, 1942, the Dominion of Canada would continue, at its own expense, the maintenance of experimental and observational work by two scientists similar to that which was established by the Tribunal under its previous decision, and has been in operation during the trial period since 1938. It seems probable that a continuance of investigations until at least December 31, 1942, would provide additional valuable data both for the purpose of testing the effective operation of the regime now prescribed and for the purpose of obtaining information as to the possibility or necessity of improvement in it.

PART FIVE.

The fourth question under Article III of the Convention is as follows: What indemnity or compensation, if any, should be paid on account of any decision or decisions rendered by the Tribunal pursuant to the next two preceding Questions?

The Tribunal is of opinion that the prescribed regime will probably remove the causes of the present controversy and … will probably result in preventing any damage of a material nature occurring in the State of Washington in the future.

PART SIX.

Since further investigations in the future may be possible under the provisions of Part Four and of Part Five of this decision, the Tribunal finds it necessary to include in its report, the following provision: "Investigators appointed by or on behalf of either Government, whether jointly or severally, and the members of the Commission provided for in Paragraph VI of Section 3 of Part Four of this decision, shall be permitted at all reasonable times to inspect the operations of the Smelter and to enter upon and inspect any of the properties in the State of Washington which may be claimed to be affected by fumes...."

The Tribunal expresses the strong hope that any investigations which the Governments may undertake in the future, in connection with the matters dealt with in this decision, shall be conducted jointly.

> (*Signed*) JAN HOSTIE
> (*Signed*) CHARLES WARREN
> (*Signed*) R. A. E. GREENSHIELDS

NUCLEAR TESTS CASE (NEW ZEALAND v. FRANCE)
I.C.J. Reports 1974, p. 457 (International Court of Justice, 1974)

BACKGROUND: From 1966 to 1972, France conducted atmospheric tests of nuclear devices in French Polynesia—in the Pacific Ocean. Its main firing site was Mururoa atoll, located about 2500 nautical miles from New Zealand and about 1050 nautical miles from the Cook Islands, a self-governing State linked in free association with New Zealand. The French Government created "Prohibited Zones" for aircraft and "Dangerous Zones" for aircraft and shipping, in order to exclude aircraft and shipping from the area of the tests; these "zones" were in effect during the testing period each year.

Reports by the U.N. Scientific Committee on the Effects of Atomic Radiation indicate that measurable quantities of radioactive matter are released into the atmosphere by such testing. New Zealand claimed that the French testing caused some fall-out of this kind on New Zealand territory. France said that the radioactive matter produced by its tests was so infinitesimal as to be negligible and that any fallout on New Zealand territory never involved any danger to the health of New Zealand's population.

New Zealand asked the International Court of Justice to rule on the legality of the French atmospheric nuclear tests. Being notified of the case filing, France responded with a letter which stated: "[T]he Government of the [French] Republic, as it has notified the Government of New Zealand, considers that the Court is manifestly not competent in this case and that [France] cannot accept its jurisdiction," and "respectfully requests the Court to be so good as to order that the case be removed from the list."

THE COURT ... *delivers the following Judgment*:

"By letters of 21 September 1973 and 1 November 1974, the Government of New Zealand informed the Court that subsequent to the Court's Order of 22 June 1973 indicating, as interim measures under Article 41 of the Statute, *(inter alia)* that the French Government should avoid nuclear tests causing the deposit of radioactive fallout on New Zealand territory, two further series of atmospheric tests, in the months of July and August 1973 and June to September 1974, had been carried out at the Centre d'experimentations du Pacifique. The letters also stated that fallout had been recorded on New Zealand territory, analysis of samples of which, according to the New Zealand Government, established conclusively the presence of fallout from these tests, and that it was 'the view of the New Zealand Government that there has been a clear breach by the French Government of the Court's Order of 22 June 1973.'...

"Since that time, certain French authorities have made a number of consistent public statements concerning future tests which provide material facilitating the Court's task of assessing the Applicant's interpretation of the earlier documents, and which indeed require to be examined in order to discern whether they embody any modification of intention as to France's future conduct. It is true that these statements have not been made before the Court, but they are in the public domain, are known to the New Zealand Government, and were commented on by its Prime Minister in his statement of 1 November 1974. It will clearly be necessary to consider all these statements, both those drawn to the Court's attention in July 1974 and those subsequently made....

"It will be convenient to take the statements referred to above in chronological order. The first statement is contained in the communique issued by the Office of the President of the French Republic on 8 June 1974, shortly before the commencement of the 1974 series of French nuclear tests: 'The Decree reintroducing the security measures in the South Pacific nuclear test zone has been published in the Official Journal of 8 June 1974. The Office of the President of the Republic takes this opportunity of stating that in view of the stage reached in carrying out the French nuclear defence programme France will be in a position to pass on to the stage of underground explosions as soon as the series of tests planned for this summer is completed.'

"The second is contained in a Note of 10 June 1974 from the French Embassy in Wellington to the New Zealand Ministry of Foreign Affairs: 'It should ... be pointed out that the decision taken by the Office of the President of the French Republic to have the opening of the nuclear test series preceded by a press communique represents a departure from the practice of previous years. This procedure has been chosen in view of the fact that a new element has intervened in the development of the programme for perfecting the French deterrent force. This new element is as follows: France, at the point which has been reached in the execution of its programme of defence by nuclear means, will be in a position to move to the stage of underground firings as soon as the test series planned for this summer is completed. Thus the atmospheric tests which will be carried out shortly will, in the normal course of events, be the last of this type. The French authorities express the hope that the New Zealand Government will find this information of some interest and will wish to take it into consideration.'

"Thus the phrase 'in the normal course of events' was regarded by New Zealand as qualifying the statement made, so that it did not meet the expectations of the Applicant, which evidently regarded those words as a form of escape clause. This is clear from the observations of counsel for New Zealand at the hearing of 10 July 1974. In a Note of 17 June 1974, the New Zealand Embassy in Paris stated that it had good reason to believe that France had carried out an atmospheric nuclear test on 16 June and made this further comment: 'The announcement that France will proceed to underground tests in 1975, while presenting a new development, does not affect New Zealand's fundamental opposition to all nuclear testing, nor does it in any way reduce New Zealand's opposition to the atmospheric tests set down for this year: the more so since the French Government is unable to give firm assurances that no atmospheric testing will be undertaken after 1974.'

"The third French statement is contained in a reply made on 1 July 1974 by the President of the Republic to the New Zealand Prime Minister's letter of 11 June: 'In present circumstances, it is at least gratifying for me to note the positive reaction in your letter to the announcement in the tests. There is in this a new element whose importance will not, I trust, escape the New Zealand Government.'

"These three statements were all drawn to the notice of the Court by the Applicant at the time of the oral proceedings....

"On 11 October 1974, the Minister of Defence held a press conference during which he stated twice, in almost identical terms, that there would not be any atmospheric tests in 1975 and that France was ready to proceed to underground tests. When the comment was made that he had not added 'in the normal course of events', he agreed that he had not. This latter point is relevant in view of the Note of 10 June 1974 from the French Embassy in Wellington to the Ministry of Foreign Affairs of New Zealand ... to the effect that the atmospheric tests contemplated 'will, in the normal course of events, be the last of this type'. The Minister also mentioned that, whether or not other governments had been officially advised of the decision, they could become aware of it through the press and by reading the communiques issued by the Office of the President of the Republic.

"In view of the foregoing, the Court finds that the communique issued on 8 June 1974 …, the French Embassy's Note of 10 June 1974 … and the President's letter of 1 July 1974 … conveyed to New Zealand the announcement that France, following the conclusion of the 1974 series of tests, would cease the conduct of atmospheric nuclear tests. Special attention is drawn to the hope expressed in the Note of 10 June 1974 'that the New Zealand Government will find this information of some interest and will wish to take it into consideration', and the reference in that Note and in the letter of 1 July 1974 to 'a new element' whose importance is urged upon the New Zealand Government. The Court must consider in particular the President's statement of 25 July 1974 … followed by the Defence Minister's statement of 11 October 1974…. These reveal that the official statements made on behalf of France concerning future nuclear testing are not subject to whatever proviso, if any, was implied by the expression 'in the normal course of events…'.

"Before considering whether the declarations made by the French authorities meet the object of the claim by the Applicant that no further atmospheric nuclear tests should be carried out in the South Pacific, it is first necessary to determine the status and scope on the international plane of these declarations.

"It is well recognized that declarations made by way of unilateral acts, concerning legal or factual situations, may have the effect of creating legal obligations. Declarations of this kind may be, and often are, very specific. When it is the intention of the State making the declaration that it should become bound according to its terms, that intention confers on the declaration the character of a legal undertaking, the State being thenceforth legally required to follow a course of conduct consistent with the declaration. An undertaking of this kind, if given publicly, and with an intent to be bound, even though not made within the context of international negotiations, is binding. In these circumstances, nothing in the nature of a *quid pro quo,* nor any subsequent acceptance of the declaration, nor even any reply or reaction from other States, is required for the declaration to take effect, since such a requirement would be inconsistent with the strictly unilateral nature of the juridical act by which the pronouncement by the State was made.

"Of course, not all unilateral acts imply obligation; but a State may choose to take up a certain position in relation to a particular matter with the intention of being bound—the intention is to be ascertained by interpretation of the act. When States make statements by which their freedom of action is to be limited, a restrictive interpretation is called for.

"With regard to the question of form, it should be observed that this is not a domain in which international law imposes any special or strict requirements. Whether a statement is made orally or in writing makes no essential difference, for such statements made in particular circumstances may create commitments in international law, which does not require that they should be couched in written form. Thus the question of form is not decisive…. '[T]he sole relevant question is whether the language employed in any given declaration does reveal a clear intention….'

"One of the basic principles governing the creation and performance of legal obligations, whatever their source, is the principle of good faith. Trust and confidence are inherent in international co-operation, in particular in an age when this co-operation in many fields is becoming increasingly essential. Just as the very rule of *pacta sunt servanda* in the law of treaties is based on good faith, so also is the binding character of an international obligation assumed by unilateral declaration. Thus interested States may take cognizance of unilateral declarations and place confidence in them, and are entitled to require that the obligation thus created be respected….

"Of the statements by the French Government now before the Court, the most essential are clearly those made by the President of the Republic. There can be no doubt, in view of his functions, that his public communications or statements, oral or written, as Head of State, are in international relations acts of the French State. His statements, and those of members of the French Government acting under his authority, up to the last statement made by the Minister of Defence (of 11 October 1974), constitute a whole. Thus, in whatever form these statements were expressed, they must be held to constitute an engagement of the State, having regard to their intention and to the circumstances in which they were made….

"In announcing that the 1974 series of atmospheric tests would be the last, the French Government conveyed to the world at large, including the Applicant, its intention effectively to terminate these tests. It was bound to assume that other States might take note of these statements and rely on their being effective. The validity of these statements and their legal consequences must be considered within the general framework of the security of international intercourse, and the confidence and trust which are so essential in the relations among States. It is from the actual substance of these statements and from the circumstances attending their making, that the legal implications of the unilateral act must be deduced. The objects of these statements are clear and they were addressed to the international community as a whole, and the Court holds that they constitute an undertaking possessing legal effect. The Court considers that the President of the Republic, in deciding upon the effective cessation of atmospheric tests, gave an undertaking to the international community to which his words were addressed. It is true that the French Government has consistently maintained that its nuclear experiments do not contravene any subsisting provision of international law, nor did France recognize that it was bound by any rule of international law to terminate its tests, but this does not affect the legal consequences of the statements examined above. The Court finds that the unilateral undertaking resulting from these statements cannot be interpreted as having been made in implicit reliance on an arbitrary power of reconsideration. The Court finds further that the French Government has undertaken an obligation the precise nature and limits of which must be understood in accordance with the actual terms in which they have been publicly expressed.

"The Court will now confront the commitment entered into by France with the claim advanced by the Applicant. Though the latter has formally requested from the Court a finding on the rights and obligations of the Parties, it has throughout the dispute maintained as its final objective the termination of the tests. It has sought from France an assurance that the French programme of atmospheric nuclear testing would come to an end. While expressing its opposition to the 1974 tests, the Government of New Zealand made specific reference to an assurance that '1974 will see the end of atmospheric nuclear testing in the South Pacific'.... On more than one occasion it has indicated that it would be ready to accept such an assurance. Since the Court now finds that a commitment in this respect has been entered into by France, there is no occasion for a pronouncement in respect of rights and obligations of the Parties concerning the past ... whatever the date by reference to which such pronouncement might be made.

"Thus the Court faces a situation in which the objective of the Applicant has in effect been accomplished, inasmuch as the Court finds that France has undertaken the obligation to hold no further nuclear tests in the atmosphere in the South Pacific....

"The Court, as a court of law, is called upon to resolve existing disputes between States. Thus the existence of a dispute is the primary condition for the Court to exercise its judicial function; it is not sufficient for one party to assert that there is a dispute, since 'whether there exists an international dispute is a matter for objective determination' by the Court.... The dispute brought before it must therefore continue to exist at the time when the Court makes its decision. It must not fail to take cognizance of a situation in which the dispute has disappeared because the final objective which the Applicant has maintained throughout has been achieved by other means. If the declarations of France concerning the effective cessation of the nuclear tests have the significance described by the Court, that is to say if they have caused the dispute to disappear, all the necessary consequences must be drawn from this finding.

"It may be argued that although France may have undertaken such an obligation, by a unilateral declaration, not to carry out atmospheric nuclear tests in the South Pacific region, a judgment of the Court on this subject might still be of value because, if the Judgment upheld the Applicant's contentions, it would reinforce the position of the Applicant by affirming the obligation of the Respondent. However, the Court having found that the Respondent has assumed an obligation as to conduct, concerning the effective cessation of nuclear tests, no further judicial action is required. The Applicant has repeatedly sought from the Respondent an assurance that the tests would cease, and the Respondent has, on its own initiative, made a series of statements to the effect that they will cease. Thus the Court concludes that, the dispute having disappeared, the claim advanced by New Zealand no longer has any object. It follows that any further finding would have no *raison d'etre* ....

"Thus the Court finds that no further pronouncement is required in the present case. It does not enter into the adjudicatory functions of the Court to deal with issues *in abstracto,* once it has reached the conclusion that the merits of the case no longer fall to be determined. The object of the claim having clearly disappeared, there is nothing on which to give judgment....

"In its above-mentioned Order of 22 June 1973, the Court stated that the provisional measures therein set out were indicated 'pending its final decision in the proceedings instituted on 9 May 1973 by New Zealand against France'. It follows that such Order ceases to be operative upon the delivery of the present Judgment, and that the provisional measures lapse at the same time.

"For these reasons, THE COURT,
by nine votes to six,
finds that the claim of New Zealand no longer has any object and that the Court is therefore not called upon to give a decision thereon.

"Done in English and in French, the English text being authoritative, at the Peace Palace, The Hague, this twentieth day of December, one thousand nine hundred and seventy-four, in three copies, one of which will be placed in the archives of the Court and the others transmitted to the Government of New Zealand and the Government of the French Republic, respectively."

(*Signed*) Manfred LACHS,
President.

(*Signed*) S. AQUARONE
Registrar.

Judges FORSTER, GROS, PETREN and IGNACIO-PINTO append separate opinions to the Judgment of the Court.

Judges ONYEAMA, DILLARD, JIMENEZ DE ARECHAGA and Sir Humphrey WALDOCK append a joint dissenting opinion, and Judge DE CASTRO and Judge *ad hoc* Sir Garfield BARWICK append dissenting opinions to the Judgement of the Court.

(*Initialed*) M.L.
(*Initialed*) S.A.

HER MAJESTY THE QUEEN IN RIGHT OF ONTARIO v.
U.S. ENVIRONMENTAL PROTECTION AGENCY
912 F.2d 1525 (DC Cir. 1990)

BACKGROUND: The U.S. Clean Air Act specifically recognizes the possibility of cross-border air pollution. Section 115 provides: "Whenever the Administrator ... has reason to believe that any air pollutant or pollutants emitted in the United States cause or contribute to air pollution which may reasonably be anticipated to endanger public health or welfare in a foreign country ... the Administrator shall give formal notification thereof to the Governor of the State in which such emissions originate." The Governor is then required to improve that State's clean air program so as to deal with the problem.

In January 1981, Environmental Protection Agency ("EPA") administrator Douglas Costle sent letters to U.S. Secretary of State Edmund Muskie and Senator George Mitchell, indicating that U.S. pollution was causing acid rain in Canada, and that the EPA staff was investigating which States should receive the required notification. When the EPA did nothing further, several States and private parties filed a lawsuit in U.S. District Court for the District of Columbia—to force the EPA to make findings and to issue the required notifications. The District Court ordered the EPA to do so within 180 days. In 1985, the Court of Appeals reversed that decision, stating that the EPA's findings were "rules" under the Administrative Procedure Act, and since the EPA had not held hearings as required by the Administrative Procedure Act, the "rules" were invalid.

In 1988, the Province of Ontario, several States, and various environmental groups filed rule-making petitions with the EPA, requesting that it take action on the acid rain problem. After several months, an EPA assistant administrator (Clay) wrote letters to the petitioners, indicating that he felt that the EPA did not have enough data to notify specific States that it was their pollution which was causing the acid rain in Ontario. Clay also said that the EPA would not hold a separate proceeding on whether Canada was "endangered," but would wait until it could identify the sources of the air pollution. Petitioners then asked the Court of Appeals to review the EPA's "non-action" decision.

JUDGE BUCKLEY:

"The question before us is whether the Environmental Protection Agency has any present obligation to take action under section 115 of the Clean Air Act, which establishes a procedure for the prevention of air pollutants in the United States from causing harm in the form of acid deposition to the public health and welfare in Canada…. We conclude, first, that section 115 does not require the EPA to initiate those procedures until it is able to identify the specific sources in the United States of pollutants that cause harm in Canada; and second, we are satisfied that the EPA is not as yet able to do so….

"Although the EPA emphasizes that it has taken no final action with respect to the petitions, 'agency inaction may represent effectively final agency action that the agency has not frankly acknowledged.'... When administrative inaction has the same impact on the rights of the parties as an express denial of relief, judicial review is not precluded…. Similarly, the absence of a formal statement of the agency's position, as here, is not dispositive. An agency may not, for example, avoid judicial review 'merely by choosing the form of a letter to express its definitive position on a general question of statutory interpretation.'...

"On applying the foregoing principles, we conclude that the Clay letters represent final agency action as to the EPA's interpretation of section 115. In other words, although ... the EPA concededly made no final decision on petitioners' request that the section 115 remedial process be initiated, it clearly and unequivocally rejected, on the basis of its construction of section 115, petitioners' requests for a separate proceeding limited to the endangerment and reciprocity findings….

"The EPA also asserts that even if it is deemed to have taken final action, the petitions are not ripe for review…. Under the Supreme Court's [test], we consider 'both the fitness of the issues for judicial decision and the hardship to the parties of withholding court consideration.' The ripeness doctrine generally prevents courts from becoming 'entangled' in 'abstract disagreements over agency policy' and from improperly interfering in the administrative decision-making process…. The EPA contends that neither part of the ripeness test is satisfied here.

"The first prong of the test, fitness for review, measures the interests of both court and agency in postponing review…. We consider such factors as whether the issue presented is purely legal, whether consideration of the issue would benefit from a more concrete setting, and whether the agency's action is sufficiently final….

"The issue presented is a purely legal question of statutory interpretation—that is, whether section 115 obliges the EPA to promulgate endangerment and reciprocity findings even when it is unable to follow through with notification to specific States. Petitioners do not challenge the technical and factual aspects of the EPA's acid rain research; they challenge only its failure to take action under section 115 on the endangerment and reciprocity issues. Our resolution of the question will not benefit from the development of further information; nor will it interfere prematurely with the EPA's own consideration of the issue, as the Clay letters represent a definitive statement of the agency's position....

"[The Acid Precipitation Act of 1980] initiated a ten-year program, commonly known as the National Acid Precipitation Assessment Program ... that is designed to identify the causes and sources of acid rain, to evaluate its environmental, social, and economic effects, and to assess potential methods of control.... We note that the final NAPAP report is due in December 1990. At oral argument the EPA pointed to this study as evidence of specific research being conducted that could enable the agency to take action under section 115; the EPA also asserted that the report should provide it with a sufficient basis to make a reasoned decision on the petitioners' rulemaking petitions.

"It is in part on the basis of this information that we conclude that the EPA's delay in acting on the petitions has been neither arbitrary, nor capricious, nor contrary to law.

"... The petitions for review are therefore
Denied."

ENVIRONMENTAL DEFENSE FUND v. MASSEY
986 F.2d 528 (DC Cir. 1993)

BACKGROUND: The USA's 1970 National Environmental Policy Act specifies that any national governmental agency must prepare an Environmental Impact Statement ("EIS") before it takes any "major action significantly affecting the quality of the human environment." The U.S. National Science Foundation ("NSF") conducts scientific research in Antarctica, operating three year-round installations there. Of the three, McMurdo Station is the largest—with over 100 buildings and about 1200 persons there during the summer. For several years, NSF had burned the food wastes at McMurdo in an open landfill. When asbestos was found in the landfill in 1991, NSF stopped the open burning and stored the food wastes temporarily. It then decided to burn them in an "interim incinerator," until a state-of-the-art incinerator could be delivered.

Environmental Defense Fund ("EDF") filed a lawsuit in U.S. District Court in the District of Columbia, alleging that NSF had failed to file the required EIS for its decision to resume burning food waste in Antarctica. The USA and 39 other nations agreed in 1961 not to assert territorial claims or sovereignty in Antarctica, although several nations are engaged in scientific research there. The continent is not, and has never been, subject to the sovereign rule of any nation. The District Court dismissed the EDF's lawsuit, since Antarctica is not part of the USA. EDF appealed to the U.S. Circuit Court for the District of Columbia.

CHIEF JUDGE MIKVA:

"There are at least three general categories of cases for which the presumption against the extraterritorial application of statutes clearly does not apply. First ... the presumption will not apply where there is an 'affirmative intention of the Congress clearly expressed' to extend the scope of the statute to conduct occurring within other sovereign nations....

"Second, the presumption is generally not applied where the failure to extend the scope of the statute to a foreign setting will result in adverse effects within the United States....

"Finally, the presumption against extraterritoriality is not applicable when the conduct regulated by the government occurs within the United States. By definition, an extraterritorial application of a statute involves the regulation of conduct beyond U.S. borders. Even where the significant effects of the regulated conduct are felt outside U.S. borders, the statute itself does not present a problem of extraterritoriality so long as the conduct which Congress seeks to regulate occurs within the United States....

"Antarctica's unique status in the international arena further supports our conclusion that this case does not implicate the presumption against extraterritoriality.... [W]here the U.S. has some real measure of legislative control over the region at issue, the presumption against extraterritoriality is much weaker.... And where there is no potential for conflict 'between our laws and those of other nations' the purpose behind the presumption is eviscerated, and the presumption ... applies with significantly less force.

"Applying the presumption against extraterritoriality here would result in a federal agency being allowed to undertake actions significantly affecting the human environment in Antarctica, an area over which the United States has substantial interest and authority, without ever being held accountable for its failure to comply with the decision-making procedures instituted by Congress—even though such accountability, if it was enforced, would result in no conflict with foreign law or threat to foreign policy. NSF has provided no support for its proposition that conduct occurring within the United States is rendered exempt from otherwise applicable statutes merely because the effects of its compliance would be felt in the global commons. We therefore reverse the District Court's decision."

JUAN ANTONIO [OPOSA], et al. v. FACTORAN, et al.
(Philippine Supreme Court, G.R. No. 101083 July 30, 1993)

BACKGROUND: Three Oposa children (represented by their parents) and several other families filed a lawsuit against Fulgencio Factoran, the Secretary of the Department of Environment and Natural Resources. (Plaintiffs were represented by "Oposa Law Office.") The complaint was instituted as a taxpayers' class suit, and alleges that the plaintiffs "are all citizens of the Republic of the Philippines, taxpayers, and entitled to the full benefit, use and enjoyment of the natural resource treasure that is the country's virgin tropical forests." It was filed for themselves and others who are equally concerned about the preservation of said resource but are "so numerous that it is impracticable to bring them all before the Court." The minors further assert that they "represent their generation as well as generations yet unborn." They ask that judgment be rendered: ". . . ordering defendant, his agents, representatives and other persons acting in his behalf to (1) cancel all existing timber license agreements in the country; (2) cease and desist from receiving, accepting, processing, renewing or approving new timber license agreements"; and granting the plaintiffs ". . . such other reliefs just and equitable under the premises."

Secretary Factoran filed a motion to dismiss the complaint based on two grounds: (1) the plaintiffs have no cause of action against him and (2) the issue raised by the plaintiffs is a political question which properly pertains to the legislative or executive branches of Government. Judge Rosario agreed with both arguments and granted the motion. He further ruled that the granting of the relief prayed for would result in the impairment of contracts which is prohibited by the fundamental law of the land. Plaintiffs petitioned for certiorari to the Philippine Supreme Court.

JUSTICE DAVIDE:

"In a broader sense, this petition bears upon the right of Filipinos to a balanced and healthful ecology which the petitioners dramatically associate with the twin concepts of 'inter-generational responsibility' and 'inter-generational justice.' Specifically, it touches on the issue of whether the said petitioners have a cause of action to 'prevent the misappropriation or impairment' of Philippine rainforests and 'arrest the unabated hemorrhage of the country's vital life support systems and continued rape of Mother Earth.'...

"The complaint starts off with the general averments that the Philippine archipelago of 7,100 islands has a land area of thirty million (30,000,000) hectares and is endowed with rich, lush and verdant rainforests in which varied, rare and unique species of flora and fauna may be found; these rainforests contain a genetic, biological and chemical pool which is irreplaceable; they are also the habitat of indigenous Philippine cultures which have existed, endured and flourished since time immemorial; scientific evidence reveals that in order to maintain a balanced and healthful ecology, the country's land area should be utilized on the basis of a ratio of fifty-four per cent (54%) for forest cover and forty-six per cent (46%) for agricultural, residential, industrial, commercial and other uses; the distortion and disturbance of this balance as a consequence of deforestation have resulted in a host of environmental tragedies, such as (a) water shortages resulting from drying up of the water table, otherwise known as the 'aquifer,' as well as of rivers, brooks and streams, (b) salinization of the water table as a result of the intrusion therein of salt water, incontrovertible examples of which may be found in the island of Cebu and the Municipality of Bacoor, Cavite, (c) massive erosion and the consequential loss of soil fertility and agricultural productivity, with the volume of soil eroded estimated at one billion (1,000,000,000) cubic meters per annum—approximately the size of the entire island of Catanduanes, (d) the endangering and extinction of the country's unique, rare and varied flora and fauna, (e) the disturbance and dislocation of cultural communities, including the disappearance of the Filipino's indigenous cultures, (f) the siltation of rivers and seabeds and consequential destruction of corals and other aquatic life leading to a critical reduction in marine resource productivity, (g) recurrent spells of drought as is presently experienced by the entire country, (h) increasing velocity of typhoon winds which result from the absence of windbreakers, (i) the floodings of lowlands and agricultural plains arising from the absence of the absorbent mechanism of forests, (j) the siltation and shortening of the lifespan of multi-billion peso dams constructed and operated for the purpose of supplying water for domestic uses, irrigation and the generation of electric power, and (k) the reduction of the earth's capacity to process carbon dioxide gases which has led to perplexing and catastrophic climatic changes such as the phenomenon of global warming, otherwise known as the 'greenhouse effect.'

"Plaintiffs further assert that the adverse and detrimental consequences of continued and deforestation are so capable of unquestionable demonstration that the same may be submitted as a matter of judicial notice. This notwithstanding, they expressed their intention to present expert witnesses as well as documentary, photographic and film evidence in the course of the trial....

"Petitioners contend that the complaint clearly and unmistakably states a cause of action as it contains sufficient allegations concerning their right to a sound environment based on Articles 19, 20 and 21 of the Civil Code (Human Relations), Section 4 of Executive Order (E.O.) No. 192 creating the DENR, Section 3 of Presidential Decree (P.D.) No. 1151 (Philippine Environmental Policy), Section 16, Article II of the 1987 Constitution recognizing the right of the people to a balanced and healthful ecology, the concept of generational genocide in Criminal Law and the concept of man's inalienable right to self-preservation and self-perpetuation embodied in natural law. Petitioners likewise rely on the respondent's correlative obligation per Section 4 of E.O. No. 192, to safeguard the people's right to a healthful environment.

"It is further claimed that the issue of the respondent Secretary's alleged grave abuse of discretion in granting Timber License Agreements (TLAs) to cover more areas for logging than what is available involves a judicial question.

"[As to] the invocation by the respondent Judge of the Constitution's non-impairment clause, petitioners maintain that the same does not apply in this case because TLAs are not contracts. They likewise submit that even if TLAs may be considered protected by the said clause, it is well settled that they may still be revoked by the State when the public interest so requires....

"Before going any further, we must first focus on some procedural matters. Petitioners instituted Civil Case No. 90-777 as a class suit. The original defendant and the present respondents did not take issue with this matter. Nevertheless, We hereby rule that the said civil case is indeed a class suit....

"This case, however, has a special and novel element. Petitioners minors assert that they represent their generation as well as generations yet unborn. We find no difficulty in ruling that they can, for themselves, for others of their generation and for the succeeding generations, file a class suit. Their personality to sue in behalf of the succeeding generations can only be based on the concept of intergenerational responsibility insofar as the right to a balanced and healthful ecology is concerned. Such a right, as hereinafter expounded, considers the 'rhythm and harmony of nature.' Nature means the created world in its entirety. Such rhythm and harmony indispensably include, inter alia, the judicious disposition, utilization, management, renewal and conservation of the country's forest, mineral, land, waters, fisheries, wildlife, off-shore areas and other natural resources to the end that their exploration, development and utilization be equitably accessible to the present as well as future generations. Needless to say, every generation has a responsibility to the next to preserve that rhythm and harmony for the full enjoyment of a balanced and healthful ecology. Put a little differently, the minors' assertion of their right to a sound environment constitutes, at the same time, the performance of their obligation to ensure the protection of that right for the generations to come....

"After a careful perusal of the complaint in question and a meticulous consideration and evaluation of the issues raised and arguments adduced by the parties, We do not hesitate to find for the petitioners and rule against the respondent Judge's challenged order for having been issued with grave abuse of discretion amounting to lack of jurisdiction....

"We do not agree with the trial court's conclusions that the plaintiffs failed to allege with sufficient definiteness a specific legal right involved or a specific legal wrong committed, and that the complaint is replete with vague assumptions and conclusions based on unverified data. A reading of the complaint itself belies these conclusions.

"The complaint focuses on one specific fundamental legal right—the right to a balanced and healthful ecology which, for the first time in our nation's constitutional history, is solemnly incorporated in the fundamental law. Section 16, Article II of the 1987 Constitution explicitly provides: Sec. 16. The State shall protect and advance the right of the people to a balanced and healthful ecology in accord with the rhythm and harmony of nature. This right unites with the right to health which is provided for in the preceding section of the same article: Sec. 15. The State shall protect and promote the right to health of the people and instill health consciousness among them.

"While the right to a balanced and healthful ecology is to be found under the Declaration of Principles and State Policies and not under the Bill of Rights, it does not follow that it is less important than any of the civil and political rights enumerated in the latter. Such a right belongs to a different category of rights altogether for it concerns nothing less than self-preservation and self-perpetuation—aptly and fittingly stressed by the petitioners—the advancement of which may even be said to predate all governments and constitutions. As a matter of fact, these basic rights need not even be written in the Constitution for they are assumed to exist from the inception of humankind. If they are now explicitly mentioned in the fundamental charter, it is because of the well-founded fear of its framers that unless the rights to a balanced and healthful ecology and to health are mandated as state policies by the Constitution itself, thereby highlighting their continuing importance and imposing upon the state a solemn obligation to preserve the first and protect and advance the second, the day would not be too far when all else would be lost not only for the present generation, but also for those to come—generations which stand to inherit nothing but parched earth incapable of sustaining life.

"The right to a balanced and healthful ecology carries with it the correlative duty to refrain from impairing the environment....

"The said right implies, among many other things, the judicious management and conservation of the country's forests. Without such forests, the ecological or environmental balance would be irreversib[l]y disrupted....

"Thus, the right of the petitioners (and all those they represent) to a balanced and healthful ecology is as clear as the DENR's duty—under its mandate and by virtue of its powers and functions under E.O. No. 192 and the Administrative Code of 1987—to protect and advance the said right....

"The last ground invoked by the trial court in dismissing the complaint is the non-impairment of contracts clause found in the Constitution....

"In Abe v. Foster Wheeler Corp. this Court stated: 'The freedom of contract, under our system of government, is not meant to be absolute. The same is understood to be subject to reasonable legislative regulation aimed at the promotion of public health, moral, safety and welfare. In other words, the constitutional guaranty of non-impairment of obligations of contract is limited by the exercise of the police power of the State, in the interest of public health, safety, moral and general welfare.'

"The reason for this is emphatically set forth in Neb[b]ia vs. New York [a 1934 decision by the U.S. Supreme Court]: 'Under our form of government the use of property and the making of contracts are normally matters of private and not of public concern. The general rule is that both shall be free of governmental interference. But neither property rights nor contract rights are absolute; for government cannot exist if the citizen may at will use his property to the detriment of his fellows, or exercise his freedom of contract to work them harm. Equally fundamental with the private right is that of the public to regulate it in the common interest.'

"In short, the non-impairment clause must yield to the police power of the state....

"WHEREFORE, being impressed with merit, the instant Petition is hereby GRANTED, and the challenged Order of respondent Judge of 18 July 1991 dismissing Civil Case No. 90-777 is hereby set aside....

"No pronouncement as to costs.

"SO ORDERED."

THE "CAMOUCO" CASE (PANAMA v. FRANCE)
No. 5 Year 2000 (International Tribunal for the Law of the Sea)

BACKGROUND: On January 14, 2000, the Tribunal received an application on behalf of Panama, against France, under article 292 of UNCLOS, seeking prompt release of the fishing vessel *Camouco* and its master. Panama asked the Tribunal, *inter alia*, to declare that the Tribunal had jurisdiction to entertain the application pursuant to article 292 of the United Nations Convention on the Law of the Sea; to find that the French Republic failed to observe the provisions of the Convention concerning prompt release of the Master of the vessel *Camouco*, and to demand that the French Republic promptly release the vessel *Camouco* and its Master, against payment of a reasonable bond of one million three hundred thousand francs (1,300,000 FF) before deduction of the price of the cargo seized (350,000 FF), i.e., a final guarantee in a maximum amount of nine hundred and fifty thousand francs (950,000 FF). The

Government of the French Republic requested the Tribunal to declare that Panama's application was not admissible; and as a subsidiary submission, if it decided that the *Camouco* is to be released upon the deposit of a bond, that the bond shall be not less than the sum of 20,000,000 francs.

The *Camouco* was a fishing vessel flying the flag of Panama and owned by Merce-Pesca S.A., a Panamanian company. Panama provided the *Camouco* with a fishing license for longline bottom fishing of "Patagonian toothfish" in "international waters" in the South Atlantic between 20° and 50° latitude South and between 20° and 80° longitude West. On September 28, 1999, the *Camouco* was boarded by the French surveillance frigate *Floréal* in the exclusive economic zone of the Crozet Islands, 160 nautical miles from the northern boundary of the zone. According to the procès-verbal of violation, drawn up by the Captain and two other officers of the *Floréal*, the *Camouco* was observed paying out a longline within the exclusive economic zone of the Crozet Islands by the Commander of the helicopter carried on board the *Floréal*. The procès-verbal of violation further recorded that the *Camouco* did not reply to calls from the *Floréal* and the helicopter, and moved away from the *Floréal* while members of the *Camouco*'s crew were engaged in jettisoning 48 bags and documents, and that one of those bags was later retrieved and found to contain 34 kilograms of fresh toothfish. The procès-verbal of violation also stated that six tons of frozen toothfish were found in the holds of the *Camouco* and that the Master of the *Camouco* was in breach of law on account of: (a) unlawful fishing in the exclusive economic zone of the Crozet Islands under French jurisdiction; (b) failure to declare entry into the exclusive economic zone of the Crozet Islands, while having six tons of frozen Patagonian toothfish on board; (c) concealment of vessel's markings, while flying a foreign flag; and (d) attempted flight to avoid verification by the maritime authority. The *Camouco* was escorted under the supervision of the French navy to Port-des-Galets, Réunion.

THE TRIBUNAL,
delivers the following JUDGMENT:

"The Tribunal will, at the outset, examine the question whether it has jurisdiction to entertain the Application. Panama and France are both States Parties to UNCLOS. Pursuant to article 113, paragraph 2, of the Rules, if the Tribunal decides that the allegation is 'well-founded' it will order the release of the vessel and its crew upon the posting of the bond or other financial security as determined by the Tribunal….

"The Respondent states that the Applicant filed the Application more than three months after the detention of the *Camouco*, that the Applicant had been completely inactive during this period, that article 292 speaks in terms of 'prompt release,' which carries with it the characteristics of dispatch and urgency that are inherent in the notion of 'prompt release,' that, by failing to act promptly, the Applicant has created, by its conduct, a situation akin to estoppel and that, consequently, the Application is not admissible.

"The Applicant states that article 292 does not impose any time-limit for making an application and that, in any event, there is no delay on its part, as alleged by the Respondent. It adds that it was only on 14 December 1999, when the court of first instance at Saint-Paul made an order confirming its earlier order, that it came to know, in a definitive manner, that the sum to be secured by a bond was 20 million FF. It states that it was then that it took a decision to approach the Tribunal. It notes that the Respondent cannot complain about delay. In its final submissions, the Applicant stated that the Respondent has failed to notify the Applicant, as required by article 73, paragraph 4, of the Convention, of the 'arrest and seizure of the *Camouco*... of the measures taken and of those which were to be taken' in respect of the vessel. The Applicant further states that, even if the communication addressed to the Ministry of Foreign Affairs of Panama by the French Embassy in Panama were to be taken as amounting to notification of the information required under article 73, paragraph 4, of the Convention, it was dated 11 November 1999, long after the date of detention....

"The Tribunal finds that there is no merit in the arguments of the Respondent regarding delay in the presentation of the Application. In any event, article 292 of the Convention requires prompt release of the vessel or its crew once the Tribunal finds that an allegation made in the Application is well-founded. It does not require the flag State to file an application at any particular time after the detention of a vessel or its crew. The 10-day period referred to in article 292, paragraph 1, of the Convention is to enable the parties to submit the question of release from detention to an agreed court or tribunal. It does not suggest that an application not made to a court or tribunal within the 10-day period or to the Tribunal immediately after the 10-day period will not be treated as an application for 'prompt release' within the meaning of article 292.

"The other objection to admissibility pleaded by the Respondent is that domestic legal proceedings are currently pending before the court of appeal of Saint-Denis involving an appeal against an order of the court of first instance at Saint Paul, whose purpose is to achieve precisely the same result as that sought by the present proceedings under article 292 of the Convention. The Respondent, therefore, argues that the Applicant is incompetent to invoke the procedure laid down in article 292 as 'a second remedy' against a decision of a national court and that the Application clearly points to a 'situation of *lis pendens* which casts doubt on its admissibility.' The Respondent draws attention in this regard to article 295 of the Convention on exhaustion of local remedies, while observing at the same time that 'strict compliance with the rule of the exhaustion of local remedies, set out in article 295 of the Convention, is not considered a necessary prerequisite of the institution of proceedings under article 292.'

"The Applicant rejects the argument of the Respondent and maintains that its taking recourse to local courts in no way prejudices its right to invoke the jurisdiction of the Tribunal under article 292 of the Convention.

"In the view of the Tribunal, it is not logical to read the requirement of exhaustion of local remedies or any other analogous rule into article 292. Article 292 of the Convention is designed to free a ship and its crew from prolonged detention on account of the imposition of unreasonable bonds in municipal jurisdictions, or the failure of local law to provide for release on posting of a reasonable bond, inflicting thereby avoidable loss on a ship owner or other persons affected by such detention. Equally, it safeguards the interests of the coastal State by providing for release only upon the posting of a reasonable bond or other financial security determined by a court or tribunal referred to in article 292, without prejudice to the merits of the case in the domestic forum against the vessel, its owner or its crew.

"Article 292 provides for an independent remedy and not an appeal against a decision of a national court. No limitation should be read into article 292 that would have the effect of defeating its very object and purpose. Indeed, article 292 permits the making of an application within a short period from the date of detention and it is not normally the case that local remedies could be exhausted in such a short period.

"At this stage, the Tribunal wishes to deal with the submissions of the Applicant requesting it to declare that the Respondent has violated article 73, paragraphs 3 and 4, of the Convention. The scope of the jurisdiction of the Tribunal in proceedings under article 292 of the Convention encompasses only cases in which 'it is alleged that the detaining State has not complied with the provisions of this Convention for the prompt release of the vessel or its crew upon the posting of a reasonable bond or other financial security.' As paragraphs 3 and 4, unlike paragraph 2, of article 73 are not such provisions, the submissions concerning their alleged violation are not admissible. It may, however, be noted, in passing, that there is a connection between paragraphs 2 and 4 of article 73, since absence of prompt notification may have a bearing on the ability of the flag State to invoke article 73, paragraph 2, and article 292 in a timely and efficient manner.

"The considerations set out in the previous paragraph also apply to the allegations of the Applicant (which are not reiterated in the Applicant's final submissions), that the Respondent has violated the provisions of the Convention on freedom of navigation and that the Respondent's laws are incompatible with the provisions of the Convention.

"Non-compliance with article 73, paragraph 2, of the Convention

"The Tribunal will now deal with the allegation that the detaining State has not complied with the provisions of the Convention for the prompt release of the vessel and its Master upon the posting of a reasonable bond or other financial security. For the application for release to succeed, the allegation that the detaining State has not complied with the provisions of the Convention for the prompt release of the vessel or its crew upon the posting of a reasonable bond should be well-founded. In the present case, the Master of the *Camouco* has been accused of violating the French laws concerning fishery resources in the exclusive economic zone of France and it is not disputed that article 73 of the Convention is thereby attracted.

"The Respondent maintains that, under article 73, paragraph 2, the posting of a bond or other security is a necessary condition to be satisfied before an arrested vessel and its crew can be released, that the Applicant has not posted any bond so far, which it is required to do promptly and immediately after the arrest of the *Camouco* and its Master, and that, consequently, the Application deserves to be dismissed as the allegation contained therein is not well-founded. In reply, the Applicant states that the posting of a bond is not a condition precedent for the submission of an application under article 292.

"The Tribunal wishes to clarify that the posting of a bond or other security is not necessarily a condition precedent to filing an application under article 292 of the Convention....

"In its Application, the Applicant contends that the bond of 20,000,000 FF fixed by the French court is not 'reasonable.' In its final submissions, the Applicant stated that the amount of a reasonable bond should be fixed at 1,300,000 FF, from which the value of the cargo seized (350,000 FF) should be deducted. The Respondent stated that the maximum total amount of fines which could be imposed on the Master of the *Camouco* and on the owners of Merce-Pesca could be more than 30 million francs and that this figure alone suffices to show the reasonableness of the amount of the bond required by the French court....

"The Tribunal considers that a number of factors are relevant in an assessment of the reasonableness of bonds or other financial security. They include the gravity of the alleged offences, the penalties imposed or imposable under the laws of the detaining State, the value of the detained vessel and of the cargo seized, the amount of the bond imposed by the detaining State and its form.

"In the present case, the Tribunal has taken note of the gravity of the alleged offences and also the range of penalties which, under French law, could be imposed for the offences charged. The Agent of France indicated that the maximum penalty which can be imposed on the Master of the *Camouco* is a fine of 5 million FF. The Tribunal notes the statement by the Agent of France that, in conformity with article 73, paragraph 3, of the Convention, the Master of the *Camouco* is not subject to imprisonment. According to the Agent of France, under French law, the company which owns the *Camouco* can also be held criminally liable, as a legal person, for the offences committed by the Master of the *Camouco* acting on its behalf to a fine up to five times that imposed on the Master. The Tribunal, however, notes that no charge has yet been made against the company.

"Regarding the value of the *Camouco*, article 111, paragraph 2(b), of the Rules requires that the application for the release of a vessel or its crew from detention contain, where appropriate, data relevant to the determination of the value of the vessel. However, the value of the vessel alone may not be the controlling factor in the determination of the amount of the bond or other financial security. In the present case, the parties differ on the value of the *Camouco*. During the oral proceedings, expert testimony was offered by the Applicant and not challenged by the Respondent to the effect that the replacement value of the *Camouco* was 3,717,571 FF. On the other hand, the value assessed by the French authorities for the purposes of the domestic proceedings is 20 million FF but there is no evidence on record to substantiate this assessment. Attention is drawn to court orders referred to in paragraphs 36 and 42. The Tribunal also notes that the catch on board the *Camouco*, which according to the Respondent is valued at 380,000 FF, has been confiscated and sold by the French authorities.

"On the basis of the above considerations, and keeping in view the overall circumstances of this case, the Tribunal considers that the bond of 20 million FF imposed by the French court is not 'reasonable.'

"That the *Camouco* has been in detention is not disputed. However, the parties are in disagreement whether the Master of the *Camouco* is also in detention. It is admitted that the Master is presently under court supervision, that his passport has also been taken away from him by the French authorities, and that, consequently, he is not in a position to leave Réunion. The Tribunal considers that, in the circumstances of this case, it is appropriate to order the release of the Master in accordance with article 292, paragraph 1, of the Convention.

"For the above reasons, the Tribunal finds that the Application is admissible, that the allegation made by the Applicant is well-founded for the purposes of these proceedings and that, consequently, France must release promptly the *Camouco* and its Master upon the posting of a bond or other financial security as determined....

"Form and amount of the bond or other financial security

"The Tribunal then comes to the task of determining the amount, nature and form of the bond or other financial security to be posted, as laid down in article 113, paragraph 2, of the Rules.

"On the basis of the foregoing considerations, the Tribunal is of the view that a bond or other security should be in the amount of 8 million FF and that, unless the parties otherwise agree, it should be in the form of a bank guarantee.

"The Applicant has requested that the Tribunal order a bank guarantee 'to be entrusted to the care of the Tribunal in order that it may be duly delivered to the French authorities.' The provisions of article 114 of the Rules lay down the procedure if a bond or other financial security were to be posted with the Tribunal. Such posting, however, requires the agreement of the parties. The bond or other financial security is to be posted with the detaining State unless the parties agree otherwise…. Since the parties have not agreed otherwise, the Tribunal cannot accede to the request of the Applicant.

"The bank guarantee should, among other things, state that it is issued in consideration of France releasing the *Camouco* and its Master, in relation to the incidents that occurred in the exclusive economic zone of the Crozet Islands on 28 September 1999 and that the issuer undertakes and guarantees to pay to France such sums, up to 8 million FF, as may be determined by a final judgment or decision of the appropriate domestic forum in France or by agreement of the parties. Payment under the guarantee would be due promptly after receipt by the issuer of a written demand by the competent authority of France accompanied by a certified copy of the final judgment or decision or agreement.

"For these reasons, THE TRIBUNAL,
(1) Unanimously,
    Finds that the Tribunal has jurisdiction under article 292 of the Convention to entertain the Application made on behalf of Panama on 17 January 2000.

(2) By 19 votes to 2,
    Finds that the Application for release is admissible; …

(3) By 19 votes to 2,
    Orders that France shall promptly release the *Camouco* and its Master upon the posting of a bond; …

(4) By 15 votes to 6,
    Determines that the bond shall be eight million French Francs (8,000,000 FF) to be posted with France; …

(5) By 19 votes to 2,
    Determines that the bond shall be in the form of a bank guarantee or, if agreed to by the parties, in any other form….

"Done in English and in French, both texts being authoritative, in the Free and Hanseatic City of

Hamburg, this seventh day of February, two thousand, in three copies, one of which will be placed in the archives of the Tribunal and the others transmitted to the Government of the Republic of Panama and the Government of the French Republic, respectively.

(*Signed*) P. CHANDRASEKHARA RAO, President.
(*Signed*) Gritakumar E. CHITTY, Registrar."

MASSACHUSETTS v. ENVIRONMENTAL PROTECTION AGENCY
549 U.S. 497 (2007)

BACKGROUND: In 1999, nineteen private organizations filed a rulemaking petition asking the Environmental Protection Agency ("EPA") to regulate "greenhouse gas emissions from new motor vehicles under S. 202 of the Clean Air Act." Section 202(a)(1) provides: "The [EPA] Administrator shall by regulation prescribe … standards applicable to the emission of any air pollutant from the class or classes of new motor vehicles or new motor vehicle engines, which in his judgment cause, or contribute to, air pollution which may reasonably be anticipated to endanger public health or welfare…." "Air pollutant" is defined in the Act as meaning "any air pollution agent or combination of such agents, including any physical, chemical, biological, radioactive … substance or matter which is emitted into or otherwise enters the ambient air." The Act says "welfare" includes "effects on … weather … and climate."

Fifteen months later, EPA requested public comment on "all the issues raised in [the] petition," particularly comments on "any scientific, technical, legal, economic or other aspect of these issues that may be relevant to EPA's consideration of this petition." EPA received more than 50,000 comments over the next five months. On September 8, 2003, EPA entered an order denying the rule-making petition. The agency gave two reasons for its decision: (1) that the Clean Air Act does not authorize EPA to issue mandatory regulations to address global climate change, and (2) that even if the agency had the authority, it would be unwise to use it at that time. Petitioner groups, with several States and local governments, sought review of the EPA's decision by the U.S. Court of Appeals for the District of Columbia Circuit. The D.C. Circuit decided, by a 2-1 vote, that "the EPA Administrator properly exercised his discretion … in denying the petition." Petitioners then asked for review by the U.S. Supreme Court.

JUSTICE STEVENS:

"EPA maintains that because greenhouse gas emissions inflict widespread harm, the doctrine of standing presents an insuperable jurisdictional obstacle. We do not agree. At bottom, 'the gist of the question of standing' is whether petitioners have 'such a personal stake in the outcome of the controversy as to assure that concrete adverseness which sharpens the presentation of issues upon which the court so largely depends for illumination.'...

"To ensure the proper adversarial presentation ... a litigant must demonstrate that it has suffered a concrete and particularized injury that is either actual or imminent, that the injury is fairly traceable to the defendant, and that it is likely that a favorable decision will redress that injury.... However, a litigant to whom Congress has 'accorded a procedural right to protect his concrete interests ... can assert that right without meeting all the normal standards for redressability and immediacy.'... When a litigant is vested with a procedural right, that litigant has standing if there is some possibility that the requested relief will prompt the injury-causing party to reconsider the decision that allegedly harmed the litigant....

"Only one of the petitioners needs to have standing to permit us to consider the petition for review.... We stress here ... the special position and interest of Massachusetts. It is of considerable relevance that the party seeking review here is a sovereign State and not ... a private individual.

"Well before the creation of the modern administrative state, we recognized that States are not normal litigants for the purposes for invoking federal jurisdiction [citing *Georgia v. Tennessee Copper Co.*, 206 U.S. 230 (1907)]....

"With that in mind, it is clear that petitioners' submissions as they pertain to Massachusetts have satisfied the most demanding standards of the adversarial process. EPA's steadfast refusal to regulate greenhouse gas emissions presents a risk of harm to Massachusetts that is both 'actual' and 'imminent.'... There is, moreover, a 'substantial likelihood that the judicial relief requested' will prompt EPA to take steps to reduce that risk....

"That these climate-change risks are 'widely shared' does not minimize Massachusetts' interest in the outcome of this litigation.... [The] rising seas have already begun to swallow Massachusetts' coastal land.... Because the Commonwealth 'owns a substantial portion of the state's coastal property' ... it has alleged a particularized injury in its capacity as a landowner....

"The scope of our review of the merits of the statutory issues is narrow. As we have repeated time and again, an agency has broad discretion to choose how best to marshal its limited resources and personnel to carry out its delegated responsibilities.... That discretion is at its height when the agency decides not to bring an enforcement action.... Some debate remains, however, as to the rigor with which we review an agency's denial of a petition for rulemaking.

"There are key differences between a denial of a petition for rulemaking and an agency's decision not to initiate an enforcement action…. In contrast to nonenforcement decisions, agency refusals to initiate rulemaking 'are less frequent, more apt to involve legal as opposed to factual analysis, and subject to special formalities … including a public explanation.'… Refusals to promulgate rules are thus susceptible to judicial review, though such review is 'extremely limited' and 'highly deferential.'…

"On the merits, the first question is whether S. 202 (a)(1) of the Clean Air Act authorizes EPA to regulate greenhouse gas emissions from new motor vehicles in the event that it forms a 'judgment' that such emissions contribute to climate change. We have little trouble concluding that it does….

"The broad language of S. 202(a)(1) reflects an intentional effort to confer the flexibility necessary to forestall [the Act's] obsolescence…. Because greenhouses gases fit well within the Clean Air Act's capacious definition of 'air pollutant,' we hold that EPA has the statutory authority to regulate the emission of such gases from new motor vehicles….

"The alternative basis for EPA's decision—that even if it does have statutory authority to regulate greenhouse gases, it would be unwise to do so at this time—rests on reasoning divorced from the statutory text. While the statute does condition the exercise of EPA's authority on its formation of a 'judgment,' … the use of the word 'judgment' is not a roving license to ignore the statutory text. It is but a direction to exercise discretion within defined statutory limits.

"If EPA makes a finding of endangerment, the Clean Air Act requires the agency to regulate emission of the deleterious pollutant from new motor vehicles…. EPA no doubt has significant latitude as to the manner, timing, content, and coordination of its regulations with those of other agencies. But once EPA has responded to a petition for rulemaking, its reasons for action or inaction must conform to the authorizing statute….

"EPA has refused to comply with this clear statutory mandate. Instead, it has offered a laundry list of reasons not to regulate….

"Although we have neither the expertise nor the authority to evaluate these policy judgments, it is evident they have nothing to do with whether greenhouse gas emissions contribute to climate change. Still less do they amount to a reasoned justification for declining to form a scientific judgment….

"Nor can EPA avoid its statutory obligation by noting the uncertainty surrounding various features of climate change and concluding that it would therefore be better not to regulate at this time…. If the scientific uncertainty is so profound that it precludes EPA from making a reasoned judgment as to whether greenhouse gases contribute to global warming, EPA must say so....

"In short, EPA has offered no reasoned explanation for its refusal to decide whether greenhouse gases cause or contribute to climate change. Its action was therefore 'arbitrary, capricious ... or otherwise not in accordance with law.'... We need not and do not reach the question whether on remand EPA must make an endangerment finding, or whether policy concerns can inform EPA's actions in the event it makes such a finding.... We hold only that EPA must ground its reasons for action or inaction in the statute....

"The judgment of the Court of Appeals is reversed, and the case is remanded for further proceedings consistent with this opinion."

DISSENT by *Chief Justice ROBERTS*:

"Global warming may be a 'crisis,' even 'the most pressing environmental problem of our time.'... Indeed, it may ultimately affect nearly everyone on the planet in some potentially adverse way, and it may be that governments have done too little to address it. It is not a problem, however, that has escaped the attention of the policymakers in the Executive and Legislative Branches of our Government, who continue to consider regulatory, legislative, and treaty-based means of addressing global climate change.

"Apparently dissatisfied with the pace of progress on the issue in the elected branches, petitioners have come to the courts claiming broad-ranging injury, and attempting to tie that injury to the Government's alleged failure to comply with a rather narrow statutory provision. I would reject these challenges as nonjusticiable. Such a conclusion involves no judgment on whether global warming exists, what causes it, or the extent of the problem. Nor does it render petitioners without recourse. This Court's standing jurisprudence simply recognizes that redress of grievances of the sort at issue here 'is the function of Congress and the Chief Executive,' not the federal courts.... I would vacate the judgment below and remand for dismissal of the petitions here for review....

"Our modern framework for addressing standing is familiar: 'A plaintiff must allege personal injury fairly traceable to the defendant's allegedly unlawful conduct and likely to be redressed by the requested relief.'... Applying that standard here, petitioners bear the burden of alleging an injury that is fairly traceable to the [EPA's] failure to promulgate new motor vehicle greenhouse gas emission standards, and that is likely to be redressed by the prospective issuance of such standards.

"Before determining whether petitioners can meet this familiar test, however, the Court changes the rules. It asserts that 'States are not normal litigants for the purposes of invoking federal jurisdiction,' and that given 'Massachusetts' stake in protecting its quasi-sovereign interests, the Commonwealth is entitled to special solicitude in our standing analysis.'...

"Relaxing Article III standing requirements because asserted injuries are pressed by a State, however, has no basis in our jurisprudence, and support for any such 'special solicitude' is conspicuously absent from the Court's opinion....

"Nor does the case law cited by the Court provide any support for the notion that Article III somehow implicitly treats public and private litigants differently. The Court has to go back a full century in an attempt to justify its novel standing rule, but even there it comes up short. The Court's analysis hinges on *Georgia v. Tennessee Copper Co.* ... a case that did indeed draw a distinction between a State and private litigants, but solely with respect to available remedies. The case had nothing to do with Article III standing....

"It is not at all clear how the Court's 'special solicitude' for Massachusetts plays out in the standing analysis, except as an implicit concession that petitioners cannot establish standing on traditional terms. But the status of Massachusetts as a State cannot compensate for petitioners' failure to demonstrate injury in fact, causation, and redressability....

"Petitioners are never able to trace their alleged injuries back through this complex web to the fractional amount of global emissions that might have been limited with EPA standards. In light of the bit-part domestic new motor vehicle greenhouse gas emissions have played in what petitioners describe as a 150-year global phenomenon, and the myriad additional factors bearing on petitioners' alleged injury—the loss of Massachusetts coastal land—the connection is far too speculative to establish causation....

"No matter, the Court reasons, because any decrease in domestic emissions will 'slow the pace of global emissions increases, no matter what happens elsewhere.'... Every little bit helps, so Massachusetts can sue over any little bit....

"The good news is that the Court's 'special solicitude' for Massachusetts limits the future applicability of the diluted standing requirements applied in this case. The bad news is that the Court's self-professed relaxation of those Article III requirements has caused us to transgress 'the proper—and properly limited—role of the courts in a democratic society.'...

"I respectfully dissent."

DISSENT by *Justice SCALIA*:

"I join THE CHIEF JUSTICE's opinion in full, and would hold that this Court has no jurisdiction to decide this case because petitioners lack standing. The Court having decided otherwise, it is appropriate for me to note my dissent on the merits....

"As the Court recognizes, the statute 'conditions the exercise of EPA's authority on its formation of a "judgment".'... There is no dispute that the Administrator has made no such judgment in this case....

"The question thus arises: Does anything require the Administrator to make a 'judgment' whenever a petition for rulemaking is filed? Without citation of the statute or any other authority, the Court says yes. Why is that so? When Congress wishes to make private action force an agency's hand, it knows how to do so....

"I am willing to assume, for the sake of argument, that the Administrator's discretion in this regard is not unbounded—that if he has no reasonable basis for deferring judgment he must grasp the nettle at once. The Court, however, with no basis in text or precedent, rejects all of EPA's stated 'policy judgments' as not 'amounting to a reasoned justification' ... effectively narrowing the universe of potentially reasonable bases to a single one: Judgment can be delayed only if the Administrator concludes that 'the scientific uncertainty is [too] profound.'... The Administrator is precluded from concluding for other reasons 'that it would ... be better not to regulate at this time.' Such other reasons—perfectly valid reasons—were set forth in the agency's statement....

"EPA's interpretation of the discretion conferred by the statutory reference to 'its judgment' is not only reasonable, it is the most natural reading of the text. The Court nowhere explains why it is not entitled to deference.... As the Administrator acted within the law in declining to make a 'judgment' for the policy reasons [stated], I would uphold the decision to deny the rulemaking petition on that ground alone....

"I simply cannot conceive of what else the Court would like EPA to say....

"The Court's alarm over global warming may or may not be justified, but it ought not distort the outcome of this litigation. This is a straightforward administrative-law case, in which Congress has passed a malleable statute giving broad discretion, not to us but to an executive agency. No matter how important the underlying policy issues at stake, this Court has no business substituting its own desired outcome for the reasoned judgment of the responsible agency."

WHALING IN THE ANTARCTIC (AUSTRALIA v. JAPAN)
(General List No. 148, International Court of Justice 2014)

BACKGROUND: On May 31, 2010, Australia filed in the Registry of the Court an Application instituting proceedings against Japan in respect of a dispute concerning: "Japan's continued pursuit of a large-scale program of whaling under the Second Phase of its Japanese Whale Research Program under Special Permit in the Antarctic ('JARPA II'), in breach of obligations assumed by Japan under the International Convention for the Regulation of Whaling ['ICRW'] . . ., as well as its other international obligations for the preservation of marine mammals and the marine environment." On November 20, 2012, New Zealand, pursuant to Article 63, paragraph 2, of the Statute, filed in the Registry of the Court a Declaration of Intervention in the case. In its Declaration, New Zealand stated that it "avail[ed] itself of the right . . . to intervene as a non-party in the proceedings brought by Australia against Japan in this case."

The ICRW is the third multi-nation agreement attempting to regulate international whaling activities. It establishes a "moratorium setting zero catch limits for the killing of whales from all stocks for commercial purposes (para. 10[e])," subject to limited exceptions. Article VIII, paragraph 1, of the Convention reads as follows:

> Notwithstanding anything contained in this Convention any Contracting Government may grant to any of its nationals a special permit authorizing that national to kill, take and treat whales for purposes of scientific research subject to such restrictions as to number and subject to such other conditions as the Contracting Government thinks fit, and the killing, taking, and treating of whales in accordance with the provisions of this Article shall be exempt from the operation of this Convention. Each Contracting Government shall report at once to the Commission all such authorizations which it has granted. Each Contracting Government may at any time revoke any such special permit which it has granted.

Australia claims that JARPA II is not really a program for purposes of scientific research, but simply a "cover" for continued commercial whaling.

THE COURT, composed as above, after deliberation, *delivers the following Judgment*:

"... Even where a Contracting Government issues a special permit 'for purposes of scientific research', it is still required to ensure that the number of whales to be killed under that permit is the lowest necessary for, and proportionate to, the scientific purpose, and takes into account the collective interests of the parties. This is a matter for objective determination in light of the facts, as evidenced through the Guidelines and Resolutions of the Scientific Committee and the Commission.

"There is, in any case, a substantive duty of meaningful co-operation on a Contracting Government which proposes to issue a special permit. This requires it to show that it has taken into account the legitimate interests of the other parties to the Convention; that it has balanced the interests of all the parties in the conservation and management of whale stocks....

"The Court first considers the arguments of the Parties and the intervening State regarding the meaning of the term 'scientific research' and then turns to their arguments regarding the meaning of the term for purposes of' in the phrase 'for purposes of scientific research.'...

"First, Australia acknowledges that Article VIII, paragraph 2, of the Convention allows the sale of whale meat that is the by-product of whaling for purposes of scientific research. That provision states: 'Any whales taken under these special permits shall so far as practicable be processed and the proceeds shall be dealt with in accordance with directions issued by the Government by which the permit was granted.'

"However, Australia considers that the quantity of whale meat generated in the course of a programme for which a permit has been granted under Article VIII, paragraph 1, and the sale of that meat, can cast doubt on whether the killing, taking and treating of whales is for purposes of scientific research....

"... In the Court's view, the fact that a programme involves the sale of whale meat and the use of proceeds to fund research is not sufficient, taken alone, to cause a special permit to fall outside Article VIII. Other elements would have to be examined, such as the scale of a programme's use of lethal sampling, which might suggest that the whaling is for purposes other than scientific research. In particular, a State party may not, in order to fund the research for which a special permit has been granted, use lethal sampling on a greater scale than is otherwise reasonable in relation to achieving the programme's stated objectives.

"Secondly, Australia asserts that a State's pursuit of goals that extend beyond scientific objectives would demonstrate that a special permit granted in respect of such a programme does not fall within Article VIII. In Australia's view, for example, the pursuit of policy goals such as providing employment or maintaining a whaling infrastructure would indicate that the killing of whales is not for purposes of scientific research....

"The JARPA II Research Plan identifies four research objectives: (1) Monitoring of the Antarctic ecosystem; (2) Modelling competition among whale species and future management objectives; (3) Elucidation of temporal and spatial changes in stock structure; and (4) Improving the management procedure for Antarctic minke whale stocks....

"Japan asserts that lethal sampling is 'indispensable' to JARPA II's first two objectives, relating to ecosystem monitoring and multi-species competition modelling. The JARPA II Research Plan explains that the third objective will rely on 'genetic and biological markers' taken from whales that have been lethally sampled in connection with the first two objectives, as well as non-lethal methods, namely biopsy sampling from blue, fin and humpback whales.

"… Australia maintains that Japan has an 'unbending commitment to lethal take' and that 'JARPA II is premised on the killing of whales.' According to Australia, JARPA II, like JARPA before it, is 'merely a guise' under which to continue commercial whaling….

"Another factor casts doubt on whether the design of JARPA II is reasonable in relation to achieving the programme's stated objectives. The overall sample sizes selected for fin and humpback whales 50 whales of each species per year are not large enough to allow for the measurement of all the trends that the programme seeks to measure. Specifically, the JARPA II Research Plan states that at least 131 whales of each species should be taken annually to detect a particular rate of change in age at sexual maturity. The Research Plan does not indicate whether the researchers decided to accept a lower level of accuracy or instead adjusted the rate of change that they sought to detect by targeting fewer whales, nor did Japan explain this in the present proceedings. In light of the calculations of its own scientists, JARPA II does not appear designed to produce statistically relevant information on at least one central research item to which the JARPA II Research Plan gives particular importance….

"The Court finds that the JARPA II Research Plan overall provides only limited information regarding the basis for the decisions used to calculate the fin and humpback whale sample size. These sample sizes were set using a 12-year period, despite the fact that a shorter six-year period is used to set the minke whale sample size and that JARPA II is to be reviewed after each six-year research phase. Based on Japan's own calculations, the sample sizes for fin and humpback whales are too small to produce statistically useful results. These shortcomings, in addition to the problems specific to the decision to take fin whales … are important to the Court's assessment of whether the overall design of JARPA II is reasonable in relation to the programme's objectives, because Japan connects the minke whale sample size … to the ecosystem research and multi-species competition objectives that, in turn, are premised on the lethal sampling of fin and humpback whales….

"Australia acknowledges that JARPA II has produced some results in the form of data that has been considered by the Scientific Committee. The Parties disagree about this output, however, in the sense that Australia argues that the data obtained from lethal sampling and provided to the Scientific Committee has not proven useful or contributed 'significant knowledge' relating to the conservation and management of whales.

"The Court notes that the Research Plan uses a six-year period to obtain statistically useful information for minke whales and a 12-year period for the other two species, and that it can be expected that the main scientific output of JARPA II would follow these periods. It nevertheless observes that the first research phase of JARPA II (2005-2006 to 2010-2011) has already been completed … but that Japan points to only two peer-reviewed papers that have resulted from JARPA II to date. These papers do not relate to the JARPA II objectives and rely on data collected from respectively seven and two minke whales caught during the JARPA II feasibility study. While Japan also refers to three presentations made at scientific symposia and to eight papers it has submitted to the Scientific Committee, six of the latter are JARPA II cruise reports, one of the two remaining papers is an evaluation of the JARPA II feasibility study and the other relates to the programme's non-lethal photo identification of blue whales. In light of the fact that JARPA II has been going on since 2005 and has involved the killing of about 3,600 minke whales, the scientific output to date appears limited.…

"Taken as a whole, the Court considers that JARPA II involves activities that can broadly be characterized as scientific research … but that the evidence does not establish that the programme's design and implementation are reasonable in relation to achieving its stated objectives. The Court concludes that the special permits granted by Japan for the killing, taking and treating of whales in connection with JARPA II are not 'for purposes of scientific research' pursuant to Article VIII, paragraph 1, of the Convention.…

"The Court therefore proceeds on the basis that whaling that falls outside Article VIII, paragraph 1, other than aboriginal subsistence whaling, is subject to the three Schedule provisions invoked by Australia. As this conclusion flows from the interpretation of the Convention and thus applies to any special permit granted for the killing, taking and treating of whales that is not 'for purposes of scientific research in the context of Article VIII, paragraph 1, the Court sees no reason to evaluate the evidence in support of the Parties' competing contentions about whether or not JARPA II has attributes of commercial whaling.…

"The moratorium on commercial whaling, paragraph 10 *(e)*, provides:
> 'Notwithstanding the other provisions of paragraph 10, catch limits for the killing for commercial purposes of whales from all stocks for the 1986 coastal and the 1985/86 pelagic seasons and thereafter shall be zero. This provision will be kept under review, based upon the best scientific advice, and by 1990 at the latest the Commission will undertake a comprehensive assessment of the effects of this decision on whale stocks and consider modification of this provision and the establishment of other catch limits.'

"From 2005 to the present, Japan, through the issuance of JARPA II permits, has set catch limits above zero for three species—850 for minke whales, 50 for fin whales and 50 for humpback whales. [T]he Court considers that all whaling that does not fit within Article VIII of the Convention (other than aboriginal subsistence whaling) is subject to paragraph 10 *(e)* of the Schedule. It follows that Japan has not acted in conformity with its obligations under paragraph 10 *(e)* in each of the years in which it has granted permits for JARPA II (2005 to the present) because those permits have set catch limits higher than zero....

"For these reasons,
THE COURT,

"(1) Unanimously,
 Finds that it has jurisdiction to entertain the Application filed by Australia on 31 May 2010;

"(2) By twelve votes to four,
 Finds that the special permits granted by Japan in connection with JARPA II do not fall within the provisions of Article VIII, paragraph 1, of the International Convention for the Regulation of Whaling; ...

"(3) By twelve votes to four,
 Finds that Japan, by granting special permits to kill, take and treat fin, humpback and Antarctic minke whales in pursuance of JARPA II, has not acted in conformity with its obligations under paragraph 10 *(e)* of the Schedule to the International Convention for the Regulation of Whaling; ...

"(4) By twelve votes to four,
 Finds that Japan has not acted in conformity with its obligations under paragraph 10 *(d)* of the Schedule to the International Convention for the Regulation of Whaling in relation to the killing, taking and treating of fin whales in pursuance of JARPA II; ...

"(5) By twelve votes to four,
 Finds that Japan has not acted in conformity with its obligations under paragraph 7 *(b)* of the Schedule to the International Convention for the Regulation of Whaling in relation to the killing, taking and treating of fin whales in the "Southern Ocean Sanctuary" in pursuance of JARPA II; ...

"(6) By thirteen votes to three,
 Finds that Japan has complied with its obligations under paragraph 30 of the Schedule to the International Convention for the Regulation of Whaling with regard to JARPA II; ...

"(7) By twelve votes to four,

Decides that Japan shall revoke any extant authorization, permit or licence granted in relation to JARPA II, and refrain from granting any further permits in pursuance of that programme....

"Done in English and in French, the English text being authoritative, at the Peace Palace, The Hague, this thirty-first day of March, two thousand and fourteen, in four copies, one of which will be placed in the archives of the Court and the others transmitted to the Government of Australia, the Government of Japan and the Government of New Zealand, respectively.

(*Signed*) Peter TOMKA, President
(*Signed*) Philippe COUVREUR, Reporter"

CHAPTER VI

International Competition Regulation and Government Expropriation

OVERVIEW:

INTERNATIONAL COMPETITION REGULATION. Too many of us seem to equate "competition law" with (and only with) U.S. antitrust law. While it's true that the USA has a rich—if mixed—heritage of competition regulation, and is still a major force for protection of competition both internally and internationally, it is not now the only player and has not been for some time. Further, U.S. antitrust law owes a considerable doctrinal debt to a number of historical sources, as Senator John Sherman of Ohio is quoted as recognizing: "[The Sherman Act] does not announce a new principle of law, but applies old and well-recognised principles of common law." (*See*, Anestis Papadopoulos, *The International Dimension of EU Competition Law,* New York: Cambridge University Press, 2010, p. 10.) The USA and the EU may have the greatest bodies of case law from which to draw examples of the application of rules, but there are now well over 100 other nations with their own national competition regimes. (The website for one "Joachim Rudo," self-identified as an attorney-at-law in Germany, lists the appropriate official "Antitrust Authorities" for 41 nations in addition to the USA and the EU; presumably, these are the ones with which he is familiar and/or where he is licensed to practice.) Examples of recent activity in some of the 100+ other nations will be discussed briefly below.

Historical Beginnings of Competition Law. The ancient world had its "Seven Wonders," including the Colossus of Rhodes—a giant statue of the sun god Helios, built in the city's harbor as thanks for Rhodes' victory over an invading Cyprian army. It turns out that the ancient world also had price-fixing conspiracies. Thanks to what has to be one of the "Wonders" of our modern world—the "colossus" called the Internet—a short sequence of electronic searches leads us to a wonderful essay by a staff member of the Antitrust Division of the U.S. Justice Department, Wayne Dunham: "Cold Case Files: The Athenian Grain Merchants 386 B.C.," EAG

07-2 (January 2007). One more search yields the text of Dunham's primary source: the Greek orator Lysias' prosecutorial speech to the Greek jury in the criminal trial of the merchants. Using the Lysias speech, Dunham describes a conspiracy of buyers attempting to lower the price of grain purchased for the Athens market. The stakes could not have been higher, since the death penalty was prescribed for conviction on such charges. (Dunham indicates that the earliest "monopsony"—dominant buyer—case in the USA occurred in 1924. *Live Poultry Dealers Protective Assn. v. U.S.,* 4 F.2d 840, U.S. Second Circuit Court of Appeals, 1924. However, *see, H.B. Marinelli, Limited v. United Booking Offices of America,* 227 F. 165, S.D. NY, 1914. Judge Learned Hand wrote both of these opinions.)

The initial link in the chain leading to Lysias and the Athenian grain conspiracy was the Roman statute *Lex Julia de Annona,* dated about 50 BC by Wikipedia and about 18 BC by another source. With Rome, like Athens, dependent on grain imports, the statute is described as providing "heavy fines" for those convicted of intentionally interfering with grain ships. Rome reportedly upped the ante on market manipulation in 301 AD, when an edict of the Emperor Diocletian imposed the death penalty for violators. A text co-authored by Lord Richard Wilburforce, *The Law of Restrictive Practices and Monopolies,* is cited for the proposition that the 1322 and 1325 laws of Florence, Italy are based on anti-monopoly legislation adopted in 483 AD, during the reign of the Byzantine Emperor Zeno.

The Wilburforce text is also cited as a source for several developments in England during the Middle Ages. Near the end of his reign (1085), William the Conqueror commissioned a massive data-collection process to determine the taxable assets in his realm. The "Domesday Book" was the result—not quite completed for the whole of England when he died in 1087. The data allegedly showed that the King could declare forfeiture of property for the offense of "forestalling"—buying up goods and reselling them at higher prices ("monopolization"?). The 1351 "Statute of Laborers" required all "sellers of victuals" to sell at a reasonable price, and provided that those who were guilty of violating the Statute should pay the injured buyer twice what the buyer had paid. (This provision was suggested as the inspiration for the treble damages provision in the USA's antitrust statutes.)

Perhaps the most closely-related common-law ancestor of the USA's antitrust regime is the so-called "covenant not to compete." Any form of business relationship—employer/employee, principal/agent, partnership, corporation/shareholder—may come to a point where at least one of the parties feels that termination of the relationship is preferable to continuation. In many instances, one or more of the associates will want to continue the existing business operation. The concern of those continuing the business is that the former associate may want to begin a new competing firm, or utilize experience gained in the previous association on behalf of an already existing competitor. Likewise, many firms build up significant customer/client "good will" by providing excellent service and product support, and that "good will" is frequently personified in the business owner. When it's time for the business owner to retire, or to "devote more time to my family"—and the business is to be sold—prospective buyers of the business want to be sure that they are in fact going to receive a major part of that firm's value: the customer/client "good will." They do not want the former owner coming back into business across the street as "The *Original* Petrov's Pizza!"

The legal solution to both of these potential business problems is the covenant not to compete: a promise by the former associate or by the business-seller not to compete with the former business for a limited period of time, within the relevant geographical area. So the rule developed that such limitations on competition were lawful and enforceable—IF there was a legitimate business purpose to be served, and IF the scope of the time and area restraints were "reasonable." Hence, the U.S. Supreme Court's 1911 *Standard Oil* decision and the antitrust enforcement "rule of reason."

Development of U.S. Antitrust Law. Very significant changes have occurred over time in the enforcement of the USA's major "antitrust" statutes. Both the Sherman Act of 1890 and the Clayton Act of 1914 contain very vague language, and are therefore susceptible of, and have in fact been subject to, widely varying interpretations. There is a striking contrast between the "per se illegality"/"power to abuse"/"big-is-bad" approach of the 1960s and early 1970s, and the more recent rule-of-reason/abuse-of-power/consumer-welfare approach. The U.S. Supreme Court reversed the horrible ("bad guy [price-gouging monopolist] wins") *Albrecht* precedent in 1997, and the nearly 100-year-old *Dr. Miles* precedent in 2007, so that both maximum and minimum resale price agreements are now tested—in USA courts, at least—under the rule of reason. On the other hand, one of the very first steps taken by the new Obama administration in 2009 was its Justice Department repudiation of the "Bush II" DOJ policy statement on single-firm competitive tactics that had just been developed after extensive oral and written commentary, from a wide variety of sources. This step was an attempt to provide some guidelines for private conduct and public agency enforcement of competition policy. The "off-the-cuff" nature of the repudiation was especially disturbing given the time, effort and resources that had gone into the preparation of the report. (So much for consistency and common sense!)

Legislators trying to regulate human conduct face a dilemma: they must identify the conduct to be prohibited with enough specificity so that those regulated can know what not to do; but that very specificity may provide an opportunity to frustrate the purpose of the law by a simple variance in behavior—just enough so that what is done does not match the terms of the prohibition. For that reason, there does need to be a degree of generality in the prohibition language. The bottom-line results are a number of "grey areas" where the dividing line between legal and illegal conduct is not exactly clear. The USA's major antitrust statutes provide some classic examples of this problem.

Section 1 of the Sherman Antitrust Act of 1890 states: "Every contract, combination in the form of trust or otherwise, or conspiracy, in restraint of trade or commerce among the several States, or with foreign nations, is hereby declared to be illegal." The definitional difficulties with that seemingly simple prohibition begin with the first word: the universal "every." Consider this scenario: I am in the market for a new car; I am therefore a business opportunity for the car dealers in my community—and in any other locations I may wish to consider. When I make a contract to buy a new car from Freedom Chevrolet, the sale opportunity that I represent is removed from the market; commerce is "restrained" by the loss of that sale opportunity. Not a big loss, to be sure; but Section 1 says "***Every*** contract"! So a literal reading of Section 1 makes every business contract illegal, since it removes that goods or services buyer from the market: clearly not what the Congress intended. What then did they intend? In the 1911 *Standard Oil* case, the U.S. Supreme Court said Congress only intended to outlaw contracts that "***unreasonably***" restrain commerce! So the multi-billion-dollar question then becomes: when does a contract "unreasonably" restrain commerce? Judges and business managers are likely to have different perspectives on this—not only as between the two groups, but even within the two groups. And if a contract is challenged as being an unreasonable restraint, and a trial results, there may be still different perspectives held by a group of jurors.

The conduct prohibited by Section 1 is the unreasonable restraint of trade or "commerce." So what is "commerce"? Since that word also appears in the U.S. Constitution as a grant of significant power to the national Congress—the "**commerce** clause"—its meaning has been litigated numerous times. Earlier courts tended to take a very narrow interpretation: insurance was not "commerce"; manufacturing was not "commerce"; et al. In 1922, with the great Justice Oliver Wendell Holmes, Jr., writing the opinion, a unanimous U.S. Supreme Court decided that organized professional baseball—selling tickets to fans who paid for the privilege of watching salaried players give baseball exhibitions—was not "commerce"! Four years earlier, again writing for the Court—in *Towne v. Eisner*—Holmes had said: "A word is not a crystal, transparent and unchanged; it is the skin of a living thought and may vary greatly in color and content according to the circumstances and time in which it is used." As Holmes might have predicted, over time the U.S. Supreme Court has greatly expanded the meaning of "commerce," so that the reach of Congress' power under the Commerce Clause was extended in 1942 to an Ohio farmer (Roscoe Filburn) growing a few acres of wheat for his own use on his farm. In the Court's 2012 decision on Obamacare, however, a majority of five Justices did rule that a person's decision not to buy health insurance could *not* be defined as "commerce." (A decision not to engage in commerce is not itself part of "commerce.")

If there are some definitional difficulties with the language of Section 1 of the Sherman

Act, they pale into insignificance when compared with the extreme fuzziness of Section 2 of the Clayton Act. It reads: "**(a) Price; selection of customers.** It shall be unlawful for any person engaged in commerce, in the course of such commerce, either directly or indirectly, to discriminate in price between different purchasers of commodities of like grade and quality, where either or any of the purchasers involved in such discrimination are in commerce … and where the effect of such discrimination may be substantially to lessen competition or tend to create a monopoly in any line of commerce…." "Commodities"?—presumably, this means only goods (tangible, movable personal property), not services and not real estate. "Like grade and quality"?—does a car dealer have to sell a new Buick at the same price as a new Dodge? Does a Firestone tire factory have to sell its brand-name tires at the same price as the "Brand X" tires it makes for sale at gasoline stations? In 1966 the U.S. Supreme Court said there was illegal price discrimination when a Borden's plant sold its brand-name condensed milk for a higher price than it charged A&P stores for their house-brand milk that was processed at the same plant and was chemically the same as the Borden's milk.

Those ambiguities in defining price discrimination are bad enough, but they are not the worst part of the problem; that's reserved for the "effects" that have to be proved to have been caused by the discrimination in order for there to be a violation. (The same loose language on "effects" is used in Clayton Section 3—prohibiting tying contracts and exclusive dealing agreements and in Clayton Section 7—prohibiting mergers.) "Where the effect … *may* be *substantially* to *lessen* competition or *tend* to *create* a monopoly in any *line* of commerce…." Does "may" mean possibly?—or probably?—or most likely? How "substantial" does the "lessening" need to be?—2%?—5%?—10%?—20%?—50%? How does the court decide that there may be a substantial lessening of *competition*? Does fewer competitors = less competition? That's what a majority of the U.S. Supreme Court decided in its silly 1966 opinion in the *Von's Grocery* merger case! The fact that there were fewer separate grocery sellers— bakeries, meat markets, dairies, produce stores—meant that there had been a lessening of competition in the retail grocery business. In the real world, of course, the grocery chains—large and small—and the many remaining independents were vigorously competing for retail grocery customers in Los Angeles. The lower total number of competitors was due to shoppers' preference for buying all their grocery (and some other) household needs at one "supermarket," rather than making six or eight stops at small specialty stores.

Multinational firms thus need to be aware that government enforcement policies in such highly political areas can change drastically—even without a violent revolution. The good (antitrust) news from the USA is that most legal challenges to competition strategies and tactics are now being judged under the "rule of reason," rather than being automatic violations with no explanations permitted—under the *per se* rule. At least for the time being, the *per se* standard seems to be confined to conspiracies between/among competitors—to fix prices, divide markets, rig bids, and the like. There may not be any conceivable justification for those sorts of blatant violations of the competition rules; but for most alleged violations, the defendant business will at least get a chance to try to justify its adoption of the challenged practice or policy. The bad news from the USA (for antitrust violators outside the country) is that its international enforcement efforts took a quantum leap in 2014, with a "first of its kind extradition on an antitrust charge": one Romano Pisciotti, an Italian national, was extradited from Germany to face criminal antitrust charges—bid rigging—in the U.S. District Court for the Southern District of Florida. (*See*, U.S. Department of Justice press release, April 4, 2014.)

Competition Regulation Outside the USA. One of the most notable features of the European Union was its adoption of a competition policy—from the beginning. The 1957 Treaty of Rome—the founding document of the European Economic Community—contained two key provisions which regulated the strategy and tactics of "undertakings" (i.e., business enterprises): Articles 85 and 86. The drafters of these provisions were certainly aware of the USA's Sherman Act and Clayton Act, and the court decisions interpreting them, so it is not surprising that Articles 85 and 86 contain some parallel concepts, even if expressed in different phraseology.

Article 85 prohibited all agreements "which may affect trade between Member States and which have as their object or effect the prevention, restriction or distortion of competition within the common market…." Specifically prohibited are "those which: (a) directly or indirectly fix purchase or selling prices or any other trading conditions; (b) limit or control production, markets, technical development, or investment; (c) share markets or sources of supply; (d) apply dissimilar conditions to equivalent transactions with other trading parties, thereby placing them at a competitive disadvantage; (e) make the conclusion of contracts subject to acceptance by the other parties of supplementary obligations which, by their nature or according to commercial usage, have no connection with the subject of such contracts." Unlike the U.S. statutes, however, Article 85 goes on in paragraph 3 to provide a possible defense to the alleged competition violation. The prohibitions in paragraph 1 "may" be "declared inapplicable" if the challenged agreement "contributes to improving the production or distribution of goods or to promoting technical or economic progress, while allowing consumers a fair share of the resulting benefit, and which does not: (a) impose on the undertakings concerned restrictions which are not indispensable to the attainment of these objectives; (b) afford such undertakings the possibility of eliminating competition in respect of a substantial part of the products in question."

Article 86 prohibited any "abuse" by "one or more undertakings" of a "dominant position" in the common market or a substantial part of it "in so far as it [the abuse] may affect trade between Member States." Specifically listed as such "abuses" were: "(a) directly or indirectly imposing unfair purchase or selling prices or other unfair trading conditions; (b) limiting production, market or technical development to the prejudice of consumers; (c) applying dissimilar conditions to equivalent transactions with other trading parties, thereby placing them at a competitive disadvantage; (d) making the conclusion of contracts subject to acceptance by the other parties of supplementary obligations which, by their nature or according to commercial usage, have no connection with the subject of such contracts."

The substantial redundancy in the listed specific offenses in the two Articles is perhaps explained by their slightly different sources: an "agreement" in Article 85 (implying at least two bad persons?), and an "abuse" in Article 86 (by one *or more* undertakings—but presumably the abuser is committing the offense against an innocent victim).

The offenses themselves have at least some parallels in the USA's version of antitrust law. Price fixing is of course one of the commonest of alleged violations. U.S. law now differentiates between horizontal (between supposed competitors) and vertical (between different levels of the distribution chain) price-fixing. The former is still treated as a *per se* violation, and generally is subject to criminal prosecution as well as civil remedies. As previously noted, vertical price-fixing (whether maximum or minimum prices are being set) is now subject to the rule of reason. Price discrimination by a seller, between buyers of "like goods," may be a U.S. violation if it is found to have the prohibited effect on competition. Articles 85 and 86 extend such discrimination to any "conditions" of the sale transaction. (The USA's Clayton Act does extend "price" discrimination to at least some "promotion" conditions.) The Articles' prohibitions on forced "supplementary obligations" may have some relationship to the "tying contract" or "full line forcing" in U.S. law: requiring the purchase of an unwanted item in order to buy the wanted item. That seems inherently unfair, and there are some interesting U.S. cases litigating the issue. (*See, e.g., Illinois Tool Works, Inc. v. Independent Ink, Inc.,* 547 U.S. 28 [2006].)

As the European Economic Community has evolved into the European Union, with an expanded membership, the Treaty provisions have been adjusted. Articles 85 and 86 were first re-numbered as Articles 81 and 82—so some competition cases will reference those numbers. Most recently, the Lisbon Treaty came into force on December 1, 2009, and the two Articles have been re-numbered again; this time as Articles 101 and 102. The references to the "common market" in the quoted sections above now read the "internal market" instead. One would not imagine that the one-word change would adversely impact the validity of earlier cases as examples of how these Articles should be interpreted.

The International Law Section of the American Bar Association publishes a yearly review of international legal developments, one subsection of which is "International Antitrust." That's a good place to see the kinds of things that have been happening in some of the other nations that have adopted competition regulations. Using the ABA reviews for two recent years—2013 and 2011—as examples, we find that twelve other nations are listed, in addition to the USA and the EU: Australia, Brazil, Canada, China, France, Germany, India, Israel, Mexico, Russia, South Africa, and the United Kingdom. Five common areas appear in both years' reviews: "Legislative Developments," "Mergers," "Cartels and Other Anticompetitive Practices," "Abuse of Dominant Position," and "Court Decisions." For 2011, neither Canada nor the USA had any reported legislative activity; but "Administrative Developments" were reported for each. Also in 2011, South Africa had a listing for "Exemptions," since it had had a number of such requests that year.

All fourteen systems had discussions on cartel activity in both years. Israel had no reported merger activity in 2013; the other thirteen had discussions on merger enforcement for both years. In addition to Canada and the USA (noted above), there was no reported legislative activity for the EU in 2011, or for Australia in 2013. Australia likewise reported no court activity for either year, as did Mexico. Brazil, India and (surprise!) the USA had no court-cases discussion for 2011; France had none for 2013. The "Abuse" topic had the most no-discussion instances: China, Germany and Israel had no such reports for either year. France, South Africa and the USA had no such discussion for 2011; India and the U.K. had none for 2013. Brazil's "Cartels" discussion for 2011 was really about an "Abuse" case—as an example of "Other Anticompetitive Practices."

Contrary to what are most probably the popular perceptions, Russia was the only one of the fourteen jurisdictions with events reported in all five areas for both years. One generally imagines more instances of competition misconduct there, but probably not more instances of enforcement efforts. Three other systems—the E.U., South Africa, and the U.K.—were "9 of 10." In any event, these little surveys indicate a considerable amount of global effort being devoted to the enforcement of competition rules. Managers of cross-border business operations surely need to be aware of these developments.

GOVERNMENTAL EXPROPRIATION. A different set of problems is presented when a country "nationalizes" property located there, including that owned by foreign persons. Historically, this has occurred when "revolutionary" regimes of one flavor or another have come to power (sometimes by violent means, sometimes not). The creation of the Russian and Chinese Communist regimes, of course, involved large-scale nationalizations of private property—both that owned by locals and that owned by foreign individuals and companies. In the U.K., extensive nationalization occurred after World War II, when the Labor Party replaced the Conservatives—much of it then undone during Prime Minister Thatcher's tenure after the Conservative Party's return to power. The end of the USSR's socialist bloc was also followed by large-scale de-nationalization in Eastern Europe, with mixed results thus far.

There has been, and to some extent still is, disagreement in the international community about the legalities involved in nationalization of private property. FCN/BIT treaties may impose an obligation on the signatory nations to protect the property of each other's nationals, and to pay "prompt and adequate" compensation if such property is taken by the government. Since international law says that change of governments does not absolve the involved nation of its treaty obligations, it would follow that the revolutionary regime would be bound to pay the required compensation. Of course, that has not always happened, but it may provide an additional argument in a subsequent lawsuit.

"SOVEREIGN IMMUNITY" AND "ACT OF STATE." Two interconnected—but different —legal doctrines immensely complicate court challenges to governmental actions: *sovereign immunity* and *act of state*. O.P.E.C.—the Organization of Petroleum Exporting Countries— provides a classic example, thus far successfully brushing off attempts to challenge the legality of its price-fixing and supply-managing activities. (*See* the *Prewitt* case in Chapter II.)

"Sovereign immunity from suit" seems a logical derivative from the "divine rights of kings": if the ruler is chosen by a supreme being, how can his or her actions be subjected to review by a body of fallible humans? If the courts derive their power from the King or Queen, how can they sit in judgment on the acts of their creator? In more legalistic terms, can an "agent" judge the actions of his or her "principal" who delegated to the agent the authority to act? Perhaps this level of analysis was a sufficient explanation at one time, but the "divine right of kings" has not been a viable notion for some time. As the concept of "popular sovereignty" has expanded, governments (particularly those democratically chosen) have accepted a rather wide range of possible "reviews"—by *their own nation's* courts—of their official actions.

More significant for our purposes, of course, is the application of "sovereign immunity" from suit of a foreign government and its officials in the courts of another nation. An injured party from Country A wants to sue the Government of Country B in Country A's courts. The doctrine of sovereign immunity is very much a live issue in that context. The debate has intensified by several degrees of magnitude in recent years, as victims of World War II atrocities—or their surviving family members—have sought court remedies. While these claims do not generally have a close connection to international commercial operations, some of them do—and others yet to be filed may also. In any event, the legalities involved are significant for the development of international law.

On the one side is the idea of sovereign immunity: one nation's courts do not have (and should not have?) the authority to sit in judgment on the governments or officials of other nations. International law assumes the sovereignty and equality of all nations. How can a nation claim to be sovereign if courts in other nations can exercise authority over it? On the other side of the current debate is the more recently-developed concept of international human rights, violations of which must be remedied—even if the violators are national governments and their officials. With two such strongly-held principles in conflict, it may not be possible to construct a general international law rule which will cover all contingencies and satisfy all interested parties. It may be necessary to simply recognize the impossibility of a universal reconciliation of the conflicting concepts, and to leave to the courts the difficult job of weighing the two conflicting interests on a case-by-case basis, in terms of the specific facts presented.

Of course, not all cases raising the sovereign immunity question involve what could fairly be classified as international "human rights." Most commercial cases involve more mundane issues of contract, property, and organization management. Most nations now apparently recognize a more "limited" version of sovereign immunity that does not apply to "commercial activities" of governments. By entering the marketplace, the sovereign impliedly agrees to be bound by market rules—like any other participant. This sort of "implied waiver" argument seems implicit in the analysis, but does not seem to be explicitly acknowledged very often. In any event, there are still some definitional difficulties in deciding which activities are truly "governmental," and which are "commercial." "Construction," for example, is clearly a commercial activity pursued by large numbers of individuals and private firms. Yet it also seems clear that construction of roads, post offices, military bases, and other official buildings is a well-recognized function of government. How about government construction of housing for aged or low-income citizens? These buildings are rented to private persons, of course—but post offices are used mostly by private persons, who pay for the privilege, and at least some roads charge tolls for their use. As governments assume more functions, the "sovereign immunity" line becomes more difficult to draw and "traditional functions" becomes a less useful test.

Waiver of Immunity. The agent or agency having authority to represent the nation in question can waive the nation's immunity and thus submit it to the court's jurisdiction for the purpose of the pending lawsuit. *Express* waiver could occur in a treaty—such as a bilateral investment treaty or a "friendship, commerce and navigation" treaty—or in a separate government agreement—a loan agreement, perhaps. The case-law seems to indicate that such express waivers are normally interpreted strictly. Implied waivers may also occur, although here again courts seem a bit hesitant to "imply" such a fundamental change in the parties' legal positions without significant indicators that it was clearly intended as part of the relationship.

Counter-Claims. Another kind of "waiver" argument can be made when it is the foreign government itself which files a lawsuit in the courts of another nation. Hasn't the plaintiff clearly consented to have its rights determined by that court when it asks that court for a remedy for its claim? Certainly the typical assumption is that when you sue me, I can not only answer you with reasons why I am not liable to you on the asserted claim, but also respond with my own affirmative claim against you—and (generally, at least) my claim against you need not arise from the same relationship as did your original claim against me. For example, you sue me for the price of your services in fixing my garage roof. I can not only present reasons why I don't owe you that money; I can counter-claim that you owe me the contract price for a used boat I sold you.

The plaintiff-government will of course argue that it only agreed to give up its sovereign immunity and to have the court determine its rights as to the claim on which it based its lawsuit. That argument does have some weight if the counter-claim is totally unconnected to the plaintiff's claim. (But *see* the *First National* case, below.) It seems much less valid if the counter-claim arises out of the same relationship as the original claim—like the *Alafoss* case in Chapter III, for instance. (*See* the *Kalamazoo Spice* case, below, as another example of this problem.)

Act of State. The "Act of State" doctrine works differently than sovereign immunity. The latter is essentially a procedural argument: the sovereign defendant simply cannot be sued. The Act of State defense says that there is no claim to be litigated: an action by a sovereign nation within its own borders is not subject to review by the courts of other nations. That principle also originates in the ideas of national sovereignty and equality of nations—basic foundations of international law.

Here again, there are complications when the governmental action within its own nation has consequences outside that nation. If the validity/legality of the action itself cannot be challenged in courts of other nations, can the acting government be held liable for the *consequences*—intended and/or unintended—of the official act? If the act itself is legally permitted, how can that same act be the basis for a legal liability? On the other hand, can it not be argued that the legality of one's action under *national* law is not necessarily a defense to a claim that the action violates *international* law? (*See* the Chapter I case *La Jeune Eugenie*, for example.) Are there not some cases where it is possible to recognize the finality/effectiveness of the act itself within that nation, and to recognize, nonetheless, that the act has produced liability consequences externally?

That last argument seemed persuasive to a unanimous U.S. Supreme Court in a 1990 case: *W.S. Kirkpatrick & Co. v. Environmental Tectonics Corp, Int'l.* ETC claimed that it had lost a large construction contract with the government of Nigeria because Kirkpatrick had bribed a Nigerian official to award the contract to them. ETC filed a civil action for damages in the U.S. District Court in New Jersey, alleging violations of the USA's Racketeering Influenced and Corrupt Organizations Act, its Robinson-Patman Act, and the New Jersey Anti-Racketeering Act. ETC did not ask the court to invalidate the contract between Nigeria and Kirkpatrick.

Kirkpatrick asked the court to dismiss the case, on the basis of the Act of State doctrine, which the court did. The U.S. Court of Appeals for the Third Circuit reversed, and the defendants asked for U.S. Supreme Court review. The Supreme Court held that the Act of State argument was operative only where a court was being asked specifically to declare the action of the foreign government invalid, or to make such a decision in order to decide the case before it, neither of which was the situation here. This more limited scope to the doctrine surely provides creative litigators with some further opportunities for gaining court remedies, even though foreign governmental actions are somehow involved in the dispute. Not to be overlooked is the possibility that the chance of a successful lawsuit might motivate the defendant government to agree to arbitration—a la *Altmann v. Austria*.

EXAMPLE CASES PREVIEW:

The focus of our rather limited selection of cases is on the application of national competition policies to multi-national business operations and of national court processes to the actions of governments, and on the international complications that may arise as a result.

TIMBERLANE: Several nations, including the USA, recognize so-called "effects" jurisdiction as a sufficient basis for applying their internal competition policies to multinational operations. The USA Ninth Circuit Court of Appeals says a more thorough analysis is required—with a number of factors considered.

PFIZER: The only issue here was whether a foreign nation that bought drugs at prices inflated by an illegal antitrust conspiracy could collect the "treble" (automatically-tripled) damages provided by USA antitrust law. The U.S. Supreme Court said yes. (This ruling was subsequently modified by amendment of the statute.)

BRITISH AIRWAYS: One of the most extreme international "conflict" examples ever occurred when USA antitrust law was being applied to UK-based airlines. The airlines had asked UK courts to enjoin the UK plaintiff airline from continuing its antitrust lawsuit in the USA. The defendants were not just asking their home nation not to enforce any resulting USA judgment; they wanted their courts to stop the plaintiff from litigating in the other nation! Thankfully, the "good-old" House of Lords appellate branch provided a common-sense solution to the dispute. (The UK plaintiff was not enjoined, since the UK airlines had agreed to be bound by USA law as part of their permission to operate there, and since the USA was the only place where the UK plaintiff could get a remedy if it proved its antitrust case.)

MATSUSHITA: USA TV manufacturers sued several Japanese competitors, claiming that the defendants had conspired in Japan to limit the number of USA dealers who could sell their products, and to charge higher prices in the USA than they charged for the same TVs in Japan (*after* shipping them half-way around the world!) After extended litigation, the case was finally dismissed, on the basis that the alleged tactics would not seem to harm the USA manufacturers, but rather give them a better chance to compete.

U.S.A. v. ANDREAS and WILSON: This case excerpt begins with an extensive quotation of the facts found by the Court, to give you a better idea of what an international price-fixing cartel looks like. There's also a rather thorough discussion of the sort of procedural issues that may come up in a USA-antitrust criminal trial, and the potential "down-side" of a conviction.

F. HOFFMAN-LA ROCHE: The issue here was the extent of the extraterritorial reach of the USA's antitrust acts. Where an international conspiracy (cartel) involving USA participants results in damages in the USA, to USA persons, there is enough connection here to justify application of our laws. But if the wrongful acts occur outside the USA, and result in damages outside the USA, to non-USA persons, those persons should not be able to participate in a class action lawsuit in the USA.

VINCENZO MANFREDI: The buyers, who paid too much for vehicle liability insurance as a result of illegal price-fixing by several insurance companies, have sued for damages. The offending insurance companies have raised various arguments as to why they should not be held liable.

COOPER TIRE: This case involves some complicated procedural rules concerning the enforcement of a EU Commission finding that there has been a violation of Article 101 of the EU Treaty. The violator-companies have filed appeals of the Commission's decision with the European Court of First Instance. Meanwhile, the buyer-victims of the illegal acts are seeking damages in national courts—choosing England. The violator-companies object to having their damages liabilities determined in England, and argue that Italian courts should hear that part of the case.

PFLEIDERER AG: A buyer, who overpaid for industrial product as a result of a price-fixing conspiracy which the German Federal Cartel Office (Bundeskartellamt) had established, requested access to the FCO's case file so that it could prepare its own lawsuit for damages. The FCO initially refused, but was ordered by the Local Court in Bonn to make the disclosure. The court, however, deferred enforcement of its disclosure order pending a decision from the EU Court of Justice on whether such disclosure would conflict with the EU's competition policy, which includes a leniency program for those who cooperate with prosecutors.

COMPETITION COMMISSION: Like the competition-regulatory regimes in several other nations, including the EU (in the prior case) and the USA, South Africa tries to encourage members of illegal conspiracies to admit their guilt and to provide evidence and assistance to government prosecutors. In return for their help, the confessors are given lighter or suspended sentences, and a promise of confidentiality as to the information provided. One of the conspirators in this case has taken advantage of that cooperation program, but the other conspirators are trying to access the disclosed information. They claim that they need the information to properly prepare their defense. The confessor has insisted that it was promised confidentiality for the information it disclosed. The court must decide which interest prevails.

U.S.A. v. HUI HSIUNG: This is another recent price-fixing case, this one involving Taiwanese and Korean manufacturers of liquid crystal display panels used on many consumer electronics products. It's a criminal case, tried in California, with significant jail time for the managers and fines for the company at stake.

BANCO NACIONAL: This is a famous nationalization case, following the Cuban revolution led by Fidel Castro (the "George Washington of Cuba," per one of my grad school professors!) The U.S. Supreme Court, applying the "Act of State" doctrine, sided with the Cuban Government. The U.S. State Department and Justice Department argued that the doctrine should be respected, and the Supreme Court agreed. Much criticism—from Congress and commentators—followed.

FIRST NATIONAL: The parties are switched in this case. An agency of the Cuban Government (the Banco) is suing to recover the surplus the USA bank (a creditor) realized when it sold the loan collateral. As a counter-claim, the USA bank argues that it is owed money for its assets that were nationalized by the Cuban Government. In this scenario, the U.S. Supreme Court changes its mind about the application of the Act of State doctrine.

HAVANA CLUB: This is a more recent chapter in the (still ongoing) saga of USA/Cuba relations. The key to the decision seems to be the continuing effect of the USA's 1963 embargo, and how it applies to the assignment of a trademark registered in the USA.

AMERICAN INT'L: This time it's the Iranian Revolution that resulted in the nationalization. The Shah had been a close ally of the USA—our "policeman in the Gulf." The USA and Iran had an FCN treaty. The USA insurance company claims that it is not violating the Act of State doctrine; it's not asking a USA court to judge the validity of Iran's nationalization of assets, only asking for compensation—per the FCN treaty. It also argues the Act of State doctrine is not applicable to commercial activity by a government. AIG did get a liability judgment; but actually collecting funds was quite a bit more complicated. A USA/Iran claims commission was eventually established, and several volumes of claims decisions resulted. Relations between the two nations remain problematic to this day (2015).

KALAMAZOO SPICE: This case has a combination of the counter-claim argument and the FCN treaty argument, as exceptions to the application of the Act of State doctrine. Kalamazoo Spice was permitted (by the U.S. 6th Circuit Court of Appeals) to offset its compensation claim for nationalized assets, so as to wipe out what it owed Ethiopia for spices delivered.

EL-SHIFA: Actor Sir Anthony Hopkins, as USA President Richard Nixon, in the movie *Nixon*: "They can't impeach me for bombing Cambodia! The President can bomb whoever he wants!" The U.S. Circuit Court for the Federal Circuit dismissed the claim brought by the pharmaceutical company whose plant had been destroyed in a bombing raid authorized by U.S. President Bill Clinton. The President's "war powers" as Commander-in-Chief of the USA's military are not subject to court review. Their use involves a "political" decision which the courts are neither equipped nor empowered to review. ("Hannibal Lecter" had it right?)

REPUBLIC OF AUSTRIA: This lawsuit is the subject-matter of the film *Woman in Gold*— Maria Altmann's struggle to recover some of the artworks that were stolen from her family by the Nazis before and during World War II. The U.S. Supreme Court's decision that she had a basis to sue the Austrian government in the USA led to Austria's agreement to have the case heard by a panel of three Austrian arbitrators—in Austria (the next case opinion).

ALTMANN: Rather amazingly, perhaps, in view of the Austrian government's repeated refusal to recognize the validity of Maria Altmann's claim, there is no indication that the arbitrators' decision was anything other than unanimous—3-0 for Maria! The US$135,000,000 sale price mentioned in the prior case was paid to Maria by the owner of a USA art gallery, and the *Woman in Gold* painting was put on permanent display in New York City. That was quite possibly the happiest ending this story could have had. The difficulties in obtaining restitution of the thousands of artworks stolen in World War II are detailed in Chapter 28, "Art in Time of War," in Richard J. Evans, *The Third Reich in History and Memory,* New York: Oxford University Press, 2015.

JURISDICTIONAL IMMUNITIES OF THE STATE: The ICJ is presented with the current controversy between the rule of sovereign immunity from suit and the need to provide remedies to victims of war crimes, torture, and the like. The opposing parties are interesting, since they were both members of the Axis coalition during World War II, and both founding members of the EU and NATO.

CASE EXAMPLES:

TIMBERLANE LUMBER CO. v. BANK OF AMERICA
549 F.2d 597 (9th Cir. 1976)

BACKGROUND: Timberlane, a USA corporation, filed an antitrust lawsuit in California, claiming that BoA officials and other persons in the USA and Honduras (including some Honduran government officials) had conspired to prevent Timberlane and its Honduran subsidiaries from processing lumber in Honduras and exporting it to the USA. Some of the defendants moved to dismiss the case. The U.S. District Court did dismiss, based on the "Act of State" doctrine, and also for lack of jurisdiction since there was "no direct and substantial effect on United States foreign commerce." Timberlane appealed the dismissal.

JUDGE CHOY:

"The classic enunciation of the act of state doctrine is found in *Underhill v. Hernandez* …: 'Every sovereign State is bound to respect the independence of every other sovereign State, and the courts of one country will not sit in judgment on the acts of the government of another done within its own territory.'…

"It is apparent that the doctrine does not bestow a blank-check immunity upon all conduct blessed with some imprimatur of a foreign government….

"While we do not wish to impugn or question the nobility of a foreign nation's motivation, we are necessarily interested in the depth and nature of its interest….

"… [W]e conclude that the court below erred in dismissing the instant suit on the authority of *Occidental Petroleum*…. The actions of the Honduran government that are involved here—including the application by its courts and their agents of the Honduran laws concerning security interests and the protection of the underlying property against diminution—are clearly distinguishable from the sovereign decrees laying claim to off-shore waters that were at issue in *Occidental Petroleum*…. Here, the allegedly 'sovereign' acts of Honduras consisted of judicial proceedings which were initiated by Caminals, a private party and one of the alleged co-conspirators, not by the Honduran government itself. Unlike the *Occidental Petroleum* plaintiffs … Timberlane does not seek to name Honduras or any Honduran officer as a defendant or co-conspirator, nor does it challenge Honduran policy or sovereignty in any fashion that appears on its face to hold any threat to relations between Honduras and the United States. In fact, there is no indication that the actions of the Honduran court or authorities reflected a sovereign decision that Timberlane's efforts should be crippled or that trade with the United States should be restrained…. Moreover … plaintiffs here apparently complain of additional agreements and actions which are totally unrelated to the Honduran government. These separate activities would clearly be unprotected even if procurement of a Honduran act of state were one part of defendants' overall scheme….

"Under these circumstances, it is clear that the 'act of state' doctrine does not require dismissal of the Timberlane action….

"There is no doubt that American antitrust laws extend over some conduct in other nations….

"That American law covers some conduct beyond this nation's borders does not mean that it embraces all, however. Extraterritorial application is understandably a matter of concern for the other countries involved. Those nations have sometimes resented and protested, as excessive intrusions into their own spheres, broad assertions of authority by American courts…. Our courts have recognized this concern and have, at times, responded to it, even if not always enough to satisfy all the foreign critics…. In any event, it is evident that at some point the interests of the United States are too weak and the foreign harmony incentive too strong to justify an extraterritorial assertion of jurisdiction.

"What that point is or how it is determined is not defined by international law…. Nor does the Sherman Act limit itself. In the domestic field the Sherman Act extends to the full reach of the commerce power. To define it somewhat more modestly in the foreign commerce area courts have generally, and logically, fallen back on a narrower construction of congressional intent….

"It is the effect on American foreign commerce which is usually cited to support extraterritorial jurisdiction. *Alcoa* set the course, when Judge Hand declared … 'It is settled law … that any state may impose liabilities, even upon persons not within its allegiance, for conduct outside its borders that has consequences within its borders which the state reprehends; and these liabilities other states will ordinarily recognize.' Despite its description as 'settled law,' *Alcoa's* assertion has been roundly disputed by many foreign commentators as being in conflict with international law, comity, and good judgment. Nonetheless, American courts have firmly concluded that there is some extraterritorial jurisdiction under the Sherman Act….

"Few cases have discussed the nature of the effect required for jurisdiction, perhaps because most of the litigated cases have involved relatively obvious offenses and rather significant and apparent effects on competition within the United States…. It is probably in part because the standard has not often been put to a real test that it seems so poorly defined….

"The effects test by itself is incomplete because it fails to consider the other nation's interests. Nor does it expressly take into account the full nature of the relationship between the actors and this country. Whether the alleged offender is an American citizen, for instance, may make a big difference; applying American laws to American citizens raises fewer problems than application to foreigners….

"A tripartite analysis seems to be indicated. [T]he antitrust laws require in the first instance that there be *some* effect—actual or intended—on American foreign commerce before the federal courts may legitimately exercise subject matter jurisdiction under those statutes. Second, a greater showing of burden or restraint may be necessary to demonstrate that the effect is sufficiently large to present a cognizable injury to the plaintiffs and, therefore, a civil *violation* of the antitrust laws…. Third, there is the additional question which is unique to the international setting of whether the interests of, and links to, the United States—including the magnitude of the effect on American foreign commerce—are sufficiently strong, vis-à-vis those of other nations, to justify an assertion of extraterritorial authority.

"It is this final issue which is both obscured by under reliance on the 'substantiality' test and complicated to resolve. An effect on United States commerce, although necessary to the exercise of jurisdiction under the antitrust laws, is alone not a sufficient basis on which to determine whether American authority *should* be asserted in a given case as a matter of international comity and fairness…. A more comprehensive inquiry is necessary….

"The elements to be weighed include the degree of conflict with foreign law or policy, the nationality or allegiance of the parties and their principal places of business of corporations, the extent to which enforcement by either state can be expected to achieve compliance, the relative significance of effects on the United States as compared with those elsewhere, the extent to which there is explicit purpose to harm or affect American commerce, the foreseeability of such effect, and the relative importance to the violations charged of conduct with the United States as compared with conduct abroad. A court evaluating these factors should identify the potential degree of conflict if American authority is asserted. A difference in law or policy is one likely sore spot, though one which may not always be present. Nationality is another; though foreign governments may have some concern for the treatment of American citizens and business residing there, they primarily care about their own nationals. Having assessed the conflict, the court should then determine whether in the face of it the contacts and interests of the United States are sufficient to support the exercise of extraterritorial jurisdiction….

"… The district court's judgment found only that the restraint involved in the instant suit did not produce a direct and substantial effect on America's foreign commerce. That holding does not satisfy any of these inquiries.

"The Sherman Act is not limited to trade restraints which have both a direct and substantial

425

effect on our foreign commerce. Timberlane has alleged that the complained of activities were intended to, and did, affect the export of lumber from Honduras to the United States—the flow of United States foreign commerce, and as such they are within the jurisdiction of the federal courts under the Sherman Act. Moreover, the magnitude of the effect alleged would appear to be sufficient to state a claim....

"The comity question is more complicated. From Timberlane's complaint it is evident that there are grounds for concern as to at least a few of the defendants, for some are identified as foreign citizens.... Moreover, it is clear that most of the activity took place in Honduras, though the conspiracy may have been directed from San Francisco, and that the most direct economic effect was probably on Honduras. However, there has been no indication of any conflict with the law or policy of the Honduran government, nor any comprehensive analysis of the relative connections and interests of Honduras and the United States. Under these circumstances, the dismissal by the district court cannot be sustained on jurisdictional grounds.

"We, therefore, reverse and remand the Timberlane action."

PFIZER INC. v. GOVERNMENT OF INDIA
434 U.S. 308 (1978)

BACKGROUND: Alleging that Pfizer and several other drug makers had engaged in illegal price-fixing and market-division, the governments of India, Iran and the Philippines filed antitrust cases in U.S. District Courts. Their cases were consolidated for trial in the U.S. District Court for Minnesota. The governments asked for treble damages for themselves and for groups of buyers in their countries. The drug makers argued that governments of foreign nations were not intended to be included as "persons" who had the right to sue for "treble" damages under Section 4 of the Clayton Antitrust Act. The U.S. District Court refused to dismiss these triple damages claims, and the U.S. Eighth Circuit Court of Appeals affirmed. The drug companies asked for U.S. Supreme Court review.

JUSTICE STEWART:

"[W]hether a foreign nation is entitled to sue for treble damages depends upon whether it is a 'person' as that word is used in S.4. There is no clear statutory provision or legislative history that provides a clear answer; it seems apparent that the question was never considered at the time the Sherman and Clayton Acts were enacted.

"Th[is] Court has previously noted the broad scope of the remedies provided by the antitrust laws. 'The Act is comprehensive in its terms and coverage, protecting all who are made victims of the forbidden practices by whomever they may be perpetrated.' ... And the legislative history of the Sherman Act demonstrates that Congress used the phrase 'any person' intending it to have its naturally broad and inclusive meaning. There was no mention in the floor debates of any more restrictive definition. Indeed, during the course of those debates the word 'person' was used interchangeably with other terms even broader in connotation. For example, Senator Sherman said that the treble-damages remedy was being given to 'any party,' and Senator Edmunds, one of the principal draftsmen of the final bill, said that it established 'the right of anybody to sue who chooses to sue.' ...

"The [plaintiffs] ... possess two attributes that could arguably exclude them from the scope of the sweeping phrase 'any person.' They are foreign, and they are sovereign nations.

"... Yet it is clear that a foreign corporation is entitled to sue for treble damages, since the definition of 'person' contained in the Sherman and Clayton Acts explicitly includes 'corporations and associations existing under or authorized by ... the laws of any foreign country.'... Moreover, the antitrust laws extend to trade 'with foreign nations' as well as among the several States of the Union.... Clearly, therefore, Congress did not intend to make the treble-damages remedy available only to consumers in our own country....

"Moreover, an exclusion of all foreign plaintiffs would lessen the deterrent effect of treble damages. The conspiracy alleged ... operated domestically as well as internationally. If foreign plaintiffs were not permitted to seek a remedy for their antitrust injuries, persons doing business both in this country and abroad might be tempted to enter into anticompetitive conspiracies affecting American consumers in the expectation that the profits they could safely extort abroad would offset any liability to plaintiffs at home. If, on the other hand, potential antitrust violators must take into account the full costs of their conduct, American consumers are benefited by the maximum deterrent effect of treble damages upon all potential violators....

"On the two previous occasions that the Court has considered whether a sovereign government is a 'person' under the antitrust laws, the mechanical rule urged by the [defendants] has been rejected....

"It is clear that ... the Court [has] rejected the proposition that the word 'person' as used in the antitrust laws excludes all sovereign states. And the [Court's] reasoning ... leads to the conclusion that a foreign nation, like a domestic State, is entitled to pursue the remedy of treble damages when it has been injured in its business or property by antitrust violations. When a foreign nation enters our commercial markets as a purchaser of goods or services, it can be victimized by anticompetitive practices just as surely as a private person or a domestic State. The antitrust laws provide no alternative remedies for foreign nations as they do for the United States [national government]....

"The result we reach does not involve any novel concept of the jurisdiction of the federal courts....

"Finally, the result we reach does not require the Judiciary in any way to interfere in sensitive matters of foreign policy....

"Accordingly, the judgment of the Court of Appeals is

"Affirmed."

BRITISH AIRWAYS BOARD v. LAKER AIRWAYS LTD. AND OTHERS
[1985] AC 58 (House of Lords 1985)

BACKGROUND: Transatlantic air services between the USA and the UK were regulated under a treaty known as "Bermuda 2" which gave each nation the right to designate airlines of its own nationality to fly particular routes between the two countries. Each nation's airline board approved fares for its carriers. British Airways ("BA"), British Caledonian ("BC"), and Laker were UK airlines competing in this market. In 1977 Laker introduced "Skytrain," a low-cost scheduled service. Laker later encountered financial difficulties and went into liquidation.

Claiming that it had been the victim of an anti-competitive conspiracy between BA and BC, Laker filed an antitrust lawsuit in the USA, asking for $350 million in damages (which would be automatically tripled if Laker proved its case), and asking for another $700 million based on "intentional tort." BA and BC sued Laker in England, asking that Laker be enjoined from continuing with the USA lawsuit. That request was denied, but the Queen's Bench did issue an interim injunction ordering Laker not to proceed with its lawsuit until BA/BC could get a ruling on their appeal from the Queen's Bench denial of the injunction. Meanwhile, pursuant to the UK's 1980 Protection of Trading Interests Act, the UK Secretary of State for Trade and Industry had issued orders prohibiting BA and BC from complying with any orders of the U.S. District Court hearing Laker's lawsuit. At the appeal, BA and BC relied on the Secretary's order, and Laker asked for judicial review of the validity of the Secretary's order. After review, the UK Court of Appeals "allowed" the appeals by BA and BC ("relief of the nature sought by BA and BC should be granted"), and dismissed Laker's application for judicial review of the

Secretary's order. Laker appealed both rulings to the House of Lords.

LORD DIPLOCK:

"My Lords, there are two propositions, one of American law and thus of fact, the other of English law, which, if correct, are in my view decisive of the appeals in both the civil actions without its being necessary for your Lordships to make detailed reference to the multitudinous documents which this litigation has already generated.

"Upon the first proposition, that of American law, not only is the expert evidence all one way but it is also common ground between the parties, that if the allegations made against B.A. and B.C. in the complaint in the American action can be proved at the trial they disclose a cause of action by Laker against B.A. and B.C. under the antitrust law of the United States ... which falls within the jurisdiction of the Federal District Court for the District of Columbia within whose territorial area both B.A. and B.C. have premises at which they carry on business. Indeed, Judge Greene, the judge of the District Court who has been in charge of the pre-trial proceedings in the American action, regards the complaint as being of a kind so commonplace that he describes it as an antitrust action of 'the garden variety,' a description which embraces the alternative was of pleading the antitrust cause of action as a count for 'intentional tort.'

"The second proposition, that of English law, was understood by your Lordships to have been common ground between the parties ... no argument casting any doubt upon it was advanced. The proposition is that, even if the allegations against B.A. and B.C. in the complaint in the American action can be proved, they disclose no cause of action on the part of Laker against B.A. or B.C. that is justiciable in an English court. The Clayton Act which creates the civil remedy with threefold damages for criminal offenses under the Sherman Act is, under English rules of conflict of laws, purely territorial in its application, while because the predominant purpose of acts of B.A. and B.C. that are complained of was the defence of their own business interests as providers of scheduled airline services on routes on which Laker was seeking to attract customers from them by operating its Skytrain policy, any English cause of action for conspiracy would be ruled out under the now well-established principle of English (as well as Scots) law laid down in a series of cases in this House spanning 50 years....

"In the result your Lordships are confronted in the civil actions [by B.A. and B.C., seeking to enjoin Laker from pursuing its USA lawsuit] with a case in which there is a single forum only that is of competent jurisdiction to determine the merits of the claim; and the single forum is a foreign court. For an English court to enjoin a claimant from having access to that foreign court is, in effect, to take upon itself a one-sided jurisdiction to determine the claim upon the merits against the claimant but also to prevent its being decided on the merits in his favour. This poses a novel problem, different in kind from that involved where there are alternative fora in which a particular civil claim can be pursued: an English court and a court of some foreign country both of which are recognised under English rules of conflict of laws as having jurisdiction to entertain proceedings against a defendant for a remedy for acts or omissions which constitute an actionable wrong under the substantive law of both England and that foreign country…

"Broadly speaking, the aim of bipartite treaties such as Bermuda 2 which are entered into by the United Kingdom with foreign states is to secure that the obligations imposed by domestic law of one state upon operators of scheduled services upon routes between the two states that are parties to the treaty shall be the same as, or, at any rate, shall not conflict with, the obligations imposed upon those operators by the domestic law of the other party to the treaty; but whether the treaty has achieved this aim so far as it applies to the operations of designated British airlines within the territorial jurisdiction of the United States is not a question that an English court has jurisdiction to determine, since Bermuda 2 forms no part of English law. What is relevant for present purposes is that the domestic law of the United States includes the U.S. antitrust laws embodied in the Sherman and Clayton Acts as those Acts of Congress have been so expansively interpreted by the U.S. courts, as well as including the Federal Aviation Act of 1958 and the Bermuda 2 treaty itself which, in contrast to the position under United Kingdom law, is under the Constitution of the United States of direct application as part of the American domestic law….

"My Lords, by obtaining an air transport license from [the U.K.'s] C.A.A. to operate scheduled services on routes between the United Kingdom and the United States as British airlines designated by the United Kingdom under Bermuda 2, B.A., B.C. and Laker alike voluntarily submitted themselves to a regulatory regime which, so far as their operations within the territorial jurisdiction of the United States were concerned, required that each of them should become subject to American domestic law including American antitrust laws. In the circumstances as I have outlined them, it seems to me to be impossible to argue plausibly either that Laker by submitting itself to such a regime precluded itself form relying upon any cause of action against B.A. or B.C. that might accrue to it under American antitrust laws as a result of what these airlines subsequently did within the territorial jurisdiction of the United States; or that there was anything so unconscionable or unjust in Laker's conduct in pursuing such cause of action in a U.S. court that an English judge, in the proper exercise of a judicial discretion, would be entitled to grant an injunction to prevent Laker from doing so….

"My Lords, I can now turn to the steps taken by the Secretary of State under the Protection of Trading Interests Act 1980, in the interval between the judgment by Parker J. and the hearing of the Court of Appeal….

"Since Laker alleged that the Order and both directions were ultra vires [outside the Secretary's power] and its application for judicial review of them was disposed of by the Court of Appeal at the same time as the appeals in the civil actions an excursus on the validity of the Order and directions seems appropriate at this point though it need only be short.

"The first submission made on behalf of Laker was that the expression 'measures … taken by or under the law of any overseas country' (Act of 1980, section 1(1)(a)) is not wide enough to include measures which take the form of legislation. This seems to me to be so plainly wrong as not to merit reasoned refutation. I content myself with expressing my agreement with what was said in the judgment of the Court of Appeal … in answer to this argument….

"… [A] decision reached by a person upon whom a statute confers a discretion to exercise coercive powers over individuals may be held by a court of law to be ultra vires if it be established to the satisfaction of the court upon an application for judicial review that the decision is one no reasonable person holding the office of minister upon whom the discretion is conferred could have reached. Where the decision is one which concerns international relations between the United Kingdom and a foreign sovereign state a very strong case needs to be made out to justify a court of law in holding the decision to be ultra vires…. In the instant case, I agree with the Court of Appeal that Laker does not come anywhere near doing so….

"For my part, I should allow Laker's appeals in both civil actions and discharge the injunction granted by the Court of Appeal. I should dismiss Laker's appeal in the application for judicial review against the Secretary of State."

MATSUSHITA ELECTRIC INDUS. v. ZENITH RADIO CORP.
475 U.S. 574 (1986)

BACKGROUND: After several years in which USA manufacturers of TVs lost significant market share to Japanese competitors, Zenith and several others filed an antitrust case in U.S. District Court in Pennsylvania in 1974. Naming twenty-one Japanese and Japanese-controlled TV makers, plaintiffs alleged a conspiracy to restrain trade in violation of the Sherman Antitrust Act, price discrimination in violation of the Clayton Act as amended by the Robinson-Patman Act, and other illegal activities. After "several years of detailed discovery," evidence showed an agreement in Japan that each Japanese manufacturer would have only five USA distributors, and that the Japanese Ministry of Trade and Industry (MITI) had established or helped to establish minimum prices for TVs exported for sale in the USA. In 1981, the U.S. District Court granted the Japanese defendants' motion for summary judgment, but the U.S. Third Circuit Court of Appeals reversed, holding that there was a material issue of fact that required a trial. Matsushita and the other defendants asked for Supreme Court review. (In support of their arguments to the Supreme Court, the parties filed a 40-*volume* "appendix" of evidence produced by the trial.)

JUSTICE POWELL:

"We begin by emphasizing what [Zenith's] claim is *not*. [Zenith] cannot recover antitrust damages based solely on an alleged cartelization of the Japanese market, because American antitrust laws do not regulate competitive conditions of other nations' economies…. Nor can [Zenith] recover damages for any conspiracy by [Matsushita] to charge higher than competitive prices in the American market. Such conduct would indeed violate the Sherman Act … but it would not injure [Zenith]: as [Matsushita's] competitors, [Zenith et al.] stand to gain from any conspiracy to raise the market price…. Finally, for the same reason, [Zenith] cannot recover for a conspiracy to impose nonprice restraints that have the effect of either raising market price or limiting output. Such restrictions, though harmful to competition, actually *benefit* competitors by making supracompetitive pricing more attractive. Thus, neither [Matsushita's] alleged supracompetitive pricing in Japan, nor the five company rule that limited distribution in this country, nor the check prices insofar as they established minimum prices in this country, can by themselves give [Zenith] a cognizable claim again [Matsushita] for antitrust damages. The Court of Appeals therefore erred to the extent that it found evidence of these alleged conspiracies to be 'direct evidence' of a conspiracy that injured [Zenith]….

"… According to [Matsushita], the alleged conspiracy is one that is economically irrational and practically infeasible. Consequently, [they] contend, they had no motive to engage in the alleged predatory pricing conspiracy; indeed, they had a strong motive *not* to conspire in the manner [Zenith et al.] allege. [They] argue that, in light of the absence of any apparent motive and the ambiguous nature of the evidence of conspiracy, no trier of fact could find that the alleged conspiracy with which [they] are charged actually existed….

"The alleged conspiracy's failure to achieve its ends in the two decades of its asserted operation is strong evidence that the conspiracy does not in fact exist. Since the losses in such a conspiracy [to engage in predatory pricing] accrue before its gains, they must be repaid with interest….

"Nor does the possibility that [Matsushita et al.] have obtained supracompetitive profits in the Japanese market change this calculation. Whether or not [defendants] have the *means* to sustain substantial losses in this country over a long period of time, they have no *motive* to sustain such losses absent some strong likelihood that the alleged conspiracy in this country will eventually pay off. The courts below have found no evidence of any such success, and … the facts are actually to the contrary: RCA and Zenith, not any of the [defendants], continue to hold the largest share of the American retail market in color television sets. More important, there is nothing to suggest any relationship between [Matsushita's] profits in Japan and the amount [they] could expect to gain from a conspiracy to monopolize the American market. In the absence of any such evidence, the possible existence of supracompetitive profits in Japan simply cannot overcome the economic obstacles to the ultimate success of this alleged predatory conspiracy….

"On remand, the Court of Appeals is free to consider whether there is other evidence that is sufficiently unambiguous to permit a trier of fact to find that [Matsushita] conspired to price predatorily for two decades despite the absence of any apparent motive to do so…. In the absence of such evidence, there is no 'genuine issue for trial' … and [Matsushita et al.] are entitled to have summary judgment reinstated….

"The decision of the Court of Appeals is reversed, and the case is remanded for further proceedings consistent with this opinion.

"*It is so ordered.*"

UNITED STATES OF AMERICA v. ANDREAS and WILSON
216 F.3d 645 (7th Cir. 2000)

FACTS: "The defendants in this case, Andreas and Wilson, were executives at Archer Daniels Midland Co., the Decatur, Illinois-based agriculture processing company. Mark E. Whitacre, the third ADM executive named in the indictment, did not join this appeal. ADM, the self-professed 'supermarket to the world,' is a behemoth in its industry with global sales of $14 billion in 1999 and 23,000 employees. Its concerns include nearly every farm commodity, such as corn, soybeans and wheat, but also the processing of commodities into such products as fuel ethanol, high-fructose sweeteners, feed additives and various types of seed oils. ADM has a worldwide sales force and a global transportation network involving thousands of rail lines, barges and trucks. The company is publicly held and listed on the New York Stock Exchange….

"The Andreas family has long controlled ADM. Dwayne Andreas is a director and the former CEO, G. Allen Andreas is the board chairman and president, and various other family members occupy other executive positions. Michael D. Andreas, commonly called 'Mick,' was vice chairman of the board of directors and executive vice president of sales and marketing. Wilson was president of the corn processing division and reported directly to Michael Andreas….

"Lysine is an amino acid used to stimulate an animal's growth. It is produced by a fermentation

433

process in which nutrients, primarily sugar, are fed to microorganisms, which multiply and metabolize. As a product of that process, the microorganisms excrete lysine, which is then harvested and sold to feed manufacturers who add it to animal feed. Feed manufacturers sell the feed to farmers who use it to raise chickens and pigs. The fermentation process tends to be very delicate, and utmost care must be used to keep the fermentation plant sterile.

"Until 1991, the lysine market had been dominated by a cartel of three companies in Korea and Japan, with American and European subsidiaries. Ajinomoto Co., Inc. of Japan, was the industry leader, accounting for up to half of all world lysine sales. Ajinomoto had 50 percent interests in two subsidiaries, Eurolysine, based in Paris, and Heartland Lysine, based in Chicago. The other two producers of lysine were Miwon Co., Ltd. (later renamed Sewon Co., Ltd.) of South Korea, and Kyowa Hakko, Ltd. of Japan. Miwon ran a New Jersey-based subsidiary called Sewon America, and Kyowa owned the American subsidiary Biokyowa, Inc., which is based in Missouri.

"Lysine is a highly fungible commodity and sold almost entirely on the basis of price. Pricing depended largely on two variables: the price of organic substitutes, such as soy or fish meal, and the price charged by other lysine producers. Together, the three parent companies produced all of the world's lysine until the 1990s, presenting an obvious opportunity for collusive behavior. Indeed the Asian cartel periodically agreed to fix prices, which at times reached as high as $3.00 per pound.

"In 1989, ADM announced that it was building what would be the world's largest lysine plant. If goals were met, the Illinois facility could produce two or three times as much lysine as any other plant and could ultimately account for up to half of all the lysine produced globally. Even before the plant became operational, ADM embarked on an ambitious marketing campaign aimed at attracting large American meat companies, such as Tyson Foods, in part by capitalizing on anti-Asia sentiment prevalent at the time. Also around 1990, another South Korean company, Cheil Jedang Co., began producing lysine. Despite some early difficulties with the fermenting process, the ADM plant began producing lysine in 1991 and immediately became a market heavyweight, possibly even the industry leader. The two new producers created chaos in the market, igniting a price war that drove the price of lysine down, eventually to about 70-cents per pound. The Asian companies understandably were greatly concerned by developments in this once profitable field.

"Against this background, Kyowa Hakko arranged a meeting with Ajinomoto and ADM in June 1992. Mexico City was chosen as the site in part because the participants did not want to meet within the jurisdiction of American antitrust laws. Ajinomoto was represented by Kanji Mimoto and Hirokazu Ikeda from the Tokyo headquarters, and Alain Crouy from its Eurolysine subsidiary. Masaru Yamamoto represented Kyowa Hakko, and Wilson and Whitacre attended for

434

ADM. Mimoto, Ikeda, Crouy and Yamamoto testified as government witnesses at trial. At this meeting, the three companies first discussed price agreements and allocating sales volumes among the market participants. Wilson, who was senior to Whitacre in the corporate hierarchy, led the discussion on behalf of ADM. The price agreements came easily, and all present agreed to raise the price in two stages by the end of 1992. According to internal Ajinomoto documents prepared after the meeting, the cartel's goal was to raise the price to $1.05 per pound in North America and Europe by October 1992 and up to $1.20 per pound by December, with other price hikes for other regions. The companies agreed to that price schedule and presumed that Ajinomoto and Kyowa would convince Sewon and Cheil to agree as well.

"The sales volume allocation, in which the cartel (now including ADM) would decide how much each company would sell, was a matter of strong disagreement. In ADM's view, ADM should have one-third of the market, Ajinomoto and its subsidiaries should have one-third and Kyowa and the Koreans should have the remaining third. Ajinomoto—the historical industry leader—disagreed vehemently and thought ADM did not deserve an equal portion of the market and could not produce that much lysine in any case. Wilson also suggested each company pick an auditor to whom sales volumes could be reported so that the cartel could keep track of each other's business. The meeting ended without a sales volume allocation agreement, but two months later, at the recommendation of Whitacre, the cartel raised prices anyway, and prices rose from $.70 to $1.05 per pound.

"Still, the cartel considered a price agreement without allocating sales volume to be an imperfect scheme because each company would have an incentive to cheat on the price to get more sales, so long as its competitors continued to sell at the agreed price. With cheating, the price ultimately would drop, and the agreement would falter. An effort had to be made to get the parties to agree to a volume agreement, and to that end, Whitacre invited Ajinomoto officials to visit ADM's Decatur lysine facility to prove that it could produce the volume ADM claimed. Mimoto, Ikeda and other Ajinomoto officials, including an engineer named Fujiwara, visited the plant in September 1992. At a meeting before the tour, Whitacre and Mimoto confirmed the price schedule to which the parties had agreed in Mexico City.

"The cartel met again in October 1992, this time in Paris. All five major lysine producers attended, along with representatives of their subsidiaries. Wilson and Whitacre again represented ADM. To disguise the purpose of the meeting, the parties created a fake agenda, and later a fictitious lysine producers trade association, so they could meet and share information without raising the suspicions of customers or law enforcement agencies. According to the agenda, the group was to discuss such topics as animal rights and the environment. In reality, they discussed something much dearer to their hearts—the price of lysine. According to internal Ajinomoto documents, the 'purpose of the meeting" was to 'confirm present price level and reaction of the market, and 2, future price schedule.'

"Shortly after this meeting … Whitacre began cooperating with the FBI in an undercover sting operation aimed at busting the price-fixing conspiracy. As a result, most of the meetings and telephone conversations involving Whitacre and other conspirators after October 1992 were audiotaped or videotaped.

"Despite the cartel's efforts to raise prices, the price of lysine dropped in 1993. According to executives of the companies who testified at trial, without a sales volume agreement, each company had an incentive to underbid the agreed price, and consequently each company had to match the lower bids or lose sales to its underbidding competitors. This resulted in the price of lysine falling in the spring of 1993. The group, calling itself 'G-5' or 'the club,' met in Vancouver, Canada, in June 1993 to deal with the disintegrating price agreement. Wilson and Whitacre again represented ADM. At this meeting, the Asian companies presented a sales volume allocation that limited each company to a certain tonnage of lysine per year. ADM, through Wilson, rejected the suggested tonnage assignment because it granted ADM less than one-third of the market. Ajinomoto still considered ADM's demands too high.

"That summer's strong commodities market permitted frequent increases in the lysine price, to which each of the companies agreed, despite the absence of a volume allocation. The cartel's continued strong interest in a volume allocation to support the price agreement led to another meeting in Paris in October 1993. The failure to reach a volume schedule in Paris finally led to a call for a meeting between the top management at Ajinomoto and ADM: Kazutoshi Yamada and Mick Andreas.

"In October 1993, Andreas and Whitacre met with Yamada and Ikeda in Irvine, California. With Whitacre's assistance, the meeting was secretly videotaped and audiotaped. Andreas threatened Yamada that ADM would flood the market unless a sales volume allocation agreement was reached that would allow ADM to sell more than it had the previous year. The four discussed the dangers of competing in a free market and hammered out a deal on volume allocations, with Andreas accepting less than a one-third share of the market in exchange for a large portion of the market's growth. Specific prices were not discussed, but Andreas acknowledged the price deal that had already been negotiated. Yamada agreed to present ADM's proposal to the other three Asian producers.

"A central concern to Andreas was the difficulty he expected the Asian producers to encounter in maintaining their agreed price level. As Andreas explained at some length, the Asian companies had a more decentralized sales system that depended on agents making deals with customers. ADM featured a very centralized system in which agents played a small role in overall sales and had no discretion over price. In such an environment, maintaining control over price was easy; for the Japanese, Andreas feared it would be difficult and suggested that Ajinomoto move to a more ADM-like centralized pricing system. Andreas also expressed concern that customers could "cheat" the producers by bargaining down the price, apparently by claiming to have received lower bids from competing producers. Ikeda and Yamada agreed that customer cheating was a problem, and the four briefly discussed a quick-response system that would allow the producers to verify with each other the prices offered to particular customers.

"After the Irvine meeting, the cartel met in Tokyo to work out the details of the Andreas-Yamada arrangement. All the companies except for Cheil now agreed to both tonnage maximums and percentage market shares. The group excluded Cheil from this discussion because it considered Cheil's volume demand unreasonable. The cartel, expecting the lysine market to grow in 1994, thought it wise to agree on percentages of the market that each company could have since it was possible that all five producers could sell more than their allotted tonnage. With a total expected market of 245,000 tons for 1994, Ajinomoto was to sell 84,000 tons, ADM would sell 67,000 tons, Kyowa would sell 46,000 tons, Miwon would sell 34,000 tons and Cheil, if it eventually accepted the deal, would get 14,000 tons, according to the deal hammered out by Yamada and Andreas in Irvine.

"As they had before the Andreas-Yamada meeting, Wilson and Whitacre attended these Tokyo meetings for ADM. In Tokyo, Wilson suggested, and the members agreed, that each producer report their monthly sales figures by telephone to Mimoto throughout the year, and if one producer exceeded its allocation, it would compensate the others by buying enough from the shorted members to even out the allocation. The producers also agreed on a new price of $1.20 for the United States market. The agreement to buy each other's unsold allocation cemented the deal by eliminating any incentive for a company to underbid the sales price. According to Mimoto: 'Since there is an agreement on the quantity allocation, our sales quantity is guaranteed by other manufacturers of the lysine. So by matching the price, to us, lowering the price is very silly. We can just keep the price.' With the agreement on prices and quantities in place, the lysine price remained at the agreed level for January and February 1994.

"On March 10, 1994, the cartel met in Hawaii. At this meeting, attended by Wilson and Whitacre on behalf of ADM, the producers discussed the progress of the volume allocation agreement, reported their sales figures and agreed on prices. They also considered letting Cheil into the allocation agreement and agreed to grant the company a market share of 17,000 tons. Cheil accepted this arrangement at a meeting later that day, at which Wilson explained that the conspiracy would operate almost identically to the scheme used to fix prices in the citric-acid market. The cartel further agreed on prices for Europe, South America, Asia and the rest of the world, and discussed how the global allocations would work on a regional basis. According to the figures reported to Mimoto through May 1994, prices were maintained, and both ADM and Ajinomoto were on track to meet their sales volume limits.

"In the summer of 1994, the producers met in Sapporo, Japan, for a routine cartel meeting. Whitacre represented ADM by himself. At this meeting, Sewon demanded a larger share of the market for 1995. This created a problem for the cartel, which necessitated another meeting between Andreas and Yamada. In October 1994, while on a separate business trip to the United States, Yamada met with Andreas in a private dining room at the Four Seasons Hotel in Chicago. Whitacre, Wilson and Mimoto also attended along with their bosses.

"The cartel met in Atlanta in January 1995, using a major poultry exposition as camouflage for the producers being in the same place at the same time. The cartel, without the presence of Sewon, decided to cut Sewon out of the agreement for 1995 because of its unrealistic volume demand. Sewon then joined the meeting and agreed to abide by the set price, if not the volume. The group discussed the year-end sales figures for 1994, comparing them to each company's allocated volume, and discussed the new allotment for 1995. According to the 1994 numbers, each company finished fairly close to its allotted volume. The cartel met once more in Hong Kong before the FBI raided the offices of ADM in Decatur and Heartland Lysine in Chicago. These raids ended the cartel. Heartland Lysine immediately notified its home office in Japan of the search, and Ajinomoto began destroying evidence of the cartel housed in its Tokyo office. Mimoto overlooked documents stored at his home and later turned these over to the FBI. Included in these saved documents were copies of internal Ajinomoto reports of the Mexico and Paris meetings.

"Mark E. Whitacre joined ADM in 1989 as president of its bioproducts division. That year, ADM announced that it would enter the lysine market dominated by Asian producers. Whitacre, who held a Ph.D. in biochemistry from Cornell University and degrees in agricultural science, answered directly to Mick Andreas. Just 32 years old when he joined the company, Whitacre's star clearly was rising fast at ADM, and some industry analysts thought he could be the next president of ADM.

"In 1992, Whitacre began working with Wilson, and the two attended the first meetings of the lysine producers in Mexico City. Also in 1992, Whitacre began embezzling large sums of money from ADM and eventually stole at least $9 million from the company by submitting to ADM phony invoices for work done by outside companies, who would then funnel the money to Whitacre's personal offshore and Swiss bank accounts. To cover up the embezzlement, Whitacre hatched a scheme in the summer of 1992 to accuse Ajinomoto of planting a saboteur in ADM's Decatur plant. Whitacre would accuse the saboteur of contaminating the delicate bacterial environment needed for the production of lysine, a story made believable because of the many early difficulties the ADM lysine plant encountered.

"In accordance with the plot, Whitacre told Mick Andreas that an engineer at Ajinomoto named Fujiwara had contacted him at his home and offered to sell ADM the name of the saboteur in exchange for $10 million. The story was a lie. However, Dwayne Andreas believed it and feared it could jeopardize relations between the United States and Japan. He called the CIA, but the CIA, considering the matter one of federal law enforcement rather than national security, directed the call to the FBI, which sent agents out to ADM to interview Whitacre and other officials about the extortion. Whitacre apparently had not expected this and realized quickly that his lie would be discovered by the FBI, particularly after Special Agent Brian Shepard asked Whitacre if he could tap Whitacre's home telephone to record the next extortion demand. Whitacre knew that when the extortionist failed to call, Shepard would know Whitacre had invented the story. Whitacre confessed the scheme to Shepard, but to save himself, he agreed to become an undercover informant to help the FBI investigate price fixing at ADM. He did not come totally clean with the FBI, however; he failed to mention the millions he embezzled and in fact continued to embezzle after he began working for the government. For the next two-and-a-half years, Whitacre acted as an undercover cooperating witness—legally a government agent—and secretly taped hundreds of hours of conversations and meetings with Wilson, Mick Andreas and the other conspirators. In addition, the FBI secretly videotaped meetings of the lysine producers.

"The jury convicted the three defendants on the single-count conspiracy indictment .... United States Sentencing Guidelines ... mandated a base-offense level of ten and a seven-level increase because the volume of commerce affected was more than $100 million.... [T]he applicable range under the Guidelines for an offense level of seventeen was twenty-four to thirty months. The Presentence Investigation Reports (PSR) recommended a four-level increase for Andreas and three-level increase for Wilson based on their leadership roles in the conspiracy, pursuant to U.S.S.G. The court rejected the leadership role enhancements because it found that Wilson and Andreas were no more culpable than their co-conspirators. The court then sentenced each defendant to twenty-four months in prison."

OPINION by *Judge KANNE*:

"For many years, Archer Daniels Midland Co.'s philosophy of customer relations could be summed up by a quote from former ADM President James Randall: 'Our competitors are our friends. Our customers are the enemy.' This motto animated the company's business dealings and ultimately led to blatant violations of U.S. antitrust law, a guilty plea and a staggering criminal fine against the company. It also led to the criminal charges against three top ADM executives that are the subject of this appeal. The facts involved in this case reflect an inexplicable lack of business ethics and an atmosphere of general lawlessness that infected the very heart of one of America's leading corporate citizens. Top executives at ADM and its Asian co-conspirators throughout the early 1990s spied on each other, fabricated aliases and front organizations to hide their activities, hired prostitutes to gather information from competitors, lied, cheated, embezzled, extorted and obstructed justice....

"On appeal, Andreas and Wilson raise ten issues including, among others, challenges to evidentiary rulings, the sufficiency of the evidence and the calculation of their sentences under the Sentencing Guidelines. The government appeals only one ruling, the denial of an upward adjustment for the defendants' leadership roles in the crime....

"The defendants claim the admission of the tapes violated their due process rights because the FBI failed to supervise Whitacre adequately, badly mismanaged the two-year taping operation and because Whitacre had ulterior motives for acting as a mole, thereby rendering the tapes so unreliable as to make them constitutionally defective.... After holding an evidentiary hearing, the trial court denied the defendants' motions to suppress the tape recordings....

"... The government established the accuracy of the recordings through witnesses who attended the meetings, and defense counsel took full advantage of the opportunity to *voir dire* and cross-examine these witnesses on the truth, accuracy and meaning of the tapes. A tape expert testified that although some of the tapes had been reused, none of the conversations on the tapes had been altered or edited in any way. We see no 'extraordinary circumstances' (in fact, no circumstances whatsoever) that would cause us to reverse the trial court's decision to admit the tapes....

"The defendants further contend that the tape recordings violated federal wiretap laws, and therefore must be excluded from trial based on 18 U.S.C. § 2515, which prohibits the evidentiary use of any illegally obtained tape recording. Two exceptions to § 2515 potentially apply. First, § 2511(2)(c) allows the use of tape recordings made by a participant to the conversation who was 'acting under color of law.'... Because we find that Whitacre acted under color of law, we do not need to reach the second possibility....

"Rather, when assessing whether someone acted under 'color of law' for the wiretap statute, the question is whether the witness was acting under the government's direction when making the recording.... No cases demand that the government's supervision of its cooperating witnesses and informants need be flawless.... What we find essential is that the government requested or authorized the taping with the intent of using it in an investigation and that they monitored the progress of the covert surveillance activities....

"To be sure, the FBI's supervision of Whitaker's surreptitious taping activities will likely never make it into the textbooks. The defendants make use of the technical errors in the supervision to paint a picture of a rogue witness, completely out of control, acting alone, throwing away tapes and manipulating evidence with callous indifference.... The FBI did not seem to follow its own internal guidelines on supervising taping activities, but this does not provide a basis for constitutional challenge....

"Still, these technical deficiencies do not show Whitacre acting independently of the FBI. FBI agents requested Whitacre begin taping his co-conspirators, instructed him on what type of conversation to record, supplied him with taping equipment and tapes, instructed him on the proper use of the equipment and met with him regularly to discuss developments in the conspiracy and collect the tapes. When possible, the FBI itself monitored the conversations by setting up remote-controlled video recorders to tape the face-to-face meetings of the conspirators and having FBI agents act as hotel staff to infiltrate the meetings. As in Craig, this evidence was sufficient to prove that Whitacre acted at the direction of the FBI in gathering the tapes, and therefore acted under color of law.

"The government and Cox entered into a use-immunity agreement to facilitate Cox's interview with the FBI and the DOJ in preparation for ADM's impending plea agreement, which would settle all charges against the corporation. At all times, the government was preparing to prosecute Wilson and Andreas criminally, which makes the defendants' request that this Court interpret the Cox immunity agreement ... to immunize them truly remarkable. They contend that this absurd result follows from a logical chain beginning with the government's *intent* to immunize Andreas and Wilson, even though Andreas and Wilson were the prime individual targets of the government's three-year investigation. The defendants contend they are third-party beneficiaries of the agreement and that because the government cannot present an entirely independent source for Cox's testimony, the indictment must be dismissed, or at the very least, Cox's testimony regarding the citric-acid conspiracy should have been suppressed. We decline to take the first step down this too clever road.

"Without deciding whether third parties can ever be immunized by another's compelled testimony, we agree with the district court that Wilson and Andreas do not have standing to enforce the terms of the Cox agreement. Immunity agreements, like plea bargains, are interpreted as ordinary contracts in light of the parties' reasonable expectations at the time of contracting.... Individuals who are not parties to a contract may enforce its terms only when the original parties intended the contract to directly benefit them as third parties.... 'The critical inquiry centers on the intention of the parties, which is to be gleaned from the language of the contract and the circumstances surrounding the parties at the time of its execution.'...

"In this case, the circumstances conclusively establish that neither the promisee (Cox) nor the promisor (the government) intended to give Andreas and Wilson any benefit of the promise since both knew Andreas and Wilson specifically would be excluded from the plea deal....

"The text of the letters and the circumstances surrounding them do not evince an intent to vest third-party rights in Andreas and Wilson. To the contrary, the evidence demonstrates an intent to exclude Andreas and Wilson from any benefit of the agreement. Because they are not parties or third-party beneficiaries, we hold that Wilson and Andreas do not have standing to enforce the terms of the immunity agreement....

"Defendant Andreas objected to the admission of Cox's testimony regarding the citric-acid conspiracy as unduly prejudicial. Andreas contends that no evidence showed he had been involved in the citric-acid conspiracy, and therefore it could not be admitted against him under Rule 404(b) of the Federal Rules of Evidence, which allows evidence of other crimes or bad acts to be used to show a defendant's motive, plan or intent in the instant crime....

"Rule 404(b) guards against the impermissible inference that because a defendant committed Crime A at some time in the past, he is more likely to have committed Crime B, the crime charged in the present. The risk that the jury may improperly comprehend and weigh evidence of prior bad acts looms so large that courts in this country have long forbidden the government from invoking it.... Yet we have carved out two important categories of cases where the rule does not apply. The first, and most common, is expressly stated in the rule itself, and that allows the use of other crimes evidence for purposes other than to show a propensity to commit the crime, such as to show the defendant's motive, plan or intent....

"The second exception, which applies here, covers acts that are so intricately interwoven with the facts of the charged crime that to omit the evidence relating to it would lead to confusion or leave an unexplainable gap in the narrative of the crime.... While not an express exception to Rule 404(b), this type of evidence is permitted by virtue of not being included within the province of the rule. 'Other crimes or acts' does not include those acts that are part and parcel of the charged crime itself; they simply are not 'other.' To omit the evidence would leave unanswered some questions regarding the charged offense. Such evidence includes acts that although not charged as crimes, 'are directly related to the charged offense.'... 'The question is whether the evidence is properly admitted to provide the jury with a complete story of the crime....'

"The evidence of the citric-acid conspiracy answered at least three relevant questions. First, the jurors heard the conspirators in tape-recorded meetings discussing the citric-acid conspiracy, and they heard Wilson explaining that certain aspects of the lysine conspiracy, such as the bogus trade association, would operate in the same way. The evidence of the citric-acid conspiracy was relevant to explain these references in the conspirators' conversations.

"Second, testimony at trial showed that in the halls of ADM's Decatur headquarters, the lysine and citric-acid conspiracies were closely related parts of a master plan to control prices and product supply through collusion with competitors. The citric-acid conspiracy, of which Andreas was aware, provided the blueprint for and motivating force behind the nascent lysine scheme. Many of the lysine cartel's meetings revolved around the need to allocate sales volume, a lesson dictated by the experience in the citric-acid conspiracy.

"Finally, omitting the citric-acid evidence would leave Wilson's participation in the lysine conspiracy unexplained. Wilson—head of the corn division—was called in to work on the bioproducts project solely because he had experience with cartels that he gained from the citric-acid conspiracy. Wilson was to tutor Whitacre in running a citric-acid type conspiracy. The inference cannot be missed that since Wilson reported directly to Andreas, Andreas must have known why his corn processing chief was working so closely and traveling so much with the bioproducts chief. Because Wilson's entire reason for getting involved in lysine was to share his criminal experience with Whitacre, it takes little imagination to see how evidence of the citric-acid conspiracy implicated Andreas. To omit this evidence would ... leave an unexplained gap in the narrative of the crime. We find the evidence of the citric-acid conspiracy was relevant to Andreas' guilt and not unfairly prejudicial....

"On appeal, Wilson and Andreas contend that the jury instruction impermissibly allowed the jury to convict them for allocating sales volumes without requiring the government to prove with economic evidence that such an allocation unreasonably restrained trade. Violations of § 1 require evidence proving that the charged practice had the effect of unreasonably restraining trade under the 'rule of reason,' except in the limited cases referred to as per se violations.... *Per se* violations are ones that 'always or almost always tend to restrict competition and decrease output' such that the court may dispense with the requirement of economic evidence.... *Per se* violations are 'naked restraints of trade with no purpose except stifling of competition ... and have been characterized as so 'plainly anti-competitive' and lacking 'any redeeming virtue' that they are presumed illegal under § 1.... The defendants do not contend that price fixing is not a *per se* violation, only that the agreement to allocate sales volumes, which according to the indictment and jury charge was a separate and independent goal of the conspiracy, should be subject to rule of reason analysis.... We will reverse jury verdicts in multiple-goal conspiracies when the potential exists that the jury convicted the defendant on an improper ground....

"The issue then is whether the agreement to divide the market among the five lysine producers constituted a *per se* violation of the Sherman Act. The defendants' argument relies heavily on the fact that neither the words 'sales volume allocation' nor any practices precisely identical to their scheme appear in the case law as a *per se* violation.... The agreement did feature some clever characteristics that the conspirators hoped would help them avoid detection, but these small differences are not sufficient to distinguish their plot from more common *per se* prohibited practices.

"[T]he fact that the lysine producers' scheme did not fit precisely the characterization of a prototypical *per se* practice does not remove it from *per se* treatment. At bottom, the lysine cartel's agreement was a conspiracy to limit the producers' output and thereby raise prices. Functionally, an agreement to restrict output works in most cases to raises prices above a competitive level ... and for this reason, output restrictions have long been treated as *per se* violations.... A prototypical output restriction raises prices by reducing supply below demand. Here, the volume division among the lysine competitors restricted competition over those sales that would lower the commodity price....

"Here, the district court found nothing in the record that rose to the level of ... special circumstances ... to warrant departure from *per se* treatment. Nothing suggests that a market allocation was necessary to maintain a competitive industry.... [E]ach lysine competitor could have continued selling its product without the others. While market demand might not support the full production of five companies at a profitable price, this fact does not distinguish lysine from many other markets. ADM's entrance into the market may have resulted in oversupply and lower prices for consumers, but this does not grant a license to violate the antitrust laws.

"Andreas and Wilson next appeal the district court's refusal to give a requested instruction highlighting their defense theory on intent. The defendants argued at trial that whenever they seemed to be agreeing and conspiring with their competitors to violate the antitrust laws, they were actually playing a clever game of deception. By pretending to agree, they sought to put the Asian companies at a disadvantage so that they would share information and fall into a false sense of security, while ADM aggressively pursued new customers. Their proposed intent instruction would have advised the jury that an agreement does not exist if 'one party did not intend to abide by the agreement.' We agree that a defendant's subjective intent is a required element of a criminal antitrust violation ... and that a defendant who pretended to agree but did not intend to honor the agreement could not be convicted of a crime.... However, we reject the defendants' claim of error for two reasons.

"First, the defendants' theory was not supported by any evidence in the record....

"Second, the jury instructions as given adequately covered this possible defense theory....

"The government's closing argument twice prompted objections related to improper comments, requiring the trial court to assess the damage done to the fairness of the proceedings. After a thorough analysis, the court refused to declare a mistrial, admonished the government and instructed the jury appropriately. The defendants appeal the denial of a mistrial on two grounds....

"The defendants contend that lead prosecutor Scott Lassar impermissibly vouched for the strength of the government's case. In closing argument, Lassar characterized the case against the three defendants as 'one of the most compelling and powerful that has ever been presented in an American courtroom.'...

"We look next to see whether the remark deprived the defendants of a fair proceeding when considered in the context of the whole trial.... To guide us in this decision, we consider five factors: (1) the nature and seriousness of the statement; (2) whether defense counsel invited it; (3) whether the district court sufficiently instructed the jury to disregard it; (4) whether defense counsel had the opportunity to respond to the improper statement; and (5) whether the weight of the evidence was against the defendant....

"First, we consider the prosecution's comment on the weight of the evidence to be less damaging than other forms of impermissible argument.... Furthermore, the prosecution made the comment only once, which considering the length of the trial and the closing argument, could not have weighed that heavily in the minds of the jury....

"Defense counsel could not have invited Lassar's comment and could not counter it directly during their own closings, so those two factors weigh in favor of reversal. However, the two remaining factors strongly support the district court's decision. The court instructed the jury before the completion of closing arguments with the following: 'During the course of Mr. Lassar's closing argument he made reference to the strength of the evidence in this case as compared to other cases. Such references to other cases are totally irrelevant. So I would instruct you that you should absolutely disregard any statements or references comparing this case to any other case, and you should decide this case solely on the evidence presented in this case without regard to any comparison to any other case.' We presume juries can and do follow curative instructions.... Considering the largely irrelevant implication of Lassar's comparison, we believe a jury could easily follow this instruction.

"Finally, the Court has reviewed all of the evidence against Andreas and Wilson and can fairly characterize it as overwhelming....

"... Lassar's missteps came at the end of a two-month trial in which the jury heard directly from co-conspirators, heard the defendants' voices and saw their faces on video making illegal deals. It would challenge credibility to say that a prosecutor's rather nugatory comment assessing the evidence at trial rendered the trial fundamentally unfair. Therefore, we cannot say that Judge Manning abused her discretion in denying the motion for mistrial.

"During closing, Lassar also discussed the defendants' interviews with the FBI in June 1995 at which they denied any knowledge of price fixing or sales volume allocation agreements. At the time of those interviews, the defendants did not know of the extensive tape-recorded evidence of their conversations detailing both agreements. That evidence severely undercut a 'no knowledge' defense, and at trial, the defendants did not deny knowledge. Rather, defense counsel argued that the agreements were pro-competitive or that they were part of a clever deception. These theories were directly inconsistent with the denials Andreas and Wilson offered in June 1995.

"Lassar suggested to the jury that they 'ask [themselves] why didn't we hear those defenses from Mr. Wilson and Mr. Andreas on June 27, 1995? That was their opportunity if they had a defense. They were confronted. That was their opportunity to give all these defenses.' He then implied that defense counsel would fabricate new explanations for their clients' behavior that their clients did not offer a year earlier and that the new explanations were lies. The defense objected on the ground that Lassar's statements punished the defendants for invoking their Fifth Amendment right not to testify. The district court agreed, finding Lassar's closing to be improper.... She instructed the jury to disregard the improper portions of Lassar's closing and not to penalize the defendants for remaining silent.

"Once a constitutional violation has been found, 'the government can only prevail if it sustains the burden of proving beyond a reasonable doubt that the defendant would have been convicted absent the prosecutor's unconstitutional remarks.'... Considering the overwhelming nature of the evidence, we agree with the district court that the error was entirely harmless....

"To determine the extent of the harm from an improper remark, we must consider the context in which it was offered....

"Here ... the context shows the government sought to point out the inconsistency between the defendants' prior statements and the current defense theories. The remarks immediately followed a discussion of the June 1995 raids and the defendants' voluntary statements at that time. The jury may have drawn no more than that from Lassar's remarks. Judge Manning properly instructed the jury to disregard any inference that the defendants should have testified at trial, and we presume juries follow proper instructions.... This curative instruction undercuts the potential that the statements caused the jury to convict the defendants.

"Finally, the evidence as a whole included statements from co-conspirators and tape-recorded conversations of both Andreas and Wilson that clearly showed they knew of and participated in the conspiracy to fix prices and restrain trade. There simply could be no doubt in the jurors' minds after hearing overwhelming evidence of the defendants' meetings with the cartel that they knowingly violated the Sherman Act. Assuming that the prosecution indirectly—although impermissibly—called to the jury's attention the lack of a defense justification for their actions, these comments amounted to a few brief words in the midst of a two-month trial. To say that these brief comments resulted in the convictions would ignore the far more plausible conclusion that the overwhelming evidence of guilt led to the jury verdict. In that context, we find the error to be harmless....

"The defendants and the government each appeal one issue related to sentencing. The first, whether 'volume of commerce' includes all sales or some subset of all sales affected by the conspiracy, is a question of law, which we review *de novo*.... However, once we determine the correct legal principle, we review deferentially the lower court's findings of fact regarding the volume of commerce affected.... The second issue is whether the district court correctly denied a sentencing enhancement based on the defendants' leadership roles in the conspiracy, a factual finding which we also review for clear error....

"The district court enhanced Andreas' and Wilson's sentences based on a volume of commerce affected by the conspiracy greater than $100 million.... After an evidentiary hearing, at which both sides presented evidence and argument regarding the amount of sales affected by the conspiracy, the court accepted the report of the U.S. Probation Office that the volume of commerce amounted to $168 million. The court ... rejected the defendants' argument that 'affected commerce' means only that quantity sold at the targeted price and determined that 'affected commerce' includes all sales made within the scope of the conspiracy, which amounted conservatively to $168 million....

"Because horizontal agreements to restrain trade, whether by price or output restrictions, naturally affect all sales during the period that the conspiracy operates, the trial court correctly determined the volume of commerce based on all sales within the scope of the conspiracy. Andreas and Wilson presented evidence at sentencing that certain sales were not affected, and the district court considered that proof. The lysine conspiracy restrained trade by allocating each market participant's output and fixing prices. Together these two methods served to raise the price beginning in the summer of 1992 and lasting for nearly three years. The price fluctuated, and cartel members cheated each other when they could, but the evidence soundly supports a volume of commerce influenced by the conspiracy of at least $168 million. Based on the evidence at trial, the court was entitled to find that the conspiracy was indeed successful at affecting more than $100 million in commerce.

"The government requested that Andreas' and Wilson's sentences be increased based on their leadership roles in the conspiracy.... The district court denied the enhancement, finding that neither man was more culpable than his co-conspirators. We review for clear error the district court's application of a sentencing enhancement under § 3B1.1.

"Section 3B1.1 enhances a defendant's sentence based on the defendant's role in the offense. An organizer or leader of a criminal activity that 'involved five or more participants or was otherwise extensive' receives a four-level increase, while a manager or supervisor earns a three-level increase…. The district court found that the conspiracy satisfied the size requirements of § 3B1.1, but that Andreas and Wilson did not control the requisite number of participants to merit the increase…. After reviewing the record, we hold that the district court erred in making this finding of fact.

"Evidence submitted at trial and during the sentencing phase indicated that at least three sales executives—Marty Allison, Alfred Jansen and John Ashley—in addition to Andreas, Wilson and Whitacre, helped to implement the pricing and volume allocation schemes. Even discounting Whitacre, who was a government agent during part of the conspiracy and therefore cannot be counted as a participant for that part … the crime still involved the requisite number of participants for an enhancement.

"Furthermore, the court should have considered Andreas' control over the foreign co-conspirators at the Irvine meeting as counting toward the minimum number of participants needed for the § 3B1.1 enhancement. A co-conspirator who used his power to guide or direct other conspirators qualifies as an organizer even though his control was not absolute…. The need to negotiate some details of the conspiracy with the cartel members also does not strip a defendant of the organizer role….

"The district court erred in focusing on the conspiracy as a union of equals, which it was only in part. Neither the Guidelines nor our cases require the 'participants' to be mere drones working for their queen…. [W]e [have] recognized the 'concept of collective leadership,' which is the case here. Evidence from the Irvine meeting showed that Andreas used coercive power to force the foreign competitors to accept ADM's leadership role in the cartel, demonstrating his control over the cartel and its participants. When the cartel had internal squabbles and disputes, Andreas was called in to resolve them. ADM's market power gave Andreas the ability to coerce the other cartel members into submission, and the evidence is clear that he used that power to lead the conspiracy. The fact that control over co-conspirators was not absolute and that he had to negotiate does not negate the conclusion that Andreas was the ultimate leader of the price-fixing cabal.

"The evidence at trial conclusively showed that Wilson engaged in the conspiracy by running the meetings and speaking for ADM. He appears on countless tapes proposing ways to run the cartel and ways to make it more efficient. His entire purpose in attending lysine meetings as the head of the corn processing division was to bring his management skills to the cartel. Neither he nor Andreas can claim in any meaningful way to be merely equally culpable with the other conspirators since it was ADM that suggested the scheme, planned it and carried it out. Therefore, we find the district court's decision to deny the four-and three-level enhancements for Andreas and Wilson, respectively, to be clearly erroneous.

"For the reasons stated above, the convictions of Andreas and Wilson are Affirmed and the cases are Remanded to the district court for resentencing in accordance with this opinion."

F. HOFFMAN-LaROCHE LTD. v. EMPAGRAN S.A.
542 U.S. 155 (2004)

BACKGROUND: Plaintiffs originally filed a class-action antitrust suit on behalf of foreign and domestic purchasers of vitamins, under s.1 of the Sherman Act and ss.4 and 16 of the Clayton Act. Their complaint alleged that defendants-petitioners, who were foreign and domestic vitamin manufacturers and distributors, had engaged in a price-fixing conspiracy, raising the price of vitamin products for the USA and foreign customers. Defendants moved to dismiss the complaint as to foreign purchasers—located in Ukraine, Australia, Ecuador, and Panama (Empagran and four other distributors)—who never did any buying in the USA. Applying the USA's Foreign Trade Antitrust Improvements Act of 1982, the U.S. District Court did dismiss the claims of those five firms. The intra-USA buyers then transferred their claims to a separate lawsuit, and the Empagran group appealed the dismissal of their claims. A panel of the U.S. Court of Appeals for the District of Columbia reversed, 2 to 1, and the entire D.C. Circuit voted 4 to 3 not to review the panel's decision. Defendants petitioned for U.S. Supreme Court review.

JUSTICE BREYER:

"The Foreign Trade Antitrust Improvements Act of 1982 (FTAIA) excludes from the Sherman Act's reach much anticompetitive conduct that causes only foreign injury. It does so by setting forth a general rule stating that the Sherman Act 'shall not apply to conduct involving trade or commerce ... with foreign nations.'... It then creates exceptions to the general rule, applicable where (generally speaking) that conduct significantly harms imports, domestic commerce, or American exporters.

"We focus here upon anticompetitive price-fixing activity that is in significant part foreign, that causes some domestic antitrust injury, and that independently causes separate foreign injury. We ask two questions about the price-fixing conduct and the foreign injury that it causes. First, does that conduct fall within FTAIA's general rule excluding the Sherman Act's application? That is to say, does the price-fixing conduct constitute 'conduct involving trade or commerce ... with foreign nations'? We conclude that it does.

"Second, we ask whether the conduct nonetheless falls within a domestic-injury exception to the general rule, an exception that applies (and makes the Sherman Act nonetheless applicable) where the conduct (1) has a 'direct, substantial, and reasonably foreseeable effect' on domestic commerce, and (2) 'such effect gives rise to a [Sherman Act] claim.'... We conclude that the exception does not apply where the plaintiff's claim rests solely on the independent foreign harm.

"To clarify: The issue before us concerns (1) significant foreign anticompetitive conduct with (2) an adverse domestic effect and (3) an independent foreign effect giving rise to the claim. In more concrete terms, this case involves vitamin sellers around the world that agreed to fix prices, leading to higher vitamin prices in the United States and independently leading to higher prices in other countries such as Ecuador. We conclude that, in this scenario, a purchaser in the United States could bring a Sherman Act claim under the FTAIA based on domestic injury, but a purchaser in Ecuador could not bring a Sherman Act claim based on foreign harm....

"The FTAIA seeks to make clear to American exporters (and to firms doing business abroad) that the Sherman Act does not prevent them from entering into business arrangements (say, joint-selling arrangements), however anticompetitive, as long as those arrangements adversely affect only foreign markets.... It does so by removing from the Sherman Act's reach, (1) export activities and (2) other commercial activities taking place abroad, *unless* those activities adversely affect domestic commerce, imports to the United States, or exporting activities of one engaged in such activities within the United States....

"We turn now to the basic question presented, that of the exception's application. Because the underlying antitrust action is complex, potentially raising questions not directly at issue here, we reemphasize that we base our decision upon the following: The price-fixing conduct significantly and adversely affects both customers outside the United States and customers within the United States, but the adverse foreign effect is independent of any adverse domestic effect. In these circumstances, we find that the FTAIA exception does not apply (and thus that the Sherman Act does not apply) for two main reasons.

"*First*, this Court ordinarily construes ambiguous statutes to avoid unreasonable interference with the sovereign authority of other nations.... This rule of construction reflects principles of customary international law—law that (we must assume) Congress ordinarily seeks to follow.... '[A]n act of Congress ought never to be construed to violate the law of nations if any other possible construction remains.'...

"This rule of statutory construction cautions courts to assume that legislators take account of the legitimate sovereign interests of other nations when they write American laws. It thereby helps the potentially conflicting laws of nations work together in harmony—a harmony particularly needed in today's highly interdependent commercial world.

"No one denies that America's antitrust laws, when applied to foreign conduct, can interfere with a foreign nation's ability independently to regulate its own commercial affairs. But our courts have long held that application of our antitrust laws to foreign anticompetitive conduct is nonetheless reasonable, and hence consistent with principles of prescriptive comity, insofar as they reflect a legislative effort to redress *domestic* antitrust injury that foreign anticompetitive conduct has caused....

"But why is it reasonable to apply those laws to foreign conduct *insofar as that conduct causes independent foreign harm and that foreign harm alone gives rise to the plaintiff's claim?* Like the former case, application of those laws creates a serious risk of interference with a foreign nation's ability independently to regulate its own commercial affairs. But, unlike the former case, the justification for that interference seems insubstantial.... Why should American law supplant, for example, Canada's or Great Britain's or Japan's own determination about how best to protect Canadian or British or Japanese customers from anticompetitive conduct engaged in significant part by Canadian or British or Japanese companies?

"We recognize that principles of comity provide Congress greater leeway when it seems to control through legislation the actions of *American* companies ... and some of the anticompetitive price-fixing conduct alleged here took place in *America*. But the higher foreign prices of which the foreign plaintiffs here complain are not the consequence of any domestic anticompetitive conduct *that Congress sought to forbid*, for Congress did not seek to forbid any such conduct insofar as it is here relevant, *i.e.*, insofar as it is intertwined with foreign conduct that causes independent foreign harm. Rather Congress sought to *release* domestic (and foreign) anticompetive conduct from Sherman Act constraints when that conduct causes foreign harm.... But any independent domestic harm the foreign conduct causes here has, by definition, little or nothing to do with the matter.

"We thus repeat the basic question: Why is it reasonable to apply this law to conduct that is significantly foreign *insofar as that conduct causes foreign harm and that foreign harm alone gives rise to the plaintiff's claim?* We can find no good answer to the question....

"[Plaintiffs] reply that many nations have adopted antitrust laws similar to our own, to the point where the practical likelihood of interference with the relevant interests of other nations is minimal. Leaving price fixing to the side, however, this Court has found to the contrary....

"Regardless, even where nations agree about primary conduct, say, price-fixing, they disagree

451

dramatically about appropriate remedies. The application, for example, of American treble damages remedies to anticompetitive conduct taking place abroad has generated considerable controversy…. And several foreign nations have filed briefs here arguing that to apply our remedies would unjustifiably permit their citizens to bypass their own less generous remedial schemes, thereby upsetting a balance of competing considerations that their own domestic antitrust laws embody….

"These briefs add that a decision permitting independently injured foreign plaintiffs to pursue private treble-damages would undermine foreign nations' own antitrust enforcement policies by diminishing foreign firms' incentive to cooperate with antitrust authorities in return for prosecutorial immunity….

"At most, [plaintiffs'] linguistic arguments might show that [their] reading is the more natural reading of the statutory language. But those arguments do not show that we *must* accept that reading. And that is the critical point. The considerations previously mentioned—those of comity and history—make clear that the [plaintiffs'] reading is not consistent with the FTAIA's basic intent. If the statute's language reasonably permits an interpretation consistent with that intent, we should adopt it. And, for the reasons stated, we believe that the statute's language permits the reading that we give it….

"For these reasons, the judgment of the Court of Appeals is vacated, and the case is remanded for further proceedings."

VINCENZO MANFREDI v. LLOYD ADRIATICO ASSICURAZIONI
C-295/04 (European Court of Justice 2006)

BACKGROUND: These cases were referred to the European Court of Justice ("ECJ") for a preliminary ruling concerning the application of Article 81 of the European Community Treaty. Damages claims were brought by Vincenzo Manfredi against Lloyd Adriatico Assicurazioni SpA, by Antonio Cannito against Fondiaria Sai SpA and by Nicolo Tricarico and Pasqualina Murgulo against Assitalia SpA. Plaintiffs sought repayment of the increases in premiums for compulsory civil liability insurance relating to motor vehicle accidents. The companies' agreement to charge the higher premiums had been declared unlawful by the national competition authority (Autorita garante per la concorrenza e del mercato—'the AGCM').

Article 2(2) of [Italian] Law No. 287 of October 10, 1990 (on the rules for the protection of competition and markets) prohibits arrangements between undertakings which have as their object or effect appreciably to prevent, restrict or distort competition in the national market or a substantial part of it. Under Article 2(3) of that Law, prohibited agreements are null and void.

The AGCM initiated the procedure for infringement laid down in Article 2 against various insurance companies, including the three defendant companies here. It was alleged that those companies had participated in an arrangement for the purpose of "the tied selling of separate products and the exchange of information between competing undertakings." In the course of its investigation, the AGCM obtained documentation showing extensive and widespread exchange of information between various civil liability auto insurance companies relating to all aspects of insurance activities. In its final decision the AGCM declared that the insurance companies involved had implemented an unlawful agreement for the purpose of exchanging information on the insurance sector. That agreement enabled those undertakings to coordinate and fix the prices of civil liability auto insurance premiums so as to charge users large increases in premiums which were not justified by market conditions and which they could not escape. The AGCM's decision was upheld by the Regional Administrative Court of Latium and by the Council of State. The applicants in the main proceedings brought their respective actions before the Giudice di pace di Bitonto to obtain damages against each insurance company concerned for the increase in the cost of premiums paid by reason of the agreement declared unlawful by the AGCM. The investigation revealed that the average price of civil liability auto insurance premiums was 20% higher than would have been the case if the competitive conduct of the insurance companies had not been distorted by the concerted practice.

The insurance companies in the main proceedings pleaded that the Giudice di pace di Bitonto did not have jurisdiction under Article 33 of Law No. 287/90 and that the right to restitution and/or compensation in damages was time-barred. The national court took the view that, in so far as insurance companies of other Member States carrying on their activities in Italy also took part in an illegal agreement, that agreement infringes not only Article 2 of Law No. 287/90 but also Article 81 EC Treaty, paragraph 2, which declares void all such prohibited agreements. Paragraph 2 considers that any third party may consider itself entitled to claim compensation in damages where there is a causal relationship between the harm suffered and the prohibited arrangement. If that is the case, a provision such as that in Article 33 of Law No. 287/90 could be regarded as contrary to Community law. The time-scales are much longer and the costs much higher in proceedings before the Corte d'appello compared to those in proceedings before the Giudice di pace, which could compromise the effectiveness of Article 81 EC. The national court is also uncertain whether the limitation period for bringing actions for damages, and the amount of damages to be paid—both of which are fixed by national law—are compatible with Article 81 EC. The ECJ was asked for a ruling on these questions.

453

THE COURT *(Third Chamber)*:

"… Articles 81 EC and 82 EC are a matter of public policy which must be automatically applied by national courts…. It follows that the questions referred for a preliminary ruling are admissible….

"By its first question, the national court asks, in essence, whether an agreement or concerted practice, such as that at issue in the main proceedings, between insurance companies, consisting of a mutual exchange of information that makes possible an increase in civil liability auto insurance premiums not justified by market conditions, which infringes national rules on the protection of competition, may also constitute an infringement of Article 81 EC in view, in particular, of the fact that undertakings from several Member States took part in the agreement or concerted practice.

"The Italian Government submits that Article 81 EC does not apply to an agreement such as that at issue in the main proceedings. In order for anti-competitive conduct to fall within Community rules, a series of criteria which go beyond the mere participation of undertakings from different Member States must be fulfilled.

"The Commission of the European Communities submits that Article 81 EC must be interpreted as prohibiting an agreement or concerted practice between undertakings which restricts competition where, on the basis of a set of factors of law or of fact, it is possible to foresee with a sufficient degree of probability that the agreement or concerted practice in question has an influence, direct or indirect, actual or potential, on the pattern of trade between Member States. The fact that certain undertakings from other Member States took part in that agreement or concerted practice is not, in itself, sufficient to conclude that that agreement or concerted practice has such an effect on trade between Member States.

"… [I]n accordance with settled case-law, Community competition law and national competition law apply in parallel, since they consider restrictive practices from different points of view. Whereas Articles 81 EC and 82 EC regard them in the light of the obstacles which may result for trade between Member States, national law proceeds on the basis of considerations peculiar to it and considers restrictive practices only in that context…. It should also be borne in mind that Articles 81(1) EC and 82 EC produce direct effects in relations between individuals and create rights for the individuals concerned which the national courts must safeguard … and that the primacy of Community law requires any provision of national law which contravenes a Community rule to be disapplied, regardless of whether it was adopted before or after that rule…. However, as is already clear from the wording of Articles 81 EC and 82 EC, in order for the Community competition rules to apply to an arrangement or abusive practice it is necessary for it to be capable of affecting trade between Member States....

"The interpretation and application of that condition relating to effects on trade between Member States must take as its starting-point the fact that its purpose is to define, in the context of the law governing competition, the boundary between the areas respectively covered by Community law and the law of the Member States. Thus, Community law covers any agreement or any practice which is capable of affecting trade between Member States in a manner which might harm the attainment of the objectives of a single market between the Member States, in particular by sealing off national markets or by affecting the structure of competition within the common market....

"For an agreement, decision or practice to be capable of affecting trade between Member States, it must be possible to foresee with a sufficient degree of probability, on the basis of a set of objective factors of law or of fact, that they may have an influence, direct or indirect, actual or potential, on the pattern of trade between Member States in such a way as to cause concern that they might hinder the attainment of a single market between Member States.... Moreover, that influence must not be insignificant.... Thus, an effect on intra-Community trade is normally the result of a combination of several factors which, taken separately, are not necessarily decisive.... In that regard it should be stated ... that the mere fact that the participants in a national arrangement also include undertakings from other Member States is an important element in the assessment, but, taken alone, it is not so decisive as to permit the conclusion that the criterion of trade between Member States being affected has been satisfied.... On the other hand, the fact that an agreement, decision or concerted practice relates only to the marketing of products in a single Member State is not sufficient to exclude the possibility that trade between Member States might be affected.... An agreement, decision or concerted practice extending over the whole of the territory of a Member State has, by its very nature, the effect of reinforcing the partitioning of markets on a national basis, thereby holding up the economic interpenetration which the Treaty is designed to bring about.... Further, in the case of services, the Court has already held that an influence on the pattern of trade between Member States may consist in the activities in question being conducted in such a way that their effect is to partition the common market and thereby restrict freedom to provide services, which constitutes one of the objectives of the Treaty....

"It is for the national court to determine whether, in the light of the characteristics of the national market at issue, there is a sufficient degree of probability that the agreement or concerted practice at issue in the main proceedings may have an influence, direct or indirect, actual or potential, on the sale of civil liability auto insurance policies in the relevant Member State by operators from other Member States and that that influence is not insignificant. However, when giving a preliminary ruling the Court may, where appropriate, provide clarification designed to give the national court guidance in its interpretation.... In that regard, according to the case-law of the Court, since the market concerned is susceptible to the provision of services by operators from other Member States, the members of a national price cartel can retain their market share only if they defend themselves against foreign competition....

"The national court's decision indicates that the AGCM observed that the market for civil liability auto insurance premiums has considerable barriers to entry which have arisen primarily due to the need to set up an efficient distribution network and a network of centres for the settlement of accident claims throughout Italy. However, the national court also points out that insurance companies from other Member States but with activities in Italy also took part in the agreement ruled unlawful by the AGCM. It therefore appears that the market concerned is susceptible to the provision of services by insurance companies from other Member States, although such barriers make the provision of those services more difficult. In such circumstances, it is a matter, in particular, for the national court to examine whether the mere existence of the agreement or concerted practice was capable of having a deterrent effect on insurance companies from other Member States without activities in Italy, in particular by enabling the coordination and fixing of civil liability auto insurance premiums at a level at which the sale of such insurance by those companies would not be profitable....

"The answer to the first question in Joined Cases C-295/04 to C-298/04 must therefore be that an agreement or concerted practice, such as that at issue in the main proceedings, between insurance companies, consisting of a mutual exchange of information that makes possible an increase in civil liability auto insurance premiums not justified by market conditions, which infringes national rules on the protection of competition, may also constitute an infringement of Article 81 EC if, in the light of the characteristics of the national market at issue, there is a sufficient degree of probability that the agreement or concerted practice at issue may have an influence, direct or indirect, actual or potential, on the sale of those insurance policies in the relevant Member State by operators established in other Member States and that that influence is not insignificant.

"The second question in Cases C-295/04 to C-297/04 and the third question in Case C-298/04

"By this question, which should be examined before the second question in Case C-298/04, the national court asks, essentially, whether Article 81 EC is to be interpreted as entitling any individual to rely on the invalidity of an agreement or practice prohibited under that article and, where there is a causal relationship between that agreement or practice and the harm suffered, to claim damages for that harm....

"First, it should be noted that Article 81(2) EC provides that any agreements or decisions

456

prohibited pursuant to Article 81 EC are void.... According to settled case-law, that principle of invalidity can be relied on by anyone, and the courts are bound by it once the conditions for the application of Article 81(1) EC are met and so long as the agreement concerned does not justify the grant of an exemption under Article 81(3) EC.... Since the invalidity referred to in Article 81(2) EC is absolute, an agreement which is null and void by virtue of this provision has no effect as between the contracting parties and cannot be invoked against third parties.... Moreover, it is capable of having a bearing on all the effects, either past or future, of the agreement or decision concerned.... Further ... Article 81(1) EC produces direct effects in relations between individuals and creates rights for the individuals concerned which the national courts must safeguard. It follows that any individual can rely on a breach of Article 81 EC before a national court ... and therefore rely on the invalidity of an agreement or practice prohibited under that article.

"Next, as regards the possibility of seeking compensation for loss caused by a contract or by conduct liable to restrict or distort competition, it should be recalled that the full effectiveness of Article 81 EC and, in particular, the practical effect of the prohibition laid down in Article 81(1) EC would be put at risk if it were not open to any individual to claim damages for loss caused to him by a contract or by conduct liable to restrict or distort competition.... It follows that any individual can claim compensation for the harm suffered where there is a causal relationship between that harm and an agreement or practice prohibited under Article 81 EC.

"In the absence of Community rules governing the matter, it is for the domestic legal system of each Member State to designate the courts and tribunals having jurisdiction and to lay down the detailed procedural rules governing actions for safeguarding rights which individuals derive directly from Community law, provided that such rules are not less favourable than those governing similar domestic actions (principle of equivalence) and that they do not render practically impossible or excessively difficult the exercise of rights conferred by Community law (principle of effectiveness)....

"Accordingly, the answer to the second question in Cases C-295/04 to C-297/04 and the third question in Case C-298/04 must be that Article 81 EC must be interpreted as meaning that any individual can rely on the invalidity of an agreement or practice prohibited under that article and, where there is a causal relationship between the latter and the harm suffered, claim compensation for that harm....

"The second question in Case C-298/04

"By this question, the national court asks, essentially, whether Article 81 EC must be interpreted as precluding a national provision such as Article 33(2) of Law No 287/90 under which third parties must bring their actions for damages for infringement of Community and national competition rules before a court other than that which usually has jurisdiction in actions for damages of similar value, thereby involving a considerable increase in costs and time....

"The answer to the second question in Case C-298/04 must therefore be that, in the absence of Community rules governing the matter, it is for the domestic legal system of each Member State to designate the courts and tribunals having jurisdiction to hear actions for damages based on an infringement of the Community competition rules and to prescribe the detailed procedural rules governing those actions, provided that the provisions concerned are not less favourable than those governing actions for damages based on an infringement of national competition rules and that those national provisions do not render practically impossible or excessively difficult the exercise of the right to seek compensation for the harm caused by an agreement or practice prohibited under Article 81 EC.

"The third question in Cases C-295/04 to C-297/04 and the fourth question in Case C-298/04

"By this question, the national court asks, in essence, whether Article 81 EC must be interpreted as precluding a national rule which provides that the limitation period for seeking compensation for harm caused by an agreement or practice prohibited under Article 81 EC begins to run from the day on which that prohibited agreement or practice was adopted....

"... [I]n the absence of Community rules governing the matter, it is for the domestic legal system of each Member State to lay down the detailed procedural rules governing actions for safeguarding rights which individuals derive directly from Community law, provided that such rules observe the principles of equivalence and effectiveness.... It is for the national court to determine whether such is the case with regard to the national rule at issue in the main proceedings....

"The fourth question in Cases C-295/04 to C-297/04 and the fifth question in Case C-298/04

"By this question, the national court asks, in essence, whether Article 81 EC must be interpreted as requiring national courts to award punitive damages, greater than the advantage obtained by the offending operator, thereby deterring the adoption of agreements or concerted practices prohibited under that article....

"As to the award of damages and the possibility of an award of punitive damages, in the absence of Community rules governing the matter, it is for the domestic legal system of each Member State to set the criteria for determining the extent of the Damages, provided that the principles of equivalence and effectiveness are observed. In that respect, first, in accordance with the principle of equivalence, it must be possible to award particular damages, such as exemplary or punitive damages, pursuant to actions founded on the Community competition rules, if such damages may be awarded pursuant to similar actions founded on domestic law....

"On those grounds, the Court (Third Chamber) hereby rules:

1. An agreement or concerted practice, such as that at issue in the main proceedings, between insurance companies, consisting of a mutual exchange of information that makes possible an increase in premiums for compulsory civil liability insurance relating to accidents caused by motor vehicles, vessels and mopeds, not justified by market conditions, which infringes national rules on the protection of competition, may also constitute an infringement of Article 81 EC if, in the light of the characteristics of the national market at issue, there is a sufficient degree of probability that the agreement or concerted practice at issue may have an influence, direct or indirect, actual or potential, on the sale of those insurance policies in the relevant Member State by operators established in other Member States and that that influence is not insignificant.

2. Article 81 EC must be interpreted as meaning that any individual can rely on the invalidity of an agreement or practice prohibited under that article and, where there is a causal relationship between the latter and the harm suffered, claim compensation for that harm. In the absence of Community rules governing the matter, it is for the domestic legal system of each Member State to prescribe the detailed rules governing the exercise of that right, including those on the application of the concept of 'causal relationship', provided that the principles of equivalence and effectiveness are observed.

3. In the absence of Community rules governing the matter, it is for the domestic legal system of each Member State to designate the courts and tribunals having jurisdiction to hear actions for damages based on an infringement of the Community competition rules and to prescribe the detailed procedural rules governing those actions, provided that the provisions concerned are not less favourable than those governing actions for damages based on an infringement of national competition rules and that those national provisions do not render practically impossible or excessively difficult the exercise of the right to seek compensation for the harm caused by an agreement or practice prohibited under Article 81 EC.

4. In the absence of Community rules governing the matter, it is for the domestic legal system of each Member State to prescribe the limitation period for seeking compensation for harm caused by an agreement or practice prohibited under Article 81 EC, provided that the principles of equivalence and effectiveness are observed. In that regard, it is for the national court to determine whether a national rule which provides that the limitation

period for seeking compensation for harm caused by an agreement or practice prohibited under Article 81 EC begins to run from the day on which that prohibited agreement or practice was adopted, particularly where it also imposes a short limitation period that cannot be suspended, renders it practically impossible or excessively difficult to exercise the right to seek compensation for the harm suffered.

5. In the absence of Community rules governing that field, it is for the domestic legal system of each Member State to set the criteria for determining the extent of the damages for harm caused by an agreement or practice prohibited under Article 81 EC, provided that the principles of equivalence and effectiveness are observed. Therefore, first, in accordance with the principle of equivalence, if it is possible to award particular damages, such as exemplary or punitive damages, in domestic actions similar to actions founded on the Community competition rules, it must also be possible to award such damages in actions founded on Community rules. However, Community law does not prevent national courts from taking steps to ensure that the protection of the rights guaranteed by Community law does not entail the unjust enrichment of those who enjoy them. Secondly, it follows from the principle of effectiveness and the right of individuals to seek compensation for loss caused by a contract or by conduct liable to restrict or distort competition that injured persons must be able to seek compensation not only for actual loss *(damnum emergens)* but also for loss of profit *(lucrum cessans)* plus interest."

COOPER TIRE & RUBBER CO. EUROPE et ors v. DOW DEUTSCHLAND INC. et ors
[2010] EWCA Civ 864 (England & Wales Court of Appeal 2010)

BACKGROUND: The decision by the Commission of the European Communities was dated November 29, 2006 and entitled *Butadiene Rubber and Emulsion Styrene Butadiene Rubber*. The Commission Decision found 13 companies (the "Addressees") guilty of an infringement of Article 81 of the EC Treaty (now Article 101 of the Treaty on the Functioning of the European Union ["TFEU"]) in relation to the market for the supply of Butadiene Rubber ("BR") and Emulsion Styrene Butadiene Rubber ("ESBR"). The Addressees were: Bayer AG ("Bayer"), The Dow Chemical Company, Dow Deutschland Inc., Dow Deutschland Anlagengesellschaft mbH, Dow Europe GmbH (collectively "Dow"), Eni SpA, Polimeri Europa SpA (collectively "Enichem"), Shell Petroleum NV, Shell Nederland BV, Shell Nederland Chemie BV (collectively "Shell"), Kaucuk a.s. and Unipetrol a.s. (collectively "Kaucuk") and Trade-Stomil Ltd. ("Stomil"). They were variously domiciled in Germany, the Netherlands, Italy, the Czech

Republic, Switzerland and Poland. None was domiciled in England. The Commission Decision held that the Addressees committed a "complex single and continuous infringement" of Article 81 of the Treaty by agreeing price targets for their products, sharing customers by non-aggression agreements and exchanging sensitive commercial information relating to prices, competitors and customers.

In considering the liability of particular companies the Commission said: "Concerning the principle of personal liability, Article 81 of the Treaty is addressed to 'undertakings' which may comprise several legal entities. In this context the principle of personal liability is not breached so long as different legal entities are held liable on the basis of circumstances which pertain to their own role and their conduct within the same undertaking. In the case of parent companies, liability is established on the basis of their exercise of effective control on the commercial policy of the subsidiaries which are materially implicated by the facts. Under these circumstances, the principle of personal liability is not breached. References to different areas of law where the principle of autonomy of a subsidiary plays a different role (such as under corporate law) is not appropriate."

The Commission Decision then imposed fines on the Addressees. In February 2007, the Addressees, with the exception of Bayer, lodged appeals against the Commission Decision with the Court of First Instance of the European Communities ("CFI"). It is worth noting the grounds of appeal submitted by Dow and Enichem. The Dow Chemical Company contends that it should not be held liable for the acts of its subsidiaries. The other Dow companies contend that the Commission identified too early a start date for the cartel and that the fine imposed on them was too high. Thus the Dow Defendants do not challenge the cartel's existence on their appeal. Nor do they challenge the participation of subsidiary companies in the Dow group in that cartel. Eni SpA contends that it should not be held liable for the acts of its subsidiaries. It also contends that the fine is too high. Polimeri Europa SA, a company in the Eni group, contends that the Commission made procedural errors in coming to its Decision, that the Commission's assessment of the market was unfair, that another company, and not it, was managing BR and ESBR, and that the fine imposed was too high. Thus Enichem also does not challenge the existence of the cartel. The appeals to the CFI were heard in October 2009. A judgment is awaited.

On or around July 29, 2007, after receiving letters before action from the Milan office of S.J.Berwin LLP, Enichem commenced proceedings in Milan against 28 defendants, all of whom were companies in the Pirelli, Michelin, Continental, Goodyear, Bridgestone and Cooper groups, which use BR and ESBR in the manufacture of tires. It is relevant to note two matters concerning these Italian proceedings: (i) Although Enichem has not sought to appeal to the CFI on the basis that the cartel did not exist, Enichem has (illegitimately) sought a declaration from the Italian court that the cartel did not exist. (ii) Enichem contends that those who bought BR or ESBR not only from it but also from other companies in the cartel suffered no loss. Thus Enichem has invited the Italian court to consider whether the cartel as a whole, not just Enichem, has caused any damage to the tire manufacturers who were made defendants to the Italian proceedings.

The claims brought in England are for damages for breach of statutory duty, in particular, breach of Article 81 of the EC Treaty which prohibits agreements between "undertakings" which may affect trade between Member States and which have as their object or effect the prevention, restriction or distortion of competition within the common market. In May 2008 the Dow Defendants (and other Dow companies) intervened in the Italian proceedings and adopted the claims made by Enichem. In June 2008, the Bayer Defendants (and other companies) intervened in the Italian proceedings, just as Dow had done. Also in June 2008 further proceedings were instituted in Italy by Enichem against fellow producers of BR and ESBR. The aim of these proceedings, in which similar negative declaratory relief was also sought, appears to have been to protect the Claimants from being exposed to possible recourse suits by fellow producers of BR and ESBR. At the same time, Enichem joined as parties to the Italian proceedings those of the Claimants in England who had not been party to the first Milan proceedings. On June 12, 2008 the Dow Defendants issued an application in England challenging the jurisdiction of the English court and, in the alternative, seeking a stay.

On January 28, 2009 Judge Paola Gandolfi of the Tribunal of Milan directed a determination of preliminary matters in the Italian proceedings and a hearing took place on February 9, 2009. The defendants to the Italian proceedings sought an order that the proceedings were inadmissible pursuant to Article 16 of the Modernisation Regulation which provides that national courts "cannot take decisions running counter to the decisions adopted by the Commission."

On April 29, 2009 Judge Paola Gandolfi gave her decision. The effect of Judge Gandolfi's decision was to dismiss the Italian proceedings *in toto*. The claimants and interveners in Italy have lodged notices of appeal against the decision. The Dow Defendants in Italy have not sought to appeal the dismissal of the first and second pleas but only the dismissal of the third plea. If that appeal succeeds the Italian Court of Appeal of Milan will also consider the merits of the case. However, before proceeding to do so, the Court of Appeal will likely issue a preliminary appeal judgment in which it will either reverse Judge Gandolfi or uphold her judgment. The experts on Italian law agreed that it was likely that a decision on the appeal would be made within two to two and a half years from September 10, 2009 (that is between September 2011 and February 2012). After the judgment of Teare J, the Court of Appeal of Milan fixed January 2014 for the next hearing of the appeal proceedings.

LORD JUSTICE LONGMORE:

"This is the judgment of the court. This appeal raises the questions (1) whether the English court has jurisdiction pursuant to Article 6(1) of EC Council Regulation 44/2001 to determine claims made by the victims of illegal cartel arrangements found by the European Commission to have been made by the Defendants and (2) whether, if so, the proceedings should be stayed pursuant to Article 28 of that Regulation (which we shall call 'the Judgments Regulation') because the proceedings are related to proceedings brought elsewhere within the EU. There is also a cross-appeal raising a distinct point about a stay.

"Once the Commission has found that there has been an infringement of Article 81 [of the EC Treaty] (now Article 101 of the Treaty on the Functioning of the European Union ('the TFEU') … on the part of participants in relevant anti-competitive conduct in any particular country, that finding cannot be challenged in the domestic courts of any Member State…. Such a finding can only be challenged on appeal to what was the Court of First Instance of the Communities and is now called the General Court and then, if appropriate, by further appeal to the European Court of Justice on a point of law. Once an infringement has been established by the Commission, therefore, the main question liable to arise in national courts in respect of any alleged civil liability of participants in the infringement is whether any alleged victim has suffered any loss or damage as a result of that infringement. One might have thought that if there has been a Europe-wide infringement, as the Commission has found in this case, it would not much matter in which Member State that question should be tried. But for reasons which it might be easier to guess than to state, the infringers are very keen that the question should be tried in Italy while the victims are very keen that it should be tried in England. Teare J has decided that the victims' claims to damages can and should be tried in England and some of the infringers (whom we shall call 'the Dow Defendants') now appeal with permission of the judge….

"As at the date of issue of the first English proceedings only two Defendants were domiciled in England. In addition, DCCL, the only Defendant to the second English proceedings, is domiciled in England. Thus, of the 24 Defendants only three are domiciled in England. Those three companies were in the Shell, Bayer and Dow groups of companies. Jurisdiction was established against those three Defendants pursuant to Article 2 of the Judgments Regulation on the basis of their domicile. We shall refer to them as 'the Anchor Defendants'.

"Although it is logical to consider this pleading point first, that can only be usefully done in the context of the point of law [considered by the judge] which we shall call 'the *Provimi* point'.

"In English domestic law, which proceeds on the basis that corporate bodies are all separate legal personalities, one cannot say that the act of one company in a group of companies, all controlled by a holding company, is automatically the act of any other company in that group. The position in EU law is, however, different at least in the area of competition law and alleged breaches of Article 81 of the EC Treaty. What concerns EU law is the activity of 'undertakings' which may comprise a number of separate corporate entities. The question under Article 81 is whether an 'undertaking' has participated in anti-competitive practices and it will not avail the undertaking to say that because a corporate entity which is part of the undertaking is a party to anti-competitive practices, either the undertaking as a whole or a parent company in the group did not participate in those practices. Otherwise evasion of Article 81 would be too easy. Since, however, the Commission, in deciding whether to exact penalties for anti-competitive behaviour, has to find corporate entities on which to impose such fines, liability has to be imposed on a particular entity in the undertaking. As the Commission wants to identify an entity with an ability to pay, it will normally wish to fine a parent company in addition to any relevant subsidiaries and the European Court has evolved a concept of what may be called presumptive decisive influence if a subsidiary company is effectively controlled by a parent company…. It does not, of course, necessarily follow, as a matter of logic that a subsidiary company is to be liable for (or to be deemed to be aware of) any anti-competitive practices of its parent or of a fellow-subsidiary, but the question is whether European law does go that far. That was the question addressed by Aikens J in *Provimi* … :

> 'It seems to me to be arguable that where two corporate entities are part of an "undertaking" (call it "Undertaking A") and one of those entities has entered into an infringing agreement with other, independent, "undertakings", then if another corporate entity which is part of Undertaking A then implements that infringing agreement, it is also infringing art 81. In my view it is arguable that it is not necessary to plead or prove any particular "concurrence of wills" between the two legal entities within Undertaking A. The EU competition law concept of an "undertaking" is that it is one economic unit. The legal entities that are a part of the one undertaking, by definition of the concept, have no independence of mind or action or will. They are to be regarded as all one. Therefore, so it seems to me, the mind and will of one legal entity is, for the purposes of art 81, to be treated as the mind and will of the other entity. There is no question of having to "impute" the knowledge or will of one entity to another, because they are one and the same.'

"With that introduction it is now appropriate to consider whether the particulars of claim assert a narrow case against the Anchor Defendants which is confined to a claim that although those Defendants made sales of BR and ESBR they did so without being party to (or being aware of) the anti-competitive conduct of relevant Addressees or whether it is a more general case which includes possible alternative cases of knowing participation and implementation….

"The Defendants to the particulars of claim, of course, included the Anchor Defendants (they were, in fact, the first and seventh defendants)....

"There then follows, in the document with which the court was provided, certain particulars which were voluntarily provided by the claimants but only after the hearing before Teare J. We agree, however ... that the question whether the claim is a narrow or general one should be decided on the material which was before the judge. It is, however, fair to add that in paragraph 90 where a claim for exemplary damages is made it is alleged that the Defendants' wrongful actions were carried out 'in the knowledge of and in willful disregard of the Claimants' rights'.

"The judge may have been correct to say ... that it is not clear whether it is being alleged that the Anchor Defendants were party to the alleged agreements or were aware of them when they made their sales. On the other hand, it would also be correct to say that it is not clear whether it is being alleged that, even if the Anchor Defendants were neither a party to the alleged agreements nor aware of them, they are nevertheless still liable for infringement of Article 81.

"But once it is alleged that representatives of (inter alia) Shell, Bayer and indeed Dow and others had discussions to co-ordinate their anti-competitive behaviour ... and that those discussions led to 'each of the Defendants' co-ordinating their anti-competitive behaviour ... and that the arrangements were implemented by 'each of the Defendants' with specific attention being drawn to sales by the First and Seventh Defendants ... that to our mind constitutes a general plea of involvement in the arrangements rather than a narrower assertion of liability in the absence of knowledge or awareness of them. It would not in our view have been open to either of the Anchor Defendants to strike out the plea on the basis that knowledge or awareness was required and had not been pleaded. To the extent that the lack of clarity was embarrassing, it would always have been possible for any Defendant to enquire whether knowledge was being alleged and, if so, what facts and matters were relied on to establish such knowledge. To give an answer to that request would not be to plead a new cause of action....

"In these circumstances it seems to us that the particulars of claim encompass both the possibility that the Anchor Defendants were parties to or aware of the anti-competitive conduct of their parent company and the other Addressees and the possibility that they were not. It is only if they were not that what we have called the *Provimi* point will arise. But it is unnecessary to decide it on this application because it is open to the claimants on the pleadings to prove that the Anchor Defendants were parties to (or aware of) the Addressees' anti-competitive conduct. The strength (or otherwise) of any such case cannot be assessed (or indeed usefully particularised) until after disclosure of documents because it is in the nature of anti-competitive arrangements that they are shrouded in secrecy. But the case that the Anchor Defendants were parties to the cartel arrangements or were aware of them when they sold BR and ESBR to the Claimants is not a case that is susceptible to being struck out at the present stage.

"In those circumstances, it is self-evident that the claims against the Dow Defendants are sufficiently closely connected with the claims against the Anchor Defendants to make it 'expedient to hear and determine them together to avoid the wish of irreconcilable judgments resulting from separate proceedings' and that there is therefore jurisdiction for the English court to determine the claims against the Dow Defendants pursuant to Article 6(1) of the Judgment Regulation. It also follows that it is not possible to distinguish between the claims against the Anchor Defendants and those against the other Defendants on the premise that the former would only relate, at most, to the modest sales of BR and ESBR by each Anchor Defendant in the UK....

"As to the *Provimi* point, we can readily agree that ... it is 'arguable'. We would, however, add that it is also arguable the other way. Although one can see that a parent company should be liable for what its subsidiary has done on the basis that a parent company is presumed to be able to exercise (and actually exercise) decisive influence over a subsidiary, it is by no means obvious even in an Article 81 context that a subsidiary should be liable for what its parent does, let alone for what another subsidiary does. Nor does the *Provimi* point sit comfortably with the apparent practice of the Commission, when it exercises its power to fine, to single out those who are primarily responsible or their parent companies rather than to impose a fine on all the entities of the relevant undertaking. If, moreover, liability can extend to any subsidiary company which is part of an undertaking, would such liability accrue to a subsidiary which did not deal in rubber at all, but another product entirely? ...

"If it had been necessary to address the *Provimi* point, we would have been inclined to say that it would be necessary to make a reference to the ECJ before coming to a conclusion on jurisdiction. It would be possible to say that, because a claimant only has to show that he has a case against an anchor defendant which cannot be struck out, the fact that the *Provimi* point is arguable should not deter the English court from assuming jurisdiction. But that would mean that the *Provimi* point could never be decided in a jurisdiction (and possibly, therefore, in any other) context. That would not be a satisfactory state of affairs.

"As it is, the need for a reference does not arise....

"The judge dismissed an application for a mandatory stay pursuant to Article 27 because the litigation in England and in Italy was not between the same parties. The Dow Defendants, however, also applied for a discretionary stay pursuant to Article 28....

"The judge was faced with a difficult balancing exercise.... He acknowledged ... that the proceedings in Italy and England were related so that there was a risk of mutually irreconcilable decisions. He was aware that the earlier proceedings were in Italy so that the Italian court was first seised (and was the only court seised) of Enichem's claim for negative relief but he was also aware that the Dow Defendants had only sought to intervene in the Italian proceedings after they had been served with the English proceedings. As against those considerations he had to weigh the fact that the prospect of a decision on the merits in Italy was contingent on a successful appeal (despite it being 'likely' that such appeal might be to a degree successful) and the fact that proceedings would, in any event, continue against those Defendants who had submitted to the jurisdiction in England…. It was also probable that the English court would, in any event, have to quantify any damage, if the Italian court considered that the cartel had caused any damage at all, since quantification was not an issue in Italy….

"He then held that, in considering the stage which the proceedings had reached in each jurisdiction, he was entitled to consider when a decision was likely to be reached…. He accepted that the connections with England were slight and that an alleged key player in the form of Enichem was domiciled in Italy but pointed out that that did not mean that Italy could be said to be the centre of gravity of the case since the conspiracy was Europe-wide…. He acknowledged that there was an element of care and deliberation in the claimants seeking out Anchor Defendants in England and said that might be important if Italy clearly was the centre of gravity but it was not….

"He balanced all these factors together and concluded that he should decline to stay the proceedings. This was a carefully considered balancing exercise and we are far from persuaded that he either erred in law or came to a decision outside the reasonable range of options open to him. We are certainly not persuaded that the fact that the Italian court was first seised of Enichem's claim can operate as a sort of trump card or even as a primary factor where there was as much care and deliberation on the part of Enichem in starting proceedings for negative declaratory relief as there was in the Claimants' decision to make their substantive claim in England…. Nor are we persuaded that some combination of events in an inevitably somewhat distant future might put difficulties in the way of the Dow Defendants making a contribution claim against Enichem. That is speculative and imponderable at best and would depend on the Italian court holding that the elaborate conspiracy found by the Commission had not caused anyone any loss at all….

"In the result, we see no error on the part of the judge and would not interfere with the way in which he exercised his discretion. Nor, since his decision was one made in his discretion, can we see any scope for a reference on this aspect of the case. We therefore dismiss this appeal….

"The cross-appeal concerns the Claimants' appeal from the decision of the Judge that the Defendant, Dow Europe, was entitled to a stay of the proceedings against it under Art. 21 of the Lugano Convention.

"It was not in dispute that Dow Europe was domiciled in Switzerland, where the Lugano Convention rather than the Judgments Regulation applies....

"There is a difference between the Lugano Convention and the Judgments Regulation in respect of determining the Court first seised of proceedings: so far as concerns English law, the Lugano Convention looks to the date of *service* of proceedings, whereas the Judgments Regulation looks to the date of *issue* of proceedings....

"Before the judge, it was common ground that the question of jurisdiction, so far as concerned Dow Europe, turned on the Lugano Convention....

"Very properly, however, the Dow Defendants drew the attention of this Court to the decision of Sir William Blackburne in *The Trademark Licensing Company Ltd. v Leofelis SA*.... [He] held that the Judgments Regulation, not the Lugano Convention, applied where the dispute involved a choice between jurisdiction in two member states.

"Upon reflection, both parties accepted the correctness of Sir William Blackburne's analysis in *Leofelis*. Accordingly, the Dow Defendants did not pursue their opposition to the cross-appeal. We are content with the stance taken by the parties and the cross-appeal is allowed on this ground alone—thus, on the basis of an argument which had not been raised before the judge. It follows that the position of Dow Europe is no longer distinguishable from the position of any of the other Dow Defendants....

"We therefore dismiss the appeal and allow the cross-appeal."

PFLEIDERER AG v. BUNDESKARTELLAMT
Case C-360/09 (European Court of Justice 2011)

BACKGROUND: On January 21, 2008, pursuant to Article 81 EC, the Bundeskartellamt imposed fines amounting in total to EUR 62 million on three European manufacturers of decor paper and on five individuals who were personally liable for agreements on prices and capacity closure. The undertakings concerned did not appeal and the decisions imposing those fines have now become final. On the conclusion of that procedure, Pfleiderer submitted an application to the Bundeskartellamt on February 26, 2008 seeking full access to the file relating to the imposition of fines in the decor paper sector, with a view to preparing civil actions for damages. Pfleiderer is a purchaser of decor paper and, more specifically, special paper for the surface treatment of engineered wood. Pfleiderer is one of the world's three leading manufacturers of engineered wood, surface finished products and laminate flooring. It stated that it had purchased goods with a value in excess of EUR 60 million over the previous three years from the manufacturers of decor paper which have been penalized. By letter of May 8, 2008 the Bundeskartellamt replied to the application for access to the file by sending three decisions imposing fines, from which identifying information had been removed, and a list of the evidence recorded as having been obtained during the search. Pfleiderer then sent a second letter to the Bundeskartellamt expressly requesting access to all the material in the file, including the documents relating to the leniency applications which had been voluntarily submitted by the applicants for leniency and the evidence seized. On October 14, 2008 the Bundeskartellamt partly rejected that application and restricted access to the file to a version from which confidential business information, internal documents and documents covered by point 22 of the Bundeskartellamt's notice on leniency had been removed, and again refused access to the evidence which had been seized. Pfleiderer thereupon brought an action before the Amtsgericht (Local Court) Bonn challenging that decision of partial rejection, pursuant to Paragraph 62(1) of the OwiG [the German Law on Administrative Offences].

On February 3, 2009 the Amtsgericht Bonn delivered a decision by which it ordered the Bundeskartellamt to grant Pfleiderer access to the file, through its lawyer, in accordance with the combined provisions of Paragraph 406e(1) of the Code of Criminal Procedure and Paragraph 46(1) of the OWiG. In the view of the Amtsgericht Bonn, Pfleiderer is an 'aggrieved party' within the meaning of those provisions, given that it may be assumed that it paid excessive prices, as a result of the cartel, for the goods which it purchased from the cartel members. Further, the Amtsgericht held, Pfleiderer had a 'legitimate interest' in obtaining access to the documents, since those were to be used for the preparation of civil proceedings for damages. However, the court stayed enforcement of its decision, pending a ruling from the ECJ on whether requiring access to such information would conflict with the EU's competition policies.

THE COURT:

"As it took the view that the resolution of the dispute before it required an interpretation of European Union law, the Amtsgericht Bonn decided to stay the proceedings and to refer the following question to [this] Court for a preliminary ruling:

'Are the provisions of Community competition law—in particular Articles 11 and 12 of Regulation No 1/2003 and the second paragraph of Article 10 EC, in conjunction with Article 3(1)(g) EC—to be interpreted as meaning that parties adversely affected by a cartel may not, for the purpose of bringing civil-law claims, be given access to leniency applications or to information and documents voluntarily submitted in that connection by applicants for leniency which the national competition authority of a Member State has received, pursuant to a national leniency programme, within the framework of proceedings for the imposition of fines which are (also) intended to enforce Article 81 EC?'

"It must be recalled at the outset that the competition authorities of the Member States and their courts and tribunals are required to apply Articles 101 TFEU and 102 TFEU, where the facts come within the scope of European Union law, and to ensure that those articles are applied effectively in the general interest....

"Neither the provisions of the EC Treaty on competition nor Regulation No 1/2003 lay down common rules on leniency or common rules on the right of access to documents relating to a leniency procedure which have been voluntarily submitted to a national competition authority pursuant to a national leniency programme.

"Within the ECN, a model leniency programme, designed to achieve the harmonisation of some elements of national leniency programmes, was also drawn up and adopted in 2006. However, that model programme likewise has no binding effect on the courts and tribunals of the Member States.

"Accordingly, even if the guidelines set out by the Commission may have some effect on the practice of the national competition authorities, it is, in the absence of binding regulation under European Union law on the subject, for Member States to establish and apply national rules on the right of access, by persons adversely affected by a cartel, to documents relating to leniency procedures.

"However, while the establishment and application of those rules falls within the competence of the Member States, the latter must none the less exercise that competence in accordance with European Union law.... In particular, they may not render the implementation of European Union law impossible or excessively difficult ... and, specifically, in the area of competition law, they must ensure that the rules which they establish or apply do not jeopardise the effective application of Articles 101 TFEU and 102 TFEU....

"However, as maintained by the Commission and the Member States which have submitted observations, leniency programmes are useful tools if efforts to uncover and bring to an end infringements of competition rules are to be effective and serve, therefore, the objective of effective application of Articles 101 TFEU and 102 TFEU.

"The effectiveness of those programmes could, however, be compromised if documents relating to a leniency procedure were disclosed to persons wishing to bring an action for damages, even if the national competition authorities were to grant to the applicant for leniency exemption, in whole or in part, from the fine which they could have imposed.

"The view can reasonably be taken that a person involved in an infringement of competition law, faced with the possibility of such disclosure, would be deterred from taking the opportunity offered by such leniency programmes, particularly when, pursuant to Articles 11 and 12 of Regulation No 1/2003, the Commission and the national competition authorities might exchange information which that person has voluntarily provided.

"Nevertheless, it is settled case-law that any individual has the right to claim damages for loss caused to him by conduct which is liable to restrict or distort competition….

"The existence of such a right strengthens the working of the Community competition rules and discourages agreements or practices, frequently covert, which are liable to restrict or distort competition. From that point of view, actions for damages before national courts can make a significant contribution to the maintenance of effective competition in the European Union….

"Accordingly, in the consideration of an application for access to documents relating to a leniency programme submitted by a person who is seeking to obtain damages from another person who has taken advantage of such a leniency programme, it is necessary to ensure that the applicable national rules are not less favourable than those governing similar domestic claims and that they do not operate in such a way as to make it practically impossible or excessively difficult to obtain such compensation … and to weigh the respective interests in favour of disclosure of the information and in favour of the protection of that information provided voluntarily by the applicant for leniency.

"That weighing exercise can be conducted by the national courts and tribunals only on a case-by-case basis, according to national law, and taking into account all the relevant factors in the case.

"In the light of the foregoing, the answer to the question referred is that the provisions of European Union law on cartels, and in particular Regulation No 1/2003, must be interpreted as not precluding a person who has been adversely affected by an infringement of European Union competition law and is seeking to obtain damages from being granted access to documents relating to a leniency procedure involving the perpetrator of that infringement. It is, however, for the courts and tribunals of the Member States, on the basis of their national law, to determine the conditions under which such access must be permitted or refused by weighing the interests protected by European Union law….

"On those grounds, the Court (Grand Chamber) hereby rules:
The provisions of European Union law on cartels, and in particular Council Regulation (EC) No 1/2003 of 16 December 2002 on the implementation of the rules on competition laid down in Articles 101 TFEU and 102 TFEU, must be interpreted as not precluding a

person who has been adversely affected by an infringement of European Union competition law and is seeking to obtain damages from being granted access to documents relating to a leniency procedure involving the perpetrator of that infringement. It is, however, for the courts and tribunals of the Member States, on the basis of their national law, to determine the conditions under which such access must be permitted or refused by weighing the interests protected by European Union law."

COMPETITION COMMISSION v. ARCELORMITTAL SOUTH AFRICA LIMITED
[2013] ZASCA 84 (Supreme Court of Appeal of South Africa 2013)

BACKGROUND: This is an appeal by the Competition Commission and cross-appeals by the first and second respondents (defendants), ArcelorMittal South Africa Limited and Cape Gate (Pty.) Limited ("AMSA"), that arise from proceedings before the Competition Appeal Court ("CAC"). There is a dispute between the Commission and the respondents over the latters' entitlement to the production of documents from the Commission. They require the documents, the respondents say, to properly consider their written responses to a complaint that the Commission has lodged against them with the Competition Tribunal. The Commission alleges they have engaged in prohibited practices as part of a steel cartel in contravention of the Competition Act 89 of 1998. It refuses to hand over the documents, saying they are privileged and also contain "restricted information" under the Commission's rules.

Scaw South Africa (Pty.) Ltd., the third respondent, which admits to being part of the alleged cartel, gave the documents to the Commission. It did so to avoid prosecution by taking advantage of the Commission's Corporate Leniency Policy ("CLP"). The rationale of the policy was recently explained, as follows: "[T]he CLP has been developed to encourage participants to break ranks and disclose information that enables the Commission to tackle cartel behaviour. This information is furnished 'in return for immunity from prosecution'...."

Unable to obtain the documents from the Commission, AMSA and Cape Gate separately applied to the tribunal for an order directing the Commission to produce them. The Commission opposed the applications, alleging both that the documents were privileged and that they constituted restricted information. Scaw was a party to the proceedings, alleging that it had a claim to have the documents kept confidential. Save for ordering limited disclosure of certain documents, the Tribunal dismissed both applications. Both respondents then appealed to the CAC against the order of the tribunal. The CAC made no order on the appeals by the respondents, considering it unnecessary to decide the issues upon which the Tribunal had pronounced. Instead it upheld Scaw's contention that the documents were protected from disclosure by a claim it had made to confidentiality. The CAC therefore remitted the matter to the Tribunal to determine Scaw's confidentiality claim. Both sides then asked for review by the Supreme Court of Appeal.

JUDGE OF APPEAL CACHALIA:

"Litigation privilege is one of two components of legal professional privilege, the other being the privilege that attaches to communications between a client and his attorney for the purpose of obtaining and giving legal advice. Litigation privilege, with which we are concerned in this case, protects communications between a litigant or his legal advisor and third parties, if such communications are made for the purpose of pending or contemplated litigation. It applies typically to witness statements prepared at a litigant's instance for this purpose. The privilege belongs to the litigant, not the witness, and may be waived only by the litigant.

"Litigation privilege has two established requirements: The first is that the document must have been obtained or brought into existence for the purpose of a litigant's submission to a legal advisor for legal advice; and second that litigation was pending or contemplated as likely at the time.

"There is some uncertainty as to whether documents prepared for litigation must have submission to legal advisers as it sole purpose, substantial purpose, definite purpose or dominant purpose. A suggestion that the document must have been prepared substantially for that purpose was rejected as having been based on a misreading of earlier authority.... [One case said] the dominant purpose test ... did not accord with our practice. The dominant purpose test has since been applied in Canadian and Australian courts. And the parties [here] appear to adopt it in their submissions.

"It is, however, not always apparent what the definite or dominant purpose is. In *Waugh*, where the two purposes of a document carried equal weight, the court found that no dominant purpose attached to the document and it was therefore not protected by litigation privilege. But the courts have also looked at these separate or dual purposes as part of a single overarching purpose related to litigation....

"Here the parties differ over the purpose for which the leniency application was brought into existence, let alone its definite or dominant purpose....

"In my view the flaw in the respondents' approach is that they incorrectly focus on Scaw's motive in composing the leniency application to determine the purpose – whether definite or dominant – instead of focusing on the Commission's reason for obtaining or procuring it. The purpose of the document is not to be ascertained by reference to its author, either at the time at which the document was prepared or at the time it is handed over to the litigant or the litigant's legal representative. Instead, the purpose of the document is to be determined by reference to 'the person or authority under whose direction, whether particular or general, it was produced or brought into existence'. In that case it is the intention of the person who procured the document, and not the author's intention, that is relevant for ascertaining the document's purpose. The author need not even have known of possible litigation when the document was prepared.

"The inquiry into whether litigation privilege attaches to the leniency application is fact-bound. In this case that inquiry must focus on the facts set out in the Commission's answering affidavits in response to the respondents' discovery applications. The Commission says that the CLP is founded upon an expectation of litigation. The commencement of discussions with a leniency applicant is always with a view to instituting prosecutions against cartelists. And the grant of immunity flows from the process. Put simply the grant of immunity, to secure the cooperation of a cartelist, is inseparable from the litigation process itself.

"I therefore consider that the circumstances under which Scaw created the document and the Commission obtained it are inseparable. The document came into existence at the instance of the Commission for the purpose of prosecuting firms alleged to be part of a cartel.... Furthermore, the accepted facts support the Commission's averment that litigation was likely when the document was procured, that its lawyers were involved in the process – including advising on the leniency application, and that the purpose for the preparation of the leniency application was to support the envisaged litigation. The leniency application was, in substance, Scaw's witness statement in the contemplated litigation. The document was therefore privileged in the hands of the Commission.

"In the light of this finding the question that arises is whether the Commission waived its privilege by referring to the leniency application in the referral affidavit, as the respondents' contend it did. Under rule 35(12) a document becomes disclosable if reference is made to it in a pleading. The tribunal dismissed this contention somewhat cursorily: waiver, it said, is not lightly inferred and the 'oblique references' to the leniency application in the referral affidavit are not sufficient to constitute a waiver. The CAC did not consider the point....

"I appreciate that a bare reference to a document in a pleading, without more, may be insufficient to constitute a waiver, whereas the disclosure of its full contents may constitute a waiver. Where the line is drawn between these extremes is a question of degree, which calls for a value judgment by the court. When that line is crossed the privilege attached to the whole document, and not just the part of the document that was referred to, is waived. The reason is that courts are loath to order disclosure of only part of a document because its meaning may be distorted. But it must also be so that it does not inevitably follow that because part of document is disclosed, privilege is lost in respect of the whole document. This would be so where a document consists of severable parts and is capable of severance. I turn to the facts here.

"The Commission referred to the leniency application in its referral affidavit in these terms:

'8.7 . . . Scaw applied for leniency in terms of the Commission's CLP for price fixing and market allocation in relation to rebar, wire rod, sections (including rounds, squares angles and profiles).

'8.8 Scaw confirmed in the application for leniency that there has been a long standing culture of cooperation amongst the steel mills regarding the prices to be charged, and discounts to be offered, for their steel products such as rebar, wire rod, sections (including rounds and squares, angels and profiles). The cooperation extended to arrangements on market division.

'8.9 In addition to information submitted by Scaw in its leniency application, the Commission conducted its own investigations which largely confirmed the allegations made by Scaw and provided further evidence of anticompetitive practices in contravention of section 4(1)(b) of the Act – involving both price fixing and market division.

'8.10 It is as a consequence of information contained in the Scaw application for leniency and that obtained from the Commission's investigations that this referral is made.'

"These paragraphs, in my view, amount to much more than a bare or oblique reference to the leniency application. The allegation in para 8.8 that a long standing culture of cooperation was 'confirmed in the application for leniency' makes it clear that the application contained a full recital of facts that supported that conclusion. Whether the application indeed contained those facts is a matter that the respondents will be called upon to respond to in their answering affidavits. It is precisely to enable it to do so that rule 35(12) requires documents referred to in pleadings to be disclosed....

"Once it is accepted that the Commission waived its privilege to the leniency application, it follows that any entitlement of the Commission to claim the information as restricted information under rule 14(1)(e) was similarly waived.

"What remains is Scaw's claim of confidentiality concerning the information that was part of the leniency application. Cape Gate contests the claim. As I understand its submission, Cape Gate contends that once Scaw and the Commission agreed that the information provided was discoverable for use in proceedings before the tribunal in terms of s 11.1.3.3, Scaw no longer had any reasonable expectation that the information provided would be treated as confidential in litigation proceedings. And so, it submits, Scaw cannot claim any of the documents provided to the Commission as confidential information....

"In my view Cape Gate's submission conflates the two senses in which the term confidentiality is dealt with in the CLP: The first concerns the confidentiality of the CLP process, and the second relates to the confidentiality of an informant's information.... Properly construed, therefore, *all* information submitted by the applicant must be treated in confidence by the Commission until it decides to use the information before the tribunal, in which case only information specifically claimed to be 'confidential information' must be dealt with in terms of the Act....

"The CAC, I think, correctly held that until the respondents apply through the legislatively prescribed procedure under s 45(1) for access to the information, and the tribunal determines whether or not the information is confidential, the documents remain confidential. I do, however, have doubts as to whether Scaw's claim to confidentiality falls within the terms of the section. In its written statement in the prescribed form explaining why the information is confidential, and under a column requiring an applicant to describe the 'nature of the economic value of the information', Scaw made no attempt to bring any of the information within the ambit of the definition. It merely stated, formulaically, and in respective of each of four categories of information claimed to be confidential, that it is '[i]nformation belonging to a private entity which is strictly private and confidential and made in pursuance of corporate leniency and which is clearly not in the public domain and which could cause irreparable harm if it becomes available to competitors or other third parties'. What Scaw describes here are the *consequences* of the information being disclosed, not the *nature* and economic value of the information. Scaw's mere assertion, in the prescribed form, that the information is confidential, does not make it so.

"But it was submitted on behalf of Scaw, and I accept the submission, that the tribunal is the proper forum in which a claim to confidentiality under the section, both in its form and its substance, is to be tested. The CAC therefore correctly remitted this question to the tribunal, and Cape Gate's submission to the contrary falls to be dismissed.

"AMSA's Rule 15 application

"As mentioned earlier, AMSA also seeks access to the Commission record (apart from the leniency application) under Commission rule 15(1) read with rule 14. Rule 15(1) allows 'any person' to have access to 'any Commission record', provided it is not 'restricted information' contemplated in rule 14(1). The Commission opposes this.

"The Commission suggested in argument that AMSA is not entitled to invoke rule 15 to obtain access to the record as the rule is aimed at providing access to information to the public, and not to a litigant. If it is correct that a member of the public may gain access to the Commission record under rule 15, subject to any restrictions under rule 14, and this must be so on a plain reading of the rule, it would be absurd to prevent a litigant from being given access. This would mean, for example, that access could be denied to the Chief Executive Officer of AMSA, but not to her relatives or friends, who are members of the public. It follows that AMSA is entitled to the Commission record subject to any claims of privilege or any restriction under rule 14....

"Rule 14(1) provides for five categories of restricted information: confidential information; information concerning the identity of a complainant; information concerning the conduct attached to a complaint until a referral or notice of non-referral is issued; the Commission's work product; and finally any document to which the Commission is 'required or entitled to restrict access in terms the Promotion of Access to Information Act, 2000 (Act No. 2 of 2000)' (PAIA), which is in issue here.

"There is no dispute that once the complaint had been referred to the tribunal for adjudication, any restriction under rule 14(1)(c) fell away because access to the record could no longer be restricted on this ground. The tribunal, however, held that the Commission was entitled to withhold access to the record because disclosure would reasonably compromise the future supply of similar information or information from the same source. The tribunal thus held that the information could be withheld from AMSA at the Commission's discretion because of its 'inherent nature'. As I have already held that the information forming part of the leniency application must be disclosed, the question whether information from the same source – i.e. the leniency applicant – may be withheld falls away. The Commission may therefore not withhold this part of the record on this ground.

"I accept though that the record may also contain similar information pertaining to the investigation that may emanate from sources other than the leniency applicant, which the Commission may well be entitled to restrict; indeed it may be obliged to restrict this information in the public interest if it reasonably believes that disclosure would prejudice the future supply of such information. But it does not follow that all information in the record may be withheld even if it does not fall into this category, or any other category, contemplated in rule 14. If the Commission seeks to prevent AMSA from gaining access to the record, it cannot do so generally but is required to identify specific documents or categories of documents to which it may wish to restrict access. In this regard AMSA has made it clear that it does not seek access to documents that may legitimately be claimed to be part of the Commission's work product as contemplated by rule 14(1)(d). Consequently AMSA's claim to the record succeeds, subject to any claim that specific documents are privileged, restricted or confidential.

"To conclude, I hold that the leniency application was privileged, but that the Commission waived its privilege by referring to it in the referral affidavit, as it did to the claim that the application was restricted under rule 14(1)(e). The leniency application must therefore be disclosed to the respondents subject to the tribunal determining Scaw's claim of confidentiality in terms of s 45(1) of the Act. In respect of AMSA's application for disclosure of the Commission record, this too is upheld, subject to any claim that the record or any part of it may be restricted under rule 14, or on the grounds of privilege, or any other ground that provides a recognised defence to the disclosure of information. Those claims are to be adjudicated by the tribunal, if any such claims arise.

"The following order is made:
'1.   The appeal by the Commission is dismissed and the cross-appeals by AMSA and Cape Gate are upheld. In each case the Commission is to pay the costs of AMSA and Cape Gate, including the costs of two counsel.

'2.   No order is made regarding the costs incurred by Scaw on appeal.

'3.   The order of the Competition Appeal Court is replaced with the following order:
(i)   The appeal by AMSA and Cape Gate is upheld and the order of the tribunal is set aside;
(ii)   The Commission is ordered to provide to AMSA the documents listed as items 3–42 in para 14 of the judgment of the Competition Appeal Court;
(iii)   The Commission is ordered to provide the leniency application and marker application to AMSA, and to provide the leniency application to Cape Gate, subject to the finding by the tribunal on Scaw's claim to confidentiality in form CC7 dated 9 July 2008. That claim to confidentiality is remitted to the tribunal for determination and the making of an appropriate order regarding access to the information;
(iv)   The Commission is ordered to provide to AMSA its record of information collected during its investigation, subject to any claims to privilege made by the Commission in relation to any of the information, and to any claims that it is restricted information, including confidential information. Should any such claims be made they are to be submitted to and determined by the tribunal;
(v)   The Commission is to pay AMSA's and Cape Gate's costs in the appeal and its costs in the proceedings before the tribunal, including the costs of two counsel where employed;
(vi)   No order is made regarding the costs of Scaw'."

UNITED STATES OF AMERICA v. HUI HSIUNG & AU OPTRONICS CORP.
778 F.3d 738 (9th Cir. 2015)

BACKGROUND: This criminal antitrust case stems from an international conspiracy between Taiwanese and Korean electronics manufacturers to fix prices for what is now ubiquitous technology, Liquid Crystal Display panels known as "TFT-LCDs." After five years of secret meetings in Taiwan, sales worldwide including in the United States, and millions of dollars in profits to the participating companies, the conspiracy ended when the FBI raided the offices of AU Optronics Corporation of America ("AUOA") in Houston, Texas.

The defendants, AU Optronics ("AUO"), a Taiwanese company, and AUOA, AUO's retailer and wholly owned subsidiary (collectively, "the corporate defendants"), and two executives from AUO, Hsuan Bin Chen, its President and Chief Operating Officer, and Hui Hsiung, its Executive Vice President, were convicted of conspiracy to fix prices in violation of the Sherman Act after an eight-week jury trial.

From October 2001 to January 2006, representatives from six leading TFT-LCD manufacturers met in Taiwan to "set the target price" and "stabilize the price" of TFT-LCDs, which were sold in the United States principally to Dell, Hewlett Packard ("HP"), Compaq, Apple, and Motorola for use in consumer electronics. This series of meetings, in which Chen, Hsiung, and other AUO employees participated, came to be known as the "Crystal Meetings."

Following each Crystal Meeting, the participating companies produced "Crystal Meeting Reports." These reports provided pricing targets for TFT-LCD sales, which, in turn, were used by retail branches of the companies as price benchmarks for selling panels to wholesale customers. More specifically, AUOA used the Crystal Meeting Reports that AUO provided to negotiate prices for the sale of TFT-LCDs to United States customers including HP, Compaq, ViewSonic, Dell, and Apple. AUOA employees and executives routinely traveled to the United States offices of Dell, Apple, and HP in Texas and California to discuss pricing for TFT-LCDs based on the targets coming out of the Crystal Meetings. Chen and Hsiung played the most "critical role[s]" in settling price disputes with executives at Dell.

The defendants were indicted in the Northern District of California and charged with one count of conspiracy to fix prices for TFT-LCDs in violation of the Sherman Act. The indictment also contained a sentencing allegation pursuant to the Alternative Fine Statute, alleging that AUO and AUOA, along with their coconspirators, "derived gross gains of at least $500,000,000."

At trial, the government presented evidence regarding the defendants' extensive involvement in the Crystal Meetings and their sales of price-fixed TFT-LCDs to customers in the United States, including evidence that the defendants specifically targeted United States technology companies, principally, Apple, Compaq, and HP. Government experts testified regarding the financial impact of those sales, specifically that the defendants derived hundreds of millions of dollars in profits from sales of price-fixed TFT-LCDs in the United States.

The jury found the defendants guilty of conspiracy to fix prices in violation of the Sherman Act. The jury also found that the "combined gross gains derived from the conspiracy by all the participants in the conspiracy" were "$500 million or more."

The district court sentenced Hsiung and Chen principally to a term of thirty-six months' imprisonment and a $200,000 fine each. The district court sentenced the corporate defendants to a three-year term of probation with conditions. The district court also imposed a $500 million fine on AUO. All of the defendants appeal their convictions, and AUO appeals its sentence.

JUDGE McKEOWN:

I. VENUE CHALLENGE

"As a preliminary matter, the defendants appeal on the basis of improper venue. Four issues are subsumed in the venue challenge: (i) our standard of review, (ii) the proper standard for proof at trial, (iii) whether the government's representation in closing arguments constituted prosecutorial misconduct, and (iv) whether the government proved venue....

"It is well established that a preponderance of the evidence is the proper standard of proof for venue.... The defendants' position that the standard is beyond a reasonable doubt has no support in the law. The district court appropriately instructed the jury on the standard of proof for venue....

"Finally, the evidence referenced by the government was sufficient to establish venue by a preponderance of the evidence. 'It is by now well settled that venue on a conspiracy charge is proper where ... any overt act committed in furtherance of the conspiracy occurred.'... In addition to the HP negotiations, the government introduced evidence that AUOA representatives negotiated sales of price-fixed TFT-LCDs with Apple in the Northern District of California and that AUOA maintained offices in the Northern District of California from which it conducted price negotiations by e-mail and phone. This evidence is sufficient to establish by a preponderance of the evidence that overt acts in furtherance of the conspiracy occurred in the Northern District of California. Thus, venue was proper.

II. JURY INSTRUCTION CHALLENGE AND EXTRATERRITORIALITY OF THE SHERMAN ACT

"The Supreme Court's seminal case on antitrust and foreign conduct is *Hartford Fire*, in which the Court held that 'the Sherman Act applies to foreign conduct that was meant to produce and did in fact produce some substantial effect in the United States.'… The district court instructed the jury to this effect: 'to convict the defendants you must find beyond a reasonable doubt one or both of the following [] (A) that at least one member of the conspiracy took at least one action in furtherance of the conspiracy within the United States, or (B) that the conspiracy had a substantial and intended effect in the United States.'

"Before trial, the defendants moved to dismiss the indictment on the basis that it did not allege adequately the *Hartford Fire* 'substantial and intended effects' test. At the jury instructions conference, the defendants urged the district court to give the *Hartford Fire* instruction, while also claiming that part A of the instruction was erroneous because it permitted the jury to convict on the basis of one domestic act. Although the defendants contested part A, they all concurred that part B 'is a correct statement of the *Hartford Fire* requirements for establishing extraterritorial jurisdiction over foreign anticompetitive conduct, and should be given.'

"In an about face, in post-trial motions, the defendants rejected the principle of *Hartford Fire* and argued for the first time that the Sherman Act cannot be used to prosecute foreign conduct because there is no affirmative indication that the Sherman Act applies extraterritorially. They cited to the Supreme Court's decision in *Morrison*, which addressed the extraterritorial reach of the federal securities laws.

"At the time of the jury instructions conference, in February 2012, *Morrison* had been on the books for more than eighteen months. Commentary about the case was extensive…. The opinion was hardly breaking news. In light of the defendants' request that the court give the *Hartford Fire* jury instruction and their untimely objection to the instruction in post-trial motions, we hold that the defendants waived the argument that *Morrison* overruled *Hartford Fire* and that an extraterritoriality defense bars their convictions.

"Because the defendants were the ones who proposed the instruction in the first place, they cannot now claim that giving the instruction was error. The defendants considered the effects of the instruction and intentionally relinquished the right to argue that the Sherman Act does not apply extraterritorially….

"We have held that the FTAIA's requirement that the defendants' conduct had a 'direct, substantial, and reasonably foreseeable effect' on domestic commerce displaced the intentionality requirement of *Hartford Fire* where the FTAIA applies…. To the extent that the prosecution was not subject to the FTAIA, the jury instructions as a whole belie the assertion that the jury could have convicted on the basis of one, unintentional domestic act….

"The effect of foreign conduct in the United States was a central point of controversy throughout the trial. Nonetheless, the conduct always was linked … to targeting for sale or delivery in the

United States. Part A of the instruction required the jury to find that the defendants fixed the prices of TFT-LCDs 'targeted' for sale or delivery in the United States. This 'targeting' language subsumed intentionality.... There is no way that the defendants could have unintentionally designated or chosen the United States market as a target of the conspiracy. Viewing the instructions as a whole, nothing misled the jury as to its task. The *Hartford Fire* jury instruction was neither a surprise nor was it improper. Part A of the instruction passes legal muster, and the defendants solicited part B.

III. *PER SE* LIABILITY FOR HORIZONTAL PRICE-FIXING

"Having determined that the prosecution was not barred by an extraterritoriality defense, we address the appropriate standard for judging liability in this price-fixing scheme. For over a century, courts have treated horizontal price-fixing as a *per se* violation of the Sherman Act.... Twice in recent years, the Supreme Court reiterated this principle. The directive in *Leegin Creative Leather*... is unequivocal: 'A horizontal cartel among competing manufacturers or competing retailers that decreases output or reduces competition in order to increase price is, and ought to be, *per se* unlawful.' And just last year, the Chief Justice emphasized that 'it is *per se* unlawful to fix prices under antitrust law.'...

IV. THE FOREIGN TRADE ANTITRUST IMPROVEMENTS ACT

"The international implications of this case are not limited to the challenges to the jury instructions or the *per se* rule. The defendants also argue that the indictment and proof did not satisfy the requirements of the FTAIA. The FTAIA provides that the Sherman Act 'shall not apply to conduct involving trade or commerce (other than import trade or import commerce) with foreign nations unless—(1) such conduct has a direct, substantial, and reasonably foreseeable effect—(A) on trade or commerce which is not trade or commerce with foreign nations....

"Although the statute is a web of words, it boils down to two principles. First, the Sherman Act applies to 'import trade or import commerce' with foreign nations.... Put differently, the FTAIA does not alter the Sherman Act's coverage of import trade; import trade is excluded from the FTAIA altogether. Second, under the FTAIA, the Sherman Act does not apply to nonimport trade or commerce with foreign nations, unless the domestic effects exception is met.... For the Sherman Act to apply to nonimport trade or commerce with foreign nations, the conduct at issue must have a 'direct, substantial, and reasonably foreseeable effect—(A) on trade or commerce which is not trade or commerce with foreign nations...'.

A. JURISDICTION VERSUS MERITS

"Whether the FTAIA 'affects the subject-matter jurisdiction of the district court or if, on the other hand, it relates to the scope of coverage of the antitrust laws,' is our first inquiry.... We start here because '[a] court has a duty to assure itself of its own jurisdiction, regardless of whether jurisdiction is contested by the parties ... and the Supreme Court has emphasized the need to draw a careful line between the jurisdictional limitations and other types of rules...'. We hold that the FTAIA is not a subject-matter limitation on the power of the federal courts but a component of the merits of a Sherman Act claim involving nonimport trade or commerce with foreign nations....

B. THE FTAIA CHALLENGES ...

"The defendants argue that (i) the indictment was insufficient because it did not name or cite the FTAIA, (ii) the indictment and evidence are insufficient as to both import trade and domestic effects, and (iii) the domestic effects exception, which was not alleged in the indictment, is an element of a Sherman Act offense that implicates the FTAIA and thus this instruction constructively amended the indictment.

1. THE FTAIA IN THE INDICTMENT

"The defendants argue that the indictment was flawed for failing to mention the FTAIA by name or statutory citation. However, as explained in detail with regard to import trade and domestic effects, the indictment contained the factual allegations necessary to establish that the FTAIA either did not apply or that its requirements were satisfied.

"In any event, there was absolutely no prejudice from the indictment's failure to cite the FTAIA. 'Unless the defendant[s] w[ere] misled and thereby prejudiced, neither an error in a citation nor a citation's omission is a ground to dismiss the indictment or information or to reverse a conviction.'... The parties raised the FTAIA requirements throughout the proceedings, and the district court record is full of briefing and argument on the FTAIA.

2. IMPORT TRADE AND THE FTAIA

"The appropriate characterization of the import trade provision of the FTAIA is essential to our analysis.... The statute provides that the Sherman Act 'shall not apply to conduct involving trade or commerce (other than import trade or import commerce),' and then goes on to provide limitations vis-a-vis nonimport commerce.... We agree with the defendants that this section should not be labeled an FTAIA exception. Rather, more accurately, import trade, as referenced in the parenthetical statement, does not fall within the FTAIA at all. It falls within the Sherman

Act without further clarification or pleading. Consequently, we disagree with the defendants' view that the indictment was insufficient because it did not allege import trade under the FTAIA.

"The indictment charged a violation of § 1 of the Sherman Act and alleged that the defendants 'entered into and engaged in a combination and conspiracy to suppress and eliminate competition by fixing the prices of thin-film transistor liquid crystal display panels ("TFT-LCD") in the United States and elsewhere.'... 'It is generally sufficient that an indictment set forth the offense in the words of the statute itself, as long as those words of themselves fully, directly, and expressly, without any uncertainty or ambiguity, set forth all the elements necessary to constitute the offence intended to be punished.'... Apart from tracking the language of the Sherman Act in the indictment, the government did, in fact, plead and prove that the defendants engaged in import trade....

"Although our circuit has not defined 'import trade' for purposes of the FTAIA, not much imagination is required to say that this phrase means precisely what it says. As the Seventh Circuit held in a case involving foreign cartel members, "transactions that are directly between the [U.S.] plaintiff purchasers and the defendant cartel members *are* the import commerce of the United States....'

"The defendants' conduct, as alleged and proven, constitutes 'import trade,' and falls outside the scope of the FTAIA....

"The indictment is replete with allegations that support the government's position that the defendants engaged in import trade. The indictment alleged that, within the conspiracy period, AUO and AUOA 'engaged in the business of producing and selling TFT-LCDs to customers in the United States.'...

"These allegations directly describe that the defendants and their coconspirators engaged in import commerce with the United States—indeed, the conspiracy's intent, as alleged, was to 'suppress and eliminate competition' by fixing the prices for panels that AUO and AUOA sold to manufacturers 'in the United States and elsewhere' for incorporation into retail technology sold to consumers in the United States and elsewhere.

"Going into trial, there was no surprise regarding the import trade allegations; likewise, the evidence at trial was ample on this aspect of the conspiracy....

"Trial testimony established that AUO imported over one million price-fixed panels per month into the United States. The Crystal Meeting participants earned over $600 million from the importation of TFT-LCDs into the United States. Although it was undisputed at trial that AUO and AUOA did not manufacture any consumer products for importation into the United States, the evidence revealed that AUO and AUOA executives and employees negotiated with United States companies in the United States to sell TFT-LCD panels at the prices set at the Crystal Meetings. Importation of this critical component of various electronic devices is surely 'import trade or import commerce.' To suggest, as the defendants do, that AUO was not an 'importer' misses the point. The panels were sold into the United States, falling squarely within the scope of the Sherman Act.

"The defendants also claim that the transactions did not 'target' the United States. Targeting is not a legal element for import trade under the Sherman Act, though it was included in the jury instructions at the defendants' request. In any event, the negotiations in the United States and the significant direct sales to the United States certainly qualify as targeting. The challenge to the sufficiency of the evidence fails.

"In sum, the FTAIA does not apply to the defendants' import trade conduct. The government sufficiently pleaded and proved that the conspirators engaged in import commerce with the United States and that the price-fixing conspiracy violated § 1 of the Sherman Act.

3. DOMESTIC EFFECTS UNDER THE FTAIA

"Unlike import trade, which is exempted from the FTAIA altogether, if the government proceeds on a domestic effects theory, which it did here, the government must plead and prove the requirements for the domestic effects exception to the FTAIA, namely that the defendants' conduct had 'a direct, substantial, and reasonably foreseeable effect' on United States commerce.... . We hold that the indictment sufficiently alleged such conduct and reject the defendants' sufficiency of the evidence challenge to the domestic effects exception....

"Looking at the conspiracy as a whole, and recognizing the standard on appeal is whether '*any* rational trier of fact could have found the essential elements of the crime beyond a reasonable doubt,' ... we conclude that the conduct was sufficiently 'direct, substantial and reasonably foreseeable' with respect to the effect on United States commerce....

"The constellation of events that surrounded the conspiracy leads to one conclusion—the impact on the United States market was direct and followed 'as an immediate consequence' of the price fixing. To begin, the TFT-LCDs are a substantial cost component of the finished products—70-80 percent in the case of monitors and 30-40 percent for notebook computers....

"Finally, we note that even disregarding the domestic effects exception, the evidence that the defendants engaged in import trade was overwhelming and demonstrated that the defendants sold hundreds of millions of dollars of price-fixed panels directly into the United States. The evidence offered in support of the import trade theory alone was sufficient to convict the defendants of price-fixing in violation of the Sherman Act....

V. THE ALTERNATIVE FINE STATUTE

"The final basis for the defendants' appeal is the $500 million fine the district court imposed on AUO pursuant to the Alternative Fine Statute.... The Alternative Fine Statute provides: 'If any person derives pecuniary gain from the offense, or if the offense results in pecuniary loss to a person other than the defendant, the defendant may be fined not more than the greater of twice the gross gain or twice the gross loss....' The jury found that the collective gain to the conspiracy members was over $500 million. We analyze the fine from two perspectives: (i) whether the fine was improper because it was based on the collective gains to all members of the conspiracy rather than the gains to AUO alone, and (ii) whether the district court, in not imposing joint and several liability, erred by failing to adhere to the 'one recovery'" rule and failing to take into account any fines paid by AUO's coconspirators. These are issues of first impression.

A. COLLECTIVE GAINS

"Whether 'gross gains' under § 3571 means gross gains to the individual defendant or to the conspiracy as a whole is an issue of statutory interpretation that we review *de novo*.... [The] instruction was proper because the statute unambiguously permits a 'gross gains' calculation based on the gain attributable to the entire conspiracy.

"The statute does not require that the gain derive from the defendant's 'own individual conduct,' as AUO reads it. Indeed, AUO's interpretation reads additional provisions into the statute.... Nor has AUO pointed to any case that supports its suggested interpretation, which is contrary to the plain text of the statute....

"AUO's offense is the conspiracy to fix prices for TFTLCDs. The jury found $500 million in gross gains from that offense. The unambiguous language of the statute permitted the district court to impose the $500 million fine based on the gross gains to all the coconspirators.

B. JOINT AND SEVERAL LIABILITY

"AUO also argues that the district court erred by failing to follow principles of joint and several liability in imposing the fine, an approach that would have required a reduction from the fine amount of the portion already paid by AUO's coconspirators. However, AUO offers no support for the proposition that § 3571(d) incorporates principles of joint and several liability. The cases it cites do not address whether the 'one recovery' rule of joint and several liability applies to § 3571(d), nor do they even discuss § 3571(d).... No statutory authority or precedent supports

AUO's interpretation of the Alternative Fine Statute as requiring joint and several liability and imposing a 'one recovery' rule.

"AFFIRMED."

BANCO NACIONAL DE CUBA v. SABBATINO
376 U.S. 398 (1964)

BACKGROUND: On July 6, 1960, the U.S. Congress amended the Sugar Act of 1948 to permit a presidential reduction in Cuba's quota for sugar exports to the USA. President Eisenhower exercised that option the same day. Also on July 6, the Cuban Council of Ministers adopted Law No. 851, which denounced the sugar quota reduction as an act of "aggression, for political purposes" and which gave the Cuban President and Prime Minister power to nationalize Cuban-located property of American nationals.

Farr, Whitlock ("F-W," a USA commodities broker) had bought Cuban sugar from a subsidiary of Compania Azucarera Vertientes-Camaguey de Cuba (C.A.V.), a Cuban corporation whose stock was primarily owned by U.S. residents. F-W had agreed to pay for the sugar in New York upon presentation of the shipping documents and a draft for the amount of the purchase price. Between August 6 and 9, the sugar was loaded on board a ship bound for the ultimate customer in Morocco. President Castro nationalized American assets on August 6, including those of C.A.V. In order to get Cuba's permission for the ship and cargo to leave, F-W was forced to enter duplicate purchase contracts with Banco Para el Comercio Exterior de Cuba, an agency of the Cuban Government. Banco P.E.C.E. assigned these duplicate bills of lading to Banco Nacional de Cuba, which instructed its New York agent (Societe General) to present them to F-W and collect the $175,250.69 contract price. F-W refused to pay Societe General, but it also received a payment demand from C.A.V. F-W agreed to pay C.A.V., which in turn promised not to pay any funds to the Cuban government's banks. Sabbatino was appointed by a New York court to manage C.A.V.'s assets there, and the court also ordered F-W not to take any action to dispose of the disputed funds.

Banco Nacional then filed a lawsuit in U.S. District Court to recover the money. The court entered a summary judgment for Sabbatino, on the basis that the Cuban decree of nationalization violated international law. The U.S. Second Circuit Court of Appeals affirmed, and Banco Nacional asked for U.S. Supreme Court review.

JUSTICE HARLAN:

"The classic American statement of the act of state doctrine, which appears to have taken root in England as early as 1674 ... and began to emerge in the jurisprudence of this country in the late eighteenth and early nineteenth centuries ... is found in *Underhill* v. *Hernandez* ...: 'Every sovereign State is bound to respect the independence of every other sovereign State, and the courts of one country will not sit in judgment on the acts of another done within its own territory. Redress of grievances by reason of such acts must be obtained through the means open to be availed of by sovereign powers as between themselves.' ...

"The outcome of this case ... turns on whether any of the contentions urged by [Sabbatino] against the application of the act of state doctrine [here] is acceptable: (1) that the doctrine does not apply to acts of state which violate international law, as is claimed to be the case here; (2) that the doctrine is inapplicable unless the Executive specifically interposes it in a particular case; and (3) that, in any event, the doctrine may not be invoked by a foreign government plaintiff in our courts....

"We do not believe that this doctrine is compelled either by the inherent nature of sovereign authority, as some of the earlier decisions seem to imply ... or by some principle of international law.... While historic notions of sovereign authority do bear upon the wisdom of employing the act of state doctrine, they do not dictate its existence.

"That international law does not require application of the doctrine is evidenced by the practice of nations. Most of the countries rendering decisions on the subject fail to follow the rule rigidly. No international arbitral or judicial decision discovered suggests that international law prescribes recognition of sovereign acts of foreign governments ... and apparently no claim has ever been raised before an international tribunal that failure to apply the act of state doctrine constitutes a breach of international obligation. If international law does not prescribe use of the doctrine, neither does it forbid application of the rule even if it is claimed that the act of state in question violated international law. The traditional view of international law is that it establishes substantive law principles for determining whether one country has wronged another. Because of its peculiar nation-to-nation character the usual method for an individual to seek relief is to exhaust local remedies and then repair to the executive authorities of his own state to persuade them to champion his claim in diplomacy or before an international tribunal.... Although it is, of course, true that United States courts apply international law as a part of our own in appropriate circumstances ... the public law of nations can hardly dictate to a country which is in theory wronged how to treat that wrong within its domestic borders....

"The act of state doctrine does, however, have 'constitutional' underpinnings. It arises out of the basic relationships between branches of government in a system of separation of powers. It concerns the competency of dissimilar institutions to make and implement particular kinds of decisions in the area of international relations. The doctrine as formulated in past decisions expresses the strong sense of the Judicial Branch that its engagement in the task of passing on the validity of foreign acts of state may hinder rather than further this country's pursuit of goals both for itself and for the community of nations as a whole in the international sphere. Many commentators disagree with this view....

"Since the act of state doctrine proscribes a challenge to the validity of the Cuban expropriation decree in this case, any counterclaim based on asserted invalidity must fail. Whether a theory of conversion or breach of contract is the proper cause of action under New York law, the presumed validity of the expropriation is unaffected. Although we discern no remaining litigable issues of fact in this case, the District Court may hear and decide them if they develop.

"The judgment of the Court of Appeals is reversed and the case is remanded to the District Court for proceedings consistent with this opinion."

DISSENT by *Justice WHITE*:

"I am dismayed that the Court has, with one broad stroke, declared the ascertainment and application of international law beyond the competence of the courts of the United States in a large and important category of cases. I am also disappointed in the Court's declaration that the acts of a sovereign state with regard to the property of aliens within its borders are beyond the reach of international law in the courts of this country. However clearly established that law may be, a sovereign may violate it with impunity, except insofar as the political branches of the government may provide a remedy. This backward-looking doctrine, never before declared by this Court, is carried a disconcerting step further: not only are the courts powerless to question acts of state proscribed by international law but they are likewise powerless to refuse to adjudicate the claim founded upon a foreign law; they must render judgment and thereby validate the lawless act. Since the Court expressly extends its ruling to all acts of state expropriating property, however clearly inconsistent with the international community, all discriminatory expropriations of the property of aliens, as for example the taking of properties belonging to certain races, religions or nationalities, are entitled to automatic validation in the courts of the United States. No other civilized country has found such a rigid rule necessary for the survival of the executive branch of its government; the executive of no other government seems to require such insulation from international law adjudications in its courts; and no other judiciary is apparently so incompetent to ascertain and apply international law....

"The reasons for nonreview, based as they are on traditional concepts of territorial sovereignty, lose much of their force when the foreign act of state is shown to be a violation of international law. All legitimate exercises of sovereign power, whether territorial or otherwise, should be exercised consistently with the rules of international law, including those rules which mark the bounds of lawful state action against aliens or their property located within the territorial confines of the foreign state. Although a state may reasonably expect that the validity of its laws operating on property within its jurisdiction will not be defined by local notions of public policy of numerous other states (although a different situation may well be presented when courts of another state are asked to lend their enforcement machinery to effectuate the foreign act), it cannot with impunity ignore the rules governing the conduct of all nations and expect that other nations and tribunals will view its acts as within the permissible scope of territorial sovereignty. Contrariwise, to refuse inquiry into the question of whether norms of the international community have been contravened by the act of state under review would seem to deny the existence or purport of such norms, a view that seems inconsistent with the role of international law in ordering the relations between nations. Finally, the impartial application of international law would not only be an affirmation of the existence and binding effect of international rules of order, but also a refutation of the notion that this body of law consists of no more than the divergent and parochial views of the capital importing and exporting nations, the socialist and free-enterprise nations.

"The Court puts these considerations to rest with the assumption that the decisions of the courts 'of the world's major capital exporting country and principal exponent of the free enterprise system' would hardly be accepted as impartial expressions of sound legal principle. The assumption, if sound, would apply to any other problem arising from transactions that cross state lines and is tantamount to a declaration excusing this Court from any future consequential role in the clarification and application of international law…. This declaration ignores the historic role which this Court and other American courts have played in applying and maintaining principles of international law.

"Of course, there are many unsettled areas of international law, as there are of domestic law, and these areas present sensitive problems of accommodating the interest of nations that subscribe to divergent economic and political systems. It may be that certain nationalizations of property for public purpose fall within this area. Also, it may be that domestic courts, as compared to international tribunals, or arbitral commissions, have a different and less active role to play in formulating new rules of international law or choosing between rules not yet adhered to by any substantial group of nations. Where a clear violation of international law is not demonstrated, I would agree that principles of comity underlying the act of state doctrine warrant recognition and enforcement of the foreign act. But none of these considerations relieve a court of the obligation to make an inquiry into the validity of the foreign act, none of them warrant a flat rule of no inquiry at all. The vice of the act of state doctrine as formulated by the Court and applied in this case, where he decree is alleged not only to be confiscatory but also retaliatory and discriminatory and has been found by two courts to be a flagrant violation of international law, is that it precludes any such examination and proscribes any decision on whether Cuban Law No. 851 contravenes an accepted principle of international law....

"The Court's rule is peculiarly inappropriate in the instant case, where no one has argued that C.A.V. can obtain relief in Cuba, where the United States has broken off diplomatic relations with Cuba, and where the United States, although protesting the illegality of the Cuban decrees, has not sought to institute any action against Cuba in an international tribunal....

"In the absence of a specific objection [by the U.S. Department of State] to an examination of the validity of Cuba's law under international law, I would have proceeded to determine the issue and resolve this litigation on the merits."

FIRST NATIONAL CITY BANK v. BANCO NACIONAL DE CUBA
406 U.S. 759 (1972)

BACKGROUND: First National City loaned $15 million to Banco Nacional's predecessor bank, also an agency of the Cuban government, in 1958. As security for the loan, U.S. government bonds were pledged as collateral. After Castro came to power, Cuba renewed the loan and then paid off $5 million. Late in 1960, foreign banks in Cuba were nationalized. First National then sold off the remaining bonds it held, paid itself the $10 million remaining on the loan, and kept the $1.8 million surplus cash. When Banco Nacional sued in U.S. District Court for the $1.8 million, First National counterclaimed for the damages it sustained when its branches in Cuba were nationalized. The District Court granted summary judgment to First National, but the Second Circuit reversed. On certiorari, the U.S. Supreme Court reversed and remanded. Reconsidering, the Second Circuit again decided that U.S. courts could not review the validity of the Cuban nationalization of banks, due to the "act of state" doctrine. First National again requested review by the U.S. Supreme Court.

JUSTICE REHNQUIST:

"We must here decide whether, in view of the substantial difference between the position taken in this case by the Executive Branch and that which it took in *Sabbatino*, the act of state doctrine prevents [First National] from litigating its counterclaim on the merits. We hold that it does not.

"The separate lines of cases enunciating both the act of state and sovereign immunity doctrines have a common source in the case of *The Schooner Exchange v. M'Faddon*…. There Chief Justice Marshall stated the general principle of sovereign immunity: sovereigns are not presumed without explicit declaration to have opened their tribunals to suits against other sovereigns. Yet the policy considerations at the root of this fundamental principle are in large part also the underpinnings of the act of state doctrine….

"Thus, both the act of state and sovereign immunity doctrines are judicially created to effectuate general notions of comity among nations and among the respective branches of the Federal Government. The history and the legal basis of the act of state doctrine are treated comprehensively in the Court's opinion in *Sabbatino*….

"The act of state doctrine represents an exception to the general rule that a court of the United States, where appropriate jurisdictional standards are met, will decide cases before it by choosing the rules appropriate for decision from among various sources of law including international law….

"The act of state doctrine is grounded on judicial concern that application of customary principles of law to judge the acts of a foreign sovereign might frustrate the conduct of foreign relations by the political branches of the government. We conclude that where the Executive Branch, charged as it is with primary responsibility for the conduct of forcign affairs, represents to the Court that application of the act of state doctrine would not advance the interests of American foreign policy, that doctrine should not be applied by the courts. In so doing, we of course adopt and approve the so-called *Bernstein* exception to the act of state doctrine….

"It bears noting that the result we reach is consonant with the principles of equity set forth in *National City Bank* v. *Republic of China*…. Here [Banco Nacional] … has sought to come into our courts and secure an adjudication in its favor, without submitting to decision on the merits of the counterclaim which [First National] asserts against it….

"The act of state doctrine, as reflected in the cases culminating in *Sabbatino*, is a judicially accepted limitation on the normal adjudicative processes of the courts, springing from the thoroughly sound principle that on occasion individual litigants may have to forgo decision on the merits of their claims because involvement of the courts in such a decision might frustrate the conduct of the nation's foreign policy. It would be wholly illogical to insist that such a rule, fashioned because of fear that adjudication would interfere with the conduct of foreign relations, be applied in the face of assurance from that branch of the Federal Government that conducts foreign relations that such a result would not obtain. Our holding confines the courts to adjudication of the case before them, and leaves to the Executive Branch the conduct of foreign relations. In so doing, it is both faithful to the principle of separation of powers and consistent with earlier cases applying the act of state doctrine where we lacked the sort of representation from the Executive Branch that we have in this case.

"We therefore reverse the judgment of the Court of Appeals, and remand the case to it for consideration of [Banco Nacional's] alternative bases of attack on the judgment of the District Court."

HAVANA CLUB HOLDING, S.A. v. GALLEON S.A. & BACARDI-MARTINI USA
203 F.3d 116 (2nd Cir. 2000)

BACKGROUND: Plaintiff-Appellant HCI is a joint stock company organized under the laws of Cuba, with its domicile and principal place of business in Cuba. Plaintiff-Appellant HCH, a Luxembourg corporation, owns the "Havana Club" trademark in certain countries outside the United States. Defendant-Appellee Bacardi & Company is a corporation organized in Liechtenstein and headquartered in the Bahamas, and Defendant-Appellee Bacardi-Martini USA is a Delaware corporation. Defendant Galleon S.A. has merged into Bacardi & Company.

Before the Cuban revolution, Jose Arechabala, S.A. ("JASA"), a Cuban corporation owned principally by members of the Arechabala family, produced "Havana Club" rum and owned the trademark "Havana Club" for use with its rum. JASA exported its rum to the United States until 1960, when the Cuban government, under the leadership of Fidel Castro, seized and expropriated JASA's assets. Neither JASA nor its owners ever received compensation for the seized assets from the Cuban government. In 1963, the United States imposed an embargo on Cuba, reflected in the Cuban Assets Control Regulations ("CACR"). The USA Treasury Secretary delegated CACR enforcement authority to the USA's Office of Foreign Asset Control ("OFAC"). From 1972 to 1993, Empresa Cubana Exportadora De Alimentos y Productos Varios ("Cubaexport"), a Cuban state enterprise, exclusively exported "Havana Club" rum, primarily to Eastern Europe and the Soviet Union. Cubaexport registered the "Havana Club" trademark with Cuban authorities in 1974, and with the United States Patent and Trademark Office ("USPTO") in 1976. In 1993, Cubaexport sought to reorganize and find a foreign partner for its "Havana Club" rum business. Havana Rum & Liquors, S.A. ("HR&L"), a newly formed Cuban company, entered into a joint venture agreement with Pernod Ricard, S.A. ("Pernod"), a French company distributing liquor internationally. Under a November 1993 agreement between Pernod and HR&L, HCI and HCH were formed. In 1994, Cubaexport assigned the USA "Havana Club" trademark, to HR&L, and in a subsequent agreement, HR&L assigned this trademark to HCH. In 1996, HCH renewed the United States registration of the "Havana Club" mark for a term of

493

ten years.

In April 1997, Bacardi & Co. purchased the Arechabala family's rights (if any) to the "Havana Club" trademark, the related goodwill of the business, and any rum business assets still owned by the Arechabala family. In 1995 OFAC issued to Cubaexport License No. C-18147, which approved the two assignments and authorized all necessary transactions incident to the assignments of the mark. However, on April 17, 1997, after the instant lawsuit was filed in the District Court, OFAC issued a Notice of Revocation, revoking License No. C-18147.

Since 1994, HCI has exported rum under the "Havana Club" trademark under an exclusive license to that mark from HCH. From 1994 to 1998, HCI sold over 38 million bottles of "Havana Club" rum, with approximately 30 percent of the sales in Cuba—including sales to Americans traveling in Cuba—and the remainder exported principally to Spain, France, Germany, Italy, Canada, Mexico, Bolivia and Panama. Under travel regulations imposed by OFAC, the class of travelers permitted to visit Cuba may reenter the United States with up to $100 in Cuban-origin goods for personal use. Havana Club rum and cigars are the most popular items brought back.

Because of the Cuban embargo, however, HCI's "Havana Club" rum has never been sold in the United States. HCI intends to export its rum to the United States as soon as legally possible. HCI anticipates using its current marketing strategy of emphasizing the quality and character of its rum based primarily upon its Cuban origin. The label on HCI's "Havana Club" rum portrays the city of Havana and contains the phrase "El Ron de Cuba" ("The Rum of Cuba"). HCI's advertising also stresses the product's Cuban origin.

Beginning in 1995, Bacardi-Martini's predecessor-in-interest, Galleon S.A., produced rum in the Bahamas bearing the "Havana Club" name, and distributed sixteen cases of this rum in the United States. From May 1996 to August 1996, Bacardi distributed an additional 906 cases of "Havana Club" rum in the United States.

In 1996 HCH and HCI filed the instant action to enjoin Bacardi from using the "Havana Club" trademark, alleging violations of sections 32 and 43(a) of the Trademark Act of 1946 ("Lanham Act"). Among Bacardi's defenses was a claim that OFAC's specific license to HCH, authorizing the assignments of the U.S. trademark, was invalid because HCH obtained the mark by fraud. In 1997, the District Court ruled that Bacardi lacked standing to challenge OFAC's specific license to HCH and that OFAC's decision to grant the specific license was unreviewable. In August 1997, the District Court ruled that HCH had no rights to the "Havana Club" trademark because the specific license to assign the mark to HCH had been nullified by OFAC's revocation of the specific license and because the CACR's general license authority did not authorize the assignment. After rejecting the Appellants' claim of rights to the "Havana Club" *mark*, the Court granted the Appellants' motion to amend their Complaint to assert rights to the "Havana Club" trade *name* under sections 44(g) & 44(h) of the Lanham Act, and Chapter III of the General Inter-American Convention for Trade Mark and Commercial Protection ("IAC"). Both Cuba and the United States are signatories to the IAC.

During the bench trial, the District Court ruled that HCH, a Luxembourg corporation, could not claim rights to trade name protection under the IAC because Luxembourg was not a party to the IAC. The District Court also ruled that HCI lacked standing to assert its claim under section 43(a) of the Lanham Act. HCI had alleged that Bacardi's use of the mark "Havana Club" and its label—which features a sketch of Malecon, a seafront boulevard in Havana—falsely designated Cuba as the place of origin of Bacardi's rum, when in fact Bacardi produced it in the Bahamas. The District Court held that HCI had no standing to pursue this claim, because the Cuban embargo prevented HCI from selling its rum in the United States, and thereby from suffering commercial injury because of Bacardi's actions. The District Court added, "Any competitive injury plaintiffs will suffer based upon their intent to enter the U.S. market once the embargo is lifted is simply too remote and uncertain to provide them with standing." An amended judgment was entered on June 28, 1999.

JUDGE NEWMAN:

"This appeal, raising issues concerning the Cuban embargo, arises from a dispute between two rum producers over the rights to the 'Havana Club' trademark and trade name. Havana Club Holding, S.A. ('HCH') and Havana Club International, S.A. ('HCI') appeal from the June 28, 1999, judgment of the United States District Court for the Southern District of New York … dismissing trademark, trade name, and false advertising claims against Defendants-Appellees Bacardi & Company Ltd. and Bacardi-Martini USA, Inc. We conclude that the Cuban embargo barred assignment to HCH of the 'Havana Club' trademark registered in the United States, that we are precluded by statute from enforcing whatever rights HCI might have to trade name protection under the General Inter-American Convention for Trade Mark and Commercial Protection, and that HCI lacks standing to assert its false advertising and unfair competition claims under the Lanham Act. We therefore affirm.…

"HCH contends that Bacardi infringed its rights to the 'Havana Club' trademark registered in the United States. The basic issue on the trademark claim is whether HCH has any rights to the mark. Although HCH purported to acquire rights by assignments from Cubaexport to HR&L and from HR&L to HCH, HCH recognizes that to have enforceable rights in the United States, it must find authority for the assignment somewhere in United States law, because in the absence of such authority, the Cuban embargo renders null and void the transfer of trademark registrations in which a Cuban national or entity has an interest....

"As authority for the assignments, HCH's Complaint in this litigation initially invoked the 'specific' license issued by OFAC in November 1995, which 'licensed' the assignments. However, after OFAC revoked the specific license in 1997, HCH has relied on the 'general' licensing authority in 31 C.F.R. § 515.527. Section 515.527(a) states: Transactions *related to* the registration and renewal in the United States Patent and Trademark Office . . . in which . . . a Cuban national has an interest are authorized.... HCH contends that, even though OFAC revoked the specific license to assign the 'Havana Club' trademark, the assignments remain valid under the general authorization of section 515.527(a)(1) as transactions 'related to' the registration and renewal of a trademark. HCH also contends that if section 515.527(a)(1) is not construed to authorize the assignments, HCH will be denied treaty rights protected by the IAC. We disagree with both arguments....

"Before considering the meaning of section 515.527(a)(1), we encounter an express prohibition against HCH's claim set forth earlier in Subpart E of Part 515, which contains section 515.527(a)(1). Section 515.502(a) provides: No . . . authorization contained in this part . . . shall be deemed to authorize or validate any transaction effected *prior* to the issuance thereof, unless such . . . authorization specifically so provides.... The assignments for which HCH claims to find authorization in section 515.527 were effected' in 1994, prior to the issuance of section 515.527 in 1995, and section 515.527(a)(1) does not 'specifically so provide[]' for authorization of transactions that occurred prior to its issuance. Therefore, whether or not section 515.527(a)(1) might be interpreted to authorize assignments occurring *after* its effective date, this provision cannot authorize the 1994 assignments of the 'Havana Club' trademark to HCH....

"... HCH contends that failure to recognize its rights as assignee of the United States registration for the 'Havana Club' trademark would nullify rights guaranteed by Article 11 of the IAC.... Since the 'Havana Club' mark registered in the United States was originally registered in Cuba and was transferred in accordance with Cuban law, Article 11 purports to assure that the transfer to HCH will be recognized in the United States. The disputed issue is whether the Cuban embargo has abrogated the rights that Section 11 of the IAC would otherwise protect.

"A 'treaty will not be deemed to have been abrogated or modified by a later statute unless such *purpose* on the part of Congress has been clearly expressed.'... Although neither the CACR nor the LIBERTAD Act refers expressly to the IAC, the question of abrogation does not turn on whether the IAC has been expressly identified for abrogation. Congress is not required to investigate the array of international agreements that arguably provide some protection that it wishes to annul and then assemble a check-list reciting each one. What is required is a clear expression by Congress of a purpose to override protection that a treaty would otherwise provide.

"With respect to the Cuban embargo, the purpose of Congress could not be more clear. Congress wished to prevent any Cuban national or entity from attracting hard currency into Cuba by selling, assigning, or otherwise transferring rights subject to United States jurisdiction. The CACR make this clear, and the LIBERTAD Act, by codifying the CACR, provides unmistakable evidence of congressional purpose. We must therefore accord primacy to the prohibition of the CACR that bars a Cuban national or entity from transferring a United States trademark....

"For all of these reasons, HCH has no enforceable rights to the 'Havana Club' trademark....

"HCI contends that Bacardi infringed its rights under the IAC to protection of the 'Havana Club' trade name. The IAC provides that any manufacturer 'domiciled or established' in a signatory country that uses a particular trade name or commercial name may enjoin the use of that name in another signatory country that is identical with or deceptively similar to' its trade name.... A trade or commercial name need not be a registered to be protected....

"Rights to trade names and commercial names arising under treaties may be asserted under section 44(b) of the Lanham Act....

"On October 21, 1998, before the bench trial in this case, Congress passed section 211 of the Omnibus Act, which provides in pertinent part: (b) No U.S. court shall recognize, enforce or otherwise validate any assertion of treaty rights by a designated national or its successor-in-interest under sections 44 (b) or (e) of the Trademark Act of 1946 (15 U.S.C. 1126 (b) or (e)) for a mark, trade name, or commercial name that is the same as or substantially similar to a mark, trade name, or commercial name that was used in connection with a business or assets that were confiscated unless the original owner of such mark, trade name, or commercial name, or the bona fide successor-in-interest has expressly consented....

"Section 211(b) applies in this case....

"Applying section 211(b), the District Court ruled that it precluded HCI's assertion of treaty rights under sections 44(b) or (e) of the Lanham Act and thereby precluded HCI's claims under the IAC....

"Since section 211 does not clearly indicate that it should be applied retroactively, the traditional presumption against retroactivity would likely apply.... In this case, however, we can apply section 211(b) to bar relief on HCI's trade name claim because when an 'intervening statute authorizes or affects the propriety of *prospective relief*, application of the new provision is not retroactive.' ('When an intervening repeal of a statute affects the propriety of prospective relief, a court should apply the law in effect at the time it renders its decision.'). Because HCI seeks only injunctive relief, this Court can properly apply section 211(b).

"Third, HCI argues that section 211(b) does not apply when the trade name at issue has been abandoned. Section 211(b) precludes enforcement of rights under section 44(b) for a trade name 'that was used in connection with a business or assets that were confiscated unless the original owner of such mark, trade name, or commercial name, or the bona fide successor-in-interest has expressly consented.... By 'confiscated' section 211(b) refers to the nationalization, expropriation, or other seizure of property by the Cuban Government on or after January 1, 1959.... It is undisputed that JASA used the 'Havana Club' name until the Cuban government expropriated the business in 1960 and has not expressly consented to HCI's use of the 'Havana Club' name....

"Fourth, HCI argues that it should be allowed to prove that the 'Havana Club' trade name was never confiscated. Section 211(d)(2) ... defines 'confiscated' ... as property nationalized, expropriated, or otherwise seized by the Cuban government on or after January 1, 1959, 'without the property having been returned or adequate and effective compensation provided.'... The District Court found that 'all of JASA's assets were taken and that it received no compensation.'...

"We disagree with HCI's premise that no compensation is 'adequate and effective' compensation under section 515.336(a)(1) where the confiscated business allegedly had no positive net value at the time of expropriation. The embargo's definition of confiscated property contemplates only three ways in which property expropriated by Cuba can avoid becoming classified as 'confiscated.' Cuba can either return the property, provide 'adequate and effective compensation,' or settle the property claim pursuant to an international claims settlement agreement or other mutually accepted settlement procedure.... Where Cuba has not returned JASA's property, not made even a gesture toward compensation, and not settled the claim, the confiscation inquiry ends.

"HCI disputes the District Court's finding that it does not have standing to assert its 'false advertising' claim. 'Although a section 43 plaintiff need not be a direct competitor, it is apparent that, at a minimum, standing to bring a section 43 claim requires the potential for a commercial or competitive injury.'...

"... Contrary to the case law on standing under section 43(a), HCI first argues that to obtain standing, it must demonstrate only that Bacardi has falsely indicated the origin of its 'Havana Club' rum as Havana, when in fact Bacardi produced its rum in the Bahamas.... Although

Congress amended section 43(a) in 1988, the Senate Report stated that standing 'should continue to be decided on a case-by-case basis, and that the amendments . . . made to the legislation with respect to [this issue] should not be regarded as either limiting or extending applicable decisional law.'...   Therefore, HCI argues, it has standing under the current version of section 43(a), because HCI does business 'in the locality falsely indicated as that of origin' by Bacardi, namely, Havana.

"We disagree.   The Senate Report indicates that Congress intended not to alter the then 'applicable decisional law' under section 43(a).   Although numerous cases prior to 1988 recognized that standing under section 43(a) required demonstrable proof that a plaintiff would be likely to suffer damage as a result of false advertising ... we have found no case decided before 1988 that recognized standing under section 43(a) based on HCI's interpretation of the pre-1988 version of section 43(a).   Since no such case existed, Congress cannot be deemed to have left unaltered, and by implication recognized, HCI's theory of standing when it amended section 43(a) in 1988....

"Second, to establish the likelihood of commercial injury for the purposes of standing, HCI argues that Bacardi's use of the 'Havana Club' name will adversely affect HCI's current and future sales of its rum to U.S. visitors to Cuba. The fact that HCI sells to Americans traveling in Cuba, however, does not necessarily demonstrate the likelihood that the distribution of Bacardi's 'Havana Club' rum in the United States will hurt HCI sales to those persons in Cuba. Although HCI presented consumer surveys ... the District Court noted that 'it is intuitively doubtful that these findings would apply to U.S. travelers authorized to visit Cuba.'... In this case, the plaintiffs' consumer surveys drew their sample from across the United States, without attempting to control for any likelihood that the participants would travel to Cuba.   Under such circumstances, the District Court's finding that these surveys did not show consumer confusion among the relevant class of travelers was not clearly erroneous....

"Third, HCI argues that the District Court erred in finding HCI's ability to enter the U.S. market to be too remote at this point to confer standing. Although this Court has conferred standing for section 43(a) claims based on a showing of *potential* commercial injury, not all potential commercial injuries are sufficient to confer standing....

"... Even if HCI competes with Bacardi in markets elsewhere in the world, standing requires that HCI demonstrate at least potential commercial injury in the United States, because Bacardi sells 'Havana Club' rum only in the United States. Because HCI's rum does not now compete with Bacardi's rum in the United States, HCI's alleged injury amounts to the present diminution in the speculative value of its sales of Cuban-origin rum in the United States market once the United States government removes the obstacle of the Cuban embargo.

"That obstacle is formidable.... At this time, the President has not determined that a 'transition government,' let alone a 'democratically elected' government, exists in Cuba. HCI points to recent efforts in Congress to pass legislation to lift portions of the Cuban embargo. However, by conferring standing to HCI based on its own prediction of Congress's actions, this Court would expand its authority well beyond any zone of twilight that might exist between legislative and judicial authority....

"Finally, HCI argues that it has standing to sue under section 44(h) of the Lanham Act for unfair competition. Section 44(h) provides: Any person designated in subsection (b) of this section as entitled to the benefits and subject to the provisions of this chapter shall be entitled to effective protection against unfair competition, and the remedies provided in this chapter for infringement of marks shall be available so far as they may be appropriate in repressing acts of unfair competition....

"Rights under Section 44(h) are co-extensive with treaty rights under section 44(b), including treaty rights 'relating to . . . the repression of unfair competition.'... HCI essentially argues that it must demonstrate less to obtain standing to assert its section 44(h) claim than is required for its section 43(a) claim. Article 21(c) of the IAC defines an act of 'unfair competition' to include 'the use of false indications of geographical origin or source of goods, by words, symbols, or other means which tend in that respect to deceive the public in the country in which these acts occur.'... We note, however, that article 21 of the IAC authorizes the prohibition of its specified acts of unfair competition 'unless otherwise effectively dealt with under the domestic laws of the Contracting States.'... ICI's section 44(h) claim amounts to little more than the re-assertion of its section 43(a) claim because article 21(c) of the IAC prohibits a subset of the conduct already effectively prohibited under American law by section 43(a). We therefore conclude as a matter of law that HCI has failed to state a viable claim under section 44(h).

"The judgment of the District Court is affirmed."

AMERICAN INTERNATIONAL GROUP, INC. v. ISLAMIC REPUBLIC OF IRAN
493 F.Supp. 522 (D. DC 1980)

BACKGROUND: Plaintiffs are three groups of insurance companies that together did all of the USA insurance business in Iran. Despite prior assurances from officials at Central Insurance of Iran (CII)—the governmental agency regulating the industry in Iran—that no nationalization was intended, the assets of USA insurance companies were in fact nationalized. A treaty in force between Iran and the USA required "prompt payment of just compensation" in such cases, but the Iranian nationalization law did not include any mechanism for such compensation. AIG and the other USA insurance companies sued the Iranian government and CII for damages.

JUDGE HART:

"Defendants' nationalization without a mechanism for adequate compensation violates the Treaty of Amity and, independently, international law. The weight of authority manifestly states that international law, as reflected in the Treaty, requires prompt, adequate, and effective compensation.... The [Iranian] 'Law of Nationalization' does not provide a mechanism for determination and payment of prompt compensation relevant to this case.... There has been no compensation either paid or offered. Though the exact scope and precise requirements of the Treaty and international law may be subject to interpretation, the defendants in this case have failed by any interpretation to meet even the minimum standards set by the Treaty and international law.

"Venue and jurisdiction is proper in this Court regardless of the fact that plaintiffs have not exhausted their remedies by seeking judicial or administrative redress in Iran. Resort to such legal means is unnecessary when such remedy is impracticable or futile.... At the time of nationalization Iran was in such a state of turmoil that recourse to the Iranian courts was impossible.... Plaintiffs' employees were in physical danger, forced out of Iran, and generally unable to perform most of their ordinary duties during the period following the nationalization decree.... Further, the United States severed all diplomatic relations on April 7, 1980, and imposed a ban on travel to and from Iran on April 17, 1980.... It is absolutely clear that the Republic of Iran has shown a complete and utter disregard for international law by its seizure and holding of diplomatic hostages for a period exceeding eight months and its disdain of all diplomatic and international efforts to obtain their release. It is well settled in international law that where local remedies would be ineffective or meaningless or would not meet the international standard of minimum justice, the alien need not subject himself, in the first instance, to the local courts or administrative tribunals....

"Plaintiffs can assert their rights to recover damages in this Court for violations of the Treaty and international law. First, the right of individuals and companies to enforce a private right of action in a United States court under the property protection provisions of a treaty of friendship, commerce, and navigation has been consistently upheld.... Second, since Article IV, paragraph 2 of the Treaty is self-executing, plaintiffs have a right of action before this Court. The Treaty clearly meets the criteria considered significant in determining whether a Treaty is self-executing and, therefore, capable of enforcement in a United States court....

"The Act of State Doctrine does not preclude this Court from awarding summary judgment in this case. First, the theory underlying the Act of State Doctrine is inapplicable in this litigation. The Court is not asked to judge the validity of defendants' expropriation of plaintiffs' interests in Iran, but rather the defendants' failure, in violation of the Treaty and international law, to make adequate provision for the determination and payment of prompt, adequate, and effective compensation. Second, the Act of State Doctrine does not preclude judicial review where, as here, there is a relevant, unambiguous treaty setting forth agreed principles of international law applicable to the situation at hand…. Third, the Act of State Doctrine does not apply since defendants' failure to compensate plaintiffs occurred in connection with a commercial activity of defendants….

"The doctrine of sovereign immunity does not preclude this Court from awarding summary judgment in this case. First … this Court [has already] decided that under the Treaty the defendants have waived any sovereign immunity…. Article XI, paragraph 4 of the Treaty eliminates sovereign immunity with respect to defendants and their property. Second, even if the narrow view of the Treaty urged by the State Department … is accepted, Article XI, paragraph 4 of the Treaty still waives immunity. Under the narrow interpretation, CII and its property are clearly subject to jurisdiction since CII is a commercial entity. Therefore, Iran which is inseparable from CII and of which CII is the alter ego with respect to matters relevant here, is subject to the jurisdiction of this Court to the same extent as CII. Iran and its instrumentality (CII) are 'in effect one person, one juridical person.'… Third, defendants and their property do not enjoy any immunity pursuant to the terms of the (USA) Foreign Sovereign Immunities Act [which exempts commercial activities of foreign nations from its coverage]….

"Thus, plaintiffs are entitled to judgment as to defendants' liability [for violation of the Treaty and of international law]…. [A] hearing on the issue of damages will follow at a later date." [Defendants were also enjoined from removing or concealing any U.S.-located property in which either had an interest, up to the amount of plaintiffs' claimed damages—$35,000,000.]

KALAMAZOO SPICE EXTRACTION CO. v.
PROVISIONAL MILITARY GOVERNMENT OF SOCIALIST ETHIOPIA
729 F.2d 422 (6th Cir. 1984)

BACKGROUND: Ethiopian Spice Extraction Company (ESECo) was organized as an Ethiopian corporation in 1966. Kalamazoo Spice (KSpice), a USA corporation, owned 80 percent of the stock; Ethiopian persons held 20 percent. A 1974 revolution in Ethiopia produced the Provisional Military Government (PMG), which then nationalized much of the nation's industry. KSpice's ownership in ESECo was reduced to 39 percent. PMG's Compensation Commission offered to pay $450,000 to settle KSpice's claim of $11,000,000; KSpice rejected the offer. ESECo shipped some $1.9 million worth of spices to KSpice, which KSpice paid for until it realized that PMG was not going to pay fair value for the nationalized property. ESECo then sued in U.S. District Court in Michigan to collect the unpaid contract price for spices already delivered. KSpice responded by filing a counter-claim for the value of its seized properties. The U.S. District Court decided in favor of ESECo and PMG. KSpice appealed to the U.S. Sixth Circuit Court of Appeals.

JUDGE KEITH:

"In *Sabbatino* the [U.S. Supreme] Court stated: 'The judicial branch will not examine the validity of a taking of property within its own territory by a foreign sovereign government, extant and recognized by this country at the time of suit, in the absence of a treaty or other unambiguous agreement regarding controlling legal principles, even if the complaint alleges that the taking violates customary international law.'…

"… The treaty in existence between the United States and Ethiopia is the 1953 Treaty of Amity and Economic Relations … [which] provides: 'Property of nationals and companies of either High Contracting Party, including interests in property, shall receive constant protection and security within the territories of the other High Contracting Party. *Such property shall not be taken … without prompt payment of just and effective compensation*' (emphasis added [by the Court]).

"The 1953 … Treaty … is one of a series of treaties, also known as the FCN Treaties, between the United States and foreign nations after World War II. As the legislative history of these treaties indicates, they were adopted to protect American citizens and their interests abroad…. Almost all of these treaties contain sections which provide for 'prompt, adequate, and effective compensation,' 'just compensation,' or similar language regarding compensation for expropriated property….

"As the [U.S.] Supreme Court stated in [the] *Sabbatino* [case]: 'It should be apparent that the greater the degree of codification or consensus concerning a particular area of international law, the more appropriate it is for the judiciary to render decisions regarding it, since the courts can then focus on the application of an *agreed principle* [emphasis by the Court] to circumstances of fact rather than on the sensitive task of establishing a principle not inconsistent with the national interest or with international justice.'… Numerous treaties employ the standard of compensation used in the 1953 Treaty…. Undoubtedly, the widespread use of this compensation standard is evidence that it is an agreed upon principle in international law.

"Nor will adjudication in this matter interfere with any efforts by the Executive branch to resolve this matter. In fact … the Departments of State, Treasury, and Justice … have filed a joint … brief urging that the 1953 Treaty makes the act of state doctrine inapplicable. Obviously, the Executive branch feels that an adjudication in this matter is appropriate. Thus, the Supreme Court's concern in *Sabbatino* for judicial interference with foreign policy activity by the Executive branch is not a consideration in this case.

"Additionally, there is a great national interest to be served in this case, i.e., the recognition and execution of treaties that we enter into with foreign nations…. Accordingly, the Supreme Court has recognized that treaties, in certain circumstances, have the 'force and effect of a legislative enactment.'… The failure of this court to recognize a properly executed treaty would indeed be an egregious error because of the position that treaties occupy in our body of laws….

"Accordingly, the decision of the district court dismissing [KZOO's] counterclaim is reversed and remanded for further proceedings not inconsistent with this opinion."

EL-SHIFA PHARM. IND. CO. v. UNITED STATES
378 F.3d 1346 (Fed.Cir. 2004)

BACKGROUND: The 1998 terrorist bombings of U.S. embassies in Kenya and Tanzania killed 224 persons and injured 5000 more. President Clinton responded by ordering cruise missile attacks on suspected terrorist sites. One target was a manufacturing plant in Khartoum, the capital of Sudan. The plant was allegedly linked to Osama bin Ladin and al-Qaeda, and making a nerve gas ingredient. The plant's owner, El-Shifa Pharmaceutical, claimed that the plant was merely making badly needed medicines, and that the destruction of the plant amounted to a "taking" of its property by the U.S. Government. El-Shifa and a major stockholder (Salah El Din Ahmed Mohammed Idris) sued in the U.S. Court of Federal Claims for $50 million compensation, as required by the "takings clause" of Fifth Amendment to the U.S. Constitution. The Court of Federal Claims dismissed the case, and the plaintiffs appealed to the U.S. Federal Circuit Court of Appeals.

JUDGE CLEVENGER:

"The role of the judiciary in much of our precedent in the area of military takings … has been to draw a 'thin line … between sovereign immunity and governmental liability.'… The instant case is unique however in military takings jurisprudence, in that we are not asked to determine on which side of that line the governmental conduct at issue falls. Indeed, under our precedent, if it were actually true in 1998, as the government then maintained, that the nation's terrorist enemies were using the Plant to manufacture chemical weapons destined for use against American citizens and interests around the globe, then the appellants' property loss would be subsumed by the enemy property doctrine, and that would be the end of it. Accordingly, today, we need not further sharpen the line that separates private property lost to the 'fortunes of war' from that the military takes pursuant to the state's power of eminent domain.

"This case asks us to draw a line of a different sort. The complaint filed by the appellants challenges the government's designation of the Plant as enemy property by, *inter alia*, suggesting that the President relied on flawed intelligence in targeting it for destruction. It is replete with allegations contradicting the government's, indeed the President's, determination that the Plant was part of Osama bin Laden's array of weapons deployed against Americans at home and abroad. For the reasons set forth more fully below, we think the power set forth in Article III, section 1 of the Constitution does not encompass judicial supervision over the President's designation as enemy property the private property belonging to aliens located outside the territory of the United States.

"Without question, 'it is emphatically the province and duty of the judicial department to say what the law is. '*Marbury v. Madison* … (1803). 'Sometimes, however, the law is that the judicial department has no business entertaining [a] claim of unlawfulness—because the question is entrusted to one of the political branches or involves no judicially enforceable rights. Such questions are said to be "nonjusticiable" or "political questions".'…

"… [W]hatever the Constitution says regarding the President's war powers, either explicitly in its text or by its structure, it need not say anything about the Takings Clause per se in order for us to conclude that it commits exclusively to the President the power to make extraterritorial enemy property designations.…

"We think consideration of the decisional law touching on the nature and scope of the President's war powers sheds important light on our present inquiry…. 'The Constitution … invests the President with the power to wage war'….

"In exercising the power to wage war, the President finds authorization in the Constitution itself to 'direct the performance of those functions which may constitutionally be performed by the military arm of the nation in time of war.'… Within these functions are 'important incidents to the conduct of war' such as 'the adoption of measures by the military command … to repel and defeat the enemy.'… They also include 'the power to seize and subject to disciplinary measures those enemies who in their attempt to thwart or impede our military effort have violated the laws of war.'…

"In our view, the President's power to wage war must also necessarily include the power to make extraterritorial enemy property designations because such designations are also an important incident to the conduct of war. As much is borne out of the history of this nation's many declared and undeclared wars, part of which is documented in the cases where courts have applied the enemy property doctrine. The cases teach that the purpose of such designations is almost always to 'repel and defeat the enemy' by diminishing the sum of material resources it has at its disposal to prosecute hostilities against the United States and its citizens.... We cannot envision how a military commander, much less the Commander-in-Chief, could wage war successfully if he did not have the inherent power to decide what targets, i.e., property, belonged to the enemy and could therefore be destroyed free from takings liability....

"... The appellants' theory of takings liability centers on the alleged inaccuracy of the President's designation of the Plant as enemy property. This must be the case, because ... if the Plant was in fact the property of al-Qaeda, the appellants would have no claim in takings against the United States for its destruction.... The appellants would have the [courts] ... provide them with an opportunity to test [the President's] contention, and in the process, require this court to elucidate the constitutional standards that are to guide a President when he evaluates the veracity of military intelligence.

"We are of the opinion that the federal courts have no role in setting even minimal standards by which the President, or his commanders, are to measure the veracity of intelligence gathered with the aim of determining which assets, located beyond the borders of the United States, belong to the Nation's friends and which belong to its enemies.... Today, we need not decide whether and to what extent the Executive and Legislative branches share that responsibility. We conclude only that the Constitution does not contemplate or support the type of supervision over the President's extraterritorial enemy property designations the appellants request in this case....

"The circumstances here, under which the Plant was targeted and destroyed, strengthen this conclusion. When the President ordered the Plant destroyed, he exercised the 'authority ... the Constitution itself gives the Commander in Chief, to direct the performance of those functions which may constitutionally be performed by the military arm of the nation in time of war.'... In 1998, the President determined that the Plant's destruction was a necessary and proper response to 'the imminent threat of further terrorist attacks against U.S. personnel and facilities.'...

"Under these conditions, where the President's own assessment of the offensive posture of the Nation's enemies overseas leads him to conclude that the Nation is at risk of imminent attack, we cannot find in the Constitution any support for judicial supervision over the process by which the President assures himself that he has in fact targeted that part of the enemy's wealth of property that he thinks, if it were destroyed, would most effectively neutralize the possibility of attack.

"For the foregoing reasons, the decision of the Court of Federal Claims to dismiss the complaint because it raises a nonjusticiable political question is affirmed."

REPUBLIC OF AUSTRIA v. MARIA V. ALTMANN
541 U.S. 677 (2004)

BACKGROUND: Maria Altmann, being informed by an Austrian journalist that certain items in the art collection of the national "Austrian Gallery" had been stolen by the German Nazis or expropriated by the Austrian government after the end of World War II, filed this lawsuit in California. Born in Austria in 1916, she had become a U.S. citizen in 1942, having escaped Austria after the German takeover of Austria in 1938. Her original intention to file suit in Austria was frustrated by that nation's court rule that required payment of a certain percentage of the value of the claim to be litigated—in this case, well over US$100,000—and also by the fact that Austria's "Statute of Limitations" (the time-period within which to file a claim) might have barred her lawsuit. She is the sole surviving heir of her uncle, Ferdinand Block-Bauer, the last legal owner of six Gustav Klimt paintings. (Maria's aunt Adele was the subject of two of these paintings—one of which, the celebrated "Woman in Gold," was sold in 2006 for US$135,000,000.)

Her uncle had also fled Austria in 1938. He never voluntarily transferred ownership of his properties to Austria or to the Austrian Gallery. He died in Zurich, Switzerland in 1945, leaving a will that named as heirs Maria, her brother Robert Bentley, and another niece. Robert had retained an Austrian lawyer in 1947, to assist in trying to recover their uncle's property. In response to the lawyer's inquiry, the Austrian Gallery had said that Aunt Adele had actually donated the paintings prior to her death and that the Gallery had merely allowed Uncle Ferdinand to retain possession temporarily. Purporting to represent all three heirs, but without any authorization from Maria, the lawyer signed a document which acknowledged the Gallery's ownership.

Claiming "sovereign immunity" from suit, Austria and the Gallery filed a motion to dismiss the lawsuit. The motion was denied by the U.S. District Court, and the U.S. Ninth Circuit affirmed the denial. The two defendants petitioned the U.S. Supreme Court for review.

JUSTICE STEVENS:

"Chief Justice Marshall's opinion in *Schooner Exchange* v. *M'Faddon* … (1812), is generally viewed as the source of our foreign sovereign immunity jurisprudence. In that case, the libellants [plaintiffs] claimed to be the rightful owners of a French ship that had taken refuge in the port of Philadelphia. The Court first emphasized that the jurisdiction of the United States over persons and property within its territory 'is susceptible of no limitation not imposed by itself,' and thus foreign sovereigns have no right to immunity in our courts.... Chief Justice Marshall went on to explain, however, that as a matter of comity, members of the international community had implicitly agreed to waive the exercise of jurisdiction over other sovereigns in certain classes of cases, such as those involving foreign ministers or the person of the sovereign. Accepting a suggestion advanced by the Executive Branch ... the Chief Justice concluded that the implied waiver theory also served to exempt the *Schooner Exchange*—'a national armed vessel ... of the emperor of France'—from United States courts' jurisdiction....

"In accordance with Chief Justice Marshall's observation that foreign sovereign immunity is a matter of grace and comity rather than a constitutional requirement, this Court has 'consistently . . . deferred to the decisions of the political branches—in particular, those of the Executive Branch—on whether to take jurisdiction' over particular actions against foreign sovereigns and their instrumentalities.... Until 1952 the Executive Branch followed a policy of requesting immunity in all actions against friendly sovereigns.... In that year, however, the State Department concluded that 'immunity should no longer be granted in certain types of cases.' In a letter to the Attorney General, the Acting Legal Adviser for the Secretary of State, Jack B. Tate, explained that the Department would thereafter apply the 'restrictive theory' of sovereign immunity....

"... [T]he change in State Department policy wrought by the 'Tate Letter' had little, if any, impact on federal courts' approach to immunity analyses.... The change did, however, throw immunity determinations into some disarray, as 'foreign nations often placed diplomatic pressure on the State Department,' and political considerations sometimes led the Department to file 'suggestions of immunity in cases where immunity would not have been available under the restrictive theory.'...

"In 1976 Congress sought to remedy these problems by enacting the FSIA, a comprehensive statute containing a 'set of legal standards governing claims of immunity in every civil action against a foreign state or its political subdivisions, agencies, or instrumentalities.'... The Act 'codifies, as a matter of federal law, the restrictive theory of sovereign immunity,' ... and transfers primary responsibility for immunity determinations from the Executive to the Judicial Branch. The preamble states that 'henceforth' both federal and state courts should decide claims of sovereign immunity in conformity with the Act's principles....

"The Act itself grants federal courts jurisdiction over civil actions against foreign states ... and over diversity actions in which a foreign state is the plaintiff ...; it contains venue and removal provisions ...; it prescribes the procedures for obtaining personal jurisdiction over a foreign state ...; and it governs the extent to which a state's property may be subject to attachment or execution.... Finally, the Act carves out certain exceptions to its general grant of immunity, including the expropriation exception on which respondent's complaint relies. These exceptions are central to the Act's functioning: 'At the threshold of every action in a district court against a foreign state ... the court must satisfy itself that one of the exceptions applies,' as 'subject-matter jurisdiction in any such action depends' on that application.

"The District Court agreed with respondent that the FSIA's expropriation exception covers petitioners' alleged wrongdoing ... and the Court of Appeals affirmed that holding.... [W]e declined to review this aspect of the courts' opinions, confining our grant of certiorari to the issue of the FSIA's general applicability to conduct that occurred prior to the Act's 1976 enactment, and more specifically, prior to the State Department's 1952 adoption of the restrictive theory of sovereign immunity.... We begin our analysis of that issue by explaining why, contrary to the assumption of the District Court ... and Court of Appeals ... the default rule announced in our opinion in *Landgraf* v. *USI Film Products* ... does not control the outcome in this case....

"To begin with, the preamble of the FSIA expresses Congress' understanding that the Act would apply to all postenactment claims of sovereign immunity. That section provides: '*Claims* of foreign states to immunity should *henceforth* be decided by courts of the United States and of the States in conformity with the principles set forth in this chapter.'...

"Though perhaps not sufficient to satisfy *Landgraf*'s 'express command' requirement ... this language is unambiguous: Immunity 'claims'—not actions protected by immunity, but assertions of immunity to suits arising from those actions—are the relevant conduct regulated by the Act; those claims are 'henceforth' to be decided by the courts. As the District Court observed ... this language suggests Congress intended courts to resolve *all* such claims 'in conformity with the principles set forth' in the Act, regardless of when the underlying conduct occurred....

"The FSIA's overall structure strongly supports this conclusion. Many of the Act's provisions unquestionably apply to cases arising out of conduct that occurred before 1976.... And there has never been any doubt that the Act's procedural provisions relating to venue, removal, execution, and attachment apply to all pending cases. Thus, the FSIA's preamble indicates that it applies 'henceforth,' and its body includes numerous provisions that unquestionably apply to claims based on pre-1976 conduct. In this context, it would be anomalous to presume that an isolated provision (such as the expropriation exception on which respondent relies) is of purely prospective application absent any statutory language to that effect.

"Finally, applying the FSIA to all pending cases regardless of when the underlying conduct occurred is most consistent with two of the Act's principal purposes: clarifying the rules that judges should apply in resolving sovereign immunity claims and eliminating political participation in the resolution of such claims. We have recognized that, to accomplish these purposes, Congress established a comprehensive framework for resolving any claim of sovereign immunity.... Quite obviously, Congress' purposes in enacting such a comprehensive jurisdictional scheme would be frustrated if, in postenactment cases concerning preenactment conduct, courts were to continue to follow the same ambiguous and politically charged 'standards' that the FSIA replaced....

"We conclude by emphasizing the narrowness of this holding. To begin with, although the District Court and Court of Appeals determined that § 1605(a)(3) covers this case, we declined to review that determination.... Nor do we have occasion to comment on the application of the so-called 'act of state' doctrine to petitioners' alleged wrongdoing. Unlike a claim of sovereign immunity, which merely raises a jurisdictional defense, the act of state doctrine provides foreign states with a substantive defense on the merits. Under that doctrine, the courts of one state will not question the validity of public acts ... performed by other sovereigns within their own borders, even when such courts have jurisdiction over a controversy in which one of the litigants has standing to challenge those acts.... But because the FSIA in no way affects application of the act of state doctrine, our determination that the Act applies in this case in no way affects any argument petitioners may have that the doctrine shields their alleged wrongdoing.

"Finally, while we reject the United States' recommendation to bar application of the FSIA to claims based on pre-enactment conduct ... nothing in our holding prevents the State Department from filing statements of interest suggesting that courts decline to exercise jurisdiction in particular cases implicating foreign sovereign immunity.... We express no opinion on the question whether such deference should be granted in cases covered by the FSIA.

"The judgment of the Court of Appeals is affirmed.

"It is so ordered."

ALTMANN, et al. v. THE REPUBLIC OF AUSTRIA
Arbitration Court (Austria), 15 January 2006

"THE ARBITRATION COURT, consisting of Dr. Andreas Nödl, lawyer; Professor Walter H. Rechberger, and Professor Peter Rummel as chairman,

has ruled as follows:

1. The Republic of Austria acquired ownership of the paintings by Gustav Klimt, *Adele Bloch-Bauer I, Adele Bloch-Bauer II, Apfelbaum, Buchenwald /Birkenwald,* **and** *Häuser in Unterach am Attersee* **by virtue of the settlement with the representative of the heirs of Ferdinand Bloch-Bauer, Dr. Gustav Rinesch, in 1948.**

2. The conditions of the Federal Act Regarding the Restitution of Artworks from Austrian Federal Museums and Collections dated 4 December 1998, Federal Law Gazette 1 No. 18111998 for the return of the five paintings indicated above without remuneration to the heirs of Ferdinand Bloch-Bauer are fulfilled.

3. Pursuant to Section B of the Arbitration Agreement, the Republic of Austria shall bear the costs of the proceedings.

"Statement of Grounds …

"The claimants asserted claims against the Republic of Austria for the surrender of five paintings by Gustav Klimt *(Adele Bloch-Bauer I, Adele Bloch-Bauer II, Apfelbaum I, Buchenwald/ Birkenwald, Häuser in Unterach am Attersee)* that are currently in the possession of the Republic and kept in the Austrian Gallery in the Belvedere. The parties ended the proceedings initiated in this matter in courts of general jurisdiction both in the USA and in Austria by means of an Arbitration Agreement, undersigned by the parties in May 2005. Based on this Arbitration Agreement, the arbitration court deciding this matter analyzed the following issues: 'whether, and in what manner, in the period between 1923 and 1949, or thereafter, Austria acquired ownership of the arbitrated paintings, *Adele Bloch-Bauer I, Adele Bloch-Bauer II, Apple Tree I, Beech Forrest (Birch Forrest),* and *Haus in Unterach am Attersee*; and whether, pursuant to Section 1 of Austria's Federal Act Regarding the Restitution of Artworks from Austrian Federal Museums and Collections dated 4 December 1998 … the requirements are met for restitution of any of the arbitrated paintings without remuneration to the heirs of Ferdinand Bloch-Bauer.'…

"The **claimants** made the following submission in their **complaint** …: Ferdinand Bloch-Bauer, died 13 November 1945 in Zurich, the claimants being his uncontested legal successors (heirs), commissioned Gustav Klimt to paint the arbitrated paintings. He paid for the paintings, and since then they were in his ownership and possession. In her will drawn up in 1923, in which she named her husband the sole heir, Ferdinand Bloch-Bauer's wife Adele, died 24 January

1925, disposed of – in addition to a series of other instructions, in particular legacies – the arbitrated paintings, two of which are portraits of her, as well as of one further painting, as follows: '*I ask my husband after his death to leave my two portraits and the four landscapes by Gustav Klimt to the Austrian State Gallery in Vienna and to leave the Vienna and Jungfer, Brezan library, which belongs to me, to the People's and Workers' Library of Vienna.*'...

"The executor appointed by the testatrix, her brother-in-law Dr. Gustav Bloch-Bauer, a lawyer and the brother of Ferdinand Bloch-Bauer, made the following statement in the Adele Bloch-Bauer probate proceedings: '*In Section III, Paragraphs 2 and 3, the testatrix makes various requests to her husband; he promises to faithfully fulfill said requests, though they do not have the binding nature of a testamentary disposition. It is important to note that the Klimt paintings are not the property of the testatrix, but rather of the testatrix's widower.*'

"Because of his Jewish descent and political convictions, in March 1938 Ferdinand Bloch-Bauer was forced to flee Austria and seek refuge in Prague. As was common practice at that time in the case of individuals who had fled the country, the Vienna-Wieden tax authorities initiated tax evasion proceedings on 27 April 1938 as an excuse to confiscate the property Ferdinand Bloch-Bauer had left behind in Austria (at that time the German Reich). In the course of these proceedings, the lawyer Dr. Friedrich Führer was appointed temporary administrator of the estate and, among other things, was ordered to liquidate and make appropriate use of the 'Bloch-Bauer collection'. Dr. Führer was quick to fulfil this task in the interests of the Nazi regime, including in the case of other significant assets belonging to Ferdinand Bloch-Bauer, for example his extensive porcelain collection and a large number of other paintings. In 1939 Ferdinand Bloch-Bauer was forced to leave Prague and settle in Zurich, and in the process lost all access of any kind to his assets. Thereafter, Dr. Führer gave the paintings *Adele Bloch-Bauer I* and *Apfelbaum I* to the gallery, which in turn gave him *Schloss Kammer am Attersee III,* which Ferdinand Bloch-Bauer had given to the gallery in 1936 in fulfilment of his promise made as part of the probate proceedings. Dr. Führer subsequently sold the latter painting for 6,000 Reichsmark to Gustav Ucicky, a son of Gustav Klimt. In 1942 Dr. Führer sold and surrendered *Buchenwald (Birkenwald)* for 5,000 Reichsmark to the City of Vienna Collection. In 1943, Dr. Führer sold *Adele Bloch-Bauer II* to the Austrian Gallery (known as the Modern Gallery at that time), and kept *Häuser in Unterach am Attersee* for himself. Ferdinand Bloch-Bauer died on 13 November 1945 in Zurich; he left a will establishing the legal succession of the claimants with regard to his estate.

"After the end of the war, Ferdinand Bloch-Bauer entrusted Viennese lawyer Dr. Rinesch with the recovery of his artworks as well as generally with restitution of his seized assets. After Ferdinand Bloch-Bauer's death, Dr. Rinesch also acted as the representative of the Ferdinand Bloch-Bauer's heirs. He tried to locate the scattered assets, in particular the paintings from

Ferdinand Bloch-Bauer's collection, and attempted to arrange for their return and export. At that time, it was common administrative practice to grant an export permit for rediscovered or restituted artworks of expelled or exiled victims of the Nazi regime only if they in turn declared that they would 'donate' to the Republic valuable parts of their restituted assets. This was what happened in the case of numerous objects from the Bloch-Bauer collection, including the five arbitrated paintings by Gustav Klimt. An attempt was made to pass off this procedure as an acknowledgment of Adele Bloch-Bauer's (in fact legally invalid) legacy.

"A request by the claimants for restitution of the five Klimt paintings pursuant to the 1998 Art Restitution Act was informally rejected by the minister under whose mandate it fell.

"In legal terms, the submitted facts lead one to conclude that Adele Bloch-Bauer's will regarding the five or respectively six paintings was merely a non-binding request; furthermore, even if it was construed as a legacy that was intended to be binding, the validity of this request was incompatible with the principle of testamentary freedom, as it was at best a reversionary legacy of an asset that did not belong to the testatrix, but rather to the heir (Ferdinand Bloch-Bauer). Furthermore, his declaration made in the Adele Bloch-Bauer probate proceedings, namely that he would faithfully fulfill the request, was neither a constitutive acknowledgment nor a valid promise to donate. Nothing regarding the legal position of the other five paintings can be derived from the donation of one painting to the gallery in 1936.

"Accordingly, Ferdinand Bloch-Bauer was, in 1938, the unencumbered owner of the paintings. The paintings, of which the Republic acquired the ownership without remuneration only as part of the export application, therefore fulfill the first element of the 1998 Art Restitution Act. *In eventu*, the second element of the 1998 Art Restitution Act is also fulfilled....

"Under the general rules of Austrian civil law, i.e. pursuant to §§ 423 ff of the General Civil Code [*ABGB*], the Republic could only have acquired ownership in this manner if there was valid title and the paintings were surrendered. The arbitration court did not consider the possibility of original acquisition by prescription, because this would have had to be determined on a subsidiary basis and was not asserted by the parties. The possibility that the paintings were acquired first by the German Reich and then subsequently (in particular, as asserted by the claimants, on the basis of the international treaty and its implementation laws) by the Republic of Austria, ultimately on the basis of Dr. Führer's activities, will be discussed later. In assessing the question of acquisition, the arbitration court based its method of procedure on the fact that under Austrian civil law, effective acquisition of the paintings by the Republic would rule out the applicability of any special rules regarding German ownership, though in fact it would not been feasible to assess the relevant provisions without clarifying the general civil law situation regarding the paintings....

"The arbitration court did not find this argument convincing. Adele Bloch-Bauer, who has named her spouse as the sole heir, asks him to dispose of the paintings and the library in a specific way, namely 'after his death to leave' them to the recipients specified by her. If he does so, as she of course expects him to, she leaves it up to the beneficiary, the People's and Workers' Library, to decide whether to keep the books or sell them and 'accept the proceeds as a legacy'. As the disposition by her husband, which she has requested and expects, would have been a legacy in all instances, it is unconvincing to argue for the desired legal nature of the separate instruction solely on the basis of this phrase (word). The release from the obligation to provide a guarantee can simply be seen as a precautionary measure to release her spouse from any current obligation.

"Another point supporting the argument that it was merely a request is the fact that as part of the probate proceedings … and therefore very probably by agreement with Ferdinand Bloch-Bauer (in whose name he promised fulfillment), the executor appointed by Adele Bloch-Bauer, the attorney Dr. Gustav Bloch-Bauer, categorized it as such, by marked contrast with the other legacies bequeathed. In view of the respect shown by the spouses to one another, as stressed repeatedly by the respondent, and as reflected in the surviving spouse's subsequent handling of the paintings (and in his statements during the probate proceedings), it is fair to assume that the spouses had discussed their thoughts on the subject with one another. If, immediately after his wife's death, the surviving spouse made it clear that it was merely a request which he nonetheless intended to faithfully fulfill, this strongly suggests that this view of matters was not attributable merely to the wording of the will (which was possibly surprising to the spouse), but rather to an earlier understanding between the spouses.

"Thus the arbitration court felt that in an overall analysis of the rather unambiguous circumstances as known today, it was more convincing to interpret the instruction as merely a legally non-binding wish. The potential objection that a mere request would not have necessitated a testamentary instruction, may be ignored, because in actual practice … testators frequently express mere wishes alongside binding instructions….

"At first glance, it is not entirely necessary for one to be fully clear about the ownership situation at the time of Adele Bloch-Bauer's death in order to be able to clarify whether the relevant passages in the will should be understood as a request or as an instruction intended to be binding…. Nevertheless, the arbitration court felt that the interpretation of Adele Bloch-Bauer's instruction as a mere request does gain additional plausibility if the testatrix assumed that the paintings belonged to her spouse rather than her.

"The aforementioned question—namely to whom did the paintings objectively belong and what subjective opinion did the testatrix (rightly or wrongly) have regarding this—is not unambiguously clear from the subject matter of the case…. There are only two decisive statements by parties directly involved concerning the ownership situation: In Adele Bloch-Bauer's letter … where she speaks of 'one of my landscapes painted by Klimt' and 'which I purchased from Klimt's estate' (during oral proceedings, it was not possible to ascertain the meaning of the statement [in the aforementioned letter] where she says that the painting in question was unfinished); and in the statement (… made by Adele Bloch-Bauer's executor, her brother-in-law Dr. Gustav Bloch-Bauer) who indicated during the probate proceedings that the paintings were owned by the husband Ferdinand Bloch-Bauer, which was then used as the basis for further proceedings. In the will itself, Adele Bloch-Bauer speaks of 'my' portrait and 'the' four landscapes, but also of the library 'belonging to me'; since it could be construed that the word 'my' before the word 'portraits' refers to the fact that she was the subject painted in the portraits, it is not possible to determine what her thoughts were on the matter solely from the wording of the disposition….

"Thus in the arbitration court's view, there was more reason to believe the paintings belonged to Ferdinand Bloch-Bauer than to Adele Bloch-Bauer. Admittedly, this does not constitute certain proof that they belonged to Ferdinand Bloch-Bauer. By contrast with for example the situation in Anglo-American civil proceedings, under Austrian law greater probability is not enough to constitute proof; instead, jurisprudence requires at least strong probability to convince the court…. Because of what the arbitration court considered lingering doubts surrounding the ownership of the paintings, strong probability of this kind that they were the property of Ferdinand Bloch-Bauer could not be deemed present.

"Under these circumstances, the *praesumptio Muciana* which applied at that time in property law (§ 1237 of the General Civil Code)—which meant that in doubtful cases 'property acquired was deemed to belong to the husband'—is applicable…. Thus the arbitration court's analysis thereof is ultimately in line with the doubt rule per § 1237 aF of the General Civil Code….

"Thus, during the period between 1938 and 1945, the Austrian Gallery … and the German Reich did not acquire ownership of *Adele Bloch-Bauer I*, *Adele Bloch-Bauer II* or *Apfelbaum* under general civil law, as the three paintings were surrendered to the gallery in fulfillment of Adele Bloch-Bauer's will, which, as explained above, did not constitute sufficient title for acquisition of ownership…. As the arbitration court categorized the instruction as a mere request, there was no need to analyze the inheritance-law question … regarding possible 'suspension' and subsequent 'healing' of the instruction that originated from the pre-war period….

"If the German Reich, and therefore the Republic of Austria as its legal successor, did not, according to general rules of civil law, acquire ownership of the paintings … in the course of Dr. Führer's activities, then it is important to analyze whether title was acquired as a consequence of

Dr. Rinesch's activities on behalf of Ferdinand Bloch-Bauer and the heirs. Dr. Rinesch's legal authority to act on behalf of Dr. Ferdinand Bloch-Bauer, and later on behalf of his heirs, was not disputed....

"Under these circumstances – i.e. in view of his own doubts about the legal situation – it is hardly surprising that Dr. Rinesch used the paintings so to speak as weapons for negotiation in connection with the matter of the export permit: The heirs, not being legal experts, some of them friends of Dr. Rinesch, were relatively easy to convince of a valid obligation; by contrast, it was possible to emphasize to the authorities that the heirs were co-operative, helpful and generous by acknowledging the binding nature of will.... [T]here was no need to file a formal export application nor to exert explicit pressure. Instead, it was clear that the heirs' concession would make the agents of the Republic more willing to grant the export permit for the other items (the fact that there were clear connections of this kind in relation to other objects is a matter of record)....

"The declarations of the executor, Dr. Gustav Bloch-Bauer, in the Adele Bloch-Bauer probate proceedings did not create a new obligation for the heir Ferdinand Bloch-Bauer, not least because of the absence of a suitable declaration addressee. Hence these declarations were neither an acknowledgment establishing an obligation, nor a legally valid promise to donate....

"In the opinion of the arbitration court, the facts explained above are sufficient to uphold the claimant's petition, according to which the conditions of the first element of § 1 of the 1998 Art Restitution Act are satisfied....

"§ 1 Section 2 of the 1998 Art Restitution Act concerns artworks which *'although they have legally passed into the ownership of the Republic, were previously the subject of a legal transaction as defined in § 1 of the Federal Act dated 15 May 1946 concerning the Annulment Declaration of Legal Transactions and Other Legal Acts Performed during the German Occupation of Austria ... and are still in the ownership of the Republic.'* ...

"As proven by the materials pertaining to the 1998 Art Restitution Act, the makers of the law had in mind 'doubtful purchases' via which items which during the Nazi regime underwent a process later covered by the Annulment Act were subsequently (in a further step) acquired by the Republic. This last step had to have been or could have been 'lawful'. The typical case presented was acquisition in the art market or at auctions; the motivating aspect for restitution per the 1998 Art Restitution Act was the fact that the objects were at the time appropriated from the owners in a manner described as follows in the Annulment Act: *'§ 1. Legal transactions with and without remuneration and other legal acts during the German occupation of Austria [are null and void] if they were carried out in the course of the political and economic penetration by the German*

Reich in order to appropriate from natural or legal persons property or property rights that they had rightfully enjoyed on 13 March 1938.'...

"In light of the reference to the Annulment Act, this basically involves items that had been the subject of dispossession prior to 1945. The element of appropriation per the Annulment Act is in fact fulfilled by all items sold by Dr. Führer in his capacity as Nazi-appointed administrator of Ferdinand Bloch-Bauer's property (or property he merely factually surrendered or even kept for himself. Re 'legal transactions' in § 1 of the Annulment Act, the arbitration court shared the opinion ... that by virtue of its purpose the reference in Section 2 of § 1 of the 1998 Art Restitution Act in fact covers the entire scope of § 1 of the Annulment Act and not just the 'legal transactions' specified therein. According to the judicial decisions of the Supreme Restitution Commission, which the arbitration court adhered to in the present case, a 'legal act' for the purposes of the Annulment Act is 'any act or omission that produces a legal effect under the rule of law'....

"Therefore it only remains to be seen whether – in addition to the undoubted fact that the appropriation had occurred – the case envisaged by the legislators who drafted the 1998 Art Restitution Act, in which a subsequent lawful acquisition by the Republic must now be reversed, is in fact an indispensable element and, if applicable, how it should be interpreted.... In the present case ... acquisition from German property, as argued by the claimants, or due to passing of the restitution law deadlines, or possibly directly from the entitled party but in a doubtful manner, were the subject of deliberation.

"The latter, at any rate in instance of acquisition without the involvement of the entitled party, struck the arbitration court as convincing. Hence if the Republic acquired the ownership of certain items directly or indirectly via the German Reich, which had itself executed the void legal transaction, then in principle the corresponding restitution element should, compared with acquisition in good faith from a third party, be deemed to have been all the more fulfilled. Moreover, one could argue that acquisition from a private third party and acquisition by the Republic pursuant to the First State Treaty Implementation Act (if the paintings were German property) were of equivalent status, in which case the fulfilment of the element of merely indirect 'lawful' acquisition would be fulfilled per the wording. The extent to which this 'if x applies, then y applies all the more' type of conclusion also applies to a doubtful acquisition *from a party entitled at the time* is an unresolved issue.

"[The] conclusion regarding this, namely that all items which were appropriated at the time and not restituted in later years, but rather passed into the ownership of the Republic, should be restituted, fails to adequately address the central question as to *why* the items were not restituted. If this happened unknowingly, or in a worse case due to the authorities' ignorance or ill will, if the affected persons were coerced into the settlement because it gave them a means to finally retrieve some of their seized assets, then all of this could lie within the spirit of Section 2, for which the Republic's good faith is of no significance. However, if the reason was that there was an 'honest' settlement between the Republic and the owners (or their heirs), reached because of serious doubts regarding the asserted claims, then in the arbitration court's view the spirit of the 1998 Art Restitution Act is not fulfilled. Section 1 of § 1 of the 1998 Art Restitution Act suggests that a settlement reached under duress is not deemed an 'honest' settlement. In view of the material distress many of the exiles suffered at the time, the term 'under duress' may be interpreted broadly (as the Republic could not have felt a similar pressure to reach a settlement, as compared with what usually happens in the case of private individuals with disputed or doubtful claims). If, however, there is no evidence of inequality of the basic positions and of a resulting lack of 'honesty', then subsequent acquisition of an item seized from the owner, into whose possession it has been returned, should be equally as legally valid as acquisition based on a settlement concerning a genuinely 'disputed' or 'doubtful' claim to surrender or restitution....

"Accordingly, the 'defect' of the items, i.e. their having been seized from their owner as defined in the Annulment Act, could (only) be cured by Dr. Rinesch's subsequent effective creation, on behalf of the heirs, of new title for the acquisition of ownership by the Republic. In light of all of the above, this was clearly what happened: Under general civil law, his acknowledgment ... is incontestable in terms of its validity ... at least today. Thus if the purpose of the settlement/ acknowledgement was solely to eliminate the uncertainty surrounding the legal validity of the will, in the arbitration court's view it is definitely incontestable with regard to Section *2* of § 1 of the 1998 Art Restitution Act.

"The apparent contradiction with the above decision concerning Section 1 § 1 of the 1998 Art Restitution Act derives from the fact that that part of the law involves politically motivated compensation for what is nowadays seen as the duress of the export proceedings, while the second section involves unobjectionable (under general civil law) acquisition of works of objectively offensive provenance....

"Thus in the arbitration court's view, the legal element of § 1 Section 2 of the 1998 Art Restitution Act is not fulfilled. Therefore the arbitration court did not have to analyze whether there was temporary ownership of some or all of the paintings by the German Reich. The prevailing opinion after 1945 was evidently that the forced transactions and legal acts carried out by the exiles, either personally or via administrators assigned to handle their assets, were or became legally effective unless, per the restitution laws, they were annulled upon request by the authorities or courts within the corresponding deadlines or actually annulled. The only exceptions were acts such robbery and theft, though it is assumed that 'German property' may also have arisen in that way. Closer examination of restitution decisions reveals that restitution claims directed at German property were decided upon unscrupulously and without regard for the facts (to some extent this was justified by arguing that restitution proceedings only involved obligatory claims), and that it was argued that the Allies' authorization requirements concerning surrender of property would only have to be fulfilled in cases of execution or land register proceedings. In the case of movable assets, restitution was evidently carried out de facto without much regard for the question of German property. As ... (Restitution Legislation), page 208f has shown, restitutions were already being approved in 1947, at least in the British occupation zone."

Vienna, 15th January 2006

[signature]   [signature]
Dr. Andreas Nödl, Lawyer   Professor Walter H. Rechberger

[signature]
Professor Peter Rummel (Chairman)

JURISDICTIONAL IMMUNITIES OF THE STATE
(GERMANY v. ITALY: GREECE intervening)
Judgment of 3 February 2012 (International Court of Justice)

BACKGROUND: On December 23, 2008, the Federal Republic of Germany filed in the Registry of the Court an Application instituting proceedings against the Italian Republic in respect of a dispute originating in "violations of obligations under international law" allegedly committed by Italy through its judicial practice "in that it has failed to respect the jurisdictional immunity which . . . Germany enjoys under international law". As a basis for the jurisdiction of the Court, Germany invoked Article 1 of the 1957 European Convention for the Peaceful Settlement of Disputes. Since the Court included upon the Bench no judge of Italian nationality, Italy exercised its right to choose a judge *ad hoc* to sit in the case. The Counter-Memorial of Italy included a counter-claim "with respect to the question of the reparation owed to Italian victims of grave violations of international humanitarian law committed by forces of the German Reich". By an Order of July 6, 2010, the Court decided that the counter-claim presented by Italy was inadmissible as such under the Rules of Court. On January 13, 2011, the Hellenic Republic (hereinafter "Greece") filed in the Registry an Application for permission to intervene in the case. In its Application, Greece indicated that it "[did] not seek to become a party to the case." By an Order of July 4, 2011, the Court authorized Greece to intervene in the case as a non-party, in so far as this intervention was limited to the decisions of Greek courts which were declared by

Italian courts as enforceable in Italy.

In its Application, Germany made the following requests: "Germany prays the Court to adjudge and declare that the Italian Republic: (1) by allowing civil claims based on violations of international humanitarian law by the German Reich during World War II from September 1943 to May 1945, to be brought against the Federal Republic of Germany, committed violations of obligations under international law in that it has failed to respect the jurisdictional immunity which the Federal Republic of Germany enjoys under international law; (2) by taking measures of constraint against 'Villa Vigoni', German State property used for government non-commercial purposes, also committed violations of Germany's jurisdictional immunity; (3) by declaring Greek judgments based on occurrences similar to those defined above in request No. 1 enforceable in Italy, committed a further breach of Germany's jurisdictional immunity. Accordingly, the Federal Republic of Germany prays the Court to adjudge and declare that (1) the Italian Republic's international responsibility is engaged; (2) the Italian Republic must, by means of its own choosing, take any and all steps to ensure that all the decisions of its courts and other judicial authorities infringing Germany's sovereign immunity become unenforceable; (3) the Italian Republic must take any and all steps to ensure that in the future Italian courts do not entertain legal actions against Germany founded on the occurrences described in request No. 1 above."

In June 1940, Italy entered the Second World War as an ally of the German Reich. In September 1943, following the removal of Mussolini from power, Italy surrendered to the Allies and, the following month, declared war on Germany. German forces, however, occupied much of Italian territory and, between October 1943 and the end of the War, perpetrated many atrocities against the population of that territory, including massacres of civilians and the deportation of large numbers of civilians for use as forced labor. In addition, German forces took prisoner, both inside Italy and elsewhere in Europe, several hundred thousand members of the Italian armed forces. Most of these prisoners were denied the status of prisoner of war and deported to Germany and German-occupied territories for use as forced labor.

In 1953, the Federal Republic of Germany adopted the Federal Compensation Law concerning Victims of National Socialist Persecution in order to compensate certain categories of victims of Nazi persecution. Many claims by Italian nationals under the Federal Compensation Law were unsuccessful, either because the claimants were not considered victims of national Socialist persecution within the definition of the Federal Compensation Law, or because they had no domicile or permanent residence in Germany, as required by that Law. The Federal Compensation Law was amended in 1965 to cover claims by persons persecuted because of their nationality or their membership in a non-German ethnic group, while requiring that the persons in question had refugee status on October 1, 1953. Even after the Law was amended in 1965, many Italian claimants still did not qualify for compensation because they did not have refugee status on October 1, 1953. Because of the specific terms of the Federal Compensation Law as originally adopted and as amended in 1965, claims brought by victims having foreign nationality were generally dismissed by the German courts.

In 1961, Germany and Italy entered into two settlement agreements, in which Germany paid compensation to Italy and to Italian citizens for claims arising between September 1, 1939 and May 8, 1945. Germany adopted a law in 2000 for the compensation of forced laborers, but it excluded P.O.W.'s as possible claimants. In its 2004 Ferrini decision, the Italian Court of Cassation upheld a compensation award despite Germany's claim of immunity, and similar claims are pending. That Court used similar reasoning in upholding a criminal conviction for war crimes.

On June 10, 1944, during the German occupation of Greece, German armed forces committed a massacre in the Greek village of Distomo, involving many civilians. In 1995, relatives of the victims of the massacre who claimed compensation for loss of life and property commenced proceedings against Germany. The Greek Court of First Instance of Livadia rendered a default judgment in 1997 against Germany and awarded damages to the successors in title of the victims of the massacre. Germany's appeal of that judgment was dismissed by the Hellenic Supreme Court. Article 923 of the Greek Code of Civil Procedure requires authorization from the Minister for Justice to enforce a judgment against a foreign State in Greece. That authorization was requested by the claimants in the *Distomo* case but was not granted. As a result, the judgments against Germany have remained unexecuted in Greece. The claimants in the *Distomo* case brought proceedings against Greece and Germany before the European Court of Human Rights, which held that the claimants' application was inadmissible, because of Germany's immunity. The German courts made the same ruling. The Italian courts ruled that they could enforce the Greek judgment, and the Greek claimants registered a claim against the Villa Vigoni—a property owned by the German Government near Lake Como. Germany filed a petition with the ICJ, claiming that Italy's enforcement violated international law.

THE COURT,
composed as above, after deliberation, renders the following *Judgment*:

"… [T]he Court must determine, in accordance with Article 38 (1) *(b)* of its Statute, the existence of 'international custom, as evidence of a general practice accepted as law' conferring immunity on States and, if so, what is the scope and extent of that immunity. To do so, it must apply the criteria which it has repeatedly laid down for identifying a rule of customary international law. In particular … the existence of a rule of customary international law requires that there be 'a settled practice' together with *opinio juris*.... Moreover, as the Court has also observed, '[i]t is of course axiomatic that the material of customary international law is to be looked for primarily in the actual practice and *opinio juris* of States, even though multilateral conventions may have an important role to play in recording and defining rules deriving from custom, or indeed in developing them.'...

"In the present context, State practice of particular significance is to be found in the judgments of national courts faced with the question whether a foreign State is immune, the legislation of those States which have enacted statutes dealing with immunity, the claims to immunity advanced by States before foreign courts and the statements made by States, first in the course of the extensive study of the subject by the International Law Commission and then in the context of the adoption of the United Nations Convention. *Opinio juris* in this context is reflected in particular in the assertion by States claiming immunity that international law accords them a right to such immunity from the jurisdiction of other States; in the acknowledgment, by States granting immunity, that international law imposes upon them an obligation to do so; and, conversely, in the assertion by States in other cases of a right to exercise jurisdiction over foreign States. While it may be true that States sometimes decide to accord an immunity more extensive than that required by international law, for present purposes, the point is that the grant of immunity in such a case is not accompanied by the requisite *opinio juris* and therefore sheds no light upon the issue currently under consideration by the Court.

"Although there has been much debate regarding the origins of State immunity and the identification of the principles underlying that immunity in the past, the International Law Commission concluded in 1980 that the rule of State immunity had been 'adopted as a general rule of customary international law solidly rooted in the current practice of States.'... That conclusion was based upon an extensive survey of State practice and, in the opinion of the Court, is confirmed by the record of national legislation, judicial decisions, assertions of a right to immunity and the comments of States on what became the United Nations Convention. That practice shows that, whether in claiming immunity for themselves or according it to others, States generally proceed on the basis that there is a right to immunity under international law, together with a corresponding obligation on the part of other States to respect and give effect to that immunity.

"The Court considers that the rule of State immunity occupies an important place in international law and international relations. It derives from the principle of sovereign equality of States, which, as Article 2, paragraph 1, of the Charter of the United Nations makes clear, is one of the fundamental principles of the international legal order. This principle has to be viewed together with the principle that each State possesses sovereignty over its own territory and that there flows from that sovereignty the jurisdiction of the State over events and persons within that territory. Exceptions to the immunity of the State represent a departure from the principle of sovereign equality. Immunity may represent a departure from the principle of territorial sovereignty and the jurisdiction which flows from it.

"The Parties are thus in broad agreement regarding the validity and importance of State immunity as a part of customary international law. They differ, however, as to whether (as Germany contends) the law to be applied is that which determined the scope and extent of State immunity in 1943-1945, i.e., at the time that the events giving rise to the proceedings in the Italian courts took place, or (as Italy maintains) that which applied at the time the proceedings themselves occurred. The Court observes that, in accordance with the principle stated in Article 13 of the International Law Commission Articles on Responsibility of States for Internationally Wrongful Acts, the compatibility of an act with international law can be determined only by reference to the law in force at the time when the act occurred. In that context, it is important to distinguish between the relevant acts of Germany and those of Italy. The relevant German acts … occurred in 1943-1945, and it is, therefore, the international law of that time which is applicable to them. The relevant Italian acts—the denial of immunity and exercise of jurisdiction by the Italian courts—did not occur until the proceedings in the Italian courts took place. Since the claim before the Court concerns the actions of the Italian courts, it is the international law in force at the time of those proceedings which the Court has to apply. Moreover, as the Court has stated … the law of immunity is essentially procedural in nature…. It regulates the exercise of jurisdiction in respect of particular conduct and is thus entirely distinct from the substantive law which determines whether that conduct is lawful or unlawful. For these reasons, the Court considers that it must examine and apply the law on State immunity as it existed at the time of the Italian proceedings, rather than that which existed in 1943-1945.

"The Parties also differ as to the scope and extent of the rule of State immunity. In that context, the Court notes that many States (including both Germany and Italy) now distinguish between *acta jure gestionis*, in respect of which they have limited the immunity which they claim for themselves and which they accord to others, and *acta jure imperii*. That approach has also been followed in the United Nations Convention and the European Convention (*see also* the draft Inter-American Convention on Jurisdictional Immunity of States drawn up by the Inter-American Juridical Committee of the Organization of American States in 1983….

"The Court is not called upon to address the question of how international law treats the issue of State immunity in respect of *acta jure gestionis*. The acts of the German armed forces and other State organs which were the subject of the proceedings in the Italian courts clearly constituted *acta jure imperii*. The Court notes that Italy, in response to a question posed by a Member of the Court, recognized that those acts had to be characterized as *acta jure imperii*, notwithstanding that they were unlawful. The Court considers that the terms *'jure imperii'* and *'jure gestionis'* do not imply that the acts in question are lawful but refer rather to whether the acts in question fall to be assessed by reference to the law governing the exercise of sovereign power *(jus imperii)* or the law concerning non-sovereign activities of a State, especially private and commercial activities *(jus gestionis)*. To the extent that this distinction is significant for determining whether or not a State is entitled to immunity from the jurisdiction of another State's courts in respect of a particular act, it has to be applied before that jurisdiction can be exercised, whereas the legality or illegality of the act is something which can be determined only in the exercise of that jurisdiction. Although the present case is unusual in that the illegality of the acts at issue has been admitted by Germany at all stages of the proceedings, the Court considers that this fact does not alter the characterization of those acts as *acta jure imperii*.

"Both Parties agree that States are generally entitled to immunity in respect of *acta jure imperii*. That is the approach taken in the United Nations, European and draft Inter-American Conventions, the national legislation in those States which have adopted statutes on the subject and the jurisprudence of national courts. It is against that background that the Court must approach the question raised by the present proceedings, namely whether that immunity is applicable to acts committed by the armed forces of a State (and other organs of that State acting in co-operation with the armed forces) in the course of conducting an armed conflict. Germany maintains that immunity is applicable and that there is no relevant limitation on the immunity to which a State is entitled in respect of *acta jure imperii*. Italy, in its pleadings before the Court, maintains that Germany is not entitled to immunity in respect of the cases before the Italian courts for two reasons: first, that immunity as to *acta jure imperii* does not extend to torts or delicts occasioning death, personal injury or damage to property committed on the territory of the forum State, and, secondly, that, irrespective of where the relevant acts took place, Germany was not entitled to immunity because those acts involved the most serious violations of rules of international law of a peremptory character for which no alternative means of redress was available. The Court will consider each of Italy's arguments in turn.

"The essence of the first Italian argument is that customary international law has developed to the point where a State is no longer entitled to immunity in respect of acts occasioning death, personal injury or damage to property on the territory of the forum State, even if the act in question was performed *jure imperii*....

"Germany maintains that ... neither Article 11 of the European Convention, nor Article 12 of the United Nations Convention reflects customary international law. It contends that, in any event, they are irrelevant to the present proceedings, because neither provision was intended to apply to the acts of armed forces. Germany also points to the fact that, with the exception of the Italian cases and the Distomo case in Greece, no national court has ever held that a State was not entitled to immunity in respect of acts of its armed forces, in the context of an armed conflict and that, by contrast, the courts in several States have expressly declined jurisdiction in such cases on the ground that the respondent State was entitled to immunity....

"The Court considers that it is not called upon in the present proceedings to resolve the question whether there is in customary international law a 'tort exception' to State immunity applicable to *acta jure imperii* in general. The issue before the Court is confined to acts committed on the territory of the forum State by the armed forces of a foreign State, and other organs of State working in co-operation with those armed forces, in the course of conducting an armed conflict.

"The Court will first consider whether the adoption of Article 11 of the European Convention or Article 12 of the United Nations Convention affords any support to Italy's contention that States are no longer entitled to immunity in respect of the type of acts specified in the preceding paragraph. As the Court has already explained ... neither Convention is in force between the Parties to the present case. The provisions of these Conventions are, therefore, relevant only in so far as their provisions and the process of their adoption and implementation shed light on the content of customary international law.

"Article 11 of the European Convention states the territorial tort principle in broad terms, 'A Contracting State cannot claim immunity from the jurisdiction of a court of another Contracting State in proceedings which relate to redress for injury to the person or damage to tangible property, if the facts which occasioned the injury or damage occurred in the territory of the State of the forum, and if the author of the injury or damage was present in that territory at the time when those facts occurred.'

"That provision must, however, be read in the light of Article 31, which provides, 'Nothing in this Convention shall affect any immunities or privileges enjoyed by a Contracting State in respect of anything done or omitted to be done by, or in relation to, its armed forces when on the territory of another Contracting State.' Although one of the concerns which Article 31 was intended to address was the relationship between the Convention and the various agreements on the status of visiting forces, the language of Article 31 makes clear that it is not confined to that matter and excludes from the scope of the Convention all proceedings relating to acts of foreign armed forces, irrespective of whether those forces are present in the territory of the forum with the consent of the forum State and whether their acts take place in peacetime or in conditions of armed conflict. The Explanatory Report on the Convention, which contains a detailed commentary prepared as part of the negotiating process, states in respect of Article 31, 'The Convention is not intended to govern situations which may arise in the event of armed conflict; *nor* can it be invoked to resolve problems which may arise between allied States as a result of the stationing of forces. These problems are generally dealt with by special agreements.... [Article 31] prevents the Convention being interpreted as having any influence upon these matters.'...

"Unlike the European Convention, the United Nations Convention contains no express provision excluding the acts of armed forces from its scope. However, the International Law Commission's commentary on the text of Article 12 states that that provision does not apply to 'situations involving armed conflicts....'

"The Court considers, however, that for the purposes of the present case the most pertinent State practice is to be found in those national judicial decisions which concerned the question whether a State was entitled to immunity in proceedings concerning acts allegedly committed by its armed forces in the course of an armed conflict. All of those cases, the facts of which are often very similar to those of the cases before the Italian courts, concern the events of the Second World War. In this context, the *Cour de cassation* in France has consistently held that Germany was entitled to immunity in a series of cases brought by claimants who had been deported from occupied French territory during the Second World War.... The Court also notes that the European Court of Human Rights held in [2009] that France had not contravened the European Convention on Human Rights, because the *Cour de cassation* had given effect to an immunity required by international law.

"The highest courts in Slovenia and Poland have also held that Germany was entitled to immunity in respect of unlawful acts perpetrated on their territory by its armed forces during the Second World War....

"The only State in which there is any judicial practice which appears to support the Italian argument, apart from the judgments of the Italian courts which are the subject of the present proceedings, is Greece....

"In the Court's opinion, State practice in the form of judicial decisions supports the proposition that State immunity for *acta jure imperii* continues to extend to civil proceedings for acts occasioning death, personal injury or damage to property committed by the armed forces and other organs of a State in the conduct of armed conflict, even if the relevant acts take place on the territory of the forum State. That practice is accompanied by *opinio juris*, as demonstrated by the positions taken by States and the jurisprudence of a number of national courts which have made clear that they considered that customary international law required immunity. The almost complete absence of contrary jurisprudence is also significant, as is the absence of any statements by States in connection with the work of the International Law Commission regarding State immunity and the adoption of the United Nations Convention or, so far as the Court has been able to discover, in any other context asserting that customary international law does not require immunity in such cases....

"In light of the foregoing, the Court considers that customary international law continues to require that a State be accorded immunity in proceedings for torts allegedly committed on the territory of another State by its armed forces and other organs of State in the course of conducting an armed conflict. That conclusion is confirmed by the judgments of the European Court of Human Rights to which the Court has referred....

"The Court therefore concludes that, contrary to what had been argued by Italy in the present proceedings, the decision of the Italian courts to deny immunity to Germany cannot be justified on the basis of the territorial tort principle....

"Italy's second argument, which, unlike its first argument, applies to all of the claims brought before the Italian courts, is that the denial of immunity was justified on account of the particular nature of the acts forming the subject-matter of the claims before the Italian courts and the circumstances in which those claims were made. There are three strands to this argument. First, Italy contends that the acts which gave rise to the claims constituted serious violations of the principles of international law applicable to the conduct of armed conflict, amounting to war crimes and crimes against humanity. Secondly, Italy maintains that the rules of international law thus contravened were peremptory norms *(jus cogens)*. Thirdly, Italy argues that the claimants having been denied all other forms of redress, the exercise of jurisdiction by the Italian courts was necessary as a matter of last resort....

"The first strand is based upon the proposition that international law does not accord immunity to a State, or at least restricts its right to immunity, when that State has committed serious violations of the law of armed conflict (international humanitarian law as it is more commonly termed today, although the term was not used in 1943-1945). In the present case, the Court has already made clear ... that the actions of the German armed forces and other organs of the German Reich giving rise to the proceedings before the Italian courts were serious violations of the law of armed conflict which amounted to crimes under international law. The question is whether that fact operates to deprive Germany of an entitlement to immunity....

"... Apart from the decisions of the Italian courts which are the subject of the present proceedings, there is almost no State practice which might be considered to support the proposition that a State is deprived of its entitlement to immunity in such a case. Although the Hellenic Supreme Court in the *Distomo* case adopted a form of that proposition, the Special Supreme Court in *Margellos* repudiated that approach two years later. As the Court has noted ... under Greek law it is the stance adopted in *Margellos* which must be followed in later cases unless the Greek courts find that there has been a change in customary international law since 2002, which they have not done. As with the territorial tort principle, the Court considers that Greek practice, taken as a whole, tends to deny that the proposition advanced by Italy has become part of customary international law.... The European Court of Human Rights has not accepted the proposition that States are no longer entitled to immunity in cases regarding serious violations of international humanitarian law or human rights law. In 2001, the Grand Chamber of that Court, by the admittedly narrow majority of nine to eight, concluded that, 'Notwithstanding the special character of the prohibition of torture in international law, the Court is unable to discern in the international instruments, judicial authorities or other materials before it any firm basis for concluding that, as a matter of international law, a State no longer enjoys immunity from civil suit in the courts of another State where acts of torture are alleged.'

"The Court concludes that, under customary international law as it presently stands, a State is not deprived of immunity by reason of the fact that it is accused of serious violations of international human rights law or the international law of armed conflict. In reaching that conclusion, the Court must emphasize that it is addressing only the immunity of the State itself from the jurisdiction of the courts of other States; the question of whether, and if so to what extent, immunity might apply in criminal proceedings against an official of the State is not in issue in the present case...."The Court now turns to the second strand in Italy's argument, which emphasizes the *jus cogens* status of the rules which were violated by Germany during the period 1943-1945. This strand of the argument rests on the premise that there is a conflict between *jus cogens* rules forming part of the law of armed conflict and according immunity to Germany. Since *jus cogens* rules always prevail over any inconsistent rule of international law, whether contained in a treaty or in customary international law, so the argument runs, and since the rule which accords one State immunity before the courts of another does not have the status of *jus cogens*, the rule of immunity must give way.

"This argument therefore depends upon the existence of a conflict between a rule, or rules, of *jus cogens*, and the rule of customary law which requires one State to accord immunity to another. In the opinion of the Court, however, no such conflict exists. Assuming for this purpose that the rules of the law of armed conflict which prohibit the murder of civilians in occupied territory, the deportation of civilian inhabitants to slave labour and the deportation of prisoners of war to slave labour are rules of *jus cogens*, there is no conflict between those rules and the rules on State immunity. The two sets of rules address different matters. The rules of State immunity are procedural in character and are confined to determining whether or not the courts of one State may exercise jurisdiction in respect of another State. They do not bear upon the question whether or not the conduct in respect of which the proceedings are brought was lawful or unlawful. That is why the application of the contemporary law of State immunity to proceedings concerning events which occurred in 1943-1945 does not infringe the principle that law should not be applied retrospectively to determine matters of legality and responsibility.... For the same reason, recognizing the immunity of a foreign State in accordance with customary international law does not amount to recognizing as lawful a situation created by the breach of a *jus cogens* rule, or rendering aid and assistance in maintaining that situation, and so cannot contravene the principle in Article 41 of the International Law Commission's Articles on State Responsibility.

"In the present case, the violation of the rules prohibiting murder, deportation and slave labour took place in the period 1943-1945. The illegality of these acts is openly acknowledged by all concerned. The application of rules of State immunity to determine whether or not the Italian courts have jurisdiction to hear claims arising out of those violations cannot involve any conflict with the rules which were violated. Nor is the argument strengthened by focusing upon the duty of the wrongdoing State to make reparation, rather than upon the original wrongful act. The duty to make reparation is a rule which exists independently of those rules which concern the means by which it is to be effected. The law of State immunity concerns only the latter; a decision that a foreign State is immune no more conflicts with the duty to make reparation than it does with the rule prohibiting the original wrongful act. Moreover, against the background of a century of practice in which almost every peace treaty or post-war settlement has involved either a decision not to require the payment of reparations or the use of lump sum settlements and set-offs, it is difficult to see that international law contains a rule requiring the payment of full compensation to each and every individual victim as a rule accepted by the international community of States as a whole as one from which no derogation is permitted....

"Accordingly, the Court concludes that even on the assumption that the proceedings in the Italian courts involved violations of *jus cogens* rules, the applicability of the customary international law on State immunity was not affected....

"For these reasons, The Court,
(1) by twelve votes to three,
    Finds that the Italian Republic has violated its obligation to respect the immunity which the Federal Republic of Germany enjoys under international law by allowing civil claims to be brought against it based on violations of international humanitarian law committed by the German Reich between 1943 and 1945;

(2) by fourteen votes to one,
    Finds that the Italian Republic has violated its obligation to respect the immunity which the Federal Republic of Germany enjoys under international law by taking measures of constraint against Villa Vigoni;

(3) by fourteen votes to one,
    Finds that the Italian Republic has violated its obligation to respect the immunity which the Federal Republic of Germany enjoys under international law by declaring enforceable in Italy decisions of Greek courts based on violations of international humanitarian law committed in Greece by the German Reich;

(4) by fourteen votes to one,

Finds that the Italian Republic must, by enacting appropriate legislation, or by resorting to other methods of its choosing, ensure that the decisions of its courts and those of other judicial authorities infringing the immunity which the Federal Republic of Germany enjoys under international law cease to have effect;

(5) unanimously,

Rejects all other submissions made by the Federal Republic of Germany.

"Done in French and in English, the French text being authoritative, at the Peace Palace, The Hague, this third day of February, two thousand and twelve, in four copies, one of which will be placed in the archives of the Court and the others transmitted to the Government of the Federal Republic of Germany, the Government of the Italian Republic and the Government of the Hellenic Republic, respectively.

(Signed) Hisashi Owada, President
(Signed) Philippe Couvreur, Registrar

"Judges Koroma, Keith and Bennouna append separate opinions to the Judgment of the Court; Judges Cançado Trindade and Yusuf append dissenting opinions to the Judgment of the Court; Judge ad hoc Gaja appends a dissenting opinion to the Judgment of the Court.

(Initialed) H.O.
(Initialed) Ph.C."

Afterword

While the nature of this text (primarily a set of edited cases) does not seem to call for a traditional chapter of conclusions or summary, it does seem to require some sort of final statement. In considering the possibilities for such a "farewell message," the last sentence of Hugo Grotius' classic treatise on International Law—*De Jure Belli ac Pacis* ("Of the Law of Wars and Peace")—stood out. The quote below is taken from the Kessenger Legacy Reprints edition of the translation by A.C. Campbell, published in 1901 under the title, *The Rights of War and Peace*:

> And may God, to whom alone it belongs to dispose the affections and desires of sovereign princes and kings, inscribe these principles upon their hearts and minds, that they may always remember that the noblest office, in which man can be engaged, is the government of men, who are the principal objects of the divine care.

Made in the USA
Middletown, DE
09 September 2018